JOHN WILLIS

SCREEN WORLD

1996

VOLUME 47

WITH FULL COLOR HIGHLIGHTS OF THE FILM YEAR

ASSOCIATE EDITOR
BARRY MONUSH

APPLAUSE
NEW YORK • LONDON

LIBRARY OF CONGRESS CARD NO. 50-3023
ISBN: 1-55783-252-8 (CLOTH)
ISBN: 1-55783-253-6 (PAPER)

1955 · 1959 · *The Apartment* · 1964

Woman Times Seven · *The Bliss of Mrs. Blossom* · *Sweet Charity* · *Desperate Characters*

The Possession of Joel Delaney · *The Turning Point* · *Being There* · *Loving Couples*

To
SHIRLEY MACLAINE

one of the truly original performers of the postwar era, whose rich gallery of motion picture characters has showcased an impressive range of vulnerability and strength, humor and pathos, eccentricity and warmth.

FILMS: *The Trouble With Harry* (debut, 1955), *Artists and Models* (1955), *Around the World in 80 Days* (1956), *Hot Spell* (1958), *The Sheepman* (1958), *The Matchmaker* (1958), *Some Came Running (1958; Academy Award nomination)*, *Ask Any Girl* (1959), *Career* (1959), *Can-Can* (1960), *Ocean's Eleven* (1960; cameo), *The Apartment* (1960; Academy Award nomination), *All in a Night's Work* (1961), *Two Loves* (1961), *The Children's Hour* (1961), *My Geisha* (1962), *Two for the Seesaw* (1962), *Irma La Douce* (1963; Academy Award nomination), *What a Way to Go!* (1964), *The Yellow Rolls-Royce* (1964), *John Goldfarb, Please Come Home* (1964), *Gambit* (1966), *Woman Times Seven* (1967), *The Bliss of Mrs. Blossom* (1968), *Sweet Charity* (1969), *Two Mules for Sister Sara* (1970), *Desperate Characters* (1971), *The Possession of Joel Delaney* (1972), *The Turning Point* (1977; Academy Award nomination), *Being There* (1979), *Loving Couples* (1980), *A Change of Seasons* (1980), *Terms of Endearment* (1983; Academy Award for Best Actress), *Cannonball Run II* (1984), *Madame Sousatzka* (1988), *Steel Magnolias* (1989), *Postcards From the Edge* (1990), *Waiting for the Light* (1990), *Defending Your Life* (1991; cameo), *Used People* (1992), *Wrestling Ernest Hemingway* (1994), *Guarding Tess* (1994), *The Celluloid Closet* (1996), *Mrs.Winterbourne* (1996), *The Evening Star* (1996).

Terms of Endearment   *Steel Magnolias*   *Waiting for the Light*   *Mrs. Winterbourne*

Mel Gibson in *Braveheart*
Academy Award Winner for Best Picture of 1995
© B.H. Finance C.V./Paramount Pictures

CONTENTS

EDITOR: JOHN WILLIS

ASSOCIATE EDITOR: BARRY MONUSH

Staff: Marco Starr Boyajian, William Camp, Jimmie Hollifield, II,

Tom Lynch, Stanley Reeves, John Sala

Acknowledgements: David Christopher, Cline & White, Tommy Crudup, Richard D'Attile, Gerard Dapena, Dennis Davidson Associates, Samantha Dean, Paola Fantini, Emily Franzosa, The Film Forum, Frank Gaffney, Richard Hampton, Felix Mariposa, David Munro, PMK Publicity, Rachel Reiss, Greg Rossi, George Scherling, Kimberly Scherling, Sony Pictures Entertainment, Sheldon Stone, Paul Sugarman, Walt Disney Pictures, Glenn Young, David Zeliff.

1. Tom Hanks

2. Jim Carrey

3. Brad Pitt

4. Harrison Ford

5. Robin Williams

6. Sandra Bullock

7. Mel Gibson

8. Demi Moore

9. John Travolta

10. Kevin Costner

11. Michael Douglas

12. Bruce Willis

13. Val Kilmer

14. Michelle Pfeiffer

15. Julia Roberts

16. Morgan Freeman

TOP BOX OFFICE STARS OF 1995

17. Pierce Brosnan   18. Anthony Hopkins   19. Robert De Niro   20. Steven Seagal

1995 RELEASES
January 1 Through December 31, 1995

21. Meg Ryan   22. Winona Ryder   23. Steve Martin   24. Tommy Lee Jones

25. Denzel Washington   Meryl Streep   Gene Hackman   Susan Sarandon

Sinbad, Mason Adams, Phil Hartman

Phil Hartman, Sinbad, Jeffrey Jones

Tony Longo, Sinbad, Paul Ben-Victor, Chauncey Leopardi, Phil Hartman, Kim Greist, Jeffrey Jones, Kim Murphy

HOUSEGUEST

(HOLLYWOOD PICTURES) Producers, Joe Roth, Roger Birnbaum; Executive Producer, Dennis Bishop; Director, Randall Miller; Screenplay, Michael J. DiGaetano, Lawrence Gay; Photography, Jerzy Zielinski; Designer, Paul Peters; Editor, Eric Sears; Co-Producers, Riley Kathryn Ellis, Jody Savin; Music, John Debney; Costumes, Jyl Moder; Casting, Rick Montgomery, Dan Parada; Distributed by Buena Vista Pictures; Presented in association with Caravan Pictures; Dolby Digital Stereo; Technicolor; Rated PG; 108 minutes; January release

CAST

Kevin Franklin	Sinbad
Gary Young	Phil Hartman
Emily Young	Kim Greist
Jason Young	Chauncey Leopardi
Sarah Young	Talia Seider
Brooke Young	Kim Murphy
Pauly Gasperini	Paul Ben-Victor
Joey Gasperini	Tony Longo
Ron Timmerman	Jeffrey Jones
Larry	Stan Shaw
Derek Bond	Ron Glass
Steve "ST-3"	Kevin Jordan
Mr. Pike	Mason Adams
Nancy Pike	Patricia Fraser
Happy Marcelli	Don Brockett
Vincent Montgomery	Kevin West
Lynn	Wynonna Smith
Stuart the Manager	Kirk Baily
Sister Mary Winters	Valerie Long
Little Kevin	Jesse Rivera
Bobby	Melvin Brentley II
Kid #1	Brandon Alexander
Local Guys	B'nard Lewis, Jonathan Floyd
Ticket Saleswoman	Vondria Bergen
Happy's Wife	Susan Richards
Myrna	Palma Greenwood
Big Spin Host	Chuck Aber
Mr. Ichabod	Larry John Meyers
Rosie the Caterer	Jody Savin
Tom Miller	Alex Coleman
Stern Man	Lee Cass
Society Woman	Marilyn Eastman
Preppy Man	John Hall
Priest	Bob Tracey
Woman in Red Dress	Vicki Ross-Norris
Waitress	Tina Benko
Jerry Jordon	William Cameron
Jane Jordon	Patti Lesniak
Michelle Castel	Kate Young
Drunk at Party	Randall Miller
Happy's Thug	Donald Joseph Freeman
Burger Counter Girl	Mindy Reynolds
Kelly	Catherine Cuppari
Ticket Vendor	Bingo O'Malley
Nurse	Susan Chapek
Dr. Kraft	Ron Newell
Dental Student	Alvin McCray
Little Girls	Nicole Armstrong, Alana Hixson
Tough Kids	Damien Luvara, Ben Hanlan, Jason Walczuk
Biker	Jan Eddy
Secretary	Lisa Davis
Security Guard	David Early
Cop	Greg Collins
Mayor	Bernie Canepari
Serious Woman	Patricia Cray
Guy in Crowd	Harold Surratt

and Donna Leichenko (Counter Girl), Robert Le (Don Woo), Dante Washington (Yogurt Store Kid), Shaft the Hamster (Himself), Thor (Carl the Dog)

On the run from loan sharks, Kevin Franklin pretends to be the old friend whom Gary Young has not seen in twenty-five years.

Michael Rapaport

Jennifer Connelly, Kristy Swanson

HIGHER LEARNING

(COLUMBIA) Producers, John Singleton, Paul Hall; Director/Screenplay, John Singleton; Photography, Peter Lyons Collister; Designer, Keith Brian Burns; Editor, Bruce Cannon; Costumes, Carol Oditz; Co-Producer, Dwight Alonzo Williams; Music, Stanley Clarke; Title Sequence, Elaine & Saul Bass; Casting, Jaki Brown-Karman, Kimberly Hardin; a New Deal Production; SDDS Dolby Digital Stereo; Technicolor; Rated R; 127 minutes; January release

CAST

Malik Williams	Omar Epps
Kristen Connor	Kristy Swanson
Remy	Michael Rapaport
Taryn	Jennifer Connelly
Fudge	Ice Cube
Wayne	Jason Wiles
Deja	Tyra Banks
Scott Moss	Cole Hauser
Professor Maurice Phipps	Laurence Fishburne
Officer Bradley	Bradford English
Monet	Regina King
Dreads	Busta Rhymez
Billy	Jay Ferguson
Knocko	Andrew Bryniarski
James	Trevor St. John
Erik	Talbert Morton
David Isaacs	Adam Goldberg
Eddie	J. Trevor Edmond
Nicole	Bridgette Wilson
Claudia	Kari Salin
Coach Davis	John Walton Smith, Jr.
Chad Shadowhill	Randall Batinkoff
Cory	Malcolm Norrington
Adam	Antonio Todd

and Tim Griffin (Orientation Advisor), Patricia Forte, Sheila Ward (Counselors), George LePorte (Starting Judge), Warren Olney (TV Reporter), D-Knowledge (Himself), Skip O'Brien, Joe Bugs, Bill Evans (Security Guards), Ernie Singleton, Dedrick Gobert, Bruce Williams (Fudge's Homies), Richard D. Alexander (Big Shorty), Michael Buchman Silver, Graham Galloway, Paul Anthony Kropfl (Frat Members), James W. Smith, Walton Greene, Mary Bakjian (Race Officials), Mista Grimm (Drunk Student), Alicia Stevenson (Monet's Friend), Colleen Ann Fitzpatrick (Festival Singer), Robby Parker (Dogman), Pola Maloles (Flyer Girl), Ingrid Walters (Party Girl), Kiante Elam (Black Pepper), Jamie Jo Medearis (White Salt), Rick Avery (Guard Beats Malik), Tony Donno, Cole McLarty (Gay Victims)

Drama follows a varying group of students at Columbus University as racial tensions escalate.

© Columbia Pictures Industries, Inc

Laurence Fishburne, Omar Epps

Omar Epps, Richard D. Alexander, Ice Cube, Busta Rhymez

FAR FROM HOME: THE ADVENTURES OF YELLOW DOG

Joel Palmer, Bruce Davison, Mimi Rogers, Jesse Bradford

(20th CENTURY FOX) Producer, Peter O'Brian; Director/Screenplay, Phillip Borsos; Photography, James Gardner; Designer, Mark S. Freeborn; Editor, Sidney Wolinsky; Music, John Scott; Costumes, Antonia Bardon; Casting, Linda Phillips Palo; Dakotah's Trainer, Frank Disesso; Dolby Digital Stereo; Alpha Cine Color; Rated PG; 81 minutes; January release

CAST

Katherine McCormick	Mimi Rogers
John McCormick	Bruce Davison
Angus McCormick	Jesse Bradford
John Gale	Tom Bower
Silas McCormick	Joel Palmer
Yellow Dog	Dakotah
David Finlay	Josh Wannamaker
Sara	Margot Finley
Ron Willick	Matt Bennett
St. Clair McColl	St. Clair McColl
Labrador Helicopter Pilot	Capt. Jennifer Weissenborn
Flight Engineer	MCPL. Gordon Neave
Nurse	Karen Kruper

and Dean Lockwood, John LeClair, Brent Stait (Sartechs)

Fourteen-year-old Angus McCormick befriends a stray dog who later becomes his only companion when the two are stranded in the wilderness following a boating accident.

© Twentieth Century Fox

Dakotah, Jesse Bradford

Ellen Barkin, Frank Langella

Ellen Barkin, Laurence Fishburne

BAD COMPANY

(TOUCHSTONE) formerly *The Tool Shed*; Producers, Amedeo Ursini, Jeffrey Chernov; Director, Damian Harris; Screenplay, Ross Thomas; Photography, Jack N. Green; Designer, Andrew McAlpine; Editor, Stuart Pappé; Costumes, Richard Shissler, Charles DeCaro; Music, Carter Burwell; Casting, Deborah Aquila; Distributed by Buena Vista Pictures; Dolby Digitial Stereo; Technicolor; Rated R; 108 minutes; January release

CAST

Margaret Wells	Ellen Barkin
Nelson Crowe	Laurence Fishburne
Vic Grimes	Frank Langella
Tod Stapp	Michael Beach
Julie Ames	Gia Carides
Judge Beach	David Ogden Stiers
Les Goodwin	Daniel Hugh Kelly
Walter Curl	Spalding Gray
Bobby Birdsong	James Hong
Al	Tegan West
John Cartwain	Fred Henderson
Wanda	Michelle Beaudoin
Mrs. Beach	Sherry Bie
Phil	Alan Robertson
Doctor	L. Harvey Gold
Cleaners Clerk	Alan C. Peterson
Detective Harrison	Larry Musser

and Brian Drummond (Ed the Doorman), Sook Yin Lee (Waitress), Marcus Youssef (Concierge), Nicholas Lea (Jake), Jill Teed (Jane), Michael Murphy

CIA operative Nelson Crowe is selected to infiltrate a secret espionage organization known as the Tool Shed.

© Buena Vista Pictures Distribution, Inc.

TALES FROM THE CRYPT PRESENTS DEMON KNIGHT

(UNIVERSAL) Producer/Crypt Keeper Sequences Director, Gilbert Adler; Executive Producers, Richard Donner, David Giler, Walter Hill, Joel Silver, Robert Zemeckis; Director, Ernest Dickerson; Screenplay, Ethan Reiff, Cyrus Voris, Mark Bishop; Based on comic magazines originally published by William M. Gaines; Photography, Rick Bota; Designer, Christiaan Wagener; Editor, Stephen Lovejoy; Music, Ed Shearmur; Main Title Theme Composer, Danny Elfman; Costumes, Warden Neil; Visual Effects, Available Light Limited, John T. Van Vliet; Casting, Jaki Brown-Karman; DTS Digital Stereo; Deluxe color; Rated R; 93 minutes; January release

CAST

Voice of the Crypt Keeper	John Kassir
The Collector	Billy Zane
Brayker	William Sadler
Jeryline	Jada Pinkett
Cordelia	Brenda Bakke
Irene	CCH Pounder
Uncle Willy	Dick Miller
Roach	Thomas Haden Church
Sheriff Tupper	John Schuck
Deputy Bob Martel	Gary Farmer
Wally Enfield	Charles Fleischer
Homer	Tim deZarn
Wanda	Sherrie Rose
Danny	Ryan Sean O'Donohue
Sirach	Tony Salome
Dickerson	Ken Baldwin

and Tiffany Anne, Reda Beebe, Te-See Bender, Traci Bingham, Ponti Butler, Veronica Culver, Tina Hollimon, Elaine Marks, Mim Parker (Party Babes), Graham Galloway (Fred), Dale Swann (Bus Driver), Mark D. Kennerly (Other Collector), Peggy Trentini (Amanda), Kathy Barbour, Tina New (Crypt Keeper Starlets), Stephanie Sain (Radio Voice/Mavis)

The Crypt Keeper

At a dingy New Mexico boarding house, two supernatural adversaries arrive to do battle: the virtuous Brayker and the evil Collector. Based on the HBO Cable TV series "Tales From the Crypt."

Billy Zane

Brenda Bakke, William Sadler

Malcolm X (l)

BROTHER MINISTER: THE ASSASSINATION OF MALCOLM X

(X-CEPTIONAL PRODUCTIONS) Producers, Jack Baxter, Lewis Kesten, Jefri Aalmuhammed; Executive Producer, Lewis Kesten; Directors, Jack Baxter, Jefri Aalmuhammed; Screenplay, Jack Baxter, Jefri Aalmuhammed, Joan Claire Chabriel; Photography, Robert Haggins; Music, Richie Havens, Frank Herrero; Editor, Mitchell Kress; Narrator, Roscoe Lee Browne; Presented in association with Illuminati Entertainment Group Inc., Why Productions Inc.; Dolby Stereo; Color/black and white; Not rated; 115 minutes; January release

WITH

Peter Bailey, Dr. John Henry Clarke, James Fox, Khalil Islam (Thomas 15X Johnson), Charles 37X Kenyatta, William Kunstler, Jack Newfield, Percy Sutton, Bill Tatum

Documentary about the assassination of black leader Malcom X at the Audobon Ballroom in Harlem on Feb. 18, 1965.

Julie Delpy, Ethan Hawke

BEFORE SUNRISE

(COLUMBIA) Producer, Anne Walker-McBay; Executive Producer, John Sloss; Director, Richard Linklater; Screenplay, Richard Linklater, Kim Krizan; Co-Producers, Ellen Winn Wendl, Gernot Schaffler, Wolfgang Ramml; Photography, Lee Daniel; Editor, Sandra Adair; Casting, Judy Henderson, Alycia Aumuller; a Detour Filmproduction in association with F.I.L.M.H.A.U.S, Wien; from Castle Rock Entertainment; Dolby Stereo; Technicolor; Rated R; 100 minutes; January release

CAST

Jesse	Ethan Hawke
Celine	Julie Delpy
Wife on Train	Andrea Eckert
Husband on Train	Hanno Pöschl
Guys on Bridge	Karl Bruckschwaiger, Tex Rubinowitz
Palm Reader	Erni Mangold
Street Poet	Dominik Castell
Bartender	Haymon Maria Buttinger
Guitarist in Club	Harold Waiglein
Belly Dancer	Bilge Jeschim
Percussionist	Kurti
Cafe Patrons	Hans Weingartner, Liese Lyon, Peter Ily Huemer, Otto Reiter, Hubert Fabian Kulterer, Branko Andric, Constanze Schweiger, John Sloss, Alexandra Seibel, Georg Schöllhammer, Christian Ankowitsch, Wilbirg Reiter
Musicians on boat	Barbara Klebel, Wolfgang Staribacher
Harpsichord Player	Wolfgang Glüxam

Jesse and Celine meet on a train and spend a night together, roaming the streets of Venice, as they fall in love.

Julie Delpy, Ethan Hawke

Julie Delpy, Ethan Hawke

MIAMI RHAPSODY

(HOLLYWOOD PICTURES) Producers, Barry Jossen, David Frankel; Executive Producers, Jon Avnet, Jordan Kerner; Director/Screenplay, David Frankel; Photography, Jack Wallner; Designer, J. Mark Harrington; Editor, Steven Weisberg; Music, Mark Isham; Costumes, Patricia Field; Casting, Renée Rousselot; Distributed by Buena Vista Pictures; Dolby Digital Stereo; Technicolor; Rated PG-13; 95 minutes; January release

Sarah Jessica Parker, Antonio Banderas

CAST

Gwyn Marcus	Sarah Jessica Parker
Matt	Gil Bellows
Antonio	Antonio Banderas
Nina Marcus	Mia Farrow
Vic Marcus	Paul Mazursky
Jordan Marcus	Kevin Pollak
Terri	Barbara Garrick
Leslie Marcus	Carla Gugino
Jeff	Bo Eason
Kaia	Naomi Campbell
Mitchell	Jeremy Piven
Zelda	Kelly Bishop
Peter	Mark Blum
Charlie	Norman Steinberg
Rabbi	Ben Stein
Derek	Donal Logue
Grandma Lil	Mary Chernoff
Antonio's Mother	Elodia Riovega
Ted	Chaz Mena
Carlos	George Tapia
Nurse	Avery Sommers
Photographer	Ed Arenas
Chinese Host	Frank Fong
Gynecologist	Lisa Banes

Gwen Marcus begins to have second thoughts about her engagement to Matt when she discovers that each member of her family is having an extra-marital affair.

Mia Farrow, Paul Mazursky

Naomi Campbell, Kevin Pollak

Sarah Jessica Parker, Gil Bellows

THE SECRET OF ROAN INISH

(FIRST LOOK PICTURES) Producers, Sarah Green, Maggie Renzi; Executive Producers, John Sloss, Glenn R. Jones, Peter Newman; Director/Screenplay/Editor, John Sayles; Based on the novella *Secret of the Ron Mor Skerry* by Rosalie K. Fry; Photography, Haskell Wexler; Designer, Adrian Smith; Costumes, Consolata Boyle; Music, Mason Daring; Casting, John and Ros Hubbard; a presentation of Jones Entertainment Group Ltd. in association with Peter Newman productions of a Skerry Movies Production; Dolby Stereo; Color; Rated PG; 102 minutes; February release

CAST

Fiona	Jeni Courtney
Tess, Grandmother	Eileen Colgan
Hugh, Grandfather	Mick Lally
Eamon	Richard Sheridan
Tadhg	John Lynch

A thirteen-year-old girl is sent to live with her grandparents in a fishing village in Northwest Ireland. There she is enchanted by stories of the mythical Selkie, creatures half-human, half-seal.

© Overseas Filmgroup/First Look Pictures

Mick Lally, Jeni Courtney

Susan Lynch

Susan Lynch

Jeni Courtney

Cillian Byrne

JOHN CARPENTER'S IN THE MOUTH OF MADNESS

(NEW LINE CINEMA) Producer, Sandy King; Director, John Carpenter; Executive Producer/Screenplay, Michael De Luca; Photography, Gary B. Kibbe; Editor, Edward A. Warschilka; Designer, Jeff Steven Ginn; Music, John Carpenter, Jim Lang; Special Make-up Effects, Robert Kurtzman, Gregory Nicotero, Howard Berger; Visual Effects Supervisor, Bruce Nicholson; Associate Producer, Artist Robinson; Dolby Stereo; Panavision; Film House color; Rated R; 94 minutes; February release

CAST

John Trent	Sam Neill
Linda Styles	Julie Carmen
Sutter Cane	Jurgen Prochnow
Jackson Harglow	Charlton Heston
Dr. Wrenn	David Warner
Saperstein	John Glover
Robinson	Bernie Casey
Paul	Peter Jason
Mrs. Pickman	Frances Bay
Simon	Wilhelm von Homburg
Guards	Kevin Rushton, Gene Mack
Axe Maniac	Conrad Bergschneider
Reporter	Marvin Scott
Receptionist	Katherine Ashby
Young Teen	Ben Gilbert
Cop	Dennis O'Connor
Scrawny Teen	Paul Brogen
Homeless Lady	Sharon Dyer
Bicycle Boy	Sean Ryan
Little Boy	Lance Paton
Little Girl	Jacelyn Holmes
Paper Boy	Hayden Christiansen

and Garry Robbins (Truck Driver), Sean Roberge (Desk Clerk), Robert Lewis Bush (Hotel Man), Louise Beaven (Old Lady), Cliff Woolner (Bus Driver), Deborah Theaker (Municipal Woman), Chuck Campbell (Customer), Carolyn Tweedle (Nurse), Thom Bell (Farmer), Mark Adriaans (Window Teen), Jack Moore-Wickham (Simon's Son—Johnny), David Austerwell, Richard Kohler, Kieran Sells, Laura Schmidt (Group of Kids)

Insurance investigator John Trent tracks down mysterious best-selling author Sutter Cane, whose horror novels seem to be inciting readers to strange and random acts of violence.

© New Line Productions, Inc.

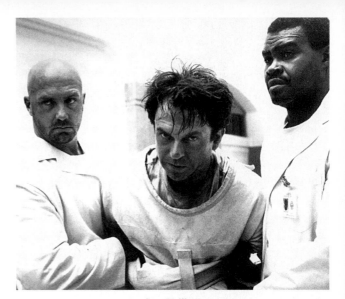

Sam Neill (c)

Charlton Heston   Jurgen Prochnow

Julie Carmen, Sam Neill

Sam Neill

Bridgette Wilson, Adam Sandler

Adam Sandler

Dina Platias, Adam Sandler

Brad Whitford, Adam Sandler

BILLY MADISON

(UNIVERSAL) Producer, Robert Simonds; Executive Producer, Fitch Cady; Director, Tamra Davis; Screenplay, Tim Herlihy, Adam Sandler; Photography, Victor Hammer; Designer, Perry Blake; Editor, Jeffrey Wolf; Music, Randy Edelman; Costumes, Marie-Bylvie Deveau; Casting, Jaki Brown-Karman, Todd Thaler, Deidre Bowen; DTS Stereo; Color; Rated PG-13; 88 minutes; February release

CAST

Bill Madison	Adam Sandler
Brian Madison	Darren McGavin
Veronica	Bridgette Wilson
Eric Gordon	Bradley Whitford
Max Anderson	Josh Mostel
Frank	Norm MacDonald
Jack	Mark Beltzman
Carl Alphonse	Larry Hankin
Juanita	Theresa Merritt
Miss Lippy	Dina Platias

and Hrant Alianak (Pete), Vincent Marino (Cook), Jack Mather (Clemens), Christopher Kelk (Janitor), Marc Donato (Nodding 1st Grader), Keith Cole, Chris Mei (Penguin), Conor Devitt (O'Doyle—Grade 1), Jared Durand (Scotty—Grade 1), Jessica Nakamura (Tricia—Grade 1), Helen Hughes (2nd Grade Teacher), Jacelyn Holmes (2nd Grader), Claire Cellucci (Attractive Lady), Shane Farberman (Clown), Al Maini (Chauffeur), Jared Cook (Ernie—Grade 3), Christian Matheson (O'Doyle—Grade 3), Kyle Bailey (Kyle), Vernon Chapman (Butler), Mandy Watts (Maid), Austin Pool (Dan—Grade 3), Gladys O'Connor (Tour Guide), Marica Bennett (4th Grade Teacher), Diane Douglas (Nurse), Tim Herlihy, Frank Nakashima (Architects), Joyce Gordon (Lunch Lady), Jordan Lerner-Ellis, Daniel Lerner-Ellis (Potheads), Robert Smigel (Mr. Oblaski), Melissa Korzenko (Nancy Connors), Colin Smith (O'Doyle—Grade 9), Jeff Moser (Paul), Amos Crawley (Rod), Tex Konig, Eduardo Gomez (Crazy Persons), Tanya Grout (Eric's Secretary), Benjamin Barrett, Matthew Ferguson (Tenth Graders), Sean Lett (O'Doyle—Grade 12), Stacey Wheal (Jennifer—Grade 3), Shanna Bresee (Susan—Grade 3), Michael Ayoub (Drama Teacher), Lawrence Nakamura (Lawn Guy), Gino Veltri (Rock Singer), James Downey (Principal), Bob Rodgers (Mr. O'Doyle), Margo Wladyka (Mrs. O'Doyle), Allison Robinson (Newswoman), Marcel Jean Gilles (Haitian Gardener), Suzanna Shebib (High School Girl), Justin Williams, Nicholas A. Catalano, Devon Codrington, Nicole Harrison, Lindsay Curran, Brandi Tower, Cassandra Forrester, Matthew Tempest, Michelle Toth, Craig MacIsaac, Tara Rooney, Robby Cavallari, Ryan Luis, Alanna Budhoo, Shomar Dejonge, Carmela Bigioni, Eric Aguilera (3rd Graders), Kevin Leroy, Kelly Childerhouse (Jet Skiers), Ken Shires (Fire-Eater), Chris Farley, Steve Buscemi

To prove that he is worthy of taking over his father's hotel chain, dim-witted Billy Madison must repeat grades 1 through 12 with no more than two weeks devoted to each grade.

© Universal City Studios, Inc.

Darren McGavin, Adam Sandler

John Leguizamo, Wesley Snipes, Patrick Swayze in *To Wong Foo Thanks for Everything, Julie Newmar*
© Universal City Studios/Amblin

Liam Neeson in *Rob Roy*
© United Artists Pictures

Alicia Silverstone in *Clueless*
© Paramount Pictures Corp.

Nicole Kidman in *To Die For*
© Columbia/Sony Pictures Entertainment

Harrison Ford, Julia Ormond in *Sabrina*
© Paramount Pictures Corp.

John Travolta in *Get Shorty*
© Metro-Goldwyn-Mayer, Inc.

Julie Delpy, Ethan Hawke in *Before Sunrise*
© Castle Rock Entertainment

Michael Douglas, Annette Bening in *The American President*
© Castle Rock Entertainment

Denzel Washington in *Devil in a Blue Dress*
© Sony Pictures Entertainment

Anthony Hopkins in *Nixon*
© Hollywood Pictures

Pierce Brosnan in *GoldenEye*
© United Artists Pictures, Inc.

Pocahontas, Meeko in *Pocahontas*
© Walt Disney Pictures

Operation Dumbo Drop
© Walt Disney Pictures

Mel Gibson in *Braveheart*
© Paramount Pictures Corp.

Ian McKellen in *Richard III*
© United Artists Pictures, Inc.

Patrick McGaw, Leonardo DiCaprio in *The Basketball Diaries*
© New Line Cinema

Sharon Stone, Robert De Niro in *Casino*
© Universal City Studios, Inc.

Olivia Hack, Jennifer Elise Cox, Christine Taylor, Christopher Daniel Barnes, Paul Sutera, Jesse Lee in *The Brady Bunch Movie*
© Paramount Pictures Corp.

Susan Sarandon, Sean Penn, Director Tim Robbins in
Dead Man Walking
© Gramercy Pictures

Robin Williams in *Jumanji*
© Sony Pictures Entertainment

Michael T. Weiss, Steven Weber in *Jeffrey*
© Orion Classics

Johnny Depp, Marlon Brando, Faye Dunaway in *Don Juan DeMarco*
© New Line Cinema

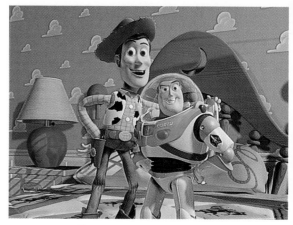

Woody, Buzz Lightyear in *Toy Story*
© Walt Disney Pictures

Richard Dreyfuss, Glenne Headly in *Mr. Holland's Opus*
© Hollywood Pictures

Elizabeth Berkeley in *Showgirls*
© United Artists Pictures Inc.

Johnny Depp, Christopher Walken in *Nick of Time*
©Paramount Pictures Corp.

Robert Downey, Jr. in *Restoration*
© Miramax Films

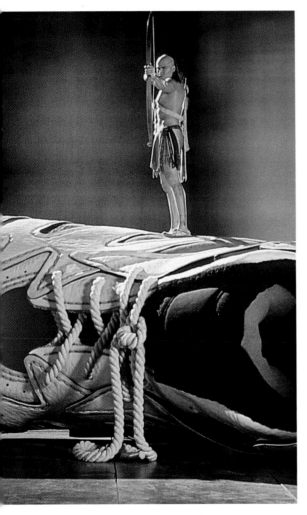

Litefoot in *The Indian in the Cupboard*
© Paramount Pictures Corp.

Debra Winger, Billy Crystal in *Forget Paris*
© Castle Rock Entertainment

Angela Bassett, Whitney Houston in *Waiting to Exhale*
© Twentieth Century Fox

Kate Winslet, Gemma Jones, Emilie Francois, Emma Thompson in
Sense and Sensibility
© Columbia Pictures

Aitana Sanchez-Gijon, Keanu Reeves in *A Walk in the Clouds*
© Twentieth Century Fox

Tom Hanks, Kevin Bacon, Bill Paxton in *Apollo 13*
© Universal City Studios, Inc.

Leonardo DiCaprio, Gene Hackman

Leonardo DiCaprio, Gene Hackman, Sharon Stone, Russell Crowe

THE QUICK AND THE DEAD

(TRISTAR) Producers, Joshua Donen, Allen Shapiro, Patrick Markey; Executive Producers, Toby Jaffe, Robert Tapert; Director, Sam Raimi; Screenplay, Simon Moore; Co-Producers, Chuck Binder, Sharon Stone; Photography, Dante Spinotti; Designer, Patrizia von Brandenstein; Editor, Pietro Scalia; Costumes, Judianna Makovsky; Music, Alan Silvestri; Casting, Francine Maisler; an IndieProd production, presented in association with Japan Satellite Broadcasting Inc.; Dolby Stereo/SDDS; Technicolor; Rated R; 103 minutes; February release

CAST

Ellen	Sharon Stone
Herod	Gene Hackman
Cort	Russell Crowe
Kid	Leonardo DiCaprio
Dog Kelly	Tobin Bell
Doc Wallace	Roberts Blossom
Eugene Dred	Kevin Conway
Sgt. Cantrell	Keith David
Ace Hanlon	Lance Henriksen
Horace the Bartender	Pat Hingle
Marshall	Gary Sinise
Scars	Mary Boone Junior
Katie	Olivia Burnette
Mattie Silk	Fay Masterson
Ratsy	Raynor Scheine
Charles Moonlight	Woody Strode
Blind Boy	Jerry Swindall
Gold Teeth Man	Scott Spiegel
Spotted Horse	Jonothon Gill
Gutzon	Sven-Ole Thorsen
Flat Nose Foy	Lennie Loftin
Foy's Boy	Matthew Gold
Carlos Montoya	Arturo Gastelum
Simp Dixon	David Cornell
Virgil Sparks	Josef Rainer
Young Ellen	Stacey Ramsower

and Tony Boggs (Zeb), Scott Ryder (Gunfighter), Timothy Patrick Quill (Man in Bar), Solomon Abrams (Man on Veranda), John Cameron (Bordello Swell), Bruce Campbell (Wedding Shemp), Michael Stone (Counselor), Butch Molina (Saloon Patron), Gergory Goossen, Mick Garris, Oliver Dear (Young Herod's Men)

Ellen arrives in the western town of Redemption to enter a gunslinger's contest, hoping to kill the town's evil ruler, Herod. This film marked the last appearance of actor Woody Strode, who died on Dec. 31, 1994.

© TriStar Pictures, Inc.

Keith David

Lance Henriksen

(top) Christine Taylor, Shelley Long, Christopher Daniel Barnes;
(middle) Jennifer Elise Cox, Henriette Mantel, Paul Sutera;
(bottom) Olivia Hack, Gary Cole, Jesse Lee

THE BRADY BUNCH MOVIE

(PARAMOUNT) Producers, Sherwood Schwartz, Lloyd J. Schwartz, David Kirkpatrick; Executive Producer, Alan Ladd, Jr.; Director, Betty Thomas; Screenplay, Laurice Elehwany, Rick Copp, Bonnie Turner, Terry Turner; Based on characters created by Sherwood Schwartz; Photography, Mac Ahlberg; Designer, Steven Jordan; Editor, Peter Teschner; Co-Producers, Barry Berg, Jenno Topping; Costumes, Rosanna Norton; Songs: The Brady Bunch by Sherwood Schwartz, Frank DeVol; Girl by Charles Fox, Norman Gimbel/performed by Davy Jones; Keep On by Tom Jenkins, Jackie Mills/performed by the Original Brady Bunch; Choreographer, Margaret T. Hickey-Perez; Dolby Digital Stereo; Deluxe color; Rated PG-13; 85 minutes; February release

CAST

Carol Brady	Shelley Long
Mike Brady	Gary Cole
Greg Brady	Christopher Daniel Barnes
Marcia Brady	Christine Taylor
Peter Brady	Paul Sutera
Jan Brady	Jennifer Elise Cox
Bobby Brady	Jesse Lee
Cindy Brady	Olivia Hack
Alice	Henriette Mantel
Sam	David Graf
Eric	Jack Noseworthy
Donna	Megan Ward
Mrs. Dittmeyer	Jean Smart
Mr. Dittmeyer	Michael McKean
Missy	Moriah Snyder
Noreen	Alanna Ubach
Doug	Shane Conrad
Holly	Marissa Ribisi
Charlie	R.D. Robb
Jason	David Leisure
Music Producer	Barry Williams
Mrs. Cummings	RuPaul
Trucker	Ann B. Davis
Themselves	Davy Jones, Micky Dolenz, Peter Tork
Coach	Christopher Knight
Grandma	Florence Henderson

and Steven Gilborn (Mr. Phillips), Alexander Pourtash (Mr. Amir), Keone Young (Mr. Watanabe), James Avery (Mr. Yeager), Yolanda Snowball (Mrs. Yeager), Robert Rothwell (Mr. Simmons), Elisa Pensler Gabrielli (Miss Lynley), David Proval (Electrician), Arnold Turner (Officer Axelrod), Darion Basco (Eddie), Gaura Vani Buchwald (Leon), Shannah Laumeister (Molly), Archie Hahn (Mr. Swanson), Beverly Archer (Mrs. Whitfield), Tammy Townsend (Danielle), Patrick Thomas O'Brien (Auctioneer), Eric Nies (Hip MC), Tully Jensen (Model), Jennifer Blanc (Valley Girl), Julie Payne (Mrs. Simmons), Tamara Mello (Stacy), Selma Archerd (Neighbor), James Randall White (Limo Driver), Lisa Sutton (Hooker), Dan Lipe, John R. Fors (Angry Neighbors), Kim Hasse (Student)

Comedy about a 1990s family, The Bradys, who are hopelessly stuck in an early 1970s timewarp when it comes to ideals and fashion. Based on the ABC comedy series which ran from 1969 through 1974. This film features original series members Florence Henderson, Ann B. Davis, Barry Williams, and Christopher Knight in cameo roles.

© Paramount Pictures

ROOMMATES

(HOLLYWOOD PICTURES) Producers, Ted Field, Scott Kroopf, Robert W. Cort; Executive Producers, Adam Leipzig, Ira Halberstadt; Director, Peter Yates; Screenplay, Max Apple, Stephen Metcalfe; Story, Max Apple; Photography, Mike Southon; Designer, Dan Bishop; Editor, John Tintori; Music, Elmer Bernstein; Costumes, Linda Donahue; Special Makeup Creator, Greg Cannom; Casting, Linda Lowy; an Interscope Communications/PolyGram Filmed Entertainment production in association with Nomura Babcock & Brown; Distributed by Buena Vista Pictures; Dolby Digital Stereo; Technicolor; Rated PG; 109 minutes; March release

Peter Falk, D.B. Sweeney

CAST

Rocky Holeczek	Peter Falk
Michael Holeczek	D.B. Sweeney
Beth	Julianne Moore
Judith	Ellen Burstyn
Bolek Krupa	Jan Rubes
Barbara	Joyce Reehling
Stash	Ernie Sabella
Burt Shook	John Cunningham

PITTSBURGH 1963

Michael (age 5)	Noah Fleiss
Betty	Lisa Davis
Kevin	Rohn Thomas
Milan Postevic	Karl Mackey
Funeral Priest	Rev. Zygmund Szarnicki
Bully at Baseball Game	Chance Marquez
Peanut Vendor	David Cutter

PITTSBURGH 1973

Michael (age 15)	David Tom
Bakery Saleswoman	Lillian Misko-Coury
Nun	Kate Young
Stavinski	Noah Abrams

Peter Falk

OHIO STATE UNIVERSITY & COLUMBUS 1983-85

E.R. Nurses	Ilana Levine, Pattie Carlson, Adrienne Wodenka
Attending Intern	Scott Cohen
Attending Physician	Daniel Corbin Cox
Toby	Joel de la Fuente
Deng	Raymond Wong
Zhang	Wanqing Wu
Liu	Zhe Sun
Fan	Mengze Shi
Cecilia	Ann Heekin
Cecilia's Son	Scott Kloes
Cecilia's Nurse	Vicki Ross-Norris
Professor Martin	Frankie Faison
Bartender	Peter Klemens
Reverend at Wedding	Rev. Donald R. Wilson
Good Morning Columbus Host	Ron Jaye

PITTSBURGH 1993

Lisa	Courtney Chase
Mo	Ryan Kelley
Papergirl	Katie Cardille-Rogal
Himself	Willard Scott
Judith's Lawyer	Bernard Canepari
Housekeeper	Dorothy Silver
Cleaning Lady	Rosa Gamarra-Thomson

THE PITTSBURGH MEDICAL CENTER

Dr. Minceberg	Gerry Becker
Surgeon	Jeffrey Howell
Recovery Room Nurse	Nelle Stokes
O.R. Nurse	Mary Marini, R.N.
Assisting Surgeon	Robert Gardner, MD
Profusionist	Robert Dyga

Drama-comedy about the relationship between feisty, unpredictable Rocky Holeczek and his grandson Michael, over a thirty-year period.

© Interscope Communications Inc./Nomura Babcock & Brown Unit One Film Partners

Ellen Burstyn, D.B. Sweeney, Julianne Moore, Peter Falk

George Wendt, Zachary Browne, Jonathan Taylor Thomas, Chevy Chase

MAN OF THE HOUSE

(WALT DISNEY PICTURES) formerly *Man 2 Man*; Producers, Bonnie Bruckheimer, Marty Katz; Executive Producer, Margaret South; Director, James Orr; Screenplay, James Orr, Jim Cruickshank; Story, David Peckinpah, Richard Jefferies; Photography, Jamie Anderson; Designer, Lawrence G. Paull; Editor, Harry Keramidas; Costumes, Tom Bronson; Music, Mark Mancina; Casting, Amy Lippens; Distributed by Buena Vista Pictures; Dolby Digital Stereo; Technicolor; Rated PG; 98 minutes; March release

CAST

Jack Sturges	Chevy Chase
Sandra Archer	Farrah Fawcett
Ben Archer	Jonathan Taylor Thomas
Chet Bronski	George Wendt
Lloyd Small	David Shiner
Red Sweeney	Art LaFleur
Joey Renda	Richard Portnow
Murray	Richard Foronjy
Tony	Peter Appel
Leonard Red Crow	Chief Leonard George
Frank Renda	George Greif
Bob Younger	Ron Canada
Hank Sweeney	Chris Miranda
Norman Bronski	Zachary Browne
Darryl Small	Spencer Vrooman
Monroe Hill	Nicholas Garrett
Young Ben	Jimmy Baker
Romeo Costanza	John DiSanti
Judges	Walter Marsh, Judith Maxie
Minister	Jim Smith
Bailiff	Sean Orr
Big Kids at School	Tony Sampson, Shane Meier

Ben Archer, jealous of his mother's fiancee, Jack Sturges, comes up with various schemes to drive Jack away.

(top) Jonathan Taylor Thomas, Chevy Chase, Farrah Fawcett; (bottom) Jonathan Taylor Thomas, Chevy Chase

Randy Quaid, Paul Reiser, Matthew Modine

Rob Reiner

Johnny Whitworth

Randy Quaid, Janeane Garofalo

BYE BYE LOVE

(20th CENTURY FOX) Producers, Gary David Goldberg, Brad Hall, Sam Weisman; Co-Producer, Michael MacDonald; Director, Sam Weisman; Screenplay, Gary David Goldberg, Brad Hall; Photography, Kenneth Zunder; Designer, Linda DeScenna; Music, J.A.C. Redford; Editor, Roger Bondelli; an UBU production; Dolby Digital Stereo; Deluxe color; Rated PG-13; 107 minutes; March release

CAST

Dave	Matthew Modine
Vic	Randy Quaid
Donny	Paul Reiser
Lucille	Janeane Garofalo
Susan	Amy Brenneman
Emma	Eliza Dushku
Walter	Ed Flanders
Kim	Maria Pitillo
Grace	Lindsay Crouse
Ben	Ross Malinger
Max	Johnny Whitworth
Hector	Wendell Pierce
Jed	Cameron Boyd
Michele	Mae Whitman
Claire	Jayne Brook
Heidi	Dana Wheeler-Nicholson
Meg	Amber Benson
Dr. Townsend	Rob Reiner
Sheila	Pamela Dillman
Phil	Brad Hall
Mikey	Danny Masterson
Waiter in Italian Restaurant	James Arone
Lindsay	Karlie M. Gavino Brown, Kirstie R. Gavino Brown
Sarah	Marguerite Weisman

and Max Ryan Ornstein (Ring Bearer at Wedding), Dean Williams (Wedding Photographer), Caroline Lagerfelt, Stephanie Shroyer (Mothers at McDonald's), Christopher Curry, Michael Bofshever (Dads at McDonald's), Daniel Weisman (Boy at McDonald's), Christina Massari (Girl at McDonald's), Brian Frank (Screener), Shang Forbes (Engineer), T.K. Meehan (T-Ball Coach), Mina Kolb (Dorothy), Geoffrey Woodhall (Gerald), Michael Spound (Mike), Joe Basile, Dennis Bowen (Fathers—Dad's Day Out), Donald Bishop (Grandfather), Kate Williamson (Grandmother), Nicholas Davey (Heidi's Son), Justin Garms (Sheila's Son), Lauren Kopit (Sheila's Daughter), Jack Black (DJ at Party), Keaton Simons (Party Dude), Juney Smith (Security Guard)

Three divorced fathers go through the weekly ritual of child custody exchange with their exes in this comedy-drama. This film was the last appearance of actor Ed Flanders, who died on Feb. 22, 1995.

© Twentieth Century Fox

Amy Brenneman, Paul Reiser

David Strathairn

Eric Bogosian, Jennifer Jason Leigh

DOLORES CLAIBORNE

(COLUMBIA) Producers, Taylor Hackford, Charles Mulvehill; Director, Taylor Hackford; Screenplay, Tony Gilroy; Based on the novel by Stephen King; Photography, Gabriel Beristain; Designer, Bruno Rubeo; Editor, Mark Warner; Costumes, Shay Cunliffe; Music, Danny Elfman; Casting, Nancy Klopper; a Castle Rock Entertainment presentation; Dolby Stereo; Panavision; Technicolor; Rated R; 131 minutes; March release

CAST

Dolores Claiborne...Kathy Bates
Selena St. George....................................Jennifer Jason Leigh
Vera Donovan ....Judy Parfitt
Detective John Mackey ....Christopher Plummer
Joe St. George...David Strathairn
Peter...Eric Bogosian
Constable Frank Stamshaw..................................John C. Reilly
Young Selena..Ellen Muth
Mr. Pease ....Bob Gunton
Magistrate ....Roy Cooper
Sammy Marchant ....Wayne Robson
Secretary...Ruth Marshall
Bartender ....Weldon Allen
Searcher ....Tom Gallant
Jack Donovan ....Kelly Burnett
Kids on Street ....Matt Appleby, Thomas Skinner
Ferry Vendor ....Vernon Steele
Young Selena (age 5) ....Taffara Jessica, Stella Murray
Crying Girl...Susan Lane
Detective Supervisors.......................Frank Adamson, Ed Rubin
Sheriff ....Sandy MacDonald
Moving Man ....Dean Eilertson

The estranged daughter of Dolores Claiborne returns to her hometown to find out why her mother has been accused of murdering the woman she took care of for years.

© Castle Rock Entertainment

Kathy Bates

Jennifer Jason Leigh, Christopher Plummer

Kathy Bates, Jennifer Jason Leigh

Judy Parfitt

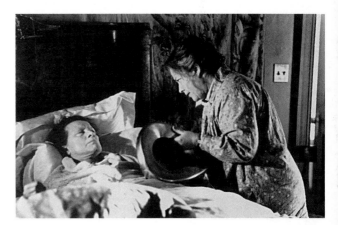

Judy Parfitt, Kathy Bates

Ellen Muth, Chistopher Plummer

LOSING ISAIAH

(PARAMOUNT) Producers, Howard W. Koch, Jr., Naomi Foner; Director, Stephen Gyllenhaal; Screenplay, Naomi Foner; Based upon the novel by Seth Margolis; Photography, Andrzej Bartkowiak; Designer, Jeannine C. Oppewall; Music, Mark Isham; Editor, Harvey Rosenstock; Costumes, Mary Malin; Casting, Aleta Chappelle; Dolby Digital Stereo; Deluxe color; Rated R; 108 minutes; March release

CAST

Margaret Lewin	Jessica Lange
Khaila Richards	Halle Berry
Charles Lewin	David Strathairn
Eddie Hughes	Cuba Gooding, Jr.
Hannah Lewin	Daisy Eagan
Isaiah	Marc John Jeffries
Kadar Lewis	Samuel L. Jackson
Marie	Joie Susannah Lee
Gussie	Regina Taylor
Caroline Jones	La Tanya Richardson
Judge Silbowitz	Jacqueline Brookes
Amir	Donovan Ian H. McKnight
Josie	Rikkia A. Smith
Ethel	Paulette McDaniels
Rehab Leader	Velma Austin
Group Leader	Glenda Starr Kelley
Toby Fredericks	Joan Kohn
Bill Fredericks	Patrick Clear
Heidi	Gabriella Santinelli
Liquor Store Clerk	Mike Bacarella
Liquor Store Cop #1	Mike Houlihan
Garbage Men	John Beasley, James "Ike" Eichling
Intern	James F. Tillett

and John Judd, Evan Lionel (Paramedics), Cheryl Hamada, Jackie Taylor (ER Nurses), Valerie Shull (Mrs. Ianelli), Laura Cerón (NICU Woman), Jackie Samuel (NICU Nurse), Deanna Dunagan (Dr. Goldfein), Mike Nussbaum (Dr. Jamison), Margaret Travolta (Sandra Harris), Eddie "Bo" Smith, Jr. (Alley Junkie), Jaqueline Fleming (File Cabinet Girl), Sibyl Offutt (Tenement Woman), Gregory Hollimon (Tenement Man), Rick Worthy, Torrence W. Murphy (Alley Men), Crystal Barnes, Sheila-Marie Robinson, La Taunya Bounds, Tamara Rutledge (Inmates), Valeri Ross (Day Care Teacher), Jacqueline Williams (Day Care Worker), Ora Jones (Day Care Woman), Nicholas Foster (Boy at Swings), Thomica Laquice Simmons (Neighbor Girl), Jennifer Crystal (Park Nanny); School Play: Matthew Brennan (Boy Singer), Denise Aguilar, Christy Lombardi, Hector Matos, Stephanie Mullin, Daniel Nudelman, Elbert Pagan, Jr., Kate Tash, Chris Tossing (Singers), Jonathan Rivera (Cymbals Player), Karen Luehne (Pianist), Brian Friedopfer, Paul Jorjorian (Ducks)

A white social worker adopts a black baby abandoned in a dumpster by its crack-addicted mother, only to have the birth mother seek custody years later.

© Paramount Pictures

Jessica Lange, La Tanya Richardson, David Strathairn

Cuba Gooding, Jr., Halle Berry

Samuel L. Jackson, Halle Berry

Halle Berry, Marc John Jeffries

Patrick Swayze, Oliver Platt

Nick Stahl, Patrick Swayze

Nick Stahl, Roger Aaron Brown

Stephen Lang, Scott Glenn

TALL TALE

(WALT DISNEY PICTURES) Producers, Joe Roth, Roger Birnbaum; Executive Producer, Bill Badalato; Director, Jeremiah Chechik; Screenplay, Steven L. Bloom, Robert Rodat; Photography, Janusz Kaminski; Designer, Eugenio Zanetti; Editor, Richard Chew; Costumes, Wayne Finkelman; Music, Randy Edelman; Visual Effects Supervisor, Erik Henry; Casting, Jackie Burch; Dolby Digital Stereo; Panavision; Technicolor; Rated PG; 96 minutes; March release

CAST

Pecos Bill ....Patrick Swayze
Paul Bunyan ....Oliver Platt
John Henry ....Roger Aaron Brown
Daniel Hackett ....Nick Stahl
J.P. Stiles ....Scott Glenn
Jonas Hackett ....Stephen Lang
Head Thug Pug ....Jared Harris
Calamity Jane ....Catherine O'Hara
Sahra Hackett ....Moira Harris
Man in Top Hat ....Joseph Grifasi
Grub ....John P. Ryan
Zeb ....Scott Wilson
Bronson ....Bert Kramer
Sheriff ....Eric Lawson
Captain of Industry ....Bill Rodgers
Hag in Alley ....Susan Barnes
Doctor ....John Nance
Bar Room Bully ....Mike Moroff
Barkeep..Richard Zobel
Farmers ....Michael J. Kosta, Timothy Glenn Riley
Lumberjacks...Darwyn Swalve, Jay S. York
Bettors ....Kevin Brown, E.B. Meyers
Spectator..James Oscar Lee
Big Jim..Sal Jenco
Logging Foreman..Burgess Meredith
and Michael, Ronnie, Niko (Widowmaker), Luke, Belle (Babe), Kit, Kate (Cold Molasses), Violet (Hairless Cat), Dudley (Dancing Dog), Sampson (Himself), Manny, Moe & Jack (Vultures)

Young Daniel Hackett is joined in his fight to save his family's land from a greedy railroad baron by three American legends: Pecos Bill, Paul Bunyan, and John Henry.

© The Walt Disney Company

Chris Farley, Rob Lowe

David Spade, Chris Farley, Brian Dennehy

TOMMY BOY

(PARAMOUNT) Producer, Lorne Michaels; Executive Producer, Robert K. Weiss; Director, Peter Segal; Screenplay, Bonnie Turner, Terry Turner; Photography, Victor J. Kemper; Designer, Stephen J. Lineweaver; Editor, William Kerr; Co-Producer, Barnaby Thompson; Associate Producer, Michael Ewing; Music, David Newman; Costumes, Patti Unger; Casting, Pamela Basker; a Lorne Michaels production; Dolby Digital Stereo; Deluxe color; Rated PG-13; 98 minutes; March release

CAST

Tommy Callahan	Chris Farley
Richard Hayden	David Spade
Big Tom Callahan	Brian Dennehy
Beverly	Bo Derek
Paul	Rob Lowe
Michelle	Julie Warner
Rittenhauer	Sean McCann
Zalinsky	Dan Aykroyd
Reilly	Zach Grenier
Gilmore	James Blendick
Young Tommy	Clinton Turnbull
Young Richard	Ryder Britton
Skittish Student	Paul Greenberg
Frat Boys	Graeme Millington, Michael Cram, Dean Marshall, Trent McMullen
Danny	Philip Williams
Sammy	David "Skippy" Ward
Louis	Roy Lewis
Obnoxious Bus Kid	Austin Pool
R.T.	William Dunlop
Priest	Jack Jessop
Singer at wedding	Michael Dunston

and David Hemblen (Archer), George Kinamis, Dov Tiefenbach, Mark Zador (Kids at Lake), Helen Hughes (Boardroom Lady), J.R. Zimmerman (Boardroom Man), Robert K. Weiss, Reg Dreger, Lloyd White ("No" Managers), David Huband (Gas Attendant), Hayley Gibbins (Little Girl at Carnival), Julianne Gillies (Brady's Receptionist), Addison Bell (Mr. Brady), Cory Sevier (Boy in Commerical), Maria Vacratsis (Helen), Colin Fox (Nelson), Lorri Bagley (Woman at Pool), Lynn Cunningham (Pretty Hitchhiker), David Calderisi, Sven Van De Ven, Errol Sitahal ("Yes" Executives), Marc Strange ("Toy Car" Executive), Michael Ewing (Ticket Agent), Adrian Truss, Christopher John (Cops), Henry Gomez (Airport Cop), Lindsay Leese (Reservationist), Camilla Scott (Stewardess), Bunty Webb (Large Woman), Marilyn Boyle (Woman with Pen), Gino Marrocco (Cabbie), Gil Filar (Kid in Bank), Jonathan Wilson (Marty), Sandi Stahlbrand (News Reporter), Ron James, Brian Kaulback (Bank Guards), Mark Ingram, Jim Codrington (Security Guards), Pat Moffatt (Mrs. Nelson), Raymond Hunt, Robbie Rox, Jerry Schaeffer (Restaurant Regulars), Taylor Segal (Flower Girl)

Affable screw-up Tommy Callahan faces his greatest challenge when the family business is left in his hands.

© Paramount Pictures

Bo Derek

Chris Farley, David Spade

Seth Gilliam, Thandie Newton

Nick Nolte, Greta Scacchi

Gwyneth Paltrow, Nick Nolte

JEFFERSON IN PARIS

(TOUCHSTONE) Producer, Ismail Merchant; Executive Producers, Donald Rosenfeld, Paul Bradley; Director, James Ivory; Screenplay, Ruth Prawer Jhabvala; Photography, Pierre Lhomme; Music, Richard Robbins; Editors, Andrew Marcus, Isabel Lorente; Designer, Guy-Claude Francois; Costumes, Jenny Beavan, John Bright; Hairdressing/Makeup, Carol Hemming; Co-Producer, Humbert Balsan; Casting, Sylvie Brocheré, Joanna Merlin, Celestia Fox; a Merchant Ivory Productions presentation; Distributed by Buena Vista Pictures; Dolby Digital Stereo; Color; Rated PG-13; 144 minutes; March release

CAST

AT JEFFERSON'S HOUSE, THE HOTEL DE LANGEAC

Thomas Jefferson..Nick Nolte
Patsy Jefferson ....Gwyneth Paltrow
Polly Jefferson ....Estelle Eonnet
Sally Hemings ....Thandie Newton
James Hemings ....Seth Gilliam
William Short..Todd Boyce
John Trumbull...Nigel Whitmey
Monsieur Petit..Nicolas Silberg
and Catherine Samie (Cook), Lionel Robert (Cook's Helper), Stanislas Carré de Malberg, Jean Rupert (Surgeons), Yvette Petit (Dressmaker), Paolo Mantini (Hairdresser), F. Van Den Driessche, Humbert Balsan, Michel Rois (Mutilated Officers), Bob Sessions (James Byrd), Jeffrey Justin Ribier (Mulatto Boy), Marc Tissot (Construction Foreman)

AT LAFAYETTE'S

Maria Cosway ....Greta Scacchi
Richard Cosway ....Simon Callow
Marquis de Lafayette...Lambert Wilson
Adrienne de Lafayette ....Elsa Zylberstein
D'Hancarville ....Jean-Pierre Aumont
and Christopher Thompson (Interpretor), Olivier Galfione (Chevalier de Saint-Colombe), Anthony Valentine (British Ambassador), Steve Kalfa (Dr. Guillotin), Jean-François Perrier, Eric Genovese, Bruno Putzulu, Philippe Mareuil, Philippe Bouclet (Liberal Aristocrats), André Julien, Jacques Herlin (Savants), Elizabeth Kaza, Agathe de la Boulaye (Card Players), Abdel Bouthegmes (Lafayette's Indian)

AT VERSAILLES

Louis XVI...Michael Lonsdale
Marie Antoinette ....Charlotte de Turckheim
and Damien Groelle (The Dauphin), Valerie Toledano (Madame Elizabeth), Vernon Dobtche (King's Translator), Mathilde Vitry, Catherine Chevalier, Laure Killing (Ladies of the Court), Felix Malinbaum (Captain of the Guard), Hervé Hiolle (King's Messenger), Christian Vurpillot (Archbishop), Philippe Girard, Eric Berg (Post Office Spies)

AT THE PANTHÉMONT ABBEY

The Abbesse...Nancy Marchand
Julia..Jessica Lloyd
and Olivia Bonamy, Sarah Mesguich, Virginie Desarnault (Schoolgirls), Sylvie Laguna (Nun), Sandrine Piau, Sophie Daneman (Singers), Denis Fouqueret (Bishop), Annie Didion (Crazed Nurse)

AT DOCTOR MESMER'S

Doctor Mesmer ....Daniel Mesguich
Assistants ....Yan Duffas, Thibault de Montalembert
and Magali Leiris, Valentine Varella (Patients), Gabrielle Islwyn (Singer with Megaphone)

PIKE COUNTY, OHIO

Madison Hemings..James Earl Jones
Mary Hemings...Beatrice Winde
Reporter ....Tim Choate

AT THE DÉSERT DE RETZ

Sylvia Berge, Philippine Leroy-Beaulieu, Martine Sarcey, Céline Samie, Jean-Marie Lhomme, Luke Pontifell, Scott Thrun (Head and Heart Game)

AT THE OPERA

William Christie (Conductor), Jean-Paul Fouchécourt (Dardanus), Ismail Merchant (Tipoo Sultan's Ambassador), Martine Chevalier (Mademoiselle Contat), Valerie Lang (Demented Woman)

AT THE PALAIS ROYAL

Vincent Cassel (Camille Desmoulins), Jean Dautremay (Shopkeeper), Alban Thierry, Alain Picard, Jean-Marc Hervé (Puppeteers)

Historical drama speculates on the intimate relationships Thomas Jefferson had with the aristocratic Maria Cosway and his daughter's nurse, Sally Hemings, during his term as American ambassador to France (1784–1789).

© Merchant Ivory Productions

TANK GIRL

(UNITED ARTISTS) Producers, Richard B. Lewis, Pen Densham, John Watson; Executive Producers, Aron Warner, Tom Astor; Director, Rachel Talalay; Screenplay, Tedi Sarafian; Based on the comic strip created by Alan Martin, Jamie Hewlett; Co-Producer, Christian L. Rehr; Photography, Gale Tattersall; Designer, Catherine Hardwicke; Editor, James R. Symons; Costumes, Arianne Philips; Music, Graeme Revell; Rippers Designer, Stan Winston; Casting, Pam Dixon Mickelson; Stunts, Walter Scott; a Trilogy Entertainment Group production; Distributed by MGM/UA; DTS Stereo; Deluxe color; Rated R; 103 minutes; March release

CAST

Tank Girl (Rebecca Buck)	Lori Petty
T-Saint	Ice-T
Jet Girl	Naomi Watts
Sergeant Small	Don Harvey
Booga	Jeff Kober
DeeTee	Reg E. Cathey
Donner	Scott Coffey
Kesslee	Malcolm McDowell
Sam	Stacy Linn Ramsower
Sub Girl	Ann Cusack
Richard	Brian Wimmer
Rat Face	Iggy Popp
Model	Dawn Robinson
Max	Billy L. Sullivan
Che'tsai	James Hong
Captain Derouche	Charles Lucia
Dr. Nikita	Roz Witt
Pilot	Braxton Karnes
Razor Ray	Will Nahkohe Strickland
Zack	Charles Robert Harden

and Harlan Clark, Doug Jones, Ata Scanlan, Alvarez Wortham (Additional Rippers), Tom Noga (Foreman), Bo Jesse Christopher (Town), John David Bland (Trooper Wayne), Jo Farkas (Sand Hermit), Stanton Davis (Father), Jillian Balch (Mother), Richard Schiff (Trooper in Trench), Kane Picoy (Trooper #1), Troy Sartoni (Jet Pilot), Beth DePatie (Prostitute), Clayton Landey (Guard at Front Entrance), Roger Bohman (Technician), Frank Walton (Trooper in Basement), Richard Scott Sarafian (Flyer Trooper), Aaron Kuhr (Trooper at Pump Hanger), Kelly Cousineau (Young Rebecca), Chief Gordon, Kelly Kerby (Troopers), Jim Sullivan (Semi Driver), William A. Doyle (Dig Site Worker), Robert "Rock" Galotti (Long Hair), Peer Ebbighausen (Flyer Pilot)

In the year 2033, Rebecca Buck and her army of rippers take on the Water and Power Company to bring water back to the dying, arid wasteland that has consumed the earth.

© United Artists Pictures Inc.

Scott Coffey, Lori Petty, Ice-T, Naomi Watts, Jeff Kober

Malcolm McDowell

BULLETPROOF HEART

(KEYSTONE/REPUBLIC) formerly Killer; Producers, Robert Vince, William Vince; Executive Producers, Robert Sigman, Gary Delfiner, Michael Strange; Director/Story, Mark Malone; Screenplay, Gordon Melbourne; Photography, Tobias Schliessler; Designer, Lynne Stopkewich; Music, Graeme Coleman; Editor, Robin Russell; Casting, Abra Edelman, Elisa Goodman, Marcia Shulman; Ultra-Stereo; Color; Rated R; 100 minutes; March release

CAST

Mick	Anthony LaPaglia
Fiona	Mimi Rogers
Archie	Matt Craven
George	Peter Boyle
Laura	Monika Schnarre
Dr. Alstricht	Joseph Maher
Hellbig	Mark Acheson
F.B.I. Agent	Philip Hayes
Partygoers	Christopher Mark Pinhey, Claudio De Victor
Masseuse	Justine Priestley

A hitman finds himself falling in love with a mysterious woman he has been ordered to kill.

© Keystone Pictures Inc.

Anthony LaPaglia, Mimi Rogers

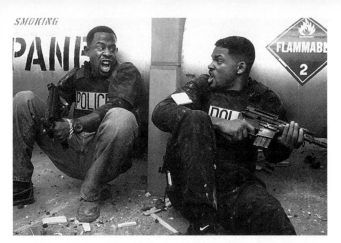

Martin Lawrence, Will Smith

Tcheky Karyo

BAD BOYS

(COLUMBIA) Producers, Don Simpson, Jerry Bruckheimer; Executive Producers, Bruce S. Pustin, Lucas Foster; Director, Michael Bay; Screenplay, Michael Barrie, Jim Mulholland, Doug Richardson; Story, George Gallo; Photography, Howard Atherton; Designer, John Vallone; Editor, Christian Wagner; Costumes, Bobbie Read; Music, Mark Mancina; Casting, Francine Maisler, Lynn Kressel; Dolby SDDS Stereo; Technicolor; Rated R; 119 minutes; April release

CAST

Marcus Burnett	Martin Lawrence
Mike Lowrey	Will Smith
Julie Mott	Téa Leoni
Fouchet	Tcheky Karyo
Captain Howard	Joe Pantoliano
Theresa Burnett	Theresa Randle
Alison Sinclair	Marg Helgenberger
Decoy	Lisa Boyle
Carjacker	Michael Taliferro
Eddie Dominguez	Emmanuel Xuereb
Noah Trafficante	Marc Macaulay
Kuni	Ralph Gonzalez
Ferguson	Vic Manni
Casper	Frank John Hughes
Andy	Mike Kirton
Officer Bill O'Fee	Will Knickerbocker
Megan Burnett	Tiffany Samuels
James Burnett	Cory Hodges
Quincy Burnett	Scott Cumberbatch
Francine	Anna Thomson
Detectives	Joey Romano, Sam Ayers
Detective Sanchez	Nestor Serrano
Detective Ruiz	Julio Oscar Mechoso
Jojo	Michael Imperioli
Max Logan	Karen Alexander
Woman at boxing gym	Fawn Reed
Lois Fields	Heather Davis
Chet the Doorman	Saverio Guerra
Yvette	Maureen Gallagher
Ether Van Driver	Juan Cejas
Ether Van Boss	Ed Amatrudo
Club Bartender	Jimmy Franzo

and Tony Bolano (Drunk Guy at Urinal), Shaun Toub (Store Clerk), Marty McSorley, Norman Max Maxwell (Henchmen), Kevin Corrigan (Elliot), Buddy Bolton (Wally), Stan Miller (News Anchor), Doug Jones (Man #1), John Spider Salley (Hacker "Fletcher"), Dana Mark (Police Technician), Mario Ernesto Sanchez (Drug Buyer)

Miami cops Marcus Burnett and Mike Lowrey investigate the theft of $100 million in heroin from the police department's evidence room.

© Columbia Pictures Industries, Inc.

Martin Lawrence, Will Smith

Martin Lawrence, Will Smith, Téa Leoni

Brian McCardie, Gilly Gilchrist, Liam Neeson, Jason Flemyng, Eric Stoltz, Ewan Stewart

Jessica Lange

John Hurt

Tim Roth

ROB ROY

(UNITED ARTISTS) Producers, Peter Broughan, Richard Jackson; Executive Producer/Director, Michael Caton-Jones; Screenplay, Alan Sharp; Photography, Karl Walter Lindenlaub; Designer, Assheton Gorton; Editor, Peter Honess; Costumes, Sandy Powell; Music, Carter Burwell; Co-Producer, Larry DeWaay; Casting, Susie Figgis; a Talisman production; Distributed by MGM/UA; DTS Digitial Stereo; J-D-C Scope; Deluxe color; Rated R; 134 minutes; April release

CAST

Robert Roy MacGregor (Rob Roy)	Liam Neeson
Mary MacGregor	Jessica Lange
Marquis of Montrose	John Hurt
Cunningham	Tim Roth
Alan McDonald	Eric Stoltz
Argyll	Andrew Keir
Killearn	Brian Cox
Alasdair	Brian McCardie
Guthrie	Gilbert Martin
Betty	Vicki Masson
Iain	Gilly Gilchrist
Gregor	Jason Flemyng
Coll	Ewan Stewart
Sibbald	David Hayman
Ranald	Brian McArthur
Duncan	David Palmer
Tinker Woman	Myra McFadyen
Ceilidh Singer	Karen Matheson
Morag	Shirley Henderson
Referee	John Murtagh
Tavern Lad	Bill Gardiner
Servant Boy	Valentine Nwanze
Gutherie's Opponent	Richard Bonehill

Robert Roy MacGregor runs afoul of the Marquis of Montrose when the money he has borrowed from him is stolen by the evil Cunningham. Previous versions of the Rob Roy legend include the 1954 Disney film Rob Roy, the Highland Rogue, *starring Richard Todd and Glynis Johns.*

Tim Roth received an Oscar nomination for his performance.

Jessica Lange, Liam Neeson

Liam Neeson

Jessica Lange, Liam Neeson

Eric Stoltz

DON JUAN DEMARCO

(NEW LINE CINEMA) Producers, Francis Ford Coppola, Fred Fuchs, Patrick Palmer; Executive Producers, Ruth Vitale, Michael DeLuca; Director/Screenplay, Jeremy Leven; Co-Executive Producers, Robert Newmyer, Brian Reilly, Jeffrey Silver; Photography, Ralf Bode; Designer, Sharon Seymour; Editor, Tony Gibbs; Costumes, Kirsten Everberg; Music, Michael Kamen; Song: "Have You Ever Really Loved a Woman" by Michael Kamen, Bryan Adams, Robert John Lang/performed by Bryan Adams; Casting, Lynn Kressel; an American Zoetrope production; Dolby Digital Stereo; Film House color; Rated PG-13; 97 minutes; April release

CAST

Dr. Jack Mickler	Marlon Brando
Don Juan DeMarco	Johnny Depp
Marilyn Mickler	Faye Dunaway
Dona Ana	Geraldine Pailhas
Dr. Paul Showalter	Bob Dishy
Dona Inez	Rachel Ticotin
Dona Julia	Talisa Soto
Woman in Restaurant	Marita Geraghty
Detective Sy Tobias	Richard Sarafian
Grandmother DeMarco	Tresa Hughes
Dr. Bill Dunsmore	Stephen Singer
Don Antonio	Franc Luz
Don Alfonzo	Carmen Argenziano
Sultana Gulbeyaz	Jo Champa
Nurse Alvira	Esther Scott
Nurse Gloria	Nada Despotovich
Judge Ryland	Gilbert Lewis
Rocco Compton	"Tiny" Lister, Jr.
Baba the Eunuch	Tom Mardirosian
Woman's Date	Al Corley
Nicholas the Doorman	Nick La Tour
Sultan	Bill Capizzi
Dona Querida	Patricia Mauceri
Delivery Man #1	Cliff Weissman
Young Don Juan	Michael Malota
Flower Girl	Renee Sicignano
Waiter	Trevor Long
Auctioneer	Sanjay
Night Duty Nurse	Diane Lee

and Joni Kramer, Shirlee Reed (Nurses), Ken Gutstein (Doctor #1), Adriana Jardini (Social Worker), Robert Polanco Rodriguez (Priest), Roberta Danza, Bridget Mariano, Christine Wolfe (Nuns), Jose Hernandez (Bandleader), Selena Perez (Singer), Rosendo Casillas, Esperanza Donlucas, Ramirez Filberto, Santiago Garcia, Ernesto V. Molina (Mariachi Band)

Psychiatrist Jack Mickler becomes fascinated by a young patient who claims to be the world's greatest seducer of women, Don Juan.

The song "Have You Ever Really Loved a Woman" received an Oscar nomination.

Johnny Depp

Geraldine Pailhas

Marlon Brando, Faye Dunaway

Talisa Soto

Johnny Depp, Talisa Soto

Faye Dunaway

Geraldine Pailhas, Johnny Depp

Johnny Depp

Faye Dunaway, Marlon Brando

Geraldine Pailhas, Johnny Depp

A GOOFY MOVIE

(WALT DISNEY PICTURES) Producer, Dan Rounds; Director, Kevin Lima; Screenplay, Jymn Magon, Chris Matheson, Brian Pimental; Story, Jymn Magon; Editor, Gregory Perler; Songs, Tom Snow & Jack Feldman, Patrick DeRemer & Roy Freeland; Music, Carter Burwell; Art Directors, Wendell Luebbe, Lawrence Leker; Designer, Fred Warter; Associate Producer, Patrick Reagan; Animation Supervisors, Nancy Beiman, Matias Marcos, Stéphane Sainte-Foi, Dominique Monfery; Distributed by Buena Vista Pictures; Dolby Digital Stereo; Technicolor; Rated G; 76 minutes; April release

VOICE CAST

Goofy	Bill Farmer
Max	Jason Marsden
Pete	Jim Cummings
Roxanne	Kellie Martin
PJ	Rob Paulsen
Principal Mazur	Wallace Shawn
Stacey	Jenna Von Oy
Bigfoot	Frank Welker
Lester	Kevin Lima
Waitress	Florence Stanley
Miss Maples	Jo Anne Worley
Powerline	Tevin Campbell
Max's Singing Voice	Aaron Lohr
Photo Studio Girl	Brittany Alyse Smith
Lester's Grinning Girl	Robyn Richards
Lisa	Julie Brown
Tourist Kid	Klée Bragger
Chad	Joey Lawrence
Possum Park Emcee	Pat Butrum
Mickey Mouse	Wayne Allwine
Security Guard	Herschel Sparber

and Dante Basco, Pat Carroll, Steve Moore, Sheryl Bernstein, E.G. Daily, Brian Pimental, Corey Burton, Carol Holliday, Jason Willinger (Additional Voices)

Goofy, hoping to bond with his son Max, takes the reluctant teenager on a fishing trip.

© The Walt Disney Company

Goofy, Max

SEARCH AND DESTROY

(OCTOBER) Producers, Ruth Charny, Dan Lupovitz, Elie Cohn; Executive Producers, Avi Lerner, Danny Dimbort, Martin Scorsese; Director, David Salle; Screenplay, Michael Almereyda; Based on the play by Howard Korder; Associate Producers, Trevor Short, Boaz Davidson, Mark Blum; Photography, Bobby Bukowski, Michael Spiller; Designer, Robin Standefer; Music, Elmer Bernstein; Costumes, Donna Zakowska; Casting, Billy Hopkins, Suzanne Smith, Kerry Barden; a Nu Image production in association with Autumn Pictures; Color; Rated R; 89 minutes; April release

CAST

Martin Mirkheim	Griffin Dunne
Marie Davenport	Illeana Douglas
Dr. Luthor Waxling	Dennis Hopper
Kim Ulander	Christopher Walken
Ron	John Turturro
Lauren Mirkheim	Rosanna Arquette
Roger	Ethan Hawke
Dorothy	Nicole Burdette
Daniel Strong	Robert Knepper
Rob	David Thornton
Pamfilo	Angel David
Young Daniel Strong	Jason Ferraro
The Accountant	Martin Scorsese
Tailor	Dan Hedaya
Dead World Girl	Tahnee Welch

and Linda Wahl (Party Guest), Laurie Godet (Model), Randy Pearlstein (Desk Clerk), Vincent Angell (Security Guard), Tanya Polkhotte (Kim's Secretary), Karole Armitage (Red River Valley Dancer), Ken Simmons (Nunez), Frank Girardeau (State Trooper)

Owing thousands of dollars in back taxes, Martin Mirkheim hopes to make a fortune turning Dr. Luthor Waxling's self-help book Daniel Strong *into a film. Griffin Dunne repeats his role from the 1992 Broadway production.*

© October Films

Griffin Dunne, John Turturro, Christopher Walken

STUART SAVES HIS FAMILY

(PARAMOUNT) Producers, Lorne Michaels, Trevor Albert; Executive Producers, C.O. Erickson, Dinah Minot; Director, Harold Ramis; Screenplay, Al Franken, based on his book *I'm Good Enough I'm Smart Enough and Doggone It People Like Me!*; Photography, Lauro Escorel; Designer, Joseph T. Garrity; Editors, Pembroke Herring, Craig Herring; Costumes, Susie DeSanto; Music, Marc Shaiman; Associate Producer, Whitney White; Casting, Nancy Foy; Presented in association with Constellation Films; Dolby Digital Stereo; Deluxe color; Rated PG-13; 98 minutes; April release

Vincent D'Onofrio, Lesley Boone, Al Franken, Shirley Knight, Harris Yulin

CAST

Stuart Smalley	Al Franken
Julia	Laura San Giacomo
Donnie Smalley	Vincent D'Onofrio
Stuart's Mom	Shirley Knight
Stuart's Dad	Harris Yulin
Jodie	Lesley Boone
Kyle	John Link Graney
Aunt Paula	Marjorie Lovett
Smalley Uncles	Walt Robles, Erik Cord, Denver Mattson
Young Stuart	Grant Hoover
Young Donnie	Cory Milano
Young Jodie	Michelle Horn
Mr. Dimmit	Harris Laskawy
Ajax Spokesman	Tom Dugan
Roz Weinstock	Camille Saviola
Laurie	Bess Meyer
Mea C.	Julia Sweeney
Makeover Artist	Patrick Kerr
Fred	Aaron Lustig
Carl	Fred Applegate
Jerry	Darrell Larson
Intervention Counselor	Dakin Matthews
Lawyer	Jeffrey Joseph

and Marte Boyle Slout (Madelyn Doyle), Joe Flaherty (Cousin Ray), Robin Duke (Cousin Denise), Lewis Arquette (Cemetery Official), Michael G. Hagerty (Cop), Peter Torokvei (Minister), Allen Garfield (Maitre D'), Pamela Brüll (Diner), Walter Olkewicz (Larry Skoag), Jeremy Roberts (Brad Skoag), Steven Kampmann (Stan Brunner), Robert Curtis-Brown (Andy), Violet Ramis (P.A.), Aloma Wright (Autograph Seeker), Rachel Miller (Woman with Subpoena), Kurt Fuller (Von Arks), Walter S. Beaver (Orville Egeberg), Michael C. McCarthy (Merl Egeberg), David Pasquesi (Tollefson), Richard Riehle (Judge), R.M. Haley (Bailiff), Theodore Rami (Hal), Rogan Wilde (Ted)

After his self-help TV show is cancelled, Stuart Smalley finds himself back home in Minneapolis for a relative's funeral, a situation which causes him to once again face his disfunctional family. Comedy based on the skits which Al Franken first performed on TV's "Saturday Night Live."

Al Franken, Laura San Giacomo

Al Franken

AMATEUR

(SONY PICTURES CLASSICS) Producers, Ted Hope, Hal Hartley; Executive Producers, Jerome Brownstein, Lindsay Law, Scott Meek, Yves Marmion; Director/Screenplay, Hal Hartley; Photography, Michael Spiller; Music, Jeff Taylor, Ned Rifle; Designer, Steve Rosenzweig; Editor, Steve Hamilton; Casting, Billy Hopkins, Suzanne Smith; a UGC in association with American Playhouse Theatrical Films/La Sept Cinema and Channel Four Films presentation of a Zenith/True Fiction Pictures production; Dolby Stereo; Color; Rated R; 105 minutes; April release

CAST

Isabelle	Isabelle Huppert
Thomas	Martin Donovan
Sofia	Elina Lowensohn
Edward	Damian Young
Jan	Chuck Montgomery
Kurt	David Simonds
Officer Melville	Pamela Stewart
Irate Woman	Erica Gimpel
Waitress	Jan Leslie Harding
Frank, the Cook	Terry Alexander
Usher	Holt McCallany
Warren	Hugh Palmer
Doorman at club	Michael Imperioli
Detective	Angel Caban
Bartender	Emmanuel Xuereb
Taxi Driver	Lennie Loftin
George, the Pornographer	David Greenspan
Kid reading *The Odyssey*	Adria Tennor
Girl Squatter	Parker Posey
Boy Squatter	Dwight Ewell

and Currie Graham (Video Store Clerk), Jamie Harrold (Pizza Guy), Patricia Scanlon (Young Irate Mother), James McCauley, Benny Nieves (Policemen), David Troup (Guard), Tim Blake Nelson (Young Detective), Marissa Copeland (Sister at Door), Dael Orlandersmith (Mother Superior), Michael Gaston (Sharpshooter), Paul Schulze (Cop who Shoots Thomas)

An ex-nun-turned-pornography-writer hooks up with an amnesiac to put together the pieces of his past.

© Sony Pictures Entertainment

Isabelle Huppert, Martin Donovan

Damian Young, Pamela Stewart

Nancy Allison Wolfe, Liza D'Agostino

BAR GIRLS

(ORION CLASSICS) Producers, Laran Hoffman, Marita Giovanni; Co-Producer, Doug Lindeman; Director, Marita Giovanni; Screenplay, Lauran Hoffman, based on her play; Photography, Michael Ferris; Editor, Carter DeHaven; Costumes, Houston Sams; Foto-Kem color; Rated R; 95 minutes; April release

CAST

Loretta	Nancy Allison Wolfe
Rachael	Liza D'Agostino
J.R.	Camila Griggs
Noah	Michael Harris
Veronica	Justine Slater
Annie	Lisa Parker
Celia	Pam Raines
Tracy	Paula Sorge
Sandy	Cece Tsou
Kimba	Caitlin Stansbury
Destiny	Patti Sheehan
Lee	Lee Everett
Cafe Waitress	Betsy Burke
Laurie	Laurie Jones
Scorp	Chastity Bono

Comedy about the lesbian dating scene in Los Angeles, focusing specifically on the relationship between Loretta and Rachael.

© Orion Pictures Corporation

Joseph Mazzello, Brad Renfro

Annabella Sciorra, Joseph Mazzello

Brad Renfro, Joseph Mazzello

Joseph Mazzello, Brad Renfro

THE CURE

(UNIVERSAL) Producers, Mark Burg, Eric Eisner; Executive Producers, Todd Baker, Bill Borden; Director, Peter Horton; Screenplay, Robert Kuhn; Photography, Andrew Dintenfass; Designer, Armin Ganz; Editor, Anthony Sherin; Music, Dave Grusin; Casting, Mali Finn; a co-presentation of Island Pictures; DTS Stereo; Deluxe color; Rated PG-13; 95 minutes; April release

CAST

Dexter	Joseph Mazzello
Erik	Brad Renfro
Linda	Annabella Sciorra
Gail	Diana Scarwid
Dr. Stevens	Bruce Davison
Pony	Nicky Katt
Tyler	Aeryk Egan
Tyler's Girlfriend	Delphine French
Tyler's Buddies	Andrew Broder, Jeremy Howard
Elderly Woman in Street	Rosemary Corman
Garbage Men	T. Mychael Rambo, David Alan Smith
Angry Woman	Delia Jurek
Jim	Craig Gierl
Angle	Renee Humphrey
Cheryl	Laurie A. Sinclair
Bus Station Clerk	Stephen D'Ambrose
Nurse Snyder	Shirley Venard
Nurse Murphy	Mary McCusker
Male Nurse	Peter Moore
Final Doctor	Rodney W. England, M.D.
Funeral Director	Bill Schoppert
Funeral Attendant	Samantah Lemole

and John Lynch, John Beasley, Raymond Nelson, Scott Stockton, Dale Handevidt (Skippers)

Young Erik finds himself being drawn to his next door neighbor, Dexter, an ostracized boy who is dying of AIDS.

© Universal City Studios, Inc.

CRUMB

(SONY PICTURES CLASSICS) Producers, Lynn O'Donnell, Terry Zwigoff; Executive Producers, Lawrence Wilkinson, Albert Berger, Lianne Halfon; Co-Producer, Neal Halfon; Director, Terry Zwigoff; Photography, Maryse Alberti; Editor, Victor Livingston; Color; Rated R; 119 minutes; April release

WITH

Robert Crumb (The Artist), Alin Kominsky (Robert's Wife), Charles Crumb (Robert's Older Brother), Max Crumb (Robert's Younger Brother), Robert Hughes (*Time Magazine* Art Critic), Martin Muller (Owner, Modernism Gallery), Don Donahue (Former Zap Comix Publisher), Dana Crumb (Robert's First Wife), Trina Robbins, Spain Rodriguez, Bill Griffith (Cartoonists), Deirdre English (Former Editor, *Mother Jones Magazine*), Peggy Orenstein (Journalist), Beatrice Crumb (Robert's Mother), Kathy Goodell (Ex-Girlfriend), Dian Hanson (*Leg Show Magazine* Editor and Ex-Girlfriend), Sophie Crumb (Robert and Aline's Daughter), Jesse Crumb (Robert's Son from his marriage with Dana).

Documentary looks at the life of controversial artist Robert Crumb and various eccentric members of his family.

Robert Crumb

Robert Crumb

Jesse Crumb, Maxon Crumb, Robert Crumb

Maxon Crumb, Robert Crumb, Charles Crumb

Robert Crumb

Leonardo DiCaprio, Lorraine Bracco

Mark Wahlberg, Leonardo DiCaprio

James Madio, Mark Wahlberg, Patrick McGaw, Leonardo DiCaprio

THE BASKETBALL DIARIES

(NEW LINE CINEMA) Producers, Liz Heller, John Bard Manulis; Executive Producers, Chris Blackwell, Dan Genetti; Director, Scott Kalvert; Screenplay, Bryan Goluboff; Based on the novel by Jim Carroll; Photography, David Phillips; Line Producer, Kathie Hersch; Costumes, David C. Robinson; Designer, Christopher Nowak; Music, Graeme Revell; Casting, Avy Kaufman; an Island Pictures presentation; Dolby Digital Stereo; Technicolor; Rated R; 102 minutes; April release

CAST

Jim Carroll	Leonardo DiCaprio
Pedro	James Madio
Neutron	Patrick McGaw
Mickey	Mark Wahlberg
Jim's Mother	Lorraine Bracco
Frankie Pinewater	Jim Carroll
Reggie Porter	Ernie Hudson
Bobby	Michael Imperioli
Swifty	Bruno Kirby
Confessional Priest	Barton Heyman
Father McNulty	Roy Cooper
Chanting Woman	Marilyn Sokol
Construction Worker	Vinnie Pastore
Iggy	Jimmy Papiris
Referees	Nick Gaetani, Lawrence Barth
Bobo	Alexander Gaberman
Tommy	Ben Jorgensen
Counterman	Josh Mostel
Diane Moody	Juliette Lewis
Stripper	Akiko Ashley
Manny	Manny Alfaro
Winkie	Cynthia Daniel
Blinkie	Brittany Daniel
Drug Dealer #1	Eric Betts
Mugging Victim	Joyce R. Korbin
Kenny	Toby Huss
Juju Johnson	William Webb
Mr. Rubin	John Vennema
Skinhead	Michael Rapaport
Policemen	Gary Iorio, Doc Dougherty
Billy the Bartender	John Hoyt

The true story of Brooklyn teenager Jim Carroll's hellish descent into the world of drug addiction.

© New Line Productions, Inc.

Leonardo DiCaprio

Lindsay J./Megan L. Wrinn, Helen Hunt, David Caruso

Nicolas Cage, David Caruso

Samuel L. Jackson

KISS OF DEATH

(20th CENTURY FOX) Producers, Barbet Schroeder, Susan Hoffman; Executive Producer, Jack Baran; Director, Barbet Schroeder; Screenplay/Co-Producer, Richard Price; Based on the 1947 screenplay by Ben Hecht, Charles Lederer; Photography, Luciano Tovoli; Designer, Mel Bourne; Editor, Lee Percy; Music, Trevor Jones; Costumes, Theadora Van Runkle; Casting, Paula Herold; Dolby Digital Stereo; Technicolor; Rated R; 101 minutes; April release

CAST

Jimmy Kilmartin	David Caruso
Calvin	Samuel L. Jackson
Little Junior Brown	Nicolas Cage
Bev Kilmartin	Helen Hunt
Rosie	Kathryn Erbe
Frank Zioli	Stanley Tucci
Ronnie	Michael Rapaport
Omar	Ving Rhames
Big Junior Brown	Philip Baker Hall
Jack Gold (Lawyer)	Anthony Heald
J.J.	Angel David
Cleary (Calvin's Partner)	John Costelloe
Corinna (toddler)	Lindsay J. Wrinn, Megan L. Wrinn
Corinna (4 yrs. old)	Katie Sagona
Bev's Mother	Anne Meara
Kid Selling Infinity	Kevin Corrigan
Naked Man Dancing	Hugh Palmer
Junior's Girlfriend	Hope Davis
City Clerk	Richard Price
U.S. Attorney	Edward McDonald
Convoy Drunk	Alex Stevens
Judge	Mark Hammer
Agent at Bungalow	Joe Lisi
Big Junior's Friend	Frank DiLeo
Johnny A.	Jason Andrews
Bobby B.	Sean G. Wallace
Calvin's Partner	Ed Trucco
Molested Dancer	Bernadette Penotti
Sioux Dancer	Debra J. Pereira
Federal Agent	Shiek Mahmud-Bey
Angry Federal Agent	John C. Vennema
Junior's Crew	Tony Cucci, Allen L. Bernstein
J.J.'s Crew	Dame, Jose DeSoto
Prison Chaplain	Lloyd Hollar

and Nicholas Falcone (Priest at Funeral), James McCauley (Cop Outside Bar), Michael Artura (Emergency Room Cop), Tom Riis Farrell (EMS Supervisor), Juliet Adair Pritner (Agent), Henry Yuk (Chinese Restaurant Owner), Chuck Margiotta, Jay Boryea (Escorts at Cemetery), Joseph Pentangelo, Alan Jeffrey Gordon (Riker's Security Officers), Dean Rader-Duval, Willie M. Watford (Sing Sing Guards), Jay O. Sanders (Federal Agent)

Ex-con Jimmy Kilmartin reluctantly agrees to help his no-good cousin Ronnie, a move that lands him back in prison and at odds with a criminal named Little Junior Brown. Remake of the 1947 20th Century Fox film which starred Victor Mature and Richard Widmark.

© Twentieth Century Fox

David Caruso, Michael Rapaport

David Caruso, Nicolas Cage

Kathryn Erbe, David Caruso

David Caruso

Nicolas Cage

Stanley Tucci, David Caruso

Nicholas Cage (c), Ving Rhames

THE LAST GOOD TIME

(SAMUEL GOLDWYN CO.) Producers, Dean Silvers, Bob Balaban; Executive Producer, Klaus Volkenborn; Director, Bob Balaban; Screenplay, Bob Balaban, John McLaughlin; Based on the novel by Richard Bausch; Photography, Claudia Raschke; Editor, Hughes Winborne; Music, Jonathan Tunick; Designer, Wing Lee; Costumes, Kimberly A. Tillman; Casting, Billy Hopkins, Suzanne Smith, Kerry Barden; DuArt color; Not rated; 95 minutes; April release

CAST

Joseph Kopple	Armin Mueller-Stahl
Ida Cutler	Maureen Stapleton
Howard Singer	Lionel Stander
Charlotte Zwicki	Olivia d'Abo
Eddie	Adrian Pasdar
Barbara	Zohra Lampert
Frank	Kevin Corrigan
Dorothy	Molly Powell
Mrs. Wilder	Jody Wilson
Nurse Westman	Beatrice Winde
Supermarket Manager	Burtt Harris
Bartender	Ken Simmons
Bus Driver	Gino Lucci

A retired violinist develops an unlikely relationship with a young woman who has been thrown out of her apartment by her abusive lover.

© The Samuel Goldwyn Company

Armin Mueller-Stahl, Maureen Stapleton

Lionel Stander, Armin Mueller-Stahl

Olivia d'Abo, Armin Mueller-Stahl

CLEAN, SHAVEN

(STRAND) Producer/Director/Screenplay, Lodge H. Kerrigan; Executive Producer, J. Dixon Byrne; Photography, Teodoro Maniaci; Editor, Jay Rabinowitz; Music, Hahn Rowe; Special Effects Make-Up Designer/Creator, Rob Benevides; Designer, Tania Ferrier; Color; Not rated; 80 minutes; April release

CAST

Peter Winter	Peter Greene
Nicole	Jennifer MacDonald
Jack McNally	Robert Albert
Mrs. Winter	Megan Owen
Melinda Frayne	Molly Castelloe
Dr. Michaels	J. Dixon Byrne
Girl with Ball	Alice Levitt
Teenager at Motel	Jill Chamberlain
Murdered Girl	Agathe Leclerc
Police Photographer	Roget Joly

and René Beaudin (Boy on Bicycle), Eliot Rockett (Man on Ladder/Man in Jeep), Angela Vibert, Karen MacDonald (Girls in rain), Lee Kayman (Bartender), Peter Lucas (Drunk), Rob Benevides (Robber), Ismael Ramirez (Psychotic Derelict), Marty Clinis, Ruth Gottheimer (Library Patrons), June Kelly (Librarian), Grace Vibert (Schoolteacher), James Hance (Man in Adoption Agency), Marti Wilkerson (Adoption Agent), Michael Benson (Man in Jeep), Cathleen Biro, Harlan Hamilton (Drunks)

Schizophrenic Peter Winter returns to his hometown to visit his daughter Nicole, while the police investigate the murder of several young girls.

© Strand Releasing

Peter Greene

Ice Cube, Chris Tucker, Paula Jai Parker

Chris Tucker, LaWanda Page, Ice Cube

Bernie Mac, Chris Tucker, Ice Cube

FRIDAY

(NEW LINE CINEMA) Producer, Patricia Charbonet; Executive Producers, Ice Cube, Bryan Turner; Director, F. Gary Gray; Screenplay, Ice Cube, DJ Pooh; Co-Executive Producer, Helena Echegoyen; Co-Producer, W.E. Baker; Associate Producers, Andre Robinson, Jr., DJ Pooh; Photography, Gerry Lively; Editor, John Carter; Dolby Stereo; Color; Rated R; 90 minutes; April release

CAST

Craig	Ice Cube
Smokey	Chris Tucker
Debbie	Nia Long
Deebo	Tiny "Zeus" Lister, Jr.
Mr. Jones	John Witherspoon
Mrs. Jones	Anna Maria Horsford
Dana	Regina King
Jol	Paula Jai Parker
Big Worm	Faizon Love
Red	DJ Pooh
Felisha	Angela Means
Joann	Vickilyn Reynolds
Stanley	Ronn Riser
Mrs. Parker	Kathleen Bradley
Mr. Parker	Tony Cox
Ezal	Anthony Johnson
Hector	Demetrius Navarro
Lil Chris	Jason Bose Smith
Pastor Clever	Bernie Mac
Kids	Justin Revoner, Meagan Good
Old Lady	LaWanda Page
China	Terri J. Vaughn
Black Man at Store	F. Gary Gray
Rita	Yvette Wilson
Shooter	William L. Calhoun, Jr.
Red's Father	Reynaldo Rey

Comedy about one Friday in the life of best friends Craig and Smokey in South Central L.A.

© New Line Productions, Inc.

Nia Long

Peter Boyle

Peter Gallagher, Sandra Bullock

Jack Warden

Glynis Johns

Bill Pullman, Sandra Bullock

Bill Pullman, Sandra Bullock

Peter Gallagher

WHILE YOU WERE SLEEPING

(HOLLYWOOD PICTURES) Producers, Joe Roth, Roger Birnbaum; Executive Producers, Arthur Sarkissian, Steve Barron; Director, Jon Turteltaub; Screenplay, Daniel G. Sullivan, Fredric Lebow; Photography, Phedon Papamichael; Designer, Garreth Stover; Editor, Bruce Green; Music, Randy Edelman; Co-Producers, Charles J.D. Schlissel, Susan Stremple; Costumes, Betsy Cox; Associate Producers, Jonathan Glickman, Elaine Johnson; Casting, Amanda Mackey, Cathy Sandrich; Presented in association with Caravan Pictures; Distributed by Buena Vista Pictures; Dolby Digital Stereo; Technicolor; Rated PG; 100 minutes; April release

Sandra Bullock, Bill Pullman

CAST

Lucy Moderatz	Sandra Bullock
Jack Callaghan	Bill Pullman
Peter Callaghan	Peter Gallagher
Ox Callaghan	Peter Boyle
Saul Tuttle	Jack Warden
Elsie	Glynis Johns
Midge Callaghan	Micole Mercurio
Jerry Wallace	Jason Bernard
Joe Jr.	Michael Rispoli
Ashley Bacon	Ally Walker
Mary Callaghan	Monica Keena
Wanda	Ruth Rudnick
Celeste	Marcia Wright
Dr. Rubin	Dick Cusack
Man in Peter's Room	Thomas Q. Morris
Doorman	Bernie Landis
Dalton Clarke	James Krag
Orderly	Rick Worthy
Intern	Marc Grapey
Priest	Joel Hatch
Mr. Fusco	Mike Bacarella
Hot Dog Vendor	Peter Siragusa
Man in Church	Gene Janson
Phyllis	Krista Lally
Cop at ICU	Kevin Gudahl
Blood Donor Nurse	Ann Whitney
Admitting Nurse	Margaret Travolta
Ashley's Husband	Shea Farrell
Beth	Kate Reinders
Celeste's Friend	Susan Messing
Lucy's Father	Richard Pickren
Young Lucy	Megan Schaiper

Sandra Bullock, Jack Warden

After rescuing the man she has secretly loved from a subway accident, a misunderstanding causes Lucy Moderatz to pose as the comatose man's fiancée.

© Hollywood Pictures Company

Sandra Bullock, Monica Keena, Jack Warden

VILLAGE OF THE DAMNED

(UNIVERSAL) Producers, Michael Preger, Sandy King; Executive Producers, Ted Vernon, Shep Gordon, Andre Blay; Director, John Carpenter; Screenplay, David Himmelstein; Based on the novel *The Midwich Cuckoos* by John Wyndham, and the 1960 screenplay by Stirling Silliphant, Wolf Rilla, George Barclay; Co-Executive Producers, James Jacks, Sean Daniel; Co-Producer, David Chackler; Photography, Gary B. Kibbe; Designer, Rodger Maus; Editor, Edward A. Warschilka; Visual Effects Supervisor, Bruce Nicholson; Music, John Carpenter, Dave Davies; Casting, Reuben Cannon; an Alphaville production; DTS Stereo; Panavision; Foto-Kem color; Rated R; 98 minutes; April release

The Children

CAST

Alan Chaffee	Christopher Reeve
Dr. Susan Verner	Kirstie Alley
Jill McGowan	Linda Kozlowski
Frank McGowan	Michael Paré
Melanie Roberts	Meredith Salenger
Reverend George	Mark Hamill
Mrs. Sarah Miller	Pippa Pearthree
Ben Blum	Peter Jason
Callie Blum	Constance Forslund
Barbara Chaffee	Karen Kahn

THE CHILDREN:

David	Thomas Dekker
Mara	Lindsey Haun
Robert	Cody Dorkin
Julie	Trishalee Hardy
Dorothy	Jessye Quarry
Isaac	Adam Robbins
Matt	Chelsea DeRidder Simms
Casey	Renée René Simms
Lily	Danielle Wiener
Mara at 1 year	Hillary Harvey
David at 9 months/1 year	Bradley Wilhelm
Mara/David at 4 months	Jennifer Wilhelm
Carlton	Buck Fowler
The Sheriff	Squire Fridell
CHP	Darryl Jones
Older Deputy	Ed Corbett
Younger Deputy	Ross Martineau
Deputy	Skip Richardson
Dr. Bush	Tony Haney
Eye Doctor	Sharon Iwai
Mr. Roberts	Robert L. Bush
Technician	Montgomery Hom

and Steve Chambers, Ron Kaell (Troopers), Lane Nishikawa (Scientist), Michael Halton (Station Attendant Harold), Julie Eccles (Eileen Moore), Lois Saunders (Doctor at Clinic), Sidney Baldwin (Labor Room Physician), Wendolyn Lee, Kathleen Turco-Lyon, Abigail Van Alyn (Nurses), Roy Conrad (Oliver), Dan Belzer (Young Husband), Dena Martinez (Young Wife), Alice Barden (Woman at Town Hall), John Brebner (Man at Town Hall), Ralph Miller (Villager), Rip Haight (Man at Gas Station Phone)

Linda Kozlowski, Thomas Dekker, Christopher Reeve

After the entire village of Midwich falls into a trance, several of the town's women discover that they inexplicably are pregnant. Remake of the 1960 MGM British film which starred George Sanders and Barbara Shelley.

Karen Kahn

Meredith Salenger

Mark Hamill

Christopher Reeve, Kirstie Alley

Alison Elliott, Willam Fichtner, Peter Gallagher

Shelley Duvall

Paul Dooley

Elisabeth Shue

THE UNDERNEATH

(GRAMERCY) Producer, John Hardy; Executive Producers, Joshua Donen, William Reid, Lionel Wigram; Director, Steven Soderbergh; Screenplay, Sam Lowry, Daniel Fuchs; Based on the novel *Criss Cross* by Don Tracy; Photography, Elliot Davis; Designer, Howard Cummings; Music, Cliff Martinez; Editor, Stan Salfas; Costumes, Karyn Wagner; Casting, Ronnie Yeskel; a Populist Pictures production; DTS Stereo; Panavision; Color; Rated R; 99 minutes; April release

CAST

Michael Chambers	Peter Gallagher
Rachel	Alison Elliott
Tommy Dundee	William Fichtner
David Chambers	Adam Trese
Clay Hinkle	Joe Don Baker
Ed Dutton	Paul Dooley
Susan	Elisabeth Shue
Mrs. Chambers	Anjanette Comer
Nurse	Shelley Duvall
Guard (Tom)	Dennis Hill
Guard (Casey)	Harry Goz
Guard (George)	Mark Feltch
Hinkle's Assistant	Jules Sharp
Mantrap Guard	Kenneth D. Harris
Michael's Partner	Vincent Gaskins
Turret Operator	Cliff Haby
Ember Waitress	Tonie Perensky
Ember Bartender	Randall Brady
Ember Doorman	Richard Linklater
Susan's Friend	Helen Cates
VIP Room Flunky	Kevin Crutchfield
Man Delivering Money	Brad Leland
Justice of the Peace	John Martin

and Rick Perkins, Paul Wright (TV Delivery Men), David Jensen (Satellite Dish Installer), Jordy Hultberg (TV Sports Reporter), Steve Shearer (Detective), Fred Ellis (Detective's Partner), Joe Chrest (Mr. Rodman), Cowboy Mouth, Wheel, Gal's Panic, Herman the German (Bands)

Michael Chambers returns to his home in Texas only to find that his ex-wife has now taken up with a rich, jealous club owner. Previous film version of the story was 1949's Criss Cross *(Universal Pictures) with Burt Lancaster and Yvonne DeCarlo.*

© Gramercy Pictures

Alison Elliot, Peter Gallagher

NEW JERSEY DRIVE

(GRAMERCY) Producers, Larry Meistrich, Bob Gosse; Executive Producer, Spike Lee; Director/Screenplay, Nick Gomez; Story, Nick Gomez, Michel Marriott; Co-Producer, Rudd Simmons; Photography, Adam Kimmel; Editor, Tracy S. Granger; Designer, Lester Cohen; Casting, Tracey Moore, Todd Thaler; a 40 Acres and a Mule Filmworks production; DTS Stereo; Color; Rated R; 100 minutes; April release

CAST

Jason Petty	Sharron Corley
Midget	Gabriel Casseus
Lt. Emil Roscoe	Saul Stein
Renee Petty	Gwen McGee
Ritchie	Andre Moore
Tiny Dime	Donald Adeosun Faison
P-Nut	Conrad Meertins, Jr.
Jamal	Devin Eggleston
Ronnie Lambs	Koran C. Thomas
Coreen	Michelle Morgan
Jackie Petty	Samantha Brown
Prosecutor	Christine Baranski
Lionel Gentry	Robert Jason Jackson
Judge	Roscoe Orman
Bo-Kane	Dwight Errington Myers
Jessy	Gary DeWitt Marshall
Tiko	Ron Brice
Reebo	Shawn McClean
Booking Sergeant	Paulie Schulze
Officer	Leslie Nipkow
Mr. Chop Shop	Arthur Nascarella
Officer Clueless	Michael Tancredi
Incarcerated Knucklehead	Ian Kelly
Young Guns	Emilio Mayes, Ian Kelly
Jury Member	Arabella Field
TV Reporter	David Butler
Ron Q.'s Dad	Oran Jones
House Rules	T.K. Kirkland

and Leslie Segar (Angry Resident), Kellie Turner (Agitated Neighbor), Maurice Carlton (Irate Friend), Monique Maxwell, Monet-Cherise Dunham (Jackie's Homegirls), James McCauley (Whiteboy in Jeep), Teisha Panley (PJ Spokesperson), Damon Chandler (Detective), Andy Radcliffe (Buff), Ellsworth "Cisco" Davis (Cisco)

Two Newark teenagers run afoul of a vengeful police lieutenant after a bungled carjacking.

© Gramercy Pictures

Sharron Corley, Michelle Morgan

Sharron Corley, Saul Stein

SWIMMING WITH SHARKS

(TRIMARK) formerly *The Buddy Factor*; Producers, Steve Alexander, Joanne Moore; Executive Producers, Jay Cohen, Stephen Israel; Co-Producers, Kevin Spacey, Buzz Hays; Director/Screenplay, George Huang; Photography, Steven Finestone; Designers, Veronika Merlin, Cecil Gentry; Music, Tom Heil; Editor, Ed Marx; Costumes, Kirsten Everberg; Casting, Andrea Guttfreund, Laurel Smith; a Cineville in association with NeoFight Film and Mama'z Boy Entertainment presentation; Dolby Stereo; Foto-Kem color; Rated R; 93 minutes; April release

CAST

Buddy Ackerman	Kevin Spacey
Guy	Frank Whaley
Dawn Lockard	Michelle Forbes
Rex	Benicio Del Toro
Foster Kane	T.E. Russell
Cyrus Miles	Roy Dotrice
Manny	Matthew Flynt
Moe	Patrick Fischler
Jack	Jerry Levine

Guy, an aspiring screenwriter, lands a job as office assistant to Buddy Ackerman, a studio executive whose abrasive mistreatment of his staff is legendary.

© Trimark Pictures

Frank Whaley, Kevin Spacey

Kadeem Hardison, Jenifer Lewis

Courtney B. Vance, Marcus Chong

Wesley Jonathan, Courtney B. Vance, Bokeem Woodbine, Marcus Chong, Tyrin Turner

PANTHER

(GRAMERCY) Producers, Preston Holmes, Mario Van Peebles, Melvin Van Peebles; Executive Producers, Eric Fellner, Tim Bevan; Director, Mario Van Peebles; Screenplay, Melvin Van Peebles, based on his novel; Photography, Eddie Pei; Designer, Richard Hoover; Costumes, Paul A. Simmons; Editor, Earl Watson; Casting, Robi Reed; a PolyGram Filmed Entertainment presentation of a Working Title production in association with Tribeca Prods. and MVP Films; Dolby Stereo; Deluxe color/black and white; Rated R; 124 minutes; May release

CAST

Judge..Kadeem Hardison
Bobby Seale ....Courtney B. Vance
Huey Newton..Marcus Chong
Alma..Nefertiti
Tyrone ....Bokeem Woodbine
Cy...Tyrin Turner
Eldridge Cleaver ....Anthony Griffith
Gene McKinney ....Lahmard Tate
Brimmer...Joe Don Baker
Rita..Jenifer Lewis
Little Bobby Hutton ....Wesley Jonathan
Rose ....Bobby Brown
Rodgers ....James Russo
Drinker #1..Chris Rock
Pruitt..Roger Guenveur Smith
Tyanan ....Michael Wincott
Hoover..Richard Dysart
Dorsett ....M. Emmet Walsh
Reverend Slocum ....Dick Gregory
Cynical Jail Bird...Melvin Van Peebles
Defense Attorney ....Jerry Rubin
Avakian..James LeGros
Charles Garry...Robert Culp
Stokley Carmichael..Mario Van Peebles
and Kahlil Nelson (Boy on Bike), Thayis Walsh (Bernadette), Anthony Jones (Sabu), Kool Moe Dee (Jamal), William Fuller (Sgt. Schreck), David Greenlee (Patrolman), Adam Powers (White Hippie), Sharrif Simmons (Poet), Emory Douglas (Bret Schaefer), Aklam (Bakar), Mark Curry (Lombard), Rob Rule, Eddie Anisko, Robbie Allen, David King (Berkeley Campus Singers), Dario Scardapane (Student), Reginald Ballard (Brother at Meeting), Ralph Ahn (Mr. Yang), James Bigwood, Martin Bright (Grove Street Cops), John "Doo Doo Brown" Gordon, Marvin Young, D-Knowledge (Recruits), Mark Buntzman (Pushy Reporter), Robert Peters (Cop at Ramparts), Shanice Wilson (Singer at Punk Panthers), Jeffrey Carr (Denzil Dowell), Ann Weldon (Mrs. Dowell), Steven Carl White (George), Brian Turk (Deputy), Charles Cooper (Sheriff), Tony Toni Tone, Dwayne P. Wiggins, Timothy C. Riley, John T. Smith, Elijah Baker, Vincent Lars, Bill Ortiz (Band at Barbeque), Jay Koch (Gov. Reagan), Tim Loughrin (Reporter at Capitol), Tony Beard (Guard at Capitol), Beau Windham (Hoover's Aide), Jamie Zozzaro (Girl Buying Drugs), Yolanda Whitaker (Pregnant Junkie), Roberto L. Santana (Matty), Arthur Reed (Blind Man), Gunnar Peterson (Cop at Gas Station), Christopher Michales (Reporter at Police Station), John Harwood (Cop at Line Up), John Knight (Cop at Panther Office), Joseph Culp (Babyfaced Cop), Erik Kohner (Nervous Cop), Preston L. Holmes (Prison Guard), Chris Tucker (Bodyguard), John Snyder (Cop), Tracey Costello (Kathleen Cleaver), Jeris Poindexte (Black Cop), Steve Gagnon (Prosecutor), Brent Sincock (Judge), Manny Perry (Shorty), James A. Earley (Angry Cop), William Brennan (Partner)

The Black Panthers are formed as a response to violence by the police against blacks in the late 1960s.

© Gramercy Pictures

Chris Rock, Bobby Brown

MY FAMILY/MI FAMILIA

(NEW LINE CINEMA) Producer, Anna Thomas; Executive Producers, Francis Ford Coppola, Guy East, Tom Luddy; Director, Gregory Nava; Screenplay, Gregory Nava, Anna Thomas; Line Producer, Larura Greenlee; Photography, Edward Lachman; Designer, Barry Robison; Editor, Nancy Richardson; Music, Mark McKenzie; Original Folkloric Music, Pepe Avila; Costumes, Tracy Tynan; Associate Producer, Nancy De Los Santos; Casting, Janet Hirshenson, Jane Jenkins, Roger Mussenden; a Francis Ford Coppola presentation in association with Majestic Films and American Playhouse Theatrical Films of an American Zoetrope-Anna Thomas-Necomm production; DTS Digital Stereo; CFI color; Rated R; 128 minutes; May release

CAST

Jimmy Sanchez	Jimmy Smits
Chucho Sanchez	Esai Morales
Toni Sanchez	Constance Marie
Jose Sanchez	Eduardo Lopez Rojas
Paco Sanchez	Edward James Olmos
Maria Sanchez	Jenny Gago
Memo "Bill" Sanchez	Enrique Castillo
Isabel Magana	Elpidia Carrillo
David Ronconi	Scott Bakula
Gloria	Mary Steenburgen
Butch Mejia	Michael Delorenzo
Roberto	Rafael Cortes
Trini	Ivette Reina
Roberto's Girlfriend	Amelia Zapata
Young Jose	Jacob Vargas
Ox Cart Drivers	Emilio Del Haro, Abel Woolrich
El Californio	Leon Singer
Maria's Employer	Rosalee Mayeux
Young Maria	Jennifer Lopez
Maria's Aunt	Alicia Del Lago
The Boatman	Thomas Rosales
Baby Paco	Anthony Gonzalez
Baby Irene	Cassandra Campos
Little Paco	Michael Gonzalez
Little Irene	Susanna Campos
Young Paco	Benito Martinez
Young Memo	Greg Albert
Young Irene	Maria Canals
Young Jimmy	Jonathan Hernandez
Young Gerardo	Cris Franco
Chucho's Friend	Valente Rodriguez
Another Friend	Eddie Ayala
Eddie	Romeo Rene Fabian
Eddie's Mom	Bel Hernandez
Rosie	Jeanette Jurado
Irene Sanchez	Lupe Ontiveros
Karen Gillespie	Dedee Pfeiffer
Mrs. Gillespie	Bibi Besch
Mr. Gillespie	Bruce Gray

and Salvador Hernandez, Samuel Hernandez, Juan Jimenez, Jesus Alberto Guzman, Jose Mario Rodriguez, Arturo Palacios (Mariachis), David Salas, Bill Mondragon, Eric Mondragon, Dennis Jimenez, Alex Tanasi (The Originals), Seidy Lopez (Lena, Chucho's Girlfriend), George Lopez Jr., Moses Saldana (Ballplayers), Brian Lally (Officer), Ernie Lively (Sergeant), Bart Johnson (Young Officer), Peter Mark Vasquez (Prison Guard), Ruben Sierra (Gerardo), Willie C. Carpenter (I.N.S. Guard), Delana Michaels (Judge), Pete Leal (Old Man on Balcony), Valerie Wildman (Sunny, Gloria's Friend), Michael Tomlinson (Dr. McNally), Saachiko (Nurse), Emilio Rivera (Tamalito), Paul Robert Langdon (Carlitos), Angelina Estrada (Woman with Groceries)

Drama traces three generations of the Sanchez family from the 1920s through the 1980s.

Constance Marie, Edward James Olmos, Elpidia Carillo, Jenny Gago, Jimmy Smits, Lupe Ontiveros, Enrique Castillo, Eduardo Lopez Rojas

Esai Morales

Scott Bakula, Constance Marie

THE PEREZ FAMILY

(SAMUEL GOLDWYN CO.) Producers, Michael Nozik, Lydia Dean Pilcher; Executive Producers, Julia Chasman, Robin Swicord; Director, Mira Nair; Screenplay, Robin Swicord; Based on the novel by Christine Bell; Photography, Stuart Dryburgh; Editor, Robert Estrin; Designer, Mark Friedberg; Music Supervisor, Jellybean Benitez; Music, Alan Silvestri; Traditional Music, Arturo Sandoval; Casting, Dinaz "Mini" Stafford; Dolby Stereo; Color; Rated R; 112 minutes; May release

CAST

Juan Raul Perez	Alfred Molina
Dottie	Marisa Tomei
Carmela	Anjelica Huston
Armando Perez	Lazaro Perez
Felipe	Jose Felipe Padron
Angel Diaz	Diego Wallraff
Teresa	Trini Alvarado
Luz Paz	Celia Cruz
Ranjit	Ranjit Chowdhry
Officer Pirelli	Chazz Palminteri
Steve	Bill Sage
Flavia	Angela Lanza
Officer Rhoades	Ellen Cleghorne
Father Aiden	Billy Hopkins
Father Martinez	Ruben Rabasa
Isabel	Melissa Anne Acosta
Hermaphrodite	Jose Manuel Cabrera
Rivera	Roberto Escobar
Gate Guard	Norman "Max" Maxwell
Josette	Sarita Choudhury
Old Guajiros	Oscar Gonzalez, Florencio Santana
Angel's Secretary	Magaly Aguero
TV Reporter	Maite Arnedo
Official	Gustavo Laborie
Giovanna	Glenda Diaz-Rigau

and Vivian Ruiz, Jody Wilson (Officials), Clarence Charles (Black Owner), Elodia Riovega (Middle-Aged Mama), Marc MacCauley (Volunteer), Eduardo Corbe (News Photographer), Antoni Corone (Security), Jorge Luis Ramone (Young Guard), Bernard Fouquet (Customer—Saks Fifth Avenue), Salvador Levy (Middle-Aged Man/Customer), Vincent Gallo (Orlando), Melissa Ramone (Young Carmela), Sandor Juan (Vendor), Mel Gorham (Vilma/Raquel)

Released from a Cuban jail, Juan Raul Perez travels to Miami to be reunited with his wife and daughter. Once there, immigration officials mistake him for the husband of an ex-prostitute named Dottie whom he met on the voyage over.

© The Samuel Goldwyn Company

Anjelica Huston, Chazz Palminteri

Alfred Molina, Marisa Tomei

Angela Lanza, Diego Wallraff

Anjelica Huston, Trini Alvarado

Alfred Molina, Marisa Tomei, Celia Cruz

Denzel Washington, Gene Hackman

Denzel Washington, Gene Hackman

Gene Hackman, George Dzundza, Denzel Washington

CRIMSON TIDE

(HOLLYWOOD PICTURES) Producers, Don Simpson, Jerry Bruckheimer; Executive Producers, Bill Unger, Lucas Foster, Mike Moder; Director, Tony Scott; Screenplay, Michael Schiffer; Story, Michael Schiffer, Richard P. Henrick; Photography, Dariusz Wolski; Designer, Michael White; Editor, Chris Lebenzon; Costumes, George L. Little; Music, Hans Zimmer; Casting, Victoria Thomas; Visual Effects Supervisor, Hoyt Yeatman; Distributed by Buena Vista Pictures; Dolby Digital Stereo; Panavision; Technicolor; Rated R; 113 minutes; May release

CAST

Lt. Comdr. Ron Hunter	Denzel Washington
Capt. Frank Ramsey	Gene Hackman
Lt. Roy Zimmer	Matt Craven
Chief of the Boat Cob	George Dzundza
Lt. Peter Ince (Weps)	Viggo Mortensen
Lt. Bobby Dougherty	James Gandolfini
Lt. Darik Westergaurd	Rocky Carroll
Ood Mahoney	Jaime P. Gomez
Hunsicker	Michael Milhoan
TSO Billy Linkletter	Scott Burkholder
Danny Rivetti	Danny Nucci
Russell Vossler	Lillo Brancato, Jr.
Bennefield	Eric Bruskotter
Lt. Paul Hellerman	Rick Schroder
William Barnes	Steve Zahn
Lawson	Marcello Thedford
Marty Sotille	R.J. Knoll
Navigator	Billy Devlin
Planesman	Matt Barry
Helmsman	Christopher Birt
Diving Officer	Jim Boyce
Sonarmen	Jacob Vargas, Kai Lennox
Radioman #1	Michael Weatherred
Admiral Williams	Tommy Bush
Rick Marichek	Earl Billings
Head Cook Rono	Mark Christopher Lawrence
Chief Kline	Michael Chieffo
Guards	Ashley Smock, James Lesure
Launcher	Trevor St. John
Fire Control Technician	Dennis Garber
Julia Hunter	Vanessa Bell Calloway
Luke Hunter	Brenden Jefferson
Robin Hunter	Ashley Calloway
Vladimir Radchenko	Daniel Von Bargen
Himself	Richard Valeriani
Anchorman	Warren Olney
Lt. Comdr. Nelson	Rad Daly
Phone Talkers	Sean O'Bryan, Brent Michael Goldberg
Sailor with Oba	Victor Togunde
Sailor #1	Troy A. Cephers
Seaman Davis	Armand Watson
Petty Officer Hilaire	Scott Grimes
Seaman Grattam	Ryan Phillippe
Firing Key Runner	Dale Andre Lee Everett
Ramsey Aide	Angela Tortu
Westergaurd Dad	Ronald Ramessar
Westergaurd Mom	Robin Faraday
Bob the Magician	Bob Stone
Henry Ince	Henry Mortensen
Additional Magician	Chris Ellis
Admiral Anderson	Jason Robards

On a mission to stop a Russian nationalist, who has seized control of a nuclear missile base, two naval officers clash aboard the submarine USS Alabama when the order comes to launch its missiles.

The film received Oscar nominations for sound and sound effects editing.

Denzel Washington, George Dzundza, Gene Hackman

Lillo Brancato, Jr.

James Gandolfini

Danny Nucci

Gene Hackman, Denzel Washington, Matt Craven, Rocky Carroll

FRENCH KISS

(20th CENTURY FOX) Producers, Tim Bevan, Eric Fellner, Meg Ryan, Kathryn F. Galan; Executive Producer, Charles Okun; Director, Lawrence Kasdan; Screenplay, Adam Brooks; Photography, Owen Roizman; Designer, Jon Hutman; Editor, Joe Hutshing; Costumes, Joanna Johnston; Music, James Newton Howard; Song: La Mer by Charles Trenet/performed by Kevin Kline; Casting, Françoise Combadiere, Jennifer Schull; a PolyGram Filmed Entertainment presentation of a Working Title production in association with Prufrock Pictures; Dolby Digital Stereo; Panavision; Deluxe color; Rated PG-13; 108 minutes; May release

Kevin Kline, Meg Ryan

CAST

Kate	Meg Ryan
Luc	Kevin Kline
Charlie	Timothy Hutton
Jean-Paul	Jean Reno
Bob	Francois Cluzet
Juliette	Susan Anbeh
Lilly	Renee Humphrey
Campbell	Michael Riley
Concierge	Laurent Spielvogel
Octave	Victor Garrivier
Claire	Elizabeth Commelin
Olivia	Julie Leibowitch
Sergeant Patton	Miquel Brown
Jean-Paul's Girl	Louise Deschamps
Jean-Paul's Boy	Olivier Curdy
Antoine	Claudio Todeschini
Herb	Jerry Harte
Mom	Thomasine Heiner
Monotonous Voiced Woman	Joanna Pavlis
Flight Attendant	Florence Soyez
Pouting Girl	Barbara Schulz
Pouting Boy	Clement Sibony
Perfect Passenger	Adam Brooks

and Marianne Anska, Phillippe Garnier, Frederic Therisod (Cops), Patrice Juiff (French Customs Official), Jean Corso (Desk Clerk), Francois Xavier Tilmant (Hotel Waiter), Williams Diols (Beach Waiter), Mike Johns (Lucien), Marie Christine Adam (Juliette's Mother), Jean-Paul Jaupart (Juliette's Father), Fausto Costantino (Beefy Doorman), Jean-Claude Braquet (Stolen Moto Owner), Dominique Regnier (Attractive Passport Woman), Ghislaine Juillot (Jean-Paul's Wife), Inge Offerman, Nicholas Hawtrey, Wolfgang Pissors, Nikola Obermann (German Family), Alain Frerot (Old Man), Dorothee Picard (Mrs. Cowen), Jean Allain (Mr. Cowen)

Meg Ryan, Kevin Kline

Hoping to win her ex-fiance away from the beautiful woman for whom he has dumped her, Kate travels to Paris, meeting en route a mysterious Frenchman named Luc.

© Twentieth Century Fox

Jean Reno, Meg Ryan

Meg Ryan, Timothy Hutton

Samuel L. Jackson, Bruce Willis

Nick Wyman, Jeremy Irons

Larry Bryggman, Graham Greene

DIE HARD WITH A VENGEANCE

(20th CENTURY FOX) Producers, John McTiernan, Michael Tadross; Executive Producers, Andrew G. Vajna, Buzz Feitshans, Robert Lawrence; Director, John McTiernan; Screenplay, Jonathan Hensleigh; Certain Original Characters by Roderick Thorp; Photography, Peter Menzies; Designer, Jackson DeGovia; Editor, John Wright; Costumes, Joseph G. Aulisi; Music, Michael Kamen; Co-Producer, Carmine Zozzora; Visual Effects Supervisor, John E. Sullivan; Visual Effects, Mass. Illusion; Stunts, Terry J. Leonard; Dolby Digital Stereo; Panavision; Color; Rated R; 128 minutes; May release

CAST

John McClane	Bruce Willis
Simon	Jeremy Irons
Zeus Carver	Samuel L. Jackson
Joe Lambert	Graham Greene
Connie Kowalski	Colleen Camp
Arthur Cobb	Larry Bryggman
Ricky Walsh	Anthony Peck
Targo	Nick Wyman
Katya	Sam Phillips
Charles Weiss	Kevin Chamberlin
Officer Jane	Sharon Washington
Dr. Schiller	Stephen Pearlman
Dexter	Michael Alexander Jackson
Raymond	Aldis Hodge
Mischa	Mischa Hausserman
Dexter's Friend	Edwin Hodge
Rolf	Rob Sedgwick
Roman	Tony Halme
Ivan	Bill Christ
Gang Members	Anthony Thomas, Glenn Herman, Kent Faulcon, Akili Prince, Ardie Fuqua, Mike Jefferson, Frank Andre Ware
Van Driver	Michael Lee Merrins
Harlem Woman	Birdie M. Hale
Livery Driver	Daryl Edwards
Phone Woman	Barbara Hipkiss
Arab Cabbie	Aasif Mandvi
Business Guy (Taxi)	Bill Kux
Transit Cop	Scott Nicholson
Businessman (Station)	Ralph Buckley
Cross	Charles Dumas
Jarvis	Michael Cristofer
Wanda Shepard	Phyllis Yvonne Stickney
Sgt. John Turley	J.R. Horne
Greek Deli Proprietor	Michael Tadross
Radio D.J.	Elvis Duran
Fisherman	John McTiernan, Sr.
Kurt	Greg A. Skoric
Karl	Sven Toorvald
Berndt	Todd A. Langenfeld
Gunther	Timothy Adams
Felix Little	John C. Vennema
Nils	Gerrit Vooren
Klaus	Willis Spark
Marshals	Tony Travis, Danny Dutton
Korean Proprietor	James Saito
Kids	Patrick Borriello, Victor Rojas
Yuppie Stockbroker	Jeffrey Dreisbach
Jerry Parks	Joe Zaloom
Foreman	John Doman
Miss Thomas	Patricia Mauceri
Principal Martinez	Franchelle Stewart Dorn

and Kharisma (Little Tina), Gerry Becker (Larry Griffith), Richard Council (Otto), John Robert Tillotson (2nd Broker), Ray Arahna (Janitor), Phil Theis (Erik), Flip (Subway Man), Dory Binyon (Reporter), David Vitt (Kid at Gas Station), John Glenn Hoyt, Bray Poor, David P. Martin (Federal Reserve Guards), Shari-Lyn Safir (Secretary), Ivan Skoric (Villain A), Faisal Hassan (FBI Agent), Richard Russell Ramos (FBI Chief), Angela Amato, Shirley J. Hatcher (Cops), Richard V. Allen (Chief Allen), James Patrick Whalen, Sr. (Fat Larry Lumis), Paul Simon (Man in Precinct), Carl Brewer (Helicopter Villain)

A mysterious terrorist named Simon sends New York police officer John McClane and his unwilling civilian partner Zeus on a wild dash throughout the city to prevent a series of random bombings.

© Twentieth Century Fox/Cinergi Pictures Entertainment

Debra Winger, Billy Crystal

David Robinson, Billy Crystal

Richard Masur, Julie Kavner

FORGET PARIS

(COLUMBIA) Producer/Director, Billy Crystal; Executive Producer, Peter Schindler; Screenplay, Billy Crystal, Lowell Ganz, Babaloo Mandel; Photography, Don Burgess; Designer, Terence Marsh; Editor, Kent Beyda; Music, Marc Shaiman; Costumes, Judy Ruskin; Co-Producer, Kelly Van Horn; Casting, Pam Dixon Mickelson; a Castle Rock Entertainment presentation of a Face Production; Dolby Stereo; Technicolor; Rated PG-13; 95 minutes; May release

CAST

Mickey Gordon	Billy Crystal
Ellen Andrews	Debra Winger
Andy	Joe Mantegna
Liz	Cynthia Stevenson
Craig	Richard Masur
Lucy	Julie Kavner
Arthur	William Hickey
Waiter	Robert Costanzo
Jack	John Spencer
Tommy	Tom Wright
Lois	Cathy Moriarty
Lou	Johnny Williams
Airline Employee	Bert Copello
Insolent Official	Ron Ross
Airline Officials	Andy Flaster, David St. James, Gregory Paul Jackson, Andreas Tessi
Laker Girl	Chris Shaver
Knicks City Dancer	Mary Oedy
Spurs Silverdancer	Joie Shettler
Sonics Dancer	Andrea Toste
Attractive Woman	Lisa Gannon
Suitcase Man	Richard Assad
Receptionist	Lisa Rieffel
Woman in Porsche	Emmy Smith
Marilyn	Margaret Nagle
Andy's Date	Janette Caldwell
Doctor	Tim Halligan
Fertility Doctor	Tim Ahern
Ivy	Judyann Elder
Nurse	Deb Lacusta
Policeman	Tom Ohmer
Detroit Fans	Robert Hunter, Jr., Marty McSorley
Dangerous Man	Richard Haje
Exterminator	Clint Howard
Organist	Beverly Piper
3-year-old Girl	Charlotte Etienne
5-year-old Boy	Zachary Eginton
7-year-old Girl	Jennifer Mickelson
French Waiter	Allan Kolman
Distinguished Business Woman	Hedwige de Mouroux
Distinguished Frenchman	Roberto Bonanni
Waitress	Jean Shum
Huge Bodyguard	Andre Rosey Brown

and Marv Albert, Bill Walton, Charles Barkley, David Robinson, Dan Majerle, Kevin Johnson, Paul Westphal, Sean Elliott, Patrick Ewing, Tim Hardaway, Kareem Abdul-Jabbar, Bill Laimbeer, Reggie Miller, Chris Mullin, Charles Oakley, Kurt Rambis, John Starks, Isiah Thomas, Spud Webb, Marcus Johnson, Rush Limbaugh, David Sanborn, Safe-T-Man (Themselves), E.E. Bell, Marty Brinton, Jo Farkas, Ken Johnson, Patrick Thomas O'Brien, Jay Rusumny (Angry Fans in Crowd), Rick Gunderson, Eric Christian (Motorcycle Cops), Liz Sheridan (Lady in the Car), Irving Wasserman (Man in Car), Genelle Lee Baumgardner (Veronique), Scooter Barry, Nathaniel Bellany Jr., Robert M. Betts, Bernard Brown, Sam Crawford, Sterling Forbes, Greg Foster, Keith Gibbs, Anthony C. Hall, Kelvin L. Hildreth, Al Joseph, Paul McCracken, Mike McGee, Nigel Miguel, Kevin Morris, Rich Porter, Cliff Reed, Charles Rochelin, Dawan Scott, Larry Spriggs, Reggie Theus, Charles Wahlheim (Basketball Team)

A group of friends exchange stories charting the bumpy course of Mickey and Ellen's relationship, which began so ideally in Paris.

© Castle Rock Entertainment

Billy Crystal

Billy Crystal, Joe Mantegna

Debra Winger, Julie Kavner

Cathy Moriarty, John Spencer

Cynthia Stevenson, Joe Mantegna

Billy Crystal, Debra Winger

LITTLE ODESSA

(FINE LINE FEATURES) Producer, Paul Webster; Executive Producers, Nick Wechsler, Claudia Lewis, Rolf Mittweg; Co-Producer, Kerry Orent; Director/Screenplay, James Gray; Photography, Tom Richmond; Designer, Kevin Thompson; Editor, Dorian Harris; Music Supervisor, Dana Sano; Costumes, Michael Clancy; Casting, Douglas Aibel; a Live Entertainment presentation of a Paul Webster/Addis-Wechsler production; Dolby Stereo; Color; Rated R; 98 minutes; May release

CAST

Joshua Shapira	Tim Roth
Reuben Shapira	Edward Furlong
Alla Shustervich	Moira Kelly
Irina Shapira	Vanessa Redgrave
Arkady Shapira	Maximilian Schell
Boris Volkoff	Paul Guilfoyle
Natasha	Natasha Andreichenko
Sasha	David Vadim
Grandma Tsilya	Mina Bern
Ivan	Boris McGiver
Pahlevi	Mohammad Ghaffari
Yuri	Michael Khumrov
Victor	Dmitry Preyers
Anatoly	David Ross
Man with One Leg	Ron Brice
Mechanic	Jace Kent
Clara	Marianna Lead
Janitor	Gene Ruffini

Joshua Shapira, a hit man for the Russian mafia, returns to his neighborhood in Brooklyn, causing his father to worry about the influence Joshua might have on his impressionable younger brother, Reuben.

© Fine Line Features

Edward Furlong, Maximillian Schell

Maximilian Schell, Vanessa Redgrave

Tim Roth, Moira Kelly

Drew Barrymore, Chris O'Donnell

MAD LOVE

(TOUCHSTONE) Producer, David Manson; Director, Antonia Bird; Screenplay, Paula Milne; Co-Producers, John Landgraf, Marcus Viscidi; Photography, Fred Tammes; Designer, David Brisbin; Costumes, Eugenie Bafaloukos; Music, Andy Roberts; Casting, Dianne Crittenden; Distributed by Buena Vista Pictures; Dolby Digital Stereo; Technicolor; Rated PG-13; 99 minutes; May release

CAST

Matt Leland	Chris O'Donnell
Casey Roberts	Drew Barrymore
Eric	Matthew Lillard
Duncan	Richard Chaim
Coach	Robert Nadir
Margaret Roberts	Joan Allen
Richard Roberts	Jude Ciccolella
Joanna Leland	Amy Sakasitz
Adam Leland	T.J. Lowther
Clifford Leland	Kevin Dunn
Housekeeper	Elaine Miles
Librarian	Sharon Collar
Club Band	7 Year Bitch
Salesman	Liev Schreiber

and Todd Sible (Bartender), Leslie Do Qui (S.A.T. Monitor), Patrick Ryals (Vice Principal), Angela Hall (Dr. Laura Genel), Hunt Holman (Nurse Barry), Sandra Singler (Orderly), Allen Galli (Medication Nurse), Greg M. Gilmore, David J. Guppy (Patients), Angelina Calderon Torres (Landlady), Stefan Enriquez (Waiter), Yvonne C. Orona, Pedro Garcia (Mechanics)

Matt Leland finds himself falling madly in love with Casey Roberts, unaware that her wild nature hides the fact that she is a manic-depressive.

© Buena Vista Pictures Distribution, Inc.

CASPER

(UNIVERSAL) Producer, Colin Wilson; Executive Producers, Steven Spielberg, Gerald R. Molen, Jeffrey A. Montgomery; Director, Brad Silberling; Screenplay, Sherri Stoner, Deanna Oliver; Based on the character Casper the Friendly Ghost created by Joseph Oriolo in the story by Joseph Oriolo and Seymour Reit; Photography, Dean Cundey; Designer, Leslie Dilley; Editor, Michael Kahn; Music, James Horner; Song: "Casper the Friendly Ghost" by Mack David and Jerry Livingston/performed by Little Richard; Digitial Character Supervision, Dennis Muren; Costumes, Rosanna Norton; Casting, Nancy Nayor; an Amblin Entertainment production in association with the Harvey Entertainment Company; DTS Stereo; Deluxe color; Rated PG; 101 minutes; May release

CAST

Kat Harvey	Christina Ricci
Dr. James Harvey	Bill Pullman
Carrigan Crittenden	Cathy Moriarty
Dibs	Eric Idle
Casper (voice)	Malachi Perason
Stretch (voice)	Joe Nipote
Stinkie (voice)	Joe Alaskey
Fatso (voice)	Brad Garrett
Amelia Harvey	Amy Brenneman
Nicky	Chauncey Leopardi
Andreas	Spencer Vrooman
Rugg	Ben Stein
Father Guido Sarducci	Don Novello
Ghostbuster	Dan Aykroyd
Himself	Mr. Rogers
Herself	Terry Murphy
Woman Being Interviewed	Ernestine Mercer
Voice of Reporter	Douglas J.O. Bruckner
Faces in the Mirror	Mel Gibson, Clint Eastwood, Rodney Dangerfield
Voice of the Crypt Keeper	John Kassir
Vic	Garette Ratliff Henson
Amber	Jessica Wesson
Mr. Curtis	Wesley Thompson
Students	Michael Dubrow, J.J. Anderson, Micah Winkelspecht
Voice of Arnold	Jess Harnell
Drunk in Bar	Michael McCarty
Phantom	Mike Simmrin
Casper on Screen	Devon Sawa

The scheming owner of Whipstaff Manor hires Dr. James Harvey to rid the place of its four ghosts so that she can locate the house's fabled buried treasure. Casper first appeared on screen in the 1945 animated short "The Friendly Ghost" and in print in the 1949 comic book Casper the Friendly Ghost.

Casper, Christina Ricci

Cathy Moriarty, Eric Idle

Stretch, Bill Pullman, Stinkie

Christina Ricci, Bill Pullman

TALES FROM THE HOOD

(SAVOY) Producer, Darin Scott; Executive Producer, Spike Lee; Director, Rusty Cundieff; Screenplay, Rusty Cundieff, Darin Scott; Photography, Anthony B. Richmond; Designer, Stuart Blatt; Editor, Charles Bornstein; Music, Christopher Young; Music Supervisor, Larry Robinson; Casting, Robi Reed-Humes; a 40 Acres and a Mule Filmworks presentation; Dolby Digital Stereo; Technicolor; Rated R; 98 minutes; May release

CAST

WELCOME TO MY MORTUARY

Mr. Simms	Clarence Williams III
Stack	Joe Torry
Ball	De'Aundre Bonds
Bulldog	Samuel Monroe, Jr.

ROGUE COP REVELATION

Strom	Wings Hauser
Martin Moorehouse	Tom Wright
Clarence	Anthony Griffith
Newton	Michael Massee
Billy	Duane Whitaker

BOYS DO GET BRUISED

Carl	David Alan Grier
Walter	Brandon Hammond
Richard	Rusty Cundieff
Sissy	Paula Jai Parker

KKK COMEUPPANCE

Duke Metger	Corbin Bernsen
Rhodie	Roger Smith
Eli	Art Evans

HARD CORE CONVERT

Dr. Cushing	Rosalind Cash
Crazy K	Lamont Bentley

A macabre undertaker tells four tales of horror to a trio of street hustlers who have come to his funeral parlor to recover a lost cache of drugs.

© Savoy Pictures

Joe Torry, De'Aundre Bonds, Samuel Monroe Jr.

Clarence Williams III

Guillermo Diaz, Parker Posey, Anthony DeSando

Parker Posey, Omar Townsend

PARTY GIRL

(FIRST LOOK PICTURES) Producers, Harry Birckmayer, Stephanie Koules; Director, Daisy von Scherler Mayer; Screenplay, Daisy von Scherler Mayer, Harry Birckmayer; Story, Daisy von Scherler Mayer, Harry Birckmayer, Sheila Gaffney; Photography, Michael Slovis; Costumes, Michael Clancy; Editor, Cara Silverman; Casting, Caroline Sinclair; a Party Pictures production; Dolby Stereo; Color; Rated R; 98 minutes; June release

CAST

Mary	Parker Posey
Mustafa	Omar Townsend
Mrs. Lindendorf	Sasha von Scherler
Leo	Guillermo Diaz
Derrick	Anthony DeSando
Rene	Donna Mitchell
Nigel	Liev Schreiber
Venus	Nicole Bobbitt

Twenty-four-year-old Mary, who lives to party, takes a job at the library where her godmother works, trying to put some order into her wild way of living.

© Overseas Filmgroup/First Look Pictures

THE GLASS SHIELD

(MIRAMAX) Producers, Tom Byrnes, Carolyn Schroeder; Executive Producer, Chet Walker; Director/Screenplay, Charles Burnett; Based partially on a screenplay *One of Us* by Ned Wels; Photography, Elliot Davis; Editor, Curtiss Clayton; Music, Stephen James Taylor; Designer, Penny Barrett; Costumes, Gaye Burnett; a CIBY 2000 and a Byrnes/Schroeder/Walker production; Ultra-Stereo; Foto-Kem color; Rated PG-13; 108 minutes; June release

CAST

J.J. Johnson	Michael Boatman
Deborah Fields	Lori Petty
Teddy Woods	Ice Cube
Baker	Michael Ironside
Massey	Richard Anderson
Locket	Bernie Casey
Mr. Greenwall	Elliott Gould
Hal	M. Emmet Walsh
Deputy Bono	Don Harvey
Roy Bush	Michael Gregory
Mr. Taylor	Sy Richardson
Judge Helen Lewis	Natalija Nogulich

Drama about the opposition J.J. Johnson faces when he becomes the first black police recruit at a tough L.A. inner city station.

© Miramax Films

Michael Boatman

Matthew Modine, Fluke

Max Pomeranc, Nancy Travis, Eric Stoltz

FLUKE

(MGM) Producers, Paul Maslansky, Lata Ryan; Executive Producers, Jon Turtle, Tom Coleman; Director, Carlo Carlei; Screenplay, Carlo Carlei, James Carrington; Based upon the novel by James Herbert; Photography, Raffaele Mertes; Designer, Hilda Stark; Editor, Mark Conte; Music, Carlo Siliotto; Costumes, Elisabetta Beraldo; Animal Trainers, Stacy Basil, William S. Grisco, Joy A. Green, Janine Aines; Visual Effects, Digital Magic; Casting, Lynn Stalmaster; a Rocket Pictures production; Distributed by MGM/UA; DTS Stereo; Deluxe color; Rated PG; 96 minutes; June release

CAST

Voice of Fluke/Thomas Johnson	Matthew Modine
Carol Johnson	Nancy Travis
Jeff Newman	Eric Stoltz
Brian Johnson	Max Pomeranc
Sylvester	Ron Perlman
Boss	Jon Polito
Bert	Bill Cobbs
Bella	Collion Wilcox Paxton
Professor Santini	Federico Pacifici
Tom's Secretary	Clarinda Ross
Night Guard	Adrian Roberts
Day Guard	Bart Hansard
Dog Pound Vet	Deborah Hobart
Housekeeper	Libby Whittemore
Voice of Rumbo	Samuel L. Jackson

and Dominique Milton (Schoolboy), Mary Ann Hagan, Yolanda King (Women), Brian Katz, Mary Holloway (Paramedics), David Dwyer (News Stand Man), Michael H. Moss, Duke Steinemann (Policemen), Georgia Allen (Rose), John Lawhorn (Farmer), Calvin Miller (Skeptical Man), Harry Pritchett (Priest), Duong Bl (Asian Dishwasher), Diego La Rosa (Security Guard), Angie Reno (Delivery Boy), Sam Gifaldi (Voice of Young Fluke), Ripley (Chimpanzee), Miss Lori (Fluke's Mother)

After being killed in a car accident, a young executive finds that he has been reincarnated as a dog, in this dramatic fantasy.

© Metro-Goldwyn-Mayer, Inc.

61

CONGO

(PARAMOUNT) Producers, Kathleen Kennedy, Sam Mercer; Executive Producer, Frank Yablans; Director, Frank Marshall; Screenplay, John Patrick Shanely; Based on the novel by Michael Crichton; Photography, Allen Daviau; Designer, J. Michael Riva; Editor, Anne V. Coates; Music, Jerry Goldsmith; Costumes, Marilyn Matthews; Associate Producers, Michael Backes, Paul Deason; Gorillas by Stan Winston; Visual Effects Supervisor, Scott Farrar; Casting, Mike Fenton, Allison Cowitt; from The Kennedy/Marshall Company; Dolby DTS Digital Stereo; Deluxe color; Rated PG-13; 108 minutes; June release

CAST

Peter Elliot	Dylan Walsh
Karen Ross	Laura Linney
Monroe Kelly	Ernie Hudson
Herkermer Homolka	Tim Curry
Richard	Grant Heslov
R.B. Travis	Joe Don Baker
Amy	Lorene Noh, Misty Rosas
Moira	Mary Ellen Trainor
Boyd	Stuart Pankin
Eleanor Romy	Carolyn Seymour
Eleanor's Assistant	Romy Rosemont
College President	James Karen
William	Bill Pugin
Arliss Wender	Lawrence T. Wrentz
Rudy	Robert Almodovar
Sally	Kathleen Connors
Travicom Employee	Joel Weiss
Bob Driscoll	John Hawkes
Mr. Janus	Peter Jason
727 Pilot	Jimmy Buffett
Transport Workers	James R. Paradise, William John Murphy
Samahani	Thom Barry
African Airport Guard	Ayo Adejugbe
Roadblock Soldier	Kahara Muhoro
Charles Travis	Bruce Campbell
Jeffrey Weems	Taylor Nichols
Kahega	Adewalé

and Kevin Grevioux (Hospital Officer/Roadblock Officer), M. Darnell Suttles (Hospital Interrogator), Michael Chinyamurindi (Claude), Willie Amayke (Lead Porter), Malang, Jay Speed Forney, Shelton Mack, David Mungai, Anthony Mutune, Sylvester Mwangi, Les Robinson, Nelson Shalita (Porters), Jackson Gitonga, Andrew Kamuyu (Mizumu Tribesman), Fidel Bateke (Witch Doctor), Shayna Fox (Amy's Voice), Frank Welker (Special Vocal Effects), Gary Hecker, Peter Elliott (Gorilla Vocalizations), David Anthony, Nicholas Kadi, Christopher "Critter" Antonucci, Brian La Rosa, John Cameron, John Alexander Lowe, Jay Caputo, Garon Michael, Peter Elliott, David St. Pierre, Eldon Jackson, Philip Tan (Gorillas), Joe Pantoliano (Eddie), Delroy Lindo (Captain)

Karen Ross commandeers a safari to the Congo to find out what happened to her fiance, whose satellite contact was abruptly cut off. Joining her is a primatologist with the mission of returning a mountain gorilla, who has been taught to "speak," to her rightful home.

© Paramount Pictures

Dylan Walsh, Amy

Tim Curry, Ernie Hudson, Laura Linney

Laura Linney

Adewalé, Ernie Hudson, Laura Linney, Dylan Walsh

THE INCREDIBLY TRUE ADVENTURE OF TWO GIRLS IN LOVE

(FINE LINE FEATURES) Producer, Dolly Hall; Director/Screenplay, Maria Maggenti; Co-Producer, A. John Rath; Photography, Tami Reiker; Designer, Ginger Tougas; Editor, Susan Graef; Costumes, Cheryl Hurwitz; Music, Terry Dame; Casting, Heidi Griffiths; a Smash Pictures production; Ultra-Stereo; Color; Rated R; 95 minutes; June release

CAST

Randy Dean	Laurel Holloman
Evie Roy	Nicole Parker
Wendy	Maggie Moore
Rebecca Dean	Kate Stafford
Vicky	Sabrina Artel
Lena	Toby Poser
Frank	Nelson Rodriguez
Regina	Dale Dickey
Hayjay	Andrew Wright
Evelyn Roy	Stephanie Berry
Waitress	Babs Davy
Ali	John Elson

and Katlin Tyler, Anna Padgett, Chelsea Cattouse (Girls), Lillian Kiesler, Maryette Charlton (Old Ladies)

High school tomboy Randy Dean finds herself falling in love with the beautiful and popular Evie Roy.

© Fine Line Features

Laurel Holloman

Nicole Parker

Xander Berkeley, Julianne Moore

SAFE

(SONY PICTURES CLASSICS) Producers, Christine Vachon, Lauren Zalaznick; Executive Producers, Lindsay Law, James Schamus, Ted Hope; Director/Screenplay, Todd Haynes; Photography, Alex Nepomniaschy; Music, Ed Tomney; Editor, James Lyons; Designer, David Bomba; Costumes, Nancy Steiner; Casting, Jakki Fink; an American Playhouse Theatrical Films presentation of a Chemical Films production in association with Good Machine/Kardana Productions/Channel Four Films and Arnold Semler; Foto-Kem color; Rated R; 120 minutes; June release

CAST

Carol White	Julianne Moore
Peter Dunning	Peter Friedman
Greg White	Xander Berkeley
Linda	Susan Norman
Claire	Kate McGregor Stewart
Nell	Mary Carver
Dr. Hubbard	Stephen Gilborn
Susan	April Grace
Dr. Reynolds	Peter Crombie
Barbara	Ronnie Farer
Hairdresser	Janel Moloney
Marilyn	Lorna Scott
Chris	James LeGros
Joyce	Jessica Harper
Steve	Brandon Cruz
Mover	Dean Norris
Aerobics Instructor	Julie Burgess
Anita	Jodie Markell
Fulvia	Martha Velez-Johnson
Rory	Chauncy Leopardi
Dry Cleaners Manager	Saachiko
Department Store Dispatcher	Tim Gardner
Waitress	Wendy Haynes
Client	Alan Wasserman
Client's Wife	Jean Pflieger
Patrolman	Brendan Dolan
Psychiatrist	John Apicella
Lynn	Dana Anderson
Baby Shower Mother	Wendy Gayle
Baby Shower Child	Cassy Friel
Video Narrator	Frank Dent
Sarah	Sarah Davis
Becky (Auditorium Speaker)	Beth Grant

and Jo Wilkinson, Gerrielani Miyazaki (Listeners), Edith Meeks, Francesca Roberts, Elinor O. Caplan (Patients), Joe Comando (Exterminator), Tricia Dong (Wrenwood Patient), James Lyons (Cab Driver), Eleanor Graham (Singer), Mitch Greenhill (Accompanist), Rio Hackford (Lester), Ravi Achar (Wrenwood Instructor)

Los Angeles housewife Carol White, hoping to find a relief from her mysterious allergies, joins Wrenwood, a treatment center for people suffering from environmental illnesses.

© Sony Pictures Entertainment, Inc.

Meeko, Pocahontas, Flit

Pocahontas, John Smith, Grandmother Willow

Meeko, Pocahontas

Percy, Governor Ratcliffe

Governor Ratcliffe

POCAHONTAS

(WALT DISNEY PICTURES) Producer, James Pentecost; Directors, Mike Gabriel, Eric Goldberg; Screenplay, Carl Binder, Susannah Grant, Philip LaZebnik; Songs, Alan Menken, Stephen Schwartz; Original Score, Alan Menken; Associate Producer, Baker Bloodworth; Art Director, Michael Giaimo; Editor, H. Lee Peterson; Artistic Supervisors: Layout, Rasoul Azadani; Background, Cristy Maltese; Story, Tom Sito; Cleanup, Renee Holt-Bird, Nancy Kniep; Visual Effects, Don Paul; Computer Graphics Imagery, Steve Goldberg; Dolby Stereo; Technicolor; Rated G; 87 minutes; June release

VOICE CAST

Lon	Joe Baker
Thomas	Christian Bale
Pocahontas	Irene Bedard
Ben	Billy Connolly
Kocoum	James Apaumut Fall
John Smith	Mel Gibson
Grandmother Willow	Linda Hunt
Meeko	John Kassir
Pocahontas (singing voice)	Judy Kuhn
Percy	Danny Mann
Powhatan	Russell Means
Governor Ratcliffe/Wiggins	David Ogden Stiers
Nakoma	Michelle St. John
Kekata	Gordon Tootoosis
Flit	Frank Welker

In the year 1607, a young Native American woman, Pocahontas, falls in love with British soldier John Smith, despite her father's wishes that she marry within her own tribe.

Academy Award winner for Best Song ("Color of the Wind") and Original Score.

Pocahontas, Chief Powhatan

Nakoma, Meeko, Flit, Pocahontas

William Hurt, Harvey Keitel

Harold Perrineau, Forest Whitaker

Stockard Channing, Harvey Keitel

Harvey Keitel

SMOKE

(MIRAMAX) Producers, Greg Johnson, Peter Newman, Hisami Koroiwa, Kenzo Horikoshi; Executive Producers, Bob Weinstein, Harvey Weinstein, Satoru Iseki; Director, Wayne Wang; Screenplay, Paul Auster; Photography, Adam Holender; Designer, Kalina Ivanov; Costumes, Claudia Brown; Music, Rachel Portman; Editor, Maysie Hoy; an NDF/Euro Space production in association with Peter Newman/Internal; Dolby Digital Stereo; Color; Rated R; 112 minutes; June release

CAST

Auggie Wren	Harvey Keitel
Paul Benjamin	William Hurt
Rashid Cole	Harold Perrineau
Cyrus Cole	Forest Whitaker
Ruby McNutt	Stockard Channing
Felicity	Ashley Judd
1st OTB Man/Tommy	Giancarlo Esposito
2nd OTB Man/Jerry	Jose Zuniga
3rd OTB Man/Dennis	Stephen Gevedon
Jimmy Rose	Jared Harris
Book Thief	Daniel Auster
Waitress	Deirdre O'Connell
Vinnie	Victor Argo
Aunt Em	Michelle Hurst
Irate Customer	Vincenzo Amelia
Doreen Cole	Erica Gimpel
Cyrus, Jr.	Gilson Heglas
Baseball Announcer	Howie Rose
April Lee	Mary Ward
Violet	Mel Gorham
Lawyers	Baxter Harris, Paul Geier
The Creeper	Malik Yoba
Roger Goodwin	Walter T. Mead
Waiter	Murray Moston
Granny Ethel	Clarice Taylor

A dramatic-comical look at the lives of several characters who interact with a Brooklyn cigar store owner, Auggie Wren.

© Miramax Films

Stephen Gevedon, Harvey Keitel, Giancarlo Esposito, Jose Zuniga

Sylvester Stallone, Armand Assante

Joan Chen

Rob Schneider

JUDGE DREDD

(HOLLYWOOD PICTURES) Producers, Charles M. Lippincott, Beau E.L. Marks; Executive Producers, Andrew G. Vajna, Edward R. Pressman; Director, Danny Cannon; Screenplay, William Wisher, Steven E. De Souza; Story, Michael De Luca, William Wisher; Photography, Adrian Biddle; Designer, Nigel Phelps; Editors, Alex Mackie, Harry Keramidas; Associate Producers, Tony Munafo, Susan Nicoletti; Visual Effects Supervisor, Joel Hynek; Visual Effects, Mass. Illusion; Costumes, Emma Porteous; Judge Dredd Armour Costume Designer, Gianni Versace; Music, Alan Silvestri; Casting, Jackie Burch; an Edward R. Pressman/Cinergi production in association with Charles M. Lippincott; Distributed by Buena Vista Pictures; Dolby Digital Stereo; Panavision; Technicolor; Rated R; 95 minutes; June release

CAST

Judge Joseph Dredd	Sylvester Stallone
Rico	Armand Assante
Herman "Fergie" Ferguson	Rob Schneider
Council Judge Griffin	Jurgen Prochnow
Chief Justice Fargo	Max von Sydow
Judge Hershey	Diane Lane
Council Judge Evelyne McGruder	Joanna Miles
Ilsa	Joan Chen
Cadet Olmeyer	Balthazar Getty
Miller	Maurice Roeves
Geiger	Ian Dury
Mean Machine	Chris Adamson
Junior Angel	Ewen Bremner
Judge Esposito	Peter Marinker
Judge Silver	Angus MacInnes
Locker Judge	Louise Delamere
Fink Angel	Phil Smeeton
Hunter Squad Leader	Steve Toussaint
Chief Judge Hunter	Bradley Savelle
Judge Killed by Robot	Mark Morghan
Barge Crew Member	Ed Stobart
Brutal Prisoner	Huggy Lever
Brisco	Alexis Daniel
Border Guard	John Blakely
Pilot	Howard Grace
Reggie	Dig Wayne
Twist	Martin McDougall
Squatters	Ashley Artus, Christopher Glover, Brendan Fleming
Zed Squatters	Stephen Lord, Phil Kingston
Aspen Guard	Ewan Bailey
Co-Pilot	Stuart Mullen
Lily Hammond	Pat Starr
Fuppie	Adam Henderson
Hammond	Mitchell Ryan
Villain Leader	James Remar
Pa Angel	Scott Wilson
Narrator	James Earl Jones

In the twenty-first century, law enforcement judge Joseph Dredd is framed for murder and sentenced to the Aspen Penal Colony.

© Cinergi Pictures Entertainment Inc.

Sylvester Stallone

Max von Sydow

Diane Lane

67

Tom Hanks, Bill Paxton, Kevin Bacon

Kevin Bacon

Gary Sinise

APOLLO 13

(UNIVERSAL) Producer, Brian Grazer; Executive Producer, Todd Hallowell; Director, Ron Howard; Screenplay, William Broyles Jr., Al Reinert; Based on the book *Lost Moon* by Jim Lovell & Jeffrey Kluger; Photography, Dean Cundey; Designer, Michael Corenblith; Editors, Mike Hill, Dan Hanley; Music, James Horner; Vocal Performance, Annie Lennox; Costumes, Rita Ryack; Associate Producer, Louisa Velis; Special Visual Effects, Digital Domain; Casting, Jane Jenkins, Janet Hirshenson; DTS Stereo; Panavision; Deluxe color; Rated PG; 140 minutes; June release

CAST

Jim Lovell	Tom Hanks
Fred Haise	Bill Paxton
Jack Swigert	Kevin Bacon
Ken Mattingly	Gary Sinise
Gene Kranz	Ed Harris
Marilyn Lovell	Kathleen Quinlan
Barbara Lovell	Mary Kate Schellhardt
Susan Lovell	Emily Ann Lloyd
Jeffrey Lovell	Miko Hughes
Jay Lovell	Max Elliott Slade
Blanch Lovell	Jean Speegle Howard
Mary Haise	Tracy Reiner
Pete Conrad	David Andrews
Jane Conrad	Michelle Little
Deke Slayton	Chris Ellis
NASA Director	Joe Spano
Henry Hurt	Xander Berkeley
Glynn Lunney	Marc McClure
John Young	Ben Marley
EECOM White	Clint Howard
EECOM Arthur	Loren Dean
EECOM Gold	Tom Wood
RETRO White	Googy Gress
RETRO Gold	Patrick Mickler
FIDO White	Ray McKinnon
FIDO Gold	Max Grodénchik
Dr. Chuck	Christian Clemenson
CAPCOM 1	Brett Cullen
CAPCOM 2	Ned Vaughn
GUIDO White	Andy Milder
GUIDO Gold	Geoffrey Blake
LEM Controller White	Wayne Duvall
TELMU White	Jim Meskimen
TELMU Gold	Joseph Culp
INCO White	John Short
INCO Gold	Ben Bodé
FAO White	Todd Louiso
GNC White	Gabriel Jarret
Booster White	Christopher John Fields
Grumman Rep	Kenneth White
Ted	Jim Ritz

and Andrew Lipschultz (Launch Director), Mark Wheeler (Neil Armstrong), Larry Williams (Buzz Aldrin), Endre Hules (Guenter Wendt), Karen Martin (Tracey), Maureen Hanley (Woman), Meadow Williams (Kim), Walter Von Huene (Technician), Brian Markinson, Steve Rankin (Pad Rats), Austin O'Brien (Whiz Kid), Louisa Marie (Whiz Kid Mom), Thom Barry (Orderly), Arthur Senzy, Carl Gabriel Yorke, Ryan Holihan (SIM Techs), Rance Howard (Reverend), J.J. Chaback (Neighbor), Todd Hallowell (Noisy Civilian), Matthew Goodall (Stephen Haise), Taylor Goodall (Fred Haise, Jr.), Misty Dickinson (Margaret Haise), Roger Corman (Congressman), Lee Anne Matusek, Mark D. Newman (Loud Reporters), Mark McKeel (Suit Room Assistant), Patty Raya (Patty), Jack Conley, Jeffrey S. Kluger (Science Reporters), Bruce Wright, Ivan Allen, Jon Bruno (Anchors), Reed Rudy (Roger Chaffee), Steve Bernie (Virgil Grissom), Steven Ruge (Edward White), Herbert Jefferson Jr., John Dullaghan, John Wheeler, Paul Mantee, Julie Donatt, Thomas Crawford, Frank Cavestani, John M. Mathews (Reporters)

The true story of the ill-fated Apollo 13 space mission of April 1, 1970, when the three astronauts aboard faced danger after an oxygen tank exploded.

Academy Award winner for Best Film Editing and Sound. The film received additional Oscar nominations for picture, supporting actor (Harris), supporting actress (Quinlan), screenplay adaptation, original dramatic score, art direction, and visual effects.

Kevin Bacon, Tom Hanks

Ed Harris

Emily Ann Lloyd, Mary Kate Schellhardt, Kathleen Quinlan, Rance Howard, Miko Hughes

Bill Paxton

Tom Hanks, Bill Paxton

David Yost, Karen Ashley, Jason David Frank, Amy Jo Johnson, Steve Cardenas, Johnny Yong Bosch

Paul Freeman, Kerry Casey, Jean Paul Bell

MIGHTY MORPHIN POWER RANGERS: THE MOVIE

(20th CENTURY FOX) Producers, Haim Saban, Shuki Levy, Suzanne Todd; Director, Bryan Spicer; Screenplay, Arne Olsen; Story, John Kamps, Arne Olsen; Photography, Paul Murphy; Designer, Craig Stearns; Editor, Wayne Wahrman; Co-Producer, David Coatsworth; Music, Graeme Revell; Costumes, Joseph Porro; Stunts, Rocky McDonald; a Saban Entertainment/Toei Company production; Dolby Digital Stereo; Deluxe color; Rated PG; 95 minutes; June release

CAST

Aisha/Yellow Ranger	Karan Ashley
Adam/Black Ranger	Johnny Yong Bosch
Rocky/Red Ranger	Steve Cardenas
Tommy/White Ranger	Jason David Frank
Kimberly/Pink Ranger	Amy Jo Johnson
Billy/Blue Ranger	David Yost
Bulk	Paul Schrier
Skull	Jason Narvy
Ivan Ooze	Paul Freeman
Dulcea	Gabrielle Fitzpatrick
Zordon	Nicholas Bell
Alpha 5	Peta-Maree Rixon
Mordant	Jean Paul Bell
Goldar	Kerry Casey
Lord Zedd	Mark Ginther
Rita Repulsa	Julia Cortez
Fred Kelman	Jamie Croft
Kids	Paul Pantano, Mitchell McMahon, Tim Valka
Mr. Kelman	Peter Mochrie
Security Guard	Scott McGregor
Reporter	Paula Morrell
Construction Workers	Paul Goddard, Robert Simper
Zombie Parent Dancer	Robyn Gol

and Kerrigan Mahan, Robert L. Manahan, Robert Axelrod, Barbara Goodson, Richard Wood, Martin G. Metcalf (Voice Characterizations)

Six teenagers, who can transform themselves into martial arts superheroes, do battle with the evil Ivan Ooze. Based on the syndicated series, with the six principles repeating their roles on screen.

© Twentieth Century Fox

Johnny Yong Bosch, David Yost, Amy Jo Johnson, Jason David Frank, Karan Ashley, Steve Cardenas

FIRST KNIGHT

(COLUMBIA) Producers, Jerry Zucker, Hunt Lowry; Executive Producers, Gil Netter, Eric Rattray, Janet Zucker; Director, Jerry Zucker; Screenplay, William Nicholson; Story, Lorne Cameron, David Hoselton, William Nicholson; Photography, Adam Greenberg; Designer, John Box; Costumes, Nana Cecchi; Editor, Walter Murch; Music, Jerry Goldsmith; Special Effects Supervior, George Gibbs; from Zucker Brothers productions; SDDS Digital Stereo; Technicolor; Rated PG-13; 132 minutes; July release

CAST

King Arthur	Sean Connery
Lancelot	Richard Gere
Guinevere	Julia Ormond
Malagant	Ben Cross
Sir Agravaine	Liam Cunningham
Sir Kay	Christopher Villiers
Sir Patrise	Valentine Pelka
Sir Mador	Colin McCormack
Ralf	Ralph Ineson
Oswald	John Gielgud
Peter	Stuart Bunce
Elise	Jane Robbins
Petronella	Jean Marie Coffey
Mark	Paul Kynman
Sir Sagramore	Tom Lucy
Sir Tor	John Blakely
Sir Gawaine	Robert Gwyn Davin
Sir Carados	Sean Blowers
Sir Gaheris	Alexis Denisof
Sir Amant	Daniel Naprous
Sir Gareth	Jonathan Cake
Jacob	Paul Bentall
Gauntlet Man	Jonty Miller
Mark's Wife	Rose Keegan
Challenger	Mark Ryan

and Jeffrey Dench, Neville Phillips (Elders), Oliver Lewis, Wolf Christian, Angus Wright (Marauders), Jonathan Jaynes, Eric Stone (Guards), Ryan Todd (Young Lancelot), Albie Woodington (Scout), Richard Claxton (Child), Dido Miles (Grateful Woman), Michael Hodgson (Young Man in Crowd), Susannah Corbett (Young Woman in Crowd), Susan Breslau (Wedding Guest), Kate Zucker (Flower Girl), Bob Zucker (Little Boy with Birds), Charlotte Zucker, Burt Zucker (Bread Vendors)

Lancelot, a fearless swordsman, joins King Arthur's roundtable to be near the King's bride Guinevere, causing a triangle which threatens the ideal world of Camelot. Previous screen versions of the King Arthur legend include Knights of the Round Table *(MGM, 1954),* Lancelot and Guenevere *(1963),* Camelot *(1967), and* Excalibur *(Orion, 1981).*

© Columbia Pictures

Julia Ormond, John Gielgud

Sean Connery, Richard Gere

Ben Cross, Julia Ormond

Richard Gere

Ben Kingsley

Michael Madsen

SPECIES

(MGM) Producers, Frank Mancuso, Jr., Dennis Feldman; Director, Roger Donaldson; Screenplay, Dennis Feldman; Photography, Andrzej Bartkowiak; Designer, John Muto; Editor, Conrad Buff; Costumes, Joe I. Tompkins; Music, Christopher Young; Executive Producer, David Streit; Visual Effects Supervisor, Richard Edlund; Creature and Special Makeup Effects Creator, Steve Johnson; "Sil" Designer, H.R. Giger; Casting, Amanda Mackey, Cathy Sandrich; a Frank Mancuso, Jr. production; DTS Stereo; Panavision; Rated R; 108 minutes; July release

CAST

Xavier Fitch	Ben Kingsley
Press Lennox	Michael Madsen
Dr. Stephen Arden	Alfred Molina
Dan Smithson	Forest Whitaker
Dr. Laura Baker	Marg Helgenberger
Sil	Natasha Henstridge
Young Sil	Michelle Williams
John Carey	Whip Hubley
Aides	Jordan Lund, Don Fischer
Train Hobo	Scott McKenna
Mother	Virginia Morris
Snack Shop Clerk	Jayne Luke
German Tourist	David K. Schroeder
Conductors	David Jensen, Esther Scott
Dr. Roth	Shirley Prestia
Colleague	William Utay
Government Man	David Selburg
Mrs. Morris	Herta Ware
Fitch's Secretary	Melissa Bickerton
Wedding Dess Saleswoman	Lucy Rodriguez
Team Driver	Scott Sproule
Cop	Stogie Kenyatta
Motel Clerk	Gary Bullock
Lab Worker	Susan Hauser
Bouncer	William Bumiller
Drunken Girl	Caroline Barclay
Guy in Club	Matthew Ashford
Robbie	Anthony Guidera

and Sarah S. Leese (Screaming Woman), Patricia Belcher (Admittance Clerk), Richard Fancy (Doctor), Leslie Ishii (Nurse), Marliese K. Schneider (Abducted Woman), Robert Mendelson (Homeless Man), Pam Cook (Commercial Model), Lisa Liberati (Bathroom Bimbo), Ed Stone (Waiter), Dendrie Taylor (Marie), Kurtis Burow (Baby Boy), Dana Hee (Creature Performer), Frank Welker (Voice of Alien Sil), Susan Bartkowiak

A deadly, scientifically created life form, which has mutated into a beautiful woman, is pursued by a special team of experts trying to stop her before she finds someone to mate with.

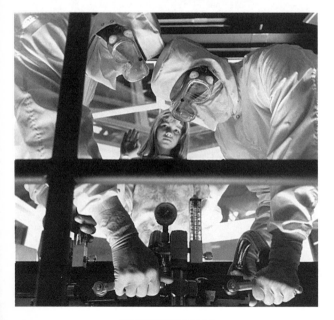

Michelle Williams (c)

Anthony Guidera, Natasha Henstridge

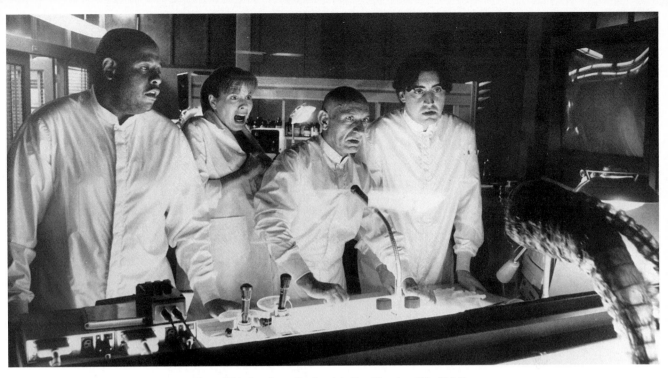

Forest Whitaker, Susan Bartkowiak, Ben Kingsley, Alfred Molina

Whip Hubley

Forest Whitaker

Sil

73

NINE MONTHS

(20th CENTURY FOX) Producers, Anne Francois, Chris Columbus, Mark Radcliffe; Executive Producers, Joan Bradshaw, Christopher Lambert; Director/Screenplay, Chris Columbus; Based on the film *Neuf Mois,* written and directed by Patrick Braoude; Photography, Donald McAlpine; Designer, Angelo P. Graham; Editor, Raja Gosnell; Music, Hans Zimmer; Costumes, Jay Hurley; Casting, Janet Hirshenson, Jane Jenkins; a 1492 Picture; Dolby Digital Stereo; Panavision; Deluxe color; Rated PG-13; 100 minutes; July release

CAST

Samuel Faulkner	Hugh Grant
Rebecca Taylor	Julianne Moore
Marty Dwyer	Tom Arnold
Gail Dwyer	Joan Cusack
Sean Fletcher	Jeff Goldblum
Dr. Kosevich	Robin Williams
Lili	Mia Cottet
Truman	Joey Simmrin
Shannon Dwyer	Ashley Johnson
Molly Dwyer	Alexa Vega
Patsy Dwyer	Aislin Roche
Older Woman	Priscilla Alden
Older Man	Edward Ivory
Bicyclist	James M. Brady
Arnie	Charles A. Martinet
Little Boy on Beach	Brendan Columbus
Little Girls in Ballet Class	Eleanor Columbus, Anna Barnathan, Zelda Williams
Tow Truck Driver	Peter Bankins
Bobbie	Betsy Monroe
Sean's Friends	Ngaio S. Bealum, Cynthia Urquhart, Tim Moffet, Mia Liban, Kumar Singh
Praying Mantis	Amanda Girard
Dr. Kosevich's Receptionist	Val Diamond
Clown Outside Toy Store	Jerry Masan
Woman in Toy Store	Irene Columbus
Baby in Toy Store	Violet Columbus
Children at Toy Store	Brittany Radcliffe, Porscha Radcliffe, Cody Lee Dorkin, Emily Gosnell, Bradley Gosnell
Tennis Attendant	Kristin Davis
Ultrasound Receptionist	Angela Hopkins
Dr. Thatcher	Emily Yancy
Baby in Ultrasound	Hayley Rose Hansen
Roller Blade Girl	Shawn Cady
Moving Man	Goerge F. Mauricio
Car Salesman	Paul Simon
Car Lot Customers	Frank P. Verducci, Barbara Olson
Kid Being Choked in Park	Morgan Miller
Maternity Floor Receptionist	Carol De Pasquale
Doctor in Hallway	Bruce Devan
Christine	Cheryl Lee Thorup
Emergency Attendants	Clarke Devereux, Tommy Banks
Delivery Room Head Nurse	Susan Ilene Johnson
Pregnant Women	Maureen McVerry, Velina Brown, Joy M. Cook, Sue Murphy, Lee Ann Manley
Rebecca's Nurse	Diane Amos
Gail's Nurse	Betsy Aidem
Anesthesiologist	Terence McGovern
Delivery Room Nurses	Geoff Bolt, Gwen Holloway

Child psychologist Samuel Faulkner finds himself less than ecstatic when his girlfriend Rebecca informs him that she is pregnant.

© Twentieth Century Fox

Julianne Moore, Hugh Grant

Jeff Goldblum

Joan Cusak, Tom Arnold

Steve Buscemi

Catherine Keener, James La Gros

Steve Buscemi

LIVING IN OBLIVION

(SONY PICTURES CLASSICS) Producers, Michael Griffiths, Marcus Viscidi; Executive Producer, Hilary Gilford; Co-Executive Producers, Frank von Zerneck, Robert Sertner; Co-Producer, Meredith Zamsky; Associate Producers, Danielle von Zerneck, Dermot Mulroney, Jane Gil; Director/Screenplay, Tom DiCillo; Photography, Frank Prinzi; Designer, Therese Deprez; Editor, Camilla Toniolo; Music, Jim Farmer; Costumes, Ellen Lutter; Casting, Marcia Shulman; a JDI productions and Lemon Sky productions presentation; Dolby Stereo; Black and white/Color; Rated R; 91 minutes; July release

CAST

Nick Reve	Steve Buscemi
Nicole	Catherine Keener
Wolf	Dermot Mulroney
Wanda	Danielle von Zerneck
Chad Palomino	James Le Gros
Cora	Rica Martens
Tito	Peter Dinklage
Script	Hilary Gilford
Sound	Michael Griffiths
Boom	Matthew Grace
Gaffer	Robert Wightman
Assistant Camera	Kevin Corrigan
Driver	Tom Jarmusch
Clapper	Ryan Bowker
Production Assistant	Francesca Dimauro

Comedy about a troubled movie set on which independent filmmaker Nick Reve attempts to maintain both his integrity and sanity.

© Sony Pictures Entertainment Inc.

THE INDIAN IN THE CUPBOARD

(PARAMOUNT/COLUMBIA) Producers, Kathleen Kennedy, Frank Marshall, Jane Startz; Executive Producers, Bernie Williams, Robert Harris, Marty Keltz; Director, Frank Oz; Screenplay, Melissa Mathison; Based upon the novel by Lynne Reid Banks; Photography, Russell Carpenter; Designer, Deborah L. Scott; Editor, Ian Crafford; Music, Randy Edelman; Special Visual Effects and Animation, Industrial Light & Magic; Supervisor of Visual Effects, Eric Brevig; Casting, Margery Simkin; a Kennedy/Marshall Production in association with Scholastic Productions; Dolby Digital Stereo; Deluxe color; Rated PG; 96 minutes; July release

CAST

Omri	Hal Scardino
Little Bear	Litefoot
Jane	Lindsay Crouse
Victor	Richard Jenkins
Patrick	Rishi Bhat
Tommy	Steve Coogan
Boone	David Keith
Lucy	Sakina Jaffrey
Gillon	Vincent Kartheiser
Teacher	Nestor Serrano
Adiel	Ryan Olson
Baby Martin	Leon Tejwani, Lucas Tejwani
Purple Mohawk	Christopher Conte
Emily	Cassandra Brown
Sam	Christopher Moritz
Ramon	Beni Malkin
Tina	Juliet Berman
Kiron	Stephen Morales
Indian Chief	George Randall
Yard Teacher	Gia Galeano
School Kid	Kevin Malaro
"Darth Vader"	Tom Bewley
"G.I. Joe"	Keii Johnston
"Robocop"	J.R. Horsting
"Cardassian"	Michael Papajohn
"Firengi"	Eric Stabenau

For his ninth birthday, Omri is given an old cupboard which magically brings a miniature plastic Indian to life.

© Paramount Pictures

Hal Scardino, Litefoot

Litefoot, David Keith

Rishi Bhat, Hal Scardino

Hal Scardino, Litefoot

KIDS

(EXCALIBUR FILMS) Producer, Cary Woods; Executive Producers, Gus Van Sant, Patrick Panzarella, Michael Chambers; Co-Producers, Cathy Konrad, Christine Vachon, Lauren Zalaznick; Director, Larry Clark; Screenplay, Harmony Korine; Photography, Eric Alan Edwards; Music, Louis Barlow; Editor, Chris Tellefson; Designer, Kevin Thomson; Costumes, Kim Druce; an Independent Pictures & the Guys Upstairs presentation; Technicolor; Not rated; 90 minutes; July release

CAST

Telly	Leo Fitzpatrick
Casper	Justin Pierce
Jennie	Chloe Sevigny
Girl #1	Sarah Henderson
Ruby	Rosario Dawson
Harold	Harold Hunter
Darcy	Yakira Peguero
Paul	Sajan Bhagat
Stanly	Billy Valdes
Zack	Billy Waldman
Javier	Javier Nunez
Luis	Luis Munoz
Christian	Christian Brums
Alex	Alex Glenn
Susan	Julia Mendoza
Linda	Gillian Goldstein
Diane	Priscilla Forsyth

and Joseph Chan (Ball Owner), Jonathan S. Kim (Korean Guy), Adriane Brown (Little Girl), Francine Fuertes (Jennie's Nurse), Deborah Draper (Ruby's Nurse), Alan Wise (Accordian Player), Billy Solomon (Dancing Boy), Johanna Ignaton (Singing Woman), Raymond Batista (Legless Man), Julia Stube-Glorhus (Telly's Mom), Dr. Henry (Rasta Drug Dealer), Joe Abrahams (Steven), Hamilton Harris (Hamilton), Jeff Pang (Jeff), Atabey Rodriguez (Misha), Giovanni Estevez, Karyn Grupski, Mike Hernandez, Peter Bici, Ryan Sikorski, Eddie Peel, Michael Arbitille, Nuri Bell, Medwin Pang, James Story, Jeff Simmons, Jam, Daniel Phillips, Jamal Simmons, Terence Oddo, Frank Natiello (Kids in Park), Tony Morales, Walter Youngblood (Couple), Ellsworth "Cisco" Davis (Hoodlum), Joseph Knofelmacher (Taxi Driver), Michele Lockwood (Kim), Carisa Glucksman (Joy), Scott Schwartz (Bennie), Sidney Prawatyotin (Sid), Carl Ly-Min (Security Guard), Avi Korine (Fidget), Darice Liguidi, Beth Waterstohn, Jason Iconstanti, Alexandra Karabell (Kids from Jersey), Zulaika Velazquez (Gertie), Nick Lockman (Nick), Joel Alvarez (Joey), Gerry Smith (Gerry), Lavar McBride (Lavar), Julie Ho (Tamara), Lila Lee, Regina Mei, Amy Moy, Lisa Acevedo, Corisa DeLeon, Johnathan Carter, Jimmy Lalpatan (Girls at Party)

Drama looks at the reckless and irresponsibile habits of a group of city teenagers as they aimlessly indulge in sex and drugs.

Yakiro Peguero, Leo Fitzpatrick

Breckin Meyer, Brittany Murphy, Donald Faison, Alicia Silverstone, Jeremy Sisto, Stacey Dash, Justin Walker, Elisa Donovan, Paul Rudd

Alicia Silverstone

Justin Walker, Alicia Silverstone

Paul Rudd, Alicia Silverstone

Stacey Dash, Brittany Murphy, Alicia Silverstone

CLUELESS

(PARAMOUNT) Producers, Scott Rudin, Robert Lawrence; Director/Screenplay, Amy Heckerling; Photography, Bill Pope; Designer, Steven Jordan; Editor, Debra Chiate; Associate Producer, Twink Caplan; Co-Producers, Adam Schroeder, Barry Berg; Music, David Kitay; Music Supervisor, Karyn Rachtman; Costumes, Mona May; Casting, Marcia S. Ross; Dolby Digital Stereo; Deluxe color; Rated PG-13; 97 minutes; July release

CAST

Cher Hamilton	Alicia Silverstone
Dionne	Stacey Dash
Tai	Brittany Murphy
Josh	Paul Rudd
Murray	Donald Faison
Amber	Elisa Donovan
Travis	Breckin Meyer
Elton	Jeremy Sisto
Mel Hamilton	Dan Hedaya
Lucy	Aida Linares
Mr. Wendell Hall	Wallace Shawn
Miss Toby Geist	Twink Caplan
Christian	Justin Walker
Paroudasm	Sebastian Rashidi
Principal	Herb Hall
Ms. Stoeger	Julie Brown
Heather	Susan Mohun
Summer	Nicole Bilderback
DMV Tester	Ron Orbach
Lawrence	Sean Holland
College Guy	Roger Kabler
Robber	Jace Alexander
Logan	Josh Lozoff
Priest	Carl Gottlieb
Student	Joseph D. Reitman
Bartender	Anthony Beninati

In this satirical comedy, rich, popular, and beautiful Beverly Hills teenager Cher decides to make it her project to give new student Tai a makeover, spark a romance between two shy teachers, and snag herself a boyfriend.

© Paramount Pictures

Justin Walker, Alicia Silverstone

Alicia Silverstone, Stacey Dash

Alicia Silverstone, Brittany Murphy, Stacey Dash

Twink Caplan, Wallace Shawn

Dennis Miller

Sandra Bullock, Jeremy Northam

Diane Baker

THE NET

(COLUMBIA) Producers, Irwin Winkler, Rob Cowan; Director, Irwin Winkler; Screenplay, John Brancato, Michael Ferris; Photography, Jack N. Green; Designer, Dennis Washington; Costumes, Linda Bass; Music, Mark Isham; Casting, Mindy Marin; SDDS Stereo; Technicolor; Rated PG-13; 118 minutes; July release

CAST

Angela Bennett ....Sandra Bullock
Jack Devlin ....Jeremy Northam
Dr. Alan Champion ....Dennis Miller
Mrs. Bennett..Diane Baker
Imposter ....Wendy Gazelle
Bergstrom..Ken Howard
Dale...Ray McKinnon
WNN Anchor ....Daniel Schorr
Public Defender ....L. Scott Caldwell
Ben Phillips ....Robert Gossett
Nurses ....Kristina Krofft, Julia Pearlstein
Resort Desk Clerk ....Juan Garcia
Mexican Doctor...Tony Perez
Mrs. Raines ....Margo Winkler
Stan Whiteman ....Gene Kirkwood
and Christopher Darga, Charles Winkler (Cops), Rick Snyder (Russ Melbourne), Gerald Berns (Jeff Gregg), Tannis Benedict (Elevator Woman), Vaughn Armstrong, Wren T. Brown (Troopers), Lynn Blades (Remote Reporter), Israel Juarbe (Thief), Julia Vera (Mexican Nun), Lewis Dix (FedEx Man), Lili Flanders (Embassy Worker), Adam Winkler (Computer Nerd), Brian Frankish (Shuttle Driver), Wanda Lee Evans (Desk Sergeant), David Winkler, John Livingston, Cam Brainard (Computer Technicians), Kerry Kilbride (WNN Reporter), Roland Gomez (Limo Driver), Melvin Thompson (Fire Official), Rich Bracco (Fireman), Lucy Butler (Officer), Dennis Richmond, Elaine Corral Kendall (Newscasters), Alfredo Lopez (Guitar Player), Thomas Crawford (Waiter), John Cappon (ICU Doctor), Barbara Abedi (CCU Nurse), Kevin Brown (The Bunny), Hope Parrish, William B. Hill (Security Officers), Danny Breen (Supervisor), Andrew Amador (Dermot Conley), Melissa Bomes (Reservation Clerk)

Computer analyst Angela Bennett is horrified to find that her identity has been electronically erased after she has stumbled upon a secret program linked to a recent politician's suicide.

Sandra Bullock, Jeremy Northam

Kevin Costner, Dennis Hopper

Kevin Costner, Jeanne Tripplehorn

WATERWORLD

(UNIVERSAL) Producers, Charles Gordon, John Davis, Kevin Costner; Executive Producers, Jeffrey Mueller, Andrew Licht, Ilona Herzberg; Director, Kevin Reynolds; Screenplay, Peter Rader, David Twohy; Photography, Dean Semler; Designer, Dennis Gassner; Editor, Peter Boyle; Music, James Newton Howard; Line Producer, Gene Levy; Costumes, John Bloomfield; Associate Producer, David Fulton; Visual Effects Supervisor, Micheal J. McAlister; Casting, David Rubin, Jakki Fink; a Lawrence Gordon presentation of a Gordon Company/Davis Entertainment Company/Licht/Mueller Film Corp. production; DTS Stereo; Eastman color; Rated PG-13; 134 minutes; July release

CAST

Mariner	Kevin Costner
Deacon	Dennis Hopper
Helen	Jeanne Tripplehorn
Enola	Tina Majorino
Gregor	Michael Jeter
Nord	Gerard Murphy
Enforcer	R.D. Call
Drifter #2	Kim Coates
Doctor	John Fleck
Ledger Guy	Robert Joy
Pilot	Jack Black
Plane Gunner	John Toles-Bey
Elder #3/Survivor #1	Zitto Kazann
Priam	Zakes Mokae
Elder #1	Sab Shimono
Drifter #1	Chaim Jeraffi
Banker	Jack Kehler
Hydroholic	Robert Silverman
Hellfire Gunner	Neil Giuntoli
Toby	David Finnegan
Sawzall Smoker	Gregory B. Goossen
Depth Gauge Guy	William Preston
Bone	Sean Whalen
Smitty	Robert LeSardo
Djeng	Lee Arenberg
Truan	Doug Spinuzza

and Ric Aviles, Henry Kapono Ka'Aihue, Tracy Anderson (Gatesmen), Leonardo Cimino (Elder #2), Luke Ka'Ili, Jr., Anthony DeMasters, Willy Petrovic (Boys), Lanny Flaherty (Trader #1), Rita Zohar, Chris Douridas (Atollers), August Neves (Old Atoller), Ari Barak (Atoll Man), Alexa Jago (Atoll Woman)

After the polar ice caps have melted and covered the earth, the various survivors live in the hope of finding land and fresh water. This sci-fi action adventure became the most expensive motion picture ever produced.

The film received an Oscar nomination for sound.

© Universal City Studios, Inc.

Kevin Costner

Jeanne Tripplehorn, Tina Majorino

OPERATION DUMBO DROP

(WALT DISNEY PICTURES) Producers, Diane Nabatoff, David Madden; Executive Producers, Ted Field, Robert W. Cort; Director, Simon Wincer; Screenplay, Gene Quintano, Jim Kouf; Story, Jim Morris; Photography, Russell Boyd; Designer, Paul Peters; Editor, O. Nicholas Brown; Costumes, Rosanna Norton; Music, David Newman; Co-Executive Producer, Edward Gold; Co-Producer, Penelope L. Foster; Tai's Trainers, Gary Johnson, Kari Johnson; Casting, Mike Fenton, Julie Ashton; an Interscope Communications production in association with PolyGram Filmed Entertainment; Distributed by Buena Vista Pictures; Dolby Digital Stereo; Panavision; Technicolor; Rated PG; 107 minutes; July release

Danny Glover, Tai, Dinh Thien Le, Ray Liotta, Doug E. Doug, Denis Leary, Corin Nemec

CAST

Capt. Sam Cahill	Danny Glover
Capt. T.C. Doyle	Ray Liotta
David Poole	Denis Leary
Harvey "H.A." Ashford	Doug E. Doug
Lawrence Farley	Corin Nemec
Linh	Dinh Thien Le
Goddard	Tcheky Karyo
Nguyen	Hoang Ly
Quang	Vo Trung Anh
Pederson	Marshall Bell
Y B'ham	James Hong
Jhon	Long Nguyen
C-123 Pilot	Tim Kelleher
C-123 Co-Pilot	Scott N. Stevens
Huey Pilot #1	Kevin La Rosa
Huey Co-Pilots	Christopher Ward, Steve Countouriotis
Huey Gunner #1	Robert Kevin Miller
Village Elder	Michael Lee
NVA Captain	Le Minh Tien
NVA Lieutenant	Mac Van Nam
Bo-Tat	Tai

and Ton Nguyen That (Feed Salesman), Somsak Hormsabat (Bike Driver), Lionel Douglas (Lieutenant), Tien Nguyen Van (NVA Anti Aircraft), Doi Chettawat Kanboon (Lihn—6 years), Chern Dao Van (Lihn's Father), Mark S. Bryant (C-130 Pilot), Jared Chandler (C-130 Co-Pilot), Nick Satriano (Red), Hing Hang Quang (Old Villager), Thanh Nguyen (NVA Soldier), Wichien Nguyen Thi (Peasant Woman)

Five Green Berets are assigned the unlikely task of transporting an elephant through the Vietnamese jungle to the villagers of Montagnard.

© The Walt Disney Company and Interscope Communications, Inc.

Corin Nemec, Tai

Ray Liotta, Danny Glover, Tai, Dinh Thien Le, Doug E. Doug

Ray Liotta, Danny Glover, Tai, Dinh Thien Le

Naomi Campbell, Isaac Mizrahi, Linda Evangelista

VIRTUOSITY

(PARAMOUNT) Producer, Gary Lucchesi; Executive Producer, Howard W. Koch, Jr.; Director, Brett Leonard; Screenplay, Eric Bernt; Photography, Gale Tattersall; Designer, Nilo Rodis; Editors, B.J. Sears, Rob Kobrin; Co-Producer, Gimel Everett; Costumes, Francine Jamison-Tanchuck; Music, Christopher Young; Visual Effects Supervisor, Jon Townley; Special Visual Effects, L² Communications; Casting, Deborah Aquila, Jane Shannon; Executive Music Producers, Tim Sexton, Richard Rudolph; A Gary Lucchesi production; Dolby Digital Stereo; Super 35 Widescreen; Deluxe color; Rated R; 105 minutes; August release

CAST

Parker Barnes	Denzel Washington
Madison Carter	Kelly Lynch
Sid 6.7	Russell Crowe
Lindenmeyer	Stephen Spinella
William Cochran	William Forsythe
Elizabeth Deane	Louise Fletcher
Wallace	William Fichtner
John Donovan	Costas Mandylor
Clyde Reilly	Kevin J. O'Connor
Karin	Kaley Cuoco
Matthew Grimes	Christopher Murray
Sheila 3.2	Heidi Schanz
Media Zone Singer	Traci Lords
Big Red	J. Gordon Noice
Linda Barnes	Mari Morrow
Christine Barnes	Miracle Unique Vincent
Beautiful Woman at Olympic Stadium	Mara Duronslet
Emcee	Michael Buffer
IS?TV Reporter	Karen Annarino
Rafael Debaca	Miguel Najera
John Symes	Danny Goldring
Ed	Randall Fontana
Surgeon	Allen Scotti

and Dwayne Chattman (Stripped Man in Media Zone), Ed Marques (Blond Punk in Media Zone), Cheryl Lawson (Pretty Woman in Media Zone), Kevin Loreque (Animatronic Bartender), Eiko Nijo (Geisha Hostess), Gauravani Buchwald (Burly Man in Video Store), Rolando Molina (Videostore Salesman), Gary Anthony Sturgis (Officer at Video Store), Monica Allison (Woman onTrain), Susan Mohun (Bystander), David Asman (Metrolink Cop), Anthony C. Hall (Locator Technician), Amy Smallman (Aide in Cochran's Office), Ahmed Ahmed (Cameraman), Marva Hicks (Onscreen Talent), Juan A. Riojas, Steven R. Barnett (Metromedia Cops), John Walcutt (Swat Captain), Michael Buchman Silver (Undercover Cop), Jordan Marder (Prison Transport Guard), Brogan Young (Monitor Prison Guard), Laura Leigh Hughes, Dustin Nguyen (Suburban Reporters), Tony Winters (Newscaster), Virginia Watson (Anchorwoman), Beverly Cohen (TV Tabloid Host), Margot Hope (Paula), Una Damon, Mary-Rachel Foot (Women with Video Cameras), Jennifer Greenhut, Lesa Noelle, Michelle Smith, Brit Thompson (Screaming Women), Alanna Ubach (Ella), Kevin La Presle (Paramedic), Daniel Anderson (Police Detective), Eric Bernt (Building Supervisor), Robert John Gomes (Swat Guy)

After virtual reality fabrication Sid 6.7, containing the traits of several noted psychopaths, escapes into the real world, ex-cop Parker Barnes is chosen to track him down and destroy him.

UNZIPPED

(MIRAMAX) Producer, Michael Alden; Executive Producers, David Pecker, Nina Santisi; Co-Producers, Paul DeBenedictis, Keith Estabrook; Director, Douglas Keeve; Photography, Ellen Kuras; Editor, Paula Heredia; Co-Executive Producer, Dori Berinstein; a Hachette Filipacchi production with *Elle Magazine*; Black and white/Color; Rated R; 76 minutes; August release; Documentary looks at the world of New York fashion designer Isaac Mizrahi, featuring Linda Evangelista, Naomi Campbell, Cindy Crawford, Kate Moss.

Louise Fletcher, Kelly Lynch, Denzel Washington

Russell Crowe

William Forsythe, Denzel Washington

Patrick Stewart, Steven Weber

Steven Weber

Olympia Dukakis, Gregory Jbara

JEFFREY

(ORION CLASSICS) Producers, Mark Balsam, Mitchell Maxwell, Victoria Maxwell; Executive Producer, Kevin McCollum; Co-Executive Producers, Dan Markley, Andrea Pines, Mike Skipper; Director, Christopher Ashley; Co-Producer/Screenplay, Paul Rudnick, based on his play; Photography, Jeffery Tufano; Designer, Michael Johnston; Editor, Cara Silverman; Music, Stephen Endelman; Line Producer, Harry Knapp; Choreographer, Jerry Mitchell; a Workin' Man Films in association with the Booking Office presentation; Ultra-Stereo; Deluxe color; Rated R; 91 minutes; August release

CAST

Jeffrey	Steven Weber
Sterling	Patrick Stewart
Steve	Michael T. Weiss
Darius	Bryan Batt
Debra Moorhouse	Sigourney Weaver
Mother Teresa	Irma St. Paule
Skip Winkley	Robert Klein
Ann Marwood Bartle	Christine Baranski
Acolyte	Kathy Najimy
Dad	Peter Maloney
Mom	Debra Monk
Father Dan	Nathan Lane
Mrs. Marcangelo	Olympia Dukakis
Angelique	Gregory Jbara
Men	Peter Jacobson, Tom Cayler, David Thornton
Crying Guy	Lee Mark Nelson
Tourist	John Ganun
Movie Theatre Guys	Joseph Dain, Jeffrey Ross
Salesman	Nicky Paraiso
Barney's Waiter	K. Todd Freeman
Cheryl the Showgirl	Patti Ann O'Connell
Waiter/Actor/Policeman	Patrick Kerr
Casting Director	Peter Bartlett
Boss	John Seidman
Tim	Victor Garber
Elderly Man	Barton Heyman
Homeboy	Darryl Theirse
Single Woman	Camryn Manheim
Sharon	J. Smith Cameron
Dave	Ethan Phillips
Thugs	Lou Sumrall, Robert Capelli Jr., Vinny Capone
Woman in the Window	Nancy Ticotin
Memorial Guest	Marcus Lovett
Young Mother	Michele Pawk
House Manager	Demetri Corbin
Child	Alexander Cohen Smith
Chuch Ladies	Mary Bond Davis, Lenka Peterson
Master	Peter B.
Slave	Albert Macklin
Sean	Michael Duvert
Network V.O.	Alison Sheehy
Nurse	Sarah Peterson
Aunt Phyllis	Marylouise Burke
Uncle Barney	Joe Ponazecki
Grandma Rose	Alice Drummond
Cousin Gary	Henry Stram

and Leroi Freeman, Scott Fowler, Christopher Harrison, Sergio A. Trujillo, J. David Elder, Christopher Davis, Richard Amaro, Andreas Niedermeier (Cater-Waiter Dancers), Kevin Nealon

Comedy about a young gay man in Manhattan, whose answer to the AIDS epidemic is swear off sex, a vow he finds more difficult than expected when he meets the man of his dreams. Bryan Batt, Patrick Kerr, and Darryl Thierse all appeared in the original 1992 Off-Broadway production.

Bryan Batt, Patrick Stewart. Steven Weber, Michael T. Weiss

Sigourney Weaver, Kathy Najimy

Nathan Lane

Christine Baranski

Steven Weber, Michael T. Weiss

Michelle Pfeiffer, George Dzundza

Renoly Santiago, Bruklin Harris, Richard Grant

Marisela Gonzales, Michelle Pfeiffer

DANGEROUS MINDS

(HOLLYWOOD PICTURES) Producers, Don Simpson, Jerry Bruck-heimer; Executive Producers, Sandra Rabins, Lucas Foster; Director, John N. Smith; Screenplay, Ronald Bass; Based upon the book *My Posse Don't Do Homework* by LouAnne Johnson; Photography, Pierre Letarte; Designer, Donald Graham Burt; Music, Wendy & Lisa; Song: "Gangsta's Paradise" by Stevie Wonder, Artis Ivey, Doug Rasheed, Lawrence Sanders/performed by Coolio featuring L.V.; Editor, Tom Rolf; Costumes, Bobbie Read; Music Supervisor, Kathy Nelson; Casting, Bonnie Timmer-mann; a Don Simpson and Jerry Bruckheimer production in association with Via Rosa Productions; Dolby Digital Stereo; Technicolor; Rated R; 98 minutes; August release

CAST

LouAnne Johnson	Michelle Pfeiffer
Hal Griffith	George Dzundza
Mr. George Grandey	Courtney B. Vance
Ms. Carla Nichols	Robin Bartlett
Mary Benton	Beatrice Winde
Waiter	John Neville
Irene Roberts	Lorraine Toussaint
Raul Sanchero	Renoly Santiago
Emilio Ramirez	Wade Dominguez
Callie Roberts	Bruklin Harris
Cornelius Bates	Marcello Thedford
Gusmaro Rivera	Roberto Alvarez
Durrell Benton	Richard Grant
Angela	Marisela Gonzales
Nikki	Toni Nichelle Buzhardt
Kareem	Norris Young
Big "G"	Rahman Ibraheem
Taiwana	Desire Galvez
Roderick	Wilson Limpo
Lionel Benton	Raymond Grant
Stephanie	Veronica Robles
Oso	Michael Archuleta
Tanyekia	Deshanda Carter
Deanne	Ebony Jerido
Grip	Brandi Younger
Pam	Asia Minor
Josy	Karina Arroyave
Alvina	Paula Garces
Huero	Ivan Sergei
P.J.	Mark Prince Edwards
Lalo	Ismael Archuleta
Jody	Skye Bassett
Warlock	Gaura Buchwald

and Cynthia Avila (Mrs. Sanchero), Roman J. Cisneros (Mr. Sanchero), Camille Winbush (Tyeisha Roberts), Al Israel (Mr. Santiago), Brian Anthony (Joey), Jason Gutman (Adam), Lara Spotts (Dianna), Danny Strong, Boris Vaks (Students), Irene Olga Lopez (Woman #1, School Office), Jeff Feringa, Sarah Marshall (Librarians), Freeze-Luv (Security Guard)

Ex-Marine LouAnne Johnson takes on the challenge of teaching English to a group of tough inner-city kids at a Northern California high school in this true-life drama.

© Hollywood Pictures Company/Don Simpson Productions Inc., and Jerry Bruckheimer, Inc.

Richard Grant, Michelle Pfeiffer, Renoly Santiago

A WALK IN THE CLOUDS

(20TH CENTURY FOX) Producers, Gil Netter, David Zucker, Jerry Zucker; Director, Alfonso Arau; Screenplay, Robert Mark Kamen, Mark Miller, Harvey Weitzman; Based on *Quattro Passi Fra le Nuvole*; Story and Screenplay material by Piero Tellini, Cesare Zavattini, Vittorio de Benedetti, by assignment of Massimo Tellini; Executive Producer, James D. Brubaker; Photography, Emmanuel Lubezki; Designer, David Gropman; Editor, Don Zimmerman; Co-Producer, Bill Johnson; Music, Maurice Jarre; Costumes, Judy L. Ruskin; Casting, John Lyons, Christine Sheaks; a Zucker Brothers production; Dolby Digital Stereo; Technicolor; Rated PG-13; 104 minutes; August release

Keanu Reeves (c)

CAST

Paul Sutton	Keanu Reeves
Victoria Aragon	Aitana Sanchez-Gijon
Don Pedro Aragon	Anthony Quinn
Alberto Aragon	Giancarlo Giannini
Marie Jose Aragon	Angelica Aragon
Guadelupe Aragon	Evangelina Elizondo
Pedro Aragon, Jr.	Freddy Rodriguez
Betty Sutton	Debra Messing
Jose Manuel	Febronio Covarrubias
Jose Luis	Roberto Huerta
Jose Marie	Juan Jimenez
Jose's Musical Son	Ismael Gallegos
Consuelo	Alejandra Flores
Maria	Gema Sandoval
Father Coturri	Don Amendolia
Armistead Knox	Gregory Martin
Bus Driver	Mary Pat Gleason
Louts	John Dennis Johnston, Joseph Lindsey
Soldiers	Mark Matheisen, Brad Rea
Conductor	Macon McCalman
Truck Driver	Ivory Ocean
Swiss Yodler	Fred Burri
USO Woman	Stephanie Maislen
Man at Gate	Joe Troconis
Ten Year Old Boy	Loren Sitomer

Pregnant and abandoned by her lover, Victoria Aragon convinces traveling salesman Paul Sutton to pose as her husband to avoid confrontation with her stern father.

© Twentieth Century Fox

Anthony Quinn, Keanu Reeves

Keanu Reeves, Aitana Sanchez-Gijon

Giancarlo Giannini, Aitana Sanchez-Gijon

Robin Shou, Talisa Soto, Christopher Lambert, Bridgette Wilson, Linden Ashby

Bridgette Wilson, Trevor Goddard

Robin Shou, Cary-Hiroyuki Tagawa

MORTAL KOMBAT

(NEW LINE CINEMA) Producer, Lawrence Kasanoff; Executive Producers, Bob Engelman, Danny Simon; Director, Paul Anderson; Screenplay, Kevin Droney; Photography, John R. Leonetti; Designer, Jonathan Carlson; Editor, Martin Hunter; Costumes, Ha Nguyen; Music, George S. Clinton; GORO Creature Effects, Alec Gillis, Tom Woodruff, Jr.; Stunts/Fight Choreographer, Pat E. Johnson; Casting, Fern Champion, Mark Paladini; a Lawrence Kasanoff/Threshold Entertainment production; Dolby Digital Stereo; Color; Rated PG-13; 95 minutes; August release

CAST

Lord Rayden	Christopher Lambert
Liu Kang	Robin Shou
Johnny Cage	Linden Ashby
Shang Tsung	Cary-Hiroyuki Tagawa
Sonya Blade	Bridgette Wilson
Kitana	Talisa Soto
Kano	Trevor Goddard
Scorpion	Chris Casamassa
Sub-Zero	Francois Petit
Reptile	Keith H. Cooke
Fighting Monk	Hakim Alston
Art Lean	Kenneth Edwards
Chief Priest	John Fujioka
Assistant Director	Daniel Haggard
Director	Sandy Helberg
Chan	Steven Ho
Master Boyd	Peter Jason
Grandfather	Lloyd Kino
Jaxx	Gregory McKinney

Three young Kombatant warriors do battle with the evil sorcerer Shang Tsung.

© New Line Productions, Inc.

Chris Casamassa

THE BABY-SITTERS CLUB

(COLUMBIA) Producers, Jane Startz, Peter O. Almond; Executive Producers, Marc Abraham, Thomas A. Bliss, Armyan Bernstein, Martin Keltz, Deborah Forte; Director, Melanie Mayron; Screenplay, Dalene Young; Based on the book series by Ann M. Martin; Co-Producer, Tina Stern; Photography, Willy Kurant; Designer, Larry Fulton; Editor, Christopher Greenbury; Costumes, Susie DeSanto; Music, David Michael Frank; Casting, Mary Artz, Barbara Cohen; a Beacon Pictures presentation of a Scholastic Production; Dolby SDDS Stereo; Technicolor; Rated PG; 85 minutes; August release

Schuyler Fisk, Brooke Adams

CAST

Kristy	Schuyler Fisk
Stacey	Bre Blair
Mary Anne	Rachael Leigh Cook
Dawn	Larisa Oleynik
Claudia	Tricia Joe
Mallory	Stacey Linn Ramsower
Jessi	Zelda Harris
Rosie Wilder	Vanessa Zima
Luca	Christian Oliver
Elizabeth Thomas Brewer	Brooke Adams
Watson	Bruce Davison
Karen	Jessica Needham
Mrs. Haberman	Ellen Burstyn
Jackie Rodowsky	Asher Metchik
Logan Bruno	Austin O'Brien
Cokie Mason	Marla Sokoloff
Bebe	Ashlee Turner
Grace	Natanya Ross
Nina Marshall	Katie Earle
Suzi Barrett	Scarlett Pomers
Becca	Kyla Pratt
Anne	Anne Costner
Lily	Lily Costner
Buddy Barrett	David Quittman
Nicky	Jonah Bliss
Ricky	Josh Berman
Emmy/Camper	Emmy Yu
Jonas	E.J. De La Peña
Beth	Madison Fisk
Cleo	Cleo Brock-Abraham
Matt	Lance O'Reilly
Vanessa	Bridget Kate Geraghty
Margie Klinger	Erica Hess
Charlotte Johannson	Samantha Alanis
Alan	Aaron Metchik
Patrick	Peter Horton
Jamie Newton	Jeffrey Quittman
Maureen McGill	Colleen Camp
David Michael	Teddy Dale
Brookes	Robin Swid
Mark	Richard Guiton
Bouncer	Peter Gregory
Cabbie	Candy Trabucco
Harold	Harris Yulin
Louise	Aixa Clemente
Sheila	Nancy Mette

Stacy Linn Ramsower, Rachael Leigh Cook, Bre Blair, Schuyler Fisk, Tricia Joe, Larisa Oleynik, Zelda Harris

In the small suburban town of Stoneybrook, Connecticut, seven teenage girls decide to set up a summer daycare center while dealing with various personal, family and dating problems.

© Columbia Pictures Industries, Inc.

Peter Horton, Schuyler Fisk

Kevin Pollak, Stephen Baldwin, Benicio Del Toro, Gabriel Byrne, Kevin Spacey

Gabriel Byrne, Kevin Pollak, Stephen Baldwin, Kevin Spacey

Dan Hedaya, Chazz Palminteri

Stephen Baldwin

Kevin Spacey, Stephen Baldwin, Benicio Del Toro

THE USUAL SUSPECTS

(GRAMERCY) Producers, Bryan Singer, Michael McDonnell; Executive Producers, Robert Jones, Hans Brockmann, Francois Duplat, Art Horan; Co-Producer, Kenneth Kokin; Director, Bryan Singer; Screenplay, Christopher McQuarrie; Photography, Newton Thomas Sigel; Designer, Howard Cummings; Costumes, Louise Mingenbach; Music/Editor, John Ottman; Casting, Francine Maisler; a PolyGram Filmed Entertainment and Spelling Films International presentation of a Blue Parrot/Bad Hat Harry production; Dolby Stereo; Super 35 Widescreen; Technicolor; Rated R; 107 minutes; August release

CAST

Michael McManus	Stephen Baldwin
Dean Keaton	Gabriel Byrne
David Kujan	Chazz Palminteri
Todd Hockney	Kevin Pollak
Kobayashi	Pete Postlethwaite
Roger "Verbal" Kint	Kevin Spacey
Edie Finneran	Suzy Amis
Fred Fenster	Benicio Del Toro
Jack Baer	Giancarlo Esposito
Jeffrey Rabin	Dan Hedaya
Smuggler	Paul Bartel
Saul Berg	Carl Bressler
Fortier	Phillip Simon
Renault	Jack Shearer
Dr. Plummer	Christine Estabrook
Dr. Walters	Clark Gregg
Arkosh Kovash	Morgan Hunter
Translator	Ken Daly
Sketch Artist	Michelle Clunie
Strausz	Louis Lombardi
Rizzi	Frank Medrano
Daniel Metzheiser	Ron Gilbert
Arresting Officer	Vito D'Ambrosio
Cop on Pier	Gene Lythgow
Keyser's Wife	Smadar Hanson
Arturro Marquez	Castulo Guerra
Arturro's Bodyguard	Peter Rocca
Old Cop	Bert Williams

and Bob Elmore, David Powledge, Bob Pennetta, Bill Bates (Bodyguards)

Three investigators interrogate a petty con-man who survived an explosion at a California pier. In flashback, he relates the events which brought him and four other criminals together to the crime scene.

Academy Award winner for Best Supporting Actor (Spacey) and Original Screenplay.

© Gramercy Pictures

Kevin Spacey, Gabriel Byrne

Pete Postlethwaite, Gabriel Byrne

Gabriel Byrne, Kevin Spacey

Stephen Baldwin, Kevin Pollack

DESPERADO

(COLUMBIA) Producers, Robert Rodriguez, Bill Borden; Director/Screenplay/Editor, Robert Rodriguez; Photography, Guillermo Navarro; Designer, Cecilia Montiel; Music, Los Lobos; Co-Producers, Elizabeth Avellán, Carlos Gallardo; Costumes, Graciela Mazón; Casting, Reuben Cannon & Associates; a Los Holigans Production; SDDS Stereo; Technicolor; Rated R; 106 minutes; August release

CAST

El Mariachi	Antonio Banderas
Carolina	Salma Hayek
Bucho	Joaquim De Almeida
Short Bartender	Cheech Marin
Buscemi	Steve Buscemi
Right Hand	Carlos Gomez
Pick-up Guy	Quentin Tarantino
Tavo	Tito Larriva
Zamira	Angel Aviles
Navajas	Danny Trejo
Nino	Abraham Verduzco
Campa	Carlos Gallardo
Quino	Albert Michel, Jr.
Buddy	David Alvarado

and Angela Lanza (Tourist Girl), Mike Moroff (Shrug), Robert Arevalo (Opponent), Gerardo Moscoso (Priest), Peter Marquardt (Moco), Consuelo Gomez (Domino), Jaime De Hoyos (Bigoton), Cristos (Cristos), Richie Gaona (Case Opener), Mark Dalton, Tommy Nix (Fighting Barflies), Patricia Vonne (Bar Girl), Elizabeth Rodriguez (Mariachi Fan)

El Mariachi searches for the drug dealer responsible for his girlfriend's death. Sequel to the 1993 Columbia film El Mariachi *which was also directed by Robert Rodriguez.*

© Columbia Pictures Industries, Inc.

Salma Hayek, Antonio Banderas

Mike McGlone, Edward Burns, Jack Mulcahy

Maxine Bahns, Edward Burns

THE BROTHERS McMULLEN

(20th CENTURY FOX) Producers, Edward Burns, Dick Fisher; Executive Producers, Edward J. Burns, Ted Hope, James Schamus; Director/Screenplay, Edward Burns; Photography/Editor, Dick Fisher; Music, Seamus Egan; a Fox Searchlight Pictures presentation of a Marlboro Road Gang/Videography/Good Machine production; Color; Rated R; 97 minutes; August release

CAST

Barry McMullen	Edward Burns
Patrick McMullen	Mike McGlone
Jack McMullen	Jack Mulcahy
Susan	Shari Albert
Audry	Maxine Bahns
Mrs. McMullen	Catharine Bolz
Molly	Connie Britton
Marty	Peter Johansen
Leslie	Jennifer Jostyn
Ann	Elizabeth P. McKay

Jack allows his younger brothers, Barry and Patrick, to move in with him and his wife while the three men attempt to sort out their romantic problems.

© Twentieth Century Fox

BEYOND RANGOON

(COLUMBIA) Producers, Barry Spikings, Eric Pleskow, John Boorman; Director, John Boorman; Screenplay/Co-Producers, Alex Lasker, Bill Rubenstein; Photography, John Seale; Designer, Anthony Pratt; Music, Hans Zimmer; Editor, Ron Davis; Costumes, Deborah La Gorce Kramer; Executive Producer, Sean Ryerson; Associate Producers, Mark Egerton, Walter Donohue; Casting, Mary Gail Artz, Barbara Cohen; a Castle Rock Entertainment presentation of a Pleskow/Spikings production; Dolby Digital Stereo; Panavision; Technicolor; Rated R; 99 minutes; August release

CAST

Laura Bowman	Patricia Arquette
U Aung Ko	U Aung Ko
Andy	Frances McDormand
Jeremy Watt	Spalding Gray
Desk Clerk	Tiara Jacquelina
Colonel (Hotel)	Kuswadinath Bujang
Mr. Scott	Victor Slezak
Sein Htoo	Jit Murad
San San	Tiara Jacquelina
Zaw Win	Ye Myint
Zabai	Cho Cho Myint
Min Han	Johnny Cheah
Karen Father	Haji Mohd Rajoli
Older Karen Boy	Azmi Hassan
Younger Karen Boy	Ahmad Fithi
Aung San Suu Kyi	Adelle Lutz
Laura's Husband	Michael Pickells
Laura's Son	Enzo Rossi
Officer Min	Ridzuan Hashim
Birdman	Samko
Woman Tourist #1	Ramona Sanchez-Waggoner
Young Woman (Sula)	Norlela Ismail
Village Headman	Nyak Osman
River Trader	Yusof Abdul Hamid
Karen Leader	Lutang Anyie
Fuel Vendor	Ali Fiji
Rapist	Dion Abu Baker

and Mohd Wan Nazri (Check Point Soldier #1 at Train), Zaidi Omar, Roslee Mansor (Check Point Officers at Train), Yeoh Keat Chye (Black Beret Major), Johari Ismail (Black Beret Sergeant), Rashidi Mohd (Secret Police Officer), William Shaw (Bandana Man), Anna Howard (Australian Doctor), Manisah Mandin (Aung Ko's Daughter), Charley Boorman (Photographer), Hani Mohsin Hanafi (Young Monk/Soldier), Ismail Din (Burmese Official), Jamaludin Rejab, Aung (Cig Soldiers), Peter Win (Aung Ko's Helper), John Mindy (Burmese Soldier), Dr. U Kyaw Win (Sule Aide & Buddha Monk), Gael d'Oliviera (French Boy #1), Pascale d'Oliviera (French Mother), Gilles d'Oliviera (French Father), Asmi Wahab (Sula Commander), Albert Thaw (Sule Officer), Mansell Rivers-Bland (Hotel Guest), Siti Abdullah (Village Woman), Satish Chand Bhandari (Aung Ko's Friend)

American tourist Laura Bowman finds herself caught in the middle of the political turmoil of 1988 Burma.

© Castle Rock Entertainment

Peter Fonda

Elina Löwensohn, Karl Geary

Aung Ko, Patricia Arquette

NADJA

(OCTOBER) Producers, Mary Sweeney, Amy Hobby; Executive Producer, David Lynch; Director/Screenplay, Michael Almereyda; Photography, Jim DeNault; Designer, Kurt Ossenfort; Costumes, Prudence Moriarty; Editor, David Leonard; Music, Simon Fisher Turner; Casting, Billy Hopkins, Suzanne Smith, Kerry Barden; Dolby Stereo; Black and white; Rated R; 92 minutes; August release

CAST

Cassandra	Suzy Amis
Lucy	Galaxy Craze
Jim	Martin Donovan
Dr. Van Helsing/Dracula	Peter Fonda
Renfield	Karl Geary
Edgar	Jared Harris
Nadja	Elina Löwensohn
Morgue Attendant	David Lynch

Dr. Van Helsing tracks the children of his nemesis Count Dracula to modern day New York in this comical horror film.

© October Films

LORD OF ILLUSIONS

(UNITED ARTISTS) Producers, JoAnne Sellar, Clive Barker; Executive Producers, Steve Golin, Sigurjon Sighvatsson; Director/Screenplay, Clive Barker, based on his short story "The Last Illusion"; Photography, Ronn Schmidt; Designer, Stephen Hardie; Editor, Alan Baumgarten; Costumes, Luke Reichle; Music, Simon Boswell; Associate Producer, Anna C. Miller; Special Make-Up & Visual Effects Supervisor, Thomas C. Rainone; Casting, Sharon Howard-Field; a Seraphim production; Distributed by MGM/UA; Digital DTS Stereo; Deluxe color; Rated R; 108 minutes; August release

CAST

Harry D'Amour	Scott Bakula
Philip Swann	Kevin J. O'Connor
Dorothea Swann	Famke Janssen
Nix	Daniel Von Bargen
Butterfield	Barry Del Sherman
Valentin	Joel Swetow
Vinovich	Vincent Schiavelli
Jennifer Desiderio	Sheila Tousey
Caspar Quaid	Joseph Latimore
Maureen Pimm	Susan Traylor
Billy Who	Lorin Stewart
Young Butterfield	Trevor Edmond
Young Dorothea	Ashley Lyn Cafagna
Nix's Mandrill	Teddy
Lead Male Cultist	Michael Angelo Stuno
Snakeman	Keith Brunsmann
Lead Female Cultist	Barbara Patrick

and Wayne Grace (Loomis), Mikey LeBeau (Exorcised Boy), Robb Humphreys (D'Amour's Demon), James Brandon Shaw (Motel Bellboy), Johnny Venokur (Tapert), Jordan Marder (Ray Miller), McNally Sagal (Det. Eddison), Joanna Sanchez (Clemenzia), Stephen Weingartner (Stage Manager), Daniel Edward Mora, Jr. (Stage Technician), Billy McComb (Walter Wilder), Barry "Shabaka" Henley (Dr. Toffler), Bergen Lynn Williams (Nurse), Mike Deak (Apparition in Repository), Carrie Ann Inaba, Sarah McAfee, Laurie Kanyok, Jason Yribar, Sebastian LaCause, Luca Tommassini, Yuri Mageoy (Dancers), Joseph Daniel Daley, Stephen Earnhart, Dana Fatigante, Nick Hunter, Tannis Kobrin, Crystal Lujan, Alan McFarland, Ava Stander, D.F. Swatter, Michael L. Swearingen, Colette J. Toomer, Rasool M. Visram, Heidi Wolfe (Cultists)

Private investigator Harry D'Amour's latest case leads him to a mysterious illusionist and his wife, whose past encounter with a diabolical cult leader is coming back to haunt them.

© United Artists Pictures Inc.

Scott Bakula, Famke Janssen

Daniel Von Bargen

Barbara Hershey, Tom Berenger

LAST OF THE DOGMEN

(SAVOY) Producer, Joel B. Michaels; Executive Producer, Mario Kassar; Director/Screenplay, Tab Murphy; Photography, Karl Walter Lindenlaub; Designer, Trevor Williams; Editor, Richard Halsey; Music, David Arnold; Costumes, Elsa Zamparelli; Associate Producer, Donald Heitzer; Casting, Amanda Mackey, Cathy Sandrich; a Mario Kassar presentation of a Joel B. Michaels production in association with Carolco Pictures; Dolby SDDS Stereo; Panavision; Deluxe color; Rated PG; 120 minutes; September release

CAST

Lewis Gates	Tom Berenger
Lillian Sloan	Barbara Hershey
Sheriff Deegan	Kurtwood Smith
Yellow Wolf	Steve Reevis
Briggs	Andrew Miller
Sears	Gregory Scott Cummins
Pharmacist	Graham Jarvis
Tattoo	Mark Boone Junior
Yellow Wolf's Wife	Helen Calahasen
Spotted Elk	Eugene Blackbear
Indian Girl	Dawn Lavand
Lean Bear	Sidel Standing Elk
Kid	Hunter Bodine
Mr. Hollis	Parley Baer

and Georgie Collins (Senior Editor), Sherwood Price (Tracker), Molly Parker (Nurse), Antony Holland (Doc Carvey), Robert Donley (Old Timer), Brian Stollery (Grad Student), Mitchell LaPlante (Wild Boy), Zip (Zip), Wilford Brimley (Narrator)

Bounty hunter Lewis Gates, tracking a group of escaped convicts in a remote region of the Rockies, stumbles upon an isolated society of Native Americans.

© Savoy Pictures

Eric Stoltz

Christopher Walken, Amanda Plummer

Christopher Walken

Viggo Mortensen, Raymie Jones

THE PROPHECY

(DIMENSION) formerly *God's Army, Daemons*; Producer, Joel Soisson; Executive Producers, W.K. Border, Don Phillips; Co-Producer, Raquel Caballes Maxwell; Director/Screenplay, Gregory Widen; Photography, Bruce Douglas Johnson, Richard Clabaugh; Editor, Sonny Baskin; Designer, Clark Hunter; Special Makeup Effects, Scott Patton; Music, David C. Williams; Casting, Don Phillips; a First Look Pictures presentation of a Neo Motion Pictures production, distributed by Miramax films; Ultra-Stereo; Widescreen; Color; Rated R; 91 minutes; September release

CAST

Gabriel	Christopher Walken
Thomas Daggett	Elias Koteas
Katherine	Virginia Madsen
Simon	Eric Stoltz
Rachel	Amanda Plummer
Jerry	Adam Goldberg
Lucifer	Viggo Mortensen
Mary	Moriah Snyder
Grandmother	Emma Sheneh
John	Nik Winterhawk
Burrows	J.C. Quinn
Grey Horse	Albert Nelson
Joseph	Steve Hytner

and Jeremy Williams-Hurner (Brian), Emily Conforto (Sandra), Nick Gomez (Jason), Christina Holmes (Allison), Sandra Lafferty (Madge), Jeff Cadiente (Usiel), John Sankovich, Bobby Lee Hayes (Deputies), William Buck Hart (Grave Keeper), Randy Adakai-Nez (High School Kid), Sioux-Z Jessup (Nurse)

Supernatural thriller about two angels, one good and one evil, who descend from heaven to start a war on earth.

© Dimension Films

Elias Koteas, Virginia Madsen

Wesley Snipes, John Leguizamo, Patrick Swayze

Patrick Swayze

Wesley Snipes

TO WONG FOO THANKS FOR EVERYTHING, JULIE NEWMAR

(UNIVERSAL) Producer, G. Mac Brown; Executive Producer, Bruce Cohen; Director, Beeban Kidron; Screenplay, Douglas Carter Beane; Photography, Steve Mason; Designer, Wynn Thomas; Editor, Andrew Mondshein; Costumes, Marlene Stewart; Music, Rachel Portman; Executive Music Producers, Happy Walters, Pilar McCurry; Choreographer, Kenny Ortega; Associate Producer, Mitchell Kohn; Casting, Billy Hopkins, Suzanne Smith, Kerry Barden; Hair and Makeup, J. Roy Helland; an Amblin Entertainment production; DTS Stereo; Deluxe color; Rated PG-13; 108 minutes; September release

CAST

Noxeema Jackson	Wesley Snipes
Vida Boheme	Patrick Swayze
Chi Chi Rodriguez	John Leguizamo
Carol Ann	Stockard Channing
Beatrice	Blythe Danner
Virgil	Arliss Howard
Bobby Ray	Jason London
Sheriff Dollard	Chris Penn
Merna	Melinda Dillon
Loretta	Beth Grant
Clara	Alice Drummond
Katina	Marceline Hugot
Bobby Lee	Jennifer Milmore
Billy Budd	Jamie Harrold
Jimmy Joe	Mike Hodge
Tommy	Michael Vartan
Rachel Tensions	RuPaul
Herself	Julie Newmar
John Jacob	Robin Williams
Little Earnest	Joel Story
Donna Lee	Abie Hope Hyatt
Sandra Lee	Jamie Leigh Wolbert
State Troopers	Shea Degan, Dean Houser, Joe Grojean
Motel Manager	Keith Reddin
Girl	Naomi Campbell
Small Guy	William P. Hopkins
Crazy Elijah	Dayton Callie
Old Man	Ron Carley
Rude Boys	Shea R. Bredenkamp, Michael A. Tushaus, Patrick Tuttle, Timothy A. Zimmerman, Tim Keller
Vida's Mother	Martha Flynn
Florist	Billie J. Diekman
Dance Teacher	Shari Shell-True

and NY Drag Queen Contestants: Alexander Heimberg (Miss Understood), Joey Arias (Justine), Allen Hidalgo (Chita Riviera), Mishell Chandler (Miss Missy), Catiria Reyes (Catiria Reyes), David Drumgold (Cappuccino Commotion), Clinton Leupp (Miss Coco Peru), Lionel Tiburcio (Laritza Dumont), Bernard A. Mosca (Olympia); Daniel T. "Sweetie" Boothe (Announcer), David Barton (Boy in Chains), Susanne Bartsch, Quentin Crisp, Kevin "Flotilla DeBarge" Joseph, Matthew Kasten, Widow Norton (NY Pageant Judges), LA Drag Queens: Carles Ching (Coco LaChine), Mike Fulk (Victoria Weston), Niasse N. Mamadou (Lola), Brendan McDanniel (Candis Cayne), Shelton McDonald (Princess Diandra), Richard Ogden (Kabuki), James Palacio (Fiona James), Steven Polito (Hedda Lettuce), Philip Stoehr (Philomena)

Three drag queens, driving cross country en route to Hollywood, are forced to stay in a small Midwestern town when their car breaks down.

© Universal City Studios Inc.

Patrick Swayze, Stockard Channing, Wesley Snipes, John Leguizamo

Alice Drummond, Wesley Snipes

Wesley Snipes

Jennifer Milmore, Marceline Hugot, Patrick Swayze, Beth Grant, Wesley Snipes, Alice Drummond

Harvey Keitel, Mekhi Phifer

Tom Byrd

Regina Taylor, Pee Wee Love

CLOCKERS

(UNIVERSAL) Producers, Martin Scorsese, Spike Lee, Jon Kilik; Executive Producers, Rosalie Swedlin, Monty Ross; Director, Spike Lee; Screenplay, Richard Price, Spike Lee; Based on the book by Richard Price; Co-Producer, Richard Price; Photography, Malik Hassan Sayeed; Editor, Sam Pollard; Music, Terence Blanchard; Designer, Andrew McAlpine; Costumes, Ruth Carter; Casting, Robi Reed-Humes; DTS Stereo; Deluxe color; Rated R; 128 minutes; September release

CAST

Rocco Klein	Harvey Keitel
Larry Mazilli	John Turturro
Rodney Little	Delroy Lindo
Ronald "Strike" Dunham	Mekhi Phifer
Victor Dunham	Isaiah Washington
Andre the Giant	Keith David
Tyrone ("Shorty")	Pee Wee Love
Iris Jeeter	Regina Taylor
Errol Barnes	Tom Byrd
Scientific	Sticky Fingaz
Go	Fredro
Horace	E.O. Nolasco
Stan	Lawrence B. Adisa
Skills	Hassan Johnson
Gloria	Frances Foster
Jo-Jo	Michael Imperioli
Sharon	Lisa Arrindell Anderson
Jesus at Hambones	Paul Calderon
Big Chief	Brendan Kelly
Thumper	Mike Starr
Mr. Herman Brown	Graham Brown
Darryl Adams	Steve White
Chucky	Spike Lee
Solo	Shawn McLean
Bartucci	Arthur Nascarella
Bill Walker	Harry Lennix
Al the Medic	John Fletcher
Frank the Medic	J.C. MacKenzie
Smart Mike	David Evanson
Reverend Paul	Norman Matlock
Charles	Isaac Fowler
Onion the Bar Patron	Leonard Thomas
Davis the Bartender	Maurice Sneed
Guard #1	Calvin Hart
Kiki	Ginny Yang
Cops	Michael Badalucco, Ricky Aiello
Earl	Scot Anthony Robinson
Moe	Richard Ziman
T	David Batiste
Ivan	Mar'Qus Sample
Mark	Mar'Rece Sample
Dead Man Begging	Ron Price
Louie	Ken Garito
"Pick Me Up" Kid	Harvey Williams
Larry the Narc	Larry Mullane
Bomb Girl	Ronda Fowler
Forensics Officer	Hal Sherman

and Bray Poor, Craig McNulty, Christopher Wynkoop, Paul Schulze, Lt. Donald Stephenson (Detectives), Anthony Nocerino, Brian Konowal, Michael McGruther, Carlo Vogel (Teens), Michael Cullen, Tim Kelleher, Skipp Sudduth (Narcs), Patrick Ferraro, L.B. Williams, Jeff Ward (Bike Cops), Marc Webster (EMS Technician), James Saxenmeyer, Paul DuBois, Jordan Brown (EMS Attendants), Michael Marchetta, Joanna Gardner (Corrections Officers), Mark Howard, Michael Shepherd, Gerald King, Ronta Davis (Baby Recruits), Lord Kayson, Orran Farmer (T's Crewmembers), Wayne Muhammad (Fruit of Islam Vendor), Martin Jaffe (Street Vendor), Freddie Velez (Pedro the Security Guard)

Brooklyn homicide detective Rocco Klein is suspicious when the brother of low life drug dealer Strike confesses to a murder Rocco is sure Strike committed.

© Universal City Studios, Inc.

Harvey Keitel, Mekhi Phifer, John Turturro

Mekhi Phifer, Isaiah Washington

Keith David, Mekhi Phifer

Pee Wee Love, Regina Taylor

Mekhi Phifer, Delroy Lindo

Kendra Krull, Andie MacDowell, Nathan Watt

Maury Chaykin, Nathan Watt, Michael Richards

John Turturro, Michael Richards

UNSTRUNG HEROES

(HOLLYWOOD PICTURES) Producers, Susan Arnold, Donna Roth, Bill Badalato; Director, Diane Keaton; Screenplay, Richard LaGravanese; Based upon the book by Franz Lidz; Photography, Phedon Papamichael; Designer, Garreth Stover; Editor, Lisa Churgin; Costumes, Jill Ohanneson; Music, Thomas Newman; Casting, Gail Levin; a Roth/Arnold production; Distributed by Buena Vista Pictures; Dolby Digital Stereo; Technicolor; Rated PG; 93 minutes; September release

CAST

Selma Lidz	Andie MacDowell
Sid Lidz	John Turturro
Danny Lidz	Michael Richards
Arthur Lidz	Maury Chaykin
Steven/Franz Lidz	Nathan Watt
Sandy Lidz	Kendra Krull
Ash	Joey Andrews
Amelia	Celia Weston
Lindquist	Jack McGee
Joanie	Candice Azzara
May	Anne DeSalvo
Aunt Estelle	Lillian Adams
Uncle Melvin	Lou Cutell
Nancy Oppenheim	Sumer Stamper
Ralph Crispi	Sean P. Donahue
Rabbi Blaustein	Rabbi Harold M. Schulewis
Mrs. Kantruitz	Zoaunne LeRoy
Inspector Marshall	Vince Melocchi
In-Crowd Boy	Charles Patrick
In-Crowd Girl	Alison Chalmers
Mr. Clements	Chris Warfield
Mr. Crispi	Wayne Duvall
Man in Line	Andrew Craig
Mrs. Harris	Becky Ann Baker
Waitress	Mary Mercier
Second Doctor	Len Costanza
Dr. Feldman	Peter Kaitlyn
Nurse Franklin	Julie Pinson

Unable to cope with his mother's illness and a distant father, twelve-year-old Steven Lidz runs off to live with his two eccentric uncles.

Nominated for an Oscar for original dramatic score.

© Hollywood Pictures Company

Nathan Watt, John Turturro

ANGUS

(NEW LINE CINEMA) Producers, Dawn Steel, Charles Roven; Executive Producers, Robert Cavallo, Gary Levinsohn, Susan B. Landau; Director, Patrick Read Johnson; Screenplay, Jill Gordon; Based on a short story by Chris Crutcher; Photography, Alexander Grusynski; Designer, Larry Miller; Editor, Janice Hampton; Costumes, Jill Ohanneson; Music, David Russo; Associate Producers, Douglas Segal, Kelley Smith-Wait; Casting, Ronnie Yeskel; a Turner Pictures presentation of an Atlas Entertainment production; Dolby DTS Stereo; Color; Rated PG-13; 90 minutes; September release

CAST

Angus Bethune	Charlie Talbert
Meg Bethune	Kathy Bates
Troy Wedberg	Chris Owen
Melissa Lefevre	Ariana Richards
Grandpa Ivan	George C. Scott
Rick Sanford	James Van Der Beek
Madame Rulenska	Rita Moreno
Principal Metcalf	Lawrence Pressman
April Thomas	Anna Thomson
Alexander	Robert Curtis-Brown
Andy	Kevin Connolly
Mike	Salim Grant
Ellen	Epatha Harris
Jody Cole	Robin Lynn Heath
Alex Immergluch	Evan Kaufman
Coach	James Keane
Mr. Stoff	Irvin Kershner
Mr. Kessler	Wesley Mann
Tuxedo Salesman	Perry Anzilotti
Science Teacher	Yvette Freeman
Minister	Monty O'Grady

and Tony Denman (Kid), Lindsay Price (Recycling Girl), Christopher Ragsdale (Boy playing football), Bob Pepper (Wedding Photographer), Steven Hartman (Rick—age 11), Grant Hoover (Angus—age 8), Michael McLeod (Rick—age 8), Tanner Lee Prairie (Rick—age 5), Bethany Richards (Melissa—age 11), Aaron Siefers (Angus—age 11), Cameron Royds (Baby Angus), Eric E. Thomas II (Kid at birthday party), Bryan Warloe (Troy—age 8), Michael Wesley (Angus—age 5)

Ariana Richards, Charlie Talbert, Chris Owen

Comedy about an overweight high school boy, Angus Bethune, who secretly loves a popular, pretty girl who doesn't seem to know he exists.

Kathy Bates

George C. Scott

James Van Der Beek, Ariana Richards

Morgan Freeman, Brad Pitt

Brad Pitt

Gwyneth Paltrow

SEVEN

(NEW LINE CINEMA) Producers, Arnold Kopelson, Phyllis Carlyle; Executive Producers, Gianni Nunnari, Dan Kolsrud, Anne Kopelson; Co-Executive Producers, Lynn Harris, Richard Saperstein; Co-Producers, Stephen Brown, Nana Greenwald, Sanford Panitch; Director, David Fincher; Screenplay, Andrew Kevin Walker; Photography, Darius Khondji; Designer, Arthur Max; Editor, Richard Francis-Bruce; Costumes, Michael Kaplan; Music, Howard Shore; Casting, Billy Hopkins, Suzanne Smith, Kerry Borden; an Arnold Kopelson production, Dolby Stereo; Super 35 Widescreen; Deluxe color; Rated R; 125 minutes; September release

CAST

Det. David Mills	Brad Pitt
Det. William Somerset	Morgan Freeman
Tracy Mills	Gwyneth Paltrow
Talbot	Richard Roundtree
Police Captain	R. Lee Ermey
Mrs. Gould	Julie Araskog
Greasy FBI Man	Mark Boone Junior
Officer Davis	John Cassini
Dr. Santiago	Reginald E. Cathey
Dr. O'Neill	Peter Crombie
George, the Night Guard at the Library	Hawthorne James
Man in Booth at Massage Parlor	Michael Massee
Crazed Man in Massage parlor	Leland Orser
Dr. Beardsley	Richard Portnow
Mark Swarr	Richard Schiff
Thin Vagrant by John Doe's Apartment	Pamala Tyson
John Doe	Kevin Spacey
Cab Driver	Endre Hules
Dead Man at 1st Crime Scene	Andy Walker
Det. Taylor at 1st murder	Daniel Zacapa
Gluttony Victim	Bob Mack
Workman at Door of Somerset's Office	George Christy
Guards at Library	Roscoe Davidson, Bob Collins
Library Janitor	Jimmy Dale Hartsell
TV News Reporters	Charline Su, Dominique Jennings
Forensic Man in Law Office	Allan Kolman
TV Anchor Woman	Beverly Burke
Eli Gould (Sin of Greed)	Gene Borkan
Fingerprint Forensic Man in Law Office	Mario Di Donato
Fingerprint Technician	Alfonso Freeman
Cops on SWAT Team	Harrison White, Robert Stephenson
Victor (Sin of Sloth)	Michael Reid Mackay
Coupon Man outside Pizza Parlor	Tudor Sherrard
Policeman who takes Statement from Vagrant	Lennie Loftin
Police Sketch Artist	Sarah Hale Reinhardt
Det. Sara at John Doe's Apartment	Emily Wagner
Wild Bill	Martin Serene
Cops at Massage Parlor	David Correia, Ron Blair
Hooker (Sin of Lust)	Cat Mueller
Beautiful Woman (Sin of Pride)	Heidi Schanz

and Lexie Bingham (Sweating Cop at Massage Parlor), Evan Miranda, Paul S. Eckstein (Paramedics at Massage Parlor), Brian Evers (Duty Sergeant), Shannon Wilcox (Woman Cop behind Desk), Jim Deeth, John Santini (Helicopter Pilots), Richmond Arquette (Delivery Man), Duffy Gaver (Marksman in Helicopter)

Retiring cop William Somerset is teamed with newcomer David Mills to investigate a series of grizzly murders patterned after the seven deadly sins.

The film received an Oscar nomination for film editing.

© New Line Productions, Inc.

Morgan Freeman, Brad Pitt

Brad Pitt

Morgan Freeman

Brad Pitt

CANADIAN BACON

(GRAMERCY) Producers, Michael Moore, David Brown, Ron Rotholz; Executive Producers, Freddy DeMann, Sigurjon Sighvatsson; Director/Screenplay, Michael Moore; Co-Producer, Kathleen Glynn; Photography, Haskell Wexler; Designer, Carol Spier; Costumes, Kathleen Glynn; Editors, Wendey Stanzler, Michael Berenbaum; Music, Elmer Bernstein, Peter Bernstein; Line Producer, Stuart M. Besser; Associate Producer/1st Assistant Director, Terry Miller; Casting, Lynn Kressell; a PolyGram Filmed Entertainment and Propaganda Films presentation of a David Brown/Maverick Picture Company production; Dolby Stereo; Deluxe color; Rated PG; 95 minutes; September release

CAST

President of the United States	Alan Alda
Bud B. Boomer	John Candy
Deputy Honey	Rhea Perlman
Stu Smiley	Kevin Pollak
General Dick Panzer	Rip Torn
Roy Boy	Kevin J. O'Connor
Kabral	Bill Nunn
R.J. Hacker	G.D. Spradlin
Niagara Mountie	Steven Wright
Charles Jackal	James Belushi
Canadian Police Officer	Dan Aykroyd
Gus	Brad Sullivan
Edwin S. Simon	Stanley Anderson
Russian President	Richard Council
Panzer's Aide	Michael Copeman
President's Aide	Bruce Hunter
Ruthie	Beth Amos
Pops	Jack Mather
Mountie Sergeant	Kenner Ames
Mountie Major	Roger Dunn
Toronto Kid	Natalie Rose
State Troopers	Michael Woods, Matt Cooke
Newswoman	Barbara Schroeder
Candy Stripers	Tara Meyer, Fab Filippo
Clarence Thomason	Carlton Watson
Secretary of State	Stan Coles

and Adrian Hough (Russian Aide), Bryan Armstrong (Auctioneer), Kelsey Binder Moore, Leah Binder Moore (Ice Cream Girls), Wally Bolland (Special Ops Soldier), Marcos Parilo (Omega Force Leader), Jim Czarnecki (Snake), Tony Proffer (Dell), Ben Hamper, Michael Moore (Redneck Guys), Linda Genovesi (Polite Canadian Woman), Sheila Gray (Voice of Hacker Hellstorm), Dana Brooks (Paulette Kalin), Wallace Shawn (Prime Minister McDonald)

The U.S. President, worried about his declining popularity, is convinced by his staff to encourage an Anti-Canadian feeling among the American people.

© Grammercy Pictures

Rhea Perlman, John Candy

Rip Torn, Alan Alda, Kevin Pollak

Rip Torn, Kevin Pollak, Michael Moore, Alan Alda, John Candy, Rhea Perlman

John Candy, Rhea Perlman

Kyle MacLachlan, Elizabeth Berkley

Elizabeth Berkley

SHOWGIRLS

(UNITED ARTISTS) Producers, Alan Marshall, Charles Evans; Executive Producer, Mario Kassar; Co-Producer, Ben Myron; Director, Paul Verhoeven; Screenplay, Joe Eszterhas; Photography, Jost Vacano; Designer, Allan Cameron; Editors, Mark Goldblatt, Mark Helfrich; Music, David A. Stewart; Choreographer, Marguerite Pomerhn-Derricks; Associate Producer, Lynn Ehrensperger; Casting, Johanna Ray, Elaine Huzzar; a Mario Kassar presentation of a Chargeurs/Charles Evans production in association with Carolco Pictures Inc., Joe Eszterhas and Ben Myron; from MGM/UA Distribution; Dolby/DTS Stereo; Clairmont-Scope; Technicolor; Rated NC-17; 131 minutes; September release

CAST

Nomi Malone	Elizabeth Berkley
Zack Carey	Kyle MacLachlan
Cristal Connors	Gina Gershon
James Smith	Glenn Plummer
Al Torres	Robert Davi
Tony Moss	Alan Rachins
Molly Abrams	Gina Ravera
Henrietta Bazoom	Lin Tucci
Phil Newkirk	Greg Travis
Mr. Karlman	Al Ruscio
Marty Jacobsen	Patrick Bristow
Andrew Carver	William Shockley
Gay Carpenter	Michelle Johnston
Jeff	Dewey Weber
Penny	Rena Riffel
Nicky	Melinda Songer
Julie	Melissa Williams
Bell Captain	Lance Davis
Jack the Stagehand	Jack McGee
Mr. Okida	Jim Ishida
Annie	Ungela Brockman
Dee	Bobbie Phillips
Carmi	Dante McCarthy
Nadia	Caroline Key Johnson

and Joan Foley (Jail Matron), Terry Beeman (Felix), Kevin Stea (Daryl), Sebastian La Cause (Sal), Lisa Boyle (Sonny), Alexander Folk (Booking Sergeant), Matt Battaglia, Teo (Andrew Carver's Bodyguards), Elaine Van Betten (Versace Salesperson), Alexander Zale (Doctor), Irene Olga Lopez (Personnel Woman), Julie Pop (Nurse), Jacob Witkin (Caesar), Jana Walker (Secretary), Christina Robinette (Receptionist), Jim Wise (Cheetah Loudmouth), Michael Shure, Geoff Calla (Cheetah Drunks), Rick Marotta (Long-Haired Drunk), Paul Bates, Gregory R. Goliath (Cheetah Bouncers), Michael Cooke (Casino Lecher), Jean Barrett (Change Girl), Gary Devaney, Gene Ellison-Jone (Texans at Spago), Fernando Celis (Hector), Robert Dunn (Chimp Trainer), Ashley Nation (Julie's Daughter), Cory Melander (Julie's Son), Sean Breen (Reporter), Elizabeth Kennedy (Photographer), Katherine Manning (Reporter), Warren Reno (Crave Club Bouncer), Ken Enomoto, Y. Hero Abe, Odney Ueno (Cheetah Customers), Kathleen McTeague, Kristen Knittl (Al Torres' Girls), Sage Peart (Paramedic), Michael Washington (Crave Club Heckler)

Young dancer Nomi bides her time working in a cheap strip joint while hoping to land a job as a Las Vegas showgirl in a lavish casino show.

© United Artists Pictures Inc.

Gina Gershon, Elizabeth Berkley

Elizabeth Berkley, Glenn Plummer

Nicole Kidman, Matt Dillon

TO DIE FOR

(COLUMBIA) Producer, Laura Ziskin; Executive Producers, Joseph M. Caracciolo, Jonathan Taplin; Director, Gus Van Sant; Screenplay, Buck Henry; Based on the book by Joyce Maynard; Photography, Eric Alan Edwards; Designer, Missy Stewart; Costumes, Beatrix Aruna Pasztor; Music, Danny Elfman; Editor, Curtiss Clayton; Title Sequence, Pablo Ferro; Casting, Howard Feuer; Presented in association with Rank Film Distributors; Dolby SDDS Stereo; Technicolor; Rated R; 100 minutes; September release

CAST

Suzanne Stone	Nicole Kidman
Larry Maretto	Matt Dillon
Jimmy Emmett	Joaquin Phoenix
Russell Hines	Casey Affleck
Janice Maretto	Illeana Douglas
Lydia Mertz	Alison Folland
Joe Maretto	Dan Hedaya
Ed Grant	Wayne Knight
Earl Stone	Kurtwood Smith
Carol Stone	Holland Taylor
Faye Stone	Susan Traylor
Angela Maretto	Maria Tucci
Mike Warden	Tim Hopper
Ben DeLuca	Michael Rispoli
Mr. Finlaysson	Buck Henry
George	Gerry Quigley
Fishermen	Tom Forrester, Alan Edward Lewis
Sexy Woman	Nadine MacKinnon
Weaselly Guy	Conrad Coates
Sal	Ron Gabriel
Detective	Nicholas Pasco
Lawyer	Joyce Maynard
Man at Lake	David Cronenberg

and Ian Heath, Graeme Millington, Sean Ryan (Students), David Collins, Eve Crawford, Janet Lo (Reporters), Tom Quinn (Skating Promoter), Peter Glenn (Priest), Amber-Lee Campbell (Suzanne at Five), Colleen Williams (Valerie Mertz), Simon Richards (Chester), Philip Williams (Babe Hines), Susan Backs (June Hines), Kyra Harper (Mary Emmett), Adam Roth, Andrew Scott (Band Members), Tamara Gorski, Katie Griffin, Carla Renee (Girls at bar), Misha (Walter), George Segal (Speaker)

Suzanne Stone, desperate to escape her small town life and establish herself as a top TV journalist, seduces a pair of high school teens into disposing of her husband.

© Columbia Pictures Industries, Inc.

Buck Henry

Matt Dillon, Nicole Kidman

Joaquin Phoenix, Casey Affleck, Alison Folland

DEVIL IN A BLUE DRESS

(TRISTAR) Producers, Jesse Beaton, Gary Goetzman; Executive Producers, Jonathan Demme, Edward Saxon; Director/Screenplay, Carl Franklin; Based on the book by Walter Mosley; Photography, Tak Fujimoto; Designer, Gary Frutkoff; Editor, Carole Kravetz; Costumes, Sharen Davis; Music, Elmer Bernstein; Associate Producers, Walter Mosley, Donna Gigliotti, Thomas A. Imperato; Title Designer, Pablo Ferro; Casting, Victoria Thomas; a Clinica Estetico and Mundy Lane Entertainment production; Dolby SDDS Digital Stereo; Technicolor; Rated R; 102 minutes; September release

Denzel Washington, Jennifer Beals

CAST

Easy Rawlins	Denzel Washington
Dewitt Albright	Tom Sizemore
Daphne Monet	Jennifer Beals
Mouse	Don Cheadle
Matthew Terell	Maury Chaykin
Todd Carter	Terry Kinney
Joppy	Mel Winkler
Odell	Albert Hall
Coretta James	Lisa Nicole Carson
Dupree Brouchard	Jernard Burks
Junior Fornay	David Wolos-Fonteno
Mason	John Roselius
Miller	Beau Starr
Benny Giacomo	Steven Randazzo
Richard McGee	Scott Lincoln
Hattie Parsons	L. Scott Caldwell
Woodcutter	Barry Shabaka Henley
Shariff	Nicky Corello
Manny	Kenny Endoso
Frank Green	Joseph Latimore
Barbara	Renee Humphrey
Herman	Robert J. Knoll
Football	Kai Lennox
Barbara's Sister	Poppy Montgomery
Terell's Chauffeur	Brendan Kelly
Carter's Secretary	Peggy Rea
Baxter	Vinny Argiro
Sophie	Deborah Lacey

and Brazylia Kotere (Neighborhood Woman), Jeris Lee Poindexter (Alphonso Jenkins), Frank Davis (Butcher), Matt Barry (Cop in Car), Mark Cotone (Cop in Station), Brian E. O'Neal (John's Band/Singer), G. Smokey Campbell (Nightclub Owner), Alan Craig Schwartz (Johnny), Steve Sekely (Abe), J.D. Smith (Pool Hall Owner), Nigel Gibbs (Bootlegger)

In 1948 Los Angeles, Easy Rawlins, eager to find work, agrees to locate a mysterious woman named Daphne Monet and soon finds himself involved with blackmail and murder.

© TriStar Pictures, Inc.

Maury Chaykin

Mel Winkler

Don Cheadle, Denzel Washington

MOONLIGHT AND VALENTINO

(GRAMERCY) Producers, Alison Owen, Eric Fellner, Tim Bevan; Co-Producer, Mary McLaglen; Director, David Anspaugh; Screenplay, Ellen Simon, based on her stageplay; Photography, Julio Macat; Designer, Robb Wilson King; Costumes, Denise Cronenberg; Associate Producer, Liza Chasin; Editor, David Rosenbloom; Music, Howard Shore; Casting, Amanda Mackey, Cathy Sandrich; a Working Title Film production; Dolby Stereo; Panavision; Technicolor; Rated R; 103 minutes; September release

Whoopi Goldberg, Elizabeth Perkins

CAST

Rebecca Trager Lott	Elizabeth Perkins
Lucy Trager	Gwyneth Paltrow
Alberta Russell	Kathleen Turner
Sylvie Morrow	Whoopi Goldberg
The Painter	Jon Bon Jovi
Steven	Jeremy Sisto
Thomas Trager	Josef Sommer
Jenny Morrow	Shadia Simmons
Drew Morrow	Erica Luttrell
Alex Morrow	Matthew Koller
Policeman	Scott Wickware
Nurse	Kelli Fox
Mr. Wong	Harrison Liu
Mr. Wong's Son	Wayne Lam
Mr. Wong's Father	Ken Wong
Henrik	Carlton Watson
Sid	Jack Jessop
Valentino	Trim
Street Vendor	Alan Clifton
Marc	Judah Katz
Hairstylist	Julian Richings
Paul Morrow	Peter Coyote

Drama about a young college professor, Rebecca Lott, who finds her life turned upside down after her husband is killed while jogging.

Jon Bon Jovi

Whoopi Goldberg, Gwyneth Paltrow, Kathleen Turner, Elizabeth Perkins

STEAL BIG, STEAL LITTLE

(SAVOY) Producers, Andrew Davis, Fred Caruso; Executive Producer, Mel Pearl; Co-Executive Producer, Larry Jackson; Director, Andrew Davis; Screenplay, Andrew Davis, Lee Blessing, Jeanne Blake, Terry Kahn; Story, Andrew Davis, Teresa Tucker-Davies, Frank Ray Perilli; Associate Producers, Teresa Tucker-Davies, Maher Ahmad; Co-Producer, Lowell Blank; Photography, Frank Tidy; Designer, Michael Haller; Editor, Don Brochu, Tina Hirsch; Costumes, Jodie Tillen; Music, William Olvis; Casting, Amanda Mackey Johnson, Cathy Sandrich; a Chicago Pacific Entertainment production; Dolby SDDS Stereo; Technicolor; Rated PG-13; 135 minutes; September release

Andy Garcia, Andy Garcia

CAST

Ruben Partida Martinez/ Robert Martin	Andy Garcia
Lou Perilli	Alan Arkin
Laura Martinez	Rachel Ticotin
Eddie Agopian	Joe Pantoliano
Mona Rowland-Downey	Holland Taylor
Bonnie Martin	Ally Walker
Judge Winton Myers	David Ogden Stiers
Sheriff Otis	Charles Rocket
Nick Zingaro	Richard Bradford
Reed Tyler	Kevin McCarthy
Harry Lordly	Nathan Davis
Maria Martinez	Dominik Garcia-Lorido
Sam Barlow	Mike Nussbaum
Autumn McBride	Rita Taggart
Yoshi Takamura	Takaaki Ishibashi
Dan McCann	Tom Wood
Tinker	Philip Arthur Ross
Buzz	Steven Robert Ross
Alice	Natalija Nogulich
Sheriff Joe	Joe Kosala
Sheriff Vic	Victor Rivers
Mauricio	Sam Vlahos
Clifford Downey	Andy Romano
Julian	Ramon Gonzales
Luis	Salvatore Basile
Angel	Fred Asparagus
Rafael	William Marquez
Emilio Campos	Nelson Marquez
Eduardo	Richard Marquez
Agatha	Leata Galloway
Rosa	Renee Victor

and Adam James (Tyler's Bodyguard), Drucilla A. Carlson (Tonya), Nina Beesley (Brandy), Candice Daly (Melissa), Cynthia Mace (Betty Myers), Karen Kondazian (Mrs. Agopian), Miguel Nino (Guardia Officer), Ron Dean, Jack Wallace (Nick's Boys), Robert Harris (Farley), Robert Langenbucher (Bailsman Aames), Time Winters (IRS Agent Cox), Tighe Barry (Glitch), Suzanne Goddard (Shakara), Joe Drago (Inmate), Duane Davis (Jailer), Roselynn Pilkington (Eddie's Secretary), Fred Lehto (Strange Man), Cody Glenn (INS Agent), Lee Debroux (INS Official), Robert Lesser (Agent Buchanan), Pamela Winslow (Melanie), Frank Ray Perilli (B.J.), Mick Pellegrino (Mission Father), Eddie Bo Smith (Bartender), Soren Hansen (Security Guard), Liz Lang (Court Clerk), Buddy the Dog (Himself)

Andy Garcia, Joe Pantoliano

When wealthy Mona Rowland-Downey dies, she leaves her lavish Santa Barbara ranch to her adopted son Ruben, much to the annoyance of Ruben's no-good twin brother, Robby.

Anthony Esquivel, Patrick Renna, Billy L. Sullivan, Olivia d'Abo, Steve Guttenberg

THE BIG GREEN

(WALT DISNEY PICTURES) Producer, Roger Birnbaum; Executive Producer, Dennis Bishop; Director/Screenplay, Holly Goldberg Sloan; Photography, Ralf Bode; Editor, John F. Link; Music, Randy Edelman; Costumes, Rondi Hillstrom Davis; Casting, Rick Montgomery, Dan Parada; Presented in association with Caravan Pictures; Distributed by Buena Vista Pictures; Dolby Digital Stereo; Technicolor; Rated PG: 100 minutes; September release

CAST

Tom Palmer	Steve Guttenberg
Anna Montgomery	Olivia d'Abo
Jay Huffer	Jay O. Sanders
Edwin V. Douglas	John Terry
Evan Schiff	Chauncey Leopardi
Larry Musgrove	Patrick Renna
Jeffrey Luttrell	Billy L. Sullivan
Marbelly Morales	Yareli Arizmendi
Newt Shaw	Bug Hall
Kate Douglas	Jessie Robertson
Juan Morales	Anthony Esquivel
Nick Anderssen	Jordan Brower
Sophia Convertino	Hayley Kolb
Polly Neilson	Haley Miller
Lou Gates	Ashley Welch
Sue Gates	Ariel Welch
Tak Yamato	Jimmy Higa

and Gil Glasgow (Cookie Musgrove), Libby Villari (Brenda Neilson), Louanne Stephens (Bomma Cole), John Bourg (Jay Huffer, Jr.), Tyler Bishop, Casey Lee (Knights), Milt Oberman (Referee), Nik Hagler (Chief Bishop), Stephen Parr (Stadium Announcer), Ernie the goat (Himself)

British school teacher Anna Montgomery arrives in the tiny Texas down of Elma and teams with a former football star to whip the kid's soccer team into shape.

Bokeem Woodbine, Freddy Rodriguez, Larenz Tate, Keith David

Larenz Tate, Rose Jackson

Larenz Tate, Freddy Rodriguez, Chris Tucker

DEAD PRESIDENTS

(HOLLYWOOD PICTURES) Producers/Directors, The Hughes Brothers (Allen & Albert Hughes); Executive Producer, Darryl Porter; Screenplay, Michael Henry Brown; Story, Allen & Albert Hughes, Michael Henry Brown; Photography, Lisa Rinzler; Designer, David Brisbin; Editor, Dan Lebental; Costumes, Paul A. Simmons; Co-Producer, Michael Bennett; Music, Danny Elfman; Casting, Risa Bramon Garcia, Mary Vernieu; an Underworld Entertainment production presented in association with Caravan Pictures; Distributed by Buena Vista Pictures; Dolby Digital Stereo; Super 35 Widescreen; Technicolor; Rated R; 118 minutes; October release

CAST

Anthony Curtis	Larenz Tate
Kirby	Keith David
Skip	Chris Tucker
Jose	Freddy Rodriguez
Juanita Benson	Rose Jackson
Delilah Benson	N'Bushe Wright
Mrs. Benson	Alvaletah Guess
Mr. Curtis	James Pickens, Jr.
Mrs. Curtis	Jenifer Lewis
Cutty	Clifton Powell
Marisol	Elizabeth Rodriguez
Cowboy	Terrence Howard
Young Revolutionary	Ryan Williams
Nicky	Larry McCoy
Mr. Warren	Rodney Winfield
Mrs. Barton	Cheryl Freeman
Martin	Sticky Fingaz
Cleon	Bokeem Woodbine
Devaughn	David Barry Gray
D'Ambrosio	Michael Imperioli
Lt. Dugan	Jaimz Woolvett
Skivvie Girls	Quynh Phann, Yen Chin Grow
Betancourt	Clifton Gonzalez Gonzalez
Ramsuer	Jean Claude La Marre
Corporal Rob	Daniel Kruse
Helicopter Pilot	Robert Smith
Protesters	Bernard Telsey, Tim Zay
Cabbie	Rik Colitti
Peaches	Heather B.
Spyder	Carlton Wilborn
Mr. Gianetti	Frank Albanese
Officer Brown	Monti Sharp
Officer Spinelli	Tony Sirico
Attorney Salvatore Rizzo	Robet LuPone
Juanita's Child (Sarah)	Joelle & Jordan Hernandez
Numbers Taker	Charles E. Lesene
Madame Minh	Cuc Dinh
Judge	Martin Sheen

Between the years 1968 and 1974, a Bronx youth finds himself shattered by his experiences in Vietnam and the harsh world back home.

© Hollywood Pictures Company

Keith David, Larenz Tate

STRANGE DAYS

(20TH CENTURY FOX) Producers, James Cameron, Steven-Charles Jaffe; Executive Producers, Rae Sanchini, Lawrence Kasanoff; Director, Kathryn Bigelow; Screenplay, James Cameron, Jay Cocks; Story, James Cameron; Photography, Matthew F. Leonetti; Designer, Lilly Kilvert; Editor, Howard Smith; Costumes, Ellen Mirojnick; Music, Graeme Revell, Deep Forest; Music Producer, Randy Gerston; Co-Producer, Ira Shuman; Special Effects Coordinator, Terry Frazee; Casting, Rick Pagano; Stunts, Doug Coleman; a Lightstorm Entertainment production; Dolby Stereo; Super 35 Widescreen; CFI color; Rated R; 140 minutes; October release

Angela Bassett, Ralph Fiennes

CAST

Lenny Nero	Ralph Fiennes
Lornette "Mace" Mason	Angela Bassett
Faith Justin	Juliette Lewis
Max Peltier	Tom Sizemore
Philo Gant	Michael Wincott
Burton Steckler	Vincent D'Onofrio
Jeriko One	Glenn Plummer
Iris	Brigitte Bako
Tick	Richard Edson
Dwayne Engelman	William Fichtner
Palmer Strickland	Josef Sommer
Keith	Joe Urla
Joey Corto	Nicky Katt
Wade Beemer	Michael Jace
Cindy "Vita" Minh	Louise LeCavalier
Duncan	David Carrera
Mr. Fumitsu	Jim Ishida
Tex Arcana	Todd Graff
Replay	Malcolm Norrington
Diamanda	Anais Munoz

and Ted Haler (Tow Truck Driver), Rio Hackford (Bobby the Bartender), Brook Susan Parker (Cecile), Brandon Hammond (Zander), Donald "Donnie" Young, B.J. Crockett (Young Zander), Dex Elliott Sanders (Curtis), Ronnie Willis (Homeboy), David Packer (Lane), Paulo Tocha (Spaz Diaz), James Muro (Nervous Pov), Ron Young (Nervous Pov Voice), Art Chudabala (Thai Restaurant Owner), Erica Kelly (Restaurant Hostess), Marlana Young (Waitress), Ray Chang (Thai Restaurant Cook), Raul Reformina (Busboy), Chris Douridas (Talk Radio Host), Billy Worley (Dan from Silverlake), Amon Bourne (Dewayne), Lisa Picotte (Lori from Encino), Kylie Ireland (Stoned Looking Girl), Nicole Hilbig (Stoned Girl's Lover), Stefan Arngrim (Skinner), Agustin Rodriguez (Eduardo), Kelly Hu (Anchor Woman), Nynno Anderson (Angry Jeriko Fan), Liat Goodson (Retinal Fetish Bouncer), Honey Labrador (Beach Beauty), Delane Vaughn (Mace's Husband), Mark Arneson (Police Officer), James Acheson (Cop in Bathroom), John Francis (Death), Zoot (Mime), Royce Minor (Angry Black Kid), Milan Reynolds (National Guard Medic #1), Russell W. Smith (National Guard #2)

Juliette Lewis

Lenny Nero is a lowlife dealer in an illict entertainment allowing viewers to vicariously experience other people's lives via visual clips. On the eve of the Millenium, he finds himself thrown into a dangerous conspiracy after a friend of his is murdered by someone trying to retrieve an explosive and incriminating "clip."

© Twentieth Century Fox

Ralph Fiennes, Tom Sizemore

Glenn Plummer

Michael Wincott

111

Jean Simmons, Winona Ryder

Alfre Woodard, Winona Ryder

Anne Bancroft, Ellen Burstyn, Winona Ryder, Alfre Woodard, Kate Nelligan

Samantha Mathis

Claire Danes

Winona Ryder, Dermot Mulroney

Anne Bancroft, Winona Ryder

Winona Ryder, Kate Nelligan

HOW TO MAKE AN AMERICAN QUILT

(UNIVERSAL) Producers, Sarah Pillsbury, Midge Sanford; Executive Producers, Walter Parkes, Laurie MacDonald, Deborah Jelin Newmyer; Director, Jocelyn Moorhouse; Screenplay, Jane Anderson; Based on the novel by Whitney Otto; Photography, Janusz Kaminski; Designer, Leslie Dilley; Editor, Jill Bilock; Music, Thomas Newman; Co-Producer, Patricia Whitcher; Costumes, Ruth Myers; Casting, Risa Bramon Garcia, Mary Vernieu; an Amblin Entertainment production; DTS Digital Stereo; Deluxe color; Rated PG-13; 110 minutes; October release

Maya Angelou, Winona Ryder, Ellen Burstyn

CAST

Young Finn	Kaelyn Craddick, Sara Craddick
Sally	Kate Capshaw
Finn's Father (photo)	Adam Baldwin
Finn	Winona Ryder
Sam	Dermot Mulroney
Hy	Ellen Burstyn
Glady Joe	Anne Bancroft
Anna	Maya Angelou
Marianna	Alfre Woodard
Sophia	Lois Smith
Em	Jean Simmons
Constance	Kate Nelligan
James	Denis Arnot
Arthur	Rip Torn
Dean	Derrick O'Connor
Leon	Johnathon Schaech
Young Sophia	Samantha Mathis
Preston	Loren Dean
Mrs. Darling	Melinda Dillon
Baby Duff	Krysten Lee Wilson, Kellie Lynn Wilson
Bay Pres	Brian McElroy, Michael McElroy
Little Evie	Paige Kettner, Ryanne Kettner
Little Duff	Annie Mae Hunter
Pres	Matt Zusser
Duff	Ari Meyers
Evie	Kaela Green
Young Em	Joanna Going
Young Dean	Tim Guinee
Em's Mother	Jane Alden
Em's Father	David Williams
Howell	Richard Jenkins
Anna's Great Grandmother	Tamala Jones
Anna's Great Grandfather	Hravey E. Lee, Jr.
Aunt Pauline	Esther Rolle
Little Anna	Rae' Ven Larrymore Kelly
The Mrs.	Gail Strickland
Guests	Debra Sticklin, Charles Parks
Beck	Jared Leto
Young Anna	Maria Celedonio
Young Glady Joe	Claire Danes
Young Hy	Alicia Goranson
Mrs. Rubens	Holland Taylor
Boys at party	Will Estes, Jonah Rooney
Winston	Mykelti Williamson

Johnathon Schaech, Winona Ryder

Undecided about her fiance's marriage proposal, Finn spends the summer at her grandmother's house where she is told varying stories about relationships from the different women gathered to make a quilt.

© Universal City Studios Inc.

Lois Smith, Kate Nelligan

THE SCARLET LETTER

(HOLLYWOOD PICTURES) Producers, Andrew G. Vajna, Roland Joffé; Executive Producers, Dodi Fayed, Tova Laiter; Co-Producer, Robert Colesberry; Director, Roland Joffé; Screenplay, Douglas Day Stewart; Based on the novel by Nathaniel Hawthorne; Associate Producer, Jonathan Cornick; Photography, Alex Thomson; Designer, Roy Walker; Editor, Thom Noble; Costumes, Gabriella Pescucci; Music, John Barry; Casting, Elisabeth Leustig, Priscilla John; an Andrew G. Vajna presentation of a Lightmotive/Allied Stars/Cinergi/Moving Pictures production; Distributed by Buena Vista Pictures; Dolby Digital Stereo; J-D-C Widescreen; Technicolor; Rated R; 135 minutes; October release

CAST

Hester Prynne	Demi Moore
Arthur Dimmesdale	Gary Oldman
Roger Prynne	Robert Duvall
Mituba	Lisa Jolliff-Andoh
John Bellingham	Edward Hardwicke
Horace Stonehall	Robert Prosky
Thomas Cheever	Roy Dotrice
Harriet Hibbons	Joan Plowright
Major Dunsmuir	Malcolm Storry
Goodman Mortimer	Jim Bearden
Goody Mortimer	Larissa Lapchinski
Goody Gotwick	Amy Wright
Johnny Sassamon	George Aguilar
Brewster Stonehall	Tim Woodward
Elizabeth Cheever	Joan Gregson
Meredith Stonehall	Dana Ivey
Margaret Bellingham	Diane Salinger
Mary Rollings	Jocelyn Cunningham
Sally Short	Francie Swift
Moskeegee	Sheldon Peters Wolfchild
Metacomet	Eric Schweig
Faith Stonehall	Kristen Fairlie
Prudence Stonehall	Sarah Campbell
Mr. Bobbin	Judd Jones
Town Beadle	Anthony Paton
Widow Wormser	Marguerite McNeil
Tarrantine Chief	Kennetch Charlette
Quaker Lady	Deborah Tennant
Female Sachem	Kateri Walker
Militia Guardsmen	Shaun R. Clarke, Jay Carmichael
First Guardsman	Jason Parkhill
Drummer Boy	Jeremy Keddy

and Nicholas Rice (The Clerk), Len Doncheff (Trader), Ashley Nolan (Goody Hunter), Stephen Aderneck (Speaking Native), Evelyn Francis (Algonquin Native), Gary Joseph (Native Rider), Stephen Micalchunk (Passenger No. 1), Jeremy Akerman (Middle Aged Passenger), Jodhi May (Voice of Pearl)

In Puritanical New England, Hester Prynne pays dearly for her adulterous affair with the Reverend Dimmesdale. Previous film adaptations starred Lilian Gish (1926), Colleen Moore (1934), and Senta Berger (1973, German). Henry B. Walthall played Roger in both the 1926 and 1934 versions.

Gary Oldman, Demi Moore

Robert Duvall

Joan Plowright

Demi Moore

Demi Moore

JADE

(PARAMOUNT) Producers, Robert Evans, Craig Baumgarten, Gary Adelson; Executive Producer, William J. MacDonald; Director, William Friedkin; Screenplay, Joe Eszterhas; Photography, Andrzej Bartkowiak; Designer, Alex Tavoularis; Editor, Augie Hess; Co-Producer, George Goodman; Music, James Horner; Costumes, Marilyn Vance; Casting, Ronnie Yeskel; a Robert Evans production of an Adelson/Baumgarten production; Dolby Stereo; Deluxe color; Rated R; 95 minutes; October release

CAST

David Corelli	David Caruso
Trina Gavin	Linda Fiorentino
Matt Gavin	Chazz Palminteri
Governor Edwards	Richard Crenna
Bob Hargrove	Michael Biehn
Karen Heller	Donna Murphy
Petey Vasko	Ken King
Bill Barrett	Holt McCallany
Pat Callendar	David Hunt
Patrice Jacinto	Angie Everhart
D.A. Arnold Clifford	Kevin Tighe
Justin Henderson	Jay Jacobus
Sandy	Victoria Smith
Executive	Drew Snyder
Justin Henderson's Brother	Bud Bostwick
Tommy Loy	Darryl Chan

and Graham Cowley (Deputy Coroner), Nellie Cravens (Governor's Secretary), Ron Ulstad (Kyle Medford), Allen Gebhardt (Forensic Man), Garrett Griffin (Police Officer), Julian Hill (Forensic), Buddy Joe Hooker, Bobby Bass, Sandra Berumen, Richard Ziker (Assistant D.A.s), Arthur Johnson, Paul Schlotfeldt, Rene Charles Laprevotte, John Loftus, Tom Walsh, Howard Weathersby, Kevin Whitfield, John Wyman (Cops), Mini Mehra (Resident), Nicholas Tarvid (Pilot), Harold Morrison (Co-Pilot), William Piletic (Priest), Olimpia Saravia (Maid), Tina J. Spangler (Secretary), Isaac Spivey (Homeless Man), Victor Talmadge (Lawyer), Kenneth Tigar (Corporate Man), Bill Tolliver (Medical Examiner), James Edwards Veurink (Executive), Victor Wong (Mr. Wong), Ron Winston Yuan (Technician), Peter Duchin & the Peter Duchin Orchestra (Black & White Ball Orchestra)

Assistant district attorney David Corelli investigates the brutal murder of a San Francisco millionaire which leads to the governor's office and implicates David's ex-lover Trina as a prime suspect.

© Paramount Pictures

Linda Florentino, Chazz Palminteri

Kenny King, Angie Everhart, David Caruso

THE ADDICTION

(OCTOBER) Producers, Denis Hann, Fernando Sulichin; Executive Producers, Russell Simmons, Preston Holmes; Director, Abel Ferrara; Screenplay, Nicholas St. John; Associate Producers, Antony Blinken, Marla Hanson; Photography, Ken Kelsch; Designer, Charles Lagola; Music, Joe Delia; Editor, Mayin Lo; Designer, Charles Lagola; Costumes, Melinda Eshelman; Dolby Stereo; Black and white; Not rated; 84 minutes; October release

CAST

Kathleen Conklin	Lili Taylor
Peina	Christopher Walken
Casanova	Annabella Sciorra
Jean	Edie Falco
Professor	Paul Calderon
Black	Fredro Starr
Anthropology Student	Kathryn Erbe
Missionary	Michael Imperioli
Black's Friend	Jamel "Redrum" Simmons
Narrator/Priest	Father Robert Castle
Mary	Lisa Casillo
Dean	Jay Julien
Cop	Michael Fella

and Dr. Louis A. Katz (Doctor), Leroy Johnson, Fred Williams (Homeless Victims), Avron Coleman (Cellist), Frank "Butchy the Hat" Aquilino (Delivery Man), Nicholas Decegli (Cabby), Chuck Jeffries (Bartender), Ed Conna (Waiter), Nancy Ellen Anzalone (Dress Victim), Susan Mitchell, Mary Ann Hannon, John Vincent McEvily, Bianca Pratt, Christina Campenella, Anthony Giangrando, Kevin Scullin (Featured Victims), Heather Bracken (Nurse)

After being bitten by a mysterious woman, philosophy student Kathleen Conklin finds herself craving blood and using any means to get it.

© October Films

Christopher Walken, Lili Taylor

Olivia d'Abo, Josh Hamilton

KICKING AND SCREAMING

(TRIMARK) Producer, Joel Castelberg; Executive Producers, Sandy Gallin, Carol Baum, Mark Amin; Co-Produces, Phillip B. Goldfine, Andrew Hersh; Associate Producers, Jeremy Kramer, Jason Blum; Director/Screenplay, Noah Baumbach; Story, Noah Baumbach, Oliver Berkman; Photography, Steven Bernstein; Editor, J. Kathleen Gibson; Music, Phil Marshall; Designer, Dan Whifler; Costumes, Mary Jane Fort; Casting, Ellie Kanner; Color; Rated R; 96 minutes; October release

CAST

Grover	Josh Hamilton
Jane	Olivia d'Abo
Otis	Carlos Jacott
Max	Chris Eigeman
Chet	Eric Stoltz
Skippy	Jason Wiles
Miami	Parker Posey
Kate	Cara Buono
Grover's Dad	Elliott Gould
Pete	Sam Gould
Gail	Catherine Kellner
Professor	Jonathan Baumbach
Louis	John Lehr
Lester	Peter Czernin
Josselyn	Eliza Roberts
Friedrich	Chris Reed
Danny	Noah Baumbach
Freddy	Jason S. Kassin
Zach	Dean Cameron
Bouncer	David Deluise
Friedrich's Date	Thea Goodman
Stephanie	Lauren Katz
Nose Ring Girl	Alexia Landau
Amy	Perrey Reeves
Ike	David Kirsch
Omar	Matthew Kaplan
Charlotte	Marissa Ribisi
Audra	Kaela Dobkin

and Anthony Giglio, Jr., Richard Tacchino (Singing Freshmen), Nico Baumbach (Random Freshman), Sal Viscuso (Bar Teacher), Jessica Hecht (Ticket Woman), Nora Perricone (Door Person), Melanie Koch (Girl at Bar)

Following graduation from college, a group of friends find themselves having difficulty coping with the real world as they stay close to the safety of campus life.

© Trimark Pictures

Jason Wiles

Cara Buono

Eric Stoltz, Carlos Jacott

Chris Eigeman, Parker Posey

Jared Harris, Michael J. Fox, Giancarlo Esposito

Harvey Keitel, Jim Jarmusch

Roseanne, Harvey Keitel

BLUE IN THE FACE

(MIRAMAX) Producers, Greg Johnson, Peter Newman, Diana Phillips; Executive Producers, Harvey Keitel, Bob Weinstein, Harvey Weinstein; Directors, Wayne Wang, Paul Auster; Situations Created by Wayne Wang and Paul Auster in collaboration with the actors; Co-Producer, Hisami Kuroiwa; Photography, Adam Holender; Designer, Kalina Ivanov; Editor, Christopher Tellefsen; Costumes, Claudia Brown; Video Segment Director, Harvey Wang; a Peter Newman/Interal production in association with NDF/Euro Space; Dolby Digital Stereo; DuArt color; Rated R; 89 minutes; October release

CAST

Auggie Wren	Harvey Keitel
Himself	Lou Reed
Dot	Roseanne
Peter	Michael J. Fox
Himself	Jim Jarmusch
Belgian Waffle Man	Lily Tomlin
Violet	Mel Gorham
Jimmy Rose	Jared Harris
Tommy	Giancarlo Esposito
Vinnie	Victor Argo
Singing Telegram Girl	Madonna
Jackie	Keith David
Blonde Woman	Mira Sorvino

and Malik Yoba, Jose Zuniga, Stephen Gevedon, The John Lurie National Orchestra, Sharif Rashed, Peggy Gormley

Auggie Wren's Brooklyn cigar store is invaded by an odd variety of characters in this improvisational follow-up to Smoke *(Miramax, 1995) which also featured Harvey Keitel, Giancarlo Esposito, Victor Argo, and Malik Yoba.*

© Miramax Films

RuPaul, Harvey Keitel, Mel Gorham

Lily Tomlin

GET SHORTY

(MGM) Producers, Danny DeVito, Michael Shamberg, Stacey Sher; Executive Producer/Director, Barry Sonnenfeld; Screenplay, Scott Frank; Based on the novel by Elmore Leonard; Photography, Don Peterman; Designer, Peter Larkin; Editor, Jim Miller; Co-Producer, Graham Place; Costumes, Betsy Heimann; Music, John Lurie; Casting, David Rubin, Debra Zane; a Jersey Films production; Distributed by MGM/UA; DTS Digital Stereo; Deluxe color; Rated R; 105 minutes; October release

CAST

Chili Palmer..John Travolta
Harry Zimm...Gene Hackman
Karen Flores...Rene Russo
Martin Weir...Danny DeVito
Ray "Bones" Barboni..Dennis Farina
Bo Catlett..Delroy Lindo
Bear...James Gandolfini
Ronnie Wingate...Jon Gries
Nicki...Renee Props
Leo Devoe..David Paymer
Tommy Carlo..Martin Ferrero
Mr. Escobar...Miguel Sandoval
Yayo Portillo...Jacob Vargas
Fay Devoe..Linda Hart
Dick Allen...Bobby Slayton
Doris..Bette Midler
Momo...Ron Karabatsos
Bear's Daughter ....Alison Waddell, Amber Waddell
Agent Curtis..John Cothran, Jr.
Agent Dunbar ....Jack Conley
Agent Morgan...Bernard Hocke
Ray Barboni's Bodyguard ....Big Daddy Wayne
Big Guy with Escobar ....Xavier Montalvo
Rental Car Attendant ....Carlease Burke
Manager at Vesuvio's..Vito Scotti
Waiter at Vesuvio's..Rino Piccolo
Ed the Barber...Alfred Dennis
Fred the Barber..Ralph Manza
Kid at Lockers...Zed Frizzelle
Limo Driver with Sign...Harry Victor
Resident Doctor...Patrick Breen
Doorman ....Barry Sonnenfeld
Themselves..Harvey Keitel, Penny Marshall
and Donna W. Scott (Screaming Woman), Zack Phifer (Ivy Restaurant Maitre d'), Gregory B. Goossen (Duke, Man at the Ivy), Stephanie Kemp (Ivy Restaurant Waitress), Rebecca Arthur (Las Vegas Waitress), Jeffrey J. Stephan, Ernest "Chili" Palmer (Bones' Buddies)

Miami loan shark Chili Palmer arrives in Hollywood to collect on a gambling debt and finds himself pitching an idea for a film to producer Harry Zimm.

© Metro-Goldwyn-Mayer Inc.

John Travolta

Delroy Lindo

Gene Hackman, Danny DeVito

John Travolta, Dennis Farina

John Travolta, Rene Russo

Rene Russo

Gene Hackman

John Travolta, Rene Russo, Danny DeVito

MALLRATS

(GRAMERCY) Producers, James Jacks, Sean Daniel, Scott Mosier; Director/Screenplay, Kevin Smith; Photography, David Klein; Line Producer, Laura Greenlee; Designer, Dina Lipton; Editor, Paul Dixon; Costumes, Dana Allyson; Music, Ira Newborn; Casting, Don Phillips; an Alphaville presentation in association with View Askew Prods.; DTS Digital Stereo; Deluxe color; Rated R; 95 minutes; October release

CAST

Rene	Shannen Doherty
T.S. Quint	Jeremy London
Brodie	Jason Lee
Brandi	Claire Forlani
Shannon	Ben Affleck
Gwen	Joey Lauren Adams
Tricia	Renee Humphrey
Jay	Jason Mewes
William	Ethan Suplee
Himself	Stan Lee
Ivannah	Priscilla Barnes
Svenning	Michael Rooker
Gill	Brian O'Halloran
Silent Bob	Kevin Smith
Security Guard	Carol Banker
Game Show Host	Art James
Roddy	Scott Mosier
La Flours	Sven Thorsen

and Steven Blackwell (Arresting Cop #2), Kyle Boe (Pull Toy Kid), David Brinkley, Jeff Gadbois (TV Executives), Walter Flanagan, David Klein (Fans at Comic Store), Ethan Flower, Ed Hapstack (Guy Contestants), Chelsea Frye (Girl with Easter Bunny), Terry Hempleman (Cop #1), Bryan Johnson (Employee at Comic Store), Mikey Kovar, Britt Swenson (Children at Kiosk), Crystal Muirhead-Manik (Saleslady at Lingerie Store), Tyson Nassauer (Kid at Poster Kiosk), Aaron Preusse (Passerby in Parking Lot), Mary Woolever (Teacher), Brad Fox, Gino Gori, Zach Perkins, Brad Giddings, Bryce Mack, Christopher O'Larkin (Team La Fours)

After they are both dumped by their girlfriends, T.S. and Brodie take off for the local mall for a series of offbeat encounters.

© Gramercy Pictures

Shannen Doherty, Jason Lee

Kevin Smith, Jason Mewes

Jason Lee, Jeremy London

Joey Lauren Adams, Claire Forlani

NOW AND THEN

(NEW LINE CINEMA) formerly *The Gaslight Edition*; Producers, Suzanne Todd, Demi Moore; Executive Producer, Jennifer Todd; Co-Producer, Eric McLeod; Director, Lesli Linka Glatter; Screenplay, I. Marlene King; Photography, Ueli Steiger; Designers, Gershon Ginsburg, Anne Kuljian; Editor, Jacqueline Cambas; Music, Cliff Eidelman; Costumes, Deena Appel; Casting, Valerie McCaffrey; a Moving Pictures production; DTS Digital Stereo; Deluxe color; Rated PG-13; 96 minutes; October release

CAST

Young Roberta	Christina Ricci
Young Teeny	Thora Birch
Young Samantha	Gaby Hoffmann
Young Chrissy	Ashleigh Aston Moore
Samantha Albertson	Demi Moore
Roberta Martin	Rosie O'Donnell
Christina Dewitt	Rita Wilson
Tina Tercell	Melanie Griffith
Angela Albertson	Willa Glen
Mrs. Dewitt	Bonnie Hunt
Scott Wormer	Devon Sawa
Roger Wormer	Travis Robertson
Eric Wormer	Justin Humphrey
Clay Wormer	Bradley Coryell
Wiladene	Janeane Garofalo
Mrs. Albertson	Lolita Davidovich
Mr. Albertson	Ric Reitz
Crazy Pete	Walter Sparrow
Grandma Albertson	Cloris Leachman
Kenny	Kellen Crosby
Outfielder	Joey Stinson
Catcher	James Paul Cleckler
Young Morton	Tucker Stone
Jimmy	Jamison B. Dowd
Bud Kent	Hank Azaria
Eda	Beverly Shelton
Tractor Driver	Geoff McKnight
Limo Driver	T.S. Morgan
Morton Williams	Carl Espy
Baby	Alice Tew

and Brendan Fraser

Four women look back on the summer of 1970 when they turned twelve and made a pact to remain friends forever.

Ashleigh Aston Moore, Gaby Hoffman, Christina Ricci, Thora Birch

Rosie O'Donnell, Rita Wilson, Demi Moore

Demi Moore, Rosie O'Donnell, Rita Wilson, Melanie Griffith

Joseph Mazzello, Patrick Swayze

Joseph Mazzello, Seth Mumy

May Elizabeth Mastrantonio, Patrick Swayze

David Marshall Grant, Mary Elizabeth Mastrantonio, Patrick Swayze

THREE WISHES

(SAVOY) Producers, Clifford Green, Ellen Green, Gary Lucchesi; Executive Producers, Keith Samples, Larry Y. Albucher; Director, Martha Coolidge; Screenplay, Elizabeth Anderson; Story, Clifford Green, Ellen Green; Photography, Johnny E. Jensen; Designer, John Vallone; Editor, Steven Cohen; Visual Effects Supervisor, Phil Tippett; Music, Cynthia Millar; Costumes, Shelley Komarov; a Rysher Entertainment presentation; Dolby Stereo; Deluxe Color; Rated PG; 115 minutes; October release

CAST

Jack McCloud...Patrick Swayze
Jeanne Holman...Mary Elizabeth Mastrantonio
Tom Holman..Joseph Mazzello
Gunny Holman...Seth Mumy
Phil...David Marshall Grant
Coach Schramka...Jay O. Sanders
Adult Tom...Michael O'Keefe
Leland's Dad...John Diehl
Joyce..Diane Venora
Little Leland...David Zahorsky
Brian...Brian Flannery
Scott...Brock Pierce
Sackin...Davin Jacob Carey
Brian's Father..David Hart
Scott's Father..Scott Patterson
Sackin's Father...Michael Laskin
Hank...Robert Starr
Brian's Mother...Simone Study
Scott's Mother..Lauren Sinclair
Leland's Mother...Annabelle Gurwitch
Katherine Holman ....Moira Harris
Policeman..Neil McDonough
Passerby...Brad Parker
Tool and Die Coach..Philip Levien
Colony Drive-In Coach ....Lawrence R. Baca
Neighbor...Bill Mumy
Neighbor's Wife ....Colleen Camp
Little Magician...Brandon Lacroix
Cindy..Jamie Cronin
Hide and Seek Boy..Alexander Roos
Neighborhood Teenager ....Garette Ratliff Hensen
Dr. Pavlick ....Jay Gerber
Dad ....D.B. Sweeney
and William G. Schilling (Doctor), Tiffany Lubran, Kathryn Lubran (Holman Daughters), Marc Shelton (X-ray Technician), Vivien Strauss, Loanne Bishop (Bystanders), John Devoe, Ethan Jensen (Teenagers on Roof), Robb Turner (Man with Rake), Rosa (Betty Jane)

A mysterious vagabond has a profound effect on the lives of Jeanne Holman and her two young sons as they start life anew after losing Jeanne's husband to the war.

© Rysher Entertainment, Inc.

Allen Payne, Angela Bassett

VAMPIRE IN BROOKLYN

(PARAMOUNT) Producers, Eddie Murphy, Mark Lipsky; Executive Producers, Marianne Maddalena, Stuart M. Besser; Director, Wes Craven; Screenplay, Charles Murphy, Michael Lucker, Christopher Parker; Story, Eddie Murphy, Vernon Lynch, Jr., Charles Murphy; Co-Producers, Ray Murphy, Jr., Dixie J. Capp; Photography, Mark Irwin; Editor, Patrick Lussier; Music, J. Peter Robinson; Costumes, Ha Nguyen; Special Makeup Effects, Kurtzman, Nicotero, Berger EFX Group; Special Visual Effects, Fantasy II Film Effects Inc.; Visual Effects Supervisor, Gene Warren; Casting, Ellen Mack Knight; an Eddie Murphy production; Dolby Stereo; Deluxe color; Rated R; 101 minutes; October release

Eddie Murphy, Kadeem Hardison

Angela Bassett, Eddie Murphy

CAST

Maximillian/Preacher Pauley/Guido	Eddie Murphy
Rita	Angela Bassett
Justice	Allen Payne
Julius	Kadeem Hardison
Silas	John Witherspoon
Dr. Zeko	Zakes Mokae
Dewey	Joanna Cassidy
Nikki	Simbi Khali
Eva	Messiri Freeman
Officer	Kelly Cinnante
Anthony	Nick Corri
Thrasher	W. Earl Brown
Bartender	Ayo Adeyemi
Choir Leader	Troy Curvey, Jr.
Mrs. Brown	Vickilyn Reynolds
Deacon Brown	William Blount
Bear	Joe Costanza
Lizzy	John La Motta
Waiter	Marcelo Tubert
Caprisi	Nick DeMauro
Woman in Park	Jerry Hall
Man in Park	Mark Haining
Zealot at Police Station	Wendy Robie
Cop	Alyse Mandel
Greeter at Church	Larry Paul Marshall
Checker Player	Vince Micelli
Game Show Host	Ray Combs

and Oren Waters, Carlton Davis, Clive Ross, Michael Hyde, Maxine Waters Willard, Josef Powell, Roy Galloway, Carmen Carter, Julie Waters Tillman, Carmen Twillie (Singers)

A Caribbean vampire arrives in Brooklyn to seek a half-human/half-vampire woman who is destined to be his bride.

Eddie Murphy

Woody Allen, Helena Bonham Carter

Mira Sorvino

Michael Rapaport, Woody Allen

MIGHTY APHRODITE

(MIRAMAX) Producer, Robert Greenhut; Executive Producers, Jean Doumanian, J.E. Beaucaire; Co-Executive Producers, Jack Rollins, Charles H. Joffe, Letty Aronson; Co-Producer, Helen Robin; Director/Screenplay, Woody Allen; Photography, Carlo DiPalma; Designer, Santo Loquasto; Editor, Susan E. Morse; Costumes, Jeffrey Kurland; Choreographer, Graciella Daniele; Casting, Juliet Taylor; from Sweetland Films; Dolby Stereo; Technicolor; Rated R; 95 minutes; October release

CAST

Greek Chorus Leader	F. Murray Abraham
Lenny Winerib	Woody Allen
Amanda's Mother	Claire Bloom
Amanda	Helena Bonham Carter
Jocasta	Olympia Dukakis
Kevin	Michael Rapaport
Linda Ash	Mira Sorvino
Laius	David Ogden Stiers
Tiresias	Jack Warden
Jerry Bender	Peter Weller
Ricky, the Pimp	Dan Moran
Bud's Wife	J. Smith Cameron
Bud	Steven Randazzo
Oedipus	Jeffrey Kurland
Infant Max	Tucker Robin
Amanda's Father	Donald Symington
Two-Year-Old Max	Nolan Tuffey
Max	Jimmy McQuaid
School Principal	Yvette Hawkins
Adoption Coordinator	Rosemary Murphy
Park Avenue Couple	Karin Haidorfer, Gary Alper
Linda's Ex-Landlord	Peter McRobbie
Ex-Landlord's Wife	Kathleen Doyle
Lenny's Secretary	Jennifer Greenhut
Operator	Sondra James
Extras Guild Researcher	Paul Giamatti
Superintendent	William Addy
Ken	Kenneth Edelson
Cassandra	Danielle Ferland
Messenger	Dan Mullane
Race Announcer	Thomas Durkin
Ricky's Friend	Paul Herman
Voice of Zeus	Kent Blocher
Porno Film Stars	Joseph P. Coleman, Georgette Pasare
On-Camera Helicopter Pilot	Bray Poor

and Pamela Blair, Rene Ceballos, Elie Chaib, George De La Pena, Joanne DiMauro, Denise Faye, Marianne Filali, Angelo Fraboni, Scott Fowler, Seth Gertsacov, Patti Karr, Fred Mann III, John Mineo, Christopher Nelson, Valda Setterfield, Sven Toorvald (Greek Chorus), Tony Sirico, Tony Darrow, Ray Garvey (Boxing Trainers), David H. Kramer, Dann Fink, Sondra James, Karen Longwell, Dominic Marcus, Craig Sechler, Bill Timoney, Lisa Vidal, Bruce Winant (Chorus Voices)

Lenny Winerib invites trouble when he decides to track down the biological mother of his adopted son.

Mira Sorvino won the Academy Award for Best Supporting Actress of 1995. The film also received an Oscar nomination for original screenplay.

© Miramax Films

Jimmy McQuaid, Woody Allen, Helena Bonham Carter

Michael Rapaport, Mira Sorvino

Woody Allen, Tony Sirico

Woody Allen, Helena Bonham Carter

Nicolas Cage, Elisabeth Shue

Nicolas Cage, Elisabeth Shue

Elisabeth Shue, Julian Sands

Steven Weber, Nicolas Cage, Richard Lewis

Elisabeth Shue, Nicolas Cage

LEAVING LAS VEGAS

(UNITED ARTISTS) Producers, Lila Cazès, Annie Stewart; Executive Producers, Paige Simpson, Stuart Regen; Director/Screenplay/Music, Mike Figgis; Based upon the novel by John O'Brien; Photography, Declan Quinn; Designer, Waldemar Kalinowski; Editor, John Smith; Costumes, Laura Goldsmith; Casting, Carrie Frazier; a Lumière Pictures presentation of a Lila Cazès production; Distributed by MGM/UA; Dolby Stereo; Foto-Kem color; Rated R; 112 minutes; October release

CAST

Ben Sanderson	Nicolas Cage
Sera	Elisabeth Shue
Yuri	Julian Sands
Peter	Richard Lewis
Marc Nussbaum	Steven Weber
Sheila	Kim Adams
Debbie	Emily Procter
Man at Bar	Stuart Regen
Terri	Valeria Golino
L.A. Bartender	Graham Beckel
Man at Strip Bar	Al Henderson
Hispanic Prostitute	Shashi Bhatia
Bank Teller	Carey Lowell
Business Colleague	Anne Lange
Mr. Simpson	Thomas Kopache
Businessmen	Vincent Ward, French Stewart
Weird Woman	Lucinda Jenney
Mobsters	Ed Lauter, Waldemar Kalinowski, Mike Figgis
Hotel Manager	David Kriegel
Midwest Man at Poolside	Bill Thompson
Pawn Shop Owner	Marek Stabrowski
Conventioneer	R. Lee Ermey
Hooker at Bar	Mariska Hargitay
Barman #2	Danny Huston
Landlady	Laurie Metcalf
Landlord	David Brisbin
Biker Girl	Shawnee Smith
Biker Guy	Paul Quinn
Bartender #3 in Biker Bar	Julian Lennon
Waitress at Mall	Tracy Thorne
Man at Mall	Bob Rafelson
Desk Clerk	Susan Barnes
Dealer	Mark Coppola
College Boys	Michael Goorjian, Jeremy Jordan, Davidlee Willson
Cynical Cabbie	Xander Berkeley
Stetson Man at Casino	Sergio Premoli
Security Guard	Gordon Michaels
Concerned Cabbie	Lou Rawls

Nicolas Cage, Elisabeth Shue

A down and out screenwriter, arriving in Las Vegas with the intention of literally drinking himself to death, finds himself forming a unique relationship with a prostitute.

Nicolas Cage received the Academy Award for Best Actor of 1995. The film received additional Oscar nominations for actress (Shue), director, and screenplay adaptation.

© United Artists Inc.

Elisabeth Shue

Julian Sands

POWDER

(HOLLYWOOD PICTURES) Producers, Roger Birnbaum, Daniel Grodnik; Executive Producers, Riley Kathryn Ellis, Robert Snukal; Director/Screenplay, Victor Salva; Photography, Jerzy Zielinski; Designer, Waldemar Kalinowski; Editor, Dennis M. Hill; Costumes, Betsy Cox; Music, Jerry Goldsmith; Co-Producer, Dennis Murphy; Special Powder Make-up Designer & Creators, Thomas R. Burman, Bari Dreiband-Burman; Visual Effects Supervisor, Stephanie Powell; Casting, Junie Lowry-Johnson; Presented in association with Caravan Pictures; Distributed by Buena Vista Pictures; Dolby Digital Stereo; Technicolor; Rated PG-13; 111 minutes; October release

Jeff Goldblum, Sean Patrick Flanery, Mary Steenburgen

CAST

Jessie Caldwell	Mary Steenburgen
Powder (Jeremy)	Sean Patrick Flanery
Sheriff Barnum	Lance Henriksen
Donald Ripley	Jeff Goldblum
Duncan	Brandon Smith
John Box	Bradford Tatum
Maxine	Susan Tyrrell
Lindsey	Missy Crider
Stipler	Ray Wise
Mitch	Esteban Louis Powell
Syke	Reed Fredrichs
Zane	Chad Cox
Brennan	Joe Marchman
Greg	Philip Maurice Hayes
Emma	Dannette McMann
Steven Barnum	Tom Tarantini
Mr. Kelloway	Woody Watson
Dr. Roth	Alex Allen Morris
Dr. Deggan	Brady Coleman
Paramedic #1	Barry Berfield
Anna	Paula Engel
Arturo	Meason Wiley
Nurses	Dee Macaluso, Bonnie Gallup
Doc. Assocs.	James Houston, Bill Grant-Minchen

Brandon Smith, Sean Patrick Flanery

Powder, a young boy kept in his grandparent's cellar because of his pale white skin and odd powers, is forced to enter society, facing fear and prejudice.

© Hollywood Pictures Company

Reed Fredrichs, Joe Marchman, Sean Patrick Flanery, Bradford Tatum, Esteban Louis Powell, Chad Cox

MAYA LIN: A STRONG CLEAR VISION

(OCEAN RELEASING) Producers, Freida Lee Mock, Terry Sanders; Director, Freida Lee Mock; Executive Producer, Eileen Harris Norton; Photography, Don Lenzer, Eddie Marritz; Music, Charles Bernstein; Editor, William T. Cartwright, Sr.; Associate Producer, Jessica Yu; from Sanders & Mock productions; Color; Not rated; 96 minutes; October release.

Documentary about how twenty-one-year-old architecture student Maya Lin was chosen to design the Vietnam Veterans Memorial in Washington, D.C.

1994 Academy Award winner for Best Feature Documentary.

© Ocean Releasing

Maya Lin

Al Pacino

TWO BITS

(MIRAMAX) formerly *A Day to Remember*; Producer, Arthur Cohn; Executive Producers, Joseph Stefano, Willi Baer, David Korda; Director, James Foley; Screenplay, Joseph Stefano; Photography, Juan Ruiz-Anchia; Designer, Jane Musky; Music, Carter Burwell; Line Producer, Larry Franco; Costumes, Claudia Brown; Editor, Howard Smith; Casting, Glenn Daniels; a Connexion prresentatin of an Arthur Cohn production; Dolby Stereo; Panavision; Color; Rated PG-13; 93 minutes; November release

CAST

Gennaro Spirito	Jerry Barone
Luisa	Mary Elizabeth Mastrantonio
Grandpa	Al Pacino
Tullio	Patrick Borriello
Dr. Bruna	Andy Romano
Mrs. Bruna	Donna Mitchell
Aunt Carmela	Mary Lou Rosato
Uncle Joe	Joe Grifasi
Mrs. Conte	Rosemary DeAngelis
Irish	Ronald McLarty
Ballyhoo Driver	Charles Scalies
Guendolina	Joanna Merlin
Dr. Wilson	Geoff Pierson
Woman in Red	Karen Shallo

and Nick Discenza (Father of Deceased), Rik Colitti (Vottima), Rose Arrick (Mother of Deceased), Joy Pinizotto (Bride), Louis Lippa (Father of the Bride), Johnny C. (Head Pallbearer), Gene D'Allesandro (Brother of Deceased), Anthony DeSando (Victor), Sheila Murphy (Mary Linguini), Jayne Haynes (Mrs. Rizzo), Joe Fersedi, Rick Faugno, Jon Napolitano (Players), Mikey Viso (Petey), Nicole Molina (Little Girl), Mario D'Elia (Petey's Dad), Mary Testa (Housewife), Ted Brunetti (Guendolina's Youngest Son), Tony Rosa (Guendolina's Eldest Son), Lynn Battaglia (Guendolina's Son's Wife), Joey Perillo (Ballyhoo Replacement Driver), Dominic Leporarti (Freddie), Skip Rose (Ball Player), Alec Baldwin (Narrator)

In 1933 Philadelphia, young Gennaro Spirito spends the day trying to obtain the quarter he needs to admit him to the grand opening of a new movie palace.

© Miramax Films

Jerry Barone, Mary Elizabeth Mastrantonio

THE NOVEMBER MEN

(NORTHERN ARTS) Producers, Paul Williams, Rodney Byron Ellis; Director, Paul Williams; Screenplay, James Andronica; Photography, Susan Emerson; Music, Scott Thomas Smith; Editor, Chip Brooks; a Rohdhouse Investments, Inc. with Robert Davi and Sun Lion Films presentation; Color; Not rated; 98 minutes; November release

CAST

Duggo	James Andronica
Elizabeth	Leslie Bevis
Chief Agent Granger	Beau Starr
Arthur Gwenlyn	P.W. Williams
Lorina	Coralissa Gines
Agent Clancy	Rod Ellis
Himself	Robert Davi
Morganna	Lexie Shine

and Shanda Cunningham (Waitress), Elsayed Badrya (Lahoud), Said Salim (Haddad), Zeri Guarino (Building Manager), Capt. Richard Daniel (Special Agent Lang), Allison Gammon (Biker Girl), Francis Grimes (Burly), Herb Nanas (Gun Merchant), Kaz Garas (Sgt. Major), Joe Perez (Aide), Billy Grillo, Jr. (Boy with Model Car), Randy McLeod (Agent—Afro-American), Dave Young (Policeman at Tape), Megan Klempa (Detective), Tony King (Agent), William Grillo (Sharpshooter Agent—Brad Lucas), James Wellington (Machinist), R.C. Johnston (Hot Dog Stand Vendor), Jeri McBride (Granger's Wife), Frank Bruynbroek (Stakeout Agent), Michael Cara, Donna Blevins (Special Agents), Jeanette Svenson (Interviewer), Lynn Sanson (Aspiring Actress), Morton Lewis ("Real" Director), Michael Adamson ("Real" Secret Service Agent)

A radical filmmaker enlists a group of malcontents to appear in his movie about the assassination of President George Bush, hoping, perhaps, that fiction will become a reality.

© Northern Arts

Paul Williams, Leslie Bevis

Christina Ricci, Anna Chlumsky

Diana Scarwid, David Keith

GOLD DIGGERS: THE SECRET OF BEAR MOUNTAIN

(UNIVERSAL) Producers, Martin Bregman, Rolf Deyhle, Michael S. Bregman; Executive Producer, Louis A. Stroller; Director, Kevin James Dobson; Photography, Ross Berryman; Designer, Michael Bolton; Editor, Stephen W. Butler; Associate Producer, Allan Wertheim; Music, Joel McNeely; Costumes, Mary McLeod; Casting, Mary Gail Artz, Barbara Cohen;a Bregman/Deyhle production; DTS Stereo; Deluxe color; Rated PG; 92 minutes; November release

CAST

Beth Easton	Christina Ricci
Jody Salerno	Anna Chlumsky
Kate Easton	Polly Draper
Matt Hollinger	Brian Kerwin
Lynette Salerno	Diana Scarwid
Ray Karnisak	David Keith
Grace Briggs	Gillian Barber
Samantha	Jewel Staite
Molly Morgan	Amy Kirk
Sgt. Weller	Dwight McFee
Hank	Andrew Wheeler

and Roger R. Cross (Paramedic), Kimberley Warnat (Girl), Jesse Moss (Adam), Scott Augustine (Doug), Steve Makaj (Deputy Ted), Betty Phillips (Mysterious Woman), Jay Brazeau (Everett Graham), Dustin Brooks, Philip Josef (Fight Boys), Carren Learning (Voice of Adult Beth)

Beth Easton, relocated with her mother to a small Northwestern town, befriends tomboy Jody Salerno, who convinces her to search for a legendary gold mine.

© Universal City Studios, Inc.

HOME FOR THE HOLIDAYS

(PARAMOUNT) Producers, Peggy Rajski, Jodie Foster; Executive Producer, Stuart Kleinman; Director, Jodie Foster; Screenplay, W.D. Richter; Based on a short story by Chris Radant; Photography, Lajos Koltai; Designer, Andrew McAlpine; Editor, Lynzee Klingman; Costumes, Susan Lyall; Music, Mark Isham; Casting, Avy Kaufman; a co-presentation PolyGram Filmed Entertainment of an Egg Pictures production; Dolby Stereo; Technicolor; Rated PG-13; 103 minutes; November release

CAST

Claudia Larson	Holly Hunter
Tommy Larson	Robert Downey, Jr.
Adele Larson	Anne Bancroft
Henry Larson	Charles Durning
Leo Fish	Dylan McDermott
Aunt Glady	Geraldine Chaplin
Walter Wedman	Steve Guttenberg
Joanne Wedman	Cynthia Stevenson
Kitt	Claire Danes
Brittany Lace	Emily Ann Lloyd
Walter Jr.	Zachary Duhame
Peter Arnold	Austin Pendleton
Russell Terziak	David Strathairn
Ginny Johnson Drewer	Amy Yasbeck
Ron Drewer	James Lecesne
Woman on Airplane	Angela Paton
Man in Car	Randy Stone
Jack	Sam Slovick
Woman at Party	Susan Lyall
Counter Boy	Shawn Wayne Hatosy
Airport Cop	Nat Benchley
Women on Airport Phones	Molly Austin, Viviene Shub, Julie Ann Mendez
Man on Airport Phone	Bus Howard
Young Henry	Johnny Tonini
Young Adele	Eva Langsdorf
Young Glady	Wilder Ferguson
Young Claudia	Stephaine Francoz
Young Tommy	Blake Hovespian
Young Joanne	Natasha Stanton

After being fired from her job in Chicago, Claudia Larson reluctantly travels to Baltimore to spend Thanksgiving with her eccentric family.

© Polygram Film Productions P.V.

Holly Hunter, Anne Bancroft

Holly Hunter, Anne Bancroft, Charles Durning

Anne Bancroft, Robert Downey, Jr., Charles Durning, Cynthia Stevenson

Dylan McDermott, Holly Hunter

Kellita Smith, Jack Nicholson, Priscilla Barnes

THE CROSSING GUARD

(MIRAMAX) Producers, Sean Penn, David S. Hamburger; Executive Producers, Bob Weinstein, Harvey Weinstein, Richard Gladstein; Director/Screenplay, Sean Penn; Photography, Vilmos Zsigmond; Designer, Michael Haller; Editor, Jay Cassidy; Costumes, Jill Ohanneson; Music, Jack Nitzsche; Song: "Missing" written and performed by Bruce Springsteen; Dolby Stereo; Color; Rated R; 114 minutes; November release

CAST

Freddy Gale	Jack Nicholson
John Booth	David Morse
Mary	Anjelica Huston
JoJo	Robin Wright
Helen Booth	Piper Laurie
Stuart Booth	Richard Bradford
Verna	Priscilla Barnes
Peter	David Baerwald
Roger	Robbie Robertson
Bobby	John Savage
Mia	Kari Wuhrer
Jennifer	Jennifer Leigh Warren
Tanya	Kellita Smith
Sunny Ventura	Richard Sarafian
Coop	Bobby Cooper
Silas	Jeff Morris
Buddy	Buddy Anderson
Eddie	Dr. Edward L. Katz
Joe at Bar	Joe Viterelli
Woman in Shop	Eileen Ryan
Jefferey	Ryo Ishabashi
Cops	Dennis Fanning, Lisa Crawford
Asian Man	Jay Koiwai
Little Asian Girl	Elizabeth Gilliam
Twin Boys	Michael Ryan, Matthew Ryan
Woman on Bus	Penny Allen
Nicky Blair	Nicky Blair
Swinger	Gene Kirkwood

and Jason Kristofer (Bus Passenger #1), Randy Meadoff (Bus Passenger's Mother), Leo Penn (Hank), Michael Abelar (Bum), Daysi Moreno (Freddy's Chicana), Christel Ehde, Kamala Petty, Millicent Sheridan, Joi Travers (Dancers), Erin Dignam (Peter's Guest #1), Jeremiah Wayne Birkett (Jefferey's Boyfriend), Hadda Brooks (Piano Player), Ruby McKoy (Deputy Sheriff), Hanna Newmaster (Little Girl), Dr. William Dignam (The Crossing Guard)

Freddy Gale, whose life fell to pieces after a drunk driver ran down his seven-year-old daughter, swears to kill the man responsible once he is released from prison. Cast members Leo Penn and Eileen Ryan are director Sean Penn's real-life parents.

© Miramax Films

David Morse, Robin Wright

Jack Nicholson, Anjelica Huston

THE JOURNEY OF AUGUST KING

(MIRAMAX) Producers, Nick Wechsler, Sam Waterston; Executive Producers, Bob Weinstein, Harvey Weinstein, Richard N. Gladstein; Director, John Duigan; Screenplay, John Ehle; Co-Producer, Kerry Orent; Photography, Slawomir Idziak; Designer/Costumes, Patricia Norris; Editor, Humphrey Dixon; Music, Stephen Endelman; Casting, Billy Hopkins, Suzanne Smith, Kerry Barden; an Addis-Wechsler production; Dolby Digital Stereo; Color; Rated PG-13; 97 minutes; November release

CAST

August King	Jason Patric
Annalees	Thandie Newton
Olaf Singletary	Larry Drake
Mooney Wright	Sam Waterston
Ida Wright	Sara-Jane Wylde
Hal Wright	Eric Mabius
Samuel	Bill Whitlock
Zimmer	Muse Watson
Bolton	John Doman
Harrison	Andrew Stahl
Felix	Danny Nelson
Mina	Collin Wilcox Paxton
Gabriel	Dean Rader Duvall
Ben	Billy Ray Reynolds
Sims	Marlus C. Harding
Meg	Lisa Roberts

and John Burnett Hall (Travis), Roy Bush Laughter (Tom), Clint Menacof (Ralph), A. Duncan Shirley III (Porter), Chase Conley (Harry—son), E. George Betz (Bridge Attendant), Nesbitt Blaisdell (Mr. Cole), Graham Paul (Wade), Joan Cope (Elsie), Terry Nienhuis (Fisher)

In nineteenth century North Carolina, widower August King breaks the law to help a runaway slave flee her owner.

© Miramax Films

Thandie Newton, Jason Patric

Thandie Newton, Jason Patric

Sam Waterston

Kimberly Flynn, Jason Andrews

RHYTHM THIEF

(STRAND) Producer, Jonathan Starch; Executive Producer/Director/Editor, Matthew Harrison; Co-Producer, Christopher Cooke; Screenplay, Christopher Grimm, Matthew Harrison; Photography, Howard Krupa; Music, Danny Brenner, Hugh O'Donovan, John L. Horn, Kevin Okerlund; Costumes, Nina Cantre; Casting, Meredith Jacobson; a Film Crash production; Black and white; Not rated; 88 minutes; November release

CAST

Simon	Jason Andrews
Marty	Eddie Daniels
Fuller	Kevin Corrigan
Cyd	Kimberly Flynn
Shayme	Sean Hagerty
Mr. Bunch	Mark Alfred
Jules	Christopher Cooke
Rat Boy	Bob McGrath

A look at the life of Simon, a Lower East Side music bootlegger, and the woman from his past who reenters his life.

© Strand Releasing

Michael Douglas, Annette Bening

Martin Sheen

Michael J. Fox

THE AMERICAN PRESIDENT

(COLUMBIA) Producer/Director, Rob Reiner; Executive Producers, Charles Newirth, Jeffrey Stott; Screenplay, Aaron Sorkin; Photography, John Seale; Designer, Lilly Kilvert; Editor, Robert Leighton; Costumes, Gloria Gresham; Music, Marc Shaiman; Casting, Jane Jenkins, Janet Hirshenson; a Castle Rock Entertainment and Universal Pictures presentation of a Wildwood Enterprises, Inc. production; Dolby DTS Stereo; Panavision; Technicolor; Rated PG-13; 113 minutes; November release

CAST

Andrew Shepherd	Michael Douglas
Sydney Ellen Wade	Annette Bening
A.J. MacInerney	Martin Sheen
Lewis Rothschild	Michael J. Fox
Robin McCall	Anna Deavere Smith
Janie Basdin	Samantha Mathis
Lucy Shepherd	Shawna Waldron
Leon Kodak	David Paymer
Mrs. Chapil	Anne Haney
Senator Rumson	Richard Dreyfuss
Beth Wade	Nina Siemaszko
Susan Sloan	Wendie Malick
Agent Cooper	Beau Billingslea
Esther MacInerney	Gail Strickland
David	Joshua Malina
President D'Astier	Clement Von Franckenstein
Madame D'Astier	Efrat Lavie
Leo Solomon	John Mahoney
Stu	Taylor Nichols
Chairman of the Joint Chiefs	John Mahon
Defense Secretary	Tom Dahlgren
General	Ralph Meyering, Jr.
Security Advisor	Kurt A. Boesen
Secret Service Agents	Joseph Latimore, Darryl Alan Reed, Andrew Steel
Carl	Jordan Lund
Rumson Staffers	Richard F. McGonagle, Frank Cavestani, Richard Stahl
Carol	Alice Kushida
Lisa	Renee Phillips
Doorkeeper	Beans Morocco
Education Secretary	Kathryn Ish
Flower Girl	Kamilah Martin
Groundskeeper	Augie Blunt
Guard	Thom Barry
Hud Secretary	Steven Gonzalez
Jeff	Gabriel Jarret
Leo's Secretary	Karen Maruyama
Leslie	Nancy Kandal
Congressman	George Murdock
Congressman Millman	Bernie McInerney
Congressman Pennybaker	Jack Gilroy
Congressional Staffer	Matthew Saks
Gil	Googy Gress
Reporter Lloyd	Ron Canada
Reporters	Brian Peitro, Rick Garcia
Aide in Bar	Aaron Sorkin
Sally	Kymberly S. Newberry
Mark	Greg Poland

and Leslie Rae Bega (White House Staffer Laura), Jennifer Crystal (White House Staffer Maria), Arthur Senzy (Deputy), Nick Toth, Jorge Noa, Maud Winchester (White House Aides), Jeffrey Anderson (TV News Anchorman), Suzanne Michaels (TV News Anchorwoman), David Drew Gallagher (New Guy), Todd Odom (Uniformed Secret Service Agent), CWO-2 Michael G. Alexander, USMC (Color Guard Officer)

Romantic comedy in which the widowed U.S. President finds himself falling in love with enviornmental lobbyist Sydney Wade.

Nominated for an Oscar for original music score.

© Castle Rock Entertainment

Michael Douglas

Anna Deavere Smith

David Paymer

Richard Dreyfuss

Anna Deavere Smith, Michael J. Fox, Samantha Mathis

LAST SUMMER IN THE HAMPTONS

(RAINBOW) Producer, Judith Wolinsky; Director/Editor, Henry Jaglom; Screenplay, Henry Jaglom, Victoria Foyt; Photography, Hanania Baer; Music, Rick Baitz; a Jagtoria Film production; Dolby Stereo; Technicolor; Not rated; 105 minutes; November release

CAST

Oona Hart	Victoria Foyt
Helena Mora	Viveca Lindfors
Jake Axelrod	Jon Robin Baitz
Suzanne	Savannah Bouchér
Freddy	Roscoe Lee Browne
Ivan Axelrod	André Gregory
George	Nick Gregory
Trish Axelrod	Melissa Leo
Thomas	Roddy McDowall
Chloe Garfield	Martha Plimpton
Eli Garfield	Ron Rifkin
Marian Mora Garfield	Diane Salinger
Lois Garfield	Brooke Smith
Nick Mora	Kristoffer Tabori Davis
Mora Axelrod	Holland Taylor
Max Berger	Henry Jaglom
Doctor	Arnold Leo
Producer	Joseph Feury
Wealthy Lady	Barbara Flood
House Guetss	Michael Emil, Alexandra Styron
Student Actor	Chris Knoblock
Chauffeur	Luis De La Garza
Waitress at Café	Michele Fleischman
Helena's Dog	Willie

Three generations of a large theatrical family gather at the East Hampton estate of the family matriarch, Helena.

© Rainbow Pictures

Victoria Foyt, Jon Robin Baitz

Nick Gregory, Jon Robin Baitz

Roddy McDowall, Jon Robin Baitz, Diane Salinger, Viveca Lindfors, Andre Gregory, Victoria Foyt, Holland Taylor

Johnny Depp, Christopher Walken

NICK OF TIME

(PARAMOUNT) Producer/Director, John Badham; Screenplay, Patrick Sheane Duncan; Executive Producer, D.J. Caruso; Photography, Roy H. Wagner; Designer, Philip Harrison; Editors, Frank Morriss, Kevin Stitt; Costumes, Mary E. Vogt; Music, Arthur B. Rubinstein; Associate Producer, Cammie Crier; Stunts, Shane Dixon; Casting, Carol Lewis; Dolby Stereo; DeLuxe color; Rated R; 89 minutes; November release

CAST

Gene Watson	Johnny Depp
Mr. Smith	Christopher Walken
Huey	Charles S. Dutton
Brendan Grant	Peter Strauss
Ms. Jones	Roma Maffia
Krista Brooks	Gloria Reuben
Governor Eleanor Grant	Marsha Mason
Lynn Watson	Courtney Chase
Officer Trust/Mr. White	Bill Smitrovich
Mystery Man	G.D. Spradlin

and Hotel Staff: Yul Vazquez (Gustino—Guest Services), Edith Diaz (Irene—Domestic Maintenance), Armando Ortega (Hector—Guest Services), C.J. Bau (Mixologist), Cynthena Sanders (Beverage Server), Dana Mackey (Transport Reception Manager), Christopher Jacobs (Comestible Server), Charles Carroll (Sanitation Engineer); Governor's Staff: Miguel Najera (Franco—Governor's Bodyguard), Jerry Tondo (Chief Aide), Lance Hunter Voorhees (Weapons Security), John Azevedo, Jr. (Security Associate), Lance August (Personal Security), Peter Mackenzie (JBN Reporter), Rick Zieff (JBN Videographer), Tom Bradley (Himself), Michael Chong (Asian Man), Cynthia Noritake (Asian Woman), Holly Kuespert (Physically Attractive Woman), Pamela Dunlap (Centerpiece Poacher), Jan Speck (Rally Orienter), Tom Lawrence (Personal Waste Facility User), Robert Buckingham (Illegal Security Access Carrier), J. Clark Johnson (Hackney Transportist), Antony Sandoval (Un Homme), Isabel Lorca (Une Femme), Nicole Mancera (Una Niña), Yolanda Gonzalez (Su Madre), Antonette Saftler (Mrs. Wentzel), Teddy Beeler (Union Station Security), Alison Stuart (Verbally Abusive Spouse)

Accountant Gene Watson is told he must assassinate Governor Eleanor Grant within a ninety-minute time period or his kidnapped daughter will die.

© Paramount Pictures

Johnny Depp, Charles S. Dutton

Johnny Depp, Marsha Mason

Courtney Chase, Johnny Depp

Sharon Stone, Robert De Niro

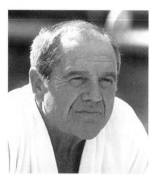

Alan King

Kevin Pollak

Sharon Stone, Robert De Niro

James Woods

Robert De Niro, Don Rickles

Frank Vincent, Joe Pesci

CASINO

(UNIVERSAL) Producer, Barbara De Fina; Director, Martin Scorsese; Screenplay, Nicholas Pileggi, Martin Scorsese; Based on the book by Nicholas Pileggi; Photography, Robert Richardson; Designer, Dante Ferretti; Editor, Thelma Schoonmaker; Title Sequence, Elaine and Saul Bass; Costumes, Rita Ryack, John Dunn; Casting, Ellen Lewis; a co-presentation of Syalis D.A. & Legende Enterprises of a De Fina/Cappa production; DTS Digital Stereo; Super 35 Widescreen; Technicolor; Rated R; 175 minutes; November release

Robert De Niro

CAST

Sam "Ace" Rothstein	Robert De Niro
Ginger McKenna	Sharon Stone
Nicky Santoro	Joe Pesci
Lester Diamond	James Woods
Billy Sherbert	Don Rickles
Andy Stone	Alan King
Phillip Green	Kevin Pollak
Pat Webb	L.Q. Jones
Senator	Dick Smothers
Frank Marino	Frank Vincent
Don Ward	John Bloom
Remo Gaggi	Pasquale Cajano
Jennifer Santoro	Melissa Prophet
John Nance	Bill Allison
Artie Piscano	Vinny Vella
Piscano's Mother	Catherine Scorsese
Dominick Santoro	Phillip Suriano
Older Amy	Erika von Tagen
Themselves	Oscar Goodman, Frankie Avalon, Steve Allen, Jayne Meadows, Jerry Vale

and Joseph Rigano (Vincent Borelli), Gene Ruffini (Vinny Forlano), Dominick Grieco (Americo Capelli), Richard Amalfitano, Richard F. Strafella (Casino Executives), Casper Molee, David Leavitt (Counters), Peter Conti (Arthur Capp), Catherine T. Scorsese (Piscano's Daughter), Steve Vignari (Beeper), Rick Crachy (Chastised Dealer), Larry E. Nadler (Lucky Larry), Paul Herman (Gambler in Phone Booth), Salvatore Petrillo (Old Man Capo), Joey DePinto (Stabbed Gambler), Heidi Keller (Blonde at Bar), Millicent Sheridan (Senator's Hooker), Nobu Matsuhisa (Ichikawa), Toru Nagai (Ichikawa's Associate), Barbara Spanjers (Ticket Agent), Dom Angelo (Craps Dealer), Joe Molinaro (Shift Manager), Ali Pirouzkar (High Roller), Frankie Allison (Craps Dealer), Jeff Scott Anderson, Frank Washko, Jr. (Parking Valets), Jennifer M. Abbott (Cashier), Christian A. Azzinaro (Little Nicky—7 yrs.), Robert C. Tetzlaff (Customs Agent), Anthony Russell (Bookie), Carol Wilson (Classroom Nun), Joe Lacoco (Det. Bob Johnson), John Manca (Wiseguy Eddy), Ronald Maccone (Wiseguy Jerry), Buck Stephens (Credit Clerk), Joseph Reidy (Winner), Joe La Due (Signaller), Fred Smith, Sonny D'Angelo, Greg Anderson (Security Guards), Stuart Nisbet (L.A. Banker), Tommy DeVito (Crooked Poker Dealer), Frank Adonis (Rocky), Joseph Bono (Moosh), Craig Vincent (Cowboy), Daniel P. Conte (Doctor Dan), Paul Dottore (Slim), Richard T. Smith (Security Guard/Cowboy), David Rose (David), Jonathan Kraft (Jonathan), Michael McKensie Pratt (Showgirls Stage Manager), Patti James, Ruth Gillis, Carol Cardwell (Country Club Women), Dean Casper (Elderly Man), Nan Brennan, Karyn Amalfitano, C.C. Carr (Wives), David Varriale (Flirting Executive), Carol Krolick (Slapping Woman), Frank Regich (Slapped Man), Herb Schwartz (Maitre d'), Max Raven (Bernie Blue), Clem Caserta (Sal Fusco), Jed Mills (Jack Hardy), Janet Denti (Receptionist), Cameron Milzer (Secretary), Leain Vashon (Bellman), Jim Morgan Williams (Pit Boss), Brian Le Baron (Valet Parker), Mortiki Yerushalmi (Jewelry Store Owner), Mufid M. Khoury, Khosrow Abrishami (Jeweler Fences), Richard Riehle (Charlie Clark), Mike Maines, Bobby Hitt (Cops in Restaurant), Shellee Renee (Showgirl in Parking Lot), Alfred Nittoli (Chastised Gambler), Carl Ciarfalio (Tony Dogs), Jack R. Orend (Baker), Linda Perri (Ace's Secretary), Ffolliott Le Coque (Anna Scott), J. Charles Thompson (Judge), Michael Paskevich, Mike Weatherford, Eric Randall (Reporters at Airport), Gwen Castaldi (Business Week Reporter), Brian Reddy, Roy Conrad (Board Investigators), Mike Bradley, Dave Curvoisier (TV Newsmen), George Comando (Piscano's Brother-in-Law), Andy Jarrell (Commissioner Bales), Robert Sidell, Tyde Kierney (Control Board Members), Paige Novodor (Newscaster), Claudia Haro (Trudy/Announcer), Sasha Semenoff (Orchestra Leader), Gil Dova (Juggler), George W. Allf (FBI Agent), Madeline Parquegte (Black Jack Dealer), Gino Bertin (Maitre 'd), Mitch Kolpan, Csaba Maczala (Detectives), Peter Sugden (Lip Reader), Rudy Guerrero (Maitre 'd at disco), Randy Sutton, Jeff Corbin (Cops at Ace's House), Sly Smith, Joe Anastasi, F. Marcus Casper, Richard Wagner, David Arcerio (FBI Agents), Jeffrey Azzinaro (Nicky Jr.—10 yrs.), Carrie Cipollini (Piscano's Wife), Loren Stevens, Gary C. Rainey (Agents—Piscano Raid), Haven Earle Haley (Judge), Sam Wilson (Ambulance Driver), Michael Toney (Fat Sally)

Sharon Stone

Sam "Ace" Rothstein looks back on how he took over control of a Vegas casino, made the mob millions of dollars, then ultimately fell from power.

Sharon Stone received an Oscar nomination for her performance.

© Universal City Studios, Inc.

Joe Pesci

Woody

Mr. Potato Head

TOY STORY

(WALT DISNEY PICTURES) Producers, Ralph Guggenheim, Bonnie Arnold; Executive Producers, Edwin Catmull, Steven Jobs; Director, John Lasseter; Screenplay, Joss Whedon, Andrew Stanton, Joel Cohen, Alec Sokolow; Story, John Lasseter, Pete Docter, Andrew Stanton, Joe Ranft; Songs Written and Performed by/Music, Randy Newman; Supervising Technical Director, William Reeves; Art Director, Ralph Eggleston; Editors, Robert Gordon, Lee Unkrich; Supervising Animator, Pete Docter; Production Supervisor, Karen Robert Jackson; a Pixar production; Dolby Digital Stereo; Technicolor; Rated G; 81 minutes; November release

VOICE CAST

Woody ....Tom Hanks
Buzz Lightyear...Tim Allen
Mr. Potato Head ....Don Rickles
Slinky Dog ....Jim Varney
Rex..Wallace Shawn
Hamm ....John Ratzenberger
Bo Peep...Annie Potts
Andy...John Morris
Sid..Erik von Detten
Mrs. Davis ....Laurie Metcalf
Sergeant...R. Lee Ermey
Hannah ....Sarah Freeman
TV Announcer ....Penn Jillette

Woody, a pull-string Cowboy, feels his status as the favorite toy of six-year-old Andy threatened by the arrival of a hi-tech action figure, Buzz Lightyear. The first feature completely animated by computers.

Recipient of a special Academy Award for computer animation. Nominated for Academy Awards for original screenplay, musical or comedy score, and original song ("You've Got a Friend").

© The Walt Disney Company

Slinky Dog, Bo Peep, Mr. Potato Head, Woody, Hamm, Rex

Buzz Lightyear, Woody

Buzz Lightyear

Buzz Lightyear, Woody

Rex, Slinky Dog, Buzz Lightyear

Woody, Bo Peep

MONEY TRAIN

(COLUMBIA) Producers, Jon Peters, Neil Canton; Executive Producers, Tracy Barone, Adam Fields, Frederick Pierce; Director, Joseph Ruben; Screenplay, Doug Richardson, David Loughery; Story, Doug Richardson; Photography, John W. Lindley; Designer, Bill Groom; Editors, George Bowers, Bill Pankow; Music, Mark Mancina; Costumes, Ruth E. Carter; Co-Producers, Doug Claybourne, Michael Steele; Casting, Francine Maisler; a Peters Entertainment production; Dolby SDDS Stereo; Super 35 Widescreen; Technicolor; Rated R; 103 minutes; November release

CAST

John	Wesley Snipes
Charlie	Woody Harrelson
Grace Santiago	Jennifer Lopez
Donald Patterson	Robert Blake
Torch	Chris Cooper
Riley	Joe Grifasi
Mr. Brown	Scott Sowers
Kowalski	Skipp Sudduth
Subway Robbers	Vincent Laresca, Nelson Vasquez
Bartender Frank	Vincent Patrick
Women on Platform	Aida Turturro, Alvaleta Guess
Gamblers	Vincent Pastore, David Tawil, Ron Ryan
Guards	Greg McKinney, Mitch Kolpan, Jeremy Roberts
Detective	John Norman Thomas
Dispatchers	Oni Faida Lampley, Jack O'Connell
Brown's Enforcers	Saul Stein, Manny Siverio, Johnny Centatiempo
Dooley	Enrico Colantoni
Guard with Dooley	Christopher Anthony Young
Motorman	Richard Grove
Guy at Bar	Steven Randazzo
Businessman	William Charlton
Young Woman	Josefina Diaz
Mickey	Moss Porter
Darryl	Keith Leon Williams
Victor	Jose Zuniga
Barricade Captain	Thomas G. Waites

and Leikili Mark (Punk Girl), Kevin Guy Brown (Punk Guy), Bill Nunn (Crash Train Motorman), Sharon Schaffer (Token Clerk), Angel Caban, Joe Bacino (Decoy Cops), Jose Soto, Larry Gilliard, Jr., Flex (Hoods), Michael Artura (Second Captain), Mark Weil (Stockbroker), Joseph Wilson Ayesu (Little Joe), Katie Gill, Cody Gill (Crosswalk Children)

A pair of New York City Transit Cops plan to rob the Money Train that collects millions from the city's subway stations.

Wesley Snipes, Woody Harrelson

Robert Blake

Woody Harrelson, Wesley Snipes, Jennifer Lopez

WHITE MAN'S BURDEN

(SAVOY) Producer, Lawrence Bender; Executive Producer, Yves Marmion; Co-Producer, Paul Hellerman; Director/Screenplay, Desmond Nakano; Photography, Willy Kurant; Designer, Naomi Shohan; Music, Howard Shore; Editor, Nancy Richardson; Music Supervisor, Happy Walters; Costumes, Isis Mussenden; a UGC presentation in association with Rysher Entertainment; Dolby Stereo; Technicolor; Rated R; 89 minutes; December release

John Travolta, Harry Belafonte

CAST

Louis Pinnock	John Travolta
Thaddeus Thomas	Harry Belafonte
Marsha Pinnock	Kelly Lynch
Megan Thomas	Margaret Avery
Stanley	Tom Bower
Donnie	Andrew Lawrence
Martin Thomas	Bumper Robinson
Lionel	Tom Wright
Roberta	Sheryl Lee Ralph
Dorothy	Judith Drake
John	Robert Gossett
Williams	Wesley Thompson
Johansson	Tom Nolan
Marcus	Willie Carpenter
Renee	Wanda Lee
Landlord	Thom Barry
Josine	Carrie Snodgress

and Michael Beach, Lee Duncan (Policemen Outside Bar), Lawrence A. Mandley, William Hendry (Sheriffs at Eviction), Brian Brophy (Bank Teller), Chelsea Lagos (Cheryl), Duane R. Shepard, Sr. (Maitre D' at Fashion Show), Bert Remsen (Hot Dog Vendor), Steve Wilcox, Jason Kristopher, Seth Green (Youths at Hot Dog Stand), Alexis Arquette (Panhandler), Larry Nash (Policeman at Gas Station), Mae Elvis (Eleven Year Old Girl), Dean Hallo (Charles), Kerry Remsen (Pregnant Woman at Bus Stop), Googy Gress (Bystander at Bus Stop), Lisa Dinkins (Shooting Policewoman), Lawrence T. Wrentz (Shooting Policeman), Steve Larson (Bottle Thrower), Lawrence Bender, Matt O'Toole, Iain Jones (Bar Patrons), Janet Hubert, Attallah Shabazz, Willette Klausner (Dinner Guests), David C. Harvey (Factory Worker), Amy Powell (Newscaster), Keith Collier, Annamarie Simmons (Dancers), Rosie Tenison (Detective), Manny Jacobson (Himself), Dondre Whitfield (Terrence), Ingrid Rogers (Taylor)

In a world where the racial roles of power are reversed, a white factory worker clashes with a successful black businessman.

Margaret Avery, Harry Belafonte

John Travolta, Andrew Lawrence, Kelly Lynch

Jeff Bridges, Ellen Barkin

Christina Applegate, David Arquette

Jeff Bridges

WILD BILL

(UNITED ARTISTS) Producers, Richard D. Zanuck, Lili Fini Zanuck; Director/Screenplay, Walter Hill; Based upon the play *Fathers and Sons* by Thomas Babe, and the novel *Deadwood* by Pete Dexter; Photography, Lloyd Ahern; Designer, Joseph Nemec III; Editor, Freeman Davies; Costumes, Dan Moore; Music, Van Dyke Parks; Co-Producer, Gary Daigler; Casting, Shari Rhodes, Joseph Middleton; Distributed by MGM/UA; DTS Digital Stereo; Deluxe color; Rated R: 97 minutes; December release

CAST

Wild Bill Hickok	Jeff Bridges
Calamity Jane	Ellen Barkin
Charley Prince	John Hurt
Susannah Moore	Diane Lane
Buffalo Bill Cody	Keith Carradine
Jack McCall	David Arquette
Lurline	Christina Applegate
Will Plummer	Bruce Dern
California Joe	James Gammon
Preacher	Marjoe Gortner
Donnie Lonigan	James Remar
Song Lew	Karen Huie
Sioux Chief Whistler	Steve Reevis
Dave Tutt	Robert Knott
Cheyenne Leader	Pato Hoffmann
Doctor	Patrick Gorman
Carl Mann	Lee deBroux
Jubal Pickett	Stoney Jackson
Mike Williams	Robert Peters
Curly	Steve Chambers
Coke	Jimmy Medearis
Pink Buford	Jason Ronard
Phil Coe	Dennis Hayden
Jessie Hazlitt	Teresa Gilmore
Ed Plummer	John Dennis Johnston
Crook-Eye Clark	Boots Southerland
Lew Scott	James Michael Taylor
Bob Rainwater	Loyd Catlett
Earlene	Janel Moloney
Tommy Drum	Ted Markland
Soldiers	Monty Stuart, Merritt Yohnka
Big Trooper	Dennis Deveaugh
Seth Beeber	Jim Wilkey
Jack Slater	Raliegh Wilson
Frank Dowder	Charles Gunning
John Harkness	Chris Doyle
Buffalo Hunter	Virgil Frye
Singer at Funeral	Lauren Abels
Fiddle Player	Ritt Henn
Women in Church	Lise Hilboldt, Trisha Munford
Citizen	Charlie Seybert
Sanitarium Woman	Luana Anders
Chinese Man	Roland Nip
Cowpoke	Mike Watson
Drover	Thomas Wilson Brown
Miner	Robert Keith
Madam	Linda Harrison
Dancer	Patricia M. Peters
Card Cheat	Anthony De Longis
Bartender at Way Station	Bill Bolenderand

and Alisa Christensen, Patricia Pretzinger (Mann's No. 10 Saloon Bargirls), Peter Jason (Dave McCandless), Joseph Crozier (Old Timer), Mikey LeBeau (Young Jack), Jaime Elysse (Young Woman with Parasol), Jamie Marsh (Young Man), Burton Gilliam (Bartender), Del Roy, Steve Brasfield (Gamblers), Juddson Keith Linn (Cheyenne Rider)

Biography tracing the latter-day period of one of the Old West's most legendary gunmen, Wild Bill Hickok (1837–1876). Previous film portrayals of Hickok include Gary Cooper (The Plainsman, 1937), Roy Rogers (Young Bill Hickok, 1940), Richard Dix (Badlands of Dakota, 1941), Howard Keel (Calamity Jane, 1953), Tom Brown (I Killed Wild Bill Hickok, 1956), Robert Culp (The Raiders, 1964), Don Murray (The Plainsman, 1966), Jeff Corey (Little Big Man, 1970), and Charles Bronson (The White Buffalo, 1976).

© United Artists Pictures Inc.

Jeff Bridges

Keith Carradine

Ellen Barkin

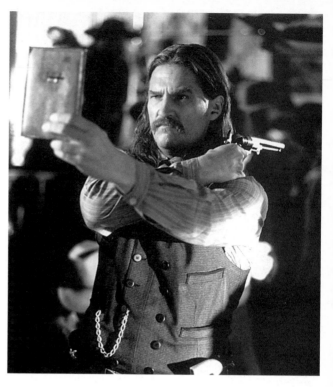

Jeff Bridges

Bruce Dern

Diane Lane

John Hurt

Jeff Bridges

THINGS TO DO IN DENVER WHEN YOU'RE DEAD

(MIRAMAX) Producer, Cary Woods; Co-Producer, Cathy Konrad; Executive Producers, Marie Cantin, Bob Weinstein, Harvey Weinstein; Director, Gary Fleder; Screenplay/Associate Producer, Scott Rosenberg; Photography, Elliot Davis; Designer, Nelson Coates; Costumes, Abigail Murray; Editor, Richard Marks; Music, Michael Convertino; Casting, Ronnie Yekel; a Woods Entertainment production; Dolby Digital Stereo; CFI Color; Rated R; 114 minutes; December release

Andy Garcia, Treat Williams

CAST

Jimmy "The Saint" Tosnia	Andy Garcia
Pieces	Christopher Lloyd
Franchise	William Forsythe
Easy Wind	Bill Nunn
Critical Bill	Treat Williams
Joe Heff	Jack Warden
Mister Shhh	Steve Buscemi
Lucinda	Fairuza Balk
Dagney	Gabrielle Anwar
The Man With The Plan	Christopher Walken
Bernard	Michael Nicolosi
Malt	Bill Cobbs
Lt. Atwater	Marshall Bell
Baby Sinister	Glenn Plummer
Gus	Don Stark
Ellie	Harris Laskawy
Cuffy	William Garson
Alex	David Stratton
Dodie	Deborah Strang
Meg	Sarah Trigger

and Jenny McCarthy (Blonde Nurse), Buddy Guy, Ray Allison, Scott Holt, Greg Rzab (House Band), Wiley Harker (Boris Carlotti), Joe Drago (Maitre D'), Chuck Bacino (Accordian Player), Dawn Cheadle (Rooster), Tiny Lister, Jr. (House), Bill Long ("The Dead Beat" Man), Cheree Jaeb (Little Girl), Sarah Levy Arbess, Larissa Michieli (Girls), Larry Raben (Young Man), Lynn Appelbaum (Young Woman), Taylor Hale (Stevie), Archie Smith (Mr. Jergen), Harriet Medin (Old Woman), Bill Bolender (Stevie's Dad), Susan Merson (Woman with Cancer), Bill Erwin (70-Year-Old Man), Nate Ingram, Jacob Bergener (Alley Hoods), Larry Curry, Jr. (Black Youth), Ruthay (Receptionist), Selina Mathews (Cynthia), Phil Boardman (Gym Teacher), William Denis (Businessman), Danny Romo (Montirez Brother)

Andy Garcia, Gabrielle Anwar

Retired gangster Jimmy the Saint is summoned by his ex-boss to do one more job on the same week he falls in love with a beautiful young woman named Dagney.

© Miramax Films

Treat Williams, Bill Nunn, William Forsythe, Christopher Lloyd

Fairuza Balk, Andy Garcia

Mare Winningham, Jennifer Jason Leigh

GEORGIA

(MIRAMAX) Producers, Ulu Grosbard, Barbara Turner, Jennifer Jason Leigh; Executive Producer, Ben Barenholtz; Director, Ulu Grosbard; Screenplay, Barbara Turner; Line Producer, Amanda DiGiulio; Photography, Jan Kiesser; Editor, Elizabeth Kling; Designer, Lester Cohen; Costumes, Carol Oditz; Music Producer, Steven Soles; Casting, Renee Rousselot; from Ciby 2000; Dolby Stereo; Technicolor; Rated R; 117 minutes; December release

CAST

Sadie Flood	Jennifer Jason Leigh
Georgia	Mare Winningham
Jake	Ted Levine
Axel	Max Perlich
Bobby	John Doe
Herman	John C. Reilly
Trucker	Jimmy Witherspoon
Chasman	Jason Carter
Erwin Flood	Tom Bower
Leland	Smokey Hormel
Clay	Jimmy Z.
Paul	Tony Marisco
Andrew	Jamian Briar
Mish	Rachel Rasco
Young Sadie	Nicole Donahoo
Young Georgia	Aisleagh Jackson
Ticket Agent	Coleen O'Hara
Dan Ferguson	Bruce Wirth
Bartender at Larry's	Thomas Kuhn
Promoter	Bill Johns
Girl with Bobby	Mina Badie
Reporter	Chris Carlson
17-Year-Old Boy	Shawn Cox
Drunk	Jeff Steitzer
Brian	Michael Shapiro

and Barbara Deering, Stephanie Shine (Nurses), Jay Keye (Gate Agent), Jo Miller (Jo Miller), Gary Lanz (Backup Singer), C.W. Huston (Drunk in Crowd)

Sadie, a self-destuctive rock star wanna-be, lives in the shadow of her successful, folk-rock singing sister, Georgia. Screenwriter/co-producer Barbara Turner is Jennifer Jason Leigh's real-life mother.

Mare Winningham received an Academy Award nomination for her performance.

© Miramax Films

John C. Reilly, Jennifer Jason Leigh, John Doe

Jennifer Jason Leigh

Ted Levine, Max Perlich, Jennifer Jason Leigh

Steve Martin, Diane Keaton, Kimberly Williams

Diane Keaton, Martin Short, Kimberly Williams

Diane Keaton, Steve Martin

FATHER OF THE BRIDE PART II

(TOUCHSTONE) Producer, Nancy Meyers; Executive Producers, Sandy Gallin, Carol Baum; Co-Producers, Cindy Williams, Bruce A. Block; Co-Executive Producers, James Orr, Jim Cruickshank; Director, Charles Shyer; Screenplay, Nancy Meyers, Charles Shyer; Based on the screenplay *Father's Little Dividend* by Albert Hackett & Frances Goodrich; Photography, William A. Fraker; Designer, Linda DeScenna; Costumes, Enid Harris; Editor, Stephen A. Rotter; Music, Alan Silvestri; Associate Producer, Julie B. Crane; Casting, Jeff Greenberg, Sheila Guthrie; Distributed by Buena Vista Pictures; Dolby Digital Stereo; Technicolor; Rated PG; 106 minutes; December release

CAST

George Banks	Steve Martin
Nina Banks	Diane Keaton
Franck Eggelhoffer	Martin Short
Annie Banks-MacKenzie	Kimberly Williams
Bryan MacKenzie	George Newbern
Matty Banks	Kieran Culkin
Howard Weinstein	B.D. Wong
John MacKenzie	Peter Michael Goetz
Joanna MacKenzie	Kate McGregor Stewart
Dr. Megan Eisenberg	Jane Adams
Mr. Habib	Eugene Levy

and Rebecca Chambers (Young Woman at Gym), April Ortiz (Olivia), Dulcy Rogers (Ava, the Beautician), Kathy Anthony (Beautician #2), Adrian Canzoneri (Justin), Lori Alan (Mrs. Habib), Stephanie Miller (Annie—Age Four), Hallie Meyers-Shyer (Annie—Age Seven), Jay Wolpert (Dr. Brooks), Ann Walker (Dr. Brooks' Nurse), Sandra Silvestri (Jogging Mom), William Akey, Jonathan Emerson (Frantic Fathers), Seth Kaplan (Wild Four Year Old), Joshua Preston (Tantrum Toddler), K.C. Colwell (Father Heading off to Work), Chase Colwell (Adorable Toddler), Tony Simotes (Construction Foreman), Annie Meyers-Shyer, Linda DeScenna, Heidi Averill (Shower Guests), Chelsea Lynn (Matty's Friend), Sue Colwell (Nina's Customer), Rodriego Botero, Vince Lozano (Gang Kids), Caroline Lagerfelt, Ilene Waterstone (Check-In Nurses), Wendy Worthington (Prostate Nurse), Dorian Spencer (E.R. Nurse), Harris Laskawy (Prostate Doctor), Roxanne Beckford, Valerie Hemmerich (Nina's Nurses), Peter Spears (Dr. Wagner), Susan Beaubian (Annie's Nurses), Mychael Bates (Hospital Orderly), Jerri Rose White, Shannon Kennedy (Baby Megan), Casey and Dylan Boersma (Baby George), Katie Pierce (Two Month Old Megan), Jonathan and Thomas Selstad (Two Month Old George)

George Banks' daughter Annie and her husband Bryan announce that they are going to have a baby shortly before George's wife Nina discovers that she too is pregnant. Sequel to the 1991 Touchstone film Father of the Bride, *with all of the principals repeating their roles. Remake of the 1951 MGM comedy* Father's Little Dividend *which starred Spencer Tracy, Elizabeth Taylor, Joan Bennett, and Don Taylor.*

© Touchstone Pictures

Peter Michael Goetz, Kate McGregor Stewart, George Newbern, Steve Martin, Kieran Culkin, Martin Short

SABRINA

(PARAMOUNT) Producers, Scott Rudin, Sydney Pollack; Executive Producers, Ronald Schwary, Lindsay Doran; Director, Sydney Pollack; Screenplay, Barbara Benedek, David Rayfiel; Based on the film written by Billy Wilder, Samuel Taylor and Ernest Lehman, from the play *Sabrina Fair* by Samuel Taylor; Photography, Giuseppe Rotunno; Designer, Brian Morris; Editor, Frederic Steinkamp; Music, John Williams; Original songs by John Williams, Alan & Marilyn Bergman; Costumes, Ann Roth; Casting, David Rubin; Dolby Stereo; Deluxe color; Rated PG; 127 minutes; December release

Harrison Ford

CAST

Linus Larrabee	Harrison Ford
Sabrina Fairchild	Julia Ormond
David Larrabee	Greg Kinnear
Maude Larrabee	Nancy Marchand
Fairchild	John Wood
Patrick Tyson	Richard Crenna
Ingrid Tyson	Angie Dickinson
Elizabeth Tyson	Lauren Holly
Mack	Dana Ivey
Rosa	Miriam Colon
Joanna	Elizabeth Franz
Irene	Fanny Ardant
Martine	Valeria Lemercier
Louis	Patrick Bruel
Linda	Becky Ann Baker
Scott	Paul Giamatti
Ron	John C. Vennema
Ron	Gregory Chase
Nurse	Margo Martindale
Carol	J. Smith-Cameron

and Christine Luneau-Lipton (Ticket Taker), Michael Dees (Singer at Larrabee Party), Denis Holmes (Butler), Jo-Jo Lowe (Red Head), Ira Wheeler (Bartender), Philippa Cooper (Kelly), Ayako (India), François Genty (Make-Up Assistant), Guillaume Gallienne (Assistant), Ines Sastre, Phina, Helena Katia, Andrea Behalikova, Jennifer Herrera, Kristina Kumlin, Eva Linderholm, Stefano Tartini (Models), Carmen Chaplin, Micheline Van De Velde, Joanna Rhodes, Alan Boone, Patrick Forster Delmas, Kentaro Matsuo (Paris Friends), J.B. Benn (Magician), Peter McKernan (Helicopter Pilot), Ed Connelly (Gulf Stream Pilot), Ronald Schwary (Sheik), Kenneth A. MacDonald (Beggar), Alvin Lum (Tyson Butler), Siching Song (Mother in Hospital), Phil Nee (Father in Hospital), Randy Becker (Trainer), Susan Browning (Secretary), Saikat Mondal (Moroccan Waiter), Peter Parks (Senator), La Compagnie Jolie Mome (Street Singers)

Sabrina, daughter of the chauffeur on the lavish Larrabee estate, is shipped off to Paris in hopes that she'll forget David Larrabee, the family's playboy son on whom she has a crush. Remake of the 1954 Paramount film which starred Humphrey Bogart (Linus), Audrey Hepburn (Sabrina), and William Holden (David).

© Paramount Pictures Corp.

Julia Ormond, Harrison Ford

Harrison Ford, Greg Kinnear

Greg Kinnear, Julia Ormond

Emma Thompson, Kate Winslet

SENSE AND SENSIBILITY

(COLUMBIA) Producer, Lindsay Doran; Executive Producer, Sydney Pollack; Co-Producers, James Schamus, Laurie Borg; Director, Ang Lee; Screenplay, Emma Thompson; Adapted from the novel by Jane Austen; Photography, Michael Coulter; Designer, Luciana Arrighi; Editor, Tim Squyres; Music, Patrick Doyle; Associate Producer, Geoff Stier; a Mirage production; SDDS Dolby Stereo; Technicolor; Rated PG; 135 minutes; December release

CAST

John Dashwood	James Fleet
Mr. Dashwood	Tom Wilkinson
Fanny Dashwood	Harriet Walter
Marianne Dashwood	Kate Winslet
Elinor Dashwood	Emma Thompson
Mrs. Dashwood	Gemma Jones
Edward Ferrars	Hugh Grant
Margaret Dashwood	Emilie François
Mrs. Jennings	Elizabeth Spriggs
Sir John Middleton	Robert Hardy
Thomas	Ian Brimble
Betsy	Isabelle Amyes
Colonel Brandon	Alan Rickman
John Willoughby	Greg Wise
Curate	Alexander John
Charlotte Palmer	Imelda Staunton
Lucy Steele	Imogen Stubbs
Mr. Palmer	Hugh Laurie
Pigeon	Allan Mitchell
Maid to Mrs. Jennings	Josephine Gradwell
Robert Ferrars	Richard Lumsden
Miss Grey	Lone Vidahl
Doctor Harris	Oliver Ford Davies
Mrs. Bunting	Eleanor McCready

When Henry Dashwood dies, leaving his estate to his son from his first marriage, his current wife and daughters are nearly left in a state of poverty.

Academy Award winner for Best Adapted Screenplay of 1995, thus making Emma Thompson the first Best Actress winner (for 1992's *Howards End*) to also win an Oscar for writing. The film received additional Oscar nominations for picture, actress (Thompson), supporting actress (Winslet), cinematography, original dramatic score, and costume design. This film also made Thompson the first actress to be nominated in the acting and writing categories in the same year.

© Columbia Pictures Industries, Inc.

Alan Rickman

Robert Hardy, Elizabeth Spriggs

Kate Winslet, Greg Wise

Emma Thompson, Kate Winslet, Gemma Jones

Emma Thompson, Imogen Stubbs, Gemma Jones, Elizabeth Spriggs,
Hugh Laurie, Imelda Staunton, Kate Winslet Greg Wise

Emma Thompson, Hugh Grant

Kate Winslet, Emma Thompson, Imogen Stubbs

Kate Winslet, Emilie François, Emma Thompson, Greg Wise

Bradley Pierce, Kirsten Dunst, Bonnie Hunt, Robin Williams

Robin Williams

Robbin Williams

Robin Williams

Robin Williams, Bonnie Hunt

David Alan Grier, Bebe Neuwirth

JUMANJI

(TRISTAR) Producers, Scott Kroopf, William Teitler; Executive Producers, Ted Field, Robert W. Cort, Larry J. Franco; Director, Joe Johnston; Screenplay, Jonathan Hensleigh, Greg Taylor, Jim Strain; Screen Story, Greg Taylor, Jim Strain, Chris Van Allsburg; Based on the book by Chris Van Allsburg; Photography, Thomas Ackerman; Designer, James Bissell; Editor, Robert Dalva; Music, James Horner; Visual Effects Supervisors, Stephen L. Price, Ken Ralston; Casting, Nancy Foy; an Interscope Communications/Teitler Film production; SDDS Dolby Stereo; Technicolor; Rated PG; 100 minutes; December release

CAST

Alan Parrish	Robin Williams
Van Pelt/Sam Parrish	Jonathan Hyde
Judy Shepherd	Kirsten Dunst
Peter Shepherd	Bradley Pierce
Sarah Whittle	Bonnie Hunt
Aunt Nora	Bebe Neuwirth
Carl Bentley	David Alan Grier
Carol Parrish	Patricia Clarkson
Young Alan	Adam Hann-Byrd
Young Sarah	Laura Bell Bundy
Exterminator	James Handy
Mrs. Thomas	Gillian Barber
Benjamin	Brandon Obray
Caleb	Cyrus Thiedeke
Billy Jessup	Gary Joseph Thorup
Cop	Leonard Zola
Bum	Lloyd Berry
Jim Shepherd	Malcolm Stewart
Martha Shepherd	Annabel Kershaw
Gun Salesman	Darryl Henriques
Paramedics	Robin Driscoll, Peter Bryant
Girls	Sarah Gilson, Florica Vlad
Baker	June Lion
Pianist	Brenda Lockmuller
Barber	Frederick Richardson
Special Vocal Effects	Frank Welker

Two children playing the board game Jumanji accidentally release Alan Parrish who has been trapped inside the game for twenty-six years.

© TriStar Pictures, Inc.

Bonnie Hunt, Robin Williams

Robin Williams

Bradley Pierce, Kirsten Dunst

Bonnie Hunt, Jonathan Hyde

Richard Harris, James Earl Jones

Richard Harris

James Earl Jones

CRY, THE BELOVED COUNTRY

(MIRAMAX) Producer, Anant Singh; Executive Producers, Harry Allan Towers, Sudhir Pragjee, Sanjeev Singh; Director, Darrell James Roodt; Screenplay, Ronald Harwood; Based on the novel by Alan Paton; Photography, Paul Gilpin; Designer, David Barkham; Costumes, Ruy Filipe; Editor, David Heitner; Music, John Barry; Associate Producer, Helena Spring; Casting, Marina Van Tonder; a Distant Horizon production in association with Videovision Entertainment/Invested Bank Limited and Alpine Films (Pty) Ltd.; Dolby Stereo; Technicolor; Rated PG-13; 108 minutes; December release

CAST

Reverend Stephen Kumalo ....James Earl Jones
James Jarvis ....Richard Harris
John Kumalo...Charles S. Dutton
Priest Theophilus Msimangu....................................Vusi Kunene
Katie ....Leleti Khumalo
Child ....Tsholofelo Wechoemang
Mrs. Kumalo ....Dolly Rathbee
Mpanza..Ramolao Makhene
Ian Jarvis...Jack Robinson
Mary Jarvis...Jennifer Steyn
Young Thief ....Somizi Mhlongo
Mafolo...Sam Ngakane
Father Vincent ....John Whiteley
Mrs. Lithebe ....Lillian Dube
Shebeen Queen...Temise Times
and Patrick Ndlovu, Darlington Michaels, King Twala (Men), Tiny Masilo (Brothel Singer), Babes Jazz Band (Jazz Band), Dambisa Kente (Gertrude Kumalo), Fats Bookholane, George Phologane (Brothel Men), Morena Sefatsa (Nephew), Sydney Chama (Dubula), Moses Rakharebe (Tomlinson), Ron Smerczak (Capt. van Jaarsveld), Tobias Sikwayo (Thomas), Anne Curteis (Mrs. Jarvis), Abigail Kubeka (Mrs. Mkize), Jerry Mofokeng (Hlabeni—Taxi Driver), Grace Mahlaba (Nurse), Ian Roberts (Evans), Jonathan Rands (Glyn Henderson), Shirley Johnston (Barbara Henderson), Ben Kruger, Dan Robbertse (Police Officers), Eric Miyeni (Absalom Kumalo), Patrick Shai (Robert Ndela), Robert Whithead (Carmichael), David Clatworthy (Clerk of the Court), Themba Ndaba (Matthew Kumalo), Louis Seboko (Johannes Pafuri), Graham Armitage (Judge), Greg Latter (Prosecutor), Thomas Hall (Court Usher), Chris Steyn, Antonio Rodrigues, Stuart Monthieth (Warders), Alfred D. Nokwe (Old Man), Lorraine Nyathikazi (Apron Woman), David Phetoe (Black Priest)

In 1940s Johannesburg, two neighbors, a black pastor, and a rich, white landowner, are brought together when one of their sons is murdered. Previously filmed in England in 1951 with Canada Lee, Charles Carson, and Sidney Poitier. Also the basis for the musical Lost in the Stars, *which was filmed in 1974 with Brock Peters, Melba Moore, and Raymond St. Jacques.*

© Miramax Films

Brad Renfro, Jonathan Taylor Thomas

Jonathan Taylor Thomas, Rachael Leigh Cook

TOM AND HUCK

(WALT DISNEY PICTURES) Producers, Laurence Mark, John Baldecchi; Executive Producers, Barry Bernardi, Stephen Sommers; Director, Peter Hewitt; Screenplay, Stephen Sommers, David Loughery; Based on the novel *The Adventures of Tom Sawyer* by Mark Twain; Photography, Bobby Bukowski; Designer, Gemma Jackson; Editor, David Freeman; Costumes, Marie France; Music, Stephen Endelman; Casting, Gail Levin, Tricia Tomey; a Laurence Mark production; Distributed by Buena Vista Pictures; Dolby Digital Stereo; Panavision; Technicolor; Rated PG; 93 minutes; December release

CAST

Tom Sawyer	Jonathan Taylor Thomas
Huck Finn	Brad Renfro
Injun Joe	Eric Schweig
Judge Thatcher	Charles Rocket
Aunt Polly	Amy Wright
Muff Potter	Michael McShane
Widow Douglas	Marian Seldes
Becky Thatcher	Rachael Leigh Cook
Emmett	Lanny Flaherty
Sid	Courtland Mead
Mr. Sneed	Peter Mackenzie
Schoolmaster Dobbins	Heath Lamberts
Doc Robinson	William Newman
Joe Harper	Joey Stinson
Ben Rodgers	Blake Heron
Defense Lawyer	Jim Aycock
Sheriff	Andy Stahl
Welshman	Adrian Roberts
Suzy Harper	Tiffany Lynn Clark
Billy Newton	Kellen Hathaway
Farmer	Mark Cabus
Mary	Bronwen Murray
Impatient Trial Spectator	Paul Anthony Kropfl

and Newell Alexander, Tommy Lamey, David Cowgill, Stuart K. Robinson (Search Party), Mitch Carter, Ike Eisenmann, Matthew Valencia, Blake Ewing (Taverners), Rosemary Alexander, Sherry Hursey, Philece Sampler, Wendy Cutler, Tamra Mellow, Edie Mirman, Toby Ganger, Austin Kottke, Courtney Pelton, Katherine Zarimba (Townsfolk)

Tom Sawyer and Huck Finn must steal a treasure map from Injun Joe in order to clear an innocent man of murder. Previous film versions of Mark Twain's novel starred Jackie Coogan (Tom Sawyer; Paramount, 1930), Tommy Kelly (UA/Selznick, 1938), Billy Cook (Tom Sawyer—Detective; Paramount, 1938), and Johnny Whitaker (Tom Sawyer; UA, 1973).

© Buena Vista Pictures Distribution Inc.

Amy Wright

Eric Schweig

Brad Renfro, Jonathan Taylor Thomas

Anthony Hopkins

Joan Allen, Anthony Hopkins

David Paymer, James Woods, Paul Sorvino, Bob Hoskins, Kevin Dunn

NIXON

(HOLLYWOOD PICTURES) Producers, Clayton Townsend, Oliver Stone, Andrew G. Vajna; Director, Oliver Stone; Screenplay, Stephen J. Rivele, Christopher Wilkinson, Oliver Stone; Photography, Robert Richardson; Designer, Victor Kempster; Editors, Brian Berdan, Hank Corwin; Co-Producers, Eric Hamburg, Dan Halsted; Music, John Williams; Costumes, Richard Hornung; Casting, Billy Hopkins, Heidi Levitt, Mary Vernieu; an Illusion Entertainment Group/Cinergi production; Dolby Stereo; Panavision; Technicolor; Rated R; 190 minutes; December release

CAST

Richard M. Nixon	Anthony Hopkins
Pat Nixon	Joan Allen
Alexander Haig	Powers Boothe
E. Howard Hunt	Ed Harris
J. Edgar Hoover	Bob Hoskins
John Mitchell	E.G. Marshall
Ron Ziegler	David Paymer
John Dean	David Hyde Pierce
Henry Kissinger	Paul Sorvino
Hannah Nixon	Mary Steenburgen
John Ehrlichman	J.T. Walsh
H.R. Haldeman	James Woods
Clyde Tolson	Brian Bedford
Charles Colson	Kevin Dunn
Murray Chotiner	Fyvush Finkel
Julie Nixon	Annabeth Gish
Harold Nixon	Tony Goldwyn
"Jack Jones"	Larry Hagman
Nelson Rockefeller	Edward Herrmann
Martha Mitchell	Madeline Kahn
Herb Klein	Saul Rubinek
Johnny Roselli	Tony Lo Bianco
Richard Nixon at 12	Corey Carrier
Frank Nixon	Tom Bower
Richard Nixon at 19	David Barry Gray
Manolo Sanchez	Tony Plana
Trini Cardoza	Dan Hedaya
Bob	John Cunningham
Earl	John C. McGinley
Gordon Liddy	John Diehl
Frank Sturgis	Robert Beltran
Bernard Barker	Lenny Vullo
James McCord	Ronald von Klaussen
Eugenio Martinez	Kamar De Los Reyes
Virgilio Gonzales	Enrique Castillo
Cuban Plumber	Victor Rivers
Moderator	Drew Snyder
Donald Nixon	Sean Stone
Arthur Nixon	Joshua Preston

and Ian Calip (Football Player), Jack Wallace (Football Coach), Julie Condra Douglas (Young Pat Nixon), Annette Helde (Happy Rockefeller), Howard Platt (Lawyer at Party), Mike Kennedy (Convention Announcer), Harry Murphy, Suzanne Schnulle Murphy, Michael Kaufman (Fans), Bridgette Wilson (Sandy), Pamela Dickerson (Girlfriend), O'Neal Compton (Texas Man), John Bedford Lloyd (Cuban Man), Dr. Christian Renna (Family Doctor), Michael Chiklis (TV Director), Wilson Cruz (Joaquin), James Pickens (Black Orator), Mikey Stone (Edward Nixon), Robert Marshall (Spiro Agnew), Marley Shelton (Tricia Nixon), James Karen (Bill Rogers), Richard Fancy (Mel Laird), Peter Carlin, Michelle Krusiec (Students), Joanna Going (Young Student), Wass Stevens (Protester), Tom Nicoletti, Chuck Pfeiffer (Secret Service Agents), Alex Butterfield (White House Staffer), Mark Steins (White House Security), Ric Young (Mao-Tse-Tung), Bai Ling (Chinese Interpreter), Peter P. Starson, Jr. (Air Force One Steward), Jon Tenney, Julie Araskog, Ray Wills, John Bellucci, Zoey Zimmerman (Reporters), Mary Rudolph (Rosemary Woods), Clayton Townsend (Floor Manager #1), Donna Dixon (Maureen Dean), John Stockwell, Charlie Haugk (Staffers), Boris Sichkin (Leonid Brezhnev), Fima Noveck (Andre Gromyko), Raissa Danilova (Russian Interpreter), Marilyn Rockafellow (Helen Smith), Bill Bolender (Bethesda Doctor), Melinda Renna (Bethesda Nurse), George Plimpton (President's Lawyer)

Biography of Richard Nixon, the thirty-seventh President of the United States, focusing most specifically on his downfall in the wake of the Watergate Scandal.

The film received Academy Award nominations for actor (Hopkins), supporting actress (Allen), original screenplay, and original dramatic score.

Joan Allen, Anthony Hopkins

Joan Allen, Anthony Hopkins

Annabeth Gish, Anthony Hopkins

Anthony Hopkins, James Woods

WAITING TO EXHALE

(20th CENTURY FOX) Producers, Ezra Swerdlow, Deborah Schindler; Executive Producers/Screenplay, Terry McMillan, Ronald Bass; Based upon the novel by Terry McMillan; Director, Forest Whitaker; Photography, Toyomichi Kurita; Designer, David Gropman; Editor, Richard Chew; Music, Kenneth "Babyface" Edmonds; Costumes, Judy L. Ruskin; Casting, Jaki Brown-Karman; a Deborah Schindler/Ezra Swerdlow production; Dolby Stereo; Deluxe color; Rated R; 123 minutes; December release

CAST

Savannah	Whitney Houston
Bernadine	Angela Bassett
Gloria	Loretta Devine
Robin	Lela Rochon
Marvin	Gregory Hines
Kenneth	Dennis Haysbert
Troy	Mykelti Williamson
John, Sr.	Michael Beach
Russell	Leon
Michael	Wendell Pierce
Tarik	Donald Adeosun Faison
James	Wesley Snipes
David	Giancarlo Esposito
Lionel	Jeffrey D. Sams
Onika	Jazz Raycole
John, Jr.	Brandon Hammond
Denise	Kenya Moore
Joseph	Lamont Johnson
Minister	Wren T. Brown
On Air D.J.	Theo
D.J. at the Hermosa	Ken Love
Fireman	Graham Galloway
Savannah's Mother	Starletta DuPois
Savannah's Assistant	Shari L. Carpenter
Interviewer	Thomas R. Leander
Group at Hermosa Table	Cordell Conway, Lee Wells, Jr., Hope Brown
Tarik's Girl Friend	Delaina Mitchell
Herbert	Luis Sharpe
Security Guard at John's Office	Joseph S. Myers
Wild Bill	Ezra Swerdlow
Hairdresser	Ellin La Var
Customer at Hair Salon	Patricia Anne Fox
Judge	Wally Bujack

Four women go through a year of trying to find the right men as various relationships arise and go sour. This film marked the theatrical directorial debut of actor Forest Whitaker.

© Twentieth Century Fox

Dennis Haysbert, Whitney Houston

Lela Rochon, Leon

Angela Bassett, Michael Beach

Loretta Devine, Gregory Hines

Loretta Devine, Whitney Houston, Angela Bassett, Lela Rochon

Boris, Balto

Muk, Luk

BALTO

(UNIVERSAL) Producer, Steve Hickner; Executive Producers, Steven Spielberg, Kathleen Kennedy, Bonnie Radford; Director, Simon Wells; Screenplay, Cliff Ruby, Elana Lesser, David Steven Cohen, Roger S.H. Schulman; Story, Cliff Ruby, Elana Lesser; Music, James Horner; Song: "Reach for the Light," music by Barry Mann and James Horner, lyrics by Cynthia Weil/performed by Steve Winwood; Associate Producer, Rich Arons; Supervising Editors, Nick Fletcher, Sim Evan-Jones; Designer, Hans Bacher; Character Designers, Carlos Grangel, Nicolas Marlet, Patrick Maté; a co-presentation of Amblin Entertainment; Dolby DTS Stereo; Eastman color; Rated G; 74 minutes; December release

VOICE CAST

Balto ....Kevin Bacon
Boris ....Bob Hoskins
Jenna...Bridget Fonda
Steele...Jim Cummings
Muk and Luk...Phil Collins
Nikki..Jack Angel
Kaltag..Danny Mann
Star..Robbie Rist
Rosy...Juliette Brewer
Sylvie and Dixie/Rosy's Mother.......................Sandra Searles Dickinson
Doc...Donald Sinden
Rosy's Father...William Roberts
Telegraph Operator..Garrick Hagon
Butcher...Bill Bailey
Town Dog..Big Al
and Mike McShane, Miriam Margolyes, Austin Tichenor, Reed Martin, Adam Long (Extra Voices)

LIVE ACTION CAST

Grandma Rosy..Miriam Margolyes
Granddaughter..Lola Bates-Campbell

True story of an Alaskan sled dog who battles the forces of nature to help save some children during a diphtheria epidemic.

© Universal Studios Inc./Amblin Entertainment

Jean-Claude Van Damme

Powers Boothe

Jean-Claude Van Damme, Dorian Harewood

SUDDEN DEATH

(UNIVERSAL) Producers, Moshe Diamant, Howard Baldwin; Executive Producers, Ash R. Shah, Sundip R. Shah, Anders P. Jensen; Director/Photography, Peter Hyams; Screenplay, Gene Quintano; Story/Associate Producer, Karen Baldwin; Designer, Philip Harrison; Editor, Steven Kemper; Co-Producers, Richard Cohen, Jason Clark, Jack Frost Sanders; Line Producer, Deborah Lee; Costumes, Dan Lester; Music, John Debney; Stunts, Gary M. Hymes; Visual Effects Supervisor, Gregory L. McMurry; Casting, Penny Perry Davis, Deborah Brown; a Signature/Baldwin Cohen production in association with Imperial Entertainment; DTS Digital Stereo; Panavision; Deluxe color; Rated R; 110 minutes; December release

CAST

Darren McCord	Jean-Claude Van Damme
Joshua Foss	Powers Boothe
Vice President	Raymond J. Barry
Emily McCord	Whittni Wright
Tyler McCord	Ross Malinger
Hallmark	Dorian Harewood
Kathi	Kate McNeil
Hickey	Michael Gaston
Mrs. Ferrara	Audra Lindley
Blair	Brian Delate

and Steve Aronson (Dooley), Michael Aubele (Ace), Karen Baldwin (TV Director), Jennifer D. Bowser (Joan), Phil Spano, Pat Brisson (Players), Glenda Morgan Brown (Mrs. Taylor), Jophery Brown (Wootton), William Cameron (Secret Serviceman), Bernard Canepari (Jefferson), Jay Caulfield (Tolliver), Alan Clement (Mr. Wirtz), Bill Clement (Pre-Game Announcer), Bill Dalzell III (Spota), Gil Combs (Secret Service #1), Jack Erdie (Scratch), Ed Evanko (Baldwin), David Flick (Spectator), Glenn Alan Gardner (Sugarman Driver), John Hall, Harold Surratt (Hallmark's Secret Service), Jeff Habbersted (Lewis), Mark Hager (Elevator SS Man), John Hateley (Briggs), Rosine "Ace" Hatem (Concessionaire), Jeff Hochendoner (Duckerman), Jeffrey Howell (Usborn), Brian Hutchison (Young Agent), Jeff Jimerson (Anthem Singer), Mark Kachowski (Beaumont), Callum Keith-King (Kitchen Assistant), Rick LeFevour (Ante Room SS Man), Tommy LaFitte (Sugarman Guard), Raymond Laine, Vinnie Sciullo (Foss Men), Mike Lange (Play by Play Announcer), Butch Luick (Fat Man), Fred Mancuso (Pratt), Anthony Marino (Vendor), Larry John Meyers (Box Secret Service #2), Ken Milchick (Coach), Faith Minton (Carla), Paul Mochnick (Andre Ferrara), Brad Moniz (Toowey), Jean-Pierre Nutini (Employee #1), Daniel R. Pagath (Assistant Coach), Manny Perry (Brody), Allan Pinsker (Older Man), Douglas Rees (Spotter), Diane Robin (Mrs. Baldwin), Luc Robitaille (Himself), Thomas Saccio (Foss Helicopter Pilot), Jack Skelly (Elderly Man), Brian Smrz (Thug #2), Paul Steigerwald (Color Commentator), John Sterling (Kitchen Secret Service Agent), Rohn Thomas (Mayor Taylor), Milton E. Thompson, Jr. (Kurtz), Dixie Tymitz (Mrs. Wirtz), Fred Waugh (Bluto), Rema D. Webb (Cindy), Dean E. Wells (Kloner)

Darren McCord desperately tries to stop a gang of extortionists who are holding his daughter and the Vice President hostage during a hockey game.

© Universal City Studios Inc.

Whittni Wright, Jean-Claude Van Damme, Ross Malinger

CUTTHROAT ISLAND

(MGM) Producers, Renny Harlin, Joel B. Michaels, Laurence Mark, James Gorman; Executive Producer, Mario Kassar; Director, Renny Harlin; Screenplay, Robert King, Marc Norman; Story, Michael Frost Beckner, James Gorman, Bruce A. Evans, Raynold Gideon; Photography, Peter Levy; Designer, Norman Garwood; Costumes, Enrico Sabbatini; Editors, Frank J. Urioste, Ralph E. Winters; Music, John Debney; Associate Producer, Jane Barteleme; Co-Producers, John Baldecchi, Lynwood Spinks; Digital & Visual Effects, Jeffrey A. Okun; Casting, Mindy Marin; a Mario Kassar presentation of a Carolco/Forge production in association with Laurence Mark productions, Beckner/Gorman productions; Distributed by MGM/UA; DTS Digital Stereo; Panavision/Technovision; Technicolor; Rated PG-13; 123 minutes; December release

Geena Davis, Matthew Modine

CAST

Morgan Adams	Geena Davis
William Shaw	Matthew Modine
Dawg Brown	Frank Langella
John Reed	Maury Chaykin
Ainslee	Patrick Malahide
Glasspoole	Stan Shaw
Mr. Blair	Rex Linn
Snelgrave	Paul Dillon
Bowen	Chris Masterson
Scully	Jimmie F. Skaggs
Black Harry	Harris Yulin
Bishop	Carl Chase
Fiddler Pirate	Peter Geeves
Captain Trotter	Angus Wright
Toussant	Ken Bones
Mandy Rickets	Mary Pegler
Ladies	Mary Peach, Lucinda Aurel
Lieutenant	Thomas Lockyer
Auctioneer	Roger Booth
Mordachai Fingers	George Murcell
Bartender	Simon Atherton
Executioner	Dickey Beer
Hastings	Christopher Halliday
Helmsman	Chris Johnston
Snake the Lookout	Richard Leaf
Fleming	Tam White
King Charles	Shayna the Monkey
Captain Perkins	Rupert Vansittart

and Nick Bartlett, David Bailie, Kwame Kwei-Armah, Ramon Tikaram, Chris Adamson (Dawg's Pirates), Thor (Pirate Dog)

Morgan Adams is given a piece of a treasure map by her dying father and sets sail on his ship, the Morning Star, to find Cutthroat Island.

Frank Langella, Geena Davis

Matthew Modine, Geena Davis

Stan Shaw, Geena Davis, Chris Masterson

Robert Downey, Jr., Sam Neill, Polly Walker

Ian McKellen, Robert Downey, Jr.

Hugh Grant

RESTORATION

(MIRAMAX) Producers, Cary Brokaw, Andy Paterson, Sarah Ryan Black; Executive Producer, Kip Hagopian; Co-Producers, Bob Weinstein, Harvey Weinstein, Donna Gigliotti; Director, Michael Hoffman; Screenplay, Rupert Walters; Based on the novel by Rose Tremain; Photography, Oliver Stapleton; Designer, Eugenio Zanetti; Music, James Newton Howard; Costumes, James Acheson; Associate Producer, Mark Bentley; Supervising Producer, Garth Thomas; Casting, Mary Selway, Patsy Pollock; a Segue Productions/Avenue Pictures production in association with Oxford Film Company; Dolby Digital Stereo; Color; Rated R; 117 minutes; December release

CAST

Robert Merivel	Robert Downey, Jr.
King Charles II	Sam Neill
John Pearce	David Thewlis
Celia	Polly Walker
Katherine	Meg Ryan
Will Gates	Ian McKellen
Finn	Hugh Grant
Ambrose	Ian McDiarmid
Midwife	Mary Macleod
Daniel	Mark Lethern
Hannah	Sandy McDade
Eleanor	Rosalind Bennett
Man With Visible Heart	Willie Ross
Chiffinch	David Gant
Merivel's Father	Benjamin Whitrow
Latin Doctor	Neville Watchurst
Watchman	Bryan Pringle
Fleeing Man	Roy Evans
The Chancellor	John Quarmby
The Secretary	John Dallimore
Mr. Bung	Roger Ashton-Griffiths
Pretty Wench	Janan Kubba
Patient	Henrietta Voigts
Second Doctor	Simon Taylor
Fair Lady	Selina Giles
Dark Lady	Susanne McKenrick
Pinworth	Nick Hutchison
Gallants	Andrew Havill, Tony Gardner
Lord Bathurst	David Ryall

Robert Merivel, a medical student in seventeenth-century England, finds his life altered when he becomes a member of the court of King Charles II.

Academy Award winner for Best Costume Design and Art Direction of 1995.

© Miramax Films

Robert Downey, Jr., Meg Ryan

Robert Downey, Jr.

Sam Neill

Ian McKellen

David Thewlis

Robert Downey, Jr.

Robert Downey, Jr. (r)

Bruce Willis, Brad Pitt

Bruce Willis

Christopher Plummer

Madeleine Stowe

Frank Gorshin

Madeleine Stowe, Bruce Willis

Bruce Willis

TWELVE MONKEYS

(UNIVERSAL) Producer, Charles Roven; Executive Producers, Robert Cavallo, Gary Levinsohn, Robert Kosberg; Director, Terry Gilliam; Screenplay, David Peoples, Janet Peoples; Inspired by the film La Jetee written by Chris Marker; Photography, Roger Pratt; Designer, Jeffrey Beecroft; Editor, Mick Audsley; Co-Producer, Lloyd Phillips; Costumes, Julie Weiss; Music, Paul Buckmaster; Associate Producers, Kelley Smith-Wait, Mark Egerton; Casting, Margery Simkin; an Atlas/Classico presentation of an Atlas Entertainment production; DTS Stereo; Eastman color; Rated R; 131 minutes; December release

Bruce Willis

CAST

James Cole	Bruce Willis
Dr. Kathryn Railly	Madeleine Stowe
Jeffrey Goines	Brad Pitt
Dr. Leland Goines	Christopher Plummer
Dr. Fletcher	Frank Gorshin
Jose	Jon Seda
Young Cole	Joseph Melito
Scarface	Michael Chance
Tiny	Vernon Campbell
Botanist	H. Michael Walls
Geologist	Bob Adrian
Zoologist	Simon Jones
Astrophysicist	Carol Florence
Microbiologist	Bill Raymond
Engineer	Ernest Abuba
Poet	Irma St. Paule
Detective Franki	Joey Perillo
Policemen	Bruce Kirkpatrick, Wilfred Williams
Billings	Rozwill Young
Ward Nurse	Nell Johnson
L.J. Washington	Fred Strother
Dr. Casey	Rick Warner
Dr. Goodin	Anthony "Chip" Brienza
Harassed Mother	Joliet Harris
Waltzing Woman Patient	Drucie McDaniel
Old Man Patient	John Blaisse
Patient at Gate	Louis Lippa
X-Ray Doctor	Stan Kang
WWI Captain	Pat Dias
WWI Sergeant	Aaron Michael Lacey
Dr. Peters	David Morse
Professor	Charles Techman
Marilou	Jann Ellis
Officer No. 1	Johnnie Hobbs, Jr.
Anchorwoman	Janet L. Zappala
Evangelist	Thomas Roy
Louie/Raspy Voice	Harry O'Toole
Thugs	Korchenko, Chuck Jeffreys
Teddy	Lisa Gay Hamilton
Fale	Felix A. Pire
Bee	Mathew Ross
Agents	Barry Price, John Panzarella, Larry Daly
Anchorman	Arthur Fennell
Pompous Man	Karl Warren
Lt. Halperin	Christopher Meloni
Detective Dalva	Paul Meshejian
Wayne	Robert O'Neill
Kweskin	Kevin Thigpen
Hotel Clerk	Lee Golden
Wallace	Joseph McKenna

Bruce Willis, Madeleine Stowe

and Jeff Tanner (Plain Clothes Cop), Faith Potts (Store Clerk), Michael Ryan Segal (Weller), Annie Golden (Cabbie), Lisa Talerico (Ticket Agent), Stephen Bridgewater (Airport Detective), Franklin Huffman (Plump Businessman), Joann S. Dawson (Gift Store Clerk), Jack Dougherty, Lenny Daniels, Herbert C. Hauls, Jr. (Airport Security), Charley Scalies (Impatient Traveler), Carolyn Walker (Terrified Traveler).

In the year 2035, James Cole is sent back in time to 1996 in hopes of finding an answer to why most of Earth's population has been wiped out and the surface of the planet made uninhabitable.

The film received Academy Award nominations for supporting actor (Pitt) and costume design.

Bruce Willis, Brad Pitt

Sean Penn, Susan Sarandon

Robert Prosky

Roberta Maxwell, Susan Sarandon

DEAD MAN WALKING

(GRAMERCY) Producers, Jon Kilik, Tim Robbins, Rudd Simmons; Executive Producers, Tim Bevan, Eric Fellner; Director/Screenplay, Tim Robbins; Based on the book by Sister Helen Prejean, C.S.J.; Photography, Roger A. Deakins; Designer, Richard Hoover; Costumes, Renée Ehrlich Kalfus; Editor, Lisa Zeno Churgin; Music, David Robbins; Title song written and performed by Bruce Springsteen; Casting, Douglas Aibel; a PolyGram Filmed Entertainment Presentation of a Working Title/Havoc production; Dolby Stereo; Color; Rated R; 120 minutes; December release

CAST

Sister Helen Prejean	Susan Sarandon
Matthew Poncelet	Sean Penn
Hilton Barber	Robert Prosky
Earl Delacroix	Raymond J. Barry
Clyde Percy	R. Lee Ermey
Mary Beth Percy	Celia Weston
Helen's Mother	Lois Smith
Chaplain Farley	Scott Wilson
Lucille Poncelet	Roberta Maxwell
Sister Colleen	Margo Martindale
Captain Beliveau	Barton Heyman
Sgt. Neal Trapp	Steve Boles
Warden Hartman	Nesbitt Blaisdell
Luis Montoya	Ray Aranha
Guy Gilardi	Larry Pine
Governor Benedict	Kevin Cooney
State Trooper	Clancy Brown
Nurse	Adele Robbins
Carl Vitello	Michael Cullen
Walter Delacroix	Peter Sarsgaard
Hope Percy	Missy Yager
Emily Percy	Jenny Krochmal
Craig Poncelet	Jack Black
Sonny Poncelet	Jon Abrahams
Troy Poncelet	Arthur Bridgers
Helene's Brother	Steve Carlisle
Helen's Sister	Helen Hester
9-Year-Old Helen	Eva Amurri
Opossum Kids	Jack Henry Robbins, Gary "Buddy" Boe, Amy Long
Henry	Dennis F. Neal
Nellie	Molly Bryant
Mirabeau	Pamela Garmon
Reporter	Adrian Colon
Supporter	John D. Wilmot

and Margaret Lane, Sally Ann Roberts, Alec Gifford, John Hurlbutt (Reporters), Mike Longman (News Anchor), Pete Burris, Joan Glover, Florrie Hathorn, Lenore Banks (Parents), Idella Cassamier (Idella), Marlon Horton (Herbie), Kenitra Singleton (Kenitra), Palmer Jackson (Palmer), Johnathan Thomas (Johnathan), Walter Breaux, Jr., Scott Sowers, Cortez Nance, Jr., Adam Nelson, Dalvin Ford, Derek Steeley, Jeremy Knaster (Guards), Mary Robbins (Aide to Governor Benedict), Miles Guthrie Robbins (Boy in Church)

The true story of Sister Helen Prejean who became spiritual advisor to Matthew Poncelet, a condemned killer awaiting execution in Louisiana.

Susan Sarandon won the Academy Award as Best Actress of 1995. The film received additional Oscar nominations for actor (Penn), director, and song ("Dead Man Walking").

© Gramercy Pictures

Susan Sarandon, Sean Penn

Susan Sarandon, Raymond J. Barry

Scott Wilson

Robert Prosky, Susan Sarandon

Steve Boles, Susan Sarandon

R. Lee Ermey, Celia Weston

Glenne Headly, Richard Dreyfuss

Jay Thomas, Richard Dreyfuss

Richard Dreyfuss, Olympia Dukakis

MR. HOLLAND'S OPUS

(HOLLYWOOD PICTURES) Producers, Ted Field, Michael Nolin, Robert W. Cort; Executive Producers, Scott Kroopf, Patrick Sheane Duncan; Director, Stephen Herek; Screenplay, Patrick Sheane Duncan; Co-Producers, William Teitler, Judith James; Photography, Oliver Wood; Designer, David Nichols; Editor, Trudy Ship; Costumes, Aggie Guerard Rodgers; Music, Michael Kamen; Casting, Sharon Bialy; an Interscope Communications/PolyGram Filmed Entertainment production in association with the Charlie Mopic Company; Distributed by Buena Vista Pictures; Dolby Digital Stereo; Panavision; Technicolor; Rated PG; 142 minutes; December release

CAST

Glenn Holland	Richard Dreyfuss
Iris Holland	Glenne Headly
Bill Meister	Jay Thomas
Principal Jacobs	Olympia Dukakis
Vice Principal Wolters	W.H. Macy
Gertrude Lang	Alicia Witt
Louis Russ	Terrence Howard
Bobby Tidd	Damon Whitaker
Rowena Morgan	Jean Louisa Kelly
Sarah Olmstead	Alexandra Boyd
Cole at 6 Years Old	Nicholas John Renner
Cole at 15 Years Old	Joseph Anderson
Cole at 28 Years Old	Anthony Natale
Adult Gertrude	Joanna Gleason
Deaf School Principal	Beth Maitland
Study Hall Student	Patrick Fong
Mr. Mims	Benjamin J. Dixon
Ms. Swedlin	Kathryn Arnett
Mr. Sullivan	Freeman O. Corbin
Ms. Godfrey	Moira Feeney
Mr. Shapiro	Joshua Minnick
Miss Reeves	Ashley Hamrick
Miss Schumaker	Janine Shouse
Mr. Hosta	Spencer Riviera
Mr. Malone	Daniel J. Vhay
Mr. McMartin	Sean Bevington
Mr. Russ	John Henry Redwood
Dr. Sorenson	Ted Roisum
Ralph	Mark Daniels
Ms. Wayne	Kaili Carlton
Mr. McKenzie	Adam Fitzhugh
Boys	Eric Michael Cole, Joe Campbell
Girls	Tomiko Peirano, Kasey Neilson, Zoe McLellan
Deaf School Teacher	Kelly M. Casey
Chaplain	Michael Mendelson
Toby Klein	Conan Doherty
Diner Waitress	Stacey Siegel
Billy Faraday	John Boyer
Secretary	Linda Williams Janke
Superintendent	David Clegg
City Official	Don Burns
Stadler	Balthazar Getty
Adult Stadler	Dennis Biasi

and Alex Dudgeon, Rachel Wooley, Jordan Carlton, Aurora J. Miller, Paul Bernard, Mary Kay O'Mealy, Dieffyd Gilman-Frederick, Tara Eng, Jay Frank (Auditioners), Nicolas Sirianni, Jacob Adams, Chris Marth, Brent Archie, Kevin Calaba, Keith Swift (Football Players)

Although his goal is to compose a piece of music which will bring him lasting fame, Glenn Holland finds that his job as a high school music teacher brings more fulfillment to him than he expected.

The film received an Academy Award nomination for best actor (Dreyfuss).

© Interscope Communications

Richard Dreyfuss

Richard Dreyfuss, Alicia Witt

Richard Dreyfuss, Joseph Anderson

Richard Dreyfuss, Glenne Headly

Richard Dreyfuss, Terrence Howard

FOUR ROOMS

(MIRAMAX) Producer, Lawrence Bender; Executive Producers, Alexandre Rockwell, Quentin Tarantino; Co-Producers, Paul Hellerman, Heidi Vogel, Scott Lambert; Directors/Screenplay, Allison Anders (*The Missing Ingredient*), Alexandre Rockwell (*The Wrong Man*), Robert Rodriguez (*The Misbehavers*), Quentin Tarantino (*The Man From Hollywood*); Photography, Rodrigo Garcia (*The Missing Ingredient*), Phil Parmet (*The Wrong Man*), Guillermo Navarro (*The Misbehavers*), Andrzej Sekula (*The Man From Hollywood*); Designer, Gary Frutkoff; Costumes, Susan Bertram (*The Missing Ingredient, The Wrong Man*), Mary Claire Hannan (*The Misbehavers, The Man From Hollywood*); Editors, Margie Goodspeed (*The Missing Ingredient*), Elena Maganini (*The Wrong Man*), Sally Menke (*The Man From Hollywood*), Robert Rodriguez (*The Misbehavers*); Music, Combustible Edison; a Band Apart production; Dolby Stereo; Color; Rated R; 93 minutes; December release

CAST

Ted the Bellhop ....Tim Roth

THE MISSING INGREDIENT
Jezebel ....Sammi Davis
Diana ....Amanda de Cadenet
Athena ....Valeria Golino
Elspeth ....Madonna
Eva..Ione Skye
Raven ....Lili Taylor
Kiva ....Alicia Witt

THE WRONG MAN
Angela..Jennifer Beals
Sigfried..David Proval

THE MISBEHAVERS
Man..Antonio Banderas
Sarah..Lana McKissack
Corpse ....Patrick Vonne Rodriguez
Wife..Tamlyn Tomita
Juancho ....Danny Verduzco

THE MAN FROM HOLLYWOOD
Angela..Jennifer Beals
Norman..Paul Calderon
Chester..Quentin Tarantino
Leo..Bruce Willis

and
Long Hair Yuppie Scum ....Lawrence Bender
Betty ....Kathy Griffin
Taxi Driver ....Paul Hellerman
Baby Bellhop..Quinn Thomas Hellerman
Sam the Bellhop..Marc Lawrence
Left Redhead ....Unruly Julie McClean
Right Redhead ....Laura Rush
Margaret ....Marisa Tomei

On New Year's Eve, at the Mon Signor Hotel, lone bellhop Ted is on call between four rooms containing: a witch coven, a psychosexual married couple, a gangster dad seeking a babysitter, and a Hollywood comedian and his entourage.

© Miramax Films

Madonna, Sammi Davis, Valeria Golino, Lili Taylor, Ione Skye

Antonio Banderas

Jennifer Beals, Tim Roth

Stephen Dorff, Reese Witherspoon in *S.F.W.*
© Gramercy Pictures

S.F.W. (Gramercy) Producer, Dale Pollock; Executive Producer, Sigurjon Sighvatsson; Co-Producer, Mike Nelson; Director, Jefery Levy; Screenplay, Danny Rubin, Jefery Levy; Based on the novel by Andrew Wellman; Photography, Peter Deming; Designer, Eve Cauley; Music, Graeme Revell; Costumes, Debra McGuire; Casting, Owens Hill, Rachel Abroms; a PolyGram Filmed Entertainment presentation of an A&M Films production in association with Propaganda Films; Dolby Stereo; Color; Rated R; 92 minutes; January release. **CAST:** Stephen Dorff (Cliff Spab), Reese Witherspoon (Wendy Pfister), Jake Busey (Morrow Streeter), Joey Lauren Adams (Monica Dice), Pamela Gidley (Janet Streeter), David Barry Gray (Scott Spab), Jack Noseworthy (Joe Dice), Richard Portnow (Gerald Parsley), Edward Wiley (Mr. Spab), Lela Ivey (Mrs. Spab), Natasha Gregson Wagner (Kristen), Annie McEnroe (Dolly), Virgil Frye (Earl), Francesca P. Roberts (Kim Martin), Soon Teck-Oh (Milt Morris), Blair Tefkin (Allison Ash), Steven Antin (Dick Zetterland), Melissa Lechner (Sandy Hooten), Lenny Wolpe (Phil Connors), Natalie Strauss (Rita Connors), Tobey Maguire (Al), Dana Allan Young (Johnny), John Roarke (Phil Donahue, Sam Donaldson, Alan Dershowitz, Ted Koppel & Larry King Clones), Amber Benson (Barbara "Babs" Wyler), China Kantner (Female Pantyhose Gunman), Kathryn Atwood (Pebbles Goren), Caroline Barclay (Mindy Lawford), Sylvia Short (Dr. Travis), Sandra Phillips, Gary Grossman (Talent Agents), Michelle Seipp (Hotel Receptionist), Frank Collison (Stoner Witness), Stephanie Friedman (Dori Smelling), Adam Small (Burger Boy Manager), Ben Slack (Madison Heights Mayor), Carol Hankins (Nervous Lady on Talkshow), Kristen Ernst (Teenage Girl on Talkshow), Mil Nicholson (Woman at Homecoming), Charles Font, John Chaidez, Corey Gunnestad (Burger Boy Workers), William Scott Brown, Lisa Dinkins, Amber Edam, Jerome Front, Susan Harney, Philip Moon, Joanne Takahashi, R.W. Wilson (Reporters), Ada Gorn, Jon Gudmundsson, Bernadette Elise (Photographers), Gary Coleman (Himself)

OBLIVION (Full Moon/R.S. Entertainment) Producers, Vlad Paunescu, Oana Paunescu; Executive Producer, Charles Band; Co-Producers, Albert Band, Debra Dion, Peter David; Director, Sam Irvin; Screenplay, Peter David; Based on a story idea by Charles Band; Story, John Rheaume, Greg Suddeth, Mark Goldstein; Photography, Adolfo Bartoli; Editor, Margaret-Anne Smith; Music, Pino Donaggio; Designer, Milo; Visual Effects, David Allen Prods.; Casting, Robert MacDonald, Perry Bullington; Ultra-Stereo; Foto-Kem color; Rated R; 94 minutes; January release. **CAST:** Richard Joseph Paul (Zack Stone), Jackie Swanson (Mattie Chase), Andrew Divoff (Redeye), Meg Foster (Stell Barr), Jimmie Skaggs (Buteo), Carel Struycken (Mr. Gaunt), Musetta Vander (Lash), George Takei (Doc Valentine), Julie Newmar (Miss Kitty)

MURDER IN THE FIRST (Le Studio Canal+/Wolper Org.) Producers, Marc Frydman, Mark Wolper; Executive Producers, David L. Wolper, Marc Rocco; Co-Producer, Deborah Lee; Director, Marc Rocco; Screenplay, Dan Gordon; Photography, Fred Murphy; Designer, Kirk M. Petruccelli; Editor, Russell Livingstone; Costumes, Sylvia Vega Vasques; Music, Christopher Young; Casting, Mary Jo Slater; a Le Studio Canal+ production in association with the Wolper Organization, distributed by

WB; Dolby Stereo; Foto-Kem color; Rated R; 122 minutes; January release. **CAST:** Christian Slater (James Stamphill), Kevin Bacon (Henri Young), Gary Oldman (Associate Warden Glenn), Embeth Davidtz (Mary McCasslin), William H. Macy (William McNeil), Stephen Tobolowsky (Mr. Henkin), Brad Dourif (Byron Stamphill), R. Lee Ermey (Judge Clawson), Mia Kirshner (Adult Rosetta Young), Ben Slack (Jerry Hoolihan), Stefan Gierasch (Warden James Humson), Kyra Sedgwick (Blanche), Alexander Bookston (Alcatraz Doc), Richie Allan (Jury Foreman), Herb Ritts (Mike Kelly), Charles Boswell (Simpson), David Sterling (Inmate Rufus "Roy" McCain), Michael Melvin (Inmate Arthur "Doc" Barker), George Maguire, Nick Scoggin, Douglas Bennett, Joseph Richards, Julius Varnado (Inmates), Tony Barr (Winthrop), Stuart Nisbet (Harve), Gary Ballard (Alcatraz Guard Swenson), Randy Pelish (Alcatraz Guard McKeon), Neil Summers (Alcatraz Guard Whitney), Sonny H. King (Alcatraz Guard Wimer), Eddie Bowz, Brian Leckner, Time Winters, James Keane, Lance Brady, Michael Merrins (Alcatraz Guards), Ray Quartermus, Lee E. Mathis, Wayne Parks (City Jail Guards), Warren Spottswood (Cable Car Conductor), Thomas Fenske, Robert Lee (Newsreel Reporter), Sheldon Flender, Fred Franklin, Danny Kovacs, Joseph Lucas, William Hall, Bill Barretta, Randall Dudley (Men on the street), Wally Rose (Shopkeeper), Amanda Borden (Rosetta Young - age 9), Eve Brenner (Winthrop's Secretary), Joseph Cole (Marshall Gates), Richard Kwong (Chinese Monk), Gary Lee Davis (Giant of a man)

Johnny Brennan, Kamal Ahmed in *The Jerky Boys*
© Touchstone Pictures

THE JERKY BOYS (Hollywood Pictures) Producers, Joe Roth, Roger Birnbaum; Executive Producers, Tony Danza, Emilio Estevez; Director, James Melkonian; Screenplay, James Melkonian, Rich Wilkes, John G. Brennan, Kamal Ahmed; Photography, Ueli Steiger; Designer, Dan Leigh; Editor, Dennis M. Hill; Co-Producer, Randy Ostrow; Music, Ira Newborn; Casting, Douglas Aibel; a Caravan Pictures presentation; Distributed by Buena Vista Pictures; Dolby Digital Stereo; Technicolor; Rated R; 81 minutes; February release. **CAST:** Johnny Brennan (Johnny), Kamal Ahmed (Kamal), Alan Arkin (Lazarro), William Hickey (Uncle Freddy), Alan North (Mickey), Brad Sullivan (Worzic), James Lorinz (Brett Weir), Suzanne Shepherd (Mrs. B), Vincent Pastore (Tony Scarboni), Brian Tarantina (Geno), Peter Appel (Sonny), Darryl Theirse (Connley), David Pittu (Doorman), Frank Senger (Bouncer), Michael Louis Wells (Roadie), Ozzy Osbourne (Band Manager), Henry Bogdan, Rob Echeverria, Page Nye Hamilton (The Band—Helmet), John Norman Thomas (Cabbie), Hope Shapiro (Tolly), Paul Bartel (Host), Danny Dennis (Comedian), Brenda Forbes (Rich Woman), David Stepkin (Old Man), Robert Weil (Quigley), Joe Lisi (Foreman), Ron Ostrow (Fast Food Family Man), Garfield! (Guard), Susan Blommaert (Sister Mary), Angela Pupello (Brett's Date), Jorjan Fox (Lazarro's Young Lady), Ronald Rand (Angry Commuter), David Klein (Young Johnny Brennan), Coach Cox (Young Kamal), Christopher Conte (Young Brett Weir), Charlotte Moore (Mrs. Weir), Dennis Hutchinson (Newsman), Maria A. Corbo (Newswoman), Jerry Dunphy (Anchorman), Tom Jones (Himself), Christopher Harrison (Sparky the Clown), John DiLeo, Marc Webster (Reporters), Michael E. Giammella (Waiter)

A Great Day In Harlem
© Castle Hill Productions, Inc.

A GREAT DAY IN HARLEM (Castle Hill) Producer/Director, Jean Bach; Co-Producer, Matthew Seig; Editor, Susan Peehl; Screenplay, Jean Bach, Susan Peehl, Matthew Seig; Narrator, Quincy Jones; Original Photograph, Art Kane; Photography, Steve Petropoulos; Color; Not rated; 60 minutes; February release. Documentary on the story behind a 1958 photograph containing some of the great jazz musicians of the time. With Dizzy Gillespie, Art Blakely, Art Farmer, Chubby Jackson, Paula Morris, Marian McPartland, Eddie Locke, Ernie Wilkins, Mona Hinton, Robert Benton, Sonny Rollins, Hank Jones, Johnny Griffin, Scoville Browne, Taft Jordan Jr., Bud Freeman, Gerry Mulligan, Elaine Lorillard, Robert Altschuler, Steve Frankfurt, Buck Clayton, Horace Silver, Milt Hinton, Felix Maxwell, Everard Powell, Max Kaminsky, Benny Golson, Nat Hentoff, Mike Lipskin

HEAVYWEIGHTS (Walt Disney Pictures) Producers, Joe Roth, Roger Birnbaum; Executive Producers, Judd Apatow, Sarah Bowman; Director, Steven Brill; Screenplay, Judd Apatow, Steven Brill; Photography, Victor Hammer; Designer, Stephen Storer; Editor, C. Timothy O'Meara; Costumes, Kimberly A. Tillman; Music, J.A.C. Redford; Casting, Judy Taylor, Lynda Gordon; presented in association with Caravan Pictures; Distributed by Buena Vista Pictures; Dolby Digital Stereo; Technicolor; Rated PG; 98 minutes; February release. **CAST:** Tom McGowan (Pat), Aaron Schwartz (Gerry Garner), Shaun Weiss (Josh), Tom Hodges (Lars), Leah Lail (Julie), Paul Feig (Tim), Kenan Thompson (Roy), David Bowe (Chris Donelly), Max Goldblatt (Phillip), Robert Zalkind (Simms), Patrick LaBrecque (Dawson), Jeffrey Tambor (Maury Garner), Jerry Stiller (Harvey Bushkin), Anne Meara (Alice Bushkin), Ben Stiller (Tony Perkis/Tony Perkis, Sr.), David Goldman (Nicholas), Joseph Wayne Miller (Sam), Cody Burger (Cody), Allen Covert (Kenny), Tim Blake Nelson (Camp Hope Salesman), Nancy Ringham (Mrs. Garner), Seth St. Laurent (Camp MVP Racer), Bobby Fain (Camp MVP Pitcher), Robert E. Spencer III (Soccer Goalie), Dustin Greer (Blob Master), Matthew R. Zboyovski

Aaron Schwartz, Tom Hodges, Kenan Thompson in *Heavyweights*
© The Walt Disney Company

(Hope Wall Climber), J.T. Alessi (Ballon Shaver), Chris Snyder (Baseball Scorekeeper), Aubrey Dollar, Mary Holt Fickes, Jamie Olson (Camp Magnolia Girls), Lauren Hill (Angelic Girl), Landry M. Constantino (Kissing Girl), Lois Yaroshefsky (Camp Magnolia Counselor), Matthew Bradley King (Gerry's School Buddy), Deena Dill (Stewardess), Tom Kelley (Man on Plane), Lars Clark (Jack Garner), Judd Apatow (Homer)

SEX, DRUGS AND DEMOCRACY (Barclay Powers Prods.) Producers/Screenplay, Barclay Powers, Jonathan Blank; Director/Photography/Editor, Jonathan Blank; Music, Philip Foxman, others; Color; Not rated; 87 minutes; February release. Documentary exploring the Netherlands' liberal attitudes on sex, drugs, and capital punishment, among other things.

JUST CAUSE (Lee Rich Prods./Fountainbridge Films) Producers, Lee Rich, Arne Glimcher, Steve Perry; Executive Producer, Sean Connery; Director, Arne Glimcher; Screenplay, Jeb Stuart, Peter Stone; Based on the novel by John Katzenbach; Photography, Lajos Koltai; Designer, Patrizia Von Brandenstein; Editor, William Anderson; Costumes, Ann Roth, Gary Jones; Music, James Newton Howard; Co-Producers, Gary Foster, Anna Reinhardt; a Lee Rich production in association with Fountainbridge Films, distributed by WB; Dolby Stereo; Panavision; Technicolor; Rated R; 105 minutes; February release. **CAST:** Sean Connery (Paul Armstrong), Laurence Fishburne (Tanny Brown), Kate Capshaw (Laurie Armstrong), Blair Underwood (Bobby Earl), Ed Harris (Blair Sullivan), Christopher Murray (Wilcox), Ruby Dee (Evangeline), Scarlett Johansson (Kate), Daniel J. Travanti (Warden), Ned Beatty (McNair), Liz Torres (Delores), Lynne Thigpen (Ida Conklin), Taral Hicks (Lena), Victor Slezak (Sgt. Rogers), Kevin McCarthy (Phil Prentiss), Hope Lange (Libby Prentiss), Chris Sarandon (Lyle Morgan), George Plimpton (Elder Phillips), Brooke Alderson (Dr. Doliveau), Colleen Fitzpatrick (Prosecutor), Richard Liberty (Chaplin), Joel E. Ehrenkranz (Judge), Barbara Jean Kane (Joanie Shriver), Maurice Jamaal Brown (Tanny's Son), Patrick Maycock, Jordan F. Vaughn (Kids Washing Car), Francisco Paz (Concierge), Marie Hyman (Clerk), S. Bruce Wilson (Party Guest), Erik Stephan (Student), Melanie Hughes (Receptionist), Megan Meinardus, Melissa Hood-Julien, Jenna Del Buono, Ashley Popelka, Marisa Perry, Ashley Council, Augusta Lunsgaard (Slumber Party Girls), Connie Lee Brown, Clarence Lark III (Prison Guards), Monte St. James, Gary Landon Mills, Shareef Malnik, Tony Bolano, Angelo Maldonado, Fausto Rodriguez (Prisoners), Karen Leeds, Dan Romero, Donn Lamkin, Stacie A. Zinn (Reporters)

THE HUNTED (Universal) Producers, John Davis, Gary W. Goldstein; Executive Producer, William Fay; Director/Screenplay, J.F. Lawton; Photography, Jack Conroy; Designer, Phil Dagort; Editors, Robert A. Ferretti, Eric Strand; Costumes, Rita Riggs; Music, Motofumi Yamaguchi; Casting, Karen Rea, Doreen Lane; Stunt Fight Coordinator, Tom Muzila; a co-presentation of Bergman/Baer of a Davis Entertainment Company production; DTS Stereo; Deluxe color; Rated R; 110 minutes; February release. **CAST:** Christopher Lambert (Paul Racine), John Lone (Kinjo), Joan Chen (Kirina), Yoshio Harada (Takeda), Yoko Shimada (Mieko), Mari Natsuki (Junko), Tak Kubota (Oshima), Masumi Okada (Lt. Wadakura), Tatsuya Irie (Hiryu), Hideyo Amamoto (Mr. Motogi), Michael Warren (Chase), Bart Anderson (John), James Saito (Nemura), Seth Sakai (Dr. Otozo Yamura), Toshishiro Obata (Ryuma), Ken Kensei (Sujin), Hiroyasu Takagi (Misato), Michio Itano (Sumato), Jason Furukawa (Bartender), Naoko Sasaki (Officer Naoko), Warren Takeuchi (Officer at Hospital), Dean Choe (Ninja #1), Victor Kimura (Medical Technician), Iris Salmon (Surgeons), Hisami Kaneta (Nurse), Anthony Towe (Fumio), Kuniharu Tamura (Noraki), Tony Lung (Detective), Reina Reyes (Small Girl), Hiroshi Nakatsuka (Taxi Driver), Jay Ono (Train Controllman), Hiro Kanagawa (Lieutenant), Mercedes Tang (Mistress), Ryoto Sakata (Officer on Train), Ken Shimizu (Rookie), Sumi Mutoh (Sumi), Chieko Sugano (Dancer)

BOYS ON THE SIDE (Le Studio Canal+/Regency Enterprises/Alcor Films) Producers, Arnon Milchan, Steven Reuther, Herbert Ross; Executive Producers, Don Roos, Patricia Karlan; Director, Herbert Ross; Screenplay, Don Roos; Co-Producer, Patrick McCormick; Photography, Donald E. Thorin; Designer, Ken Adam; Editor, Michael R. Miller; Music, David Newman; Costumes, Gloria Gresham; Songs performed by Whoopi Goldberg: "Piece of My Heart" (Jerry Rogovoy, Bert Burns), "Superstar" (Leon Russell, Bonnie Bramlett), "You Got It" (Jeff Lynne, Roy Orbison, Tom Petty); Casting, Hank McCann; a Le Studio Canal+. Regency Enterprises and Alcor Films presentation of a New Regency/Hera production, distributed by WB; Dolby Digital Stereo;

Panavision; Technicolor; Rated R; 115 minutes; February release. **CAST:** Whoopi Goldberg (Jane DeLuca), Mary-Louise Parker (Robin Nickerson), Drew Barrymore (Holly), Matthew McConaughey (Abe Lincoln), James Remar (Alex), Billy Wirth (Nick), Anita Gillette (Elaine), Dennis Boutsikaris (Massarelli), Estelle Parsons (Louise), Amy Aquino (Anna), Stan Egi (Henry), Stephen Gevedon (Johnny Figgis), Amy Ray, Emily Saliers (Indigo Girls), Jude Ciccolella (Jerry), Gede Watanabe (Steve), Jonathan Seda (Pete), Mimi Toro (Carrie), Lori Alan (Girl with Attitude), Mary Ann McGarry (Dr. Newbauer), Michael Storm (Tommy), Danielle Shuman (Young Robin), Julian Neil (Nightclub Owner), Niecy Nash (Woman at Diner),Ted Zerkowski (Drug Buyer), Jill Klein (Waitress), Marnie Crossen (Nurse), Aaron Lustig (Judge), Terri White (Guard), George Georgiadis (Cab Driver), Cheryl A. Kelly (Hotel Clerk), Adria Contreras (Mary Todd—5 months), Malika Edwards (Mary Todd—10 months), Pablo Espinosa, Kevin La Presle (New Mexico Police), Dr. John F. Manfredonia (Obstetrician), Dr. James Shuffield (Gynecologist), Thomas Kevin Danaher, Richard Lowell McDole (Tucson Police), Don Hewitt, Andy Duppin (Tow Trucker Drivers), Alan Mirikitani, Joe Pyles, Worthy Davis, Stephen Gevedon (Jane's Band), Josh Segal, Breta La Von , Patrice Jones, Tito Larriva, Gary Montemer (Indigo Girls' Band), Vernon Francisco, Fidelis Manuel, Sylvester Oliver, Bendict Martinez (Desert Suns Band), New Kiva Motions Puppet Theatre Inc. (Day of the Dead Dancers & Puppeteers), Ballet Folklorico Azteca (Folkloric Dancers)

MARTHA & ETHEL (Sony Pictures Classics) Producers/Screenplay, Jyll Johnstone, Barbara Ettinger; Director, Jyll Johnstone; Photography, Joseph Friedman; Editor, Toby Shimin; Color; Rated G; 80 minutes; February release. Documentary by narrators Jyll Johnstone and Barbara Ettinger examining their nannies Martha Kneifel and Ethel Edwards

Joan Chen, Christopher Lambert in *The Hunted*
© Universal City Studios

THE WALKING DEAD (Savoy) Producers, George Jackson, Douglas McHenry, Frank Price; Director/Screenplay, Preston A. Whitmore, II; Photography, John L. Demps, Jr.; Designer, George Costello; Editors, Don Brochu, William C. Carruth; Costumes, Ileane Meltzer; Music, Gary Chang; Casting, Jaki Brown-Karman, Kimberly Kardin; Co-Producer, Bill Carraro; a Price Entertainment/Jackson-McHenry production presented in association with Rank Film Distributors; Dolby Digital Stereo; Technicolor; Rated R; 90 minutes; February release. **CAST:** Allen Payne (Pfc. Cole Evans), Eddie Griffin (Pvt. Hoover Branche), Joe Morton (Sgt. Barkley), Vonte Sweet (Pfc. Joe Brooks), Roger Floyd (Cpl. Pippens), Ion Overman (Shirley Evans), Kyley Jackman (Sandra Evans), Bernie Mac (Ray), Jean Lamarre (Pvt. Earl Anderson), Lena Sang (Barbara Jean), Wendy Raquel Robinson (Celeste), Dana Point (Edna), Doil Williams (Harold), Damon Jones (2nd Lt. Duffy), Kevin Jackson (Deuce), Vivienne Sendaydiego (Vietnamese Woman), Hank Stone (1st Sgt. Hall), Velma Thompson (Brenda), Wilmer Calderon (Angelo), Carlos Joshua Agrait (Carlos), Frank Price (Mr. Dutkiewicz), Susan Ursitti (Ms. Glusac), Sharon Parra (Zarla), Frank Eugene Matthews, Jr. (Mr. Lake), Joshua Armstrong (Marine Recruiter), Terrence King (Brenda's Lover), Nicole Avant (Rhonda), Lisa Walker (Pippen's Girlfriend)

THE KKK BOUTIQUE AIN'T JUST REDNECKS (Public Theatre/Independent) Producers/Directors/Screenplay, Camille Billops, James V. Hatch; Photography, Dion Hatch; Editor, S.A. Burns; Music, George Brooker, Christa Victoria; Color; Not rated; 76 minutes; March release. Satirical documentary.

Allen Payne, Joe Morton, Vonte Sweet, Eddie Griffin in *The Walking Dead* © Savoy Pictures

OUTBREAK (Arnold Kopelson/Punch Prods.) Producers, Arnold Kopelson, Wolfgang Petersen, Gail Katz; Executive Producers, Duncan Henderson, Anne Kopelson; Co-Producers, Stephen Brown, Nana Greenwald, Sanford Panitch; Director, Wolfgang Petersen; Screenplay, Laurence Dworet, Robert Roy Pool; Photography, Michael Ballhaus; Designer, William Sandell; Music, James Newton Howard; Editors, Neil Travis, Lynzee Klingman, William Hoy; Costumes, Erica Edell Phillips; Casting, Jane Jenkins, Janet Hirshenson; an Arnold Kopelson production in association with Punch Productions, Inc., distributed by WB; Dolby Stereo; Technicolor; Rated R; 127 minutes; March release. **CAST:** Dustin Hoffman (Sam Daniels), Rene Russo (Robby Keough), Morgan Freeman (Gen. Billy Ford), Kevin Spacey (Casey Schuler), Cuba Gooding, Jr. (Maj. Salt), Donald Sutherland (Gen. Donald McClintock), Patrick Dempsey (Jimbo Scott), Zakes Mokae (Dt. Benjamin Iwabi), Malick Bowens (Dr. Raswani), Susan Lee Hoffman (Dr. Lisa Aronson), Benito Martinez (Dr. Julio Ruiz), Bruce Jarchow (Dr. Mascelli), Leland Hayward, III (Henry Seward), Daniel Chodos (Rudy Alvarez), Dale Dye (Col. Briggs), Cara Keough (Kate Jeffries), Gina Menza (Mrs. Jeffries), Per Didrik Fasmer (Mr. Jeffries), Michelle Joyner (Sherry Mauldin), Donald Forrest (Mack Mauldin), Julie Pierce (Erica Mauldin), Tim Ransom (Tommy Hull), Michelle M. Miller (Darla Hull), Maury Sterling (Sandman One), Michael Emanuel (Sandman One Co-Pilot), Lucas Dudley (Viper One Pilot), Robert Alan Joseph (Viper Two Pilot), Joseph Latimore (Viper Two Co-Pilot), Michael Sottile (Gunner Pilot), Ed Beechner (Gunner), Matthew Saks (Sergeant Wolf), Diana Bellamy (Mrs. Pananides), Lance Kerwin (American Mercenary), Brett Oliver (Belgian Mercenary), Eric Mungai Nguku (African Nurse), Larry Hine (Young McClintock), Nickolas H. Marshall (Young Ford), Douglas Hebron (Ju-Ju Man), Jae Woo Lee (Korean Captain), Derek Kim (Seaman Chulso Lee), Bill Stevenson (Biotest Guard), Kellie Overbey (Alice), Dana Andersen (Corinne), Patricia Place (Mrs. Foote), Nicholas Pappone (Little Boy on Plane), Traci Odom (Little Boy's Mother), Herbert Jefferson, Jr., Thomas Crawford, Buzz Barbee (Boston Doctors), Jenna Byrne (Tracy), Brian Reddy (Tracy's Father), Ina Romeo (Mrs. Logan), Teresa Velarde (Nurse Emma), J.J. Chaback (Nurse Jane), Carmela Rappazzo (Hospital Receptionist), Kurt Boesen (Mayor Gaddis), Jack Rader (Police Chief Fowler), Robert Rigamonte (County Health Official), Mimi Doyka (Frightened Mother), C. Jack Robinson (Biotest Manager), Robert Alan Beuth (George Armistead), Gordon Michaels (Man in Line), Peter Looney (White House Counsel), Conrad Bachmann (California Governor), Cary J. Pitts (Anchorman), Cynthia Harrison (Co-Anchor), Marcus Hennessy (Station Manager), Albert Owens (Broadcast Director), David Silverbrand (TV Reporter), Julie Araskog (Janet Adams), Frank Rositani (Senator Rosales), George Christy (Senator), Bruce Isacson (Jaffe), Marilyn Brandt (Ford's Secretary), Philip Handy (Sergeant Meyer), Tim Frazee, Moses Williams, Roland Tsui, Keith Butler, David Lee Phillips (MPs), Ralph Miller, Mark Drown (Officers), Jim Antonio (Dr. Drew Reynolds), J.T. Walsh

Tony Todd, Veronica Cartwright, in *Candyman: Farewell to the Flesh*
© Gramercy Pictures

CANDYMAN: FAREWELL TO THE FLESH (Gramercy) Producers, Sigurjon Sighvatsson, Gregg D. Fienberg; Executive Producer/Story, Clive Barker; Director, Bill Condon; Screenplay, Rand Ravich, Mark Kruger; Photography, Tobias Schliessler; Designer, Barry Robison; Editor, Virginia Katz; Music, Philip Glass; Costumes, Bruce Finlayson; Casting, Carol Lewis; Special Effects, Ultimate Effects; a PolyGram Filmed Entertainment Presentation; Dolby Stereo; Deluxe color; Rated R; 99 minutes; March release. **CAST:** Tony Todd (Candyman), Kelly Rowan (Annie Tarrant), Timothy Carhart (Paul McKeever), Veronica Cartwright (Octavia), William O'Leary (Ethan Tarrant), Fay Hauser (Pam Carver), Joshua Gibran Mayweather (Matthew), Matt Clark (Thibideaux), Bill Nunn (Rev. Ellis), Caroline Barclay (Caroline Sullivan), Michael Bergeron (Coleman Tarrant), Brianna Blanchard (Young Caroline), Clotiel Bordeltier (Liz), Russell Buchanan (Voice of Kingfish), Nate Bynum, Daniel Dupont, Monica L. Monica (Reporters), Sandy Byrd, Patricia Sansone (Women in Bookstore), Eric Cadora (Man in Bookstore), Carl N. Ciafalio (Bartender), Michael Culkin (Phillip Purcell), Stephen Dunn, Brian Joseph Moore (Thugs), David Gianopoulos (Det. Ray Levesque), Glen Gomez (Kingfish), Steven Hartman (Young Boy), Margaret Howell (Clara), Ralph Joseph (Mr. Jeffries), Erin Labranche (Little Girl Doctor), Carl LeBlanc (Little Boy King), George Lemore (Drew), Maria Mason (Befuddled Teacher), Randy Oglesby (Heyward Sullivan), Steve Picerni (Police Guard), Eric Pierson (Ben the Busboy), Terrence Rosemore (Suspicious Man at Matthew's House), Amy Ryder (Hostile Woman at Cabrini Green), Hunt Scarritt (Scraggly Vagrant), Carol Sutton (Angry Woman at Matthew's House)

Lisa Morris, Robert Englund in *The Mangler*
© New Line Productions

THE MANGLER (New Line Cinema) Producer, Anant Singh; Executive Producers, Harry Alan Towers, Sudhir Pragjee, Sanjeev Singh, Helena Spring; Director, Tobe Hooper; Screenplay, Tobe Hooper, Stephen Brooks, Peter Welbeck; Based on the short story by Stephen King; Photography, Amnon Salomon; Designer, Dave Barkham; Editor, David Heitner; Music, Barrington Pheloung; Visual Effects Supervisor, Stephen Brooks; "The Mangler" Creator, William Hooper; Make-Up Effects, Scott Wheeler; a Distant Horizon and Filmex (Pty) Ltd. production in association with Allied Film productions; Dolby Digital Stereo; Technicolor; Rated R; 105 minutes; March release. **CAST:** Robert Englund (Bill Gartley), Ted Levine (John Hunton), Daniel Matmor (Mark Jackson), Jeremy Crutchley (Pictureman/Mortician), Vanessa Pike (Sherry Ouelette), Demetre Phillips (Stanner), Lisa Morris (Lin Sue), Vera Blacker (Mrs. Frawley), Ashley Hayden (Annette Gillian), Danny Keogh (Herb Diment), Ted Leplat (Dr. Ramos), Todd Jensen (Roger Martin), Sean Taylor (Derrick Gates), Gerrit Schoonhoven (Aaron Rodriguez), Nan Hamilton (Mrs. Ellenshaw), Adrian Waldron (Mr. Ellenshaw), Norman Coombes (Judge Bishop), Larry Taylor (Sheriff Hughes), Irene Frangs (Mrs. Smith), Megan Wilson (Ginny Jason), Odile Rault (Alberta), Ron Smerczak (Officer Steele)

Christine Lahti, Jeff Goldblum in *Hideaway*
© TriStar Pictures, Inc.

HIDEAWAY (TRISTAR) Producers, Jerry Baerwitz, Agatha Hanczakowski, Gimel Everett; Director, Brett Leonard; Screenplay, Andrew Kevin Walker, Neal Jimenez; Based on the novel by Dean R. Koontz; Photography, Gale Tattersall; Designer, Michael Bolton; Editor, B.J. Sears; Visual Effects Supervisor, Tim McGovern; Music, Trevor Jones; Casting, Amanda Mackey, Cathy Sandrich; an S/Q production; SDDS/Dolby Stereo; Super 35 Widescreen; Technicolor; Rated R; 103 minutes; March release. **CAST:** Jeff Goldblum (Hatch Harrison), Christine Lahti (Lindsey Harrison), Alicia Silverstone (Regina Harrison), Jeremy Sisto (Vassago), Alfred Molina (Dr. Jonas Nyebern), Rae Dawn Chong (Rose Orwetto), Kenneth Welsh (Det. Breech), Suzy Joachim (Dr. Kari Dovell), Shirley Broderick (Miss Dockridge), Tom McBeath (Morton Redlow), Joely Collins (Linda), Roger R. Cross (Harry), Michael McDonald (Young Cop), Don S. Davis (Dr. Martin), Rebecca Toolan (Doctor), Hiro Kanagawa (Nurse Nakamura), Jayme Knox (Mother of Baby), Norma Wick (TV Announcer), Michelle Skalnik, Gaetana Korbin (Victims), Tiffany Foster (Samantha), Mara Duronslet (Zoe), Iris Quinn Bernard (Jonas' Wife), Natasha Morley (Jonas' Daughter), Sarah Strange (Second Girlfriend)

BALLET (Zipporah Films) Producer/Director/Editor, Frederick Wiseman; Photography, John Davey; Color; Not rated; 170 minutes; March release. Documentary on the American Ballet Theatre with Agnes DeMille, Irina Koplokova, David Richardson, Michael Somes (Choreographers/Ballet Masters), Alessandra Ferri, Cynthia Harvey, Susan Jaffe, Christine Dunham, Julio Bocca, Wes Chapman (Principal Dancers)

BORN TO BE WILD (Outlaw/Fuji) Producers, Robert Newmyer, Jeffrey Silver; Executive Producer, Brian Reilly; Director, John Gray; Screenplay, John Bunzel, Paul Young; Story, Paul Young; Photography, Donald W. Morgan; Designer, Roy Forge Smith; Editor, Maryann Brandon; Music, Mark Snow; Costumes, Ingrid Ferrin; Associate Producer, Tony Gardner; Casting, Debi Manwiller;an Outlaw Production, presented in association with Fuji Entertainment, distributed by WB; Dolby Stereo; Technicolor; Rated PG; 100 minutes; March release. **CAST:** Wil

Horneff (Rick Heller), Jean Marie Barnwell (Lacey Carr) Helen Shaver (Margaret Heller), John C. McGinley (Max Carr), Marvin J. McIntyre (Bob—Paramedic), Peter Boyle (Gus Charnley), Gregory Itzin (Walter Mallinson), Titus Welliver (Sgt. Markle), Tom Wilson (Det. Lou Greenberg), Alan Ruck (Dan Woodley), Janet Carroll (Judge Billings), John Procaccino (Ed Price), Obba Babatunde (Interpreter), David Wingert (Gary James), John Pleshette (Donald Carr), Keith Swift (Dino), Michael MacRae (Country Store Cop), Bruce Wright (Jack Graham), David MacIntyre, Rob Cea (Charnley's Guards), John Billingsly (Daryl), Sarah Brooke (Lacey's Mom), Jordan Michelman (Lacey's Brother), Burton Gilliam (Dwayne), Troy Evans (Farmer), Sandra Lee Dejong (Farmer's Wife), Larry Albert (Plain Clothes Officer), Amy Scott (Burger Girl), Chad Lindberg (Burger Boss), Drake Collier (Anchorman), Monica Hart (Anchorwoman), Peter Abrahamson, Bill Barretta, Debbie Carrington, Don McLeod, Karen Malchus, Talia Paul (Gorilla Team), Don Brady (Search Cop), Doris Bloom (Country Store Cashier), Leif Tilden, Frank Welker, Danny Mann (Special Vocal Effects)

FOR BETTER OR WORSE (Columbia) Producer, David Rotman; Executive Producer/Screenplay, Jeff Nathanson; Director, Jason Alexander; Photography, Wayne Kennan; Designer, William Elliott; Editor, Michael Jablow; Music, Miles Goodman, featuring The Bobs; Costumes, Charmaine Nash Simmons; Casting, Mary Gail Artz, Barbara Cohen; from Castle Rock Entertainment; Dolby Stereo; Color; Rated PG-13; 100 minutes; March release. **CAST:** Jason Alexander (Michael Makeshift), Lolita Davidovich (Valeri Carboni), James Woods (Reggie Makeshift), Joe Mantegna (Stone), Robert Costanzo (Ranzier), Beatrice Arthur (Beverly Makeshift), Eda Reiss Merin (Rose), John Amos (Gray), Rob Reiner (Dr. Plotner), Haley Joe Osment (Danny), Tiffany Salerno (Cindy), Beau Gravitte (Bob), Una Damon (Bartender), Steven Wright (Cabbie), Jerry Adler (Morton Makeshift), Zoaunne LeRoy (Mrs. Gelder), Greg Lewis (Bank Manager), Rip Torn (Captain Cole), Ken Lerner (Sgt. Moss), Jonathan Penner, Daena Title (Cops), Kelly Wellman (Barbara Wellman), Lynne Felderman (Screaming Woman), Brian Herskowitz (Bakery Cart Man)

Alessandra Ferri in *Ballet*
© Zipporah Films

NINA TAKES A LOVER (Triumph) Producers, Jane Hernandez, Alan Jacobs; Executive Producers, Graeme Bretall, Shelby Notkin; Director/Screenplay, Alan Jacobs; Photography, Phil Parmet; Editor, John Nutt; Designer, Don De Fina; Music, Todd Boekelheide; Color; Rated R; 100 minutes; March release. **CAST:** Laura San Giacomo (Nina), Paul Rhys (Photographer), Michael O'Keefe (Journalist), Cristi Conway (Friend), Fisher Stevens (Paulie), Alan Lightner, Vincent Lars, Carter Collins (Caribbean Musicians), Michelle Koeppe (Shoe Store Assistant), Marianna Åström-De Fina (Customer)

Paul Rhys, Laura San Giacomo in *Nina Takes a Lover*
© Triumph Releasing

MAJOR PAYNE (Universal) Producers, Eric L. Gold, Michael Rachmil; Executive Producers, Damon Wayans, Harry Tatelman; Director, Nick Castle; Screenplay, Dean Lorey, Damon Wayans, Gary Rosen; Based on a story by Joe Connelly & Bob Mosher, and the screenplay for the 1955 film *The Private War of Major Benson* by William Roberts and Richard Alan Simmons; Photography, Richard Bowen; Designer, Peter Larkin; Editor, Patrick Kennedy; Co-Producer, Tracy Carness; Music, Craig Safan; Casting, Aleta Chappelle; a Wife 'n Kids production; DTS Stereo; Deluxe color; Rated PG-13; 97 minutes; March release. **CAST:** Damon Wayans (Major Benson Winifred Payne), Karyn Parsons (Dr. Emily Walburn), Stephen Martini (Cadet Alex Stone), Andrew Harrison Leeds (Cadet Dotson), Joda Blaire-Hershman (Cadet Bryan), Steven Coleman (Cadet Leland), Damien Wayans (Cadet Williams), Chris Owen (Cadet Wuliger), Orlando Brown (Cadet Tiger), R. Stephen Wiles (Cadet Heathcoat), Mark M. Madison (Cadet Fox), Michael Ironside (Lt. Col. Stone), William Hickey (Dr. Phillips), Albert Hall (Gen. Decker), Rodney P. Barnes (Weight Lifter), Peyton Chesson Fohl (Cadet Johnson), Ross Bickell (Col. Braggart), Scott "Bam Bam" Bigelow (Huge Biker), Mark Conway (Police Sgt.), David DeHart (Wellington Cadet Captain), Joshua Todd Diveley (New Cadet), Robert Faraoni, Jr. (Smart-Ass Soldier), Michael Gabel (Lt. Wiseman), R.J. Knoll (Blind Kid), Dean Lorey (Mr. Shipman), Mark W. Madison (Cadet Fox), Brad Martin (MP), Seymour Swan (Soldier), Leonard Thomas (Bleeding Soldier), Hechter Ubarry (Guerilla Leader), Carolyn L.A. Walker (Woman), Tommy Wiles (Cadet), Christopher James Williams (Marksman)

Damon Wayans, Stephen Martini in *Major Payne*
© Universal City Studios

Max Elliott Slade, Chad Power, Michael Treanor in *3 Ninjas Knuckle Up*
© TriStar Pictures, Inc.

3 NINJAS KNUCKLE UP (TriStar) Producer, Martha Chang; Executive Producer, James Kang; Director, Simon S. Sheen; Screenplay, Alex S. Kim; Photography, Eugene Shlugleit; Designer, Don Day; Editor, Pam Choules; Costumes, Scillia A. Hernandez; Music, Gary Stevan Scott; Casting, Gary Oberst; a Sheen production; Dolby Stereo; Foto-Kem color; Rated PG-13; 85 minutes; March release. **CAST:** Victor Wong (Grandpa), Charles Napier (Jack), Michael Treanor (Rocky), Max Elliott Slade (Colt), Chad Power (Tum Tum), Crystle Lightning (Jo), Patrick Kilpatrick (J.J.), Donald L. Shanks (Charlie), Sheldon Peters Wolfchild (Lee), Nickolas G. Ramus (Chief Roundcreek), Pat Van Ingen (Granny), Donald Logue (Jimmy), Scott MacDonald (Eddy), Vincent Schiavelli (Mayor), Selina Jayne (Jo's Mother), Kait Lyn Mathews (Theresa), Don Stark (Sheriff), Dennis Holahan (EPA Man), Michael Hungerford (Truck Driver), Cathy Perry (Reporter), Wayne Collins Jr., Jamie Melissa Gunderson, Danuel Pipoly, Amanda Nicole Power (Kids), Erin Treanor (Pizza Parlor Girl), Gary Epper, Eric Mansker (Bikers), Ted Pitsis (Town Man), Stuart "Proud Eagle" Grant, Jeff Cadiente (Indians)

THE PEBBLE AND THE PENGUIN (MGM) Producer, Russell Boland; Executive Producer, James Butterworth; Screenplay, Rachel Koretsky, Steve Whitestone; Music, Mark Watters; Songs, Barry Manilow, Bruce Sussman; Layout Supervisor, Edward Gribbin; Supervising Editor, Thomas V. Moss; Designer, David Goetz; a Don Bluth Limited Film; DTS Stereo; Technicolor; Rated G; 74 minutes; April release. **VOICE CAST:** Shani Wallis (Narrator), Scott Bullock (Chubby/Gentoo), Martin Short (Hubie), Annie Golden (Marina), Louise Vallance (Priscilla/Chinstrap 2), Pat Musick (Pola/Chinstrap 1), Angeline Ball (Gwynne/Chinstrap 3), Kendall Cunningham (Timmy), Alissa King (Petra), Michael Nunes (Beany), Tim Curry (Drake), Neil Ross (Scrawny), Philip Clarke (King), B.J. Ward, Hamilton Camp (Magellenics), Will Ryan (Royal/Tika), Stanley Jones (McCallister), James Belushi (Rocko)

BLESSING (Starr Valley) Producers, Melissa Powell, Paul Zehrer; Executive Producer, Christopher A. Cuddihy; Director/Screenplay, Paul Zehrer; Photography, Stephen Kazmierski; Designer, Steve Rosenzweig;

Hubie, Rocko in *The Pebble and the Penguin*
© Metro-Goldwyn-Mayer/Invicom Ltd.

Carlin Glynn in *Blessing*
© Starr Valley Films

Editors, Andrew Morreale, Paul Zehrer; Music, Joseph S. DeBeasi; Color; Not rated; 90 minutes; April release. **CAST:** Melora Griffis (Randi), Carlin Glynn (Arlene), Guy Griffis (Jack), Clovis Siemon (Clovis), Gareth Williams (Lyle), Randy Sue Latimer (Fran), Tom Carey (Snuff), Frank Taylor (Early)

FUN (Independent/Film Forum) Producer/Director, Rafael Zelinsky; Screenplay, James Bosley, based on his play; Photography, Jens Sturup; Music, Marc Tschanz; Color; Not rated; 105 minutes; April release. **CAST:** Alicia Witt (Bonnie), Renée Humphrey (Hillary), William R. Moses (John), Leslie Hope (Jane), Ania Suli (Mrs. Farmer)

REFLECTIONS IN THE DARK (Concorde) Producers, Gwen Field, Barbara Klein, Alida Camp; Executive Producers, Roger Corman, Mike Elliott, Lance H. Robbins; Director/Screenplay, Jon Purdy; Foto-Kem color; Rated R; 95 minutes; April release. **CAST:** Mimi Rogers (Regina), Billy Zane (Colin Reeves), John Terry (Terry), Kurt Fuller (Howard), Lee Garlington (Tina), Nancy Fish (Ellen), Frank Birney (Doctor), Adrienne Regard (Lynn Meyers), Ina Parker (Prison Matron), Alain Ohanian (Daniel)

DESTINY TURNS ON THE RADIO (Savoy) Producer, Gloria Zimmerman; Executive Producers, Keith Samples, Peter Martin Nelson; Director, Jack Baran; Screenplay, Robert Ramsey, Matthew Stone; Co-Producers, Robert Ramsey, Matthew Stone, Raquel Carreras; Photography, James Carter; Designer, Jean-Philippe Carp; Editor, Raul Davalos; Costumes, Beverly Klein; Music, Steve Soles; Casting, Nicole Arbusto, Joy Dickson; a Rysher Entertainment presentation; Dolby Digital Stereo; CFI color; Rated R; 102 minutes; April release. **CAST:** James LeGros (Thoreau), Dylan McDermott (Julian Goddard), Quentin Tarantino (Destiny), Nancy Travis (Lucille), James Belushi (Tuerto), Janet Carroll (Escabel), David Cross (Ralph Dellaposa), Richard Edson (Gage), Bobcat Goldthwait (Mr. Smith), Barry "Shabaka" Henley (Dravec), Lisa Jane Persky (Katrina), Sarah Trigger (Francine), Tracey Walter (Pappy), Allen Garfield (Vinnie Vidivici), Ralph Brannen, Robert Sparks (Henchmen), Gordon Michaels (Motorist), Che Lujan (Jose), Michael O'Connell (Stage

Renee Humphrey, Alicia Witt in *Fun*

Nancy Travis, Dylan McDermott in *Destiny Turns on the Radio*
© Rysher Entertainment

Liu Liu (l) in *Moving the Mountain*
© October Films

Gordon Michaels (Motorist), Che Lujan (Jose), Michael O'Connell (Stage Manager), Michael Matthys (Lighting Technician)

TRUE BELIEVERS: THE MUSICAL FAMILY OF ROUNDER RECORDS (Dakin Film) Producer/Director/Editor, Robert Mugge; Executive Producer, David Steffen; Photography, Bill Burke; a Mug-Shot production; Color; Not rated; 86 minutes; April release. Documentary on the independent record company, Rounder Records, and some of their musical acts.

JURY DUTY (TriStar) Producers, Yoram Ben-Ami, Peter M. Lenkov; Director, John Fortenberry; Screenplay, Neil Tolkin, Barbara Williams, Samantha Adams; Story, Barbara Williams, Samantha Adams; Co-Producers, Stephen L. Bernstein, Richard M. Heller; Line Producer, Udi Nedivi; Photography, Avi Karpick; Editor, Stephen Semel; Designers, Deborah Raymond, Dorian Vernaccio; Music, David Kitay; Costumes, Terry Dresbach; Casting, Ferne Cassell; a Triumph Films presentation in association with Weasel Productions Inc.; Dolby Digital Stereo; Technicolor; Rated PG-13; 86 minutes; April release. CAST: Pauly Shore (Tommy Collins), Tia Carrere (Monica Lewis), Stanley Tucci (Frank), Brian Doyle-Murray (Harry), Abe Vigoda (Judge Powell), Charles Napier (Jed), Richard Edson (Skeets), Richard Riehle (Principal Beasely), Alex Datcher (Sarah), Richard T. Jones (Nathan), Sharon Barr (Libby Starling), Jack McGee (Murphy), Nick Bakay (Richard Hertz), Ernie Lee Banks (Ray), Shelley Winters (Mrs. Collins), Dick Vitale (Hal Gibson), Billie Bird (Rose), Jorge Luis Abreu (Jorge), Siobhan Fallon (Heather), Gregory Cooke (Reece Fishburn), Mark L. Taylor (Russell Cadbury), Sean Whalen (Carl Wayne Bishop), Laurelyn Scharkey (Harry's Bombshell), Steven Hy Landau (Tuna Salad Guy), Melissa Samuels (Club Announcer), Paul Stork (Transvestite), William Newman (Judge D'Angelo), Susan Lentini (Judge Swartz), Tom Booker (Press Runner), Jay Kogen (Russell's Assistant), Paul Thorpe (Goliath), Michael Reid Mackay (Steer Shack Employee), David McMillan (Friendly Falafel Employee), Saemi Nakamura (Wiener Boy Employee), Efren Ramirez (Pirate Pete's Employee), J.D. Hall, Bruce Economou (Guards), Lynn Ziegler (Mrs. Woodall), Yolanda Miro (Spanish Reporter), Y. Hero Abe (Japanese Reporter), Michael Feresten (Folk Singer), Fritz Mashimo (Japanese Suicide Man), George Christy (Dr. Brookings), Gizmo (Peanut)

MOVING THE MOUNTAIN (October) Producer, Trudie Styler; Director, Michael Apted; Photography, Maryse Alberti; Editor, Susanne Rostock; Music, Liu Sola; a Xingu Films presentation; Color; Not rated; 83 minutes; April release. Documentary on Beijing students involved in China's Tiananmen Square massacre, with Li Lu, Wang Dan, Wang Chaohua, Wu'er Kaixi, Chai Ling.

A PYROMANIAC'S LOVE STORY (Hollywood Pictures) Producer, Mark Gordon; Co-Producers, Allison Lyon Segan, Barbara Kelly; Director, Joshua Brand; Screenplay, Morgan Ward; Photography, John Schwartzman; Designer, Dan Davis; Editor, David Rosenbloom; Costumes, Bridget Kelly; Music, Rachel Portman; Casting, Amanda Mackey, Cathy Sandrich; Distributed by Buena Vista Pictures; Dolby Stereo; Color; Rated PG; 94 minutes; April release. **CAST:** William Baldwin (Garet Lumpke), John Leguizamo (Sergio Cuccio), Sadie Frost (Hattie), Erika Eleniak (Stephanie), Michael Lerner (Perry), Joan Plowright (Mrs. Linzer), Armin Mueller-Stahl (Mr. Linzer), Mike Sarr (Sgt. Žikowski), Julio Oscar Mechoso (Jerry), Floyd Vivino (Ass Pincher), Babz Chula (Ass Pincher's Wife), Tony Perri (Man in Car), Randy Butcher (Driver), Lesley Kelly (Jail Police Woman/Desk Officer), Jennifer Roblin (Maid), Elena Kudaba (Mrs. Olden), Michael McCullough (Bartender), Derrick Patterson, Rob Wilson (Men in Bar), Louis Strauss (Old Man), Phillip Williams (Officer in Car), Ann Holloway (Nurse), Gene Mack (Police Officer), Jonathan Allora (Man at Party), Michael Tait (Mr. Potts), Barbara Franklin (Garden Party Woman), Doug Hoyle (Biker), Richard Crenna (Mr. Lumpke)

Pauly Shore, Tia Carrere, Stanley Tucci in *Jury Duty*
© TriStar Pictures, Inc.

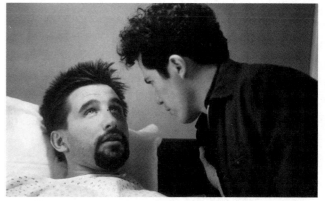

William Baldwin, John Leguizamo in *A Pyromaniac's Love Story*
© Buena Vista Pictures Distribution, Inc.

177

Reno, Chuck Norris in *Top Dog*
© Live Entertainment

Gordy, Kristy Young in *Gordy*
© Miramax Films

TOP DOG (MGM/UA) Producer, Andy Howard; Executive Producers, Tom Steinmetz, Seth Willenson; Director, Aaron Norris; Screenplay, Ron Swanson; Photography, Joao Fernandes; Designer, Norm Baron; Editor, Peter Schink; Costumes, Vernika Flower-Crow; a Live Entertainment presentation of a Tanglewood Entertainment Group production; Dolby Stereo; Foto-Kem color; Rated PG-13; 85 minutes; April release. **CAST:** Chuck Norris (Jake Wilder), Clyde Kusatsu (Capt. Callahan), Michele Lamar Richards (Savannah Boyette), Peter Savard Moore (Karl Koller), Erik von Detten (Matthew Swanson), Carmine Caridi (Lou Swanson), Herta Ware (Jake's Mother), Kai Wulff (Otto Dietrich), Francesco Quinn (Mark Curtains), Timothy Bottoms (Nelson Houseman), Reno (Himself)

A LITTLE PRINCESS (Baltimore Pictures) Producer, Mark Johnson; Executive Producers, Alan C. Blomquist, Amy Ephron; Director, Alfonso Cuaron;Screenplay,Richard LaGravenese, Elizabeth Chandler; Based on the novel by Frances Hodgson Burnett; Photography, Emmanuel Lubezki; Designer, Bo Welch; Editor, Steven Weisberg; Music, Patrick Doyle; Costumes, Judianna Makovsky; Co-Producer, Dalisa Cohen; Casting, Jill Greenberg Sands; a Mark Johnson/Baltimore Pictures production, distributed by WB; Dolby Stereo; Technicolor; Rated G; 97 minutes; May release. **CAST:** Eleanor Bron (Miss Minchin), Liam Cunningham (Captain Crewe/Prince Rama), Liesel Matthews (Sara Crewe), Rusty Schwimmer (Amelia Minchin), Arthur Malet (Charles Randolph), Vanessa Lee Chester (Becky), Errol Sitahal (Ram Dass); School Girls: Heather DeLoach (Ermengarde),Taylor Fry (Lavinia), Darcie Bradford (Jesse), Rachael Bella (Betsy), Alexandra Rea-Baum (Gertrude), Camilla Belle (Jane), Lauren Blumenfeld (Rosemary), Kelsey Mulrooney (Lottie), Kaitlin Cullum (Ruth); Alison Moir (Princess Sita), Time Winters (Frances the Milkman), Lomax Study (Monsieur Dufarge), Vincent Schiavelli (Mr. Barrow), Pushpa Rawal (Maya), Rahi Azizi (Laki), Ken Palmer (John Randolph), Helen Greenberg (Flower Lady), Norman Merrill (Doctor in hospital), Peggy Miley (Mabel the Cook), Robert P. Cohen (Ermengarde's Father), William Blomquist (Rich Boy in street), David Fresco (Beggar Man in fantasy forest), Judith D. Drake (Bakery Woman), Chris Ellis (Policeman)

DIRTY MONEY (Northern Arts) Producer/Director, James Bruce; Co-Producer/Writer, Frederick Deane; Photography, Christian Faber, Rick DiGregorio, Michael Mayers; Music, Paul Barrere, Bill Payne; Editors, James Bruce, Robert Barrere; Costumes, Alexandra Welker; Color; Not rated; 82 minutes; May release. **CAST:** Frederick Deane (Sam Reed), Timothy Patrick Cavanaugh (Frank), Biff Yeagher (Tommy), Dagmar Stansova (Maria), Charmagne Eckert (Det. Walker), David Jean Thomas (Det. Stone), Jorge "Maromero" Paez (Jorge), Delauné Michele (Cece), Taylor Nichols (Herb), Larned Fowler (Jerry), Jennifer Fowler (Carol), Elizabeth Fowler (Lizze/Girl on Tricycle), Christian Faber (Gunstore Red Neck), Josephine Wallace (Hooker in black Mustang), Melissa Smith (Tough Girl on Train), Martin Slusser (TV Reporter), Popeye (Homeless Man in Park), Cesar Garcia (Bartender), John Luessenhop (Man in White Mustang), James Bruce (Beatnik in Train Station), David Snyder (Hotel Receptionist), Arturo Gonzalez (Det. Perez), Jorge Alberto (Officer Fuentes)

GORDY (Miramax) Producer, Sybil Robson; Director, Mark Lewis; Screenplay, Leslie Stevens; Story, Jay Sommers, Dick Chevillat; Co-Producer, Frederic Brost; Photography, Richard Michalak; Designer, Philip Messina; Editor, Lindsay Frazer; Music, Charles Fox; Costumes, Barcie Waite; Casting, Shari Rhodes; a Miramax Family Films presentation in association with RAS Entertainment Ltd.of a Robson Entertainment production; Color; Rated G; 89 minutes; May release. **CAST:** Doug Stone (Luke MacAllister), Kristy Young (Jinnie Sue MacAllister), Michael Roescher (Hanky Royce), Deborah Hobart (Jessica Royce), Ted Manson (Henry Royce), James Donadio (Gilbert Sipes), Tom Lester (Cousin Jake), Tom Key (Brinks)

AND THE EARTH DID NOT SWALLOW HIM (American Playhouse Theatrical Films) Producer, Paul Espinosa; Executive Producers, Lindsay Law, Paul Espinosa; Director/Screenplay, Severo Perez; Based on the novel by Tomas Rivera; Photography, Virgil Harper; Editor, Susan Heick; Music, Marcos Loya; Designer, Armin Ganz; Associate Producer/Casting, Bob Morones; a KPBS/Severo Perez production; Ultra-Stereo; Color; Not rated; 99 minutes; May release. **CAST:** Jose Alcala (Marcos), Daniel Valdez (Bartolo), Rose Portillo (Florentina), Marco Rodriguez (Joaquin), Lupe Ontiveros (Dona ROsa), Evelyn Guerrero (Lupita), Sam Vlahos (Don Cleto), Art Bonilla (Lalo), Sal Lopez (El Mohado), Miguel Rodriguez (Narrator)

RUNNING WILD (Independent) Producer/Director, Phillippe Blot; No other credits available; Color; Rated R; 91 minutes; May release. **CAST:** Jennifer Barker (Carlotta), Daniel Dupont, Daniel Spector

BATMAN FOREVER (Tim Burton Prod./DC Comics) Producers, Tim Burton, Peter MacGregor-Scott; Executive Producers, Benjamin Melniker, Michael E. Uslan; Director, Joel Schumacher; Screenplay, Lee Batchler, Janet Scott Batchler, Akiva Goldsman; Story, Lee Batchler, Janet Scott Batchler; Based upon Batman characters created by Bob Kane and published by DC Comics; Photography, Stephen Goldblatt; Designer, Barbara Ling; Music, Elliot Goldenthal; Editor, Dennis Virkler; Costumes, Bob Ringwood, Ingrid Ferrin; Visual Effects Supervisor, John Dykstra; Special Makeup Designer/Creator, Rick Baker; Casting, Mali Finn; a Tim Burton production, distributed by WB; Dolby SDDS Stereo; Technicolor;

Timothy Patrick Cavanaugh, Frederick Deane in *Dirty Money*
© Bruce Deane Productions

Rated PG-13; 121 minutes; June release. **CAST:** Val Kilmer (Batman/Bruce Wayne), Tommy Lee Jones (Harvey Two-Face/Harvey Dent), Jim Carrey (Riddler/Edward Nygma), Nicole Kidman (Dr. Chase Meridian), Chris O'Donnell (Robin/Dick Grayson), Michael Gough (Alfred Pennyworth), Pat Hingle (Commissioner Gordon), Drew Barrymore (Sugar), Debi Mazar (Spice), Elizabeth Sanders (Gossip Gerty), Rene Auberjonois (Dr. Burton), Joe Grifasi (Bank Guard), Ed Begley, Jr. (Fred Stickley), Philip Moon, Jessica Tuck (Newscasters), Dennis Paladino (Crime Boss Moroni), Kimberly Scott (Margaret), Michael Paul Chan (Executive), Jon Favreau (Assistant), Greg Lauren (Aide), Ramsey Ellis (Young Bruce Wayne), Michael Scranton (Thomas Wayne), Eileen Seeley (Martha Wayne), David U. Hodges (Shooter), Jack Betts (Fisherman), Tim Jackson (Municipal Police Guard), Daniel Reichert (Ringmaster), Glory Fioramonti (Mom Grayson), Larry A. Lee (Dad Grayson), Bruce Roberts (Handsome Reporter), George Wallace (Mayor), Bob Zmuda (Eletronic Store Owner), Rebecca Budig (Teenage Girl), Don "The Dragon" Wilson (Gang Leader), Sydney D. Minckler (Teen Gang Member), Maxine Jones, Terry Ellis, Cindy Herron, Dawn Robinson (Girls on corner), Gary Kasper (Pilot), Amanda Trees (Paparazzi Reporter), Andrea Fletcher (Reporter), Ria Coyne (Socialite), Jed Curtis (Chubby Businessman), William Mesnik (Bald Guy), Marga Gomez (Journalist), Kelly Vaughn (Showgirl), John Fink (Deputy), Noby Arden, Marlene Bologna, Danny Castle, Troy S. Wolfe (Trapeze Act), Christopher Caso, Gary Clayton, Oscar Dillon, Keith Graham, Kevin Grevioux, Mark A. Hicks, Corey Jacoby, Randy Lamb, Maurice Lamont, Sidney S. Liufau, Brad Martin, Deron McBee, Mario Mugavero, Joey Nelson, Jim Palmer, Robert Pavell, Peewee Piemonte, Peter Radon, Francois Rodriguez, Joe Sabatino, Mike Sabatino, Ofer Samra, Matt Sigloch, Mike Smith (Harvey's Thugs)

THE BRIDGES OF MADISON COUNTY (Amblin/Malpaso)
Producers, Clint Eastwood, Kathleen Kennedy; Director, Clint Eastwood; Screenplay, Richard LaGravenese; Based on the novel by Robert James Waller; Photography, Jack N. Green; Designer, Jeannine Oppewall; Editor, Joel Cox; Music, Lennie Niehaus; Costumes, Colleen Kelsall; Casting, Ellen Chenoweth; an Amblin/Malpaso production distributed by WB; Dolby Stereo; Panavision; Technicolor; Rated PG-13; 135 minutes; June release. **CAST:** Clint Eastwood (Robert Kincaid), Meryl Streep (Francesca Johnson), Annie Corley (Carolyn), Victor Slezak (Michael), Jim Haynie (Richard), Sarah Kathryn Schmitt (Young Carolyn), Christopher Kroon (Young Michael), Phyllis Lyons (Betty), Debra Monk (Madge), Richard Lage (Lawyer), Michelle Benes (Lucy Redfield), Alison Wiegert, Brandon Bobst (Children), Pearl Faessler (Wife), R.E. "Stick" Faessler (Husband), Tania Mishler, Billie McNabb (Waitresses), Art Breese (Cashier), Lana Schwab (Saleswoman), Larry Loury (UPS Driver)

WIGSTOCK: THE MOVIE (Samuel Goldwyn Co.)
Producers, Dean Silver, Marlen Hecht; Executive Producers, Klaus Volkenborn, Susan Ripps, Barry Shils; Co-Producers, David Sweeney, Tom Parziale; Director, Barry Shils; Photography, Wolfgang Held, Michael Barrow; Music, Peter Fish, Robert Reale; Editors, Marlen Hecht, Tod Scott Brody; Ultra-Stereo; Color; Not rated; 80 minutes; June release. Documentary on New York's annual drag festival, with RuPaul, Lypsinka, Crystal Waters, The "Lady" Bunny, Dee-Lite, Alexis Arquette, Jackie Beat, John Kelly, Mistress Formika

LIABILITY CRISIS (FilmHaus)
Executive Producer, Andrew Wilkes; Co-Executive Producers, Gregory Hatanaka, Dale Gasteiger; Director/Screenplay/Editor, Richard Brody; Photography, James Maxtone-Graham; Music, Francine Trester; a Wilkesfilms production; Color; Not rated; 78 minutes; June release. **CAST:** Mirjana Jokovic (Dunia), Jim Helsinger (Paul), Shari Meg Seidman (Wendy), R. Ward Duffy (Larry), Caren Alpert (Susie), Sylvia Weber (Mother), Sidney Annis (Father), Claudia Kaye (Woman on Train), Solomon Cobitt, Henry Steen, Mac Beers (Witnesses)

LIE DOWN WITH DOGS (Miramax)
Producers, Anthony Bennett, Wally White; Executive Producer, John Pierson; Director/Screenplay, Wally White; Photography, George Mitas; Art Director, Reno Dakota; Editor, Hart F. Faber; Associate Producers, Carijn Lau, Jennifer Ryan Cohen, Eli Kabillo; Color; Rated R; 84 minutes; June release. **CAST:** Wally White (Tommie), Randy Becker (Tom), Bash Halow (Guy), James Sexton (Eddie), Darren Dryden (Ben), Reno Dakota (Square Joe), Jonathan Pauldick, Anthony Bennett (Political Guys), Devin Quigley (Political Woman), Raymond Capuana, Dennis Davis, Eli Kabillio, Eddie Encarnacion (Dick Guys), Roberto H. Fantauzzi, Clifton Lively Jr., Mark

Daisy, Christy Love in *Wigstock: The Movie*
© The Samuel Goldwyn Company

Irish (Underwear and Sex Boys), Ricardo Angelico (Underwear Boy), Kevin Mayes (Toby), David Matwljkow (Charlie), Darren Anthony (Jose), Chester Hinsfield (Flyerman), Al Marz (Scalper), Nevada Belle (Church Lady), Christine Hull (Tourist Lady), J.D. Cerna (Peter & Sal), Hans Hoppenbrouwers (Dan), Nonny Kulecza (Bob), Hart F. Faber (Bob's Voice), Vann Jones (Glen & Herbert), Ty-Ranne Grimsted (Carmelota Pessums), Jack Hazan (Simon), Wendy Adams (Sally), Michel Richoz (Michi), Richard B. Olson (Jeffrey), Brian Quirk (Ru), Julie Wheeler (Prep-Girl), Kevin Shenk (Waitress), Scott James Jordan (Driver & Groper), Ken Bonnin (Chris), Denis Gawley, Paul Rex Pierson (Sex Boys), Jesus Cortez (Stripper), Tim McCarthy (Dorothy Stratten Killer), Carol McDonald (Margaret), Martha J. Cooney (Doctor), Rob Cardazone ("Trip"), Steve Lent (Benjamin), Charlie Fieran (Anthony), Deborah Auer (Dubbing)

THE PROS AND CONS OF BREATHING (Leisure Time)
Producer, Steve Hart; Director/Screenplay, Robert Munic; Photography, Steve Adcock; Designer, Donna Kaczmarek; Editor, Michael Waterhouse; a Chi-Boy production; Ultra-Stereo; Technicolor; Not rated; 89 minutes; June release. **CAST:** Joey Lauren Adams (Shirley), Phillip Brock (Tippy), Joey Dedeo (Tony), Ira Heiden (Bradley), Philip Tanzini (Troy), Barry Sobel (Ira), Noelle Parker (Canbi), Robert Munic (Homeless Vet)

BALLOT MEASURE 9 (Zeitgeist)
Producer/Director, Heather MacDonald; Photography, Ellen Hansen; Editors, Heather MacDonald, B.B. Jorissen; Music, Julian Dylan Russell, Sunny McHale Skyedancer, Linda and the Family Values; Color; Not rated; 72 minutes; June release. Documentary about the battle over Oregon's 1992 anti-gay ballot initiative, featuring Donna Red Wing, Kathleen Saadat, Scott Seibert, Jim Self, Elise Self, Cindy Patterson, Ann Sweet, Tom Potter, Lon Mabon, Bonnie Mabon, Scott Lively, Oren Camenish

RIFT (Curb Entertainment Intl.)
Producers, Gabriel Fischbarg, Edward S. Barkin, Tryan George; Director/Screenplay, Edward S. Barkin; Photography, Lee Daniel; Editor, Tryan George; Music, Tryan George, Eric Masunaga, Edward S. Barkin; Color; Not rated; 87 minutes; June release. **CAST:** William Sage (Tom), Timothy Cavanaugh (Bill), Jennifer Bransford (Lisa), Alan Davidson (Dr. Myron Messers)

Randy Becker (c) in *Lie Down with Dogs*
© Miramax Films

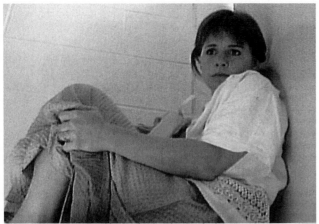

Jennifer Taylor in *The Crude Oasis*
© Miramax Films

THE WACKY ADVENTURES OF DR. BORIS AND NURSE SHIRLEY (Seventh Art) Producers, Liam Naughton, Paul Leder; Co-Producer, Vladek Juszkievicz; Director, Paul Leder; Screenplay, Liam Naughton; Photography, Francis Grumman; Music, Jan Castor; a Cordish Media presentation of a Poor Robert production; Color; Not rated; 84 minutes; June release. **CAST:** Paul Bartel (Dr. Boris), Karen Black (Evelyn), Mitch Hara (Nurse Shirley), Clive Revill (Morgenfeller)

THE CRUDE OASIS (Miramax) Producer/Director/Screenplay/Editor, Alex Graves; Photography, Steven Quale; Music, Steven Bramson; Art Director, Tom Mittlestadt; a Bluestream Films production; Dolby Stereo; Color; Rated R; 80 minutes; July release. **CAST:** Jennifer Taylor (Karen Webb), Aaron Shields (Harley Underwood), Robert Peterson (Jim Webb), Mussef Sibay (Earp), Lynn Bieler (Stone), Roberta Eaton (Cheri), Kirk Kinsinger (Radio Voice)

ROOSTERS (I.R.S.) Producers, Susan Block-Reiner, Norman I. Cohen; Executive Producers, Lindsay Law, Hans Brockman, Sandra Schulberg, Justin Ackerman; Director, Robert M. Young; Screenplay, Milcha Sanchez-Scott; Photography, Reynaldo Villalobos; Editor, Arthur Coburn; a KCET Theatrical Production, a presentation of American Playhouse Theatrical Films and WMG, in association with Olmos Productions; Color; Rated R; 95 minutes; July release. **CAST:** Edward James Olmos (Gallo), Sonia Braga (Juana), Maria Conchita Alonso (Chata), Danny Nucci (Hector), Mark Dacasco (Filipino's Son), Valente Rodriguez (Adan), Sarah Lassez (Angela), L. Ignacio Gameros (Priest), Arin Pasquel Real (ten-year-old Hector), Grace Keagy (Ms. Arganda), James Robert Lee (Filipino Father), Frank Soto (Abuelo), William Warren (Filipino's Friend), Maud Winchester (Waitress)

Danny Nucci, Edward James Olmos in *Roosters*
© I.R.S. Releasing

POSTCARDS FROM AMERICA (Strand) Producers, Craig Paull, Christine Vachon; Executive Producer, Mark Nash; Director/Screenplay, Steve McLean; Photography, Ellen Kuras; Designer, Therese Deprez; Editor, Elizabeth Gazzara; Music, Stephen Endelman; Costumes, Sara Slotnick; Casting, Daniel Haughey; an Islet Production in association with Channel Four Films; a Normal Production; Color; Not rated; 95 minutes; July release. **CAST:** James Lyons (Adult David), Michael Tighe (Teenage David), Olmo Tighe (Young David), Michael Imperioli (The Hustler), Michael Ringer (Father), Maggie Low (Mother), John Ventimiglia, David Strickland, Brad Hung, Jason Emard, Joe Marshall, Jeffrey Steele (The Drivers), Paul Germaine-Brown, Dick Gallahan, Dennis Carrig, John Corrigan, Steven Mark Friedman (The "Johns"), Les "Linda" Simpson (Trippy), Dean "Sissy Fit" Novotny (Porn Theatre Drag Queen), Tom Gilroy (Adult David's Friend), Peter Byrne (St. Sebastian), Bob Romano (Art Dealer), Danny Fass, Tony Urbina (The Porn Stars), Patti DiLeo, Maureen Goldfedder, Prudence Wright Holmes, Coco McPherson (Suburban Moms), Oona Brangam-Snell (Little Girl), Colin Blair Fisher (Young David's Friend), Rick Bolton (Uncle), Lane Burgess (Aunt), Zachary Asher Katz, Dimitri Strathas, Matthew Kuran (Little Boys), Joyce George (Ideal Mom), Jay Nickeron (Ideal Dad), Jonathan Turner, Les Gulino (David's Neighbors), Stephen M. Leach (Paperboy), Thom Milano (Policeman), Crosby Romberger (David's Brother), Allyson Anne Buckley (David's Sister), Augustus Goertz (Mugged Man), Todd Marsh (Son with AIDS)

Bob Romano, Michael Tighe in *Postcards from America*
© Strand Releasing

FREE WILLY 2: THE ADVENTURE HOME (Le Studio Canal+/Regency/Alcor) Producers, Lauren Shuler-Donner, Jennie Lew Tugend; Executive Producers, Richard Donner, Arnon Milchan, Jim Van Wyck; Director, Dwight Little; Screenplay, Karen Janszen, Corey Blechman, John Mattson; Co-Producer, Richard Solomon; Photography, Laszlo Kovacs; Designer, Paul Sylbert; Editors, Robert Brown, Dallas Puett; Music, Basil Poledouris; Costumes, Erica Edell Phillips; Casting, Judy Taylor, Lynda Gordon; a Shuler-Donner/Donner production, presented in association with Le Studio Canal+, Regency Enterprises and Alcor Films; Distributed by WB; Dolby SDDS Stereo; Panavision; Technicolor; Rated PG; 98 minutes; July release. **CAST:** Jason James Richter (Jesse), Francis Capra (Elvis), Mary Kate Schellhardt (Nadine), August Schellenberg (Randolph), Michael Madsen (Glenn), Jayne Atkinson (Annie), Mykelti Williamson (Dwight), Elizabeth Peña (Kate Haley), Jon Tenney (John Milner), Paul Tuerpe (Milner's Assistant), M. Emmet Walsh (Wilcox), John Considine (Comdr. Blake), Steve Kahan (Capt. Nilson), Neal Matarazzo (Helmsman Kelly), Al Sapienza, Wally Dalton, Cliff Fetters (Engineers), Julie Inouye, Basil Wallace, Janet Wu (Reporters), Doug Ballard, June Christopher (Veterinarians), Marguerite Moreau (Julie), Christina Orchid (Donut Shop Lady), Edward J. Rosen (Environmental Man), Isaac T. Arnett, Jr. (Camper), Scott Stuber (Policemen), Chanel Capra (Teenage Girl at Ferry), Laura Gary (Whale Spotter), John Harms, Susan Brooks, Jeff Brooks (Protesters)

SHE LIVES TO RIDE (Artistic License Films) Producer/Director/Editor, Alice Stone; Photography, Maryse Alberti; Music, Mason Daring; Color; Not rated; 75 minutes; July release. Documentary about women motorcyclists with Jo Giovannoni, Dot Robinson, Jacqui Sturgess, Becky Brown, Amy Berry

Duncan Hannah, Caitlin Grace McDonnell in *Art for the Teachers of Children* © Zeitgeist

Andrew McCarthy, Elizabeth Peña in *Dead Funny* © A-Pix Entertainment

UNDER SIEGE 2: DARK TERRITORY (Milchan-Seagal/Nasso/Regency) Producers, Steven Seagal, Steve Perry, Arnon Milchan; Executive Producers, Jeffrey Neuman, Martin Wiley, Gary Goldstein; Director, Geoff Murphy; Screenplay, Richard Hatem, Matt Reeves; Photography, Robbie Greenberg; Designer, Albert Brenner; Editor, Michael Tronick; Music, Basil Poledouris; Co-Producer, Julius R. Nasso; Associate Producer, Edward McDonnell; Visual Effects Supervisor, Richard Yuricich; Costumes, Richard Bruno; Casting, Louis Di Giaimo; an Arnon Milchan-Segal/Nasso production, presented in association with Regency Enterprises, distributed by WB; Dolby SDDS Stereo; Technicolor; Rated R; 100 minutes; July release. **CAST:** Steven Seagal (Casey Ryback), Eric Bogosian (Dane), Everett McGill (Penn), Katherine Heigl (Sarah Ryback), Morris Chestnut (Bobby Zachs), Peter Greene, Patrick Kilpatrick, Scott Sowers, Afifi (Mercs), Andy Romano (Admiral Bates), Brenda Bakke (Gilder), Sandra Taylor (Kelly), Jonathan Banks (Scotty), David Gianopoulos (David Trilling), Royce D. Applegate (Ryback's Cook), Nick Mancuso (Breaker), Christopher Darga, Don Blakely (Cooks), Dale Dye (Col. Darza), Jim Clark, Stan Garner (Train Consultants), Silan Smith (Friendly Faced Engineer #1), Rick Wiles (Conductor), Kurtwood Smith (Gen. Cooper), Denis L. Stewart (Holy-Merc), Jim Dirker, Ken Vieira (Helicopter Pilot), Todd O. Russell (Ryback's Driver), Warren Tabata (Bartender), Julius R. Nasso, Phyllis Davis, James V. Caciola, Ginger Lewis (Hostages), Greg Collins (Huey Pilot), Wren T. Brown, Al Sapienza (Captains), D.C. Douglas, Thom Adcox Hernandez (Technicians), Catherine MacNeal (Assistant), Frank Roman (Aide), Jennifer Starr (ATAC Asst. #2), Ping Wu (SYSOS Officer)

ART FOR TEACHERS OF CHILDREN (Zeitgeist) Director/Screenplay/Photography/Editor, Jennifer Montgomery; Black and White; Not rated; 82 minutes; August release. CAST: Caitlin Grace McDonnell (Jennifer), Duncan Hannah (John), Coles Burroughs (Molly), Bryan Keane (Counselor), Jennifer Williams (Alex)

SOMETHING TO TALK ABOUT (Spring Creek Prod.) Producers, Anthea Sylbert, Paula Weinstein; Executive Producer, Goldie Hawn; Director, Lasse Hallstrom; Screenplay, Callie Khouri; Photography, Sven Nykvist; Designer, Mel Bourne; Editor, Mia Goldman; Co-Producer, William Beasley; Music, Hans Zimmer, Graham Preskett; Costumes, Aggie Guerard Rodgers; Casting, Marion Dougherty; a Spring Creek production, distributed by WB; Dolby SDDS Stereo; Technicolor; Rated R; 105 minutes; August release. **CAST:** Julia Roberts (Grace King Bichon), Dennis Quaid (Eddie Bichon), Robert Duvall (Wyly King), Gena Rowlands (Georgia King), Kyra Sedgwick (Emma Rae King), Brett Cullen (Jamie Johnson), Haley Aull (Caroline), Muse Watson (Hank Corrigan), Anne Shropshire (Aunt Rae), Ginnie Randall (Eula), Terrence P. Currier (Dr. Frank Lewis), Rebecca Koon (Barbaranelle), Rhoda Griffis (Edna), Lisa Roberts (Kitty), Deborah Hobart (Lorene Tuttle), David Huddleston (Jack Pearce), Amy Parrish (Lucy), Helen Baldwin (Mary Jane), Libby Whittemore (Nadine), Punky Leonard (Norma Leggett), Michael Flippo (Sonny), Beau Holden (Frank), Noreen Reardon (June), Bennie L. Jenkins (Dub), Rusty Hendrickson (Harry), J. Don Ferguson (Announcer), Mary Nell Santacroce (Mrs. Pinkerton), Shannon Eubanks (Jessie Gaines), Jamye Price (Anne), Brinley Arden Vickers (College Friend)

DEAD FUNNY (A-Pix) Producers, Richard Abramowitz, David Hannay; Executive Producers, Paul L. Newman, James M. Gould, Robert Baruc, David Marlow; Director/Screenplay, John Feldman; Photography, Todd Crockett; Designer, Mike Shaw; Costumes, Sara Slotnick; Editor, Einar Westerlund; Music, Sheila Silver; Casting, Susan Shopmaker; an Avondale Pictures and MovieScreen Entertainment in association with Film Four International production; Color; Rated R; 96 minutes; July release. **CAST:** Elizabeth Peña (Vivian Saunders), Andrew McCarthy (Reggie Barker), Paige Turco (Louise), Blanche Baker (Barbara), Allison Janney (Jennifer), Adelle Lutz (Maria), Lisa Jane Persky (Sarah), Michael Mantell (Harold), Kristen Wilson (Cards), Lianna Pai (Knives), Jorjan Fox (Threads), Tanya Berezin (Mrs. Hause), Ken Kensei (Yosh), Patty Scanlon (Carmen), Bai Ling (Norriko), Carol Schneider (Clare), Edward Seamon (Viv's Father), Michael Mastrototaro (Man with Carriage), Samuel Baird (Know It All Man)

WORLD AND TIME ENOUGH (Strand) Producers, Julie Hartley, Andrew Peterson; Director/Screenplay, Eric Mueller; Photography, Kyle Bergersen; Designer, Heather McElhatton; Editor, Laura Stokes; Music, Eugene Huddleston; a 1 in 10 presentation; Color; Not rated; 90 minutes; August release. **CAST:** Matt Guidry (Mark), Gregory G. Giles (Joey), Kraig Swartz (David), Peter Macon (Mike), Bernadette Sullivan (Marie), John Patrick Martin (Mr. Quincy), Adam Mikelson (Young Mark), Kathleen Fuller (Mrs. Quincy), Carla Pavich (TV Reporter), Jennifer Campbell (Smiling Woman in Office), David Fields, Peter Breitmayer (Suits), Barbara Patterson (Old Health Teacher), Mez Van Oppen (Rich Woman), Shirley Venard (Adoption Caseworker), Mary Rehbein (Young Teacher), Joe Mikelson (Young Joey), Barbara Davidson (Mrs. Brown), Michael Tezla (Mr. Brown), Kyle Christopherson (Frat Boy), Natasha Grudnoske (Big Hair Girlfriend), Louis Markert (Sleazy Office Guy), Claudia Wilkens (Aunt), Johanna Stein (Katie), Clyde Lund (Farmer)

Gregory G. Giles, Matt Guidry in *World and Time Enough* © Strand Releasing

Daniel Stern in *Bushwacked*
© Twentieth Century Fox

Thomas Ian Nicholas, Joss Ackland in *A Kid in King Arthur's Court*
© Alpine Releasing Corp./Trimark Pictures

BUSHWHACKED (20th Century Fox) Producers, Charles B. Wessler, Paul Schiff; Executive Producer, Daniel Stern; Director, Greg Beeman; Screenplay, John Jordan, Danny Byers, Tommy Swerdlow, Michael Goldberg; Story, John Jordan, Danny Byers; Photography, Theo Van de Sande; Designers, Mark W. Mansbridge, Sandy Veneziano; Editor, Ross Albert; Co-Producer, David Wisnievitz; Music, Bill Conti; Costumes, Mary Zophres; Casting, Linda Lowy, John Brace; Dolby Digital Stereo; Clairmont-Scope; Deluxe color; Rated PG-13; 90 minutes; August release.
CAST: Daniel Stern (Max Grabelski), Jon Polito (Agent Palmer), Brad Sullivan (Jack Erickson), Ann Dowd (Mrs. Patterson), Anthony Heald (Bragdon), Tom Wood (Agent McMurrey), Blake Bashoff (Gordy), Corey Carrier (Ralph), Michael Galeota (Dana), Max Goldblatt (Barnhill), Ari Greenberg (Fishman), Janna Michaels (Kelsey Jordan), Natalie West (Mrs. Fishman), Michael P. Byrne (Mr. Fishman), Michael O'Neill (Jon Jordan), Jane Morris (Beth Jordan), Christopher Curry (Trooper), Kenneth Johnson (State Patrolman), Robert Donley (Proprietor), Sue Kwon (TV Newscaster), Reed Clark Means (Kid), Harley Kelsey (Forest Ranger), Cesarina Vaughn (Business Woman), Cory Buck (Tricycle Kid), Theodor Scott Owens (Business Man)

JUPITER'S WIFE (Artistic License Films) Producer/Director/Photography/Editor,Michel Negroponte; Co-Producers, Doug Block, Jane Weiner; Screenplay, Gabriel Morgan, Michel Negroponte; Music, Beo Morales, Brooks Williams; Color; Not rated; 78 minutes; August release. Documentary of Maggie, a schizophrenic homeless woman who lives in Central Park, with Bobbi, Dr. James Krumenauer, Katina Pendleton,Audrey Pendleton, Joan Culpepper, Joanne Bergbom, Charles and Lynn, Edwige Val, Peter and Ramona Negroponte.

A KID IN KING ARTHUR'S COURT (Walt Disney Pictures) Producers, Robert L. Levy, Peter Abrams, J.P. Guerin; Director, Michael Gottlieb; Screenplay, Michael Part, Robert L. Levy; Photography, Elemér Ragályi; Editors, Michael Ripps, Anita Brandt-Burgoyne; Music, J.A.C. Redford; Designer, László Gárdonyi; Co-Producers, Andrew Hersh,

Jonathon Komack Martin; Executive Producer, Mark Amin; Casting, Allison Gordon-Kohler, John & Ros Hubbard; Presented in association with Trimark Pictures and Tapestry Films; Distributed by Buena Vista Pictures; Dolby Digital Stereo; Color; Rated PG; 91 minutes; August release.
CAST: Thomas Ian Nicholas (Calvin Fuller), Joss Ackland (King Arthur), Art Malik (Lord Belasco), Paloma Baeza (Princess Katey), Kate Winslet (Princess Sarah), Daniel Craig (Master Kane), David Tysall (Ratan), Ron Moody (Merlin), Barry Stanton (Blacksmith), Michael Mehlnan (Shop Owner), Melani Eoettinger (Washer Woman), Michael Kelly (Apprentice), Louise Rosner (Lady in Waiting), Paul Rosner (Peasant Boy), Béla Unger (Head Guard), Shane Rimmer (Coach), Tim Wickham (Ricky Baker), Daniel Bennett (Howell), Debora Weston (Mom), Vincent Marzello (Dad), Catherine Blake (Maya), J.P. Guerin (Umpire)

RIVER OF GRASS (Strand) Producers/Story, Jesse Hartman, Kelly Reichardt; Director/Screenplay, Kelly Reichardt; Photography, Jim Denault; Editor, Larry Fessenden; Designer, David Doernberg; Costumes, Sara Slotnick; Color; Not rated; 81 minutes; August release. CAST: Lisa Bowman (Cozy), Larry Fessenden (Lee Ray Harold), Dick Russell (Jimmy Ryder), Stan Kaplan (J.C.), Michael Buscemi (Doug)

DR. JEKYLL AND MS. HYDE (Savoy) Producers, Robert Shaprio, Jerry Leider; Executive Producer, John Morrissey; Director/Story, David Price; Screenplay, Tim John, Oliver Butcher, William Davies, WilliamOsborne; Suggested by Robert Louis Stevenson's novel *The Strange Case of Dr. Jekyll & Mr. Hyde*; Photography, Tom Priestley; Designer, Gregory Melton; Editor, Tony Lombardo; Costumes, Molly Maginnis; Music, Mark McKenzie; Make-Up Effects Creator, Kevin Yagher; Co-Producer, Frank K. Isaac; Visual Effects, Dream Quest Images; Casting, Mike Fenton, Allison Cowitt; a Rastar/Leider-Shapiro production presented in association with Rank Film Distributors; Dolby SDDS Digital Stereo; Technicolor; Rated PG-13; 92 minutes; August release. **CAST:** Sean Young (Helen Hyde), Tim Daly (Richard Jacks), Lysette Anthony (Sarah Carver), Stephen Tobolowsky (Oliver Mintz), Harvey Fierstein (Yves DuBois), Thea Vidale (Valerie), Jeremy Piven (Pete), Polly Bergen (Mrs. Unterveldt), Stephen Shellen (Larry), Sheena Larkin (Mrs. Mintz), John Franklyn-Robbins (Prof. Manning), Aron Tager (Lawyer), Jane Connell (Aunt Agatha), Julie Cobb (DuBois' Psychiatrist),

Maggie in *Jupiter's Wife*
© Cinemax Productions

Lysette Anthony, Tim Daly, Sean Young in *Dr. Jekyll and Ms. Hyde*
© Savoy Pictures

Brian Wilson in *I Just Wasn't Made for These Times*
© Palomar Pictures

Prof. Leon Theremin in *Theremin: An Electronic Odyssey*
© Orion Pictures Corp.

Kim Morgan Greene (Paparazzi Lady/Party Lady), Victor Knight (Bill), Mark Camacho (Waiter), Robert Wuhl (Man with Lighter), Susan Trustman (Cocktail Party Woman), Manon Deschenes, Jean-Claude Page (Gorgeous Models), Maria Stanton (Dress Admirer 1&2), Donna Barnes (Young Woman), Rachel Bertrand (Pneumatic Young Woman), Herb Goldstein, Michael Rudder, Susan Glover (Noses), Kate Asner (Admirer), Liz Larson (Carson), Mike Hodge (Eagleton), Stephane Lefebvre (Bus Boy), Don Jordan (Driver), Donna Sarrasin (Mintz' Secretary)

ROY COHN/JACK SMITH (Strand) Producers, Ted Hope, James Schamus, Marianne Weems; Director, Jill Godmilow; Director of Original Theatrical Production, Gregory Mehrten; *Roy Cohn* written by Gary Indiana, *What's Underground About Marshmallows* written by Jack Smith; Photography, Ellen Kuras; Editor, Merril Stern; Music, Michael Sahl; a Jonathan Demme presentation of a production of Good Machine/Pomodori Foundation and the Library for Icon & Idiom; Color; Not rated; 91 minutes; August release. A filmed record of the Off-Broadway production with Ron Vawter (Roy Cohn/Jack Smith), Coco McPherson (Chica)

BRIAN WILSON: I JUST WASN'T MADE FOR THESE TIMES (Palomar Pictures) Producers, Don Was, Larry Shapiro, David Passick, Ken Kushnick; Executive Producers, Anne-Marie Mackay, Jonathon Ker; Director, Don Was; Photography, Wyatt Troll; Editor, Helen Lowe; Color; Not rated; 69 minutes; August release. Documentary on Beach Boys leader Brian Wilson, featuring Tom Petty, Lindsey Buckingham, Thurston Moore, David Crosby, Stephen Stills, Graham Nash, Linda Ronstadt.

THE AMAZING PANDA ADVENTURE (Lee Rich/Gary Foster Prod.) Producers, Lee Rich, John Wilcox, Gary Foster, Dylan Sellers; Executive Producer, Gabriella Martinelli; Director, Christopher Cain; Screenplay, Jeff Rothberg, Laurice Elehwany; Story, John Wilcox, Steven Alldredge; Photography, Jack N. Green; Designer, John Willett; Editor, Jack Hofstra; Costumes, Marjorie Chan; Music, William Ross; Panda Trainer, Mark Weiner; Casting, Marion Dougherty; a Lee Rich/Gary Foster production, distributed by WB; Dolby SDDS Stereo; Technicolor; Rated PG; 84 minutes; August release. **CAST:** Stephen Lang (Michael Tyler), Ryan Slater (Ryan Tyler), Yi Ding (Ling), Wang Fei (Chu), Zhou Jian Zhong (Po), Yao Er Ga (Shong), O Mi Jia Can (Village Elder), Cheu Gang (Chang), He Yu (Lei), Yeh Hui (Official #1), Shou Wei (Worker), Isabella Hoffman (Beth), Brian Wagner (Johnny), Joanne Dorian (Teacher), Doug Abrahams (Ticket Agent), John Willett (Man in Line), Za Xi Wan Dui (Tibetan Man), Yu Lang (Committee Member), Li Zhen Dou (Mr. Hsu), Moon, Shema (The Little Panda), Ying Ying-Wuhan Circus (Adult Panda), Ding San An (Reserve Worker), Lang Ping (Tibetan Kid)

THEREMIN: AN ELECTRONIC ODYSSEY (Orion Classics) Producer/Director/Screenplay, Steven M. Martin; Photography, Frank De Marco; Editor, David Greenwald; Music, Hal Willner; a Kaga Bay Production in association with Channel 4; Dolby Stereo; Color; Rated PG-13; 85 minutes; August release. Documentary on Leon Theremin inventor of the self-named electromagnetic musical instrument.

ARABIAN KNIGHT (Miramax) Producers, Imogen Sutton, Richard Williams; Executive Producer, Jake Eberts; Director, Richard Williams; Screenplay, Richard Williams, Margaret French; Art Director, Roy Naisbitt; Master Animator, Ken Harris; Background Stylist, Errol Le Cain; Photography, John Leatherbarrow; Songs, Robert Folk, Norman Gimbel; an Allied Filmmakers presentation; Dolby Stereo; Panavision; Deluxe color; Rated G; 72 minutes; August release. **VOICE CAST:** Vincent Price (Zigzag), Matthew Broderick (Tack, the Cobbler), Jennifer Beals (Princess Yum Yum), Eric Bogosian (Phido), Toni Collette (Nurse/Witch), Jonathan Winters (Thief), Clive Revill (King Nod), Kevin Dorsey (Mighty One-Eye), Stanley Baxter (Gofer/Slap), Kenneth Williams (Goblet/Tickle), Clinton Sunberg (Dying Soldier), Windsor Davies (Roofless), Frederick Shaw (Goolie), Thick Wilson (Sgt. Hook), Eddie Byme (Hoof), Peter Clayton, Geoff Golden, Derek Hinson, Declan Mulholland, Mike Nash, Tony Scannell, Dermot Walsh, Ramsay Williams (Other Brigands)

THE SHOW (Savoy) Producers, Mike Tollin, Brian Robbins, Robert A. Johnson; Executive Producers, Stan Lathan, Rob Kenneally; Director, Brian Robbins; Photography, Dasal Banks, Larry Banks, Steven Consentino, Ericson Core, John Demps, Todd A Dos Reis, Johnny Simmons; a Rysher Entertainment presentation, in association with Russell Simmons; DTS Stereo; Color; Rated R; 89 minutes; August release. Concert film featuring rap performers Craig Mack, Dr. Dre, Naughty by Nature, Run DMC, Slick Rick, The Dogg Pound, The Notorious B.I.G., Warren G, Wu-Tang Clan.

ZigZag, King Nod in *Arabian Knight*
© Miramax Films

Tie-Died: Rock 'n Roll's Most Deadicated Fans
© ISA Releasing Ltd.

TIE-DIED: ROCK 'N ROLL'S MOST DEADICATED FANS (ISA Releasing) Producers, Marsha Oglesby, James Deutch; Executive Producers, Joseph A. Kim, Sara Sackner, Jennifer Fish; Line Producer, Catherine Pellow; Director, Andrew Behar; Photography, Hamid Shams; Music, Peter Fish; Songs, Heads on the Lot; Editors, Andrew Behar, Sara Sackner; Color; Rated R; 88 minutes; September release. Documentary on the Deadheads, the loyal fans of the rock group the Grateful Dead.

HACKERS (United Artists) Producers, Michael Peyser, Ralph Winter; Executive Producer/Director, Iain Softley; Screenplay, Rafael Moreu; Photography, Andrzej Sekula; Designer, John Beard; Editors, Christopher Blunden, Martin Walsh; Costumes, Roger Burton; Music, Simon Boswell; Co-Producer, Janet Graham; Casting, Dianne Crittenden; Visual Effects Supervisor, Peter Chiang; Distributed by MGM/UA; DTS Digital Stereo; Panavision; Deluxe color; Rated PG-13; 105 minutes; September release. **CAST:** Jonny Lee Miller (Dade Murphy—"Zero Cool"), Angelina Jolie (Kate Libby—"Acid Burn"), Jesse Bradford (Joey), Matthew Lillard (Cereal Killer), Laurence Mason (Lord Nikon), Renoly Santiago (Phantom Phreak), Fisher Stevens (Eugene, a.k.a. The Plague), Alberta Watson (Lauren Murphy), Darren Lee (Razor), Peter Y. Kim (Blade), Ethan Browne (Curtis), Lorraine Bracco (Margo), Wendell Pierce (Agent Dick Gill), Michael Gaston (Agent Bob), Marc Anthony (Agent Ray), Penn Jillette (Hal), Liza Walker (Laura), Bob Sessions (Mr. Ellingson), Blake Willett (S.S. Agent, Seattle), Max Ligosh (Young Dade), Felicity Huffman (Attorney), Paul Klementowicz (Michael Murphy), Richard Ziman (Judge), Bill Maul (Norm), William DeMeo (Jock), Denise George (Denise), Jeb Handwerger, Mitchell Nguyen-McCormick (Freshmen on Roof), Gary Klar (Mr. Simpson), Terry Porter (Joey's Mom), Johnny Myers, Kevin Brewerton (Sysops Technicians), Sam Douglas (English

Teacher), Kal Weber, Jeff Harding, Yoshinori Yamamoto, Ralph Winter (V.P.s), Tom Hill (2nd S.S. Agent), Jennifer Rice, Ricco Ross (Reporters), Douglas W. Iles (Addict Hank), Annemarie Zola (Addict Vickie), Michael Potts (Tow Trucker Driver), Nancy Ticotin (Phreak's Mom), Mike Cicchetti (Ellingson Guard), Mick O'Rourke (Phone Repairman), Dave Stewart (London Hacker), Naoko Mori (Tokyo Hacker), Roberta Gotti (Italian Hacker), Ravil Isyanov, Olegario Fedoro (Russian Hackers), Eric Loren (News Technician), Kristin Moreu (Flight Attendant), Tony Sibbald (Jail Guard), Richard Purro (Talkshow Host), Enzo Junior (Da Vinci Virus), Kimbra Standish (Receptionist), Steven Angiolini (Rollerblader)

THE TIE THAT BINDS (Hollywood Pictures) Producers, David Madden, Patrick Markey, John Morrissey, Susan Zachary; Executive Producers, Ted Field, Jon Brown, Robert W. Cort; Director, Wesley Strick; Screenplay, Michael Auerbach; Photography, Bobby Bukowski; Designer, Marcia Hinds-Johnson; Editor, Michael N. Knue; Costumes, Betsy Heimann; Music, Graeme Revell; Casting, Marci Liroff; an Interscope Communications/PolyGram Filmed Entertainment production; Distributed by Buena Vista Pictures; Dolby Digital Stereo; Panavision; Technicolor; Rated R; 98 minutes; September release. **CAST:** Daryl Hannah (Leann Netherwood), Keith Carradine (John Netherwood), Moira Kelly (Dana Clifton), Vincent Spano (Russell Clifton), Julia Devin (Janie), Ray Reinhardt (Sam Bennett), Kerrie Cullen, Bob Minor (Police Officers), George Marshall Ruge, Tommy Rosales, Jr. (Detectives), Laura Lee Kelly (Aide), Marquis Nunley (Boy Russell), Jenny Gago (Maggie), Carmen Argenziano (Phil Hawkes), Laurie Lathem (Alex), Willie Garson (Ray Tanton), Cynda Williams (Lisa-Marie Chandler), Bruce A. Young (Gil Chandler), Benjamin Mouton (Father in Restaurant), Jack Johnson (Boy in Restaurant), Melanie MacQueen (Waitress), Greg Collins (Bartender), Dana Gladstone (Dr. Bradford), Jesse Hays (Boy in School), Andrea Sandahl (Tina), Chris Ellis, Coleen Maloney (Security Guards), Shawne Rowe (Ogre's Wife), Melissa Hays (Princess), Steve Rosenbaum (The Ogre), Suzanne Krull (The Fox), Kevin Bourland (Man in Range Rover), Taylor Allbright (Girl in Schoolyard), Gene Lythgow (Det. Lorenz), Lynn Wanlass (Nurse), Kenny Alexander (Officer Wright)

THE REGGAE MOVIE (Trimedia Prods.) Producers, Randy Rovins, Ricardo Chin; Executive Producers, Louis Rosenbaum, Mark Shebshiaevitz; Director, Randy Rovins; Music Supervisor, Stephen Stewart; Color; Rated PG-13; 90 minutes; September release. Concert film with Shaggy and Rayvon, Inner Circle, Steel Pulse, Ziggy Marley and the Melody Makers, Maxi Priest

Daryl Hannah, Keith Carradine in *The Tie That Binds*
© Interscope Communications

THE BREAK (Trimark) Producers, Vincent Van Patten, James Van Patten; Executive Producer, Sid Craig; Director, Lee H. Katzin; Screenplay, Vincent Van Patten, Stephanie Warren; Story, Vincent Van Patten, Tom Caffrey; Photography, Frank P. Flynn; Music, Kim Bullard; Color; Rated PG-13; 104 minutes; September release. **CAST:** Vincent Van Patten (Nick Irons), Martin Sheen (Gil Robbins), Rae Dawn Chong (Jennifer Hudson), Valerie Perrine (Delores), Ben Jorgensen (Joel Robbins), Betsy Russell (Candy), Gerritt Graham (Cowens), Fred Stolle (Fred), Cliff Drysdale (Cliff), Vitas Gerulitas (Vitas)

Laurence Mason, Jesse Bradford, Renoly Santiago, Mathew Lillard, Angelina Jolie, Jonny Lee Miller in *Hackers*
© United Artists Pictures Inc.

Nic Knight, Truan Munro in *Prince Brat and the Whipping Boy*
© Jones Entertainment Groun

James Belushi, Linda Hamilton in *Separate Lives*
© Trimark Pictures

THE STARS FELL ON HENRIETTA (Malpaso) Producers, Clint Eastwood, David Valdes; Director, James Keach; Screenplay, Philip Railsback; Photography, Bruce Surtees; Designer, Henry Bumstead; Music, David Benoit; Editor, Joel Cox; Costumes, Van Broughton Ramsey; Associate Producer, Steven Railsback; Casting, Phyllis Huffman; a Malpaso production, distributed by WB; Dolby Stereo; Panavision; Technicolor; Rated PG; 111 minutes; September release. **CAST:** Robert Duvall (Mr. Cox), Aidan Quinn (Don Day), Frances Fisher (Cora Day), Brian Dennehy (Big Dave), Lexi Randall (Beatrice Day), Kaytlyn Knowles (Pauline Day), Francesca Ruth Eastwood (Mary Day), Joe Stevens (Big Dave's Driver), Billy Bob Thornton (Roy), Victor Wong (Henry Nakai), Paul Lazar (Seymour), Spencer Garrett (Delbert Tims), Park Overall (Shirl the Waitress), Zach Grenier (Larry Ligstow), Wayne DeHart (Robert), Woody Watson (Jack Sterling), Rodger Boyce (P.G. Pratt), George Haynes (Startmeyer), Robert Westenberg (Mr. Rumsfelk), Landon Peterson (Raymond Rumsfelk), Richard Lineback (Les Furrow), Dylan Baker (Alex Wilde), Cliff Stephens (Arnold Humphries), Rob Campbell (Kid), Tom Aldredge (Grizzled Old Man), Jennifer Griffin (Brotherl Madame), Laura Poe (Prostitute), Bill Streater (Poker Oilman), Danny Wantland (Hotel Clerk Cecil), Craig Erickson (Terry - Farmer #1), Jerry Haynes (George - Farmer #2), Robert A. Burns (Franklin -Farmer #3), Blue Deckert (Contractor), Stephen N. Berger (Roustabout), Monty Stuart (Gas Station Attendant), Lou Hancock (Old Tent Lady), Richard Reyes (Hotel Handyman), Richard L. Gray (Roughneck), Marietta Marich (Adult Pauline Narrator), David Sanders (Henchman)

PRINCE BRAT AND THE WHIPPING BOY (Gemini Films/Jones Entertainment Group) Producer, Ellen Freyer; Executive Producers, Philip D. Fehrle, Glenn R. Jones, Gerhard Schmidt; Director, Syd MacCartney; Screenplay, Max Brindle; Based on the novella *The Whipping Boy* by Sid Fleischman; Photography, Clive Tickner; Designers, John Blezard, Norbert Scherer; Music, Lee Holdridge; Editor, Sean Barton; Color; Rated G; 96 minutes; September release. **CAST:** Truan Munro (Jemmy), Nic Knight (Prince Horace), George C. Scott (Blind George), Kevin Conway (Hold-Your-Nose-Billy), Vincent Schiavelli (Cutwater), Karen Salt (Annyrose), Andrew Bicknell (The King), Jean Anderson (Queen Mother), Christoph M. Orth (The Ambassador), Mathilda May (Betsy). (This film debuted on the Disney Channel in July 1994 under the title *The Whipping Boy*)

A REASON TO BELIEVE (Castle Hill) Producers, Ged Dickersin, Douglas Tirola; Co-Producer, Christopher Trela; Director/Screenplay, Douglas Tirola; Photography, Sarah Cawley; Editor, Sabine Hoffman; Designer, Carol O'Neil; Costumes, Yvens de Thelismond; Casting, Laura Adler; a Pioneer Pictures presentation; Color; Panavision; Rated R; 100 minutes; September release. **CAST:** Allison Smith (Charlotte Byrne), Jay Underwood (Jim Current), Danny Quinn (Wesley Grant), Georgia Emelin (Linda Berryman), Kim Walker (Judith), Keith Coogan (Potto), Lisa Lawrence (Alison), Christopher Birt (Gary), Obba Babatunde (Prof. Thurman), Mark Metcalf (Dean Kirby), Robin Riker (Constance), Holly Marie Combs (Sharon), Afton Smith (Becky), Joe Flanigan (Eric Sayles), David Overlund (Frehley), Jim Keiffer (Dave Brown), Michelle Stratton (Amy), Mary Thomas (Tracy), Rachel Parker (Donna), Sally Kenyon (Daisy), Andy Holcomb (Harvey), Cary Spadafori (Nancy), Terek Puckett (Lazy

Student), Matt Johnson (Hippie Student), Heather Weber (CJ's Happy Girl), Christopher Trela (Kinko's Brother), Don Handfield (Nuj), Claire Cundiff (Captain Pepper), Christian Meinhardt (Editor), Tulane Chartock (Dean's Secretary), Carol O'Neil (Feminist), Alex Wolfe (Asshole in Quad), Noah Lanich (Puking Brother), Amy Smith (Bartender), Frank Martana (Scared Brother), Jeff Niles (Treefort Brother), Doug Devine (Tequila Shot Brother), Dave Trachtenberg (Biggest Brother), Jon Huffman (Dean), Fathers of the Id (Bar Band), Material Issue (Band at Viking Party)

SEPARATE LIVES (Trimark) Producers, Diane Nabatoff, Guy Reidel, Andrew Hersh; Executive Producer, Mark Amin; Director, David Madden; Screenplay, Steven Pressfield; Photography, Kees Vab Oostrum; Designer, Bernt Capra; Costumes, Jacqueline G. Arthur; Music, William Olvis; Color; Rated R; 102 minutes; September release. **CAST:** James Belushi (Tom Beckwith), Linda Hamilton (Lauren Porter), Vera Miles (Dr. Ruth Goldin), Elisabeth Moss (Ronni Beckwith), Drew Snyder (Robert Porter), Mark Lindsay Chapman (Keno Sykes), Marc Poppel (Det. Joe Gallo), Elizabeth Arlen (Dee Harris), Josh Taylor (Charles Duffy), Ken Kerman (Det. Boyle), Michael Whaley (Det. Miller), Jackie Debatin (Darlene), Joshua Malina (Randall), Lisa Vanderpump (Heidi Porter), Ray Quartermus (Guard), Joseph Gallison (Paul), Craig Stepp (David Mills), Lisa Chess (Margaret Porter-Mills), Ara Maxwell (Young Lauren Porter), Pat Delany (Jane Weiss), John Rubano (Gyp), Beverly Castaldo (Redhead), Christine Devine (News Reporter), Joseph Briski (Arresting Cop), Logan Clarke (Big Ben), Athan Maroulis, Rob Morton, Matt Green (Band Members)

Danny Quinn, Allison Smith in *A Reason to Believe*
© Castle Hill Productions, Inc.

Tommy Chong in *National Lampoon's Senior Trip*
© New Line Productions ,Inc.

NATIONAL LAMPOON'S SENIOR TRIP (New Line Cinema) Producer, Wendy Grean; Executive Producers, Peter Morgan, Michel Roy, Neil Stearns; Co-Executive Producer, Stephane Reichel; Director, Kelly Makin; Screenplay, Roger Kumble, I. Marlene King; Photography, Francois Protat; Designer, Gregory Keen; Costumes, Sharon Purdy; Editor, Stephen Lawrence; Music, Steve Bartek; Casting, Ross Clydesdale; an Alliance Production; Dolby Stereo; Deluxe color; Rated R; 94 minutes; September release. **CAST:** Matt Frewer (Principal Todd Moss), Valerie Mahaffey (Miss Tracy Milford), Lawrence Dane (Sen. John Lerman), Tommy Chong (Red), Jeremy Renner (Dags), Rob Moore (Reggie), Eric "Sparky" Edwards (Miosky), Kevin McDonald (Travis Lindsey), Michael Blake (Herbert Jones), Tara Charendoff (Carla Morgan), Nicole deBoer (Meg Smith), Sergio Di Zio (Steve Nisser), Fiona Loewi (Lisa Perkins), Kathryn Rose (Wanda Baker), Danny Smith (Virus), Lori Anne Alter (Shirley), Jack Jessop (Mr. Bloom), Kay Tremblay (Mrs. Winston), Jack Newman (Larry Diplo), Simon Sinn (Mr. Woo), Grace Armas (Mrs. Woo), Daniel Lee (Wong Woo), Paris Chong (Pablo), Carol Ng (Du Mi Wong), Wayne Robson (Frank Hardin), George R. Robertson (President Davis), Rachel Wilson (Teen Girl—Susie), Philip DeWilde (Teen Boy—Fast Eddie), Richard Partington (Doctor), David Sparrow (Lerman's Limo Driver), Marvin Ishmael (Ish), Jim Warren (Detective), Lindsay Leese (Hotel Registration Clerk—Peggy), Monique Kavelaars (Mandy), Ingrid Kavelaars (Candy), James Millington (Sen. Johnson), Warren Davis (Sen. Duffield), Gerry Quigley (Congressional Aide), Michael Kohut (Honor Guard), Addison Bell (Congressional Chairman), Matt Piche (Teen Boy—Rick), Kim Schraner (Teen Girl—Caroline), Joanne Reece (Press Member), Robert Bidman (Gus Freely—TV Reporter), Megan Kitchen (Scared Little Girl), C.J. Fidler (Nurse)

COLDBLOODED (I.R.S.) Producers, Brad Krevoy, Steve Stabler, Brad Jenkel, Michael J. Fox, Matt Tolmach; Executive Producer, Larry Estes; Director/Screenplay, M. Wallace Wolodarsky; Photography, Robert Yeoman; Designer, Rae Fox; Music, Steve Bartek; Editor, Craig Bassett; Costumes, Matthew Jacobson; a PolyGram Film International Ltd./Motion Picture Corporation of America presentation of a Brad Krevoy & Steve Stabler production, a Snowback production; Dolby Stereo; Foto-Kem color; Rated R; 92 minutes; September release. **CAST:** Jason Priestley (Cosmo Reif), Kimberly Williams (Jasmine), Peter Riegert (Steve), Robert Loggia (Gordon), Jay Kogen (John), Janeane Garofalo (Honey), Josh Charles (Randy), David Anthony Higgins (Lance), Doris Grau (Rose), Ann Carroll (Receptionist), Buck McDancer (Fleeing Man), Marcos A. Ferraez (Man with Uzi), Gilbert Rosales (Man with Briefcase), Jim Turner (Doctor), Michael J. Fox (Tim Alexander), Talia Balsam (Jean Alexander), Marc Wolodarsky (Creepy Guy), Kay O'Connell (Yoga Woman), Cecile Krevoy (Waitress)

HALLOWEEN: THE CURSE OF MICHAEL MYERS (Dimension) Producer, Paul Freeman; Executive Producer, Moustapha Akkad; Director, Joe Chappelle; Screenplay, Daniel Farrands; Photography, Bill Dickson; Designer, Bryan Ryman; Editor, Randy Bricker; Music, Alan Howarth; *Halloween* Theme, John Carpenter; Costumes, Ann Lambert; Special Effects, Larry Fioritto; Special Effects Make-Up, John Buechler; a Nightfall production; Distributed by Miramax Films; Ultra-Stereo; CFI color; Rated R; 88 minutes; September release. **CAST:** Donald Pleasence (Dr. Loomis), Mitch Ryan (Dr. Wynn), Marianne Hagan (Kara Strode), Paul Rudd (Tommy Doyle), Mariah O'Brien (Beth), Keith Bogart (Tim Strode), Devin Gardner (Danny Strode), Kim Darby (Debra Strode), Bradford English (John Strode), George P. Wilbur (Mike Myers), Leo Geter (Barry Simms), Susan Swift (Mary)

LOTTO LAND (CFP) Producer/Director/Screenplay, John Rubino; Executive Producers, Michael J. Rubino, Carlos Hernandez; Photogrphy, Rufus Standefer; Editor, Jack Haigis; Music, The Holmes Brothers; Designer, Paola Ridolfi; Color; Not rated; 87 minutes; September release. **CAST:** Larry Gilliard (Hank), Wendell Holmes (Milton), Barbara Gonzalez (Joy), Suzanne Costallos (Florence), Jaime Tirelli (Papi), Luis Guzman, Paul Calderon

RAVE REVIEW (Gnu/Wildebeast Co.) Producers, Jeff Seymour, Ram Bergman, Dana Lustig; Executive Producers, Marcy Lafferty Shatner, William T. Elston, Dawn Tilman; Director/Screenplay, Jeff Seymour; Photography, Richard Crudo; Editor, Terry Kelley; Music, Amotz Plessner, Tal Bergman; Designer, John Marshall; Color; Not rated; 92 minutes; September release. **CAST:** Jeff Seymour (Steve Maletti), Carmen Argenziano (Abe Weinstein), Ed Begley, Jr. (Bert), Robert Costanzo (Peter Watki), James Handy (James), Bruce Kirby (Milton Mandler), Leo Rossi (Brian), Joe Spano (Lou)

EMPIRE RECORDS (Regency Enterprises) Producers, Arnon Milchan, Michael Nathanson, Alan Riche, Tony Ludwig; Director, Allan Moyle; Screenplay, Carol Heikkinen; Photography, Walt Lloyd; Designer, Peter Jamison; Editor, Michael Chandler; Co-Producer, Paul Kurta; Costumes, Susan Lyall; Music Supervisor, Mitchell Leib; Casting, Gail Levin; a Regency Enterprises presentation of a New Regency/Alan Riche and Tony Ludwig production, distributed by WB Dolby Stereo; Super 35 Widescreen; Technicolor; Rated PG-13; 100 minutes; September release. **CAST:** Anthony LaPaglia (Joe), Maxwell Caulfield (Rex), Debi Mazar (Jane), Rory Cochrane (Lucas), Johnny Whitworth (A.J.), Robin Tunney (Debra), Renee Zellweger (Gina), Ethan Randall (Mark), Coyote Shivers (Berko), Brendan Sexton (Warren), Liv Tyler (Corey), James "Kimo" Wills (Eddie), Ben Bode (Mitchell), Gary Bolen (Croupier), Kimber Monroe (Woman at Craps Table), Tony Zaar (High Roller), Patt Noday (Reporter), Julia Howard (Kathy), Kessia Randall (Autograph Girl), Michele Seidman, Diana Taylor, Bernard Granger, Mike Harding (Cops), Oderus Urungus (Lead Singer), Gwar (Band in Mark's Daydream), Kawan Rojanatavorn (Flower Delivery Guy), Corey Joshua Taylor (Roulette Table Man), Melissa Caulfield (Ballet Dancer), Lara Travis (Veronica), Dianna Miranda (Lilly), Rico Fleming, Brandon Crawford (Couch Kids), Elizabeth Grapentien ("Say No More" Woman), Pandora J. Nousianen (CD Customer), Nello Tare (Mello), Kelley Carruth (Girl on Couch), Mark Menchhofer (Clapton Customer), Tobey Maguire (Andre), Anthony Hemingway (Boom Box Kid), Paizhe Pressley, Joanna Canton (Girls), Lee Etta Sutton (Button Customer), Craig Edwards (Rex Manning Fan), Jesse Bechtel, Karen Brigman, David Myers Gray, Bob Sayer (Customers), David Lenthall (Meg Ryan Customer), Andrea Powell (Maria Carey Customer)

THE RETURN OF THE TEXAS CHAINSAW MASSACRE (CFP) Producer, Robert Kuhn; Director/Screenplay, Ken Henkel; Photography,

Kimberly Williams, Jason Priestly in *Coldblooded*
© I.R.S. Releasing

Levie Isaacks; Editor, Sandra Adair; Designer, Debbie Pastor; A Return Prods. presentation; Color; Rated R; 102 minutes; September release. **CAST:** Renee Zellweger (Jenny), Matthew McConaughey (Vilmer), Robert Jacks (Leatherface), Tony Perenski (Darla), Joe Stevens (W.E.), Lisa Newmeyer (Heather), John Harrison (Sean), Tyler Cone (Barry), Vince Brock (Eric), Susan Loughran (Amanda), David Laurence (Jack), James Gale (Rothman)

ASSASSINS (Silver Pictures) Producers, Richard Donner, Joel Silver, Bruce Evans, Raynold Gideon, Andrew Lazar, Jim Van Wyck; Executive Producers, Lauren Shuler-Donner, Dino De Laurentiis; Director, Richard Donner; Screenplay, Andy Wachowski, Larry Wachowski, Brian Helgeland; Story, Andy Wachowski, Larry Wachowski; Photography, Vilmos Zsigmond; Designer, Tom Sanders; Editor, Richard Marks; Co-Producers, Alexander Collett, Richard Solomon, Dan Cracchiolo; Music, Mark Mancina; Costumes, Elizabeth McBride; Casting, Marion Dougherty; a Silver Pictures production in association with Donner/Shuler-Donner productions, distributed by WB; Dolby SDDS Stereo; Technicolor; Rated R; 132 minutes; October release. **CAST:** Sylvester Stallone (Robert Rath), Antonio Banderas (Miguel Bain), Julianne Moore (Electra), Anatoly Davydov (Nicolai), Muse Watson (Ketcham), Stephen Kahan (Alan Branch), Kelly Rowan (Jennifer), Reed Diamond (Bob), Kai Wulff (Remy), Kerry Skalsky, James Douglas Haskins, David Shark "Fralick" (Buyers), Stephen Liska, John Harms, Bob Minor, Barbara Anne Klein, Whitey Shapiro, Stefan Enriquez, Fulvio Cecere, Shirley Oliver, Ernie Hall, Calli Medved (Cops), Edward J. Rosen (Cemetery Caretaker), Christina Orchid (Dowager), Bruce R. Orchid, Ainbal O. Lleras, Michael DeCourcey (Cabbies), James Louis Oliver (Customs Officer), Sue Carolyn Wise (Obnoxious Woman), Ron Ben Jarrett (Maintenance Man), Marian Collier (Pet Shop Lady), Dave Young, Ragna Sigrun (Guards), Mark Woodford (Room Service Waiter), Marta Labatut, Choco Orta (Cemetery Women), Ivonne Piazza (Bank Teller), Angel Vazquez (Bank Official), Axel Anderson (Bank President), David Dollase, Jim Graham (Bodyguards), Wally Dalton (Priest), Paul Tuerpe, John Procaccino, Nerissa E. Williams (Reporters), Juan Manuel Lebron (Puerto Rican Cafe Waiter), Eddie Bellaflores (Fruit Vendor), Thomas Helgeland (Soloist), James W. Gavin (Police Helicopter Pilot), Scott Stuber (Parking Attendant), Richard Blum (Watcher), Eric Sather (Cab Customer), Wally Gudgell (Upset Passenger), J. Mills Goodloe (Newlywed Man), Peter Sebastian Lackaff (Singer), John Lamar (Money Hungry Man), Robert Sanders (Monorail Driver), Rhonda J. Osborne (Police Dispatcher), Christina Herrera (Pro Choice Woman), Cary Sanchez (Bank Receptionist), Frankie R. Jimenez, Jr. (Towel Boy), Jeff King (Helicopter Pilot #3), Pearl the Cat (Cat)

Donald Pleasence, Paul Rudd in *Halloween: The Curse of Michael Myers* © Dimension Films

KILIAN'S CHRONICLE (Capstone) Producers, Pamela Berger, Mark Donadio; Executive Producer, Barbara Hartwell; Director/Screenplay, Pamela Berger; Photography, John Hoover; Designer, John Demeo; Costumes, Dena Popienko; Music, R. Carlos Nakai, Bevan Manson; a Lara Classics presentation; Color; Not rated; 112 minutes; October release. **CAST:** Christopher Johnson (Kilian), Robert McDonough (Ivar), Eva Kim (Turtle), Jonah Ming Lee (Kitchi), Gino Montesinos, Robert Mason Ham

Jonah Ming Lee, Christopher Johnson in *Kilian's Chronicle* © Marsha Cohen

BLACK IS ... BLACK AIN'T (Tara) Producer/Director, Marlon Riggs; Co-Producer, Nicole Atkinson; Photography, Robert Shepard; Editors, Christiane Badgley, Bob Paris; from California Newsreel; Color; Not rated; 87 minutes; October release. Late filmmaker Marlon Riggs' look at his own indentity as both a black and gay man.

DEAD BEAT (Northern Arts) Producers, George Moffly, Christopher Lambert; Executive Producer, Anant Singh; Screenplay, Janice Shapiro, Adam Dubov; Photography, Nancy Schreiber; Editor, Lorraine Salk; Music, Anton Sanko; Casting, Johanna Ray; an Anant Singh and Distant Horizon presentation in association with Christopher Lambert and STTM Corporation; Color; Rated R; 92 minutes; October release. **CAST:** Bruce Masey (Kit), Balthazar Getty (Rudy), Natasha Gregson Wagner (Kirsten), Meredith Salenger (Donna), Deborah Harry (Mrs. Kurtz), Sara Gilbert (Martha), Max Perlich (Jimmie), Alex Cox (English Teacher)

NEVER TALK TO STRANGERS (TriStar) Producers, Andras Hamori, Jeffrey R. Neuman, Martin J. Wiley; Executive Producer, Rebecca DeMornay; Co-Producers, Jean Desormeaux, Ralph S. Dietrich; Director, Peter Hall; Screenplay, Lewis Green, Jordan Rush; Photography, Elemer Ragalyi; Designers, Linda Del Rosario, Richard Paris; Editor, Roberto Silvi; Music, Pino Donaggio; Casting, Jon Comerford; an Alliance production; Dolby Digital Stereo; Deluxe color; Rated R; 102 minutes; October release. **CAST:** Rebecca DeMornay (Dr. Sarah Taylor), Antonio Banderas (Tony Ramirez), Dennis Miller (Cliff Raddison), Len Cariou (Henry Taylor), Harry Dean Stanton (Max Cheski), Eugene Lipinski (Dudakoff), Martha Burns (Maura), Beau Starr (Grogan), Phillip Jarrett (Spatz), Tim Kelleher (Wabash), Emma Corosky (Young Sarah), Susan Coyne (Alison), Joseph R. Gannascoli (Carnival Attendant), Reg Dreger (Flight Attendant), Frances Hyland (Mrs. Slotnick), John Bourgeois (Uniformed Cop), Kevin Rushton (Corridor Guard), Kelley Grando (Young Girl), Bruce Beaton (Taxi Driver), Tony Meyler (Cop #1), Rodger Barton (Plain Clothes Cop), Nolan Jennings (Waiter), Bret Pearson (Accomplice), Teresa Hergert (Anchorwoman)

Rebecca DeMornay, Antonio Banderas in *Never Talk to Strangers* © TriStar Pictures, Inc.

James Duval, Rose McGowan, Johnathon Schaech in *The Doom Generation* © Vidmark Entertainment

MESSENGER (Norman Loftis Prods.) Director/Screenplay, Norman Loftis; No other credits available; Color; Not rated; 80 minutes; October release. **CAST:** Richard Barbosa (Jeff), Carolyn Kinebrew (Tina)

THE DOOM GENERATION (Trimark) Producers, Andrea Sperling, Gregg Araki; Director/Screenplay/Editor, Gregg Araki; Executive Producers, Nicole Arbib, Pascal Caucheteux, Gregoire Sorlat; Photography, Jim Fealy; Designer, Therese Deprez; a UGC and the Teen Angst Movie Company presentation in association with Desperate Pictures, Blurco and Why Not Productions (France); U.S.-French; Color; Not rated; 90 minutes; October release. **CAST:** James Duval (Jordan White), Rose McGowan (Amy Blue), Johnathon Schaech (Xavier Red), Cress Williams (Peanut), Skinny Puppy (Gang of Goons), Dustin Nguyen (Quickie Mart Clerk), Margaret Cho (Clerk's Wife), Lauren Tewes (TV Anchorwoman), Christopher Knight (TV Anchorman), Nicky Katt (Carno Burger Cashier), Johanna Went (Carno Burger Co-Worker), Perry Farrell (Stop'n'Go Clerk), Amanda Bearse (Barmaid), Parker Posey (Brandi), Salvator Xuereb (Biker), Heidi Fleiss (Liquor Store Clerk), Don Galloway (FBI Guy), Dewey Weber (George), Khristofor Rossianov (Dan), Paul Fow (Pat)

DELTA OF VENUS (New Line Cinema) Producer, Evzen Kolar; Director, Zalman King; Screenplay, Elisa Rothstein, Patricia Louisianna Knop; Based on the writings of Anais Nin; Photography, Eagle Egilsson; Designer, Zdenek Fleming; Costumes, Jolie Jimenez; Music, George S. Clinton; Editor, James Bedford; Color; Rated NC-17; 101 minutes; October release. **CAST:** Costas Mandylor (Lawrence), Audie England (Elena), Bernard Zette (Donald), Rory Campbell (Miguel), Raven Snow (Leila), Emma Moore (Ariel), Eric Da Silva (Marcel)

Audie England in *Delta of Venus* © New Line Productions

PHARAOH'S ARMY (CFP) Producers, Robby Henson, Doug Lodato; Director/Screenplay/Editor, Robby Henson; Photography, Doron Schlair; Designer/Costumes, Jana Rosenblatt; Music, Vince Emmett, Charles Ellis, Michael Stamper, Robert Friedmen; Associate Producers, Elizabeth Rodgers, Tracy Kristofferson; a presentation of the Independent Television Service; Color; Not rated; 90 minutes; October release. **CAST:** Chris Cooper (Captain John Hull Abston), Patricia Clarkson (Sarah Anders), Kris Kristofferson (Preacher), Richard Tyson (Rodie), Robert Joy (Chicago), Frank Clem (Neely), Huckleberry Fox (Newt), Will Lucas (Boy)

DEAR BABE (Stratton Films) Producers, Rosanne Ehrlich, David J. Wilson; Director/Screenplay, Rosanne Ehrlich; Photography, Greg Andrake; Editor, David J. Wilson; Black and white/color; Not rated; 82 minutes; October release. Director Rosanne Ehrlich's documentary chronicling her father's letters home to her mother during World War II.

FRANK AND OLLIE (Walt Disney Pictures) Producer, Kuniko Okubo, Theodore Thomas; Director/Screenplay, Theodore Thomas; Photography, Erik Daarstad; Editor, Kathryn Camp; Music, James Wesley Stemple; Foto-Kem color; Rated G; 89 minutes; October release. Documentary on Disney Studio animations Frank Thomas and Ollie Johnston who worked for the company for some 40 years.

Chris Cooper in *Pharaoh's Army* © CFP Distribution

COPYCAT (Regency Enterprises) Producers, Arnon Milchan, Mark Tarlov; Executive Producers, Michael Nathanson, John Fiedler; Co-Producer, Joseph M. Caracciolo, Jr.; Director, Jon Amiel; Screenplay, Ann Biderman, David Madsen; Photography, Laszlo Kovacs; Editors, Alan Heim, Jim Clark; Music, Christopher Young; Designer, Jim Clay; Costumes, Claudia Brown; Casting, Billy Hopkins, Suzanne Smith, Kerry Barden; a Regency Enterprises presentation of an Arnon Milchan production, distributed by WB; Dolby Stereo; Panavision; Technicolor; Rated R; 123 minutes; October release. **CAST:** Sigourney Weaver (Helen Hudson), Holly Hunter (M.J. Monahan), Dermot Mulroney (Ruben Goetz), William McNamara (Peter Foley), Harry Connick, Jr. (Daryll Lee Cullum), J.E. Freeman (Quinn), Will Patton (Nicoletti), John Rothman (Andy), Shannon O'Hurley (Susan Schiffer), Bob Greene (Pachulski), Tony Haney (Kerby), Danny Kovacs (Kostas), Tahmus Rounds (Landis), Scott De Venney (Cop 1), David Michael Silverman (Mike),Diane Amos (Gigi), Richard Conti (Harvey), Nick Scoggin (Conrad), Bert Kinyon (Burt), Dennis Richmond (KXBU Anchorman), Rob Nilsson (SWAT Commander), Kenny Kwong (Chinese Kid), Charles Branklyn (Doc), Kelly De Martino (Festival Girl), Rebecca Jane Klingler (Peter's Wife), Terry Brown (Cop 2), Corie Henninger (Jogger), Bill Bonham (Photographer), Kathleen Stefano (Peter's Mother), Chris Beale (Tech Guy 1), Hansford Prince (Fred), Don West (Attorney), Jay Jacobus (Judge), John Charles Morris (Young Peter), Keith Phillips (Felix Mendoza), Johnetta Shearer (Paramedic), Ron Kaell (Mac), Kelvin Han Yee (Chinese Detective), James Cunningham (Hal), Victor Talmadge (Head Waiter), Brian Russell (Coroner's Man), Damon Lawner (Festival Dude), Russ Christoff (Commissioner Petrillo), Doug Morrisson (SWAT 1), Edith Bryson (Landlady), Jeni Chua (Michelle), William Oates (Man in Corridor), Lee Kopp (Haircut Man), Thomas J. Fieweger (Bodger the Cop), Floyd Gale Holland (L. Bottemy), Anthony

Moore (Uniformed Policeman), Stephanie Smith, S.J. Spinali, Katherine Fitzhugh, Robert Benscoter (Disturbed Tenants), Arlon G. Greene (Jogger), Stuart W. Yee (Thug), Vincenetta Gunn (Screaming Woman), David Ferguson (Dock On-Looker), Eleva Singleton (Paramedic), Gen Bingham (Victim in Car at Gas Station)

HARLEM DIARY: NINE VOICES OF RESILIENCE (Discovery Channel) Producer/Director, Jonathan Stack; Screenplay, Terry Williams; Photography, Maryse Alberti, Samuel Henriques; Editor, Susanne Szabo Rostock; Music, John Hicks; Co-Producers, Terry Williams, Mary Beth Mann; Produced in association with Gabriel Films; Black and White/Color; Not rated; 95 minutes; October release. Interviews with nine Harlem youths: Jermaine Ashwood, Amir Williams-Foster, Barr Elliot, Nikki Matos, Kahlil Hicks, Christina Head, Damon Williams, Rasheem Swindell, Akida Bailey.

FAIR GAME (Silver Pictures) Producer, Joel Silver; Executive Producer, Thomas M. Hammel; Director, Andrew Sipes; Screenplay, Charles Fletcher; Based on the novel by Paula Gosling; Photography, Richard Bowen; Designer, James Spencer; Music, Mark Mancina; Editors, David Finfer, Christian Wagner, Steven Kemper; Costumes, Louise Frogley; Associate Producer, Alan Schechter; Stunts, Charles Picerni; Casting, Jackie Burch; a Silver Pictures production distributed by WB; Dolby Stereo; Technicolor; Rated R; 90 minutes; November release. **CAST:** William Baldwin (Max), Cindy Crawford (Kate), Steven Berkoff (Kazak), Christopher McDonald (Meyerson), Miguel Sandoval (Juantorena), Johann Carlo (Jodi), Salma Hayek (Rita), John Bedford Lloyd (Louis), Olek Krupa (Zhukov), Jenette Goldstein (Rosa), Marc Macaulay (Navigator), Sonny Carl Davis (Baker), Frank Medrano (Guaybera), Don Yesso (Beanpole), Paul Dillon (Hacker), Gustav Vintas (Stefan), Christian Bodegaard (Farm Boy), Gary Francis Hope (Smiler), Hank Stone (Ratso), Ski Zawaski (Bail Bondsman), Nancy Nahra (Forensics), Anthony Giaimo (Cafe Romano Manager), Carmen Lopez (Angry Mother), Erika Navarro (4-Year-Old Girl), Pamela Berrard (Hotel Desk Clerk), Mark Wheatle (Stop & Shop Clerk), Bubba Baker (Hog Truck Driver), Scott Michael Campbell (Adam), Ruben Rabasa (Computer Store Mgr.), Jim Greene (Tow Truck Driver), Antoni Corone (Codebreaker)

Ally Sheedy in *One Night Stand*
© New Horizons Pictures

ONE NIGHT STAND (Concorde) Producer, Alida Camp; Executive Producers, Jack Schwartzman, Roger Corman; Photography, Arthur Albert; Music, David Shire; Editor, Jim Prior; Co-Producer, Mike Elliott; Director, Talia Shire; Screenplay, Marty Casella; a Francis Ford Coppola presentation from New Horizons; Ultra-Stereo; Foto Kem Color; Rated R; 90 minutes; November release. **CAST:** Ally Sheedy (Mickey Sanderson), A Martinez (Jack Gilman), Frederick Forrest (Michael Joslyn), Diane Salinger (Barbara Joslyn), Gina Hecht (Cy Watson), Don Novello (Warren Miller), Elsa Raven, Millie Slavin

THE BABYSITTER (Spelling Films Intl.) Producers, Kevin J. Messick, Steve Perry; Executive Producer, Joel Schumacher; Director/Screenplay, Guy Ferland; Based on a story by Robert Coover; Photography, Rick Bota; Music, Loek Dikker; Designer, Phil Leonard; Editor, Jim Prior; Color; Rated R; 90 minutes; November release. **CAST:** Alicia Silverstone (The Babysitter), J.T. Walsh (Harry Tucker), Lee Garlington (Dolly Tucker), Nicky Katt (Mark), Jeremy London (Jack), George Segal (Bill), Lois Chiles (Bernice)

Alicia Silverstone, Jeremy London in *The Babysitter*
© Spelling Films Intl.

RECKLESS (Samuel Goldwyn Co.) Producer, Amy J. Kaufman; Executive Producer, Lindsay Law; Director, Norman René; Screenplay, Craig Lucas; Photography, Frederick Elmes; Designer, Andrew Jackness; Editor, Michael Berenbaum; Music, Stephen Endelman; Costumes, Walker Hicklin; Music Supervisor, Randy Poster; Casting, Billy Hopkins, Suzanne Smith, Kerry Barden; a Playhouse International Pictures co-presentation; Dolby Stereo; Color; Rated PG-13; 92 minutes; November release. **CAST:** Mia Farrow (Rachel), Scott Glenn (Lloyd), Mary-Louise Parker (Pooty), Tony Goldwyn (Tom), Eileen Brennan (Sister Margaret), Giancarlo Esposito (Host Tim Timko), Stephen Dorff (Tom, Jr.), Juana Barrios (Reporter Re: Fire), Mike Heibeck (Fireman), Vee Brown (Anchor Person Re: Jogger), Jack Gilpin (Weatherman), William Duell (Roy), Deborah Rush (Trish), Anthony Pagano (Small Boy in Therapy), Debra Monk (Therapist), Joanne Krispin, Lisa Krispin (Beautiful Twins), Mary Beth Peil (Bartender), Lindsay Mae Sawyer (Little Rachel), William Fichtner (Rachel's Father), William Preston (Porter), John Magill (Cashier at Liquor Store), Zach Grenier (Anchor Person Re: Trish), Lisa Louise Langford (Anne Lacher-Holden), Walter Bryant (Doctor), Doug Barron (TV Director), Maureen Silliman (Shelter Reporter), Ron Bagden (Young Shelter Volunteer), Ladd Patellis (Man in Mask), Pat DiStefano (TV Technician), Elijah Nicole Rosello (Granddaughter), Nancy Marchand (Grandmother), Nesbitt Blaisdell (Grandfather)

RAGING ANGELS (Mark Borde Films) Producer/Story, Chako Van Leeuwen; Co-Producer, Peter Maris; Director, Alan Smithee; Screenplay, Kevin Rock, David Markov, Chris Bittler; Story, Chako Van Leeuwen, Stens Christensen; Photography, Bryan England; Editor, Neil Grieve; Music, Terry Plumeri; Designer, Brooke Wheeler; Costumes, Warden Neil; Speical Effects Supervisor, Larry Fioritti; a Nu Image presentation of a Chako Film Lt. production; Dolby Stereo; Deluxe color; Rated R; 96 minutes; November release. **CAST:** Sean Patrick Flannery (Chris), Diane Ladd (Sister Kate), Monet Mazur (Lila), Michael Pare (Coiln), Arielle Dombasle (Megan), Shelley Winters (Grandma Ruth)

Mary-Louise Parker, Mia Farrow, Scott Glenn in *Reckless*
© The Samuel Goldwyn Company

Frank Whaley, Sheryl Lee in *Homage*
© Arrow Releasing Inc.

HOMAGE (Arrow) Producers, Elan Sassoon, Mark Medoff; Director, Ross Kagen Marks; Screenplay, Mark Medoff, based on his play *The Homage That Follows*; Photography, Tom Richmond; Editor, Kevin Tent; Music, W.G. Snuffy Walden; Designer, Amy Ancona; Casting, Shari Rhodes, Joseph Middleton; a Skyline Entertainment presentation; Ultra-Stereo; Foto-Kem Color; Not rated; 96 minutes; November release. **CAST:** Blythe Danner (Katherine Samuel), Frank Whaley (Archie Landrum), Sheryl Lee (Lucy Samuel), Bruce Davison (Joseph), Danny Nucci (Gilbert)

IT TAKES TWO (Rysher Entertainment) formerly *Me and My Shadow*; Producers, James Orr, Jim Cruickshank; Executive Producers, Keith Samples, Mel Efros; Director, Andy Tennant; Screenplay, Deborah Dean Davis; Photography, Kenneth D. Zunder; Designer, Edward Pisoni; Editor, Roger Bondelli; Co-Producers, Laura Friedman, Andy Cohen; Music, Sherman and Ray Foote; Costumes, Molly McGuiness; Casting, Amy Lippens; a Rysher Entertainment presentation of an Orr & Cruickshank production in association with Dualstar productions distributed by WB; Dolby Stereo; Deluxe color; Rated PG; 101 minutes; November release. **CAST:** Kirstie Alley (Diane Barrows), Steve Guttenberg (Roger Callaway), Mary-Kate Olsen (Amanda Lemmon), Ashley Olsen (Alyssa Callaway), Philip Bosco (Vincenzo), Jane Sibbett (Clarice Kensington), Michelle Grisom (Carmen), Desmond Robertson (Frankie), Tiny Mills (Tiny), Shanelle Henry (Patty), Anthony Aiello (Anthony), La Tonya Borsay (Wanda), Michelle Lonsdale-Smith (Michelle), Sean Orr (Jerry), Elizabeth Walsh (Emily), Michael Vollans (Blue Team Kid), Paul O'Sullivan (Bernard Louffier), Lawrence Dane (Mr. Kensington), Gerrard Parkes (St. Bart's Priest), Gina Clayton (Muffy Bilderberg), Doug O'Keefe (Craig Bilderberg), Mark Huisman (Waiter at Party), Marilyn Boyle (Miss Van Dyke), Ernie Grunwald (Harry Butkis), Ellen Ray Hennessey (Fanny Butkis), Dov Tiefenbach (Harry Butkis, Jr.), Annick Obonsawin (Brenda Butkis), Austin Pool (Billy Butkis), Andre Lorant (Bobby Butkis), Philip Williams (Airport Tractor Driver), Vito Rezza (Butkis' Neighbor)

Gumby, Gumby Robot in *Gumby: The Movie*
© Arrow Releasing Inc.

WHEN BILLY BROKE HIS HEAD...AND OTHER TALES OF WONDER (ITVS) Producers/Directors, David E. Simpson, Billy Golfus; Screenplay, Billy Golfus; Photography, Billy Golfus, Slawomir Grunberg; Editor, David E. Simpson; Color; Not rated; 60 minutes; November release. Documentary on disability and civil rights.

UNDER THE HULA MOON (Trident) Producer, Stacy Codikow; Executive Producer, Jim B. Hodge; Director, Jeff Celentano; Screenplay, Jeff Celentano, Gregory Webb; Photography, Phil Parmet; Designer, Randal P. Earnest; Music, Hidden Faces; Editor, Donald Likovich; Costumes, Susanna Puisto; a Periscope Pictures production; Dolby Stereo; Foto-Kem color; Rated R; 94 minutes; December release. **CAST:** Stephen Baldwin (Buzz Wall), Emily Lloyd (Betty Wall), Chris Penn (Turk Dickson), Musetta Vander (Maya Gundinger), Pruitt Taylor Vince (Bob Brunswick), Edie McClurg (Dolly Brunswick), Robert Madrid (Juan), James Staszkiel (Trucker), Carel Struycken (Clyde), Ray Bumatai (King Kamehameha), Tina Naughton (News Reporter), Debra Christofferson (Kim Jones), Bill Campbell (Marvin), Molly McClure (Grandmother), Deep Roy (Bus Driver), Eric Welch (Young Man), Bobby McGee (Leon), Willard Pugh (Duane), Gary Cervantes, Luis Contreras (Bandito), Patrick Dollaghan (Agent Kepner), Craig Reay (Agent), Dennis Sharp, Doug McCurry (FBI Agents), Gregory Webb (Military Operative), R. Lee Ermey (Marine Lieutenant), Ken Wright (Dan Gilmartin), Justin McLeod Wright (Buzz Jr.)

ACE VENTURA: WHEN NATURE CALLS (Morgan Creek Prods.) Producer, James G. Robinson; Executive Producer, Gary Barber; Director/Screenplay, Steve Oedekerk; Photography, Donald E. Thorin; Designer, Stephen J. Lineweaver; Editor, Malcolm Campbell; Co-Producer, Andrew G. La Marca; Music, Robert Folk; Costumes, Elsa Zamparelli; Casting, Ferne Cassel; a Morgan Creek production, distributed by WB; Dolby Stereo; Super 35 Widescreen; Color; Rated PG-13; 105 minutes; November release. **CAST:** Jim Carrey (Ace Ventura), Ian McNeice (Fulton Greenwall), Simon Callow (Vincent Cadby), Maynard Eziashi (Ouda), Bob Gunton (Burton Quinn), Sophie Okonedo (The Princess), Tommy Davidson (Tiny Warrior), Adewale (Hitu), Danny D. Daniels (Wachootoo Witch Doctor), Sam Motoana Phillips (Wachootoo Chief), Damon Standifer (The Wachati Chief), Andrew Steel (Mick Katie), Bruce Spence (Gahjii), Thomas Grunke (Derrick McCane), Arsenio "Sonny" Trinidad (Ashram Monk), Kristen Norton (Pompous Woman), Michael Reid MacKay (Skinny Husband), Kayla Allen (Airplane Stewardess), Ken Kirzinger (Helicopter Pilot), Dev Kennedy (Dad Tourist), Patti Tippo (Mom Tourist), Sabrinah Christie (Girl Tourist), Warren Sroka (Boy Tourist), Noel De Souza (Elephant Trainer), Gene Williams (Polestander), Leif Tilden (Gorilla Performer)

GUMBY THE MOVIE (Arrow) Producers/Screenplay, Art Clokey, Gloria Clokey; Director/Storyboard, Art Clokey; Editors, Lynn Stevenson, Marilyn McCoppen; Model Sculpturing, Tom Robalcava; Set Breakdowns, Gloria Clokey, Holly Harman; Trimensional Animation, Stephen Buckley, Tony Laudati, Dan Mason, Ken Willard, Mike Belzer, Art Clokey, Angie Glocka, Kurt Hanson, Peter Kleinow, Harry Walton; Music, Jerry Gerber; a Premavision production; Color; Rated G; 90 minutes; December release. **VOICE CAST:** Dallas McKennon (Gumby/Claybert/Fatbuckle/Kapp), Art Clokey (Pokey/Prickle/Gumbo), Gloria Clokey (Goo), Manny LaCarruba (Thinbuckle), Alice Young (Ginger), Janet MacDuff (Gumba), Patti Morse (Tara), Bonnie Randolph (Lowbelly/Farm Lady), Ozzie Ahler (Radio Announcer)

LIVE NUDE GIRLS (Republic) Producers, Cara Tapper, Steve White, Barry Bernardi; Executive Producers, Heather Bernt, Mel Layton; Co-Producers, Christopher De Faria, Christopher Taylor; Director/Screenplay, Julianna Lavin; Photography, Christopher Taylor; Designer, Jerry Fleming; Editor, Kathryn Himoff; Music, Anton Sanko; Casting, Gary M. Zuckerbrod, Marcia Ross; a Steve White Properties production; Ultra-Stereo; Foto-Kem Color; Rated R; 92 minutes; December release. **CAST:** Dana Delany (Jill), Kim Cattrall (Jamie), Cynthia Stevenson (Marcy), Laila Robins (Rachel), Lora Zane (Georgina), Olivia d'Abo (Chris), Glenn Quinn (Randy), Tim Choate (Jerome), Jeremy Jordan (Greenpeace Boy), V.C. Davis (Pool Man), Simon Templeman (Bob), Julianna Lavin, Jerry Spicer (Fighting Neighbors), Joshua Beckett (Richard Silver), Brian Markinson, Paul Perri, Alex Cohen (Jerome's Friends), Amber Rose Tamblyn (Young Jill), Jennifer Fenton (Young Jamie), Lisa Wilhoit (Young Marcy), Chelsea Harrington (Young Rachel), Ara Maxwell (Young Georgina), Eric Tecosky (Pizza Boy), Sheila Travis (Marcy's Mother), Don Paul (Marcy's Father), Blake Bailey (Biker), Bob Harvey

(Bartender), Adele Sparks (Stripper), Adam Ozturk (Sous Chef), John Craig (Neighbor Boy), Gladys Jennett (Sunbathing Woman), Michael Bonnabel (Cretin Supervisor), Jason Jackson (Jeep Washer), Laurent Malaquis (Mobster Don's Son)

DRACULA: DEAD AND LOVING IT (Columbia) Producer/Director, Mel Brooks; Executive Producer, Peter Schindler; Screenplay, Mel Brooks, Rudy De Luca, Steve Haberman; Story, Rudy De Luca, Steve Haberman; Photography, Michael D. O'Shea; Designer, Roy Forge Smith; Editor, Adam Weiss; Music, Hummie Mann; Associate Producers, Robert Latham Brown, Leah Zappy; Costumes, Dodie Shepard; Casting, Lindsay D. Chag, Bill Shepard; a Castle Rock Entertainment presentation of a Brooksfilms production; SDDS Dolby Stereo; Technicolor; Rated PG-13; 89 minutes; December release. **CAST:** Leslie Nielsen (Dracula), Peter MacNicol (Renfield), Steven Weber (Harker), Amy Yasbeck (Mina), Lysette Anthony (Lucy), Harvey Korman (Dr. Seward), Mel Brooks (Prof. Van Helsing), Mark Blankfield (Martin), Megan Cavanagh (Essie), Clive Revill (Sykes), Chuck McCann (Innkeeper), Avery Schreiber, Cherie Franklin (Peasant Couple in Coach), Ezio Greggio (Coach Driver), Leslie Sachs (Usherette), Matthew Porretta (Handsome Lieutenant at Ball), Rudy De Luca (Guard), Jennifer Crystal (Nurse), Darla Haun (Brunette Vampire), Karen Roe (Blonde Vampire), Charlie Callas (Man in Straight Jacket), Anne Bancroft (Gypsy Woman), Phillip Connery (Ship Captain), Tony Griffin, Casey King, Nick Rempel (Crewmen), Zale Kessler (Orchestra Leader), Thea Nielsen, Barbaree Earl, Maura Nielsen, Robin Shepard, Elaine Ballace, Maude Winchester (Ballroom Guests), Lisa Cordray (Hat Check Girl), Cindy Marshall-Day, Benjamin Livingston (Young Lovers at Picnic), Gregg Binkley (Woodbridge), David DeLuise, Tommy Koenig, Grinnell Morris, Vince Grant, Johnny Cocktails, Ric Coy, Michael Connors, Stephen Wolfe Smith, Richard Alan Stewart (Interns), Carol Arthur, Sonje Fortag, Henry Kaiser, Loraine Shields, Derek Mark Lochran, Ira Miller, Kathleen Kane (Villagers), David and Sharon Savoy (Specialty Dancers), Audrey Baranishyn, Jeffrey Broadhurst, Kevin Crawford, John Frayer, Sandi Johnson, Shirley Kirkes, Manette LaChance, Stan Mazin, Tricia McFarlin-Mattson, Anne McVey, Delores Nemiro, Jim Peace, Jody Peterson, Dennon Rawles, Sandra Rovetta, Alton Ruff, Blane Savage, Ted Sprague, Jude Van Wormer, Alan Walls (Ballroom Dancers)

HEAT (Forward Pass/New Regency Prods.) Producers, Michael Mann, Art Linson; Executive Producers, Arnon Milchan, Pieter Jan Brugge; Director/Screenplay, Michael Mann; Photography, Dante Spinotti; Editors, Dov Hoenig, Pasquale Buba, William Goldenberg; Music, Elliot Goldenthal; Designer, Neil Spisak; Costumes, Deborah L. Scott; Stunts, Joel Kramer; a Forward Pass production presented in association with New Regency Prods., distributed by WB; Dolby SDDS Stereo; Panavision; Technicolor; Rated R; 172 minutes; December release. **CAST:** Al Pacino (Vincent Hanna), Robert De Niro (Neil McCauley), Val Kilmer (Chris Shiherlis), Jon Voight (Nate), Tom Sizemore (Michael Cheritto), Diane Venora (Justine), Amy Brenneman (Eady), Ashley Judd (Charlene), Mykelti Williamson (Drucker), Wes Studi (Casalas), Ted Levine (Bosko), Dennis Haysbert (Breedan), William Fichtner (Van Zant), Natalie Portman (Lauren), Tom Noonan (Kelso), Kevin Gage (Waingro), Hank Azaria (Marciano), Susan Traylor (Elaine Cheritto), Kim Staunton (Lillian), Danny Trejo (Trejo), Henry Rollins (Hugh Benny), Jerry Trimble (Schwartz), Marty Ferrero (Construction Clerk), Ricky Harris (Albert Torena), Tone Loc (Ricard Torena), Begonya Plaza (Anna Trejo), Hazelle Goodman (Hooker's Mother), Ray Buktenica (Timmons), Jeremy Piven (Dr. Bob), Xander Berkeley (Ralph), Bud Cort (Coffee Shop Boss), Rick Avery, Bill McIntosh (Armored Guards), Brad Baldridge (Children's Hospital Doctor), Andrew and Brian Camuccio (Dominick), Max Daniels (Shooter at Drive-In), Vince Deadrick, Jr. (Driver at Drive-In), Charles Duke (Cop #5), Thomas Elfmont (Desk Clerk Cop), Kenny Endoso (Bartender), Kimberly Flynn (Casals' Date), Steve Ford (Officer Bruce), Farrah Forke (Claudia), Hannes Fritsch (Miracle Mile Bartender), Amanda Graves (Linda Cheritto), Emily Graves (Anita Cheritto), Niki Harris (Marcia Drucker), Ted Harvey, Daniel O'Haco (Detectives), Patricia Healy (Bosko's Date), Paul Herman (Sgt. Heinz), Cindy Katz (Rachel), Brian Libby (Captain Jackson), Dan Martin (Harry Dieter), Rick Marzan (Basketball Player), Terry Miller (Children's Hospital Nurse), Paul Moyer (News Anchorman), Mario Roberts (Bank Guard #1), Phillip Robinson (Alphonse), Thomas Rosales, Jr. (Armored Truck Driver), Rainell Saunders (Dead Hooker), Kai Soremekun (Prostitute), Rey Verdugo (Vegas Cop), Wendy L. Walsh (News Anchorwoman), Yvonne Zima (Hostage Girl)

Lora Zane, Laila Robins, Dana Delany, Kim Cattrall, Cynthia Stevenson in *Live Nude Girls* © Republic Entertainment Inc.

GRUMPIER OLD MEN (John Davis/Lancaster Gate Prod.) Producers, John Davis, Richard C. Berman; Co-Producers, George Folsey, Jr., John J. Smith; Director, Howard Deutch; Screenplay, Mark Steven Johnson; Photography, Tak Fujimoto; Designer, Gary Frutkoff; Editors, Billy Weber, Seth Flaum, Maryann Brandon; Music, Alan Silvestri; Costumes, Lisa Jensen; Associate Producer, Elena Spiotta; Casting, Sharon Howard-Field; a John Davis/Lancaster Gate Production, distributed by WB; Dolby Digital Stereo; Technicolor; Rated PG-13; 105 minutes; December release. **CAST:** Walter Matthau (Max Goldman), Jack Lemmon (John Gustafson), Ann-Margret (Ariel Gustafson), Sophia Loren (Maria), Burgess Meredith (Grandpa Gustafson), Daryl Hannah (Melanie), Kevin Pollak (Jacob Goldman), Katie Sagona (Allie), Ann Guilbert (Mama), James Andelin (Sven), Marcus Klemp (Assistant Manager Eddie), Max Wright (Health Inspector), Cheryl Hawker (Lena), Wayne A. Evenson (Handsome Hans), Allison Levine (Dog Pound Assistant), John Patrick Martin (Reverend), Adam Ward (Skeleton), Ryan Waldoch (Power Ranger #1), James Cada (Husband Shopper), Jaclyn Ross (Wife Shopper), Kyle Christopherson (Stockboy), Michelle Johnston (Sears Salesperson), Jeffrey L. Smith (The Frugal Gourmet), Geraldo Rivera (Himself), Warren Schueneman, Jack Mitsch, Sterling Robson (Old Men), Gregory Schuneman (Pizza Kid), Michelle Johnston (Chicken Polka Girl), Denny Schusted (Limo Driver), Wallace Olson, Carl Johnson, Eugene Karels, Lawrence Grivna (Polka Musicians)

Leslie Nielsen, Mel Brooks in *Dracula: Dead and Loving It* © Castle Rock Entertainment

TOP 100 BOX OFFICE FILMS OF 1995

1. Toy Story (BV/Nov).....................................$191,340,000
2. Batman Forever (Jun) $184,100,000
3. Apollo 13 (Univ/Jun)................................. $171,850,000
4. Pocahontas (BV/Jun)................................$141,480,000
5. Ace Ventura: When Nature Calls (Nov) $108,270,000
6. Goldeneye(UA/Nov)....................................$103,800,000
7. Jumanji (TriS/Dec)....................................$100,300,000
8. Casper (Univ/May) $100,290,000
9. Seven (NLC/Sep)......................................$100,100,000
10. Die Hard With a Vengeance (20th/May)..........................$99,970,000

Bill Paxton in *Apollo 13*
© Universal City Studios Inc.

11. Crimson Tide (BV/May)..................................$91,370,000
12. Waterworld (Univ/Jul) $88,100,000
13. Dangerous Minds (BV/Aug)............................$84,730,000
14. Mr. Holland's Opus (BV/Dec) $82,520,000
15. While You Were Sleeping (BV/Apr)...............................$80,990,000
16. Congo (Par/Jun) $80,100,000
17. Braveheart (Par/May)..................................$75,570,000
18. Father of the Bride Part II (BV/Dec) $75,420,000
19. Get Shorty (MGM/Oct).................................$72,000,000
20. The Bridges of Madison County (Jun)...........................$71,110,000

Catherine McCormack, Mel Gibson in *Braveheart*
© B.H. Finance C.V.

21. Grumpier Old Men (Dec)...................................$71,100,000
22. Mortal Kombat (NLC/Aug) $70,310,000
23. Nine Months (20th/Jul) $69,670,000
24. Outbreak (Mar) $67,830,000
25. Heat (Dec)...$67,170,000
26. Waiting to Exhale (20th/Dec) $66,320,000
27. Bad Boys (Col/Apr) $65,660,000
28. Babe (Univ/Aug)..$63,210,000
29. Species (MGM/Jul).....................................$60,100,000
30. The American President (Col/Nov) $59,800,000
31. Twelve Monkeys (Univ/Dec)............................$56,660,000
32. Clueless (Par/Jul).....................................$56,360,000
33. Sabrina (Par/Dec)......................................$53,490,000
34. Something to Talk About (Aug).......................$50,670,000
35. The Net (Col/Jul) $50,500,000
36. A Walk in the Clouds (20th/Aug) $49,920,000
37. Under Siege 2: Dark Territory (Jul).................$48,670,000
38. The Brady Bunch Movie (Par/Feb) $46,550,000
39. Sense and Sensibility (Col/Dec) $42,940,000
40. Casino (Univ/Nov).....................................$42,430,000

Dennis Hopper in *Waterworld*
© Universal City Studios

41. Man of the House (BV/Mar)...............................$40,100,000
42. Dead Man Walking (Gram/Dec) $39,340,000
43. French Kiss (20th/May) $38,870,000
44. Higher Learning (Col/Jan) $37,960,000
45. Mighty Morphin Power Rangers (20th/Jun)....................$37,790,000
46. First Knight (Col/Jul).................................$37,370,000
47. Leaving Las Vegas (UA/Oct)...........................$36,990,000
48. Just Cause (Feb).......................................$36,860,000
49. To Wong Foo Thanks for Everything (Univ)...................$35,930,000
50. The Indian in the Cupboard (Par/Jul) $35,390,000

51. Judge Dredd (BV/Jun) $34,670,000
52. Money Train (Col/Nov) $33,860,000
53. Forget Paris (Col/May) $32,900,000
54. Tommy Boy (Par/Mar) $32,650,000
55. Rob Roy (UA/Apr) $32,510,000
56. Copycat (Oct)..$32,100,000
57. Powder (BV/Oct) $30,680,000
58. Assassins (Oct) $30,310,000
59. Major Payne (Univ/Mar).....................................$29,420,000
60. Free Willy 2: The Adventure Home (Jul) $29,100,000
61. Friday (NLC/May) $27,400,000
62. Now and Then (NLC/Oct) $27,100,000
63. Houseguest (BV/Jan) $26,330,000
64. Desperado(Col/Aug)...$25,540,000
65. Billy Madison (Univ/Feb)...................................$25,470,000

Samantha Mathis, Michael Douglas, Martin Sheen in
The American President © Castle Rock Entertainment

82. It Takes Two (Nov) $19,480,000
83. Johnny Mnemonic (TriS/May)............................$18,980,000
84. The Quick and the Dead (TriS/Feb)...................$18,560,000
85. The Big Green (BV/Sep) $17,690,000
86. Heavyweights (BV/Feb) $17,680,000
87. Home for the Holidays (Par/Nov).......................$17,470,000
88. Murder in the First (Jan) $17,430,000
89. Jury Duty (TriS/Apr) $16,950,000
90. Devil in a Blue Dress (TriS/Sep) $16,110,000
91. The Prophecy (Mir/Sep).....................................$16,100,000
92. Mad Love (BV/May) $15,450,000
93. Muriel's Wedding (Mir/Mar) $15,120,000
94. Kiss of Death (20th/Apr) $14,950,000
95. Halloween:The Curse of Michael Myers (NLC/Sep).......$14,120,000
96. Nixon (BV/Dec)..$13,500,000

John Leguizamo in *To Wong Foo, Thanks For Everything! Julie Newmar*
© Universal City Studios Inc.

66. Operation Dumbo Drop (BV/Jul) $24,500,000
67. Dolores Claiborne (Col/Mar).............................$24,270,000
68. Virtuosity (Par/Aug)...$24,000,000
69. Dead Presidents (BV/Oct)..................................$23,960,000
70. Tom and Huck (BV/Dec) $23,770,000
71. How to Make an American Quilt (Univ/Oct) $23,530,000
72. Boys on the Side (Feb) $23,400,000
73. Circle of Friends (Savoy/Mar)...........................$23,390,000
74. The Usual Suspects (Gram/Aug) $23,300,000
75. Don Juan DeMarco (NLC/Apr) $22,100,000
76. Tales From the Crypt: Demon Knight (Univ/Jan) $20,990,000
77. The Postman (Mir/Jun) $20,900,000
78. To Die For (Col/Sep)..$20,860,000
79. Showgirls (UA/Sep)..$20,260,000
80. Sudden Death (Univ/Dec)...................................$20,250,000
81. Vampire in Brooklyn (Par/Oct)..........................$19,500,000

Debra Winger, Billy Crystal in *Forget Paris*
© Castle Rock Entertainment

97. A Kid in King Arthur's Court (BV/Aug).........................$13,330,000
98. Lord of Illusions (UA/Aug) $13,250,000
99. Clockers (Univ/Sep)...$13,000,000
100. Candyman: Farewell to the Flesh (Gram/Mar)...............$12,920,000

PROMISING NEW ACTORS OF 1995

AMY BRENNEMAN
(Bye Bye Love, Heat)

DON CHEADLE
(Devil in a Blue Dress)

MATT KEESLAR
(The Run of the Country)

MINNIE DRIVER
(Circle of Friends)

MICHELLE FORBES
(Swimming With Sharks)

GREG KINNEAR
(Sabrina)

MEKHI PHIFER
(Clockers)

GWYNETH PALTROW
(Moonlight and Valentino, Seven)

LINUS ROCHE
(Priest)

ALICIA SILVERSTONE
(Hideaway, Clueless, The Babysitter)

REGINA TAYLOR
(Clockers)

FREDDY RODRIGUEZ
(A Walk in the Clouds, Dead Presidents)

Sophie Marceau, Mel Gibson, in *Braveheart*
© B.H. Finance C.V./Paramount Pictures

Mel Gibson

Patrick McGoohan

Mel Gibson (c)

BRAVEHEART

(PARAMOUNT) Producers, Mel Gibson, Alan Ladd, Jr.; Bruce Davey; Executive Producer, Stephen McEveety; Director, Mel Gibson; Screenplay, Randall Wallace; Photography, John Toll; Designer, Tom Sanders; Costumes, Charles Knode; Editor, Steven Rosenblum; Music, James Horner; Associate Producers, Dean Lopata, Elizabeth Robinson; Casting, Patsy Pollock; Stunts, Simon Crane, Mic Rodgers; an Icon Productions/Ladd Company production; Dolby/DTS Digital Stereo; Panavision; Deluxe color; Rated R; 170 minutes; May release

CAST

William Wallace	Mel Gibson
Princess Isabelle	Sophie Marceau
Longshanks—King Edward I	Patrick McGoohan
Murron	Catherine McCormack
Hamish	Brendan Gleeson
Campbell	James Cosmo
Stephen	David O'Hara
Robert the Bruce	Angus McFadyen
Prince Edward	Peter Hanly
Argyle Wallace	Brian Cox
The Leper	Ian Bannen
Young William	James Robinson
Malcolm Wallace	Sean Lawlor
John Wallace	Sandy Nelson
MacClannough	Sean McGinley
Elder Stewart	Alan Tall
Young Hamish	Andrew Weir
Mother MacClannough	Gerda Stevenson
Priests	Ralph Riach, Robert Paterson
Young Murron	Mhairi Calvey
Phillip	Stephen Billington
King's Advisor No. 2	Barry McGovern
Craig	John Kavanagh
Mornay	Alun Armstrong
Morrison	Tommy Flanagan
Mrs. Morrison	Julie Austin
Bride's Father	Alex Norton
Toothless Girl	Joanne Bett
Lord Bottoms	Rupert Vansittart
Smythe	Michael Byrne
Magistrate	Malcolm Tierney
Corporal	William Masson
Madbaker/Flagman	Dean Lopata
MacGregor	Tam White
Stewart	Donal Gibson
Nicolette	Jeanne Marine

and Martin Dunne (Lord Dolecroft), Fred Chiverton (Leper's Caretaker), Jimmy Chisholm (Faudron), John Murtagh (Lochlan), David McKay (Young Soldier), Peter Mullan (Veteran), Martin Murphy (Lord Talmadge), Gerard McSorley (Cheltham), Bernard Horsfall (Balliol), Richard Leaf (Governor of York), Daniel Coli (York Captain), Niall O'Brien (English General No. 2), Liam Carney (Sean), Bill Murdoch (Villager), Phil Kelly (Farmer), Martin Dempsey, Jimmy Keogh ((Drinkers), Joe Savino (Chief Assassin), David Gant (Royal Magistrate), Mal Whyte (Jailor), Paul Tucker (English Commander).

The true story of William Wallace who, in 13th century Scotland, rallied his people to fight against the tyrany of the King of England, Edward Longshanks.

Academy Award winner for Best Picture, Director, Cinematography, Makeup, and Sound Effects Editing. The film received additional Oscar nominations for original screenplay, film editing, original dramatic score, costume design, and sound.

Golden Globe Award winner for Best Director.

© B.H. Finance C.V./Paramount Pictures

Angus McFadyen   Sophie Marceau   David O'Hara

James Cosmo (2nd from left), Brendan Gleeson, Mel Gibson, David O'Hara

Peter Hanly   Catherine McCormack   James Cosmo

NICOLAS CAGE
in *Leaving Las Vegas*
© United Artists Inc.
ACADEMY AWARD FOR BEST ACTOR OF 1995

SUSAN SARANDON
in *Dead Man Walking*
© Gramercy Pictures
ACADEMY AWARD FOR BEST ACTRESS OF 1995

201

KEVIN SPACEY
in *The Usual Suspects*
© Gramercy Pictures
ACADEMY AWARD FOR BEST SUPPORTING ACTOR OF 1995

MIRA SORVINO
in *Mighty Aphrodite*
© Miramax Films
ACADEMY AWARD FOR BEST SUPPORTING ACTRESS OF 1995

ACADEMY AWARD NOMINEES FOR BEST ACTOR

Richard Dreyfuss in *Mr. Holland's Opus*

Anthony Hopkins in *Nixon*

Sean Penn in *Dead Man Walking*

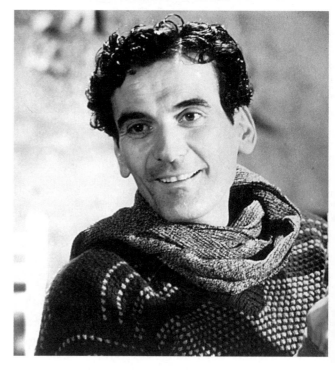

Massimo Troisi in *The Postman*

ACADEMY AWARD NOMINEES FOR BEST ACTRESS

Elisabeth Shue in *Leaving Las Vegas*

Sharon Stone in *Casino*

Meryl Streep in *The Bridges of Madison County*

Emma Thompson in *Sense and Sensibility*

ACADEMY AWARD NOMINEES FOR BEST SUPPORTING ACTOR

James Cromwell in *Babe*

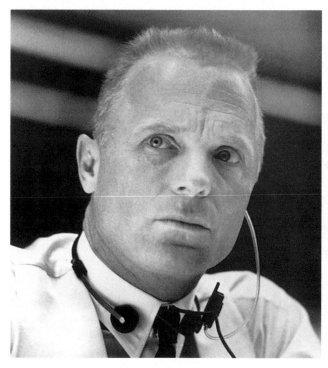

Ed Harris in *Apollo 13*

Brad Pitt in *Twelve Monkeys*

Tim Roth in *Rob Roy*

ACADEMY AWARD NOMINEES FOR BEST SUPPORTING ACTRESS

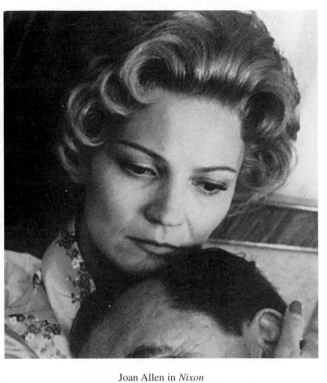

Joan Allen in *Nixon*

Kathleen Quinlan in *Apollo 13*

Mare Winningham in *Georgia*

Kate Winslet in *Sense and Sensibility*

ANTONIA'S LINE

(FIRST LOOK PICTURES) Producer, Hans de Weers; Co-Producers, Antonino Lombardo, Judy Counihan, Wim Louwrier; Director/Screenplay, Marleen Gorris; Photography, Willy Stassen; Editors, Michiel Reichwein, Wim Louwrier; Music, Ilona Sekacz; Bergen Film/Prime Time/Bard Entertainment in association with the Dutch Film Fund, the Flemish Community Fund, the European Co-Production Fund, Investco S.A., NPS/Dutch Cultural Broadcasting Promotion Fund, the Dutch Co-Production Fund & the Eurimages Fund; Dutch; Color; Not rated; 105 minutes; February 1996 release

CAST

Antonia	Willeke van Ammelrooy
Danielle	Els Dottermans
Bas	Jan Decleir
Crooked Finger	Mil Seghers
DeeDee	Marina de Graaf
Loony Lips	Jan Steen
Therese	Veerle Van Overloop
Lara	Elsie de Brauw
Sarah	Thyrza Ravesteijn
Letta	Wimie Wilhelm
The Curate	Flip Filz
Fran	Waller Zeper
Simon	Reinout Bussemaker
Allegonda	Dora van der Groen
Farmer Daan	Jakob Beks
Pitte	Filip Peeters
Janne	Michael Pas
Mad Madonna	Catherine ten Bruggencate
The Protestant	Paul Kooij
The Village Priest	Leo Hogenboom
Therese, age 13	Esther Vriesendorp
Therese, age 6	Carolien Spoor

On the day she will die, Antonia looks back on her life, beginning with her return to the village of her birth following World War I.

© First Look Pictures

Willeke van Ammelrooy, Els Dottermans

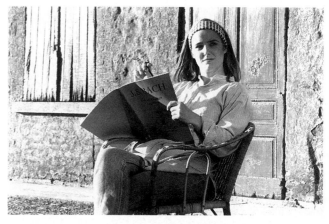

Veerle Van Overloop

Willeke van Ammelrooy

Willeke van Ammelrooy, Jan Decleir

ACADEMY AWARD FOR BEST FOREIGN LANGUAGE FILM OF 1995

FOREIGN FILMS RELEASED IN THE U.S. IN 1995

Jorge Perrugoria, Vladimir Cruz

STRAWBERRY AND CHOCOLATE

(MIRAMAX) Executive Producer, Miguel Mendoza; Directors, Tomás Gutiérrez Alea, Juan Carlos Tabio; Screenplay, Senel Paz; Photography, Mario Garcia Joya; Designer, Fernando O'Reylly; Costumes, Miriam Duenas; Editors, Miriam Talavera, Osvaldo Donatien; a production of the Cuban Institute of the Arts and Film Industry (KAIC), co-produced by Imcine and Tabasco Films—Mexico, Telemadrid and SGAE—Spain; Cuban-Spanish-Mexican; Ultra-Stereo; Color; Rated R; 110 minutes; January release

CAST

Diego..Jorge Perrugoria
David..Vladimir Cruz
Nancy..Mirta Ibarra
Miguel...Francisco Gatorno

In Havana, an unlikely friendship develops between a gay counterrevolutionary and a heterosexual Communist.

© Miramax Films

Jorge Perrugoria

Vladimir Cruz

MAMMA ROMA

(MILESTONE) Producer, Alfredo Bini; Director, Pier Paolo Pasolini; Screenplay, Pier Paolo Pasolini, Sergio Citti; Photography, Tonino Delli Colli; Art Director, Flavio Mogherini; Editor, Nino Baragli; Italian, 1962; Black and white; Not rated; 110 minutes; January release

CAST

Mamma Roma	Anna Magnani
Ettore	Ettore Garofolo
Carmine	Franco Citti
Bruno	Silvana Corsini
Biancofiore	Luisa Orioli
Priest	Paolo Volponi
Zacaria	Luciano Gonini
Signor Pellissier	Vittorio La Paglia
Piero	Piero Morgia
Carletto	Franco Ceccarelli
Tonino	Marcello Sorrentino
Pasquale	Sandro Meschino
Augusto	Franco Tovo

and Pasquale Ferrarese (Lino from La Spezia), Leandro Santarelli (Begalo, the Redhead), Emanuele di Bari (Gennario, the Troubedor), Antonio Spoletini (The Fireman), Nino Bionci (The Painter), Nino Venzi (A Client), Roberto Venzi (The Airman), Maria Bernardini (The Bride), Santino Citti (Father of the Bride), Lamberto Maggiorani (Patient), Elena Cameron, Maria Benati (Prostitutes), Renato Montabano, Enzo Fioravanti (Male Nurses), Loreto Ranalli, Mario Ferraguti (Male Prostitutes), Renato Capogna, Fulvio Orgitano, Renato Troiani, Mario Cipriani, Paolo Provenzale (Thugs)

A former prostitute hopes to leave her past behind and become a member of the middle class.

Ettore Garofolo, Anna Magnani

Agnes Soral, Serguej Dontsov

Seguej Donstov (r)

WINDOW TO PARIS

(SONY PICTURES CLASSICS) Producer, Guy Seligmann; Director, Yuri Mamin; Screenplay, Yuri Mamin, Arkadi Tigai; Photography, Sergei Nekrasov, Anatoli Lapchov; Set Designer, Vera Zelinskaia; Costumes, Natalya Zamakhina; Editors, Olga Andrianova, Joele Van Effenterre; Music, Yuri Mamin, Aleksei Zalivalov; a co-production of Films du Bouloi/Fontaine/La SEPT Cinema; Russian-French; Color; Rated PG-13; 87 minutes; February release

CAST

Nicole	Agnes Soral
Tchijov	Serguej Dontsov
Gorokhov	Viktor Michailov
Véra	Nina Oussatova
Gorokhov's Mother-in-Law	Kira Kreylis-Petrova
Gorokhov's Daughter	Natalja Ipatova
Kouzmitch	Viktor Gogolev
Maria Olégovna	Tamara Timofeeva
Gouliaiév	Andrej Ourgante
M. Prévost	Jean Rupert

Tchijov and Gorokhov discover a secret window in Tchijov's apartment which leads them to the rooftops of Paris.

Temuera Morrison, Rena Owen

Julian Arahanga (r)

Rena Owen, Temuera Morrison

Rena Owen

ONCE WERE WARRIORS

(FINE LINE FEATURES) Producer, Robin Scholes; Director, Lee Tamahori; Screenplay, Riwia Brown; Based on the novel by Alan Duff; Photography, Stuart Dryburgh; Editor, Michael Horton; Designer, Michael Kane; Music, Murray McNabb, Murray Grindaly; a Communicado Film in association with the New Zealand Film Commission, Avalon Studios and New Zealand on Air; New Zealand; Dolby Stereo; Color; Rated R; 108 minutes; February release

CAST

Beth Heke	Rena Owen
Jake Heke	Temuera Morrison
Grace Heke	Mamaengaroa Kerr-Bell
Nig Heke	Julian "Sonny" Arahanga
Boogie	Taungaroa Emile
Polly Heke	Rachael Morris
Huata Heke	Joseph Kairau
Bully	Clifford Curtis
Dooley	Pete Smith
Bennet	George Henare
Mavis	Mere Boyton
Toot	Shannon Williams

Drama about a contemporary Maori family in New Zealand and the physical abuse endured by Beth Heke from her volatile, hard-drinking husband Jake.

© Fine Line Features

Temuera Morrison, Rena Owen

SHALLOW GRAVE

(GRAMERCY) Producer, Andrew Macdonald; Executive Producer, Allan Scott; Director, Danny Boyle; Screenplay, John Hodge; Photography, Brian Tufano; Designer, Kave Quinn; Editor, Masahiro Hirakubo; Music, Simon Boswell; Title Music, Leftfield; Costumes, Kate Carin; Casting, Sarah Trevis; a Film Four International in association with the Glasgow Film Fund presentation, from PolyGram Filmed Entertainment; Scottish; Dolby Stereo; Color; Rated R; 92 minutes; February release

CAST

Juliet Miller	Kerry Fox
David Stephens	Christopher Eccleston
Alex Law	Ewan McGregor
Detective Inspector McCall	Ken Stott
Hugo	Keith Allen
Cameron	Colin McCredie
Visitors	Victoria Nairn, Gary Lewis
Goth	Jean Marie Coffey
Andy	Peter Mullan
Tim	Leonard O'Malley
Cash Machine Victim	David Scoular
Bath Victim	Grant Glendinning
Lumdsen	Robert David MacDonald
Doctor	Frances Low
Master of Ceremonies	Bill Denistoun
Brian McKinley	John Bett

and Tony Curren (Travel Agent), Elspeth Cameron (Elderly Woman), Paul Doonan (Newspaper Office Boy), Billy Riddoch (Newspaper Editor), Kenneth Bryans (Police Officer), John Hodge (D.C. Mitchell), John Carmichael and His Band

When their new roommate dies of a drug overdose, David, Alex, and Juliet are faced with moral decision of what to do with the suitcase full of cash the dead man has left behind.

© Gramercy Pictures

Kerry Fox, Ewan McGregor, Christopher Eccleston

Ewan McGregor

Christopher Eccleston

Christopher Eccleston, Kerry Fox, Ewan McGregor

Katrin Cartlidge, Rade Serbedzija

Katrin Cartlidge

Gregoire Colin

BEFORE THE RAIN

(GRAMERCY) Producers, Judy Counihan, Cedomir Kolar, Sam Taylor, Cat Villiers; Director/Screenplay, Milcho Manchevski; Co-Producers, Frederique Dumas-Zajdela, Marc Baschet, Gorjan Tozija, Vardar Films; Photography, Manuel Teran; Editor, Nicolas Gaster; Music, Anastasia; Designers, Sharon Lamofsky, David Munns; Casting, Moni Damevski, Liora Reich; an AIM Productions, NOE Productions and Vardar Film with the participation of British Screen and the European Co-Production Fund in association with Polygram Audiovisuel & the Ministry of Culuture for the Republic of Macedonia presentation; Macedonian-British-French; Dolby Stereo; Technovision; Color; Not rated; 115 minutes; February release

CAST

Aleksander	Rade Serbedzija
Anne	Katrin Cartlidge
Kiril	Gregoire Colin
Zamira	Labina Mitevska
Nick	Jay Villiers
Anne's Mother	Phyllida Law
Mitre	Ljupco Bresliski
Trajce	Vladimir Endrovski
Stojan	Igor Madzirov
Zekir	Abdurahman Salja
Hana	Silvija Stojanovska
Dr. Saso	Meto Jovanovski
Father Marko	Josif Josifovski
Petre	Boris Delcevski
Mate	Dejan Velkov
Father Damjan	Kiril Ristoski
Trifun	Mladen Krstevski
Kuzman	Dzemail Maksut
Aunt Cveta	Milica Stojanova
Zdrave	Petar Mircevski
Mome	Kiril Psaltirov
Tome	Metodi Psaltirov

and Mile Jovanovski (Priest Singing at Funeral), Ilko Stefanovski (Bojan), Blagoja Spirkovski-Dzumerko (Gang Leader), Sando Monev (Blagoj), Suzana Kirandziska (Neda), Katerina Kocevska (Kate), Atila Klince (Sefer), Vladimir Jacev (Alija), Arben Kastrati (Ramiz), Danny Newman (Ian), Gabrielle Hamilton (Woman in Cab), Moni Damevski (George), Ljupco Todorovski (Kizo), Peter Needham (Maitre D), Melissa Wilkes (Retarded Child), Joe Gould (Redhead Waiter), Rod Woodruff (Waiter in Fight), Aleksander Mikic (Atanas), Cvetko Mareski (Boy with Gun), Goran (Goran), Nino Levi (Mailman), Lence Delova (Bossy Clerk), Jordan Vitanov (Policeman)

A three part story involving a Macedonian monk and his feelings for a mysterious Albanian girl found at his monastery; a London photo editor and her relationship with her husband and Aleksander, a passionate photographer; and Aleksander's return to his childhood village in Macedonia.

Nominated for an Academy Award for best foreign-language film, 1994.

© Gramercy Pictures

Labina Mitevska

213

SON OF THE SHARK

(SEVENTH ART RELEASING) Producer, Francois Fries; Director/Screenplay, Agnes Merlet; Story, Agnes Merlet, Santiago Amigorena; Photography, Gerard Simon; Music, Bruno Coulais; Art Director, Laurent Allaire; Editors, Guy Lecorne, Pierre Choukroun; Color; Cinemascope; French-Belgian-Luxembourgian; Not rated; 88 minutes; March release

CAST

Martin Vanderhoes	Ludovic Vandendaele
Simon Vanderhoes	Erick Da Silva
Marie	Sandrine Blancke
Father	Maxime Leroux

Two young brothers are a constant menace to a small coastal French town, where they perpetually cause vandalism and trouble.

© Seventh Art

I Am Cuba

MINA TANNENBAUM

(NEW YORKER) Director/Screenplay, Martine Dugowson; Photography, Dominique Chapuis; Art Director, Philippe Chiffre; Costumes, Yan Tax; Editors, Martine Barraqué, Dominique Gallieni; Music, Peter Chase; Paintings, Zwy Milshtein; French; Color; Not rated; 128 minutes; March release

CAST

Mina Tannenbaum	Romane Bohringer
Ethel Bénégui	Elsa Zylberstein
The Cousin	Florence Thomassin
François	Nils Tavernier
Didier	Stéphane Slima
Daisy	Chantal Krief
Gisèle	Jany Gastaldi
Henri	Dimitri Furdui
Serge	Eric Defosse
Jacques	Dana Jean-Philippe Ecoffey
Gérard	Harry Cleven
Devas	Alexandre von Sivers
Naschich	Artus de Penguern
Mina (age 10)	Elise Benroubi
Ethel (age 10)	Shirley Kleinman
Mina (age 5)	Sabrina Germeau
Ethel (age 5)	Elodie Grosbois

Drama-comedy about the twenty-five-year friendship between two Jewish women in Paris: Mina, a painter, and Ethel, a journalist.

© New Yorker Films

Ludovic Vandendaele, Erick Da Silva

I AM CUBA

(MILESTONE) Director, Mikhail Kalatozov; Screenplay, Yevgeny Yevtushenko, Enrique Pineda Barnet; Photography, Sergei Urusevsky; Music, Carlos Fariñas; Presented by Francis Ford Coppola and Martin Scorsese; Cuban-Russian, 1964; Black and white; Not rated; 141 minutes; March release. Documentary on Bastista's early 1960's Cuba.

© Milestone Film

Romane Bohringer, Elsa Zylberstein

Stéfano Dionisi, Jacques Boudet, Elsa Zylberstein

Jeroen Krabbe

Enrico Lo Verso

FARINELLI

(SONY PICTURES CLASSICS) Producers, Vera Belmont, Linda Gutenberg, Aldo Lado, Dominique Janne, Stephane Thenoz; Director, Gérard Corbiau; Original Screenplay, Andree & Gerard Corbiau; Adapted for the screen by Marcel Beaulieu, Andree & Gérard Corbiau; Screenplay, Andree Corbiau; Photography, Walther Vanden Ende; Designer, Maria Cristina Reggio; Costumes, Olga Berlutti, Anne De Laugardiere; Makeup, Hair & Special Effects, Kuno Schlegelmilch; Editor, Joelle Hache; Belgian-Italian; Dolby Stereo; Color; Rated R; 110 minutes; March release

CAST

Farinelli (Carlo Broschi) ....Stéfano Dionisi
Riccardo Broschi..Enrico Lo Verso
Alexandra ....Elsa Zylberstein
Margaret Hunter ....Caroline Cellier
Countess Mauer ....Marianne Basler
Philip V ....Jacques Boudet
The Prince of Wales ....Graham Valentine
The Father ....Pier Paolo Capponi
The Young Admirer..Delphine Zentout
Porpora..Omero Antonutti
Handel ....Jeroen Krabbe
The Child ....Renaud du Peloux de Saint Romain

Celebrated eighteenth-century castrato singer Farinelli serves as the voice of his brother Riccardo's music; in a somewhat more bizarre partnership Riccardo follows through on the love trysts his castrated brother can not complete.

The film received an Academy Award nomination for foreign-language film.

Winner of the Hollywood Foreign Press Association (Golden Globes) Award for Best Foreign-Language Film of 1994.

Stéfano Dionisi

Mia Kirshner, Bruce Greenwood

Elias Koteas, Mia Kirshner

EXOTICA

(MIRAMAX) Producers, Atom Egoyan, Camelia Frieberg; Director/ Screenplay, Atom Egoyan; Photography, Paul Sarossy; Designers, Linda Del Rosario, Richard Paris; Costumes, Linda Muir; Editor, Susan Shipton; Music, Mychael Danna; Produced with the participation of Telefilm Canada and the Ontario Film Development Corporation; from Alliance International; Canadian; Dolby Digital Stereo; Color; Rated R; 103 minutes; March release

CAST

Francis	Bruce Greenwood
Christina	Mia Kirshner
Thomas	Don McKellar
Zoe	Arsinée Khanjian
Eric	Elias Koteas
Tracey	Sarah Polley
Harold	Victor Garber
Inspector	David Hemblen
CustomsOfficer	Calvin Green
Man in Taxi	Peter Krantz
Men at Opera	Damon D'Oliveira, Billy Merasty
Scalper	Jack Blum
Doorman	Ken McDougall

Drama about the relationships and desires of several employees and patrons of the upscale stripclub Exotica.

© Miramax Films

Russell Crowe, Jack Thompson

John Polson, Russell Crowe

MARTHA AND I

(CINEMA FOUR/ORIGINAL CINEMA) Producers, Sabine Tettenborn, Marius Schwartz; Director/Screenplay, Jiri Weiss; Photography, Viktor Ruzicka; Editor, Gisela Haller; Music, Jiri Stivin; a Maurice Kanbar presentation; Czech-German; Color; Not rated; 107 minutes; March release

CAST

Martha	Marianne Sägebrecht
Ernst Paul Fuchs	Michel Piccoli
Emil as a Youth	Vaclov Chalupa
Emil as an Adult	Ondrej Vetchy
Rosa	Bozidara Turzonova
Ida	Jana Brezinova

In mid-1930s Germany, Dr. Ernst Fuchs, a Czech Jew, stuns his family by marrying his German maid.

© Cinema Four, Inc.

THE SUM OF US

(SAMUEL GOLDWYN CO.) Producer, Hal McElroy; Executive Producers, Errol Sullivan, Hal McElroy; Co-Executive Producers, Hal "Corky" Kessler, Donald Scatena, Kevin Dowling; Directors, Kevin Dowling, Geoff Burton; Screenplay, David Stevens, based on his play; Photography, Geoff Burton; Editor, Frans Vandenburg; Music, Dave Faulkner; Designer, Graham "Grace" Walker; Casting, Faith Martin & Associates; a Southern Star in association with Australian Film Finance Corporation presentation; Australian; Dolby Stereo; Color; Not rated; 95 minutes; March release

CAST

Harry Mitchell	Jack Thompson
Jeff Mitchell	Russell Crowe
Greg	John Polson
Joyce Johnson	Deborah Kennedy
Young Jeff	Joss Moroney
Gran Mitch	Mathews
Mary Julie	Herbert
Football Coach	Des James
Footballer	Mick Campbell
Ferry Captain	Donny Muntz
Barmaid	Jan Adele
Jenny	Rebekah Elmaloglou
Desiree	Lola Nixon
Greg's Mother	Sally Cahill
Greg's Father	Bob Baines
George	Paul Freeman
Barman	Walter Kennard

and Stuart Campbell, Graham Drake (Leather Men), Elaine Lee (Woman on Train), Ross Anderson (Gardener), Michael Burgess (Foreman), John Rhall (Dad's Brother), Helen Williams (Brother's Wife), Jan Merriman (Nurse)

Jeff Mitchell finds that his father's opened-minded attitude about Jeff's homosexuality has its drawbacks where his son's dating is concerned. David Stevens' original play opened Off-Broadway in 1990 and starred Tony Goldwyn and Richard Venture.

© The Samuel Goldwyn Company

Vaclov Chalupa, Michel Piccoli, Marianne Sägebrecht

MURIEL'S WEDDING

(MIRAMAX) Producers, Lynda House, Jocelyn Moorhouse; Director/Screenplay, P.J. Hogan; Photography, Martin McGrath; Designer, Patrick Reardon; Costumes, Terry Ryan; Editor, Jill Bilcock; Music, Peter Best; Associate Producers, Michael D. Aglion, Tony Mahood; Casting, Alison Barrett; a CIBY 2000 presentation in association with the Australian Film Finance Corporation of a House and Moorhouse Films production; Australian; Color; Rated R; 105 minutes; March release

Toni Collette

CAST

Muriel Heslop	Toni Collette
Bill Heslop	Bill Hunter
Rhonda	Rachel Griffiths
Betty	Jeanie Drynan
Deidre	Gennie Nevinson
Brice	Matt Day
David Van Arkle	Daniel Lapaine
Tania	Sophie Lee
Janine	Belinda Jarrett
Cheryl	Rosalind Hammond
Nicole	Pippa Grandison
Ken Blundell	Chris Haywood
Perry Daniel	Wyllie
Joanie	Gabby Millgate
Penelope	Katie Saunders
Malcolm	Dene Kermond
Girl at Wedding	Susan Prior
Chook	Nathan Kaye
Tania's Mother	Cecily Polson
Higgins	Rob Steele
Store Detective	Genevieve Picot
Constable Saunders	Richard Sutherland
Constable Gillespie	Steve Smith
Chinese Waitress	Jeamin Lee
Chinese Maitre D'	Jon-Claire Lee
Akira	Kuni Hashimoto
Victor Keinosuke	Ken Senga
Island MC	Des Rodgers

and Rohan Jones, Scott Hall-Watson, Craig Olson, Justin Witham (Restaurant Boys), Rodney Arnold (Ejected Diner), Barry Crocker, Richard Morecroft (Themselves), Steve Cox (Cruise Taxi Driver), Kevin Copeland, James Schramko (Sailors), Richard Carter (Federal Policeman), John Gaden (Doctor), Heather Mitchell, Penne Hackforth-Jones (Bridal Manageresses), Heidi Lapaine, Kirsty Hinchcliffe (Bridal Assistants), Diane Smith (Physiotherapist), Darrin Klimek (Rhonda's Taxi Driver), Robert Alexander (Barrister), Troy Hardy (Young Boy), Robyn Pitt Owen (Singer at Muriel's Wedding), Annie Byron (Rhonda's Mother), Jacqueline Linke, Alvaro Marques, Fiona Sullivan, Ineke Rapp, Julian Garner (Press at Muriel's Wedding), Vincent Ball (Priest), John Hoare (Well Wisher at Muriel's Wedding), Frankie Davidson (Sergeant), Louise Cullen (Deidre's Friend), Basil Clarke (Funeral Priest), John Walton (Taxi Driver)

A frumpish, unpopular girl finds her life changing for the better after she makes friends with an old high schoolmate while on vacation.

Toni Collette

Rachel Griffith

Daniel Lapaine, Toni Collette

Rachel Griffith, Daniel Lapaine, Toni Collette, Bill Hunter

Rachel Griffith, Toni Collette, Matt Day

FUNNY BONES

(HOLLYWOOD PICTURES) Producers, Simon Fields, Peter Chelsom; Executive Producer, Nicholas Frye; Director, Peter Chelsom; Screenplay, Peter Chelsom, Peter Flannery; Photography, Eduardo Serra; Designer, Caroline Hanania; Editor, Martin Walsh; Music, John Altman; Costumes, Lindy Hemming; Casting, Janey Fothergill, Maggie Lunn, Mary Gail Artz, Barbara Cohen, Kate Dowd; Co-Producer, Laurie Borg; Distributed by Buena Vista Pictures; Dolby Digital Stereo; Technicolor; Rated R; 128 minutes; March release

Ruta Lee, Jerry Lewis, Amir Fawzi, Leslie Caron

CAST

Tommy Fawkes	Oliver Platt
Jack Parker	Lee Evans
Jim Minty	Richard Griffiths
Dolly Hopkins	Oliver Reed
Stanley Sharkey	Ian McNeice
Billy Mann	Terence Rigby
Al	William Hootkins
Battiston	Ticky Holgado
Thomas Parker	George Carl
Bruno Parker	Freddie Davies
Hal Dalzell	Harold Nicholas
Laura Fawkes	Ruta Lee
Katie Parker	Leslie Caron
George Fawkes	Jerry Lewis
Bellows	Richard Platt
Canavan	Peter McNamara
Skipper	Peter Martin
Pirard	Francois Domange
Barre	Olivier Py
Poquelin	Mouss
Jenny	Peter Pamela Rose
Gofor	Peter Morgan
Nicky	Peter Gunn
Policemen	Phil Atkinson, Nick Coppin
Steve Campbell	Gavin Millar
Lawrence Berger	Christopher Greet
Francesco	George Khan
Little Tommy	Amir Fawzi
Toast	"Sniff"
Backward Talking Man	Frank Harvey
Poodle Lady	Sadie Corre
Bag-Pipe Playing Dwarf	Rusty Goffe
Cox Twins	Freddie & Frank Cox
Doggyduo	Eileen Bell
Little Firewater	Brian Webb
Leo the Leprechaun	Andy Thompson & Peter Brande
Paper Tearer	Terri Carol
Bastard Son of Louis XIV	Shane Robinson
Themselves	Lee Jellyhead & the Ballet Hooligans
Plastic Cup Smasher	Benji Ming
Musical Saw Player	Maudie Blake
The Iceman	Anthony Irvine
Mr. Pearce	Fred Evans
Camilla Powell	Ruth Kettlewell
Puppeteer	Zipporah Simon
Himself	Phil Kelly
Comedians	Tony Barton, Mike Newman
Club Owner	George Raistrick
Security Guard	Jona Jones
Mayor	Mickey Baker
The Wychwoods	Mr. & Mrs. Mark Raffles
Ringmaster	Ian Rowe
Juggler	Laci Endresz Junior
Themselves	Bobbie Roberts & His Elephants
Ring Boy	Andras Banlak

and Chloe Treend, Andrea Bretherick, Lisa Henson, Rebecca Metcalfe, Camilla Simson, Tina Yoxall (Tropicana Dancers), Reg Griffiths, Duggie Chapman, Tony Peers, Andy Rashleigh (Reporters)

Oliver Platt

After his act bombs in Las Vegas, Tommy Fawkes, son of legendary comedian George Fawkes, heads to the seaside resort of Blackpool, England, hoping to buy some comedy material to ensure him greater success.

© Hollywood Pictures Company

Freddie Davies, George Carl, Lee Evans

CIRCLE OF FRIENDS

(SAVOY) Producers, Arlene Sellers, Alex Winitsky, Frank Price; Executive Producer, Terence Clegg; Director, Pat O'Connor; Screenplay, Andrew Davies; Based upon the novel by Maeve Binchy; Photography, Ken MacMillan; Editor, John Jympson; Designer, Jim Clay; Music, Michael Kamen; Costumes, Anushia Nierdazik; Co-Producer, Kenith Trodd; Casting, Mary Selway, Simone Ireland; a Price Entertainment/Lantana production presented in association with Rank Film Distributors; British-Irish; Dolby Digital Stereo; Technicolor; Rated PG-13; 112 minutes; March release

Chris O'Donnell, Minnie Driver

CAST

Jack Foley	Chris O'Donnell
Benny	Minnie Driver
Eve	Geraldine O'Rawe
Nan	Saffron Burrows
Sean	Alan Cumming
Simon Westward	Colin Firth
Aidan	Aidan Gillen
Dan Hogan	Mick Lally
Mrs. Hogan	Britta Smith
Brian Mahon	John Kavanagh
Emily Mahon	Ruth McCabe
Professor Flynn	Ciaran Hinds
Dr. Foley	Tony Doyle
Mrs. Foley	Marie Mullen
Mrs. Healy	Marie Conmee
Mr. Flood	Gerry Walsh
Mr. Duggan	Sean McGinley
Professor Maclure	Tom Hickey
Parish Priest	Seamus Forde
Celia Westward	Ingrid Craigie
Major Westward	Major Lambert
Big House Maid	Pauline Delany
Nasey Mahon	Jason Barry
Paul Mahon	Edward Manning
Hibernian Waiter	Phil Kelly
Rosemary	Gwynne McElveen
Sheila	Marguerite Drea
Bill Dunne	Stephen Rooney
Moaning Girl	Cathy Belton
Sobbing Girl	Elizabeth Keller
Rugby Girl	Tanya Cawley
Dancing Girl	Niamh O'Byrne
Benny (10 years old)	Dervla O'Farrell
Nan (10 years old)	Pamela Cardillo
Eve (10 years old)	Louise Maher

and Karen O'Neill, Elaine Dunphy, Emma Lannon (Little Girls), Margaret O'Neill, Maureen Lyster, Eliza Dear (Nuns), Brendan Conroy (Priest)

Romantic drama set in 1957 Ireland. Benny, a plain and shy girl, joins her friends Eve and Nan at college in Dublin where she falls in love with Jack Foley, a handsome rugby player.

© Savoy Pictures

Alan Cumming

Colin Firth, Saffron Burrows

Saffron Burrows, Minnie Driver, Chris O'Donnell, Geraldine O'Rawe

Minnie Driver, Geraldine O'Rawe, Saffron Burrows

PRIEST

(MIRAMAX) Producers, George Faber, Josephine Ward; Executive Producer, Mark Shivas; Director, Antonia Bird; Screenplay, Jimmy McGovern; Photography, Fred Tammes; Designer, Raymond Langhorn; Costumes, Jill Taylor; Music, Andy Roberts; Editor, Susan Spivey; Casting, Janet Goddard; a BBC Films production; British; Dolby Stereo; Color; Rated R; 97 minutes; March release

CAST

Father Greg Pilkington	Linus Roache
Father Matthew Thomas	Tom Wilkinson
Maria Kerrigan	Cathy Tyson
Graham	Robert Carlyle
Father Ellerton	James Ellis
Mrs. Unsworth	Lesley Sharp
Mr. Unsworth	Robert Pugh
Lisa Unsworth	Christine Tremarco
Charlie	Paul Barber
Bishop	Rio Fanning
Funeral Director	Jimmy Coleman
Altar Boy	Bill Dean
Ellie Molloy	Gilly Coman
Patrick	Fred Pearson
Mick Molloy	Jimmy Gallagher
Tommy	Tony Booth
Tommy's Children	Charley Wilde, Euan Blair
Man in Lift	Giuseppe Murphy
Mrs. Gobshite	Kim Johnson
Mr. Gobshite	Keith Cole
Jehovah's Witness	Adrian Luty
Bobby	Bobby Martino
Man on Skateboard	Rupert Pearson

and Mandy Walsh, Stephanie Roscoe, Ann Haydn-Edwards, Mike Haydn (Guests at Wake), Victoria Arnold (Girl in Confessional), Gareth Potsig (Boy Car Thief), Ray Williams (Boy with Stutter), Valerie Lilley (Sister Kevin), Kevin Jones (Boy at Beach), Michael Ananins (Charge Sergeant), Mickey Poppins (Reporter), Marsha Thomason (Nurse), Matyelok Gibbs (Housekeeper), John Bennett (Father Redstone), Gareth Milne (Fight Arranger), Mauricio Venegas (Chilean Band Leader)

Father Greg, a priest newly assigned to a poor parish in Liverpool, finds his religious ideals challenged in light of his own homosexuality and the dilemma of a child molestation case he has learned of in the confessional.

Linus Roche

Linus Roche, Christine Tremarco

Linus Roche

Tom Wilkinson, Linus Roche

Linus Roche, Tom Wilkinson, Cathy Tyson

THE WILD REEDS

(STRAND) Producers, Alain Sarde, Georges Benayoun; Director, Andre Techine; Screenplay, Andre Techine, Gilles Taurand, Olivier Massart; Photography, Jeanne Lapoirie; Editor, Martine Giordano; Casting, Michel Nasri; a co-production of IMA Films/Films Alain Sarde/Canal+/La SEPT/Arte/IMA Productions/SFP Productions; French; Color; Not rated; 110 minutes; April release.

CAST

Henri	Frederic Gorny
François	Gael Morel
Maité	Elodie Bouchez
Serge	Stephane Rideau
Mme. Alvarez	Michele Moretti
The Bride	Nathalie Vigne
The Photographer	Laurent Groulout

In 1962 France, young François finds himself falling in love with class-mate Serge.

© Strand Releasing

Gael Morel, Elodie Bouchez

Youki Kudoh, Tamlyn Tomita

Gael Morel

Youki Kudoh, Akira Takayama

PICTURE BRIDE

(MIRAMAX) Producers, Lisa Onodera, Diana Mei Lin Mark; Director, Kayo Hatta; Screenplay, Kayo Hatta, Mari Hatta; Photography, Claudio Rocha; Editors, Lynzee Klingman, Mallory Gottlieb; Presented in association with Thousand Cranes Filmworks; Japanese; Dolby Digital Stereo; Color; Rated PG-13; 95 minutes; April release

CAST

Riyo	Youki Kudoh
Matsuji	Akira Takayama
Kana	Tamlyn Tomita
Kanzaki	Cary-Hiroyuki Tagawa
The Benshi	Toshiro Mifune
Aunt Sode	Yoko Sugi

Orphaned Riyo reluctantly sets sail for Hawaii to become the bride of a Japanese man who emigrated to the Hawaiian Islands to become a sugar-cane worker.

© Miramax Films

Naoto Takenaka, Michiko Hada

Masahiro Motoki, Michiko Hada

THE MYSTERY OF RAMPO

(SAMUEL GOLDWYN CO.) Producer, Yoshihisa Nakagawa; Executive Producer/Director, Kazuyoshi Okuyama; Screenplay, Kazuyoshi Okuyama, Yuhei Enoki; Story, Rampo Edogawa; Photography, Yasushi Sasakibara; Designer, Kyoko Heya; Music, Akira Senju; Costumes, Sachico Ito; Editor, Akimasa Kawashima; Japanese; a Team Okuyama presentation of a Shochiku/Rampo Project production; Dolby Digital Stereo; Color; Not rated; 100 minutes; May release

CAST

Kogoro Akechi	Masahiro Motoki
Edogawa Rampo	Naoto Takenaka
Shizuko/Marquess	Michiko Hada
Masashi Yokomizo	Teruyuki Kagawa
Marquis Ogawara	Mikijiro Hira

Edogawa Rampo, a mystery writer, finds his imagination so vivid that his writings and characters become a part of the real world.

© The Samuel Goldwyn Company

John Hargreaves, Joan Plowright

HOTEL SORRENTO

(CASTLE HILL) a.k.a. *Sorrento Beach*; Producer/Director, Richard Franklin; Co-Producer, Helen Watts; Screenplay, Richard Franklin, Peter Fitzpatrick; Based on the play by Hannie Rayson; Photography, Geoff Burton; Designer, Tracey Watt; Editor, David Pulbrook; Costumes, Lisa Meagher; Music, Nerida Tyson Chew; Casting, Greg Apps; Australian; Dolby Stereo; Color; Not rated; 112 minutes; May release

CAST

Meg Moynihan	Caroline Goodall
Hilary Moynihan	Caroline Gillmer
Pippa Moynihan	Tara Morice
Marge Morrisey	Joan Plowright
Wal Moynihan	Ray Barrett
Edwin	Nicholas Bell
Troy Moynihan	Ben Thomas
Dick Bennett	John Hargreaves

At a family reunion, conflict errupts between three sisters after one of them publishes a thinly disguised autobiography.

© Castle Hill Productions, Inc.

Tara Morice, Caroline Goodall, Joan Plowright, Caroline Gillmer

Hugh Grant

Colm Meaney, Kenneth Griffith

Tara Fitzgerald, Hugh Grant

THE ENGLISHMAN WHO WENT UP A HILL BUT CAME DOWN A MOUNTAIN

(MIRAMAX) Producer, Sarah Curtis; Executive Producers, Sally Hibbin, Robert Jones, Bob Weinstein, Harvey Weinstein; Director/Screenplay, Christopher Monger; Photography, Vernon Layton; Editor, David Martin; Music, Stephen Endelman; Designer, Charles Garrad; Costumes, Janty Yates; Casting, Michelle Guish; Special Mountain Building, Jack Jones; a Parallax Pictures Production; British; Dolby Digital Stereo; Panavision; Color; Rated PG; 99 minutes; May release

CAST

Reginald Anson	Hugh Grant
Betty of Cardiff	Tara Fitzgerald
Morgan the Goat	Colm Meaney
George Garrad	Ian McNeice
Johnny Shellshocked	Ian Hart
Reverend Jones	Kenneth Griffith
Thomas Twp	Tudor Vaughn
Thomas Twp, Too	Hugh Vaughn
Williams the Petroleum	Robert Pugh
Ivor the Grocer	Robert Blythe
Davies the School	Garfield Morgan
Blod	Lisa Palfrey
Tommy Twostrokes	Dafydd Wyn Roberts
Sergeant	Iuean Rhys
Mavis	Anwen Williams
Jones the JP	David Lloyd Meredith
Evans the End of the World	Fraser Cains
Grandfather	Jack Walters
Young Boy	Harry Kretchmer
Thomas the Trains	Howell Evans
Girl in Classroom	Maisie McNeice

During World War I, the townspeople of the Welsh village of Ffynnon Garw are dismayed when a pair of English cartographers inform them that their local peak falls fifteen feet short of qualifying as a mountain.

© Miramax Films

A PURE FORMALITY

(SONY PICTURES CLASSICS) Producers, Mario & Vittorio Cecchi Gori; Executive Producers, Bruno Altissimi, Claudio Saranceni; Director/Story/Editor, Giuseppe Tornatore; Screenplay, Giuseppe Tornatore, Pascale Quignard; Photography, Blasco Giurato; Music, Ennio Morricone; Designer, Andrea Crisanti; Costumes, Beatrice Bordone; Italian-French; Dolby Stereo; Cinemascope; Color; Rated PG-13; 108 minutes; May release

CAST

Onoff	Gerard Depardieu
The Inspector	Roman Polanski
Andre, the Young Policeman	Sergio Rubini
The Captain	Nicola Di Pinto
The Warrant Officer	Paolo Lombardi
The Old Attendant	Tano Cimarosa
Paula	Maria Rosa Spagnolo

A police inspector is confronted by a man who claims to be the noted poet Onoff, but believes he might actually be the person responsible for a murder committed near Onoff's home.

© Sony Pictures Entertainment Inc.

Roman Polanski, Gerard Depardieu

Jodhi May, Joely Richardson

Gerard Depardieu, Roman Polanski

SISTER MY SISTER

(SEVENTH ART) Producer, Norma Heyman; Director, Nancy Meckler; Screenplay, Wendy Kesselman; Photography, Ashley Rowpe; Music, Stephen Warbeck; Editor, David Stiven; a Film Four International and British Screen presentation of an NFH production; British; Color; Not Rated; 89 minutes; June release

CAST

Madame Danzard	Julie Walters
Christine	Joely Richardson
Lea	Jodhi May
Isabelle Danzard	Sophie Thursfield
Visitors	Amelda Brown, Lucita Pope
Sister Veronica	Kate Gartside
Young Lea	Aimee Schmidt
Young Christine	Gabriella Schmidt

A pair of sisters working as maids for the overbearing Madame Danzard find themselves becoming obsessed with one another, both emotionally and sexually.

© Seventh Art

Jodhi May, Joely Richardson, Sophie Thursfield, Julie Walters

Massimo Troisi, Philippe Noiret, Maria Grazia Cucinotta

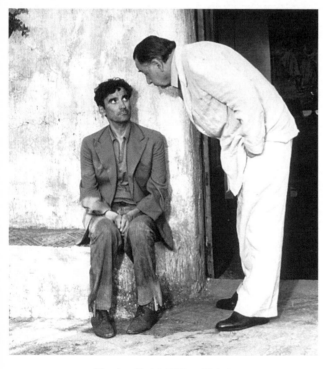

Massimo Troisi, Philippe Noiret

THE POSTMAN *(IL POSTINO)*

(MIRAMAX) Producers, Mario & Vittorio Cecchi Gori, Gaetano Daniele; Executive Producer, Albert Passone; Director, Michael Radford; Screenplay, Anna Pavignano, Michael Radford, Furio Scarpelli, Giacomo Scarpelli, Massimo Troisi; Based on the novel *Burning Patience* by Antonio Skarmeta; Photography, Franco Di Giacomo; Editor, Roberto Perpignani; Music, Luis Enrique Bacalov; Designer, Lorenzo Baraldi; Costumes, Gianni Gissi; Italian-French; Dolby Stereo; Color; Rated PG; 113 minutes; June release

CAST

Mario Ruoppolo ....Massimo Troisi
Pablo Neruda ....Philippe Noiret
Beatrice Russo......................................Maria Grazia Cucinotta
Rosa...Linda Moretti
Telegraph Operator ....Renato Scarpa
Matilde ....Anna Bonaiuto
Di Cosimo..Mariano Rigillo

On a small Italian island, a shy, lonely postman's life changes when he befriends an exiled Chilean poet. Actor Massimo Troisi died shortly after the completion of this film.

Academy Award winner for Best Original Dramatic Score. The film received additional Oscar nominations for picture, actor (Troisi), director, and screenplay adaptation.

© Miramax Films

Philippe Noiret, Massimo Troisi

Maria Grazia Cucinotta, Massimo Troisi

Thomas Gibson, Matthew Ferguson

Matthew Ferguson, Cameron Bancroft, Ruth Marshall, Thomas Gibson,
Joanne Vannicola, Mia Kirshner, Rick Roberts

Rick Roberts, Ruth Marshall

Cameron Bancroft

LOVE AND HUMAN REMAINS

(SONY PICTURES CLASSICS) Producer, Roger Frappier; Director, Denys Arcand; Screenplay, Brad Fraser, based on his play *Unidentified Human Remains and the True Nature of Love*; Co-Producer, Peter Sussman; Executive Producers, Roger Frappier, Pierre Latour; Photography, Paul Sarossy; Designer, Francois Seguin; Editor, Alain Baril; Music, John McCarthy; Costumes, Denis Sperdouklis; Casting, Deirdre Bowen, Lynn Kressel, Lucie Robitaille, Stuart Aikins; a Max Films Inc. in co-production with Atlantis Films Limited production; Canadian; Color; Rated R; 99 minutes; June release

CAST

David	Thomas Gibson
Candy	Ruth Marshall
Bernie	Cameron Bancroft
Benita	Mia Kirshner
Robert	Rick Roberts
Jerri	Joanne Vannicola
Kane	Matthew Ferguson

Roommates and ex-lovers David and Candy search for sex and love in the 1990s while a serial killer stalks the city.

© Sony Pictures Entertainment

Joanne Vannicola, Thomas Gibson, Ruth Marshall

BANDIT QUEEN

(ARROW) Producer, Sundeep S. Bedi; Director, Shekhar Kapur; Screenplay, Mala Sen; Photography, Ashok Mehta; Designer, Eve Mavrakis; Music, Nusrat Fateh Ali Khan; Editor, Renu Saluja; Costumes, Dolly Ahluwalia; Casting, Tigmanshu Dhulia; a Film Four International and Kaleidoscope presentation; Indian; Dolby Stereo; Color; Not rated; 119 minutes; June release

CAST

Phoolan Devi	Seema Biswas
Vikram Mallah	Nirmal Pandey
Man	Singh Manoj Bajpai
Mustaquim	Rajesh Vivek
Madho	Raghuvir Yadav
Sriram	Govind Namdeo
Kailash	Saurabh Shukla
Puttilal	Aditya Srivastava
Young Phoolan	Sunita Bhatt

True story of Phoolan Devi, a bandit who becomes a hero to India's lower-caste citizens.

© Arrow Releasing Inc.

Seema Biswas

Carole Bouquet

Michel Blanc, Philippe Noiret

Michel Blanc (c)

GROSSE FATIGUE

(MIRAMAX ZOË) a.k.a. *Dead Tired*; Producer, Patrice Ledoux; Director/Screenplay, Michel Blanc; From an original idea by Bertrand Blier; Photography, Eduardo Serra; Music, Rene-Marc Bini; Set Decorator, Carlos Conti; Costumes, Elizabeth Tavernier; Editor, Maryline Monthieux; Special Effects, George Demetrau; Gaumont-TFI Films production; French; Dolby Stereo; Color; Rated R; 84 minutes; July release

CAST

Michel Blanc	Michael Blanc
Carole Bouquet	Carole Bouquet
Phillipe Noiret	Phillipe Noiret
The Inspector	Jacques Buron
The Deputy	Francois Morel
Michel Blanc's Agent	Dominique Besnehard
The Psychiatrist	Jean-Louis Richard
Michel Blanc's Father	Raoul Billerey

and Josiane Balasko, Marie Anne Chazel, Christian Clavier, Guillaume Durand, Charlotte Gainsbourg, David Halliday, Estelle Halliday, Gerard Jugnot, Dominique Lavanant, Thierry Lhermitte, Mathilda May, Roman Polanski, Regine, Gilles Jacob (Themselves)

Actor Michel Blanc is alarmed to discover that a look-alike has been passing himself off as Blanc, ruining the performer's reputation.

© Miramax Films

Hugh Grant, Peter Firth, Georgina Cates

Alan Rickman, Georgina Cates

Alan Cox, Hugh Grant

AN AWFULLY BIG ADVENTURE

(FINE LINE FEATURES) Producers, Hilary Heath, Philip Hinchcliffe; Executive Producers, John Kelleher, Mark Shivas, John Sivers; Director, Mike Newell; Screenplay, Charles Wood; Based on the novel by Beryl Bainbridge; Photography, Dick Pope; Editor, Jon Gregory; Designer, Mark Geraghty; Costumes, Joan Bergin; Music, Richard Hartley; Associate Producer, Andrew Warren; Casting, Susie Figgis; from Portman Prods., with the participation of British Screen in association with BBC Films and Wolfhound Films; British; Dolby Stereo; Color; Rated R; 110 minutes; July release

CAST

P.L. O'Hara	Alan Rickman
Meredith Potter	Hugh Grant
Stella Bradshaw	Georgina Cates
Uncle Vernon	Alun Armstrong
Bunny	Peter Firth
Rose	Prunella Scales
Aunt Lily	Rita Tushingham
Geoffrey	Alan Cox
St. Ives	Edward Petherbridge
Dotty Blundell	Nicola Pagett
Dawn Allenby	Carol Drinkwater
Desmond Fairchild	Clive Merrison
George	Gerard McSorley
Grace Bird	Ruth McCabe
John Harbour	James Frain
Mr. Harcourt	Pat Laffan
Mary Deare	Patti Love
Babs Osbourne	Hilary Reynolds
Freddie Reynalde	Tom Hickey
Reporter	Robbie Doolan
Disley	Brendan Conroy
One Eye	Johnny Murphy

In postwar Liverpool, sixteen-year-old Stella lands a job as stage manager for a second rate theatrical troupe run by the callous Meredith Potter.

© Fine Line Features

COUNTRY LIFE

(MIRAMAX) Producer, Robin Dalton; Director/Screenplay, Michael Blakemore; Photography, Stephen Windon; Designer, Laurence Eastwood; Music, Peter Best; Editor, Nicholas Beauman; Line Producer, Adrienne Read; Costumes, Wendy Chuck; the Austrlialian Film Finance Corporation presentation of a Dalton Films production; Australian; Dolby Stereo; Color; Rated PG-13; 107 minutes; July release

CAST

Max Askey	Sam Neill
Deborah Voysey	Greta Scacchi
Jack Dickens	John Hargreaves
Sally Voysey	Kerry Fox
Alexander Voysey	Michael Blakemore
Hannah	Googie Withers
Fred Livingstone	Maurie Fields
Maud Dickens	Robyn Cruze
Wally	Ron Blanchard

In 1919 Australia, a young woman and her uncle are visited on their sheep ranch by various relatives and friends, in this comical revision of Anton Chekhov's Uncle Vanya.

© Miramax Films

Greta Scacchi, Michael Blakemore

Greta Scacchi, Kerry Fox, Sam Neill

DOUBLE HAPPINESS

(FINE LINE FEATURES) Producers, Steve Hegyes, Rose Lam Waddell; Director/Screenplay, Mina Shum; Photography, Peter Wunstorf; Designer, Michael Bjornson; Costumes, Cynthia Summers; Editor, Alison Grace; Music, Shadowy Men on a Shadowy Planet; a First Generation Films Inc. & New Views presentation; Canadian; Dolby Stereo; Color; Rated PG-13; 87 minutes; July release

CAST

Jade Li	Sandra Oh
Mom Li	Alannah Ong
Dad Li	Stephen Chang
Pearl Li	Frances You
Andrew Chau	Johnny Mah
Mark	Callum Rennie
Sau Wan Chin	Donald Fong
Lisa Chan	Claudette Carracedo
Mrs. Mar	Barbara Tse
Robert Chu	Nathan Fong
Carmen	Lesley Ewen
Auntie Bing	So Yee Shum
Uncle Bing	Greg Chan

Comedy about a Chinese-Canadian aspiring actress, Jade Li, who falls in love with a white university student just after her parents have set her up with a Chinese lawyer.

© Fine Line Features

Stephen Chang, Alannah Ong, Sandra Oh, Frances You

Sandra Oh, Callum Rennie

James Cromwell, Babe

Magda Szubanski, James Cromwell

Babe, Sheep

James Cromwell, Babe

BABE

(UNIVERSAL) Producers, George Miller, Doug Mitchell, Bill Miller; Director, Chris Noonan; Screenplay, George Miller, Chris Noonan; Based on the book *The Sheep-Pig* by Dick King-Smith; Photography, Andrew Lesnie; Designer, Roger Ford; Editors, Marcus D'Arcy, Jay Friedkin; Music, Nigel Westlake; Song: "If I Had Words" (adapted from Camille Saint Saens' Symphony No. 3) with lyrics by Johnathon Hodge/performed by James Cromwell, Mice Chorus; Animatronic Characters, Jim Henson's Creature Shop; Sheep Characters, John Cox & Robotechnology; Animation and Visual Effects, Rhythm & Hues; Animal Action/Babe's Trainer, Karl Lewis Miller; Casting, Liz Mullinar Casting & Valerie McCaffrey; Australian; a Kennedy Miller Film; Dolby DTS Stereo; Color; Rated G; 91 minutes; August release

VOICE CAST

Babe	Christine Cavanaugh
Fly	Miriam Margolyes
Ferdinand	Danny Mann
Rex	Hugo Weaving
Maa	Miriam Flynn
Cat	Russie Taylor
Old Ewe	Evelyn Krape
Horse	Michael Edward-Stevens
Cow	Charles Bartlett
Rooster	Paul Livingston
Narrator	Roscoe Lee Browne

CAST

Farmer Hoggett	James Cromwell
Esme Hoggett	Magda Szubanski
Daughter	Zoe Burton
Son-in-Law	Paul Goddard
Grandson	Wade Hayward
Granddaughter	Britany Byrnes
Valda	Mary Acres
Country Women	Janet Foye, Pamela Hawken, Karen Gough
The Vet	David Webb
Chairman of Judges	Marshall Napier
Lion's Club Men	Hec MacMillan, Ken Gregory
Sheep Rustler	Nicholas Lidstone
Electrical Linesman	Trevor Read, Nicholas Blake
Sheepdog Trial Officer	Matthew Long
TV Commentators	John Doyle, Mike Harris

and: Additional Voices: Ross Bagley, Gemini Barnett, Rachel Davey, Debi Derryberry, Jazzmine Dillingham, Courtland Mead, Kevin Woods (Puppies), Jane Alden, Kimberly Bailey, Patrika Darbo, Michelle Davison, Julie Forsyth, Maeve Germaine, Rosanna Huffman, Carlyle King, Tina Lifford, Genni Nevinson, Linda Phillips, Paige Pollack, Kerry Walker (Sheep)

Babe, an orphaned pig, ends up on the Hoggett farm where he aspires to become a sheep herder.

Academy Award winner for Best Visual Effects. The film received additional Oscar nominations for picture, supporting actor (Cromwell), director, screenplay adaptation, film editing, and art direction.

© Universal City Studios Inc.

James Cromwell, Babe

Babe, Fly

Babe

Sheep, Babe

I CAN'T SLEEP

(NEW YORKER) Executive Producer, Bruno Pesery; Director, Claire Denis; Screenplay, Claire Denis, Jean-Pol Fargeau; Photography, Agnes Godard; Designers, Thierry Flammand, Arnaud De Moleron; Editor, Nelly Quettier; Costumes, Claire Fraisse; French; Color; Not rated; 110 minutes; August release

CAST

Mona	Beatrice Dalle
Ninon	Line Renaud
Théo	Alex Descas
The Doctor	Laurent Grevill
Daïga	Katerina Golubeva
Camille	Richard Courcet
Raphaël	Vincent Dupont
Harry	Ira Mandella-Paul
Mina	Irina Grjebina
Vassili	Tolsty
Abel	Patrick Grandperret
Alice	Sophie Simon

Thriller based on a true story about two homosexuals in Paris who are randomly murdering elderly women.

° New Yorker Films

Anthony Hopkins, Isabella Rossellini

Campbell Scott, Isabella Rossellini

NICO ICON

(ROXIE RELEASING) Producers, Thomas Mertens, Annette Pisacane; Director/Screenplay, Susanne Ofteringer; Photography, Judith Kaufmann, Katarzyna Remin, Martin Baer; Editors, Elfe Brandenburger, Guido Krajewski; a Clak Filmproduktion presentation; German; Color; Not rated; 70 minutes; September release. Documentary on Velvet Underground singer Nico.

° Roxie Releasing

Laurent Grevill, Richard Courcet

THE INNOCENT

(MIRAMAX) Producers, Norma Heyman, Chris Sievernich, Wieland Schulz-Keil; Executive Producer, Anne Dubinet; Director, John Schlesigner; Screenplay, Ian McEwan, based on his novel; Photography, Dietrich Lohmann; Designer, Lucianna Arrighi; Music, Gerald Gouriet; Editor, Richard Marden; Line Producer, Ingrid Windisch; British, 1993; Dolby Digital Stereo; Color; Rated R; 118 minutes; September release

CAST

Bob Glass	Anthony Hopkins
Maria	Isabella Rossellini
Leonard Marnham	Campbell Scott
Otto	Ronald Nitschke
Russell	Hart Bochner
MacNamee	James Grant
Lofting	Jeremy Sinden
Black	Richard Durden
Lou	Corey Johnson

Leonard Marnham, a British electronics expert in Berlin in the mid-1950s for a classified government operation, falls in love with the mysterious Maria.

° Miramax Films

Nico

A MONTH BY THE LAKE

(MIRAMAX) Producer, Robert Fox; Executive Producers, Bob Weinstein, Harvey Weinstein, Donna Gigliotti; Director, John Irvin; Screenplay, Trevor Bentham; Based on the novella by H.E. Bates; Photography, Pasqualino de Santis; Designer, Giovanni Giovagnoni; Costumes, Lia Morandini; Music, Nicola Piovani; Editor, Peter Tanner; British; Dolby Stereo; Color; Rated PG; 94 minutes; September release

Vanessa Redgrave, Edward Fox

CAST

Miss Bentley	Vanessa Redgrave
Major Wilshaw	Edward Fox
Miss Beaumont	Uma Thurman
Mrs. Fascioli	Alida Valli
Vittorio	Alessandro Gassman
Mr. Bonizzoni	Carlo Cartier
Mrs. Bonizzoni	Natalia Bizzi
Enrico	Paola Lombardi
Maria	Sonia Maertinelli
American Ladies	Frances Nacman, Veronica Wells
Guido	Riccardo Rossi
Italian Girl	Anjanta Barilli
Angels	Bianca Tognocchi, Caroltta Bresciani

A middle-aged spinster, Miss Bentley, taking her annual vacation to Lake Como, Italy, finds herself attracted to another visitor at her hotel, Major Wilshaw.

© Miramax Films

Vanessa Redgrave

Vanessa Redgrave, Uma Thurman

Vanessa Redgrave, Edward Fox

Alessandro Gassman, Vanessa Redgrave

Matt Keeslar, Albert Finney

Matt Keeslar, Anthony Brophy

Matt Keeslar, Victoria Smurfit

THE RUN OF THE COUNTRY

(COLUMBIA) Producers, Peter Yates, Ruth Boswell; Executive Producer, Nigel Wooll; Director, Peter Yates; Screenplay, Shane Connaughton, based on his novel; Photography, Mike Southon; Art Director, David Wilson; Music, Cynthia Millar; Editor, Paul Hodgson; a Castle Rock Entertainment presentation of a One Two Nine production; British-Irish; Dolby Stereo; Panavision; Technicolor; Rated R; 109 minutes; September release

CAST

Father	Albert Finney
Danny	Matt Keeslar
Annagh	Victoria Smurfit
Prunty	Anthony Brophy
Father Gaynor	David Kelly
Mother	Dearbhla Molloy
Mrs. Prunty	Carole Nimmons
Annagh's Uncle	Vinnie McCabe
Barman	Trevor Clark
Big Man	Kevin Murphy
Bouncer Patterson	Michael O'Reilly
Carolan	P.J. Brady
Dolan	Miche Doherty
Farmer	Declan Mulholland
Daphne	Dawn Bradfield
Lookout	Paddy McGuinness
Man	Christy Mahon
McQuade	Pat Kinevane
Monkey	Joe Hanley
Mrs. McKenna	Maureen Dow
Mrs. Lee	Eileen Ward
Rennicks	Thomas Lappin
Soldier	Robin Hines
Wench	Antoine Byrne
Man at Annagh's	Seamus O'Rourke
Widdy McGinn	Joan Sheehy

and Noel Smith (Goblin Gilmour), Hugh B. O'Brien (Danny's Uncle), Aine Ni Mhuiri (Danny's Aunt), Sissy Connolly (Elderly Lady), Mary Reilly (Woman), The Titanic Cinq (Band)

In a small village on the Northern Ireland border, eighteen-year-old Danny runs away from his staid life with his father after his mother dies.

© Castle Rock Entertainment

I, THE WORST OF ALL

(FIRST RUN FEATURES) Producer, Lita Stantic; Director, Maria Luisa Bemberg; Screenplay, Maria Luisa Bemberg, Antonio Larreta; Based on the novel *The Traps of Faith* by Octavio Paz; Photography, Felix Monti; Designer, Voytek; Editor, Juan Calros Maclas; Music, Luis Maria Serra; from CEO Cinematografica; Spanish, 1990; Color; Not rated; 100 minutes; September release

CAST

Juana Inés de la Cruz	Assumpta Serna
Maria Luisa	Dominique Sanda
Archbishop Sejas	Lautaro Murua
The Viceroy	Héctor Alterio

During the time of the Inquisition, a free-thinking nun comes into conflict with the newly appointed archbishop.

© First Run Features

Assumpta Serna

THE OLD LADY WHO WALKED IN THE SEA

(CFP DISTRIBUTION) Director, Laurent Heynemann; Screenplay, Dominique Roulet; Adaptation, Dominique Roulet, Laurent Heynemann; Based on the novel by San Antonio; Photography, Robert Alazraki; Set Decorator, Valerie Grail; Music, Phillippe Sarde; Costumes, Catherine Leterrier; Editor, Jacques Comets; Casting, Shula Siegfried; a co-production with Blue Dahlia Production/Societe Financiere de Coproduction/Films A2/Little Bear/J.M. Productions with the participation of Canal+/Les Soficas Sofiarp & Investimages 3/de Grupo Bema (Rome) & du Centre National de la Cineatographie; French; Color; Not rated; 95 minutes; September release.

CAST

Lady M	Jeanne Moreau
Pompilius	Michel Serrault
Lambert	Luc Thullier
Noemie	Geraldine Danon
Mazurier	Jean Bouchard
Muriel	Marie-Dominique Aumont
Principal's Daughter	Hester Wilcox
Girl in blue	Lea Gabriele
Librarian	Lara Guirao
Stern	Mattia Sbragia

A pair of aging con-artists and ex-lovers, Lady M and Pompilius, arrive in Guadelupe where Lady M sets her sights on a young and handsome towel boy, Lambert, hoping to make him her new protégé in crime.

© CFP Distribution

Jeanne Moreau, Michel Serrault

MUTE WITNESS

(SONY PICTURES CLASSICS) Producers, Alexander Buchman, Norbert Soentgen, Anthony Waller; Executive Producer, Richard Claus; Director/Screenplay, Anthony Waller; Co-Producers, Grigory Riazhsky, Alexander Atanesjan; Photography, Egon Werdin; Art Director, Barbara Becker; Editor, Peter Adam; Music, Wilbert Hirsch; a Comet Film and Avrora Media presentation in association with Cobblestone Pictures and Patmos Film; British; Dolby Stereo; Color; Rated R; 94 minutes; September release.

CAST

Billy	Marina Sudina
Karen	Fay Ripley
Andy	Evan Richards
Larsen	Oleg Jankowskij
Arkadi	Igor Volkow
Lyosha	Sergei Karlenkov
Strohbecker	Alex Bureew

Billy, a mute makeup artist, accidentally locked inside a film studio one night, thinks she may have witnessed a snuff film being made.

© Sony Pictures Entertainment Inc.

Marina Sudina, Fay Ripley

PERSUASION

(SONY PICTURES CLASSICS) Producer, Fiona Finlay; Executive Producers, George Faber, Rebecca Eaton; Director, Roger Michell; Screenplay, Nick Dear; Based on the novel by Jane Austen; Photography, John Daly; Designers, William Dudley, Brian Sykes; Music, Jeremy Sams; Editor, Kate Evans; Costumes, Alexandra Byrne; Associate Producer, Margot Hayhoe; a BBC Films, WGBH/Mobil Masterpiece Theatre, Millesime Productions presentation; British; Dolby Stereo; Color; Rated PG; 103 minutes; September release

Amanda Root, Ciaran Hinds

CAST

Anne Elliot	Amanda Root
Captain Wentworth	Ciaran Hinds
Lady Russell	Susan Fleetwood
Sir Walter Elliot	Corin Redgrave
Mrs. Croft	Fiona Shaw
Admiral Croft	John Woodvine
Elizabeth Elliot	Phoebe Nicholls
Mr. Elliot	Samuel West
Mary Musgrove	Sophie Thompson
Mrs. Musgrove	Judy Cornwell
Charles Musgrove	Simon Russell Beale
Mrs. Clay	Felicity Dean
Mr. Musgrove	Roger Hammond
Louisa Musgrove	Emma Roberts
Henrietta Musgrove	Victoria Hamilton
Captain Harville	Robert Glenister
Captain Benwick	Richard McCabe
Mrs. Smith	Helen Schlesinger
Nurse Rooke	Jane Wood
Mr. Shepherd	David Collings
Lady Dalrymple	Darlene Johnson
Miss Carteret	Cinnamon Faye
Henry Havter	Isaac Maxwell-Hunt
Sir Henry Willoughby	Roger Llewellyn
Mrs. Harville	Sally George
Naval Officers	David Acton, Justin Avoth
Jemima	Lonnie James
Landlord	Roger Watkins

and David Plummer (Apothecary), Richard Brenner (Coachman), Bill McGuirk, Niall Refoy (Tradesman), Ken Shorter (Lady Dalrymple's Butler), Dermot Kerrigan (Footman), Tom Rigby (Little Charles), Alex Wilman (Little Walter), Rosa Mannion (Concert Opera Singer)

Eight years after Anne Elliot had broken off her engagement with a young naval officer because of his lack of fortune, she finds her own family financially strapped and the officer reappearing in her life, a wealthy man.

© Sony Pictures Entertainment Inc.

Emma Roberts, Victoria Hamilton, Ciaran Hinds

Emma Roberts, Victoria Hamilton, Simon Russell Beale

Victoria Hamilton, Emma Roberts, Sophie Thompson

Embeth Davidtz, Ben Chaplin

Tom Bell, James Purefoy, Gemma Jones, Embeth Davidtz

Embeth Davidtz, Ben Chaplin

FEAST OF JULY

(TOUCHSTONE) Producers, Henry Herbert, Christopher Neame; Executive Producers, Ismail Merchant, Paul Bradley; Director, Christopher Menaul; Screenplay, Christopher Neame; Based on the novel *The Feast of July* by H.E. Bates; Photography, Peter Sova; Designer, Christopher Robilliard; Editor, Chris Wimble; Associate Producers, Jane Cussons, Donald Rosenfeld; Music, Zbigniew Preisner; Costumes, Phoebe De Gaye; Casting, Kathleen Mackie; Distributed by Buena Vista Pictures; a Merchant Ivory production in association with Peregrine Productions; British; Dolby Digital Stereo; Panavision; Eastman color; Rated R; 118 minutes; October release

CAST

Bella Ford	Embeth Davidtz
Ben Wainwright	Tom Bell
Mrs. Wainwright	Gemma Jones
Jedd Wainwright	James Purefoy
Con Wainwright	Ben Chaplin
Matty Wainwright	Kenneth Anderson
Arch Wilson	Greg Wise
Mitchy Mitchell	David Neal
Mrs. Mitchell	Daphne Neville
Clerk at Shoe Factory	Mark Heal
Bowler-Hatted Man	Julian Protheroe
Preacher	Tim Preece
Billy Swaine	Charles De'Ath
Man in Pub	Colin Prockter
Squire Wyman	Richard Hope
Harvest Girl	Kate Hamblyn
Tom	Paddy Ward
Ticket Clerk	Alan Perrin
Rowing Youths	Dominic Gover, Richard Hicks
Game Keeper	Arthur Kelly
Seaman	Colin Mayes
Man in Restaurant	Mark Bazeley
Tubby Man	Stephen Frost
Second Man	David Belcher
Captain Rogers	Frederick Warder
Hangman	Tim Perrin
Assistant Hangman	Mark Whelehan
Prison Warders	Rupert Bates, Tom Marshall

In Victorian England, Bella Ford seeks the scoundrel who not only abandoned her but left her pregnant.

© Feast Productions, Ltd

James Purefoy, Ben Chaplin

NOBODY LOVES ME

(CFP) Producers, Gerd Huber, Renate Seefeldt; Director/Screenplay, Doris Dörrie, based on her short story; Photography, Helge Weindler; Designer, Tom Schlesinger; Music, Niki Reiser; Costumes, Siegbert Kammerer; Editor, Inez Regnier; Casting, An Dorthe Braker, Horst D. Scheel; a Cobra Film production in association with ZPF presentation; German; Dolby Stereo; Color; Not rated; 104 minutes; November release

CAST

Fanny Fink	Maria Schrader
Orfeo de Altamar	Pierre Sanoussi-Bliss
Lothar Sticker	Michael von Au
Madeleine	Elisabeth Trissenaar
Lasse Längsfeld	Ingo Naujoks
Anton	Joachim Król
Mrs. Radebrecht	Peggy Parnass
Zsa Zsa	Lorose Keller
Charlotte	Anya Hoffmann
Mr. Kokkinos	Erwin Grosche
Mr. Findeis	Roland Kabelitz
Benno Kügler	Steffen Gräbner
Mr. Froh	Oliver Nägele
Sevgi	Ute Maria Lerner
Lisa	Laura Medinger

and Stefan Gebelhoff (Young Man in Cafe), Birgit Stein (Lover I), Gruschenka Stevens (Lover II), Claudia Matschulla (Business Woman), Ömer Simsek (Bank Teller), Ruth Brück (Elderly Woman), Karin Johnson (Waitress), Klaus Köhler (Herbert), Peter Böhlke (Old Man in Church)

Lonely Fanny Fink consults her neighbor, a spiritual adviser, who forsees the arrival of a potential lover in the person of the new building manager, Lothar.

© CFP Distribution

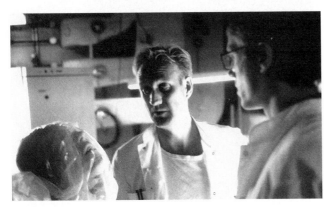

Ghita Nørby, Ernst-Hugo Järegård

Søren Pilmark, Peter Mygind

Maria Schrader, Pierre Sanoussi-Bliss

Pierre Sanoussi-Bliss, Maria Schrader

THE KINGDOM

(OCTOBER) Producer, Ole Reim; Executive Producers, Svend Abrahamsen, Peter Aalbaek Jensen; Director, Lars von Trier; Screenplay, Lars von Trier, Niels Vørsel, Tomas Gislason; Photography, Eric Kress; Art Director, Jette Lehmann; Music, Joachim Holbek; Editors, Jacob Thuesen, Molly Marleen Stensgaard; a Zentropa Entertainments APS & Denmarks Radio production; Danish; Color; Not rated; 279 minutes (shown in 2 parts); November release

CAST

Stig Helmer	Ernst-Hugo Järegård
Mrs. Drusse	Kirsten Rolffes
Rigmor	Ghita Nørby
Krogen	Søren Pilmark
Dr. Moesgaard	Holger Juul Hansen
Mary	Annevig Schelde Ebbe
Bulder	Jens Okking
Porter Hansen	Otto Brandenburg
Bondo	Baard Owe
Camilla	Solbjørg Højfeldt
Judith	Birgitte Raaberg
Sanne	Louise Fribo
Mogge	Peter Mygind
Christian	Ole Boisen
Aage Kruger	Udo Kier

and Vita Jensen, Morten Rotne Leffers (Dishwashers), Michael Simpson (Man from Haiti), Bente Eskesen (Night Nurse), Nis Bank-Mikkelsen (Priest), Dick Kaysø (Security Manager), Søren Lenander (Young Man), Finn Nielsen (Madsen), Mette Munk Plum (Mona's Mother), Solveig Sundborg (Miss Kruger), Helle Virkner (Mrs. Mogensen), Else Petersen (Old Lady), Claus Strandberg (Hypnotized Patient), Tova Maes (Mrs. Zakariasen (Kurt Ravn), Svend Ali Hamann (Haman), Morten Elsner (Mechanic), Claus Nissen (Jensen), Gunnvør Nolsøe (Charlady), Henning Jensen (Hospital Manager), Lars Lunøe (Minister of Health), Lea Brøgger (Mary' Mother), Laura Christensen (Mona), Søren Elung Jensen (Man in Top Hat), Paul Huttel (Dr Stenbaek), Holger Perfort (Prof. Ulrich)

Sprawling drama involving various staff members and patients at The Kingdom, Copenhagen's largest hospital. Taken from four segments of the Danish television series.

© October Films

David Thewlis, Leonardo DiCaprio

David Thewlis, Leonardo DiCaprio

Leonardo DiCaprio, David Thewlis

TOTAL ECLIPSE

(FINE LINE FEATURES) Producer, Jean-Pierre Ramsay Levi; Executive Producers, Jean-Yves Asselin, Staffan Ahrenberg, Pascale Faubert; Co-Producers, Philip Hinchcliffe, Cat Villiers; Director, Agnieszka Holland; Screenplay, Christopher Hampton; Photography, Yorgos Arvanitis; Designer, Dan Weil; Editor, Isabel Lorente; Costumes, Pierre-Yves Gayraud; Music, Jan A.P. Kaczmarek; a Fit-Portman production with the participation of the European Co-Production Fund (U.K.) and the Eurimages Fund of the Council of Europe; French-British-Belgian; Dolby Stereo; Color; Rated R; 110 minutes; November release

CAST

Arthur Rimbaud	Leonardo DiCaprio
Paul Verlaine	David Thewlis
Mathilde Verlaine	Romane Bohringer
Isabelle Rimbaud	Dominique Blanc
Isabelle (as a Child)	Felicie Pasotti Cabarbaye
Rimbaud's Mother	Nita Klein
Frédéric	James Thieree
Vitalie	Emmanuelle Oppo
Mrs. Mauté de Fleurville	Denise Chalem
Mr. Mauté de Fleurville	Andrzej Seweryn
Carjat	Christopher Thompson
Aicard	Bruce van Barthold
Charles Cros	Christopher Chaplin
The Judge	Christopher Hampton
André	Mathias Jung
Somalian Woman	Kettly Noel
Djami	Cheb Han

True story of the tempestuous relationship between two of France's most noted nineteenth-century poets, Arthur Rimbaud and Paul Verlaine.

Romane Bohringer, Leonardo DiCaprio

GOLDENEYE

(UNITED ARTISTS) Producers, Michael G. Wilson, Barbara Broccoli; Executive Producer, Tom Pevsner; Director, Martin Campbell; Screenplay, Jeffrey Caine, Bruce Feirstein; Story, Michael France; Photography, Phil Meheux; Designer, Peter Lamont; Music, Eric Serra; Song: "Goldeneye" by Bono and The Edge/performed by Tina Turner; Editor, Terry Rawlings; Costumes, Lindy Hemming; Associate Producer, Anthony Waye; Special Effects Supervisor, Chris Corbould; Main Title Designer, Daniel Kleinman; Stunts, Simon Crane; Casting, Debbie McWilliams; an Albert R. Broccoli presentation; Distributed by MGM/UA; British; Dolby Digital Stereo; Panavision; Deluxe/Rank color; Rated PG-13; 130 minutes; November release

Sean Bean, Pierce Brosnan

CAST

James Bond	Pierce Brosnan
Alec Trevelyan	Sean Bean
Natalya Simonova	Izabella Scorupco
Xenia Onatopp	Famke Janssen
Jack Wade	Joe Don Baker
M	Judi Dench
Valentin Zukovsky	Robbie Coltrane
Dimitri Mishkin	Tcheky Karyo
General Ourumov	Gottfried John
Boris Grishenko	Alan Cumming
Q	Desmond Llewelyn
Moneypenny	Samantha Bond
Bill Tanner	Michael Kitchen
Caroline	Serena Gordon
Severnaya Duty Officer	Simon Kunz
French Warship Captain	Pavel Douglas
French Warship Officer	Cmdt. Olivier Lajous
Admiral Chuck Farrel	Billy J. Mitchell
Computer Store Manager	Constantine Gregory
Irina	Minnie Driver
Anna	Michelle Arthur
MIG Pilot	Ravil Isyanov
Croupier	Vladimir Milanovich
Train Driver	Trevor Byfield
Valentin's Bodyguard	Peter Majer

Judi Dench

James Bond investigates the theft of a powerful nuclear missile control from a Soviet satellite station. The seventeenth James Bond film distributed by United Artists, with Pierce Brosnan making his first appearance as Bond; Desmond Llewelyn returns as Q for the fifteenth time; Joe Don Baker appeared in an earlier Bond entry, The Living Daylights, *as an all together different character.*

© Danjaq, Inc./United Artists Corp.

Famke Janssen, Pierce Brosnan

Pierce Brosnan, Joe Don Baker

Sean Bean, Izabella Scorupco

Pierce Brosnan, Izabella Scorupco

Izabella Scorupco, Pierce Brosnan

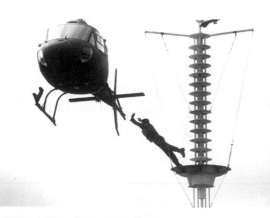

Desmond, Llewelyn, Pierce Brosnan

Emma Thompson, Jonathan Pryce

Emma Thompson, Steven Waddington

Samuel West, Emma Thompson, Steven Waddington

CARRINGTON

(GRAMERCY) Producers, Ronald Shedlo, John McGrath; Executive Producers, Francis Boespflug, Philippe Carcassonne, Fabienne Vonier; Director/Screenplay, Christopher Hampton; Based on the book *Lytton Strachey* by Michael Holroyd; Photography, Denis Lenoir; Designer, Caroline Amies; Music, Michael Nyman; Editor, George Akers; Costumes, Penny Rose; Associate Producer, Chris Thompson; Makeup/Hair Designer, Chrissie Beveridge; Casting, Fothergill & Lunn Casting; a PolyGram Filmed Entertainment presentation of a Shedlo/Freeway production in association with Cinea & Orsans & Le Studio Canal+; British-French; Dolby Stereo; Technicolor; Rated R; 123 minutes; November release

CAST

Carrington	Emma Thompson
Lytton Strachey	Jonathan Pryce
Ralph Partridge	Steven Waddington
Gerald Brenan	Samuel West
Mark Gertler	Rufus Sewell
Lady Ottoline Morrell	Penelope Wilton
Vanessa Bell	Janet McTeer
Phillip Morrell	Peter Blythe
Beacus Penrose	Jeremy Northam
Frances Partridge	Alex Kingston
Roger Senhouse	Sebastian Harcombe
Clive Bell	Richard Clifford
Mayor	David Ryall
Military Rep	Stephen Boxer
Mary Hutchinson	Annabel Mullion
Duncan Grant	Gary Turner
Marjorie Gertler	Georgiana Dacombe
Nurse	Helen Blatch
Court Usher	Neville Phillips
Dr. Starkey Smith	Christopher Birch
Porter	Daniel Betts
Fly Driver	Simon Bye
Gondolier	Marzio Idoni

True story of the unconventional relationship between painter Dora Carrington and writer Lytton Strachey from World War I to the early 1930s.

The film received awards at the 1995 Cannes Film Festival for Jonathan Pryce (Best Actor) and Christopher Hampton (Special Jury Prize).

© Gramercy Pictures

Jonathan Pryce, Emma Thompson

FRANKIE STARLIGHT

(FINE LINE FEATURES) Producer, Noel Pearson; Director, Michael Lindsay-Hogg; Screenplay, Chet Raymo, Ronan O'Leary; Based on the novel *The Dork of Cork* by Chet Raymo; Photography, Paul Laufer; Designer, Frank Conway; Editor, Ruth Foster; Costumes, Joan Bergin; Music, Elmer Bernstein; a Ferndale Films production in association with Channel Four Films; Irish; Dolby Stereo; Color; Rated R; 100 minutes; November release

CAST

Bernadette Bois	Anne Parillaud
Terry Klout	Matt Dillon
Jack Kelly	Gabriel Byrne
Emma Kelly	Rudi Davies
Young Emma	Georgina Cates
Frank Bois	Corban Walker
Young Frank	Alan Pentony
Handy Paige	Niall Toibin
Effa Kelly	Dearbhla Molloy
Albert Bois	Jean Claude Frissung
Anne Marie Bois	Victoria Begeja
Marcia	Barbara Alyn Woods
Tobin	John Davies
Charleen	Amber Hibler
Lisa	Ulrich Funke

and Guy Verama (Interpreter), Julian Negulesco (Bernadette's Uncle), Corinne Blue (Bernadette's Aunt), Sage Allen (Bar Proprietress), Ann Weakley (Midwife), Elizabeth Keller (TV Interviewer), David Parnell (Photographer), Aidan Grennell (Bookshop Manager), Tristin Gribbin (Bookshop Assistant), Christopher Casson (Bookshop Gentleman), Owen Roe (Senior Customs Officer), Aisling Leyne (Girl in Gallery), Pauline Cadell (Prostitute), Alan Devine, Edward Naessens, Laurent Mellet (Bernadette's Friends on Beach), Christine Keane (Mother of Scabious Child), Darren Monks (Young Man in Cinema), Kit Kincannon (Man in Bar), Martin Murphy (Guest at Wedding), Martin Dunne, Derry Power (Friends at Wedding)

Dwarf Frank Bois tells his life story of growing up in Ireland after World War II.

© Fine Line Features

Anne Parillaud, Alan Pentony

Anne Parillaud, Matt Dillon

Henry Czerny, Pascale Bussieres

Pascale Bussiéres, Rachael Crawford

WHEN NIGHT IS FALLING

(OCTOBER) Producer, Barbar Tranter; Director/Screenplay, Patricia Rozema; Photography, Douglas Koch; Designer, John Dondertman; Costumes, Linda Muir; Editor, Susan Shipton; an Alliance Communications Corporation presentation of a Crucial Pictures Inc production; Produced with the participation of Telefilm Canada and the Ontario Film Development Corp.; Canadian; Dolby Stereo; Color; Not rated; 82 minutes; November release

CAST

Camille	Pascale Bussières
Petra	Rachael Crawford
Martin	Henry Czerny
Reverend DeBoer	David Fox
Timothy	Don McKellar
Tory	Tracy Wright
Tillie	Clare Coulter
Trapeze Artists	Karyne Steben, Sarah Steben
Hang Gliders	Jonathan Potts, Tom Melissis, Stuart Clow
Board President	Richard Farrell

and Fides Krucker (Roaring Woman), Thom Sokoloski (Man with Goatee), Jennifer Roblin (Waitress), Jacqueline Casey, Sigrid Johnson (Iron Swingers)

Camille, unsure of her upcoming marriage to fellow professor Martin, finds herself falling in love with Petra, a flamboyant circus performer.

© October Films

THE CONVENT

(STRAND) Producer, Paulo Branco; Director/Screenplay, Manoel de Oliveira; Story, Agustina Bessa-Luis; Photography, Mario Barroso; Set Designer, Ze Branco, Ana Vaz da Silva; Costumes, Isabel Branco; Editors, Manoel de Oliveira, Valerie Loiseleux; a co-production of Madragoa Films (Lisbon)/Gemini Films (Paris)/La Sept-Cinema (Paris); Portuguese-French; Kodak color; Not rated; 90 minutes; December release

CAST

Helene Padovic	Catherine Deneuve
Michael Padovic	John Malkovich
Baltar	Luis Miguel Cintra
Piedade	Leonor Silveira
Baltazar	Duarte D'Almeida
Berta	Heloisa Miranda
Pescador	Gilberto Goncalves

Professor Michael Padovic and his wife Helene travel to Arrabida to work on his thesis that Shakespeare was of Spanish ancestry.

© Strand Releasing

Catherine Deneuve, John Malkovich

LAMERICA

(NEW YORKER) Producers, Mario & Vittorio Cecchi Gori; Executive Producer, Enzo Porcelli; Director, Gianni Amelio; Screenplay, Gianni Amelio, Andrea Porporati, Alessandro Sermoneta; Photography, Luca Bigazzi; Set Designer, Giuseppe M. Gaudino; Costumes, Liliana Sotira, Claudia Tenaglia; Editor, Simona Paggi; Music, Franco Piersanti; from C.G. Group Tiger/Alia Film; Italian-French; Technovision; Color; Not rated; 120 minutes; December release

CAST

Gino	Enrico Lo Verso
Fiore	Michele Placido
Spiro	Carmelo Di Mazzarelli
Selimi	Piro Milkani
Selimi's Cousin	Elida Janushi
Prison Warden	Sefer Pema
Boy Who Dies	Nikolin Elezi
Ismail	Artan Marina
Policeman	Besim Kurti
Little Girl	Esmeralda Ara

Italian con-men Gino and Fiore come to Albania to get rich by creating a dummy corporation, appointing a traumatized seventy-year-old political prisoner as the figurehead president.

© Petro Domenigg

Christoph Dostal

FOR GOD AND COUNTRY

(DOR FILM) Producers, Danny Krausz, Milan Dor; Director/Screenplay, Wolfgang Murnberger; Photography, Fabian Eder; Art Directors, Renate Martin, Andreas Donhauser; Editor, Maria Homolkova; Austrian; Color; Not rated; 115 minutes; December release

CAST

Private Berger	Christoph Dostal
Rumpler	Andreas Lust
Moser	Andreas Simma
Kernstock	Marcus J. Carney
Tomschitz	Leopold Altenburg

Eighteen-year-old Private Berger, sent to fight on Austrian's Eastern border, escapes from the tedium of military life through bizarre sexual fantasies.

© New Yorker Films

Carmello Di Mazzarelli, Enrico Lo Verso

Shun Chun, Gong Li

Li Baotian

Gong Li

Gong Li

Gong Li (c)

SHANGHAI TRIAD

(SONY PICTURES CLASSICS) Producer, Jean Louis Piel; Producer for UGC, Yves Marmion; Producer for Shanghai Film Studios, Wu Yigon; Executive Producers, Wang Wei, Zhu Yongde; Director, Zhang Yimou; Screenplay, Bi Feiyu; Adapted from the novel *Men gum (Gang Law)* by Li Xiao; Photography, Lu Yue; Art Director, Cao Jiuping; Editor, Tu Yuan; Costumes, Tong Huamiao; Music, Zhang Guangtian; a Shanghai Studios/Alpha Films/UGC Images/La Sept Cinema in co-operation with the participation of the Ministry of Foreign Affairs (France) production; Chinese-French; Dolby Stereo; Color; Rated R; 108 minutes; December release

CAST

Xiao Jinbao (Bijou) ....Gong Li
The Godfather ....Li Baotian
Liu Shu..Li Xuejian
Song, the Number Two ....Shun Chun
Tang Shuisheng ....Wang Xiao Xiao
Widow ....Jiang Baoying

Fourteen-year-old Tang Shuisheng enters the Shanghai underworld when his uncle asks him to keep an eye on the beautiful prostitute-singer Xiao Jinbao.

Laurence Fishburne, Kenneth Branagh

Michael Maloney, Kenneth Branagh

Andre Oumansky, Indra Ove, Anna Patrick, Kenneth Branagh,
Michael Sheen

OTHELLO

(COLUMBIA) Producers, Luc Roeg, David Barron; Executive Producer, Jonathan Olsberg; Director/Adaptation, Oliver Parker; Based on the play by William Shakespeare; Photography, David Johnson; Designer, Tim Harvey; Editor, Tony Lawson; Music, Charlie Mole; Costumes, Caroline Harris; Casting, Debbie McWilliams; a Castle Rock Entertainment presentation of a Dakota Films/Imminent Films production; British; Dolby SR; Technicolor; Rated R; 125 minutes; December release

CAST

Othello	Laurence Fishburne
Desdemona	Irene Jacob
Iago	Kenneth Branagh
Cassio	Nathaniel Parker
Roderigo	Michael Maloney
Emilia	Anna Patrick
Montano	Nicholas Farrell
Bianca	Indra Ove
Lodovico	Michael Sheen
Gratiano	Andre Oumansky
Senators	Philip Locke, John Savident
The Duke of Venice	Gabriele Ferzetti
Brabantio	Pierre Vaneck

As revenge for being passed over for a military promotion, Iago tells his superior, Othello, that his wife, Desdemona, may well have been unfaithful to him.

© Castle Rock Entertainment

Irene Jacob, Laurence Fishburne

Nathaniel Parker, Anna Patrick, Nicholas Farrell

THE CITY OF LOST CHILDREN

(SONY PICTURES CLASSICS) Producer, Claudie Ossard; Director (Artistic), Marc Caro; Director, Jean-Pierre Jeunet; Screenplay, Gilles Adrien (dialogue), Jean-Pierre Jeunet, Marc Caro; Photography, Darius Khondji; Music, Angelo Badalamenti; Song: "Who Will Take Your Dreams Away?" by Marianne Faithful and Angelo Badalamenti/performed by Marianne Faithful; Set Designer, Jean Rabasse; Costumes, Jean-Paul Gaultier; Line Producer, Daniel Szuster; Editor, Herve Schneid; Digital Special Effects, Pitof/Duboi; Special Effects, Yves Domenjoud, Jean-Baptiste Bonetto, Olivier Gleyze, Jean-Christophe Spadaccini; Makeup, Nathalie Tissier; Casting, Pierre-Jacques Benichou; French-Spanish-German; a Lumiere/Le Studio Canal+/France 3 Cinema presentation; Dolby DTS Stereo; Technovision; Color; Rated R; 111 minutes; December release

Dominique Pinon

CAST

One	Ron Perlman
Krank	Daniel Emilfork
Miette	Judith Vittet
The Clones/The Diver	Dominique Pinon
Marcello, the Flea-Tamer	Jean-Claude Dreyfus
The Octopus	Genevieve Brunet, Odile Mallet
Miss Bismuth	Mireille Mosse
Denree	Joseph Lucien
Cyclops Leader	Serge Merlin
The Killer (Cyclops)	Francois Hadji-Lazaro
The Peeler	Rufus
The Ex-Acrobat	Ticky Holgado
Irvin's Voice	Jean-Louis Trintignant
Bogdan	Dominique Bettenfeld
Melchior	Lotfi Yahyajedidi
Brutus	Thierry Gibault
Brother Ange-Joseph	Marc Caro
Lune	Mapi Galan
Bottle	Briac Barthelemy
Tadpole	Alexis Pivot
Jeannot	Leo Rubion
Pipo	Pierre Quentin-Faesch
The Barmaid	Frankie Pain
FIrst Child	Guillaume Billod-Morel
The Tattoo Artist	Ham-Chau Luong
The Tattoo Artist's Wife	Hong-Mai Thomas
A Cyclops	Daniel Adric
The Spaniard	Enrique Villanueva
Father Christmas	Chris Huerta

Genevieve Brunet, Odile Mallet

Krank, a crazed scientist who is aging prematurely because of his inability to dream, orders his Cyclops henchmen to kidnap children so he can tap into their dreams and hopefully make them his own.

© Sony Pictures Entertainment Inc.

Judith Vittet, Ron Perlman

Daniel Emilfork, Dominique Pinon

RICHARD III

(UNITED ARTISTS) Producers, Lisa Katselas Paré, Stephen Bayly; Executive Producers, Ellen Dinerman Little, Ian McKellen, Joe Simon, Maria Apodiacos; Director, Richard Loncraine; Screenplay, Ian McKellen, Richard Loncraine; Based on a stage production by Richard Eyre, from the play by William Shakespeare; Photography, Peter Biziou; Designer, Tony Burrough; Costumes, Shuna Harwood; Editor, Paul Green; Associate Producers, Mary Richards, Michele Tandy; Line Producer, David Lascelles; Casting, Irene Lamb; a Bayly/Paré production, developed in association with First Look Pictures, presented with the participation of British Screen; Distributed by MGM/UA; British; DTS Digital Stereo; Super 35 Widescreen; Technicolor; Rated R; 104 minutes; December release

Ian McKellen (c)

CAST

Richard III	Ian McKellen
Queen Elizabeth	Annette Bening
Buckingham	Jim Broadbent
Rivers	Robert Downey, Jr.
Clarence	Nigel Hawthorne
Lady Anne	Kristin Scott Thomas
Duchess of York	Maggie Smith
King Edward	John Wood
Hastings	Jim Carter
Tyrell	Adrian Dunbar
Stanley	Edward Hardwicke
Catesby	Tim McInnerny
Ratcliffe	Bill Paterson
Brackenbury	Donald Sumpter
Richmond	Dominic West
Prince Edward	Christopher Bowen
King Henry	Edward Jewesbury
Young Prince	Matthew Groom
Princess Elizabeth	Kate Steavenson-Payne
Air Hostess	Tres Hanley
Ballroom Singer	Stacey Kent
Archbishop	Roger Hammond
Lord Mayor	Dennis Lill
George Stanley	Ryan Gilmore
Jailer	Andy Rashleigh
Prince of Wales	Marco Williamson
City Gentleman	Bruce Purchase
Subalterns	James Dreyfus, David Antrobus

The deformed and wicked Richard of Gloucester plots to eliminate those who stand in the way of the throne. Based on the Royal National Theatre's world tour of Shakespeare's drama in which the story is updated to the 1930s. Ian McKellen repeats his role from that production. A previous 1955 film adaptation of the play starred Laurence Olivier.

© United Artists Pictures Inc.

Maggie Smith

Nigel Hawthorne, Andy Rashleigh, Adrian Dunbar

Donald Sumpter, Edward Hardwicke, Dominic West, Roger Hammond

Ian McKellen, Kate Steavenson-Payne, John Wood, Matthew Groom, Annette Bening, Nigel Hawthorne, Maggie Smith

Robert Downey, Jr.

Ian McKellen

Jim Broadbent, Ian McKellen

Kristin Scott Thomas

Lambert (Connor MacLeod), Mario Van Peebles (Kane), Deborah Unger (Alex Johnson/Sarah), Mako (Nokono), Raoul Trujillo, Jean-Pierre Perusse (Warriors), Martin Neufeld (Stenn), Frederick Y. Okimura (Old Japanese Man), Daniel Do (Takamura), Gabriel Kakon (John), Louis Bertignac (Pierre Bouchet), Michael Jayston (Jack Donovan), Zhenhu Han (Innkeeper), Akira Inoue (Innkeeper's Son), Darcy Laurie, Georges Vitetzakis (Bangers), David Francis (Dr. Malloy), Lisa Vitello (Nurse), Matt Holland (Intern), Richard Jutras (Uniform), Liz Macrae (Interviewer), Emidio Michetti (Detective), Andre Oumansky (Marquis de Condorcet), Charles S. Doucet, Garth Gilker (Cowboys), Paul Hopkins (Tommy), Michael McGill (Medical Examiner), Chip Chuipka (Charlie), Patrick Fierry (Captain), Clifford Spenser (Guillotine Man), John Dunn-Hill (Loony Napoleon), Morven Cameron (Receptionist), Vlasta Vrana (Vorisek), Aron Tager (Stosh), Sheena Larkin (Immigration Woman), Roberto Ozores (Paramedic #1), Lawrence Tsuji (Japanese Guard), Joe De Paul (Legless Man), Richard Raybourne, Gouchy Boy (Hustlers), Chris Heyerdahl (Ponytail), Bonnie Mac (Hooker), Jean-Marie Ribere (Sarah's Companion)

The Congress of Penguins © Ariane Film

THE CONGRESS OF PENGUINS (Ariane Film AG) Director, Hans-Ulrich Schlumpf; Screenplay, Franz Hohler, Hans-Ulrich Schlumpf; Photography, Pio Corradi, Patrick Lindenmaier, Luc Jacquet; Music, Sergei Rachmaninow, Camille Saint-Saens, Bruno Spoerri; Swiss-German, 1993; Color; Not rated; 91 minutes; January release. **CAST:** Gentoo penguins, adelie penguins, king penguins, emperor penguins

GERMANY YEAR 90 NINE ZERO (Brainstorm Prods.) Producer, Nicole Ruellé; Director/Screenplay, Jean-Luc Godard; Based on *Nos Solitudes* by Michel Hanoun; Photography, Christophe Pollock, Andreas Erben, Stepan Benda; French-German; Color; Not rated; 62 minutes; January release. **CAST:** Eddie Constantine (Lemmy Caution), Hanns Zischler (Comte Zelten), Claudia Michelsen (Charlotte/Dora), Andre Labarthe (La Narrateur), Nathalie Kadem (Delphine de Stael), Robert Wittmers (Don Quixote), Kim Kashkashian (Concertiste), Anton Mossine (Le Russe)

J.L.G. BY J.L.G. (Independent/Public Theatre) Director/Screenplay, Jean-Luc Godard; French; Color; Not rated; 65 minutes; January release. A self-portrait by French director Jean-Luc Godard

HIGHLANDER: THE FINAL DIMENSION (Dimension) Producer, Claude Léger; Executive Producers, Guy Collins, Charles L. Smiley; Co-Producers, Jean Cazes, Eric Altmayer, James Daly; Director, Andy Morahan; Screenplay, Paul Ohl; Story, William Panzer, Brad Mirman; Based on characters created by Gregory Widen; Photography, Steven Chivers; Editor, Yves Langlois; Designers, Gilles Aird, Ben Morahan; Visual Effects Supervisor, Brian Johnson; Costumes, Jackie Budin, Mario Davignon; Music, J. Peter Robinson; Casting, Nadja Rona, Vera Miller; a Transfilm/Lumiere/Falling Cloud production, Distributed by Miramax; Canadian-French-British; Dolby Digital Stereo; Super 35 Widescreen; Color; Rated PG-13; 96 minutes; January release. **CAST:** Christopher

Chang Shih, Wang Lan in *The Wooden Man's Bride* © Arrow Releasing

TSAHAL (New Yorker) Executive Producer, Bertrand Dussart; Director, Claude Lanzmann; Photography, Dominique Chapuis, Pierre-Laurent Chenieux, Jean-Michel Humeau; Editor, Sabine Mamou; Israeli-French; Color; Not rated; 300 minutes; January release. Documentary on the Israeli Defense Forces, with Sgt. Avi Yaffe, Lt. Col. Yuval Neria, Maj. Meir Weisel, Brig. Gen. Avigdor Kahalani, Maj. Gen. Yanush Ben-Gal, Lt. Col. Zvika Greengold, Maj. Gen. Yossi Ben-Hanan, Adam Gen-Tolila, Ilan Leibovitch, Maj. Gen. Israel Tal, Maj. Gen. Arik Sharon

THE WOODEN MAN'S BRIDE (Arrow) Producer, Wang Ying Hsiang; Executive Producers, Yu Shu, Li Xudong; Director, Huang Jianxin; Screenplay, Yang Zhengguang; Based on the novelette *Wu Kui* by Jia Pingau; Photography, Zhang Xiaoguang; Art Director, Teng Jie; Editor, Lei Qin; Music, Zhang Dalong; Costumes, Du Longxi; a Long Shong Production Co. Ltd. production; Chinese; Color; Not rated; 113 minutes; February release. **CAST:** Chang Shih (Kui), Wang Lan (Young Mistress), Ku Paoming (Brother), Wang Yumei (Madame Liu), Wang Fuli (Sister Ma), Kao Mingjun (Chief Tang)

Mario Van Peebles, Christopher Lambert in *Highlander: The Final Dimension* © Dimension Films

Tahereh Ladaniah in *Through the Olive Trees* © Miramax Films

Alena Mihulová, Radek Holub in *The Cow*
© Public Theatre

THROUGH THE OLIVE TREES (Miramax) Director/Screenplay/Editor, Abbas Kiarostami; Photography, Hossein Djafarian, Farhad Saba; from CIBY 2000; Iranian; Color; Rated G; 108 minutes; February release. **CAST:** Hossein Rezai (The Man), Mohamad Ali Keshavarz (The Director), Tahereh Ladania (The Woman), Mahbanou Darabin (The Grandmother), Ahmad Ahmadpour, Babak Ahmadpour (Brothers), Farhad Kheradmand, Zarifeh Shiva

THE COW (Czech TV/Public Theater) Producer, Karel Skop; Director, Karyl Kachyna; Screenplay, Karyl Kachyna, Karel Cabradek; Based on the novel by Jan Prochazka; Photography, Petri Hojda; Editor, Jan Svoboda; Music, Petr Hapka; Czech, 1993; Color; Not rated; 94 minutes; February release. **CAST:** Radek Holub (Adam), Alena Mihulová (Roza), Valérie Zawadská, Viktorie Knotková, Antonín Molcík, Zdenek Dusek, Frantisek Peterka, Vlastimil Zavrel

Liam Neeson, Hugh O'Conor in *Lamb*
© Capitol Entertainment

LAMB (Capitol Entertainment) Producer, Neil Zeiger; Executive Producer, Al Burgess; Director, Colin Gregg; Screenplay, Bernard MacLaverty, based on his novel; Photography, Mike Garfath; Music, Van Morrison; a Flickers Production and Limehouse Pictures Film in association with Film Four International; British, 1986; Color; Not rated; 110 minutes; February release. **CAST:** Liam Neeson (Michael Lamb), Hugh O'Conor (Owen Kane), Ian Bannen (Brother Benedict), Ronan Wilmot (Brother Fintan), Frances Tomelty (Mrs. Kane), Dudley Sutton (Haddock), Denis Carey (Mr. Lamb), David Gorry (O'Donnell), Stuart O'Connor (O'Halloran)

MEET THE FEEBLES (Greycat) Producers, Jim Booth, Peter Jackson; Director, Peter Jackson; Screenplay, Danny Mulheron, Frances Walsh, Stephen Sinclair, Peter Jackson; Photography, Murray Milne; Music, Peter Dasent; Editor, Jamie Selkirk; Designer, Mike Kane; Puppet Designer, Cameron Chittock; Supervising Puppeteers, Jonathon Acorn, Ramon

Aguilar; a Wingnut Films presentation; New Zealand; Color; Not rated; 96 minutes; February release. **Puppet cast with voices by** Donna Akersten, Stuart Devenie, Mark Hadlow, Ross Jolly, Brian Sergent, Peter Vere Jones, Mark Wright

SUPER 8 1/2 (Strand Releasing) Producers, Jurgen Bruning, Bruce LaBruce, Jon Gerrans, Marcus Hu, Mike Thomas; Director/Screenplay, Bruce LaBruce; Photography, Donna Mobbs; Editors, Manse James, Robert Kennedy; Canadian; Color; Not rated; 99 minutes; March release. **CAST:** Bruce LaBruce (Bruce), Liza LaMonica (Googie), Chris Teen (Wednesday Friday), Dirty Pillows (Jane Friday), Mikey Mike (Johnny Eczema), Klaus von Brucker (Pierce), Kate Ashley (Amy Nitrate), Buddy Cole, Ben Weasel, Vaginal Creme Davis, Richard Kern (Themselves)

Wynard the Frog in *Meet the Feebles*
© Greycat

NAKED KILLER (RIM) Producer/Screenplay, Wong Jing; Director, Clarence Fok; Photography, Yim Wai Lun; Art Director, Fong Ying; Hong Kong; Color; Not rated; 95 minutes; February release. **CAST:** Simon Yam (Tinman), Chingmy Yau (Kitty), Carrie Ng (Princess), Kelly Yao (Baby), Svenwara Madoka (Sister Cindy)

EROTIQUE (Group 1 Films/Odyssey Film Group) U.S./German/Hong-Kong; Color; Not rated (no one under 17 admitted); 93 minutes; March release. *Let's Talk About Sex*: Producers, Christopher Wood, Vicky Herman; Director, Lizzie Borden; Executive Producer, Marianne Chase; Screenplay, Lizzie Borden, Susie Bright; Story, Lizzie Borden; Photography, Larry Banks; Music, Andrew Belling; Editor, Richard Fields; **CAST:** Kamala Lopez-Dawson (Rosie), Bryan Cranston (Dr. Robert Stern), Ron Orbach (Nikki), Ray Oriel (Eddie), Liane Curtis (Officer Murphy). *Taboo Parlor*: Producers, Monika Treut, Michael Sombetzki; Director/Screenplay, Monika Treut; Photography, Elfi Mikesch; Editor, Steve Brown; **CAST:** Priscilla Barnes (Claire), Camilla Soeberg (Julia), Michael Carr (Victor), Marianne Sägebrecht (Hilde), Peter Kern (Fanz), Tanita Tikaram (Azian). *Wonton Soup*: Producers, Teddy Robin Kwan, Eddie Ling-Ching Fong; Director, Clara Law; Screenplay, Eddie Ling-Ching Fong; Photography, Arthur Wong; Editor, Jill Bilcock; Music, Tats Lau; **CAST:** Tim Lounibos (Adrian), Hayley Man (Ann), Choi Hark-kin (The Uncle)

Tim Lounibos, Hayley Man in *Erotique*
© Race the Wild Wind, Inc.

Svetozar Cvetkovic in *Gorilla Bathes at Noon*
© Public Theatre

GORILLA BATHES AT NOOON (Public Theatre/Independent)
Producers, Alfred Hurmer, Bojana Marijan, Joachim von Vietinghoff; Director/Screenplay, Dusan Makavejev; Photography, Aleksandar Petovic, Miodrag Milosevic; Music, Brynmer Llewelyn Jones; Editor, Vuksan Lukovac; a co-production of Alert Film/Von Vietinghoff Filmproduktion/Ekstaza; German-Russian; Color/black and white; Not rated; 83 minutes; March release. **CAST:** Svetozar Cvetkovic (Victor Borisovich), Anita Mancic (Miki Miki/Lenin), Alexandra Rohmig (German Girl), Peter Bozovic (Trandert), Andreas Lucius (Policeman), Aleksander Dovic (Dealer), Eva Rio (Mother), Suleyman Boyriz (Turk), Natzev Babie-Zoric (Frau Schmidt)

STARTING PLACE (Interama)
Director/Screenplay/Photography, Robert Kramer; Editors, Christine Benoit, Robert Kramer, Marie-Helen Mora; British-French-Vietnamese; Color; Not rated; 80 minutes; April release. Documentary on the current state of Vietnam.

METAL AND MELANCHOLY (Ariel Films)
Producer, Suzanne van Voorst; Directors, Heddy Honigmann, Peter Delpeut; Photography, Stef Tijdink; Editors, Jan Hendriks, Danniel Danniel; Spanish-Dutch, 1993; Color; Not rated; 80 minutes; Documentary on taxicab drivers of Lima, Peru.

THE CORMORANT (BBC/Public Theater)
Producer, Ruth Kenley-Letts; Executive Producers, Ruth Caleb, Andrew Holmes, Mark Shivas; Director, Peter Markham; Screenplay, Peter Ransley; Based on the novel by Stephen Gregory; Photography, Ashley Rowe; Designer, Ray Price; Music, John Lunn; Editor, Tim Kruydenberg; British, 1993; Color; Not

rated; 90 minutes; April release. **CAST:** Ralph Fiennes (John), Helen Schlesinger (Mary), Thomas Williams (Tom), Buddug Morgan (Jenny), Derek Hutchinson (Dave), Karl Francis (Uncle Ian), Dyfan Roberts (Glyn), Mici Plwm (Brian), Ray Gravell (Michael), Stewart Jones (Aled Owen), Gwilym Evans (Young John)

RED FIRECRACKER, GREEN FIRECRACKER (October)
Producers, Chen Chunkeung, Yung Naiming; Executive Producer, Weng Naiming; Director, He Ping; Screenplay, Da Ying; Based on the novel by Feng Jicai; Photography, Yang Lun; Editor, Yuan Hong; Music, Zhao Jiping; Art Director, Qian Yunxiu; Costumes, Ma Defan; a Yung & Associate Co. production, in association with Xi'an Film Studio, Beijing Salon Films; Hong Kong; Color; Not rated; 116 minutes; April release. **CAST:** Ning Jing (Chun Zhi), Wu Gang (Niu Bao), Zhao Xiaorui (Man Dihong), Gao Yang (Old Butler)

Ning Jing in *Red Firecracker, Green Firecracker*
© October Films

THE DAY THE SUN TURNED COLD (Kino)
Producer/Director/Screenplay, Yim Ho; Executive Producer/Costumes, Ann Hui; Photography, Hou Young; Art Director, Jessinta Liu; Editor, Wong Yee-shun; Music, Otomo Yoshihide; a Pineast Production presentation; Chinese; Color; Not rated; 99 minutes; April release. **CAST:** Siqin Gowa (The Mother), Tuo Zhong Hua (The Son), Ma Jing Wu (The Father), Wai Zhi (The Lover), Shu Zhong (The Son - when young), Li Hu (The Captain)

DREAMING OF RITA (First Run Features)
Producers, Borje Hansson, FilmLance International; Director, Jon Lindström; Screenplay, Rita Holst, Jon Lindström; Photography, Kjell Lagerros; Swedish, 1993; Dolby Stereo; Color; Not rated; 108 minutes; April release. **CAST:** Per Oscarsson (Bob), Marika Lagercrantz (Rita), Philip Zanden (Steff), Yaba Holst (Sandra)

THE BROKEN JOURNEY (Filmhaus)
Producer/Director/Music, Sandip Ray; Screenplay/Story, Satyajit Ray; Photography, Barun Raha; Designer, Ashoke Bose; Editor, Dulal Dutt; Indian; Color; Not rated; 82 minutes; May release. **CAST:** Soumitra Chatterji (Dr. Nihar Sengupta),

Ralph Fiennes in *The Cormorant*
© BBC/Public Theatre

Marika Lagercrantz, Per Oscarsson in *Dreaming of Rita*
© First Run Features

Alia in *Ermo*
© Arrow Releasing Inc.

Sadhu Meher (Jatin Kundu), Subhalakshmi Munshi (Manashi), Bina (Mrs. Urmila Sengupta), Minaka Goswami (Mrs. Sinha), Debotosh Ghosh (Haladhar), Masood Akhtar (Santosh), Pallavi Roy (Chumki), Subhendu Chatterji (Pankaj Basu), Lily Chakravarty (Ranjana)

THE STRANGER (Filmhaus) Director/Screenplay/Story/Music, Satyajit Ray; Photography, Barun Raha; Editor, Dulal Dutt; a C.E.G. Worldwide presentation; Indian; Eastman color; Not rated; 120 minutes; May release. **CAST:** Utpal Dutt (Manmohan Mitra), Deepanker De (Sudhindra Bose), Mamata Shankar (Anila Bose), Dhritiman Chatterjee (Lawyer Sen Gupta), Rabi Gosh (Ranjan Rakshit), Subrota Chatterji (Chhandra Rakshit)

PROFESSION: NEO-NAZI (Drift Releasing) Director/Screenplay, Winfried Bonengel; Photography, Johann Feindt; Editor, Wolfram Kohler; an OST-Film and Hoffman & Loesser Produktion; German, 1993; Color; Not rated; 87 minutes; May release. Documentary on Ewald Althans, leader of Germany's neo-Nazi movement.

ERMO (Arrow) Producers, Chen Kunming, Jimmy Tan; Director, Zhou Xiaowen; Screenplay, Lang Yun; Photography, Lu Gengxin; Editor, Zhong Furong; Music, Zhou Xiaowen; an Ocean Film Co. Ltd. presentation; Chinese; Color; Not rated; 93 minutes; May release. **CAST:** Alia (Ermo), Liu Peiqi (Blindman), Ge Zhijun (Chief), Zhang Haiyan (Fat Woman)

Elena Mandalis, Dora Kaskanis in *Only the Brave*
© First Run Features

ONLY THE BRAVE (First Run Features) Producer, Fiona Eagger; Director, Ana Kokkinos; Screenplay, Ana Kokkinos, Mira Robertson; Photography, Jaems Grant; Art Director, Georgina Campbell; Music, Philip Brophy; Editor, Mark Atkin; a Pickpocket Film produced in association with the Australian Film Commission and the Independent Filmmakers Fund of Film Victoria; Australian; Color; Not rated; 60 minutes; May release. **CAST**: Elena Mandalis (Alex), Dora Kaskanis (Vicki), Maude Davey (Miss Kate Groves), Helen Athanasiadis (Maria), Tina Zerella (Sylvie), Bob Bright (Reg), Mary Sitarenos (Athena), Peta Brady (Tammy)

STALINGRAD (Strand) Producers, Hanno Huth, Gunther Rohrbach, Joseph Vilsmaier; Director/Photography, Joseph Vilsmaier; Screenplay, Johannes Heide, Jurgen Buscher, Joseph Vilsmaier; Music, Norbert Schneider; Editor, Hannes Nikel; German; Color; Not rated; 138 minutes; May release. **CAST:** Dominique Horwitz (Fritz), Thomas Kretschmann (Hans), Jochen Nickel (Rollo), Sebastian Rudolph (GeGe)

Stalingrad © Strand Releasing

JOHNNY MNEMONIC (TriStar) Producer, Don Carmody; Executive Producers, Staffan Ahrenberg, B.J. Rack, Victoria Hamburg, Robert Lantos; Director, Robert Longo; Screenplay, William Gibson, based on his short story; Photography, Francois Protat; Designer, Nilo Rodis Jamero; Music, Brad Fiedel; Editor, Ronald Sanders; Costumes, Olga Dimitrov; Cyberspace Sequence Designers/Producers, Sony Pictures Imageworks; Special Visual Effects, Fantasy II Film Effects; an Alliance production; Canadian; SDDS Stereo; Color; Rated R; 98 minutes; May release. **CAST:** Keanu Reeves (Johnny), Dina Meyer (Jane), Ice-T (J-Bone), Takeshi (Takahashi), Denis Akiyama (Shinji), Dolph Lundgren (Street Preacher), Henry Rollins (Spider), Barbara Sukowa (Anna K), Udo Kier (Ralfi), Tracy Tweed (Pretty), Falconer Abraham (Yomamma), Don Francks (Hooky), Diego Chambers (Henson), Sherry Miller (Takahashi's Secretary), Arthur Eng, Von Flores (Viets), Victoria Tengelis (Pharmakom Receptionist), Warren Sulatycky (Yakuza Operator), Celina Wu (Mikiyo), Gene Mack (Laslo), Jamie Elman (Toad), Simon Sinn (Man in Hotel Lobby), Caitlin & Erin Carmody (Twins in Hotel Lobby), Doug O'Keefe (Pharmakom Security), Marlow Vella (Lotek Kid), Howard Szafer (Strike), Paul Brogren (Stump), Arthi Sambasivan (Nurse), Silvio Oliviero (Stick), Coyote Shivers (Buddy), Lynne Adams (Rocket Launcher Yakuza), Mike Shearer (Yakuza Partner), Susan Tsagkaris (Opera Singer), Christopher Comrie (Beijing Riot Newscaster), Robin Crosby (Girl in Hotel Room)

Keanu Reeves in *Johnny Mnemonic*
© TriStar Pictures

Deb Snyder, Sihung Lung in *Pushing Hands*
© CFP Distribution

Milena Gulbe, Ivo Uukivi in *City Unplugged*
© FilmHaus

PUSHING HANDS (CFP) Producers, Ted Hope, James Schamus, Emily Liu, Ang Lee; Executive Producer, Jiang Feng-Chyi; Director, Ang Lee; Screenplay, Ang Lee, James Schamus; Photography, Jong Lin; Music, Xiao-Song Qu; Editor, Tim Squyres; a Central Motion Pictures Corporation presentation in association with Ang Lee Productions and Good Machine; Taiwanese; Color; Not rated; 100 minutes; June release. **CAST:** Sihung Lung (Mr. Chu), Lai Wang (Mrs. Chen), Bo Z. Wang (Alex Chu), Deb Snyder (Martha Chu), Haan Lee (Jeremy)

BAB EL-OUED CITY (Jane Balfour Films) Director/Screenplay, Merzak Allouache; Photography, Jean-Jacques Mrejen; Music, Rachid Bahri; Editor, Marie Colonna; from Les Matins Films, Flash Back Audiovisuel, La Sept Cinema, Z.D.F. and Thelma Film AG; Algerian-French; Color; Not rated; 90 minutes; June release. **CAST:** Nadia Kaci (Yamina), Mohammed Ourdache (Said), Hassan Abdou (Boualem), Mourad Khen (Rachid), Mabrouk Ait Amara (Mabrouk), Nadia Samir (Ouardya), Amned Benaissa (Imam)

Thomas Arklie in *Heaven's a Drag*
© First Run Features

EXECUTIONERS (Rim Films) Producers/Directors, Johnny To, Ching Siu-Tung; Screenplay, Chan Suk-Win; Photography, Poon Hang-Sang; Music, Wong Ka-Sin; Hong Kong; Color; Not rated; 95 minutes; June release. **CAST:** Michelle Khan (Chan Sam), Anita Mui (Wonder Woman Tung), Maggie Cheung (Chan Chut), Anthony Wong (Black Warrior), Damian Lau (Tung's Husband)

HEAVEN'S A DRAG (First Run Features) formerly *To Die For*; Producer, Gary Fitzpatrick; Co-Producer, Ian Johnson; Director, Peter Mackenzie Litten; Screenplay, Johnny Byrne; Photography, John Ward; Editor, Jeffrey Arsenault; Music, Roger Bolton; a Victor Film Company production; British; Dolby Stereo; Color; Not rated; 96 minutes; June re

lease. **CAST:** Thomas Arklie (Simon), Ian Williams (Mark), Tony Slattery (Terry), Dilly Keane (Siobhan), Jean Boht (Mrs. Downs), John Altman (Dogger)

CITY UNPLUGGED (Filmhaus) formerly *Darkness in Tallinn*; Producer, Lasse Saarinen; Executive Producer/Director, Ilkka Jarvilaturi; Photography, Rein Kotov; Screenplay, Paul Kolsby; Editor, Christopher Tellefsen; Music, Mader; a Filmzolfo and Upstream Pictures production; Finnish-Estonian-Swedish-U.S.; Color; Not rated; 99 minutes; June release. **CAST:** Ivo Uukkivi (Toivo), Milena Gulbe (Maria), Monika Mäger (Terje), Enn Klooren (Mihhail), Väino Laes (Andres), Peeter Oja (Dmitri), Jüri Järvet (Anton), Villem Indrikson (Officer Kallas), Andres Raag (Kallas' Partner), Tonu Kark (Stub), Ain Lutsepp (Ernst)

CARMEN MIRANDA: BANANAS IS MY BUSINESS (International Cinema Inc.) Producers, David Meyer, Helena Solberg; Director/Narrator, Helena Solberg; Photography, Tomasz Magierski; Editors, David Meyer, Amanda Zinoman; Brazilian-U.S.; Color; Not rated; 90 minutes; July release. A look at the life of performer Carmen Miranda (1909-55), including interviews with Aurora Miranda, Caribe da Rocha, Synval Silva, Estela Romero, Cesar Romero, Alice Faye, Rita Moreno; reenactments: Cynthia Adler (Luella Hopper), Erick Barreto (Carmen Miranda, fantasy sequences), Leticia Monte (Carmen Miranda, teen-ager)

MY LIFE AND TIMES WITH ANTONIN ARTAUD (Leisure Time Features) Producer, Denis Freyd; Director, Gérard Mordillat; Screenplay, Gérard Mordillat, Jérôme Prieur; Based on the diaries of Jacques Prevel; Photography, François Catonné; Music, Jean-Claude Petit; Editor, Sophie Rouffio; French; Color; Not rated; 93 minutes; July release. **CAST:** Sami Frey (Antonin Artaud), Marc Barbé (Jacques Prevel), Julie Jézéquel (Jany), Valérie Jeannet (Rolande)

Carmen Miranda in *Carmen Miranda: Bananas Is My Business*
© International Cinema Inc.

MIDNIGHT DANCERS (First Run Features) Executive Producer, Richard Wong Tang; Director, Mel Chionglo; Screenplay, Richard Lee; Photography, George Tutanes; Editor, Jess Navarro; Designer, Edgar Martin Littaua; Music, Nonong Buenoamino; from Tangent Films; Filipino; Color; Not rated; 115 minutes; July release. **CAST:** Alex Del Rosario (Joel), Gandong Cervantes (Dennis), Lawrence David (Sonny), Perla Bautista (The Mother), Nonie Buencamino (Dave), Soxy Topacio (Dominic, Bar Manager), R.S. Francisco (Michelle)

CHRONICLE OF THE WARSAW GHETTO UPRISING ACCORDING TO MAREK EDELMAN (Independent/Film Forum) Producer/Director/Screenplay/Photography, Jolanta Dylewska; Music, Jan Kanty Pawluskiewicz; Editor, Wanda Lemon; Polish; Black and white; Not rated; 72 minutes; August release. Documentary on the Jews forced by the Nazis to live in the Warsaw ghetto and their eventual transport to the nearby Treblinka death camp.

Sami Frey in *My Life and Times with Antonin Artaud*
© Leisure Time Features

MAGIC IN THE WATER (TriStar) formerly Glenorky; Producers, Matthew O'Connor, Rick Stevenson; Executive Producers, Karen Murphy, Tony Allard; Director, Rick Stevenson; Screenplay, Rick Stevenson, Icel Dobell Massey; Story, Ninian Dunnett, Rick Stevenson, Icel Dobell Massey; Photography, Thomas Burstyn; Designer, Errol Clyde Klotz; Editor, Allan Lee; Costumes, Monique Prudhomme; Music, David Schwartz; Casting, Debra Zane, Stuart Aikins; a Triumph Films presentation of an Oxford Film Company/Pacific Motion Pictures production; Dolby Digital Stereo; Filmhouse color; Rated PG; 98 minutes; August release. **CAST:** Mark Harmon (Jack Black), Joshua Jackson (Joshua Black), Harley Jane Kozak (Dr. Wanda Bell), Sarah Wayne (Ashley Black), Willie Nark-Orn (Hiro), Frank Sotonoma Salsedo (Uncle Kipper), Morris Panych (Mack Miller), Ben Cardinal (Joe Pickled Trout), Adrien Dorval (Wright Hardy), Marc Acheson (Lefty Hardy), Anthony Towe (Taka), John Proccacino (Frank), Thomas Cavanaugh (Simon—1st Patient), Garrett Bennett (Christian—2nd Patient), Brian Finney (Bug-Eyes—3rd Patient), David Rasche (Phillip—4th Patient), Tamsin Kelsey

Joshua Jackson, Sarah Wayne, Mark Harmon in *Magic in the Water*
© Tri Star Pictures, Inc.

(Sheriff Stevenson), Benjamin Ratner (FX Man), Lesley Ewen (Private Nurse), William Sasso (Shy Young Orderly), Teryl Rothery (Beth), Norma Wick (Reporter), Nathan Begg (Kid in cowboy hat), Philip Baer, Peter Baer (Boys in boat), Elisa Wayne (Girl in tutu), Cole Halleran (Boy on leash)

HYENAS (Kino Intl.) Producers, Alain Rozanes, Pierre-Al;ain Meier; Director/Screenplay, Djibril Diop Mambety; Based upon the play *The Visit* by Friedrich Dürrenmatt; Photography, Matthias Kälin; Music, Wasis Diop; Editor, Loredana Cristelli; a production of ADR Productions (Paris)–Thelma Film AG (Zurich)–Maag Daan (Dakar)–MK2 Productions SA (Paris); Senegalese-French-Swiss; Color; Not rated; 113 minutes; August release. **CAST:** Mansour Diouf (Dramaan Drameh), Ami Diakhate (Linguère Ramatou), Mamadou Mahouredia Gueye (The Mayor), Issa Ramagelissa Samb (The Headmaster), Omar Ba dit "Baye Peul" (The Chief of Police), Calgou Fall (The Priest), Abdoulaye Yama Diop (The Doctor), Faly Gueye (Madame Drameh), Rama Tiaw (The Mayor's Wife), Kaoru Egushi (Toko), Hanny Tchelley (An Amazon), Abdul Mama Diouf (Train Conductor), Soulaymane Ndiaye, Dickel Mbaye (Captive Witnesses), Oumy Samb (Dancer), Djibril Diop Mambéty (Gaana Mbow, Former Chief Justice)

THE JAR (Artistic License) Producer, Alireza Zarrin; Director/Screenplay, Ebrahim Foruzesh; Photography, Iraj Safavi; Editor, Changiz Sayad; Music, Mohammad Reza Aligholi; Iranian; Color; Not rated; 85 minutes; September release. **CAST:** Behzad Khodaveisi (Teacher), Fatemah Azrah (Khavar)

NO MERCY (Inca Films) Producer/Director, Francisco J. Lombardi; Screenplay, Augusto Cabada; Based on the novel *Crime and Punishment* by Fyodor Dostoyevsky; Photography, Pili Flores Guerra; Music, Leopoldo La Rosa; Editor, Luis Barrios; Peruvian-Mexican-French; Color; Not rated; 117 minutes; September release. CAST: Diego Bertie (Ramón), Adriana Davila (Sonia), Jorge Chiarella (Inspector Portillo), Hernán Romero (Alejandro), Marcello Rivera (Julián), Mariella Trejos (Mrs. Aliaga)

Midnight Dancers © First Run Features

The Jar © Artistic License Films

Meret Becker, Anian Zollner in *The Promise*
© Fine Line Features

1-900 (Zeitgeist) Producer/Director, Theo van Gogh; Screenplay, Johan Doesburg, Marcel Otten, Ad van Kempen, Ariane Schluter; Based on the stageplay 06 by Johan Doesburg; Photography, Tom Erisman; Editor, Ot Louw; Music, Ruud Bos; Art Director, Ruud van Dijk; Dutch; Color; Not rated; 80 minutes; September release. **CAST:** Ariane Schluter (Sara Wever), Ad van Kempen (Wilbert Venema)

THE PROMISE (Fine Line Features) Producer, Eberhard Junkersdorf; Director, Margarethe von Trotta; Screenplay, Peter Schneider, Margarethe von Trotta, Felice Laudadio; Photography, Franz Rath; Costumes, Petra Kray, Yoshi o Yabara; Editor, Suzanne Baron; Music, Juergen Knieper; a Bioskop-Film (Munich)/Odessa Film (Paris)/WDR (Cologne)/Les Productions JMH (Lausanne) production; German; Dolby Stereo; Color; Rated R; 115 minutes; September release. **CAST:** Corinna Harfouch (Sophie), Meret Becker (Sophie, as a young woman), August Zirner (Konrad), Anian Zollner (Konrad, as a young man), Jean-Yves Gaultier (Gerard), Eva Mattes (Barbara), Susanne Ugé (Barbara, as a young woman), Hans Kremer (Harald), Pierre Besson (Harald, as a young man), Tina Engel (Sophie's Aunt), Otto Sander (Prof. Lorenz), Hark Bohm (Mueller), Dieter Mann (Konrad's Father), Simone von Zglinicki (Konrad's Mother), Ulrike Krumbiegel (Elisabeth), Monika Hansen (Sophie's Mother), Klaus Piontek (Sophie's Stepfather), Christian Herrschmann (Alexander, 12 years old), Joerg Meister (Alexander, 20 years old), Heiko Senst (Wolfgang), Anka Baier (Monika), Sven Lehmann (Max), Udo Kroschwald (Secret Police Agent)

WAR OF THE BUTTONS (Fujisankei/Enigma) Producer, David Puttnam; Executive Producers, Xavier Gelin, Stephane Marsil, David Nichols; Director, John Roberts; Screenplay, Colin Welland; Adapted from the 1962 film *La Guerre des Boutons,* directed by Yves Roberts, from the novel by Louis Pergaud; Photography, Bruno De Keyzer; Editor, David Freeman; Music, Rachel Portman; Designer, Jim Clay; Costumes, Louise Frogley; Casting, Ros and John Hubbard; a Fujisankei Communications Group presentation of an Enigma production, in association with La Gueville and Hugo Films, distributed by WB.; British-French-Japanese; Dolby Stereo; Technicolor; Rated PG; 90 minutes; September release. **CAST:** Liam Cunningham (Schoolmaster), Gregg Fitzgerald (Fergus), Colm Meaney (Geronimo's Dad), John Coffey (Geronimo), Eveanna Ryan

Greg Ellwand, Matthew Ferguson in *Eclipse*
© Strand Releasing

(Marie), Paul Batt (Gorilla), Thomas Kavanagh (Riley), John Murphy (Jonjo), Devla Kirwan (Adult Marie's Voice), Brendan McNamara, Gerard Kearney, Kevin O'Malley, Anthony Cunningham, John Cleere, Daragh Naughton, John Crowley, Stuart Dannell-Foran, Karl Byrne, Barry Walsh, Derek O'Lear, Niall Collins

THE BLUE VILLA (Nomad Films) Producer, Jacques de Clerq; Directors/Adaptation, Alain Robbe-Grillet, Dimitri de Clerq; Screenplay, Alain Robbe-Grillet; Photography, Hans Meier; Music, Nikos Kypourgos; Editor, France Duez; Belgian; Color; Widescreen; Not rated; 100 minutes; September release. **CAST:** Fred Ward (Frank), Arielle Dombasle (Sarah-la-Blonde), Charles Tordjman (Edouard Nordmann), Sandrine Le Berre (Santa), Dimitri Poulikakos (Thieu), Christian Maillet (The Father), Muriel Jacobs (Kim), Michalis Maniatis (Mars)

HALFAOUINE (BOY OF THE TERRACES) (Intl. Film Circuit) Producers, Ahmed Baha Attia, Eliane Stutterheim, Hassen Daldoul; Director/Screenplay, Ferid Boughedir; Adaptation, Maryse Leon Garcia, Nourid Bouzid; Dialog, Taoufik Jebali; Photography, Georges Barsky; Editor, Moufida Tlatli; Music, Anouar Braham; Tunisian-French, 1990; Color; Not rated; 98 minutes; September release. **CAST:** Selima Boughedir (Noura), Mustapha Adouani (Si Azzouz), Rabia Ben Abdallah (Djamila), Mohammed Driss (Salih), Helene Catzaras (Latifa), Fatma Ben Saidane (Salouah), Abdelhamid Gayess (Cheikh Mokhtar), Carolyn Chelby (Leila), Kemal Touati (Le Hooligan)

Darren McHugh, Joy Florish in *Broken Harvest*
© Kit Parker Films

LES MISÉRABLES (Les Films 13/TFI/Canal+) Producer/Director/ Screenplay/ Photography, Claude Lelouch; Art Director, Jacques Bufnoir; Costumes, Dominique Borg; Music, Francis Lai, Philippe Servain, Erik Berchot, Michel Legrand, Didier Barbelivien; Editor, Helene De Luze; presented in association with Les Films 13/TFI Films production, with the participation of Canal+; French, distributed by WB/Arriscope; Color; Rated R; 174 minutes; October release. **CAST:** Jean-Paul Belmondo (Henri Fortin/Jean Valjean), Michel Boujenah (André Ziman), Alessandra Martines (Elise Ziman), Salome (Salomé Ziman), Annie Girardot (Théardière Farmer-Woman), Philippe Léotard (Thénardier Farmer), Clémentine Célarié (Catherine/Fantine), Philippe Khorsand (Policeman/ Javert), Ticky Holgado (The Kind Hoodlum), Rufus (Thénardier Father and Son), Nicole Croisille (Thénardière 1830/1900), William Leymergie (Toureiffel), Jean Marais, (Bishop Myriel), Micheline Presle (The Mother Superior), Darryl Cowl (The Book Seller)

ECLIPSE (Strand) Producers, Camelia Frieberg, Jeremy Podeswa; Executive Producer, Wolfram Tichy; Director/Screenplay, Jeremy Podeswa; Photography, Miroslaw Baszak; Editor, Susan Maggi; Music, Ernie Tollar; Art Director, Tamara Deverell; Canadian; Color; Not rated; 95 minutes; October release. **CAST:** Von Flores (Henry), John Gilbert (Brian), Pascale Montpetit (Sylvie), Manuel Aranguiz (Gabriel), Maria Del Mar (Sarah), Greg Ellwand (Norman), Matthew Ferguson (Angelo), Earl Pastko (Michael), Daniel MacIvor (Jim), Kirsten Johnson (Carlotta)

Jean-Chretin Sibertin-Blanc in *Augustin*
© Kino Intl.

Victoria Longley, Angie Milliken in *Talk*
© Filmopolis Pictures Inc.

BROKEN HARVEST (Kit Parker Films) Producer, Jerry O'Callaghan; Director, Maurice O'Callaghan; Screenplay, Maurice O'Callaghan, Kate O'Callaghan; Photography, Jack Conroy; Editor, Pat Duffner; Music, Patrick Cassidy; Costumes, Maeve Paterson; Produced with the assistance of the Irish Film Board; Irish; Color; Not rated; 98 minutes; October release. **CAST:** Colin Lane (Arthur O'Leary), Marian Quinn (Catherine O'Leary), Niall O'Brien (Josie McCarthy), Darren McHugh (Jimmy O'Leary), Joe Jeffers, Joy Florish, Jim Queally, Michael Twomey, Christy O'Sullivan.

AUGUSTIN (Kino Intl.) Producers, Philippe Jacquier, Brigitte Faure; Co-Producer, Philippe Carcassonne; Director/Screenplay, Anne Fontaine; Photography, Jean-Marie Dreujou; Editor, Sylvie Gadmer; a Pan-Europeenne release of a Sepia/Cinea Coproduction; French; Color; Not rated; 61 minutes; October release. **CAST:** Jean-Chretien Sibertin-Blanc (Augustin), Stephanie Zhang (Caroline), Guy Casabonne (Cyril Cachones), Nora Habib (Shula), Claude Pecher (Monsieur Poirier), James Lord (Hotel Guest), Jacqueline Vimpierre (Madame Batavoine), Rahim Mazioud (Hotel Manager), Rene Boulet (Monsieur Liviescu), Thierry Lhermitte (Himself)

WHALE MUSIC (Seventh Art) Producers, Raymond Massey, Steven DeNure; Executive Producers, Robert Lantos, David Hakuna; Director, Richard J. Lewis; Screenplay, Paul Quarrington, Richard J. Lewis; Based on the novel by Paul Quarrington; Photography, Vic Sarin; Designer, Rex Raglan; Music, George Blondheim; Whale Music composed and performed by Rheostatics; Costumes, Toni Burroughs-Rutter; Editor, Richard Martin; an Alliance Communications Corporation/Cape Scott Motion Pictures Inc. production; Canadian; Color; Not rated; 110 minutes; October release. **CAST:** Maury Chaykin (Desmond Howl), Cyndy Preston (Claire Lowe), Paul Gross (Daniel Howl), Jennifer Dale (Fay Ginzburg-Howl), Kenneth Welsh (Kenneth Sexstone), Blu Mankuma (Mookie Saunders), Alan Jordan (Sal Goneau), Tom Lavin (Monty Mann), Jim Byrnes (Dewey

Moore), Deborah Duchene (Bobby Sue), Paul Quarrington (Pete the Bartender), Janne Mortil (Star), Suzanne Ristic (Monty's Wife), Roman Podhora (Prison Guard), Sherrie Wong, Arlene Warren (Groupies), Jacqueline A. Gauthier (Waitress), Stephanie Blumer (Dancer)

TALK (Filmopolis) Producer, Megan McMurchy; Director, Susan Lambert; Screenplay, Jan Cornall; Photography, Ron Hagen Acs; Designer, Lissa Coote; Editor, Henry Dangar; Music, John Clifford White; Costumes, Clarrissa Patterson; Casting, Liz Mullinar Casting Consultants; Australian; Color; Not rated; 90 minutes; October release. **CAST:** Victoria Longley (Julia/Detective Julia), Angie Milliken (Stephanie/Detective Stephanie), Richard Roxburgh (Jack/Detective Harry), John Jarratt (Mac), Jacqueline McKenzie (The Girl), Ella-Mei Wong, Tenzing Tsewang, Kee Chan (Witnesses), Aaron James (Detective), Skye Wansey, Marianne Bryant (Mothers with Kids), Rose (Waitress in Cafe), Muroyama Kazuhiro (Comic Bookshop Assistant), Lindy Davies (Taxi Driver), Emily Simpson (Woman in Sportscar), Paul Alexander (Man in Sportscar), Pam Sharp, May Pusey (Old Ladies in Car), Toula Tzoras, Jo Thomas (Photo Shop Assistants), Fiona Shannon (Pregnant Woman at Train Station), Meliss Sachs (Toddler at Train Station), Georgina Kay (Old Lady on Phone), Donald McKinnon (Flowerseller)

A BUSINESS AFFAIR (Castle Hill) Producers, Xavier Larere, Clive Parsons, Davina Belling; Executive Producers, Martha Wansbrough, Willi Baer; Director, Charlotte Brandstrom; Screenplay, William Stadiem; Story, William Stadiem, Charlotte Brandstrom; Additional Dialogue, Lucy Flannery; Inspired by the books *Tears Before Bedtime* and *Weep No More* by Barbara Skelton; Photography, Willy Kurant; Designer, Sophie Becher; Music, Didier Vasseur; Editor, Laurence Mery-Clark; British; Dolby Stereo; Color; Rated R; 101 minutes; November release. **CAST:** Christopher Walken (Vanni Corso), Carole Bouquet (Kate Swallow), Jonathan Pryce (Alec Bolton), Sheila Hancock (Judith), Anna Manahan (Bianca), Fernando Guillen Guervo (Angel), Tom Wilkinson (Bob)

Cyndy Preston, Maury Chaykin in *Whale Music*
© Seventh Art Releasing

Jonathan Pryce, Carole Bouquet in *A Business Affair*
© Castle Hill Productions, Inc.

Alida Valli in *Eyes Without a Face*
© Interama

The Dancer © Svensk/Feuer

JOHNNY 100 PESOS (IRS Releasing) Producer/Director, Gustavo Graef-Marino; Screenplay, Gustavo Graef-Marino, Gerardo Caceres; Photography, Jose Luis Arredondo; Designer, Juan Carlos Castillo; Music, Andres Pollak; Editor, Danielle Fillios; a Quality Films release; Chilean; Color; Not rated; 90 minutes; November release. **CAST:** Armando Araiza (Johnny Garcia), Patricia Rivera (Gloria), Willy Semler (Freddy), Paulina Urrutia (Patty), Sergio Hernandez (Journalist), Luis Alarcon (Judge), Luis Gnecco (Alfonso), Armando Silvestre (Loco)

EYES WITHOUT A FACE (Interama) Director, Georges Franju; Screenplay, Boileau-Narcejac, Jean Redon, Claude Sautet; Based on the novel *Les Yeux Sans Visage* by Jean Redon; Photography, Eugen Shufftan; Editor, Gilbert Natot; Music, Maurice Jarre; French, 1959; Black and white; Not rated; 88 minutes; November release. **CAST:** Pierre Brasseur (Professor Génessier), Alida Valli (Louise), Edith Scob (Christiane), Juliette Mayniel

THE SILENCES OF THE PALACE (Amorces Diffusion) Producers, Ahmed Baha Eddine Attia, Richard Magnien; Director/Editor, Moufida Tlatli; Screenplay, Moufida Tlatli, Nouri Bouzid; Photography, Youssef Ben Youssef; Music, Anouar Brahem; a CInetelefilms & Magfilm/Mat Films production; Tunisian-French; Color; Not rated; 128 minutes; November release. **CAST:** Amel Hedhili (Khedija), Hend Sabri (Young Alia), Najia Ouerghi (Khalti Hadda), Ghalia Lacroix (Adult Alia), Kamel Fazaa (Sidi Ali)

TRAPS (Filmopolis) Producer, Jim McElroy; Director, Pauline Chan; Screenplay, Robert Carter, Pauline Chan; Based on the novel *Dreamhouse* by Kate Grenville; Photography, Kevin Hayward; Editor, Nicholas Beauman; Music, Stephen Rae; Australian; Dolby Stereo; Color; Rated R; 97 minutes; December release. CAST: Saskia Reeves (Louise Duffield), Robert Reynolds (Michael Duffield), Kiet Lam (Tuan), Nguyen Minh Tri (Thief), Thierry Marquet (Captain Brochard), Hoa To (Tatie Chi), Jacqueline McKenzie (Viola Renouard), Sami Frey (Daniel Renouard), Tran Duy An (Bao), Ho Thu Nga (Kim), Vu T. Le Thi (Bao's Mother), Nguyen Ngoc Dang (Bao's Grandfather), Jean Louis Beaulieu (French

Officer), Claude Holweger (French Soldier), Tat Binh (Vietminh Captain), Trieu Xuan Sam (Vietminh in Hut), Ly Thai Dung (Vietminh Executioner)

THE DANCER (Svenska Filminstitutet/Feuer Prods.) Producers, Lisbet Gabrielsson, Gerd Edwards; Director/Screenplay, Donya Feuer; Photography, Gunnar Kallstrom; Editor, Kerstin Eriksdotter; Swedish; Color; Not rated; 100 minutes; December release. Documentary following three years of ballet training for teenager Katja Bjorner, with Anneli Alhanko, Erland Josephson, Valentina Savina, Aleksandr Khmelnitski

PIGALLE (Seventh Art Releasing) Producers, Romain Bremond, Patric Haddad; Director/Screenplay, Karim Dridi; Photography, John Mathieson; Editor, Lise Beaulieu; Art Director, Gilles Bontemps; Costumes, Jean-Louis Mazabraud; a Premiere Heure/UGC Images/FCC, and Delfilm production; French-Swiss; Color; Cinemascope; Not rated; 93 minutes; December release. **CAST:** Vera Briole (Vera), Francis Renaud (Fifi), Raymond Gil (Fernande), Philippe Ambrosini (Le Malfait), Blanca Li (Divine), Jean-Claude Grenier (L'Empereur), Bobby Pacha (Le Pacha), Younesse Boudache (Mustaf), Patrick Chauvel (Le Gitan), Jacky Baps (Forceps), Roger Desprez (Roger L'Elegant), Jean-Michel Fete (P'Tit Fred), Olindo Cavadini (Polo), Christian Auger (Rene), Jean-Jacques Jauffret (Marc-Antoine), Philippe Nahon (Lezzi), Christian Saunier (Cri-Cri), Ursula Deuker (Marlene), Anne Carole (Pauline), Mostefa Zerguine (Hamad), Gerard Lebrun (L'Africain)

A SHORT FILM ABOUT KILLING (Cinema Village) Director, Krzysztof Kieslowski; Screenplay, Krzysztof Kieslowski, Krzysztof Piesiewicz; Photography, Slawomir Idziak; Music, Zbigniew Preisner; Polish, 1987: Color; Not rated; 84 minutes; December release. **CAST:** Miroslaw Baka (Jacek), Krzysztof Globisz (Piotr), Jan Tesarz (Taxi Driver)

A SHORT FILM ABOUT LOVE (Cinema Village) Director, Krzysztof Kieslowski; Screenplay, Krzysztof Kieslowski, Krzysztof Piesiewicz; Photography, Witold Adamek; Music, Zbigniew Preisner; Polish, 1988; Color; Not rated; 85 minutes; December release. **CAST:** Olaf Lubaszenko (Tomik), Grazyna Szapolowska (Magda)

Saskia Reeves, Jacqueline McKenzie in *Traps*
© Filmopolis Pictures Inc.

Olaf Luabszenko in *A Short Film About Love*

Norma Aleandro

Dan Aykroyd

Kirstie Alley

Scott Bakula

Biographical Data

(Name, real name, place and date of birth, school attended)

AAMES, WILLIE (William Upton): Los Angeles, CA, July 15, 1960.
AARON, CAROLINE: Richmond, VA, Aug. 7, 1954. Catholic U.
ABBOTT, DIAHNNE: NYC, 1945.
ABBOTT, JOHN: London, June 5, 1905.
ABRAHAM, F. MURRAY: Pittsburgh, PA, Oct. 24, 1939. UTx.
ACKLAND, JOSS: London, Feb. 29, 1928.
ADAMS, BROOKE: NYC, Feb. 8, 1949. Dalton.
ADAMS, CATLIN: Los Angeles, Oct. 11, 1950.
ADAMS, DON: NYC, Apr. 13, 1926.
ADAMS, EDIE (Elizabeth Edith Enke): Kingston, PA, Apr. 16, 1927. Juilliard, Columbia.
ADAMS, JULIE (Betty May): Waterloo, IA, Oct. 17, 1926. Little Rock, Jr. College.
ADAMS, MASON: NYC, Feb. 26, 1919. UWi.
ADAMS, MAUD (Maud Wikstrom): Lulea, Sweden, Feb. 12, 1945.
ADDY, WESLEY: Omaha, NE, Aug. 4, 1913. UCLA.
ADJANI, ISABELLE: Germany, June 27, 1955.
AGAR, JOHN: Chicago, IL, Jan. 31, 1921.
AGUTTER, JENNY: Taunton, England, Dec. 20, 1952.
AIELLO, DANNY: NYC, June 20, 1933.
AIMEE, ANOUK (Dreyfus): Paris, France, Apr. 27, 1934. Bauer-Therond.
AKERS, KAREN: NYC, Oct. 13, 1945, Hunter College.
ALBERGHETTI, ANNA MARIA: Pesaro, Italy, May 15, 1936.
ALBERT, EDDIE (Eddie Albert Heimberger): Rock Island, IL, Apr. 22, 1908. U of Minn.
ALBERT, EDWARD: Los Angeles, Feb. 20. 1951. UCLA.
ALBRIGHT, LOLA: Akron, OH, July 20, 1925.
ALDA, ALAN: NYC, Jan. 28, 1936. Fordham.

ALEANDRO, NORMA: Buenos Aires, Dec. 6, 1936.
ALEJANDRO, MIGUEL: NYC, Feb. 21, 1958.
ALEXANDER, ERIKA: Philadelphia, PA, 1970.
ALEXANDER, JANE (Quigley): Boston, MA, Oct. 28, 1939. Sarah Lawrence.
ALEXANDER, JASON (Jay Greenspan): Newark, NJ, Sept. 23, 1959. Boston U.
ALICE, MARY: Indianola, MS, Dec. 3, 1941.
ALLEN, DEBBIE (Deborah): Houston, TX, Jan. 16, 1950. Howard U.
ALLEN, JOAN: Rochelle, IL, Aug. 20, 1956. EastIllU.
ALLEN, KAREN: Carrollton, IL, Oct. 5, 1951. UMd.
ALLEN, NANCY: NYC, June 24, 1950.
ALLEN, REX: Wilcox, AZ, Dec. 31, 1922.
ALLEN, STEVE: NYC, Dec. 26, 1921.
ALLEN, TIM: Denver, CO, June 13, 1953. W. MI. Univ.
ALLEN, WOODY (Allen Stewart Konigsberg): Brooklyn, Dec. 1, 1935.
ALLEY, KIRSTIE: Wichita, KS, Jan. 12, 1955.
ALLYSON, JUNE (Ella Geisman): Westchester, NY, Oct. 7, 1917.
ALONSO, MARIA CONCHITA: Cuba, 1957.
ALT, CAROL: Queens, NY, Dec. 1, 1960. HofstraU.
ALVARADO, TRINI: NYC, Jan. 10, 1967.
AMIS, SUZY: Oklahoma City, OK, Jan. 5, 1958. Actors Studio.
AMOS, JOHN: Newark, NJ, Dec. 27, 1940. Colo. U.
ANDERSON, KEVIN: Waukeegan, IL, Jan. 13, 1960.
ANDERSON, LONI: St. Paul, MN, Aug. 5, 1946.

ANDERSON, MELODY: Edmonton, Canada, 1955. Carlton U.
ANDERSON, MICHAEL, JR.: London, England, Aug. 6, 1943.
ANDERSON, RICHARD DEAN: Minneapolis, MN, Jan. 23, 1950.
ANDERSSON, BIBI: Stockholm, Sweden, Nov. 11, 1935. Royal Dramatic Sch.
ANDES, KEITH: Ocean City, NJ, July 12, 1920. Temple U., Oxford.
ANDRESS, URSULA: Bern, Switzerland, Mar. 19, 1936.
ANDREWS, ANTHONY: London, Dec. 1, 1948.
ANDREWS, JULIE (Julia Elizabeth Wells): Surrey, England, Oct. 1, 1935.
ANGLIM, PHILIP: San Francisco, CA, Feb. 11, 1953.
ANNABELLA (Suzanne Georgette Charpentier): Paris, France, July 14, 1912/1909.
ANN-MARGRET (Olsson): Valsjobyn, Sweden, Apr. 28, 1941. Northwestern U.
ANSARA, MICHAEL: Lowell, MA, Apr. 15, 1922. Pasadena Playhouse.
ANSPACH, SUSAN: NYC, Nov. 23, 1945.
ANTHONY, LYSETTE: London, 1963.
ANTHONY, TONY: Clarksburg, WV, Oct. 16, 1937. Carnegie Tech.
ANTON, SUSAN: Yucaipa, CA, Oct. 12, 1950. Bemardino College.
ANTONELLI, LAURA: Pola, Italy, Nov. 28, 1941.
ANWAR, GABRIELLE: Lalehaam, England, Feb. 4, 1970
APPLEGATE, CHRISTINA: Hollywood CA, Nov. 25, 1972.
ARCHER, ANNE: Los Angeles, Aug. 25, 1947.
ARCHER, JOHN (Ralph Bowman): Osceola, NB, May 8, 1915. USC.
ARDANT, FANNY: Monte Carlo, Mar 22, 1949
ARKIN, ADAM: Brooklyn, NY, Aug. 19, 1956.

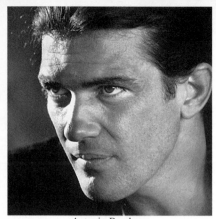

Antonio Banderas

ARNAZ, DESI, JR.: Los Angeles, Jan. 19, 1953.

ARNAZ, LUCIE: Hollywood, July 17, 1951.

ARNESS, JAMES (Aurness): Minneapolis, MN, May 26, 1923. Beloit College.

ARQUETTE, PATRICIA: NYC, Apr. 8, 1968.

ARQUETTE, ROSANNA: NYC, Aug. 10, 1959.

ARTHUR, BEATRICE (Frankel): NYC, May 13, 1924. New School.

ASHER, JANE: London, Apr. 5, 1946.

ASHLEY, ELIZABETH (Elizabeth Ann Cole): Ocala, FL, Aug. 30, 1939.

ASHTON, JOHN: Springfield, MA, Feb. 22, 1948. USC.

ASNER, EDWARD: Kansas City, KS, Nov. 15, 1929.

ASSANTE, ARMAND: NYC, Oct. 4, 1949. AADA.

ASTIN, JOHN: Baltimore, MD, Mar. 30, 1930. U Minn.

ASTIN, MacKENZIE: Los Angeles, May 12, 1973.

ASTIN, SEAN: Santa Monica, Feb. 25, 1971.

ATHERTON, WILLIAM: Orange, CT, July 30, 1947. Carnegie Tech.

ATKINS, CHRISTOPHER: Rye, NY, Feb. 21, 1961.

ATKINSON, ROWAN: England, Jan. 6, 1955. Oxford.

ATTENBOROUGH, RICHARD: Cambridge, England, Aug. 29, 1923. RADA.

Maria Conchita Alonso

AUBERJONOIS, RENE: NYC, June 1, 1940. Carnegie Tech.

AUDRAN, STEPHANE: Versailles, France, Nov. 8, 1932.

AUGER, CLAUDINE: Paris, France, Apr. 26, 1942. Dramatic Cons.

AULIN, EWA: Stockholm, Sweden, Feb. 14, 1950.

AUMONT, JEAN PIERRE: Paris, France, Jan. 5, 1909. French Nat'l School of Drama.

AUTRY, GENE: Tioga, TX, Sept. 29, 1907.

AVALON, FRANKIE (Francis Thomas Avallone): Philadelphia, PA, Sept. 18, 1939.

AYKROYD, DAN: Ottawa, Canada, July 1, 1952.

AYRES, LEW: Minneapolis, MN, Dec. 28, 1908.

AZNAVOUR, CHARLES (Varenagh Aznourian): Paris, France, May 22, 1924.

AZZARA, CANDICE: Brooklyn, NY, May 18, 1947.

BACH, CATHERINE: Warren, OH, Mar. 1, 1954.

BACALL, LAUREN (Betty Perske): NYC, Sept. 16, 1924. AADA.

BACH, BARBARA: Queens, NY, Aug. 27, 1946.

BACKER, BRIAN: NYC, Dec. 5, 1956. Neighborhood Playhouse.

BACON, KEVIN: Philadelphia, PA, July 8, 1958.

BAIN, BARBARA: Chicago, IL, Sept. 13, 1934. U Ill.

BAIO, SCOTT: Brooklyn, NY, Sept. 22, 1961.

BAKER, BLANCHE: NYC, Dec. 20, 1956.

BAKER, CARROLL: Johnstown, PA, May 28, 1931. St. Petersburg, Jr. College.

BAKER, DIANE: Hollywood, CA, Feb. 25, 1938. USC.

BAKER, JOE DON: Groesbeck, TX, Feb.12, 1936.

BAKER, KATHY: Midland, TX, June 8, 1950. UC Berkley.

BAKULA, SCOTT: St. Louis, MO, Oct. 9, 1955. KansasU.

BALABAN, BOB: Chicago, IL, Aug. 16, 1945. Colgate.

BALDWIN, ADAM: Chicago, IL, Feb. 27, 1962.

BALDWIN, ALEC: Massapequa, NY, Apr. 3, 1958. NYU.

BALDWIN, STEPHEN: Long Island, NY, 1966.

BALDWIN, WILLIAM: Massapequa, NY, Feb. 21, 1963.

BALE, CHRISTIAN: Pembrokeshire, West Wales, Jan. 30, 1974.

BALLARD, KAYE: Cleveland, OH, Nov. 20, 1926.

BALSAM, MARTIN: NYC, Nov. 4, 1919. Actors Studio.

BANCROFT, ANNE (Anna Maria Italiano): Bronx, NY, Sept. 17, 1931. AADA.

BANDERAS, ANTONIO: Malaga, Spain, Aug. 10, 1960.

BANERJEE, VICTOR: Calcutta, India, Oct. 15, 1946.

BANES, LISA: Chagrin Falls, OH, July 9, 1955. Juilliard.

BANNEN, IAN: Airdrie, Scotland, June 29, 1928.

BARANSKI, CHRISTINE: Buffalo, NY, May 2, 1952. Juilliard.

BARBEAU, ADRIENNE: Sacramento, CA, June 11, 1945. Foothill College.

Ann-Margret

BARDOT, BRIGITTE: Paris, France, Sept. 28, 1934.

BARKIN, ELLEN: Bronx, NY, Apr. 16, 1954. Hunter College.

BARNES, BINNIE (Gitelle Enoyce Barnes): London, Mar. 25, 1906.

BARNES, C. B. (Christopher): Portland, ME, 1973.

BARR, JEAN-MARC: San Diego, CA, Sept. 1960.

BARRAULT, JEAN-LOUIS: Vesinet, France, Sept. 8, 1910.

BARRAULT, MARIE-CHRISTINE: Paris, France, Mar. 21, 1944.

BARREN, KEITH: Mexborough, England, Aug. 8, 1936. Sheffield Playhouse.

BARRETT, MAJEL (Hudec): Columbus, OH, Feb. 23. Western Reserve U.

BARRIE, BARBARA: Chicago, IL, May 23, 1931.

BARRY, GENE (Eugene Klass): NYC, June 14, 1919.

BARRY, NEILL: NYC, Nov. 29, 1965.

BARRYMORE, DREW: Los Angeles, Feb. 22, 1975.

BARRYMORE, JOHN DREW: Beverly Hills, CA, June 4, 1932. St. John's Military Academy.

BARTEL, PAUL: Brooklyn, NY, Aug. 6, 1938. UCLA.

BARTY, BILLY: (William John Bertanzetti) Millsboro, PA, Oct. 25, 1924.

John Beal

BARYSHNIKOV, MIKHAIL: Riga, Latvia, Jan. 27, 1948.

BASINGER, KIM: Athens, GA, Dec. 8, 1953. Neighborhood Playhouse.

BASSETT, ANGELA: NYC, Aug. 16, 1958.

BATEMAN, JASON: Rye, NY, Jan. 14, 1969.

BATEMAN, JUSTINE: Rye, NY, Feb. 19, 1966.

BATES, ALAN: Allestree, Derbyshire, England, Feb. 17, 1934. RADA.

BATES, JEANNE: San Francisco, CA, May 21. RADA.

BATES, KATHY: Memphis, TN, June 28, 1948. S. Methodist U.

BAUER, STEVEN (Steven Rocky Echevarria): Havana, Cuba, Dec. 2, 1956. U Miami.

BAXTER, KEITH: South Wales, England, Apr. 29, 1933. RADA.

BAXTER, MEREDITH: Los Angeles, June 21, 1947. Intelochen Acad.

BAYE, NATHALIE: Maineville, France, July 6, 1948.

BEACHAM, STEPHANIE: Casablanca, Morocco, Feb. 28, 1947.

BEAL, JOHN (J. Alexander Bliedung): Joplin, MO, Aug. 13, 1909. PA U.

BEALS, JENNIFER: Chicago, IL, Dec. 19, 1963.

BEAN, ORSON (Dallas Burrows): Burlington, VT, July 22, 1928.

BEAN, SEAN: Sheffield, Yorkshire, England, Apr. 17, 1958.

BEART, EMMANUELLE: Gassin, France, Aug. 14, 1965.

BEATTY, NED: Louisville, KY, July 6, 1937.

BEATTY, ROBERT: Hamilton, Ont., Canada, Oct. 19, 1909. U of Toronto.

BEATTY, WARREN: Richmond, VA, Mar. 30, 1937.

BECK, JOHN: Chicago, IL, Jan. 28, 1943.

BECK, MICHAEL: Memphis, TN, Feb. 4, 1949. Millsap College.

BEDELIA, BONNIE: NYC, Mar. 25, 1946. Hunter College.

BEDI, KABIR: India, 1945.

BEGLEY, ED, JR.: NYC, Sept. 16, 1949.

BELAFONTE, HARRY: NYC, Mar. 1, 1927.

BEL GEDDES, BARBARA: NYC, Oct. 31, 1922.

BELL, TOM: Liverpool, England, 1932.

BELLER, KATHLEEN: NYC, Feb. 10, 1957.

BELLWOOD, PAMELA (King): Scarsdale, NY, June 26.

BELMONDO, JEAN PAUL: Paris, France, Apr. 9, 1933.

BELUSHI, JAMES: Chicago, IL, June 15, 1954.

BELZER, RICHARD: Bridgeport, CT, Aug. 4, 1944.

BENEDICT, DIRK (Niewoehner): White Sulphur Springs, MT, March 1, 1945. Whitman College.

BENEDICT, PAUL: Silver City, NM, Sept. 17, 1938.

BENIGNI, ROBERTO: Tuscany, Italy, Oct. 27, 1952.

BENING, ANNETTE: Topeka, KS, May 29, 1958. SFSt. U.

BENJAMIN, RICHARD: NYC, May 22, 1938. Northwestern U.

BENNENT, DAVID: Lausanne, Sept. 9, 1966.

Harry Belafonte

Gabrielle Anwar

Kenneth Branagh

BENNETT, ALAN: Leeds, England, May 9, 1934. Oxford.

BENNETT, BRUCE (Herman Brix): Tacoma, WA, May 19, 1909. U Wash.

BENNETT, HYWEL: Garnant, So. Wales, Apr. 8, 1944.

BENSON, ROBBY: Dallas, TX, Jan. 21, 1957.

BERENGER, TOM: Chicago, IL, May 31, 1950, U Mo.

BERENSON, MARISA: NYC, Feb. 15, 1947.

BERG, PETER: NYC, 1964. Malcalester College.

BERGEN, CANDICE: Los Angeles, May 9, 1946. U PA.

BERGEN, POLLY: Knoxville, TN, July 14, 1930. Compton, Jr. College.

BERGER, HELMUT: Salzburg, Austria, May 29, 1942.

BERGER, SENTA: Vienna, Austria, May 13, 1941. Vienna Sch. of Acting.

BERGER, WILLIAM: Austria, Jan. 20, 1928. Columbia.

BERGERAC, JACQUES: Biarritz, France, May 26, 1927. Paris U.

BERGIN, PATRICK: Dublin, Feb. 4, 1951.

BERKOFF, STEVEN: London, England, Aug. 3, 1937.

BERLE, MILTON (Berlinger): NYC, July 12, 1908.

BERLIN, JEANNIE: Los Angeles, Nov. 1, 1949.

BERLINGER, WARREN: Brooklyn, Aug. 31, 1937. Columbia.

BERNHARD, SANDRA: Flint, MI, June 6, 1955.

BERNSEN, CORBIN: Los Angeles, Sept. 7, 1954. UCLA.

BERRI, CLAUDE (Langmann): Paris, France, July 1, 1934.

BERRIDGE, ELIZABETH: Westchester, NY, May 2, 1962. Strasberg Inst.

BERRY, HALLE: Cleveland, OH, Aug. 14, 1968.

BERRY, KEN: Moline, IL, Nov. 3, 1933.

BERTINELLI, VALERIE: Wilmington, DE, Apr. 23, 1960.

BESCH, BIBI: Vienna, Austria, Feb. 1, 1942.

BEST, JAMES: Corydon, IN, July 26, 1926.

BETTGER, LYLE: Philadelphia, PA, Feb. 13, 1915. AADA.

BEY, TURHAN: Vienna, Austria, Mar. 30, 1921.

BEYMER, RICHARD: Avoca, IA, Feb. 21, 1939.

BIALIK, MAYIM: Dec. 12, 1975.

BIEHN, MICHAEL: Anniston, AL, July 31, 1956.

BIKEL, THEODORE: Vienna, May 2, 1924. RADA.

BILLINGSLEY, PETER: NYC, 1972.

BINOCHE, JULIETTE: Paris, France, Mar. 9, 1964.

BIRKIN, JANE: London, Dec. 14, 1947

BIRNEY, DAVID: Washington, DC, Apr. 23, 1939. Dartmouth, UCLA.

BIRNEY, REED: Alexandria, VA, Sept. 11, 1954. Boston U.

BISHOP, JOEY (Joseph Abraham Gotlieb): Bronx, NY, Feb. 3, 1918.

BISHOP, JULIE (Jacqueline Wells): Denver, CO, Aug. 30, 1917. Westlake School.

BISSET, JACQUELINE: Waybridge, England, Sept. 13, 1944.

BLACK, KAREN (Ziegler): Park Ridge, IL, July 1, 1942. Northwestern.

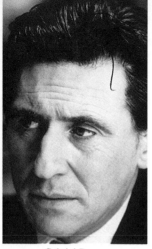
Gabriel Byrne

Christina Applegate

Keith Carradine

Anne Archer

BLACKMAN, HONOR: London, 1926.
BLADES, RUBEN: Panama City, July 16, 1948. Harvard.
BLAIR, BETSY (Betsy Boger): NYC, Dec. 11, 1923.
BLAIR, JANET (Martha Jane Lafferty): Blair, PA, Apr. 23, 1921.
BLAIR, LINDA: Westport, CT, Jan. 22, 1959.
BLAKE, ROBERT (Michael Gubitosi): Nutley, NJ, Sept. 18, 1933.
BLAKELY, SUSAN: Frankfurt, Germany, Sept. 7, 1950. U TX.
BLAKLEY, RONEE: Stanley, ID, 1946. Stanford U.
BLOOM, CLAIRE: London, Feb. 15, 1931. Badminton School.
BLOOM, VERNA: Lynn, MA, Aug. 7, 1939. Boston U.
BLOUNT, LISA: Fayettville, AK, July 1, 1957. UAk.
BLUM, MARK: Newark, NJ, May 14, 1950. UMinn.
BLYTH, ANN: Mt. Kisco, NY, Aug. 16, 1928. New Waybum Dramatic School.
BOCHNER, HART: Toronto, Canada, Oct. 3, 1956. U San Diego.
BOCHNER, LLOYD: Toronto, Canada, July 29, 1924.
BOGARDE, DIRK: London, Mar. 28, 1921. Glasgow & Univ. College.
BOGOSIAN, ERIC: Woburn, MA, Apr. 24, 1953. Oberlin College.
BOHRINGER, RICHARD: Paris, France, 1942.
BOLKAN, FLORINDA (Florinda Soares Bulcao): Ceara, Brazil, Feb. 15, 1941.
BOLOGNA, JOSEPH: Brooklyn, NY, Dec. 30, 1938. Brown U.
BOND, DEREK: Glasgow, Scotland, Jan. 26, 1920. Askes School.
BONET, LISA: San Francisco, CA, Nov. 16, 1967.
BONHAM-CARTER, HELENA: London, England, May 26, 1966.
BONO, SONNY (Salvatore): Detroit, MI, Feb. 16, 1935.
BOONE, PAT: Jacksonville, FL, June 1, 1934. Columbia U.

BOOTHE, JAMES: Croydon, England, Dec.19, 1930
BOOTHE, POWERS: Snyder, TX, June 1, 1949. So. Methodist U.
BORGNINE, ERNEST (Borgnino): Hamden, CT, Jan. 24, 1917. Randall School.
BOSCO, PHILIP: Jersey City, NJ, Sept. 26, 1930. CatholicU.
BOSLEY, TOM: Chicago, IL, Oct. 1, 1927. DePaul U.
BOSTWICK, BARRY: San Mateo, CA, Feb. 24, 1945. NYU.
BOTTOMS, JOSEPH: Santa Barbara, CA, Aug. 30, 1954.
BOTTOMS, SAM: Santa Barbara, CA, Oct. 17, 1955.
BOTTOMS, TIMOTHY: Santa Barbara, CA, Aug. 30, 1951.
BOULTING, INGRID: Transvaal, So. Africa, 1947.
BOUTSIKARIS, DENNIS: Newark, NJ, Dec. 21, 1952. CatholicU.
BOVEE, LESLIE: Bend, OR, 1952.
BOWIE, DAVID (David Robert Jones): Brixton, South London, England, Jan. 8, 1947.
BOWKER, JUDI: Shawford, England, Apr. 6, 1954.
BOXLEITNER, BRUCE: Elgin, IL, May 12, 1950.
BOYLE, LARA FLYNN: Davenport, IA, Mar. 24, 1970.
BOYLE, PETER: Philadelphia, PA, Oct. 18, 1933. LaSalle College.
BRACCO, LORRAINE: Brooklyn, NY, 1955.
BRACKEN, EDDIE: NYC, Feb. 7, 1920. Professional Children's School.
BRAEDEN, ERIC (Hans Gudegast): Kiel, Germany, Apr. 3, 1942.
BRAGA, SONIA: Maringa, Brazil, June 8, 1950.
BRANAGH, KENNETH: Belfast, No. Ireland, Dec. 10, 1960.
BRANDAUER, KLAUS MARIA: Altaussee, Austria, June 22, 1944.
BRANDIS, JONATHAN: CT, Apr. 13, 1976.
BRANDO, JOCELYN: San Francisco, Nov. 18, 1919. Lake Forest College, AADA.
BRANDO, MARLON: Omaha, NB, Apr. 3, 1924. New School.

BRANDON, CLARK: NYC, 1959.
BRANDON, MICHAEL (Feldman): Brooklyn, NY.
BRANTLEY, BETSY: Rutherfordton, NC, 1955. London Central Sch. of Drama.
BRENNAN, EILEEN: Los Angeles, CA, Sept. 3, 1935. AADA.
BRIALY, JEAN-CLAUDE: Aumale, Algeria, 1933. Strasbourg Cons.
BRIDGES, BEAU: Los Angeles, Dec. 9, 1941. UCLA.
BRIDGES, JEFF: Los Angeles, Dec. 4, 1949.
BRIDGES, LLOYD: San Leandro, CA, Jan. 15, 1913.
BRIMLEY, WILFORD: Salt Lake City, UT, Sept. 27, 1934.
BRINKLEY, CHRISTIE: Malibu, CA, Feb. 2, 1954.
BRISEBOIS, DANIELLE: Brooklyn, NY, June 28, 1969.
BRITT, MAY (Maybritt Wilkins): Sweden, Mar. 22, 1936.
BRITTANY, MORGAN (Suzanne Cupito): Los Angeles, Dec. 5, 1950.
BRITTON, TONY: Birmingham, England, June 9, 1924.
BRODERICK, MATTHEW: NYC, Mar. 21, 1962.
BROLIN, JAMES: Los Angeles, July 18, 1940. UCLA.
BROMFIELD, JOHN (Farron Bromfield): South Bend, IN, June 11, 1922. St. Mary's College.
BRON, ELEANOR: Stanmore, England, 1934.
BRONSON, CHARLES (Buchinsky): Ehrenfield, PA, Nov. 3, 1920.
BROOKES, JACQUELINE: Montclair, NJ, July 24, 1930. RADA.
BROOKS, ALBERT (Einstein): Los Angeles, July 22, 1947.
BROOKS, MEL (Melvyn Kaminski): Brooklyn, NY, June 28, 1926.
BROSNAN, PIERCE: County Meath, Ireland. May 16, 1952.
BROWN, BLAIR: Washington, DC, Apr. 23, 1947. Pine Manor.
BROWN, BRYAN: Panania, Australia, June 23, 1947.

Bess Armstrong   Max Casella   Rosanna Arquette   John Cusack

BROWN, GARY (Christian Brando): Hollywood, CA, 1958.

BROWN, GEORG STANFORD: Havana, Cuba, June 24, 1943. AMDA.

BROWN, JAMES: Desdemona, TX, Mar. 22, 1920. Baylor U.

BROWN, JIM: St. Simons Island, NY, Feb. 17, 1935. Syracuse U.

BROWNE, LESLIE: NYC, 1958.

BROWNE, ROSCOE LEE: Woodbury, NJ, May 2, 1925.

BUCHHOLZ, HORST: Berlin, Germany, Dec. 4, 1933. Ludwig Dramatic School.

BUCKLEY, BETTY: Big Spring, TX, July 3, 1947. TxCU.

BUJOLD, GENEVIEVE: Montreal, Canada, July 1, 1942.

BULLOCK, SANDRA: Arlington, VA, 1967.

BURGHOFF, GARY: Bristol, CT, May 24, 1943.

BURGI, RICHARD: Montclair, NJ, July 30, 1958.

BURKE, PAUL: New Orleans, July 21, 1926. Pasadena Playhouse.

BURNETT, CAROL: San Antonio, TX, Apr. 26, 1933. UCLA.

BURNS, CATHERINE: NYC, Sept. 25, 1945. AADA.

BURNS, GEORGE (Nathan Birnbaum): NYC, Jan. 20, 1896.

BURROWS, DARREN E.: Winfield, KS, Sept. 12, 1966

BURSTYN, ELLEN (Edna Rae Gillhooly): Detroit, MI, Dec. 7, 1932.

BURTON, LeVAR: Los Angeles, CA, Feb. 16, 1958. UCLA.

BUSCEMI, STEVE: Brooklyn, NY, Dec. 13, 1957.

BUSEY, GARY: Goose Creek, TX, June 29, 1944.

BUSFIELD, TIMOTHY: Lansing, MI, June 12, 1957. E. Tenn. St. U.

BUSKER, RICKY: Rockford, IL, 1974.

BUTTONS, RED (Aaron Chwatt): NYC, Feb. 5, 1919.

BUZZI, RUTH: Westerly, RI, July 24, 1936. Pasadena Playhouse.

BYGRAVES, MAX: London, Oct. 16, 1922. St. Joseph's School.

BYRNE, DAVID: Dumbarton, Scotland, May 14, 1952.

BYRNE, GABRIEL: Dublin, Ireland, May 12, 1950.

BYRNES, EDD: NYC, July 30, 1933. Haaren High.

CAAN, JAMES: Bronx, NY, Mar. 26,1939.

CAESAR, SID: Yonkers, NY, Sept. 8, 1922.

CAGE, NICOLAS (Coppola): Long Beach, CA, Jan.7, 1964.

CAINE, MICHAEL (Maurice Micklewhite): London, Mar. 14, 1933.

CAINE, SHAKIRA (Baksh): Guyana, Feb. 23, 1947. Indian Trust College.

CALHOUN, RORY (Francis Timothy Durgin): Los Angeles, Aug. 8, 1922.

CALLAN, MICHAEL (Martin Calinieff): Philadelphia, Nov. 22, 1935.

CALLOW, SIMON: London, June 15, 1949. Queens U.

CALVERT, PHYLLIS: London, Feb. 18, 1917. Margaret Morris School.

CALVET, CORRINE (Corinne Dibos): Paris, France, Apr. 30, 1925. U Paris.

CAMERON, KIRK: Panorama City, CA, Oct. 12, 1970.

CAMP, COLLEEN: San Francisco, CA, 1953.

CAMPBELL, BILL: Chicago, IL, 1960.

CAMPBELL, GLEN: Delight, AR, Apr. 22, 1935.

CAMPBELL, TISHA: Newark, NJ, 1969.

CANALE, GIANNA MARIA: Reggio Calabria, Italy, Sept. 12, 1927.

CANNON, DYAN (Samille Diane Friesen): Tacoma, WA, Jan. 4, 1937.

CANTU, DOLORES: San Antonio, TX, 1957.

CAPERS, VIRGINIA: Sumter, SC, 1925. Juilliard.

CAPSHAW, KATE: Ft. Worth, TX, Nov. 3, 1953. UMo.

CARA, IRENE: NYC, Mar. 18, 1958.

CARDINALE, CLAUDIA: Tunis, N. Africa. Apr. 15, 1939. College Paul Cambon.

CAREY, HARRY, JR.: Saugus, CA, May 16, 1921. Black Fox Military Academy.

CAREY, PHILIP: Hackensack, NJ, July 15, 1925. U Miami.

CARIOU, LEN: Winnipeg, Canada, Sept. 30, 1939.

CARLIN, GEORGE: NYC, May 12, 1938.

CARMEN, JULIE: Mt. Vernon, NY, Apr. 4, 1954.

CARMICHAEL, IAN: Hull, England, June 18, 1920. Scarborough College.

CARNE, JUDY (Joyce Botterill): Northampton, England, 1939. Bush-Davis Theatre School.

CARNEY, ART: Mt. Vernon, NY, Nov. 4, 1918.

CARON, LESLIE: Paris, France, July 1, 1931. Nat'l Conservatory, Paris.

CARPENTER, CARLETON: Bennington, VT, July 10, 1926. Northwestern.

CARRADINE, DAVID: Hollywood, Dec. 8, 1936. San Francisco State.

CARRADINE, KEITH: San Mateo, CA, Aug. 8, 1950. Colo. State U.

CARRADINE, ROBERT: San Mateo, CA, Mar. 24, 1954.

CARREL, DANY: Tourane, Indochina, Sept. 20, 1936. Marseilles Cons.

CARRERA, BARBARA: Managua, Nicaragua, Dec. 31, 1945.

CARREY, JIM: Jacksons Point, Ontario, Canada, Jan. 17, 1962.

CARRIERE, MATHIEU: West Germany, 1950.

CARROLL, DIAHANN (Johnson): NYC, July 17, 1935. NYU.

CARROLL, PAT: Shreveport, LA, May 5, 1927. Catholic U.

CARSON, JOHN DAVID: California, 1951. Valley College.

CARSON, JOHNNY: Corning, IA, Oct. 23, 1925. U of Neb.

CARSTEN, PETER (Ransenthaler): Weissenberg, Bavaria, Apr. 30, 1929. Munich Akademie.

CARTER, NELL: Birmingham, AL, Sept. 13, 1948.

CARTWRIGHT, VERONICA: Bristol, England, Apr 20, 1949.

CARUSO, DAVID: Forest Hills, NY, 1956.

CARVEY, DANA: Missoula, MT, Apr. 2, 1955. SFST.CoI.

CASELLA, MAX: Washington D.C., June 6, 1967

Danny DeVito

Blanche Baker

Matt Dillon

CASEY, BERNIE: Wyco, WV, June 8, 1939.

CASS, PEGGY (Mary Margaret Cass): Boston, MA, May 21, 1924.

CASSAVETES, NICK: NYC, 1959, Syracuse U, AADA.

CASSEL, JEAN-PIERRE: Paris, France, Oct. 27, 1932.

CASSEL, SEYMOUR: Detroit, MI, Jan. 22, 1935.

CASSIDY, DAVID: NYC, Apr. 12, 1950.

CASSIDY, JOANNA: Camden, NJ, Aug. 2, 1944. Syracuse U.

CASSIDY, PATRICK: Los Angeles, CA, Jan. 4, 1961.

CATES, PHOEBE: NYC, July 16, 1962.

CATTRALL, KIM: Liverpool, England, Aug. 21, 1956. AADA.

CAULFIELD, MAXWELL: Glasgow, Scotland, Nov. 23, 1959.

CAVANI, LILIANA: Bologna, Italy, Jan. 12, 1937. U Bologna.

CAVETT, DICK: Gibbon, NE, Nov. 19, 1936.

CHAKIRIS, GEORGE: Norwood, OH, Sept. 16, 1933.

CHAMBERLAIN, RICHARD: Beverly Hills, CA, March 31, 1935. Pomona.

CHAMPION, MARGE (Marjorie Belcher): Los Angeles, Sept. 2, 1923.

CHAN, JACKIE: Hong Kong, Apr. 7, 1954

CHANNING, CAROL: Seattle, WA, Jan. 31, 1921. Bennington.

CHANNING, STOCKARD (Susan Stockard): NYC, Feb. 13, 1944. Radcliffe.

CHAPIN, MILES: NYC, Dec. 6, 1954. HB Studio.

CHAPLIN, GERALDINE: Santa Monica, CA, July 31, 1944. Royal Ballet.

CHAPLIN, SYDNEY: Los Angeles, Mar. 31, 1926. Lawrenceville.

CHARISSE, CYD (Tula Ellice Finklea): Amarillo, TX, Mar. 3, 1922. Hollywood Professional School.

CHARLES, WALTER: East Strousburg, PA, Apr. 4, 1945. Boston U.

CHASE, CHEVY (Cornelius Crane Chase): NYC, Oct. 8, 1943.

CHAVES, RICHARD: Jacksonville, FL, Oct. 9, 1951. Occidental College.

CHAYKIN, MAURY: July 27, 1954

CHEN, JOAN: Shanghai, 1961. CalState.

CHER (Cherilyn Sarkisian): El Centro, CA, May 20, 1946.

CHILES, LOIS: Alice, TX, 1950.

CHONG, RAE DAWN: Vancouver, Canada, 1961.

CHONG, THOMAS: Edmonton, Alberta, Canada, May 24, 1938.

CHRISTIAN, LINDA (Blanca Rosa Welter): Tampico, Mexico, Nov. 13, 1923.

CHRISTIE, JULIE: Chukua, Assam, India, Apr. 14, 1941.

CHRISTOPHER, DENNIS (Carrelli): Philadelphia, PA, Dec. 2, 1955. Temple U.

CHRISTOPHER, JORDAN: Youngstown, OH, Oct. 23, 1940. Kent State.

CILENTO, DIANE: Queensland, Australia, Oct. 5, 1933. AADA.

CLAPTON, ERIC: London, Mar. 30, 1945.

CLARK, CANDY: Norman, OK, June 20, 1947.

CLARK, DANE: NYC, Feb. 18, 1915. Cornell, Johns Hopkins U.

CLARK, DICK: Mt. Vernon, NY, Nov. 30, 1929. Syracuse U.

CLARK, MATT: Washington, DC, Nov. 25, 1936.

CLARK, PETULA: Epsom, England, Nov. 15, 1932.

CLARK, SUSAN: Sarnid, Ont., Canada, Mar. 8, 1943. RADA.

CLAY, ANDREW DICE: Brooklyn, NY, 1958, Kingsborough College.

CLAYBURGH, JILL: NYC, Apr. 30, 1944. Sarah Lawrence.

CLEESE, JOHN: Weston-Super-Mare, England, Oct. 27, 1939, Cambridge.

CLERY, CORRINNE: Italy, 1950.

CLOONEY, ROSEMARY: Maysville, KY, May 23, 1928.

CLOSE, GLENN: Greenwich, CT, Mar. 19, 1947. William & Mary College.

COBURN, JAMES: Laurel, NB, Aug. 31, 1928. LACC.

COCA, IMOGENE: Philadelphia, Nov. 18, 1908.

CODY, KATHLEEN: Bronx, NY, Oct. 30, 1953.

COFFEY, SCOTT: HI, 1967.

COLBERT, CLAUDETTE (Lily Chauchoin): Paris, France, Sept. 15, 1903. Art Students League.

COLE, GEORGE: London, Apr. 22, 1925.

COLEMAN, GARY: Zion, IL, Feb. 8, 1968.

COLEMAN, DABNEY: Austin, TX, Jan. 3, 1932.

COLEMAN, JACK: Easton, PA, 1958. Duke U.

COLIN, MARGARET: NYC, 1957.

COLLET, CHRISTOPHER: NYC, Mar. 13, 1968. Strasberg Inst.

COLLINS, JOAN: London, May 21, 1933. Francis Holland School.

COLLINS, PAULINE: Devon, England, Sept. 3, 1940.

COLLINS, STEPHEN: Des Moines, IA, Oct. 1, 1947. Amherst.

COLON, MIRIAM: Ponce, PR., 1945. UPR.

COLTRANE, ROBBIE: Ruthergien, Scotland, Mar. 30, 1950.

COMER, ANJANETTE: Dawson, TX, Aug. 7, 1942. Baylor, Tex. U.

CONANT, OLIVER: NYC, Nov. 15, 1955. Dalton.

CONAWAY, JEFF: NYC, Oct. 5, 1950. NYU.

CONNELLY, JENNIFER: NYC, Dec. 12, 1970

CONNERY, SEAN: Edinburgh, Scotland, Aug. 25, 1930.

CONNERY, JASON: London, 1962.

CONNICK, HARRY, JR.: New Orleans, LA, Sept. 11, 1967.

CONNORS, MIKE (Krekor Ohanian): Fresno, CA, Aug. 15, 1925. UCLA.

CONRAD, ROBERT (Conrad Robert Falk): Chicago, IL, Mar. 1, 1935. Northwestern U.

CONROY, KEVIN: Westport, CT, 1956. Juilliard.

CONSTANTINE, MICHAEL: Reading, PA, May 22, 1927.

CONTI, TOM: Paisley, Scotland, Nov. 22, 1941.

CONVERSE, FRANK: St. Louis, MO, May 22, 1938. Carnegie Tech.

CONWAY, GARY: Boston, Feb. 4, 1936.

CONWAY, KEVIN: NYC, May 29, 1942.

CONWAY, TIM (Thomas Daniel): Willoughby, OH, Dec. 15, 1933. Bowling Green State.

COOGAN, KEITH (Keith Mitchell Franklin): Palm Springs, CA, Jan. 13, 1970.

Christine Baranski

Stephen Dorff

Halle Berry

Griffin Dunne

COOPER, BEN: Hartford, CT, Sept. 30, 1930. Columbia U.

COOPER, CHRIS: Kansas City, MO, July 9, 1951. UMo.

COOPER, JACKIE: Los Angeles, Sept. 15, 1921.

COPELAND, JOAN: NYC, June 1, 1922. Brooklyn College, RADA.

CORBETT, GRETCHEN: Portland, OR, Aug. 13, 1947. Carnegie Tech.

CORBIN, BARRY: Dawson County, TX, Oct. 16, 1940. Texas Tech. U.

CORBY, ELLEN (Hansen): Racine, WI, June 13, 1913.

CORCORAN, DONNA: Quincy, MA, Sept. 29, 1942.

CORD, ALEX (Viespi): Floral Park, NY, Aug. 3, 1931. NYU, Actors Studio.

CORDAY, MARA (Marilyn Watts): Santa Monica, CA, Jan. 3, 1932.

COREY, JEFF: NYC, Aug. 10, 1914. Fagin School.

CORLEY, AL: Missouri, 1956. Actors Studio.

CORNTHWAITE, ROBERT: St. Helens, OR, Apr. 28, 1917. USC.

CORRI, ADRIENNE: Glasgow, Scot., Nov. 13, 1933. RADA.

CORT, BUD (Walter Edward Cox): New Rochelle, NY, Mar. 29, 1950. NYU.

CORTESA, VALENTINA: Milan, Italy, Jan. 1, 1924.

COSBY, BILL: Philadelphia, PA, July 12, 1937. Temple U.

COSTER, NICOLAS: London, Dec. 3, 1934. Neighborhood Playhouse.

COSTNER, KEVIN: Lynwood, CA, Jan. 18, 1955. CalStaU.

COURTENAY, TOM: Hull, England, Feb. 25, 1937. RADA.

COURTLAND, JEROME: Knoxville, TN, Dec. 27, 1926.

COX, BRIAN: Dundee, Scotland, June 1, 1946. LAMDA.

COX, COURTENEY: Birmingham, AL, June 15, 1964.

COX, RONNY: Cloudcroft, NM, Aug. 23, 1938.

COYOTE, PETER (Cohon): NYC, 1942.

CRAIG, MICHAEL: Poona, India, Jan. 27, 1929.

CRAIN, JEANNE: Barstow, CA, May 25, 1925.

CRAVEN, GEMMA: Dublin, Ireland, June 1, 1950.

CRAWFORD, MICHAEL (Dumbel-Smith): Salisbury, England, Jan. 19, 1942.

CREMER, BRUNO: Paris, France, 1929.

CRENNA, RICHARD: Los Angeles, Nov. 30, 1926. USC.

CRISTAL, LINDA (Victoria Moya): Buenos Aires, Feb. 25, 1934.

CRONYN, HUME (Blake): Ontario, Canada, July 18, 1911.

CROSBY, DENISE: Hollywood, CA, 1958.

CROSBY, HARRY: Los Angeles, CA, Aug. 8, 1958.

CROSBY, MARY FRANCES: Los Angeles, CA, Sept. 14, 1959.

CROSS, BEN: London, Dec. 16, 1947. RADA.

CROSS, MURPHY (Mary Jane): Laurelton, MD, June 22, 1950.

CROUSE, LINDSAY: NYC, May 12, 1948. Radcliffe.

CROWE, RUSSELL: New Zealand, 1964.

CROWLEY, PAT: Olyphant, PA, Sept. 17, 1932.

CRUISE, TOM (T. C. Mapother, IV): July 3, 1962, Syracuse, NY.

CRYER, JON: NYC, Apr. 16, 1965, RADA.

CRYSTAL, BILLY: Long Beach, NY, Mar. 14, 1947. Marshall U.

CULKIN, MACAULAY: NYC, Aug. 26, 1980.

CULLUM, JOHN: Knoxville, TN, Mar. 2, 1930. U Tenn.

CULLUM, JOHN DAVID: NYC, Mar. 1, 1966.

CULP, ROBERT: Oakland, CA, Aug. 16, 1930. U Wash.

CUMMINGS, CONSTANCE: Seattle, WA, May 15, 1910.

CUMMINGS, QUINN: Hollywood, Aug. 13, 1967.

CUMMINS, PEGGY: Prestatyn, N. Wales, Dec. 18, 1926. Alexandra School.

CURRY, TIM: Cheshire, England, Apr. 19, 1946. Birmingham U.

CURTIN, JANE: Cambridge, MA, Sept. 6, 1947.

CURTIS, JAMIE LEE: Los Angeles, CA, Nov. 22, 1958.

CURTIS, KEENE: Salt Lake City, UT, Feb. 15, 1925. U Utah.

CURTIS, TONY (Bernard Schwartz): NYC, June 3, 1924.

CUSACK, JOAN: Evanston, IL, Oct. 11, 1962.

CUSACK, JOHN: Chicago, IL, June 28, 1966.

CUSACK, SINEAD: Ireland, Feb. 18, 1948

DAFOE, WILLEM: Appleton, WI, July 22, 1955.

DAHL, ARLENE: Minneapolis, Aug. 11, 1928. U Minn.

DALE, JIM: Rothwell, England, Aug. 15, 1935.

DALLESANDRO, JOE: Pensacola, FL, Dec. 31, 1948.

DALTON, TIMOTHY: Colwyn Bay, Wales, Mar. 21, 1946. RADA.

DALTREY, ROGER: London, Mar. 1, 1944.

DALY, TIM: NYC, Mar. 1, 1956. Bennington College.

DALY, TYNE: Madison, WI, Feb. 21, 1947. AMDA.

DAMONE, VIC (Vito Farinola): Brooklyn, NY, June 12, 1928.

DANCE, CHARLES: Plymouth, England, Oct. 10, 1946.

D'ANGELO, BEVERLY: Columbus, OH, Nov. 15, 1953.

DANGERFIELD, RODNEY (Jacob Cohen): Babylon, NY, Nov. 22, 1921.

DANIELS, JEFF: Athens, GA, Feb. 19, 1955. EMichSt.

DANIELS, WILLIAM: Brooklyn, NY, Mar. 31, 1927. Northwestern.

DANNER, BLYTHE: Philadelphia, PA, Feb. 3, 1944. Bard College.

DANNING, SYBIL: Vienna, Austria, 1950.

Stockard Channing   Albert Finney   Jennifer Connelly   Laurence Fishburne

DANSON, TED: San Diego, CA, Dec. 29, 1947. Stanford, Carnegie Tech.
DANTE, MICHAEL (Ralph Vitti): Stamford, CT, 1935. U Miami.
DANZA, TONY: Brooklyn, NY, Apr. 21, 1951. UDubuque.
D'ARBANVILLE-QUINN, PATTY: NYC, 1951.
DARBY, KIM (Deborah Zerby): North Hollywood, CA, July 8, 1948.
DARCEL, DENISE (Denise Billecard): Paris, France, Sept. 8, 1925. U Dijon.
DARREN, JAMES: Philadelphia, PA, June 8, 1936. Stella Adler School.
DARRIEUX, DANIELLE: Bordeaux, France, May 1, 1917. Lycee LaTour.
DAVENPORT, NIGEL: Cambridge, England, May 23, 1928. Trinity College.
DAVID, KEITH: NYC, June 4, 1954. Juilliard.
DAVIDOVICH, LOLITA: Toronto, Ontario, Canada, July 15, 1961.
DAVIDSON, JOHN: Pittsburgh, Dec. 13, 1941. Denison U.
DAVIS, CLIFTON: Chicago, IL, Oct. 4, 1945. Oakwood College.
DAVIS, GEENA: Wareham, MA, Jan. 21, 1957.
DAVIS, JUDY: Perth, Australia, Apr. 23, 1955.
DAVIS, MAC: Lubbock, TX, Jan. 21, 1942.
DAVIS, NANCY (Anne Frances Robbins): NYC, July 6, 1921. Smith College.
DAVIS, OSSIE: Cogdell, GA, Dec. 18, 1917. Howard U.
DAVIS, SAMMI: Kidderminster, Worcestershire, England, June 21, 1964.
DAVIS, SKEETER (Mary Frances Penick): Dry Ridge, KY, Dec. 30, 1931.
DAVISON, BRUCE: Philadelphia, PA, June 28, 1946.
DAWBER, PAM: Detroit, MI, Oct. 18, 1954.
DAY, DORIS (Doris Kappelhoff): Cincinnati, Apr. 3, 1924.
DAY, LARAINE (Johnson): Roosevelt, UT, Oct. 13, 1917.
DAY LEWIS, DANIEL: London, Apr. 29, 1957. Bristol Old Vic.
DAYAN, ASSEF: Israel, 1945. U Jerusalem.
DEAKINS, LUCY: NYC, 1971.

DEAN, JIMMY: Plainview, TX, Aug. 10, 1928.
DEAN, LOREN: Las Vegas, NV, July 31, 1969.
DECAMP, ROSEMARY: Prescott, AZ, Nov. 14, 1913.
DeCARLO, YVONNE (Peggy Yvonne Middleton): Vancouver, B.C., Canada, Sept. 1, 1922. Vancouver School of Drama.
DEE, FRANCES: Los Angeles, Nov. 26, 1907. Chicago U.
DEE, JOEY (Joseph Di Nicola): Passaic, NJ, June 11, 1940. Patterson State College.
DEE, RUBY: Cleveland, OH, Oct. 27, 1924. Hunter College.
DEE, SANDRA (Alexandra Zuck): Bayonne, NJ, Apr. 23, 1942.
DeHAVEN, GLORIA: Los Angeles, July 23, 1923.
DeHAVILLAND, OLIVIA: Tokyo, Japan, July 1, 1916. Notre Dame Convent School.
DELAIR, SUZY: Paris, France, Dec. 31, 1916.
DELANY, DANA: NYC, March 13, 1956. Wesleyan U.
DELPY, JULIE: Paris. 1969.
DELON, ALAIN: Sceaux, France, Nov. 8, 1935.
DELORME, DANIELE: Paris, France, Oct. 9, 1927. Sorbonne.
DeLUISE, DOM: Brooklyn, NY, Aug. 1, 1933. Tufts College.
DeLUISE, PETER: Hollywood, CA, 1967.
DEMONGEOT, MYLENE: Nice, France, Sept. 29, 1938.
DeMORNAY, REBECCA: Los Angeles, Aug. 29, 1962. Strasberg Inst.
DEMPSEY, PATRICK: Lewiston, ME, Jan. 13, 1966.
DeMUNN, JEFFREY: Buffalo, NY, Apr. 25, 1947. Union College.
DENCH, JUDI: York, England, Dec. 9, 1934.
DENEUVE, CATHERINE: Paris, France, Oct. 22, 1943.
DeNIRO, ROBERT: NYC, Aug. 17, 1943. Stella Adler.
DENISON, MICHAEL: Doncaster, York, England, Nov. 1, 1915. Oxford.
DENNEHY, BRIAN: Bridgeport, CT, Jul. 9, 1938. Columbia.

DENVER, BOB: New Rochelle, NY, Jan. 9, 1935.
DENVER, JOHN: Roswell, NM, Dec. 31, 1943.
DEPARDIEU, GERARD: Chateauroux, France, Dec. 27, 1948.
DEPP, JOHNNY: Owensboro, KY, June 9, 1963.
DEREK, BO (Mary Cathleen Collins): Long Beach, CA, Nov. 20, 1956.
DEREK, JOHN: Hollywood, Aug. 12, 1926.
DERN, BRUCE: Chicago, IL, June 4, 1936. UPA.
DERN, LAURA: Los Angeles, Feb. 10, 1967.
DeSALVO, ANNE: Philadelphia, Apr. 3.
DEVANE, WILLIAM: Albany, NY, Sept. 5, 1939.
DEVINE, COLLEEN: San Gabriel, CA, June 22, 1960.
DeVITO, DANNY: Asbury Park, NJ, Nov. 17, 1944.
DEXTER, ANTHONY (Walter Reinhold Alfred Fleischmann): Talmadge, NB, Jan. 19, 1919. U Iowa.
DEY, SUSAN: Pekin, IL, Dec. 10, 1953.
DeYOUNG, CLIFF: Los Angeles, CA, Feb. 12, 1945. Cal State.
DIAMOND, NEIL: NYC, Jan. 24, 1941. NYU.
DICAPRIO, LEONARDO: Hollywood, CA, Nov. 11, 1974.
DICKINSON, ANGIE (Angeline Brown): Kulm, ND, Sept. 30, 1932. Glendale College.
DILLER, PHYLLIS (Driver): Lima, OH, July 17, 1917. Bluffton College.
DILLMAN, BRADFORD: San Francisco, Apr. 14, 1930. Yale.
DILLON, KEVIN: Mamaroneck, NY, Aug. 19, 1965.
DILLON, MATT: Larchmont, NY, Feb. 18, 1964. AADA.
DILLON, MELINDA: Hope, AR, Oct. 13, 1939. Goodman Theatre School.
DIXON, DONNA: Alexandria, VA, July 20, 1957.
DOBSON, KEVIN: NYC, Mar. 18, 1944.
DOBSON, TAMARA: Baltimore, MD, 1947. MD Inst. of Art.
DOHERTY, SHANNEN: Memphis, TN, Apr. 12, 1971.

DOLAN, MICHAEL: Oklahoma City, OK, June 21, 1965.

DOMERGUE, FAITH: New Orleans, June 16, 1925.

DONAHUE, TROY (Merle Johnson): NYC, Jan. 27, 1937. Columbia U.

DONAT, PETER: Nova Scotia, Jan. 20, 1928. Yale.

DONNELLY, DONAL: Bradford, England, July 6, 1931.

D'ONOFRIO, VINCENT: Brooklyn, NY, June 30, 1959.

DONOHOE, AMANDA: London, June 29 1962.

DONOVAN, TATE: NYC, 1964.

DOOHAN, JAMES: Vancouver, BC, Mar. 3, 1920. Neighborhood Playhouse.

DOOLEY, PAUL: Parkersburg WV, Feb. 22, 1928. U WV.

DORFF, STEPHEN: July 29, 1973.

DOUGLAS, DONNA (Dorothy Bourgeois): Baywood, LA, Sept. 26, 1935.

DOUGLAS, KIRK (Issur Danielovitch): Amsterdam, NY, Dec. 9, 1916. St. Lawrence U.

DOUGLAS, MICHAEL: New Brunswick, NJ, Sept. 25, 1944. U Cal.

DOUGLASS, ROBYN: Sendai, Japan, June 21, 1953. UCDavis.

DOURIF, BRAD: Huntington, WV, Mar. 18, 1950. Marshall U.

DOVE, BILLIE: NYC, May 14, 1904.

DOWN, LESLEY-ANN: London, Mar. 17, 1954.

DOWNEY, ROBERT, JR.: NYC, Apr. 4, 1965.

DRAKE, BETSY: Paris, France, Sept. 11, 1923.

DREW, ELLEN (formerly Terry Ray): Kansas City, MO, Nov. 23, 1915.

DREYFUSS, RICHARD: Brooklyn, NY, Oct. 19, 1947.

DRILLINGER, BRIAN: Brooklyn, NY, June 27, 1960. SUNY/Purchase.

DRU, JOANNE (Joanne LaCock): Logan, WV, Jan. 31, 1923. John Robert Powers School.

DRYER, JOHN: Hawthorne, CA, July 6, 1946.

DUCHOVNY, DAVID: NYC, Aug. 7, 1960. Yale.

DUDIKOFF, MICHAEL: Torrance, CA, Oct. 8, 1954.

DUGAN, DENNIS: Wheaton, IL, Sept. 5, 1946.

DUKAKIS, OLYMPIA: Lowell, MA, June 20, 1931.

DUKE, BILL: Poughkeepsie, NY, Feb. 26, 1943. NYU.

DUKE, PATTY (Anna Marie): NYC, Dec. 14, 1946.

DUKES, DAVID: San Francisco, June 6, 1945.

DULLEA, KEIR: Cleveland, NJ, May 30, 1936. SF State College.

DUNAWAY, FAYE: Bascom, FL, Jan. 14, 1941, Fla. U.

DUNCAN, SANDY: Henderson, TX, Feb. 20, 1946. Len Morris College.

DUNNE, GRIFFIN: NYC, June 8, 1955. Neighborhood Playhouse.

DUPEREY, ANNY: Paris, France, 1947.

DURBIN, DEANNA (Edna): Winnipeg, Canada, Dec. 4, 1921.

DURNING, CHARLES S. : Highland Falls, NY, Feb. 28, 1923. NYU.

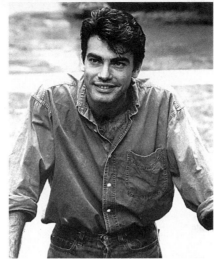
Peter Gallagher

Jamie Lee Curtis

Andy Garcia

DUSSOLLIER, ANDRE: Annecy, France, Feb. 17, 1946.

DUTTON, CHARLES: Baltimore, MD, Jan. 30, 1951. Yale.

DUVALL, ROBERT: San Diego, CA, Jan. 5, 1931. Principia College.

DUVALL, SHELLEY: Houston, TX, July 7, 1949.

DYSART, RICHARD: Brighton, ME, Mar. 30, 1929.

DZUNDZA, GEORGE: Rosenheim, Germ., July 19, 1945.

EASTON, ROBERT: Milwaukee, WI, Nov. 23, 1930. U Texas.

EASTWOOD, CLINT: San Francisco, May 31, 1931. LACC.

EATON, SHIRLEY: London, 1937. Aida Foster School.

EBSEN, BUDDY (Christian, Jr.): Belleville, IL, Apr. 2, 1910. U Fla.

ECKEMYR, AGNETA: Karlsborg, Sweden, July 2. Actors Studio.

EDELMAN, GREGG: Chicago, IL, Sept. 12, 1958. Northwestern U.

EDELMAN, HERB: Brooklyn, NY, Nov. 5, 1933.

EDEN, BARBARA (Huffman): Tucson, AZ, Aug. 23, 1934.

EDWARDS, ANTHONY: Santa Barbara, CA, July 19, 1962. RADA.

EDWARDS, VINCE: NYC, July 9, 1928. AADA.

EGGAR, SAMANTHA: London, Mar. 5, 1939.

EICHHORN, LISA: Reading, PA, Feb. 4, 1952. Queens Ont. U RADA.

EIKENBERRY, JILL: New Haven, CT, Jan. 21, 1947.

EILBER, JANET: Detroit, MI, July 27, 1951. Juilliard.

EKBERG, ANITA: Malmo, Sweden, Sept. 29, 1931.

EKLAND, BRITT: Stockholm, Sweden, Oct. 6, 1942.

ELDARD, RON: NYC, 1964.

ELIZONDO, HECTOR: NYC, Dec. 22, 1936.

ELLIOTT, CHRIS: NYC, May 31, 1960.

ELLIOTT, PATRICIA: Gunnison, CO, July 21, 1942. UCol.

ELLIOTT, SAM: Sacramento, CA, Aug. 9, 1944. U Ore.

ELWES, CARY: London, Oct. 26, 1962.

ELY, RON (Ronald Pierce): Hereford, TX, June 21, 1938.

ENGLISH, ALEX: USCar, 1954.

ENGLUND, ROBERT: Glendale, CA, June 6, 1949.

ERDMAN, RICHARD: Enid, OK, June 1, 1925.

ERICSON, JOHN: Dusseldorf, Ger., Sept. 25, 1926. AADA.

ERMEY, R. LEE (Ronald): Emporia, KS, Mar. 24, 1944

ESMOND, CARL: Vienna, June 14, 1906. U Vienna.

ESPOSITO, GIANCARLO: Copenhagen, Denmark, Apr. 26, 1958.

ESTEVEZ, EMILIO: NYC, May 12, 1962.

ESTRADA, ERIK: NYC, Mar. 16, 1949.

EVANS, DALE (Francis Smith): Uvalde, TX, Oct. 31, 1912.

EVANS, GENE: Holbrook, AZ, July 11, 1922.

EVANS, JOSH: NYC, Jan. 16, 1971.

EVANS, LINDA (Evanstad): Hartford, CT, Nov. 18, 1942.

EVERETT, CHAD (Ray Cramton): South Bend, IN, June 11, 1936.

EVERETT, RUPERT: Norfolk, England, 1959.

EVIGAN, GREG: South Amboy, NJ, Oct. 14, 1953.

FABARES, SHELLEY: Los Angeles, Jan. 19, 1944.

FABIAN (Fabian Forte): Philadelphia, Feb. 6, 1943.

FABRAY, NANETTE (Ruby Nanette Fabares): San Diego, Oct. 27, 1920.

FAHEY, JEFF: Olean, NY, Nov. 29, 1956.

FAIRBANKS, DOUGLAS, JR.: NYC, Dec. 9, 1907. Collegiate School.

FAIRCHILD, MORGAN (Patsy McClenny): Dallas, TX, Feb. 3, 1950. UCLA.

FALK, PETER: NYC, Sept. 16, 1927. New School.

FARENTINO, JAMES: Brooklyn, NY, Feb. 24, 1938. AADA.

FARGAS, ANTONIO: Bronx, NY, Aug. 14, 1946.

FARINA, DENNIS: Chicago, IL, Feb. 29, 1944.

FARINA, SANDY (Sandra Feldman): Newark, NJ, 1955.

FARLEY, CHRIS: Madison, WI, 1960. MarquetteU.

FARNSWORTH, RICHARD: Los Angeles, Sept. 1, 1920.

FARR, FELICIA: Westchester, NY, Oct. 4. 1932. Penn State College.

FARROW, MIA (Maria): Los Angeles, Feb. 9, 1945.

FAULKNER, GRAHAM: London, Sept. 26, 1947. Webber-Douglas.

FAWCETT, FARRAH: Corpus Christie, TX, Feb. 2, 1947. TexU.

FAYE, ALICE (Ann Leppert): NYC, May 5, 1912.

FEINSTEIN, ALAN: NYC, Sept. 8, 1941.

FELDMAN, COREY: Encino, CA, July 16, 1971.

FELDON, BARBARA (Hall): Pittsburgh, Mar. 12, 1941. Carnegie Tech.

FELDSHUH, TOVAH: NYC, Dec. 27, 1953, Sarah Lawrence College.

FELL, NORMAN: Philadelphia, PA, Mar. 24, 1924.

FELLOWS, EDITH: Boston, May 20, 1923.

FENN, SHERILYN: Detroit, MI, Feb. 1, 1965.

FERRELL, CONCHATA: Charleston, WV, Mar. 28, 1943. Marshall U.

FERRER, MEL: Elbeton, NJ, Aug. 25, 1912. Princeton U.

FERRER, MIGUEL: Santa Monica, CA, Feb. 7, 1954.

FERRIS, BARBARA: London, 1940.

FERZETTI, GABRIELE: Italy, 1927. Rome Acad. of Drama.

FIEDLER, JOHN: Plateville, WI, Feb. 3, 1925.

FIELD, SALLY: Pasadena, CA, Nov. 6, 1946.

FIELD, SHIRLEY-ANNE: London, June 27, 1938.

FIENNES, RALPH: Suffolk, England, Dec. 22, 1962. RADA.

FIERSTEIN, HARVEY: Brooklyn, NY, June 6, 1954. Pratt Inst.

FIGUEROA, RUBEN: NYC, 1958.

FINCH, JON: Caterham, England, Mar. 2, 1941.

FINLAY, FRANK: Farnworth, England, Aug. 6, 1926.

FINNEY, ALBERT: Salford, Lancashire, England, May 9, 1936. RADA.

FIORENTINO, LINDA: Philadelphia, PA, Mar. 9, 1960.

FIRESTONE, ROCHELLE: Kansas City, MO, June 14, 1949. NYU.

FIRTH, COLIN: Grayshott, Hampshire, England, Sept. 10, 1960.

FIRTH, PETER: Bradford, England, Oct. 27, 1953.

FISHBURNE, LAURENCE: Augusta, GA, July 30, 1961.

FISHER, CARRIE: Los Angeles, CA, Oct. 21, 1956. London Central School of Drama.

FISHER, EDDIE: Philadelphia, PA, Aug. 10, 1928.

FITZGERALD, BRIAN: Philadelphia, PA, 1960. West Chester U.

FITZGERALD, TARA: England, 1960.

FITZGERALD, GERALDINE: Dublin, Ireland, Nov. 24, 1914. Dublin Art School.

FLAGG, FANNIE: Birmingham, AL, Sept. 21, 1944. UAl.

FLANNERY, SUSAN: Jersey City, NJ, July 31, 1943.

FLEMING, RHONDA (Marilyn Louis): Los Angeles, Aug. 10, 1922.

FLEMYNG, ROBERT: Liverpool, England, Jan. 3, 1912. Haileybury College.

FLETCHER, LOUISE: Birmingham, AL, July 22 1934.

FOCH, NINA: Leyden, Holland, Apr. 20, 1924.

FOLDI, ERZSEBET: Queens, NY, 1967.

FOLLOWS, MEGAN: Toronto, Canada, 1967.

FONDA, BRIDGET: Los Angeles, Jan. 27, 1964.

FONDA, JANE: NYC, Dec. 21, 1937. Vassar.

FONDA, PETER: NYC, Feb. 23, 1939. U Omaha.

FONTAINE, JOAN: Tokyo, Japan, Oct. 22, 1917.

FOOTE, HALLIE: NYC, 1953. UNH.

FORD, GLENN (Gwyllyn Samuel Newton Ford): Quebec, Canada, May 1, 1916.

FORD, HARRISON: Chicago, IL, July 13, 1942. Ripon College.

FOREST, MARK (Lou Degni): Brooklyn, NY, Jan. 1933.

FORREST, FREDERIC: Waxahachie, TX, Dec. 23, 1936.

FORREST, STEVE: Huntsville, TX, Sept. 29, 1924. UCLA.

FORSLUND, CONNIE: San Diego, CA, June 19, 1950. NYU.

FORSTER, ROBERT (Foster, Jr.): Rochester, NY, July 13, 1941. Rochester U.

FORSYTHE, JOHN (Freund): Penn's Grove, NJ, Jan. 29, 1918.

FORSYTHE, WILLIAM: Brooklyn, NY, June 7, 1955

FOSSEY, BRIGITTE: Tourcoing, France, Mar. 11, 1947.

FOSTER, JODIE (Ariane Munker): Bronx, NY, Nov. 19, 1962. Yale.

FOSTER, MEG: Reading, PA, May 14, 1948.

FOX, EDWARD: London, Apr. 13, 1937. RADA.

FOX, JAMES: London, May 19, 1939.

Rebecca DeMornay

Terry Gilliam

Nina Foch

Jeff Goldblum

Bridget Fonda

John Goodman

Melanie Griffith

Frank Gorshin

FOX, MICHAEL J.: Vancouver, BC, June 9, 1961.

FOXWORTH, ROBERT: Houston, TX, Nov. 1, 1941. Carnegie Tech.

FRAKES, JONATHAN: Bethlehem, PA, 1952. Harvard.

FRANCIOSA, ANTHONY (Papaleo): NYC, Oct. 25, 1928.

FRANCIS, ANNE: Ossining, NY, Sept. 16, 1932.

FRANCIS, ARLENE (Arlene Kazanjian): Boston, Oct. 20, 1908. Finch School.

FRANCIS, CONNIE (Constance Franconero): Newark, NJ, Dec. 12, 1938.

FRANCKS, DON: Vancouver, Canada, Feb. 28, 1932.

FRANK, JEFFREY: Jackson Heights, NY, 1965.

FRANKLIN, PAMELA: Tokyo, Feb. 4, 1950.

FRANZ, ARTHUR: Perth Amboy, NJ, Feb. 29, 1920. Blue Ridge College.

FRANZ, DENNIS: Chicago, IL, Oct. 28, 1944.

FRASER, BRENDAN: Indianapolis, IN, 1968.

FRAZIER, SHEILA: NYC, Nov. 13, 1948.

FRECHETTE, PETER: Warwick, RI, Oct. 1956. URI.

FREEMAN, AL, JR.: San Antonio, TX, Mar. 21, 1934. CCLA.

FREEMAN, KATHLEEN: Chicago, IL, Feb. 17, 1919.

FREEMAN, MONA: Baltimore, MD, June 9, 1926.

FREEMAN, MORGAN: Memphis, TN, June 1, 1937. LACC.

FREWER, MATT: Washington, DC, Jan. 4, 1958, Old Vic.

FRICKER, BRENDA: Dublin, Ireland, Feb. 17, 1945.

FRIELS, COLIN: Glasgow, Sept. 25, 1952.

FULLER, PENNY: Durham, NK, 1940. Northwestern U.

FUNICELLO, ANNETTE: Utica, NY, Oct. 22, 1942.

FURLONG, EDWARD: Glendale, CA, Aug. 2, 1977.

FURNEAUX, YVONNE: Lille, France, 1928. Oxford U.

FYODOROVA, VICTORIA: Russia, 1946.

GABLE, JOHN CLARK: Los Angeles, Mar. 20, 1961. Santa Monica College.

GABOR, ZSA ZSA (Sari Gabor): Budapest, Hungary, Feb. 6, 1918.

GAIL, MAX: Derfoil, MI, Apr. 5, 1943.

GAINES, BOYD: Atlanta, GA, May 11, 1953. Juilliard.

GALLAGHER, PETER: NYC, Aug. 19, 1955. Tufts U.

GALLIGAN, ZACH: NYC, Feb. 14, 1963. ColumbiaU.

GAM, RITA: Pittsburgh, PA, Apr. 2, 1928.

GAMBON, MICHAEL: Dublin, Ireland, Oct. 19, 1940.

GANZ, BRUNO: Zurich, Switzerland, Mar. 22, 1941.

GARBER, VICTOR: Montreal, Canada, Mar. 16, 1949.

GARCIA, ANDY: Havana, Cuba, Apr. 12, 1956. FlaInt.

GARFIELD, ALLEN (Allen Goorwitz): Newark, NJ, Nov. 22, 1939. Actors Studio.

GARFUNKEL, ART: NYC, Nov. 5, 1941.

GARLAND, BEVERLY: Santa Cruz, CA, Oct. 17, 1926. Glendale College.

GARNER, JAMES (James Baumgarner): Norman, OK, Apr. 7, 1928. Okla. U.

GAROFALO, JANEANE: NJ, Sept. 28, 1964.

GARR, TERI: Lakewood, OH, Dec. 11, 1949.

GARRETT, BETTY: St. Joseph, MO, May 23, 1919. Annie Wright Seminary.

GARRISON, SEAN: NYC, Oct. 19, 1937.

GARSON, GREER: County Down, Ireland, Sept. 29, 1908.

GARY, LORRAINE: NYC, Aug. 16, 1937.

GASSMAN, VITTORIO: Genoa, Italy, Sept. 1,1922. Rome Academy of Dramatic Art.

GAVIN, JOHN: Los Angeles, Apr. 8, 1935. Stanford U.

GAYLORD, MITCH: Van Nuys, CA, 1961. UCLA.

GAYNOR, MITZI (Francesca Marlene Von Gerber): Chicago, IL, Sept. 4, 1930.

GAZZARA, BEN: NYC, Aug. 28, 1930. Actors Studio.

GEARY, ANTHONY: Coalsville, UT, May 29, 1947. UUt.

GEDRICK, JASON: Chicago, IL, Feb. 7, 1965. Drake U.

GEESON, JUDY: Arundel, England, Sept. 10, 1948. Corona.

GEOFFREYS, STEPHEN: Cincinnati, OH, Nov. 22, 1964. NYU.

GEORGE, SUSAN: West London, England, July 26, 1950.

GERARD, GIL: Little Rock, AR, Jan. 23, 1940.

GERE, RICHARD: Philadelphia, PA, Aug. 29, 1949. U Mass.

GERROLL, DANIEL: London, Oct. 16, 1951. Central.

GERTZ, JAMI: Chicago, IL, Oct. 28, 1965.

GETTY, BALTHAZAR: CA, Jan. 22, 1975.

GETTY, ESTELLE: NYC, July 25, 1923. New School.

GHOLSON, JULIE: Birmingham, AL, June 4, 1958.

GHOSTLEY, ALICE: Eve, MO, Aug. 14, 1926. Okla U.

GIAN, JOE: North Miami Beach, FL, 1962.

GIANNINI, CHERYL: Monessen, PA, June 15.

GIANNINI, GIANCARLO: Spezia, Italy, Aug. 1, 1942. Rome Acad. of Drama.

GIBB, CYNTHIA: Bennington, VT, Dec. 14, 1963.

GIBSON, HENRY: Germantown, PA, Sept. 21, 1935.

GIBSON, MEL: Peekskill, NY, Jan. 3, 1956. NIDA.

GIELGUD, JOHN: London, Apr. 14, 1904. RADA.

GIFT, ROLAND: Birmingham, England, May 28 1962.

GILBERT, MELISSA: Los Angeles, CA, May 8, 1964.

GILES, NANCY: NYC, July 17, 1960, Oberlin College.

GILLETTE, ANITA: Baltimore, MD, Aug. 16, 1938.

GILLIAM, TERRY: Minneapolis, MN, Nov. 22, 1940.

GILLIS, ANNE (Alma O'Connor): Little Rock, AR, Feb. 12, 1927.

GINTY, ROBERT: NYC, Nov. 14, 1948. Yale.

Hugh Grant

Daryl Hannah

GINTY, ROBERT: NYC, Nov. 14, 1948. Yale.

GIRARDOT, ANNIE: Paris, France, Oct. 25, 1931.

GIROLAMI, STEFANIA: Rome, 1963.

GISH, ANNABETH: Albuquerque, NM, Mar. 13, 1971. DukeU.

GIVENS, ROBIN: NYC, Nov. 27, 1964.

GLASER, PAUL MICHAEL: Boston, MA, Mar. 25, 1943. Boston U.

GLASS, RON: Evansville, IN, July 10, 1945.

GLEASON, JOANNA: Winnipeg, Canada, June 2, 1950. UCLA.

GLEASON, PAUL: Jersey City, NJ, May 4, 1944.

GLENN, SCOTT: Pittsburgh, PA, Jan. 26, 1942. William and Mary College.

GLOVER, CRISPIN: NYC, Sept 20, 1964.

GLOVER, DANNY: San Francisco, CA, July 22, 1947. SFStateCol.

GLOVER, JOHN: Kingston, NY, Aug. 7, 1944.

GLYNN,CARLIN: Cleveland, Oh, Feb. 19, 1940. Actors Studio.

GOLDBERG, WHOOPI (Caryn Johnson): NYC, Nov. 13, 1949.

GOLDBLUM, JEFF: Pittsburgh, PA, Oct. 22, 1952. Neighborhood Playhouse.

GOLDEN, ANNIE: Brooklyn, NY, Oct. 19, 1951.

GOLDSTEIN, JENETTE: Beverly Hills, CA, 1960.

GOLDTHWAIT, BOB: Syracuse, NY, May 1, 1962.

GOLDWYN, TONY: Los Angeles, May 20, 1960. LAMDA.

GOLINO, VALERIA: Naples, Italy, Oct. 22, 1966.

GONZALEZ, CORDELIA: Aug. 11, 1958, San Juan, PR. UPR.

GONZALES-GONZALEZ, PEDRO: Aguilares, TX, Dec. 21, 1926.

GOODALL, CAROLINE: London, Nov. 13, 1959. BristolU.

GOODING, CUBA, JR.: Bronx, N.Y., 1968.

GOODMAN, DODY: Columbus, OH, Oct. 28, 1915.

GOODMAN, JOHN: St. Louis, MO, June 20, 1952.

GORDON, KEITH: NYC, Feb. 3, 1961.

GORMAN, CLIFF: Jamaica, NY, Oct. 13, 1936. NYU.

GORSHIN, FRANK: Pittsburgh, PA, Apr. 5, 1933.

GORTNER, MARJOE: Long Beach, CA, Jan. 14, 1944.

GOSSETT, LOUIS, JR.: Brooklyn, NY, May 27, 1936. NYU.

GOULD, ELLIOTT (Goldstein): Brooklyn, NY, Aug. 29, 1938. Columbia U.

GOULD, HAROLD: Schenectady, NY, Dec. 10, 1923. Cornell.

GOULD, JASON: NYC, Dec. 29, 1966.

GOULET, ROBERT: Lawrence, MA, Nov. 26, 1933. Edmonton.

GRAF, DAVID: Lancaster, OH, Apr. 1950. OhStateU.

GRAFF, TODD: NYC, Oct. 22, 1959. SUNY/Purchase.

GRANGER, FARLEY: San Jose, CA, July 1, 1925.

GRANT, DAVID MARSHALL: Westport, CT, June 21, 1955. Yale.

GRANT, HUGH: London, Sept. 9, 1960. Oxford.

GRANT, KATHRYN (Olive Grandstaff): Houston, TX, Nov. 25, 1933. UCLA.

GRANT, LEE: NYC, Oct. 31, 1927. Juilliard.

GRANT, RICHARD E: Mbabane, Swaziland, May 5, 1957. Cape Town U.

GRAVES, PETER (Aurness): Minneapolis, Mar. 18, 1926. U Minn.

GRAVES, RUPERT: Weston-Super-Mare, England, June 30, 1963.

GRAY, CHARLES: Bournemouth, England, 1928.

GRAY, COLEEN (Doris Jensen): Staplehurst, NB, Oct. 23, 1922. Hamline.

GRAY, LINDA: Santa Monica, CA, Sept. 12, 1940.

GRAY, SPALDING: Barrington, RI, June 5, 1941.

GRAYSON, KATHRYN (Zelma Hedrick): Winston-Salem, NC, Feb. 9, 1922.

GREEN, KERRI: Fort Lee, NJ, 1967. Vassar.

GREENE, ELLEN: NYC, Feb. 22, 1950. Ryder College.

GREENE, GRAHAM: Six Nations Reserve, Ontario, June 22, 1952

GREER, JANE: Washington, DC, Sept. 9, 1924.

GREER, MICHAEL: Galesburg, IL, Apr. 20, 1943.

GREGORY, MARK: Rome, Italy, 1965.

GREIST, KIM: Stamford, CT, May 12, 1958.

GREY, JENNIFER: NYC, Mar. 26, 1960.

GREY, JOEL (Katz): Cleveland, OH, Apr. 11, 1932.

GREY, VIRGINIA: Los Angeles, Mar. 22, 1917.

GRIECO, RICHARD: Watertown, NY, 1966.

GRIEM, HELMUT: Hamburg, Germany, 1940. HamburgU.

GRIER, DAVID ALAN: Detroit, MI, June 30, 1955. Yale.

GRIER, PAM: Winston-Salem, NC, May 26, 1949.

GRIFFITH, ANDY: Mt. Airy, NC, June 1, 1926. UNC.

GRIFFITH, MELANIE: NYC, Aug. 9, 1957. Pierce College.

GRIMES, GARY: San Francisco, June 2, 1955.

GRIMES, SCOTT: Lowell, MA, July 9, 1971.

GRIMES, TAMMY: Lynn, MA, Jan. 30, 1934. Stephens College.

GRIZZARD, GEORGE: Roanoke Rapids, NC, Apr. 1, 1928. UNC.

GRODIN, CHARLES: Pittsburgh, PA, Apr. 21, 1935.

GROH, DAVID: NYC, May 21, 1939. Brown U, LAMDA.

GROSS, MARY: Chicago, IL, Mar. 25, 1953.

Julie Hagerty

Robert Guillaume

Lukas Haas

Nicole Kidman

GROSS, MICHAEL: Chicago, IL, June 21, 1947.

GUEST, CHRISTOPHER: NYC, Feb. 5, 1948.

GUEST, LANCE: Saratoga, CA, July 21, 1960. UCLA.

GUILLAUME, ROBERT (Williams): St. Louis, MO, Nov. 30, 1937.

GUINNESS, ALEC: London, Apr. 2, 1914. Pembroke Lodge School.

GULAGER, CLU: Holdenville, OK, Nov. 16 1928.

GUTTENBERG, STEVE: Massapequa, NY, Aug. 24, 1958. UCLA.

GWILLIM, DAVID: Plymouth, England, Dec. 15, 1948. RADA.

GUY, JASMINE: Boston, Mar. 10, 1964.

HAAS, LUKAS: West Hollywood, CA, Apr. 16, 1976.

HACK, SHELLEY: Greenwich, CT, July 6, 1952.

HACKETT, BUDDY (Leonard Hacker): Brooklyn, NY, Aug. 31, 1924.

HACKMAN, GENE: San Bernardino, CA, Jan. 30, 1930.

HADDON, DALE: Montreal, Canada, May 26, 1949. Neighborhood Playhouse.

HAGERTY, JULIE: Cincinnati, OH, June 15, 1955. Juilliard.

HAGMAN, LARRY (Hageman): Weatherford, TX, Sept. 21, 1931. Bard.

HAID, CHARLES: San Francisco, June 2, 1943. CarnegieTech.

HAIM, COREY: Toronto, Canada, Dec. 23, 1972.

HALE, BARBARA: DeKalb, IL, Apr. 18, 1922. Chicago Academy of Fine Arts.

HALEY, JACKIE EARLE: Northridge, CA, July 14, 1961.

HALL, ALBERT: Boothton, AL, Nov. 10, 1937. Columbia.

HALL, ANTHONY MICHAEL: Boston, MA, Apr. 14, 1968.

HALL, ARSENIO: Cleveland, OH, Feb. 12, 1959.

HALL, HUNTZ: Boston, MA, Aug. 15, 1920.

HAMEL, VERONICA: Philadelphia, PA, Nov. 20, 1943.

HAMILL, MARK: Oakland, CA, Sept. 25, 1952. LACC.

HAMILTON, CARRIE: NYC, Dec. 5, 1963.

HAMILTON, GEORGE: Memphis, TN, Aug. 12, 1939. Hackley.

HAMILTON, LINDA: Salisbury, MD, Sept. 26, 1956.

HAMLIN, HARRY: Pasadena, CA, Oct. 30, 1951.

HAMPSHIRE, SUSAN: London, May 12, 1941.

HAMPTON, JAMES: Oklahoma City, OK, July 9, 1936. NTexasStU.

HAN, MAGGIE: Providence, RI, 1959.

HANDLER, EVAN: NYC, Jan. 10, 1961. Juillard.

HANKS, TOM: Concord, CA, Jul. 9, 1956. CalStateU.

HANNAH, DARYL: Chicago, IL, Dec. 3, 1960. UCLA.

HANNAH, PAGE: Chicago, IL, Apr. 13, 1964.

HARDIN, TY (Orison Whipple Hungerford, II): NYC, June 1, 1930.

HAREWOOD, DORIAN: Dayton, OH, Aug. 6, 1950. U Cinn.

HARMON, MARK: Los Angeles, CA, Sept. 2, 1951. UCLA.

HARPER, JESSICA: Chicago, IL, Oct. 10, 1949.

HARPER, TESS: Mammoth Spring, AK, 1952. SWMoState.

HARPER, VALERIE: Suffern, NY, Aug. 22, 1940.

HARRELSON, WOODY: Midland, TX, July 23, 1961. Hanover College.

HARRINGTON, PAT: NYC, Aug. 13, 1929. Fordham U.

HARRIS, BARBARA (Sandra Markowitz): Evanston, IL, July 25, 1935.

HARRIS, ED: Tenafly, NJ, Nov. 28, 1950. Columbia.

HARRIS, JULIE: Grosse Point, MI, Dec. 2, 1925. Yale Drama School.

HARRIS, MEL (Mary Ellen): Bethlehem, PA, 1957. Columbia.

HARRIS, RICHARD: Limerick, Ireland, Oct. 1, 1930. London Acad.

HARRIS, ROSEMARY: Ashby, England, Sept. 19, 1930. RADA.

HARRISON, GEORGE: Liverpool, England, Feb. 25, 1943.

HARRISON, GREGORY: Catalina Island, CA, May 31, 1950. Actors Studio.

HARRISON, NOEL: London, Jan. 29, 1936.

HARROLD, KATHRYN: Tazewell, VA, Aug. 2, 1950. Mills College.

HARRY, DEBORAH: Miami, IL, July 1, 1945.

HART, ROXANNE: Trenton, NJ, 1952, Princeton.

HARTLEY, MARIETTE: NYC, June 21, 1941.

HARTMAN, DAVID: Pawtucket, RI, May 19, 1935. Duke U.

HARTMAN, PHIL: Ontario, Canada, Sept. 24, 1948.

HASSETT, MARILYN: Los Angeles, CA, Dec. 17, 1947.

HATCHER, TERI: Sunnyvale, CA, Dec. 8, 1964.

HAUER, RUTGER: Amsterdam, Holland, Jan. 23, 1944.

HAVER, JUNE: Rock Island, IL, June 10, 1926.

HAVOC, JUNE (Hovick): Seattle, WA, Nov. 8, 1916.

HAWKE, ETHAN: Austin, TX, Nov. 6, 1970.

HAWN, GOLDIE: Washington, DC, Nov. 21, 1945.

HAYES, ISAAC: Covington, TN, Aug. 20, 1942.

HAYS, ROBERT: Bethesda, MD, July 24, 1947, SD State College.

HEADLY, GLENNE: New London, CT, Mar. 13, 1955. AmCollege.

Barbara Hershey

Gregory Harrison

Ethan Hawke

Diane Ladd

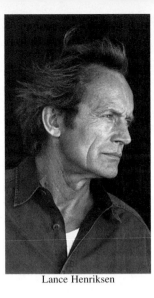
Lance Henriksen

Kelly Lynch

HEALD, ANTHONY: New Rochelle, NY, Aug. 25, 1944. MIStateU.

HEARD, JOHN: Washington, DC, Mar. 7, 1946. Clark U.

HEATHERTON, JOEY: NYC, Sept. 14, 1944.

HECKART, EILEEN: Columbus, OH, Mar. 29, 1919. Ohio State U.

HEDAYA, DAN: Brooklyn, NY, July 24, 1940.

HEDISON, DAVID: Providence, RI, May 20, 1929. Brown U.

HEDREN, TIPPI (Natalie): Lafayette, MN, Jan. 19, 1931.

HEGYES, ROBERT: NJ, May 7, 1951.

HELMOND, KATHERINE: Galveston, TX, July 5, 1934.

HEMINGWAY, MARIEL: Ketchum, ID, Nov. 22, 1961.

HEMMINGS, DAVID: Guilford, England, Nov. 18, 1941.

HEMSLEY, SHERMAN: Philadelphia, PA, Feb. 1, 1938.

HENDERSON, FLORENCE: Dale, IN, Feb. 14, 1934.

HENDRY, GLORIA: Jacksonville, FL, 1949.

HENNER, MARILU: Chicago, IL, Apr. 6, 1952.

HENRIKSEN, LANCE: NYC, May 5, 1940.

HENRY, BUCK (Henry Zuckerman): NYC, Dec. 9, 1930. Dartmouth.

HENRY, JUSTIN: Rye, NY, May 25, 1971.

HEPBURN, KATHARINE: Hartford, CT, May 12, 1907. Bryn Mawr.

HERMAN, PEE-WEE (Paul Reubenfeld): Peekskill, NY, Aug. 27, 1952.

HERRMANN, EDWARD: Washington, DC, July 21, 1943. Bucknell, LAMDA.

HERSHEY, BARBARA (Herzstein): Hollywood, CA, Feb. 5, 1948.

HESSEMAN. HOWARD: Lebanon, OR, Feb. 27, 1940.

HESTON, CHARLTON: Evanston, IL, Oct. 4, 1922. Northwestern U.

HEWITT, MARTIN: Claremont, CA, 1960. AADA.

HEYWOOD, ANNE (Violet Pretty): Birmingham, England, Dec. 11, 1932.

HICKEY, WILLIAM: Brooklyn, NY, Sept 19, 1928.

HICKMAN, DARRYL: Hollywood, CA, July 28, 1933. Loyola U.

HICKMAN, DWAYNE: Los Angeles, May 18, 1934. Loyola U.

HICKS, CATHERINE: NYC, Aug. 6, 1951. Notre Dame.

HIGGINS, ANTHONY (Corlan): Cork City, Ireland, May 9, 1947. Birmingham Sch. of Dramatic Arts.

HIGGINS, MICHAEL: Brooklyn, NY, Jan. 20, 1926. AmThWing.

HILL, ARTHUR: Saskatchewan, Canada, Aug. 1, 1922. U Brit. College.

HILL, BERNARD: Manchester, England, Dec. 17, 1944.

HILL, STEVEN: Seattle, WA, Feb. 24, 1922. U Wash.

HILL, TERRENCE (Mario Girotti): Venice, Italy, Mar. 29, 1941. U Rome.

HILLER, WENDY: Bramhall, Cheshire, England, Aug. 15, 1912. Winceby House School.

HILLERMAN, JOHN: Denison, TX, Dec. 20, 1932.

HINES, GREGORY: NYC, Feb.14, 1946.

HINGLE, PAT: Denver, CO, July 19, 1923. Tex. U.

HIRSCH, JUDD: NYC, Mar. 15, 1935. AADA.

HOBEL, MARA: NYC, June 18, 1971.

HODGE, PATRICIA: Lincolnshire, England, 1946. LAMDA.

HOFFMAN, DUSTIN: Los Angeles, Aug. 8, 1937. Pasadena Playhouse.

HOGAN, JONATHAN: Chicago, IL, June 13, 1951.

HOGAN, PAUL: Lightning Ridge, Australia, Oct. 8, 1939.

HOLBROOK, HAL (Harold): Cleveland, OH, Feb. 17, 1925. Denison.

HOLLIMAN, EARL: Tennesas Swamp, Delhi, LA, Sept. 11, 1928. UCLA.

HOLM, CELESTE: NYC, Apr. 29, 1919.

HOLM, IAN: Ilford, Essex, England, Sept. 12, 1931. RADA.

HOMEIER, SKIP (George Vincent Homeier): Chicago, IL, Oct. 5, 1930. UCLA.

HOOKS, ROBERT: Washington, DC, Apr. 18, 1937. Temple.

HOPE, BOB (Leslie Townes Hope): London, May 26, 1903.

HOPKINS, ANTHONY: Port Talbot, So. Wales, Dec. 31, 1937. RADA.

HOPPER, DENNIS: Dodge City, KS, May 17, 1936.

HORNE, LENA: Brooklyn, NY, June 30, 1917.

HORSLEY, LEE: Muleshoe, TX, May 15, 1955.

HORTON, ROBERT: Los Angeles, July 29, 1924. UCLA.

HOSKINS, BOB: Bury St. Edmunds, England, Oct. 26, 1942.

HOUGHTON, KATHARINE: Hartford, CT, Mar. 10, 1945. Sarah Lawrence.

HOUSER, JERRY: Los Angeles, July 14, 1952. Valley, Jr. College.

HOWARD, ARLISS: Independence, MO, 1955. Columbia College.

HOWARD, KEN: El Centro, CA, Mar. 28, 1944. Yale.

HOWARD, RON: Duncan, OK, Mar. 1, 1954. USC.

HOWARD, RONALD: Norwood, England, Apr. 7, 1918. Jesus College.

HOWELL, C. THOMAS: Los Angeles, Dec. 7, 1966.

HOWELLS, URSULA: London, Sept. 17, 1922.

HOWES, SALLY ANN: London, July 20, 1930.

HOWLAND, BETH: Boston, MA, May 28, 1941.

HUBLEY, SEASON: NYC, May 14, 1951.

HUDDLESTON, DAVID: Vinton, VA, Sept. 17, 1930.

HUDDLESTON, MICHAEL: Roanoke, VA. AADA.

HUDSON, ERNIE: Benton Harbor, MI, Dec. 17, 1945.

HUGHES, BARNARD: Bedford Hills, NY, July 16, 1915. Manhattan College.

HUGHES, KATHLEEN (Betty von Gerkan): Hollywood, CA, Nov. 14, 1928. UCLA.

HULCE, TOM: Plymouth, MI, Dec. 6, 1953. N.C. Sch. of Arts.

HUNNICUT, GAYLE: Ft. Worth, TX, Feb. 6, 1943. UCLA.

HUNT, HELEN: Los Angeles, June 15, 1963.

HUNT, LINDA: Morristown, NJ, Apr. 1945. Goodman Theatre.

HUNT, MARSHA: Chicago, IL, Oct. 17, 1917.

HUNTER, HOLLY: Atlanta, GA, Mar. 20, 1958. Carnegie-Mellon.

HUNTER, KIM (Janet Cole): Detroit, Nov. 12, 1922.

HUNTER, TAB (Arthur Gelien): NYC, July 11, 1931.

HUPPERT, ISABELLE: Paris, France, Mar. 16, 1955.

HURT, JOHN: Lincolnshire, England, Jan. 22, 1940.

HURT, MARY BETH (Supinger): Marshalltown, IA, Sept. 26, 1948. NYU.

HURT, WILLIAM: Washington, DC, Mar. 20, 1950. Tufts, Juilliard.

HUSSEY, RUTH: Providence, RI, Oct. 30, 1917. U Mich.

HUSTON, ANJELICA: Santa Monica, CA, July 9, 1951.

HUTTON, BETTY (Betty Thornberg): Battle Creek, MI, Feb. 26, 1921.

HUTTON, LAUREN (Mary): Charleston, SC, Nov. 17, 1943. Newcomb College.

HUTTON, TIMOTHY: Malibu, CA, Aug. 16, 1960.

HYER, MARTHA: Fort Worth, TX, Aug. 10, 1924. Northwestern U.

ICE CUBE (O'Shea Jackson): Los Angeles, 1969.

IDLE, ERIC: South Shields, Durham, England, Mar. 29, 1943. Cambridge.

INGELS, MARTY: Brooklyn, NY, Mar. 9, 1936.

IRELAND, KATHY: Santa Barbara, CA, Mar. 8, 1963.

IRONS, JEREMY: Cowes, England, Sept. 19, 1948. Old Vic.

IRVING, AMY: Palo Alto, CA, Sept. 10, 1953. LADA.

IRWIN, BILL: Santa Monica, CA, Apr. 11, 1950.

ISAAK, CHRIS: Stockton, CA, June 26, 1956. UofPacific.

IVANEK, ZELJKO: Lujubljana, Yugo., Aug. 15, 1957. Yale, LAMDA.

IVEY, JUDITH: El Paso, TX, Sept. 4, 1951.

JACKSON, ANNE: Alleghany, PA, Sept. 3, 1926. Neighborhood Playhouse.

JACKSON, GLENDA: Hoylake, Cheshire, England, May 9, 1936. RADA.

JACKSON, JANET: Gary, IN, May 16, 1966.

JACKSON, KATE: Birmingham, AL, Oct. 29, 1948. AADA.

JACKSON, MICHAEL: Gary, IN, Aug. 29, 1958.

JACKSON, SAMUEL L.: Atlanta, Dec. 21, 1948.

JACKSON, VICTORIA: Miami, FL, Aug. 2, 1958.

JACOBI, DEREK: Leytonstone, London, Oct. 22, 1938. Cambridge.

JACOBI, LOU: Toronto, Canada, Dec. 28, 1913.

JACOBS, LAWRENCE-HILTON: Virgin Islands, 1954.

JACOBY, SCOTT: Chicago, IL, Nov. 19, 1956.

JAECKEL, RICHARD: Long Beach, NY, Oct. 10, 1926.

JAGGER, MICK: Dartford, Kent, England, July 26, 1943.

JAMES, CLIFTON: NYC, May 29, 1921. Ore. U.

JAMES, JOHN (Anderson): Apr. 18, 1956, New Canaan, CT. AADA.

JARMAN, CLAUDE, JR.: Nashville, TN, Sept. 27, 1934.

JASON, RICK: NYC, May 21, 1926. AADA.

JEAN, GLORIA (Gloria Jean Schoonover): Buffalo, NY, Apr. 14, 1927.

JEFFREYS, ANNE (Carmichael): Goldsboro, NC, Jan. 26, 1923. Anderson College.

JEFFRIES, LIONEL: London, 1927. RADA.

JERGENS, ADELE: Brooklyn, NY, Nov. 26, 1922.

JETER, MICHAEL: Lawrenceburg, TN, Aug. 26, 1952. Memphis St.U.

JETT, ROGER (Baker): Cumberland, MD, Oct. 2, 1946. AADA.

JILLIAN, ANN (Nauseda): Cambridge, MA, Jan. 29, 1951.

JOHANSEN, DAVID: Staten Island, NY, Jan. 9, 1950.

JOHN, ELTON (Reginald Dwight): Middlesex, England, Mar. 25, 1947. RAM.

JOHNS, GLYNIS: Durban, S. Africa, Oct. 5, 1923.

JOHNSON, BEN: Pawhuska, OK, June 13, 1918.

JOHNSON, DON: Galena, MO, Dec. 15, 1950. UKan.

JOHNSON, PAGE: Welch, WV, Aug. 25, 1930. Ithaca.

JOHNSON, RAFER: Hillsboro, TX, Aug. 18, 1935. UCLA.

JOHNSON, RICHARD: Essex, England, July 30, 1927. RADA.

JOHNSON, ROBIN: Brooklyn, NY, May 29, 1964.

JOHNSON, VAN: Newport, RI, Aug. 28, 1916.

JONES, CHRISTOPHER: Jackson, TN, Aug. 18, 1941. Actors Studio.

JONES, DEAN: Decatur, AL, Jan. 25, 1931. Actors Studio.

JONES, GRACE: Spanishtown, Jamaica, May 19, 1952.

JONES, JACK: Bel-Air, CA, Jan. 14, 1938.

JONES, JAMES EARL: Arkabutla, MS, Jan. 17, 1931. U Mich.

JONES, JEFFREY: Buffalo, NY, Sept. 28, 1947. LAMDA.

JONES, JENNIFER (Phyllis Isley): Tulsa, OK, Mar. 2, 1919. AADA.

JONES, L.Q. (Justice Ellis McQueen): Aug 19, 1927.

JONES, SAM J.: Chicago, IL, Aug. 12, 1954.

JONES, SHIRLEY: Smithton, PA, March 31, 1934.

JONES, TERRY: Colwyn Bay, Wales, Feb. 1, 1942.

JONES, TOMMY LEE: San Saba, TX, Sept. 15, 1946. Harvard.

JOURDAN, LOUIS: Marseilles, France, June 19, 1920.

JOY, ROBERT: Montreal, Canada, Aug. 17, 1951. Oxford.

Bill Irwin

Andrea Martin

Derek Jacobi

Mary Stuart Masterson

JURADO, KATY (Maria Christina Jurado Garcia): Guadalajara, Mex., Jan. 16, 1927.

KACZMAREK, JANE: Milwaukee, WI, Dec. 21.

KAHN, MADELINE: Boston, MA, Sept. 29, 1942. Hofstra U.

KANE, CAROL: Cleveland, OH, June 18, 1952.

KAPLAN, MARVIN: Brooklyn, NY, Jan. 24, 1924.

KAPOOR, SHASHI: Bombay, India, 1940.

KAPRISKY, VALERIE: Paris, France, 1963.

KARRAS, ALEX: Gary, IN, July 15, 1935.

KATT, WILLIAM: Los Angeles, CA, Feb. 16, 1955.

KAUFMANN, CHRISTINE: Lansdorf, Graz, Austria, Jan. 11, 1945.

KAVNER, JULIE: Burbank, CA, Sept. 7, 1951. UCLA.

KAYE, STUBBY: NYC, Nov. 11, 1918.

KAZAN, LAINIE (Levine): Brooklyn, NY, May 15, 1942.

KAZURINSKY, TIM: Johnstown, PA, March 3, 1950.

KEACH, STACY: Savannah, GA, June 2, 1941. U Cal., Yale.

KEATON, DIANE (Hall): Los Angeles, CA, Jan. 5, 1946. Neighborhood Playhouse.

KEATON, MICHAEL: Coraopolis, PA, Sept. 9, 1951. KentStateU.

KEDROVA, LILA: Leningrad, 1918.

KEEL, HOWARD (Harold Leek): Gillespie, IL, Apr. 13, 1919.

KEITEL, HARVEY: Brooklyn, NY, May 13, 1939.

KEITH, BRIAN: Bayonne, NJ, Nov. 15, 1921.

KEITH, DAVID: Knoxville, TN, May 8, 1954. UTN.

KELLER, MARTHE: Basel, Switzerland, 1945. Munich Stanislavsky Sch.

KELLERMAN, SALLY: Long Beach, CA, June 2, 1936. Actors Studio West.

KELLEY, DeFOREST: Atlanta, GA, Jan. 20, 1920.

KELLY, GENE: Pittsburgh, PA, Aug. 23, 1912. U Pittsburgh.

KEMP, JEREMY (Wacker): Chesterfield, England, Feb. 3, 1935. Central Sch.

KENNEDY, GEORGE: NYC, Feb. 18, 1925.

KENNEDY, LEON ISAAC: Cleveland, OH, 1949.

KENSIT, PATSY: London, Mar. 4, 1968.

KERR, DEBORAH: Helensburg, Scotland, Sept. 30, 1921. Smale Ballet School.

KERR, JOHN: NYC, Nov. 15, 1931. Harvard, Columbia.

KERWIN, BRIAN: Chicago, IL, Oct. 25, 1949.

KEYES, EVELYN: Port Arthur, TX, Nov. 20, 1919.

KHAMBATTA, PERSIS: Bombay, Oct. 2, 1950.

KIDDER, MARGOT: Yellow Knife, Canada, Oct. 17, 1948. UBC.

KIDMAN, NICOLE: Hawaii, June 20, 1967.

KIEL, RICHARD: Detroit, MI, Sept. 13, 1939.

KIER, UDO: Germany, Oct. 14, 1944.

KILEY, RICHARD: Chicago, IL, Mar. 31, 1922. Loyola.

KILMER, VAL: Los Angeles, Dec. 31, 1959. Juilliard.

KINCAID, ARON (Norman Neale Williams, III): Los Angeles, June 15, 1943. UCLA.

Stacy Keach

Mary Elizabeth Mastrantonio

Brian Kerwin

KING, ALAN (Irwin Kniberg): Brooklyn, NY, Dec. 26, 1927.

KING, PERRY: Alliance, OH, Apr. 30, 1948. Yale.

KINGSLEY, BEN (Krishna Bhanji): Snaiton, Yorkshire, England, Dec. 31, 1943.

KINSKI, NASTASSJA: Berlin, Ger., Jan. 24, 1960.

KIRBY, BRUNO: NYC, Apr. 28, 1949.

KIRK, TOMMY: Louisville, KY, Dec.10 1941.

KIRKLAND, SALLY: NYC, Oct. 31, 1944. Actors Studio.

KITT, EARTHA: North, SC, Jan. 26, 1928.

KLEIN, ROBERT: NYC, Feb. 8, 1942. Alfred U.

KLEMPERER, WERNER: Cologne, Mar. 22, 1920.

KLINE, KEVIN: St. Louis, MO, Oct. 24, 1947. Juilliard.

KLUGMAN, JACK: Philadelphia, PA, Apr. 27, 1922. Carnegie Tech.

KNIGHT, MICHAEL: Princeton, NJ, 1959.

KNIGHT, SHIRLEY: Goessel, KS, July 5, 1937. Wichita U.

KNOX, ELYSE: Hartford, CT, Dec. 14, 1917. Traphagen School.

KOENIG, WALTER: Chicago, IL, Sept. 14, 1936. UCLA.

KOHNER, SUSAN: Los Angeles, Nov. 11, 1936. U Calif.

KORMAN, HARVEY: Chicago, IL, Feb. 15, 1927. Goodman.

KORSMO, CHARLIE: Minneapolis, MN, 1978.

KORVIN, CHARLES (Geza Korvin Karpathi): Czechoslovakia, Nov. 21, 1907. Sorbonne.

KOTEAS, ELIAS: Montreal, Quebec, Canada, 1961. AADA.

KOTTO, YAPHET: NYC, Nov. 15, 1937.

KOZAK, HARLEY JANE: Wilkes-Barre, PA, Jan. 28, 1957. NYU.

KRABBE, JEROEN: Amsterdam, The Netherlands, Dec. 5, 1944.

KREUGER, KURT: St. Moritz, Switzerland, July 23, 1917. U London.

KRIGE, ALICE: Upington, So. Africa, June 28, 1955.

KRISTEL, SYLVIA: Amsterdam, The Netherlands, Sept. 28, 1952.

KRISTOFFERSON, KRIS: Brownsville, TX, June 22, 1936, Pomona College.

KRUGER, HARDY: Berlin, Germany, April 12, 1928.

KUNTSMANN, DORIS: Hamburg, Germany, 1944.

KURTZ, SWOOSIE: Omaha, NE, Sept. 6, 1944.

KWAN, NANCY: Hong Kong, May 19, 1939. Royal Ballet.

LaBELLE, PATTI: Philadelphia, PA, May 24, 1944.

LACY, JERRY: Sioux City, IA, Mar. 27, 1936. LACC.

LADD, CHERYL (Stoppelmoor): Huron, SD. July 12, 1951.

LADD, DIANE (Ladner): Meridian, MS, Nov. 29, 1932. Tulane U.

LaGRECA, PAUL: Bronx, NY, June 23, 1962. AADA.

LAHTI, CHRISTINE: Detroit, MI, Apr. 4, 1950. U Mich.

LAKE, RICKI: NYC, Sept. 21, 1968.

Harvey Keitel

LAMARR, HEDY (Hedwig Kiesler): Vienna, Sept. 11, 1913.

LAMAS, LORENZO: Los Angeles, Jan. 28, 1958.

LAMBERT, CHRISTOPHER: NYC, Mar. 29, 1958.

LAMOUR, DOROTHY (Mary Dorothy Slaton): New Orleans, LA, Dec. 10, 1914. Spence School.

LANDAU, MARTIN: Brooklyn, NY, June 20, 1931. Actors Studio.

LANDRUM, TERI: Enid, OK, 1960.

LANE, ABBE: Brooklyn, NY, Dec. 14, 1935.

LANE, DIANE: NYC, Jan. 22, 1963.

LANE, NATHAN: Jersey City, NJ, Feb. 3, 1956.

LANG, STEPHEN: NYC, July 11, 1952. Swarthmore College.

LANGE, HOPE: Redding Ridge, CT, Nov. 28, 1931. Reed College.

LANGE, JESSICA: Cloquet, MN, Apr. 20, 1949. U Minn.

LANGELLA, FRANK: Bayonne, NJ, Jan. 1, 1940. SyracuseU.

LANSBURY, ANGELA: London, Oct. 16, 1925. London Academy of Music.

LaPAGLIA, ANTHONY: Adelaide, Australia. Jan 31, 1959.

LaPLANTE, LAURA: St. Louis, MO, Nov. 1, 1904.

Samantha Mathis

LARROQUETTE, JOHN: New Orleans, LA, Nov. 25, 1947.

LASSER, LOUISE: NYC, Apr. 11, 1939. Brandeis U.

LATIFAH, QUEEN (Dana Owens): East Orange, NJ, 1970.

LAUGHLIN, JOHN: Memphis, TN, Apr. 3.

LAUGHLIN, TOM: Minneapolis, MN, 1938.

LAUPER, CYNDI: Astoria, Queens, NYC, June 20, 1953.

LAURE, CAROLE: Montreal, Canada, 1951.

LAURIE, PIPER (Rosetta Jacobs): Detroit, MI, Jan. 22, 1932.

LAUTER, ED: Long Beach, NY, Oct. 30, 1940.

LAVIN, LINDA: Portland, ME, Oct. 15 1939.

LAW, JOHN PHILLIP: Hollywood, CA, Sept. 7, 1937. Neighborhood Playhouse, U Hawaii.

LAWRENCE, BARBARA: Carnegie, OK, Feb. 24, 1930. UCLA.

LAWRENCE, CAROL (Laraia): Melrose Park, IL, Sept. 5, 1935.

LAWRENCE, VICKI: Inglewood, CA, Mar. 26, 1949.

LAWRENCE, MARTIN: Frankfurt, Germany, 1965.

LAWSON, LEIGH: Atherston, England, July 21, 1945. RADA.

LEACHMAN, CLORIS: Des Moines, IA, Apr. 30, 1930. Northwestern U.

LEAUD, JEAN-PIERRE: Paris, France, 1944.

LEDERER, FRANCIS: Karlin, Prague, Czech., Nov. 6, 1906.

LEE, CHRISTOPHER: London, May 27, 1922. Wellington College.

LEE, MARK: Australia, 1958.

LEE, MICHELE (Dusiak): Los Angeles, June 24, 1942. LACC.

LEE, PEGGY (Norma Delores Egstrom): Jamestown, ND, May 26, 1920.

LEE, SPIKE (Shelton Lee): Atlanta, GA, Mar. 20, 1957.

LEGROS, JAMES: Minneapolis, MN, Apr. 27, 1962.

LEGUIZAMO, JOHN: Columbia, July 22, 1965. NYU.

LEIBMAN, RON: NYC, Oct. 11, 1937. Ohio Wesleyan.

LEIGH, JANET (Jeanette Helen Morrison): Merced, CA, July 6, 1926. ColofPacific.

LEIGH, JENNIFER JASON: Los Angeles, Feb. 5, 1962.

LeMAT, PAUL: Rahway, NJ, Sept. 22, 1945.

LEMMON, CHRIS: Los Angeles, Jan. 22, 1954.

LEMMON, JACK: Boston, Feb. 8, 1925. Harvard.

LENO, JAY: New Rochelle, NY, Apr. 28, 1950. Emerson College.

LENZ, KAY: Los Angeles, Mar. 4, 1953.

LENZ, RICK: Springfield, IL, Nov. 21, 1939. U Mich.

LEONARD, ROBERT SEAN: Westwood, NJ, Feb. 28, 1969.

LEONARD, SHELDON (Bershad): NYC, Feb. 22, 1907, Syracuse U.

LERNER, MICHAEL: Brooklyn, NY, June 22, 1941.

LEROY, PHILIPPE: Paris, France, Oct. 15, 1930. U Paris.

LESLIE, BETHEL: NYC, Aug. 3, 1929. Brearley School.

LESLIE, JOAN (Joan Brodell): Detroit, Jan. 26, 1925. St. Benedict's.

Mary McDonnell

LESTER, MARK: Oxford, England, July 11, 1958.

LEVELS, CALVIN: Cleveland. OH, Sept. 30, 1954. CCC.

LEVIN, RACHEL: NYC, 1954. Goddard College.

LEVINE, JERRY: New Brunswick, NJ, Mar. 12, 1957, Boston U.

LEVY, EUGENE: Hamilton, Canada, Dec. 17, 1946. McMasterU.

LEWIS, CHARLOTTE: London, 1968.

LEWIS, GEOFFREY: San Diego, CA, Jan. 1, 1935.

LEWIS, JERRY (Joseph Levitch): Newark, NJ, Mar. 16, 1926.

LEWIS, JULIETTE: Los Angeles CA, June 21, 1973.

LIGON, TOM: New Orleans, LA, Sept. 10, 1945.

LINCOLN, ABBEY (Anna Marie Woolridge): Chicago, IL, Aug. 6, 1930.

LINDEN, HAL: Bronx, NY, Mar. 20, 1931. City College of NY.

LINDSAY, ROBERT: Ilketson, Derby-shire, England, Dec. 13, 1951, RADA.

LINN-BAKER, MARK: St. Louis, MO, June 17, 1954, Yale.

LIOTTA, RAY: Newark, NJ, Dec. 18, 1955. UMiami.

LISI, VIRNA: Rome, Nov. 8, 1937.

Christopher Lambert

LITHGOW, JOHN: Rochester, NY, Oct. 19, 1945. Harvard.

LLOYD, CHRISTOPHER: Stamford, CT, Oct. 22, 1938.

LLOYD, EMILY: London, Sept. 29, 1970.

LOCKE, SONDRA: Shelbyville, TN, May, 28, 1947.

LOCKHART, JUNE: NYC, June 25, 1925. Westlake School.

LOCKWOOD, GARY: Van Nuys, CA, Feb. 21, 1937.

LOGGIA, ROBERT: Staten Island, NY, Jan. 3, 1930. UMo.

LOLLOBRIGIDA, GINA: Subiaco, Italy, July 4, 1927. Rome Academy of Fine Arts.

LOM, HERBERT: Prague, Czechoslovakia, Jan. 9, 1917. Prague U.

LOMEZ, CELINE: Montreal, Canada, 1953.

LONDON, JULIE (Julie Peck): Santa Rosa, CA, Sept. 26, 1926.

LONE, JOHN: Hong Kong, Oct 13, 1952. AADA.

LONG, SHELLEY: Ft. Wayne, IN, Aug. 23, 1949. Northwestern U.

LOPEZ, PERRY: NYC, July 22, 1931. NYU.

LORD, JACK (John Joseph Ryan): NYC, Dec. 30, 1928. NYU.

LOREN, SOPHIA (Sophia Scicolone): Rome, Italy, Sept. 20, 1934.

LOUIS-DREYFUS, JULIA: NYC, Jan. 13, 1961.

LOUISE, TINA (Blacker): NYC, Feb. 11, 1934, Miami U.

LOVETT, LYLE: Klein, TX, Nov. 1, 1957.

LOVITZ, JON: Tarzana, CA, July 21, 1957.

LOWE, CHAD: Dayton, OH, Jan. 15, 1968.

LOWE, ROB: Charlottesville, VA, Mar. 17, 1964.

LOWITSCH, KLAUS: Berlin, Apr. 8, 1936, Vienna Academy.

LUCAS, LISA: Arizona, 1961.

LUCKINBILL, LAURENCE: Fort Smith, AK, Nov. 21, 1934.

LUFT, LORNA: Los Angeles, Nov. 21, 1952.

LULU (Marie Lawrie): Glasgow, Scotland, Nov. 3, 1948.

LUNA, BARBARA: NYC, Mar. 2, 1939.

LUNDGREN, DOLPH: Stockolm, Sweden, Nov. 3, 1959. Royal Inst.

LuPONE, PATTI: Northport, NY, Apr. 21, 1949, Juilliard.

LYDON, JAMES: Harrington Park, NJ, May 30, 1923.

LYNCH, KELLY: Minneapolis, MN, 1959.

LYNLEY, CAROL (Jones): NYC, Feb. 13, 1942.

LYON, SUE: Davenport, IA, July 10, 1946.

MacARTHUR, JAMES: Los Angeles, Dec. 8, 1937. Harvard.

MACCHIO, RALPH: Huntington, NY, Nov. 4, 1961.

MacCORKINDALE, SIMON: Cambridge, England, Feb. 12, 1953.

MacDOWELL, ANDIE (Rose Anderson MacDowell): Gaffney, SC, Apr. 21, 1958.

MacGINNIS, NIALL: Dublin, Ireland, Mar. 29, 1913. Dublin U.

MacGRAW, ALI: NYC, Apr. 1, 1938. Wellesley.

MacLACHLAN, KYLE: Yakima, WA, Feb. 22, 1959. UWa.

MacLAINE, SHIRLEY (Beaty): Richmond, VA, Apr. 24, 1934.

MacLEOD, GAVIN: Mt. Kisco, NY, Feb. 28, 1931.

MacNAUGHTON, ROBERT: NYC, Dec. 19, 1966.

MACNEE, PATRICK: London, Feb. 1922.

MacNICOL, PETER: Dallas, TX, Apr. 10, 1954. UMN.

MacPHERSON, ELLE: Sydney, Australia, 1965.

MACY, W. H. (William): Miami, FL, Mar. 13, 1950. Goddard College.

MADIGAN, AMY: Chicago, IL, Sept. 11, 1950. Marquette U.

MADISON, GUY (Robert Moseley): Bakersfield, CA, Jan. 19, 1922. Bakersfield, Jr. College.

MADONNA (Madonna Louise Veronica Cicone): Bay City, MI, Aug. 16, 1958. UMi.

MADSEN, MICHAEL: Chicago, IL, 1958.

MADSEN, VIRGINIA: Winnetka, IL, Sept. 11, 1963.

MAGNUSON, ANN: Charleston, WV, Jan. 4, 1956.

MAHARIS, GEORGE: Astoria, NY, Sept. 1, 1928. Actors Studio.

MAHONEY, JOHN: Manchester, England, June 20, 1940, WUIll.

MAILER, KATE: NYC, 1962.

MAILER, STEPHEN: NYC, Mar. 10, 1966. NYU.

MAJORS, LEE: Wyandotte, MI, Apr. 23, 1940. E. Ky. State College.

MAKEPEACE, CHRIS: Toronto, Canada, Apr. 22, 1964.

MAKO (Mako Iwamatsu): Kobe, Japan, Dec. 10, 1933. Pratt.

MALDEN, KARL (Mladen Sekulovich): Gary, IN, Mar. 22, 1914.

MALET, PIERRE: St. Tropez, France, 1955.

MALKOVICH, JOHN: Christopher, IL, Dec. 9, 1953, IllStateU.

MALONE, DOROTHY: Chicago, IL, Jan. 30, 1925.

MANN, KURT: Roslyn, NY, July 18, 1947.

MANN, TERRENCE: KY, 1945. NCSchl Arts.

MANOFF, DINAH: NYC, Jan. 25, 1958. CalArts.

MANTEGNA, JOE: Chicago, IL, Nov. 13, 1947. Goodman Theatre.

MANZ, LINDA: NYC, 1961.

MARAIS, JEAN: Cherbourg, France, Dec. 11, 1913, St. Germain.

MARCHAND, NANCY: Buffalo, NY, June 19, 1928.

MARCOVICCI, ANDREA: NYC, Nov. 18, 1948.

MARIN, CHEECH (Richard): Los Angeles, July 13, 1946.

MARIN, JACQUES: Paris, France, Sept. 9, 1919. Conservatoire National.

MARINARO, ED: NYC, 1951. Cornell.

MARS, KENNETH: Chicago, IL, 1936.

MARSH, JEAN: London, England, July 1, 1934.

MARSHALL, E. G.: Owatonna, MN, June 18, 1910. U Minn.

MARSHALL, KEN: NYC, 1953. Juilliard.

MARSHALL, PENNY: Bronx, NY, Oct. 15, 1942. UN. Mex.

MARSHALL, WILLIAM: Gary, IN, Aug. 19, 1924. NYU.

MARTIN, ANDREA: Portland, ME, Jan. 15, 1947.

MARTIN, DICK: Battle Creek, MI Jan. 30, 1923.

MARTIN, GEORGE N.: NYC, Aug. 15, 1929.

MARTIN, MILLICENT: Romford, England, June 8, 1934.

MARTIN, PAMELASUE: Westport, CT, Jan. 15, 1953.

MARTIN, STEVE: Waco, TX, Aug. 14, 1945. UCLA.

MARTIN, TONY (Alfred Norris): Oakland, CA, Dec. 25, 1913. St. Mary's College.

MASON, MARSHA: St. Louis, MO, Apr. 3, 1942. Webster College.

MASON, PAMELA (Pamela Kellino): Westgate, England, Mar. 10, 1918.

MASSEN, OSA: Copenhagen, Denmark, Jan. 13, 1916.

MASSEY, DANIEL: London, Oct. 10, 1933. Eton and King's Coll.

MASTERS, BEN: Corvallis, OR, May 6, 1947. UOr.

MASTERSON, MARY STUART: Los Angeles, June 28, 1966, NYU.

MASTERSON, PETER: Angleton, TX, June 1, 1934. Rice U.

MASTRANTONIO, MARY ELIZABETH: Chicago, IL, Nov. 17, 1958. UIll.

MASTROIANNI, MARCELLO: Fontana Liri, Italy, Sept. 28, 1924.

MASUR, RICHARD: NYC, Nov. 20, 1948.

MATHESON, TIM: Glendale, CA, Dec. 31, 1947. CalState.

MATHIS, SAMANTHA: NYC, 1971.

MATLIN, MARLEE: Morton Grove, IL, Aug. 24, 1965.

MATTHAU, WALTER (Matuschanskayasky): NYC, Oct. 1, 1920.

MATTHEWS, BRIAN: Philadelphia, Jan. 24. 1953. St. Olaf.

MATURE, VICTOR: Louisville, KY, Jan. 29, 1915.

MAY, ELAINE (Berlin): Philadelphia, Apr. 21, 1932.

MAYO, VIRGINIA (Virginia Clara Jones): St. Louis, MO, Nov. 30, 1920.

MAYRON, MELANIE: Philadelphia, PA, Oct. 20, 1952. AADA.

MAZURSKY, PAUL: Brooklyn, NY, Apr. 25, 1930. Bklyn College.

MAZZELLO, JOSEPH: Rhinebeck, NY, Sept. 21, 1983.

McCALLUM, DAVID: Scotland, Sept. 19, 1933. Chapman College.

McCAMBRIDGE, MERCEDES: Jolliet, IL, Mar. 17, 1918. Mundelein College.

McCARTHY, ANDREW: NYC, Nov. 29, 1962, NYU.

McCARTHY, KEVIN: Seattle, WA, Feb. 15, 1914. Minn. U.

McCARTNEY, PAUL: Liverpool, Eng- land, June 18, 1942.

McCLANAHAN, RUE: Healdton, OK, Feb. 21, 1934.

McCLORY, SEAN: Dublin, Ireland, Mar. 8, 1924. U Galway.

McCLURE, MARC: San Mateo, CA, Mar. 31, 1957.

McCLURG, EDIE: Kansas City, MO, July 23, 1950.

McCOWEN, ALEC: Tunbridge Wells, England, May 26, 1925. RADA.

McCRANE, PAUL: Philadelphia, PA, Jan. 19. 1961.

McCRARY, DARIUS: Walnut, CA, 1976.

McDERMOTT, DYLAN: Waterbury, CT, Oct. 26, 1962. Neighborhood Playhouse.

McDONNELL, MARY: Wilkes Barre, PA, 1952.

Nathan Lane

Elizabeth McGovern

John Leguizamo

Andie MacDowell

McDORMAND, FRANCES: Illinois, June 23, 1957.

McDOWALL, RODDY: London, Sept. 17, 1928. St. Joseph's.

McDOWELL, MALCOLM (Taylor): Leeds, England, June 19, 1943. LAMDA.

McENERY, PETER: Walsall, England, Feb. 21, 1940.

McENTIRE, REBA: McAlester, OK, Mar. 28, 1955. SoutheasternStU.

McGAVIN, DARREN: Spokane, WA, May 7, 1922. College of Pacific.

McGILL, EVERETT: Miami Beach, FL, Oct. 21, 1945.

McGILLIS, KELLY: Newport Beach, CA, July 9, 1957. Juilliard.

McGINLEY, JOHN C.: NYC, Aug. 3, 1959. NYU.

McGOOHAN, PATRICK: NYC, Mar. 19, 1928.

McGOVERN, ELIZABETH: Evanston, IL. July 18, 1961. Juilliard.

McGOVERN, MAUREEN: Youngstown, OH, July 27, 1949.

McGREGOR, JEFF: Chicago, IL, 1957. UMn.

McGUIRE, BIFF: New Haven, CT, Oct. 25. 1926. Mass. Stale College.

McGUIRE, DOROTHY: Omaha, NE, June 14, 1918.

McHATTIE, STEPHEN: Antigonish, NS, Feb. 3. Acadia U AADA.

McKAY, GARDNER: NYC, June 10, 1932. Comell.

McKEAN, MICHAEL: NYC, Oct. 17, 1947.

McKEE, LONETTE: Detroit, MI, July 22, 1955.

McKELLEN, IAN: Burnley, England, May 25, 1939.

McKENNA, VIRGINIA: London, June 7, 1931.

McKEON, DOUG: Pompton Plains, NJ, June 10, 1966.

McKERN, LEO: Sydney, Australia, Mar. 16, 1920.

McKUEN, ROD: Oakland, CA, Apr. 29, 1933.

McLERIE, ALLYN ANN: Grand Mere, Canada, Dec. 1, 1926.

McMAHON, ED: Detroit, MI, Mar. 6, 1923.

McNAIR, BARBARA: Chicago, IL, Mar. 4, 1939. UCLA.

McNAMARA, WILLIAM: Dallas, TX, 1965.

McNICHOL, KRISTY: Los Angeles. CA, Sept. 11, 1962.

McQUEEN, ARMELIA: North Carolina, Jan. 6, 1952. Bklyn Consv.

McQUEEN, CHAD: Los Angeles, CA, Dec. 28, 1960. Actors Studio.

McRANEY, GERALD: Collins, MS, Aug. 19, 1948.

McSHANE, IAN: Blackburn, England, Sept. 29, 1942. RADA.

MEADOWS, AUDREY: Wuchang, China, 1926. St. Margaret's.

MEADOWS, JAYNE (formerly Jayne Cotter): Wuchang, China, Sept. 27, 1924. St. Margaret's.

MEARA, ANNE: Brooklyn, NY, Sept. 20, 1929.

MEAT LOAF (Marvin Lee Aday): Dallas, TX, Sept. 27, 1947.

MEDWIN, MICHAEL: London, 1925. Instut Fischer.

MEISNER, GUNTER: Bremen, Germany, Apr. 18, 1926. Municipal Drama School.

MEKKA, EDDIE: Worcester, MA, 1932. Boston Cons.

MELATO, MARIANGELA: Milan, Italy, 1941. Milan Theatre Acad.

MELL, MARISA: Vienna, Austria, Feb. 25, 1939.

MERCADO, HECTOR JAIME: NYC, 1949. HB Studio.

MEREDITH, BURGESS: Cleveland, OH, Nov. 16, 1907. Amherst.

MEREDITH, LEE (Judi Lee Sauls): Oct. 22, 1947. AADA.

MERKERSON, S. EPATHA: Saganaw, MI, Nov. 28, 1952. Wayne St. Univ.

MERRILL, DINA (Nedinia Hutton): NYC, Dec. 29, 1925. AADA.

METCALF, LAURIE: Edwardsville, IL, June 16, 1955., IllStU.

METZLER, JIM: Oneonda, NY, June 23. Dartmouth.

MICHELL, KEITH: Adelaide, Australia, Dec. 1, 1926.

MIDLER, BETTE: Honolulu, HI, Dec. 1, 1945.

MIFUNE, TOSHIRO: Tsingtao, China, Apr. 1, 1920.

MILANO, ALYSSA: Brooklyn, NY, 1975.

MILES, JOANNA: Nice, France, Mar. 6, 1940.

MILES, SARAH: Ingatestone, England, Dec. 31, 1941. RADA.

MILES, SYLVIA: NYC, Sept. 9, 1934. Actors Studio.

MILES, VERA (Ralston): Boise City, OK, Aug. 23, 1929. UCLA.

MILLER, ANN (Lucille Ann Collier): Chireno, TX, Apr. 12, 1919. Lawler Professional School.

MILLER, BARRY: Los Angeles, CA, Feb. 6, 1958.

MILLER, DICK: NYC, Dec. 25, 1928.

MILLER, JASON: Long Island City, NY, Apr. 22, 1939. Catholic U.

MILLER, LINDA: NYC, Sept. 16, 1942. Catholic U.

MILLER, PENELOPE ANN: Santa Monica, CA, Jan. 13, 1964.

MILLER, REBECCA: Roxbury, CT, 1962. Yale.

MILLS, DONNA: Chicago, IL, Dec. 11, 1945. UIl.

MILLS, HAYLEY: London, Apr. 18, 1946. Elmhurst School.

MILLS, JOHN: Suffolk, England, Feb. 22, 1908.

MILLS, JULIET: London, Nov. 21, 1941.

MILNER, MARTIN: Detroit, MI, Dec. 28, 1931.

MIMIEUX, YVETTE: Los Angeles, Jan. 8, 1941. Hollywood High.

MINNELLI, LIZA: Los Angeles, Mar. 19, l946.

MIOU-MIOU (Sylvette Henry): Paris, France, Feb. 22, 1950.

MIRREN, HELEN: London, 1946.

MITCHELL, JAMES: Sacramento, CA, Feb. 29, 1920. LACC.

MITCHELL, JOHN CAMERON: El Paso, TX, Apr. 21, 1963. NorthwesternU.

MITCHUM, JAMES: Los Angeles, CA, May 8, 1941.

MITCHUM, ROBERT: Bridgeport, CT, Aug. 6, 1917.

Ron Liebman

Penelope Ann Miller

Ray Liotta

Cathy Moriarty

MODINE, MATTHEW: Loma Linda, CA, Mar. 22, 1959.

MOFFAT, DONALD: Plymouth, England, Dec. 26, 1930. RADA.

MOFFETT, D. W.: Highland Park, IL, Oct. 26, 1954. Stanford U.

MOKAE, ZAKES: Johannesburg, So. Africa, Aug. 5, 1935. RADA.

MOLINA, ALFRED: London, May 24, 1953. Guildhall.

MOLL, RICHARD: Pasadena, CA, Jan. 13, 1943.

MONTALBAN, RICARDO: Mexico City, Nov. 25, 1920.

MONTGOMERY, BELINDA: Winnipeg, Canada, July 23, 1950.

MONTGOMERY, GEORGE (George Letz): Brady, MT, Aug. 29, 1916. U Mont.

MOODY, RON: London, Jan. 8, 1924. London U.

MOOR, BILL: Toledo, OH, July 13, 1931. Northwestern.

MOORE, CONSTANCE: Sioux City, IA, Jan. 18, 1919.

MOORE, DEMI (Guines): Roswell, NM, Nov. 11, 1962.

MOORE, DICK: Los Angeles, Sept. 12, 1925.

MOORE, DUDLEY: Dagenham, Essex, England, Apr. 19, 1935.

MOORE, FRANK: Bay-de-Verde, Newfoundland, 1946.

MOORE, KIERON: County Cork, Ireland, 1925. St. Mary's College.

MOORE, MARY TYLER: Brooklyn, NY, Dec. 29, 1936.

MOORE, ROGER: London, Oct. 14, 1927. RADA.

MOORE, TERRY (Helen Koford): Los Angeles, Jan. 7, 1929.

MORALES, ESAI: Brooklyn, NY, 1963.

MORANIS, RICK: Toronto, Canada, Apr. 18, 1954.

MOREAU, JEANNE: Paris, France, Jan. 23, 1928.

MORENO, RITA (Rosita Alverio): Humacao, P.R., Dec. 11, 1931.

MORGAN, HARRY (HENRY) (Harry Bratsburg): Detroit, Apr. 10, 1915. U Chicago.

MORGAN, MICHELE (Simone Roussel): Paris, France, Feb. 29, 1920. Paris Dramatic School.

MORIARTY, CATHY: Bronx, NY, Nov. 29, 1960.

MORIARTY, MICHAEL: Detroit, MI, Apr. 5, 1941. Dartmouth.

MORISON, PATRICIA: NYC, 1915.

MORITA, NORIYUKI "PAT": Isleton, CA, June 28, 1932.

MORRIS, GARRETT: New Orleans, LA, Feb. 1, 1937.

MORRIS, GREG: Cleveland, OH, Sept. 27, 1934. Ohio State.

MORRIS, HOWARD: NYC, Sept. 4, 1919. NYU.

MORROW, ROB: New Rochelle, NY, Sept. 21, 1962.

MORSE, DAVID: Hamilton, MA, Oct. 11, 1953.

MORSE, ROBERT: Newton, MA, May 18, 1931.

MORTON, JOE: NYC, Oct. 18, 1947. Hofstra U.

MOSES, WILLIAM: Los Angeles, Nov. 17, 1959.

MOSTEL, JOSH: NYC, Dec. 21, 1946. Brandeis U.

MOUCHET, CATHERINE: Paris, France, 1959. Ntl. Consv.

MOYA, EDDY: El Paso, TX, Apr. 11, 1963. LACC.

MUELLER-STAHL, ARMIN: Tilsit, East Prussia, Dec. 17, 1930.

MULDAUR, DIANA: NYC, Aug. 19, 1938. Sweet Briar College.

MULGREW, KATE: Dubuque, IA, Apr. 29, 1955. NYU.

MULHERN, MATT: Philadelphia, PA, July 21, 1960. Rutgers Univ.

MULL, MARTIN: N. Ridgefield, OH, Aug. 18, 1941. RISch. of Design.

MULLIGAN, RICHARD: NYC, Nov. 13, 1932.

MULRONEY, DERMOT: Alexandria, VA, Oct. 31, 1963. Northwestern.

MUMY, BILL (Charles William Mumy, Jr.): San Gabriel, CA, Feb. 1, 1954.

MURPHY, EDDIE: Brooklyn, NY, Apr. 3, 1961.

MURPHY, MICHAEL: Los Angeles, CA, May 5, 1938. UAz.

MURRAY, BILL: Wilmette, IL, Sept. 21, 1950. Regis College.

MURRAY, DON: Hollywood, CA, July 31, 1929.

MUSANTE, TONY: Bridgeport, CT, June 30, 1936. Oberlin College.

MYERS, MIKE: Scarborough, Canada, 1964.

NABORS, JIM: Sylacauga, GA, June 12, 1932.

NADER, GEORGE: Pasadena, CA, Oct. 19, 1921. Occidental College.

NADER, MICHAEL: Los Angeles, CA, 1945.

NAMATH, JOE: Beaver Falls, PA, May 31, 1943. UAla.

NAUGHTON, DAVID: Hartford, CT, Feb. 13, 1951.

NAUGHTON, JAMES: Middletown, CT, Dec. 6, 1945.

NEAL, PATRICIA: Packard, KY, Jan. 20, 1926. Northwestern U.

NEESOM, LIAM: Ballymena, Northern Ireland, June 7, 1952.

NEFF, HILDEGARDE (Hildegard Knef): Ulm, Germany, Dec. 28, 1925. Berlin Art Acad.

NEILL, SAM: No. Ireland, Sept. 14, 1947. U Canterbury.

NELL, NATHALIE: Paris, France, Oct. 1950.

NELLIGAN, KATE: London, Ont., Canada, Mar. 16, 1951. U Toronto.

NELSON, BARRY (Robert Nielsen): Oakland, CA, Apr. 16, 1920.

NELSON, CRAIG T.: Spokane, WA, Apr. 4, 1946.

NELSON, DAVID: NYC, Oct. 24, 1936. USC.

NELSON, GENE (Gene Berg): Seattle, WA, Mar. 24, 1920.

NELSON, JUDD: Portland, ME, Nov. 28, 1959. Haverford College.

NELSON, LORI (Dixie Kay Nelson): Santa Fe, NM, Aug. 15, 1933.

NELSON, TRACY: Santa Monica, CA, Oct. 25, 1963.

NELSON, WILLIE: Abbott, TX, Apr. 30, 1933.

NEMEC, CORIN: Little Rock, AK, Nov. 5, 1971.

NERO, FRANCO: Parma, Italy, 1941.

NESMITH, MICHAEL: Houston, TX, Dec. 30, 1942.

NETTLETON, LOIS: Oak Park, IL, 1931. Actors Studio.

NEWHART, BOB: Chicago, IL, Sept. 5, 1929. Loyola U.

Joe Mantegna

Elizabeth Perkins

Rosie Perez

Kyle MacLachlan

NEWLEY, ANTHONY: Hackney, London, Sept. 24, 1931.

NEWMAN, BARRY: Boston, MA, Nov. 7, 1938. Brandeis U.

NEWMAN, LARAINE: Los Angeles, Mar. 2, 1952.

NEWMAN, NANETTE: Northampton, England, 1934.

NEWMAN, PAUL: Cleveland, OH, Jan. 26, 1925. Yale.

NEWMAR, JULIE (Newmeyer): Los Angeles, Aug. 16, 1933.

NEWTON-JOHN, OLIVIA: Cambridge, England, Sept. 26, 1948.

NGOR, HAING S.: Cambodia, 1947.

NGUYEN, DUSTIN: Saigon, 1962.

NICHOLAS, DENISE: Detroit, MI, July 12, 1945.

NICHOLAS, PAUL: London, 1945.

NICHOLS, NICHELLE: Robbins, IL, 1936.

NICHOLSON, JACK: Neptune, NJ, Apr. 22, 1937.

NICKERSON, DENISE: NYC, 1959.

NICOL, ALEX: Ossining, NY, Jan. 20, 1919. Actors Studio.

NIELSEN, BRIGITTE: Denmark, July 15, 1963.

NIELSEN, LESLIE: Regina, Saskatchewan. Canada, Feb. 11, 1926. Neighborhood Playhouse.

NIMOY, LEONARD: Boston, MA, Mar. 26, 1931. Boston College, Antioch College.

NIXON, CYNTHIA: NYC, Apr. 9, 1966. Columbia U.

NOBLE, JAMES: Dallas, TX, Mar. 5, 1922, SMU.

NOIRET, PHILIPPE: Lille, France, Oct. 1, 1930.

NOLAN, KATHLEEN: St. Louis, MO, Sept. 27, 1933. Neighborhood Playhouse.

NOLTE, NICK: Omaha, NE, Feb. 8, 1940. Pasadena City College.

NORRIS, CHRISTOPHER: NYC, Oct. 7, 1943. Lincoln Square Acad.

NORRIS, CHUCK (Carlos Ray): Ryan, OK, Mar. 10, 1940.

NORTH, HEATHER: Pasadena, CA, Dec. 13, 1950. Actors Workshop.

NORTH, SHEREE (Dawn Bethel): Los Angeles. Jan. 17, 1933. Hollywood High.

NORTON, KEN: Jacksonville, Il, Aug. 9, 1945.

NOURI, MICHAEL: Washington, DC, Dec. 9, 1945.

NOVAK, KIM (Marilyn Novak): Chicago, IL, Feb. 13, 1933. LACC.

NOVELLO, DON: Ashtabula, OH, Jan. 1, 1943. UDayton.

NUYEN, FRANCE (Vannga): Marseilles, France, July 31, 1939. Beaux Arts School.

O'BRIAN, HUGH (Hugh J. Krampe): Rochester, N,. Apr. 19, 1928. Cincinnati U.

O'BRIEN, CLAY: Ray, AZ, May 6, 1961.

O'BRIEN, MARGARET (Angela Maxine O'Brien): Los Angeles, Jan. 15, 1937.

O'BRIEN, VIRGINIA: Los Angeles, Apr. 18, 1919.

O'CONNOR, CARROLL: Bronx, NY, Aug. 2, 1924. Dublin National Univ.

O'CONNOR, DONALD: Chicago, IL, Aug. 28, 1925.

O'CONNOR, GLYNNIS: NYC, Nov. 19, 1955. NYSU.

O'DONNELL, CHRIS: Winetka, IL, June 27, 1970.

O'DONNELL, ROSIE: Commack, NY, 1961.

O'HARA, CATHERINE: Toronto, Canada, Mar. 4, 1954.

O'HARA, MAUREEN (Maureen Fitz-Simons): Dublin, Ireland, Aug. 17, 1920.

O'HERLIHY, DAN: Wexford, Ireland, May 1, 1919. National U.

O'KEEFE, MICHAEL: Larchmont, NY, Apr. 24, 1955. NYU, AADA.

OLDMAN, GARY: New Cross, South London, England, Mar. 21, 1958.

OLIN, KEN: Chicago, IL, July 30, 1954. UPa.

OLIN, LENA: Stockholm, Sweden, Mar. 22, 1955.

OLMOS, EDWARD JAMES: Los Angeles, Feb. 24, 1947. CSLA.

O'LOUGHLIN, GERALD S.: NYC, Dec. 23, 1921. U Rochester.

OLSON, JAMES: Evanston, IL, Oct. 8, 1930.

OLSON, NANCY: Milwaukee, WI, July 14, 1928. UCLA.

O'NEAL, GRIFFIN: Los Angeles, 1965.

O'NEAL, RON: Utica, NY, Sept. 1, 1937. Ohio State.

O'NEAL, RYAN: Los Angeles, Apr. 20, 1941.

O'NEAL, TATUM: Los Angeles, Nov. 5, 1963.

O'NEIL, TRICIA: Shreveport, LA, Mar. 11, 1945. Baylor U.

O'NEILL, ED: Youngstown, OH, 1946.

O'NEILL, JENNIFER: Rio de Janeiro, Feb. 20, 1949. Neighborhood Playhouse.

ONTKEAN, MICHAEL: Vancouver, B.C., Canada, Jan. 24, 1946.

O'QUINN, TERRY: Newbury, MI, July 15, 1952.

ORBACH, JERRY: Bronx, NY, Oct. 20, 1935.

O'SHEA, MILO: Dublin, Ireland, June 2, 1926.

O'SULLIVAN, MAUREEN: Byle, Ireland, May 17, 1911. Sacred Heart Convent.

O'TOOLE, ANNETTE (Toole): Houston, TX, Apr. 1, 1953. UCLA.

O'TOOLE, PETER: Connemara, Ireland, Aug. 2, 1932. RADA.

OVERALL, PARK: Nashville, TN, Mar. 15, 1957. Tusculum College.

OZ, FRANK (Oznowicz): Hereford, England, May 25, 1944.

PACINO, AL: NYC, Apr. 25, 1940.

PACULA, JOANNA: Tamaszow Lubelski, Poland, Jan. 2, 1957. Polish Natl. Theatre Sch.

PAGE, TONY (Anthony Vitiello): Bronx, NY, 1940.

PAGET, DEBRA (Debralee Griffin): Denver, Aug. 19, 1933.

PAIGE, JANIS (Donna Mae Jaden): Tacoma, WA, Sept. 16, 1922.

PALANCE, JACK (Walter Palanuik): Lattimer, PA, Feb. 18, 1920. UNC.

PALIN, MICHAEL: Sheffield, Yorkshire, England, May 5, 1943. Oxford.

PALMER, BETSY: East Chicago, IN, Nov. 1, 1926. DePaul U.

PALMER, GREGG (Palmer Lee): San Francisco, Jan. 25, 1927. U Utah.

PAMPANINI, SILVANA: Rome, Sept. 25, 1925.

PANEBIANCO, RICHARD: NYC, 1971.

PANKIN, STUART: Philadelphia, Apr. 8, 1946.

PANTOLIANO, JOE: Jersey City, NJ, Sept. 12, 1954.

PAPAS, IRENE: Chiliomodion, Greece, Mar. 9, 1929.

PAQUIN, ANNA: Wellington, NZ, 1982.

PARE, MICHAEL: Brooklyn, NY, Oct. 9, 1959.

PARKER, COREY: NYC, July 8, 1965. NYU.

PARKER, ELEANOR: Cedarville, OH, June 26, 1922. Pasadena Playhouse.
PARKER, FESS: Fort Worth, TX, Aug. 16, 1925. USC.
PARKER, JAMESON: Baltimore, MD, Nov. l8, 1947. Beloit College.
PARKER, JEAN (Mae Green): Deer Lodge, MT, Aug. 11, 1912.
PARKER, MARY-LOUISE: Ft. Jackson, SC, Aug. 2, 1964. Bard College.
PARKER, NATHANIEL: London, 1963.
PARKER, SARAH JESSICA: Nelsonville, OH, Mar. 25, 1965.
PARKER, SUZY (Cecelia Parker): San Antonio, TX, Oct. 28, 1933.
PARKER, TREY: Auburn, AL, May 30, 1972.
PARKER, WILLARD (Worster Van Eps): NYC, Feb. 5, 1912.
PARKINS, BARBARA: Vancouver, Canada, May 22, 1943.
PARKS, MICHAEL: Corona, CA, Apr. 4, 1938.
PARSONS, ESTELLE: Lynn, MA, Nov. 20, 1927. Boston U.
PARTON, DOLLY: Sevierville, TN, Jan. 19, 1946.
PATINKIN, MANDY: Chicago, IL, Nov. 30, 1952. Juilliard.
PATRIC, JASON: NYC, June 17, 1966.
PATRICK, DENNIS: Philadelphia, Mar. 14, 1918.
PATTERSON, LEE: Vancouver, Canada, Mar. 31, 1929. Ontario College.
PATTON, WILL: Charleston, SC, June 14, 1954.
PAULIK, JOHAN: Prague, Czech., 1975.
PAVAN, MARISA (Marisa Pierangeli): Cagliari, Sardinia, June 19, 1932. Torquado Tasso College.
PAXTON, BILL: Fort Worth, TX, May. 17, 1955.
PAYS, AMANDA: Berkshire, England, June 6, 1959.
PEACH, MARY: Durban, S. Africa, 1934.
PEARL, MINNIE (Sarah Cannon): Centerville, TN, Oct. 25, 1912.
PEARSON, BEATRICE: Dennison, TX, July 27, 1920.
PECK, GREGORY: La Jolla, CA, Apr. 5, 1916. U Calif.
PEÑA, ELIZABETH: Cuba, Sept. 23, 1961.
PENDLETON, AUSTIN: Warren, OH, Mar. 27, 1940. Yale U.
PENHALL, BRUCE: Balboa, CA, Aug. 17, 1960.
PENN, SEAN: Burbank, CA, Aug. 17, 1960.
PEREZ, JOSE: NYC, 1940.
PEREZ, ROSIE: Brooklyn, NY, Sept. 6, 1964.
PERKINS, ELIZABETH: Queens, NY, Nov. 18, 1960. Goodman School.
PERKINS, MILLIE: Passaic, NJ, May 12, 1938.
PERLMAN, RHEA: Brooklyn, NY, Mar. 31, 1948.
PERLMAN, RON: NYC, Apr. 13, 1950. UMn.
PERREAU, GIGI (Ghislaine): Los Angeles, Feb. 6, 1941.
PERRINE, VALERIE: Galveston, TX, Sept. 3, 1943. U Ariz.
PERRY, LUKE (Coy Luther Perry, III)**:** Fredricktown, OH, Oct. 11, 1966.
PESCI, JOE: Newark, NJ. Feb. 9, 1943.

Liam Neeson

Joan Plowright

Nick Nolte

PESCOW, DONNA: Brooklyn, NY, Mar. 24, 1954.
PETERS, BERNADETTE (Lazzara): Jamaica, NY, Feb. 28, 1948.
PETERS, BROCK: NYC, July 2, 1927. CCNY.
PETERS. JEAN (Elizabeth): Caton, OH, Oct. 15, 1926. Ohio State U.
PETERS, MICHAEL: Brooklyn, NY, 1948.
PETERSEN, PAUL: Glendale, CA, Sept. 23, 1945. Valley College.
PETERSEN, WILLIAM: Chicago, IL, Feb. 21, 1953.
PETERSON, CASSANDRA: Colorado Springs, CO, Sept. 17, 1951.
PETTET, JOANNA: London, Nov. 16, 1944. Neighborhood Playhouse.
PETTY, LORI: Chattanooga, TN, 1965.
PFEIFFER, MICHELLE: Santa Ana, CA, Apr. 29, 1958.
PHILLIPS, LOU DIAMOND: Phillipines, Feb. 17, 1962, UTx.
PHILLIPS, MacKENZIE: Alexandria, VA, Nov. 10, 1959.
PHILLIPS, MICHELLE (Holly Gilliam): Long Beach, CA, June 4, 1944.
PHILLIPS, SIAN: Bettws, Wales, May 14, 1934. UWales.
PICARDO, ROBERT: Philadelphia, PA, Oct. 27, 1953. Yale.
PICERNI, PAUL: NYC, Dec. 1, 1922. Loyola U.
PIGOTT-SMITH, TIM: Rugby, England, May 13, 1946.
PINCHOT, BRONSON: NYC, May 20, 1959. Yale.
PINE, PHILLIP: Hanford, CA, July 16, 1925. Actors' Lab.
PISCOPO, JOE: Passaic. NJ, June 17, 1951.
PISIER, MARIE-FRANCE: Vietnam, May 10, 1944. U Paris.
PITILLO, MARIA: Mahwah, NJ, 1965.
PITT, BRAD (William Bradley Pitt): Shawnee, OK, Dec. 18, 1963.
PLACE, MARY KAY: Tulsa OK, Sept. 23, 1947. U Tulsa.
PLAYTEN, ALICE: NYC, Aug. 28, 1947. NYU.
PLESHETTE, SUZANNE: NYC, Jan. 31, 1937. Syracuse U.
PLIMPTON, MARTHA: NYC, Nov. 16, 1970.
PLOWRIGHT, JOAN: Scunthorpe, Brigg, Lincolnshire, England, Oct. 28, 1929. Old Vic.
PLUMB, EVE: Burbank, CA, Apr. 29, 1958.
PLUMMER, AMANDA: NYC, Mar. 23, 1957. Middlebury College.
PLUMMER, CHRISTOPHER: Toronto, Canada, Dec. 13, 1927.
PODESTA, ROSSANA: Tripoli, June 20, 1934.
POITIER, SIDNEY: Miami, FL, Feb. 27, 1927.
POLANSKI, ROMAN: Paris, France, Aug. 18, 1933.
POLITO, JON: Philadelphia, PA, Dec. 29, 1950. Villanova U.
POLITO, LINA: Naples, Italy, Aug. 11, 1954.
POLLACK, SYDNEY: South Bend, IN, July 1, 1934.
POLLAK, KEVIN: San Francisco, Oct. 30, 1958.
POLLAN, TRACY: NYC, June 22, 1960.

POLLARD, MICHAEL J.: Passaic, NJ, May 30, 1939.

PORTER, ERIC: London, Apr. 8, 1928. Wimbledon College.

POTTS, ANNIE: Nashville, TN, Oct. 28, 1952. Stephens College.

POWELL, JANE (Suzanne Burce): Port-land, OR, Apr. 1, 1928.

POWELL, ROBERT: Salford, England, June 1, 1944. Manchester U.

POWER, TARYN: Los Angeles, CA, 1954.

POWER, TYRONE, IV: Los Angeles, CA, Jan. 1959.

POWERS, MALA (Mary Ellen): San Francisco, CA, Dec. 29, 1921. UCLA.

POWERS, STEFANIE (Federkiewicz): Hollywood, CA, Oct. 12, 1942.

PRENTISS, PAULA (Paula Ragusa): San Antonio, TX, Mar. 4, 1939. Northwestern U.

PRESLE, MICHELINE (Micheline Chassagne): Paris, France, Aug. 22, 1922. Rouleau Drama School.

PRESLEY, PRISCILLA: Brooklyn, NY, May 24, 1945.

PRESNELL, HARVE: Modesto, CA, Sept. 14, 1933. USC.

PRESTON, KELLY: Honolulu, HI, Oct. 13, 1962. USC.

PRESTON, WILLIAM: Columbia, PA, Aug. 26, 1921. PaStateU.

PRICE, LONNY: NYC, Mar. 9, 1959. Juilliard.

PRIESTLEY, JASON: Vancouver, Canada, Aug, 28, 1969.

PRIMUS, BARRY: NYC, Feb. 16, 1938. CCNY.

PRINCE (P. Rogers Nelson): Minneapolis, MN, June 7, 1958.

PRINCE, WILLIAM: Nicholas, NY, Jan. 26, 1913. Cornell U.

PRINCIPAL, VICTORIA: Fukuoka, Japan, Jan. 3, 1945. Dade, Jr. College.

PROCHNOW, JURGEN: Berlin, June 10, 1941.

PROSKY, ROBERT: Philadelphia, PA, Dec. 13, 1930.

PROVAL, DAVID: Brooklyn, NY, 1943.

PROVINE, DOROTHY: Deadwood, SD, Jan. 20, 1937. U Wash.

PROWSE, JULIET: Bombay, India, Sept. 25, 1936.

PRYCE, JONATHAN: Wales, UK, June 1, 1947, RADA.

PRYOR, RICHARD: Peoria, IL, Dec. 1, 1940.

PULLMAN, BILL: Delphi, NY, Dec. 17, 1954. SUNY/Oneonta, UMass.

PURCELL, LEE: Cherry Point, NC, June 15, 1947. Stephens.

PURDOM, EDMUND: Welwyn Garden City, England, Dec. 19, 1924. St. Ignatius College.

PYLE, DENVER: Bethune, CO, May 11, 1920.

QUAID, DENNIS: Houston, TX, Apr. 9, 1954.

QUAID, RANDY: Houston, TX, Oct. 1, 1950. UHouston.

QUINLAN, KATHLEEN: Mill Valley, CA, Nov. 19, 1954.

QUINN, AIDAN: Chicago, IL, Mar. 8, 1959.

QUINN, ANTHONY: Chihuahua, Mex., Apr. 21, 1915.

RAFFERTY, FRANCES: Sioux City, IA, June 16, 1922. UCLA.

Chris O'Donnell

Diana Rigg

Ed O'Neill

RAFFIN, DEBORAH: Los Angeles, Mar. 13, 1953. Valley College.

RAGSDALE, WILLIAM: El Dorado, AK, Jan. 19, 1961. Hendrix College.

RAILSBACK, STEVE: Dallas, TX, 1948.

RAINER, LUISE: Vienna, Austria, Jan. 12, 1910.

RALSTON, VERA (Vera Helena Hruba): Prague, Czech., July 12, 1919.

RAMIS, HAROLD: Chicago, IL, Nov. 21, 1944. WashingtonU.

RAMPLING, CHARLOTTE: Surmer, England, Feb. 5, 1946. U Madrid.

RAMSEY, LOGAN: Long Beach, CA, Mar. 21, 1921. St. Joseph.

RANDALL, TONY (Leonard Rosenberg): Tulsa, OK, Feb. 26, 1920. Northwestern U.

RANDELL, RON: Sydney, Australia, Oct. 8, 1920. St. Mary's College.

RASCHE, DAVID: St. Louis, MO, Aug. 7, 1944.

RAYMOND, GENE (Raymond Guion): NYC, Aug. 13, 1908.

REA, STEPHEN: Belfast, No. Ireland, Oct. 31, 1949.

REAGAN, RONALD: Tampico, IL, Feb. 6, 1911. Eureka College.

REASON, REX: Berlin, Ger., Nov. 30, 1928. Pasadena Playhouse.

REDDY, HELEN: Melbourne, Australia, Oct. 25, 1942.

REDFORD, ROBERT: Santa Monica, CA, Aug. 18, 1937. AADA.

REDGRAVE, CORIN: London, July 16, 1939.

REDGRAVE, LYNN: London, Mar. 8, 1943.

REDGRAVE, VANESSA: London, Jan. 30, 1937.

REDMAN, JOYCE: County Mayo, Ireland, 1919. RADA.

REED, OLIVER: Wimbledon, England, Feb. 13, 1938.

REED, PAMELA: Tacoma, WA, Apr. 2, 1949.

REEMS, HARRY (Herbert Streicher): Bronx, NY, 1947. U Pittsburgh.

REES, ROGER: Aberystwyth, Wales, May 5, 1944.

REESE, DELLA: Detroit, MI, July 6, 1932.

REEVE, CHRISTOPHER: NYC, Sept. 25, 1952. Cornell, Juilliard.

REEVES, KEANU: Beiruit, Lebanon, Sept. 2, 1964.

REEVES, STEVE: Glasgow, MT, Jan. 21, 1926.

REGEHR, DUNCAN: Lethbridge, Canada, 1954.

REID, ELLIOTT: NYC, Jan. 16, 1920.

REID, TIM: Norfolk, VA, Dec, 19, 1944.

REILLY, CHARLES NELSON: NYC, Jan. 13, 1931. UCt.

REINER, CARL: NYC, Mar. 20, 1922. Georgetown.

REINER, ROB: NYC, Mar. 6, 1947. UCLA.

REINHOLD, JUDGE (Edward Ernest, Jr.): Wilmington, DE, May 21, 1957. NCSchool of Arts.

REINKING, ANN: Seattle, WA, Nov. 10, 1949.

REISER, PAUL: NYC, Mar. 30, 1957.

REMAR, JAMES: Boston, MA, Dec. 31, 1953. Neighborhood Playhouse.

REMSEN, BERT: Glen Cove, NY, Feb. 25, 1925. Ithaca.

RETTIG, TOMMY: Jackson Heights, NY, Dec. 10, 1941.

Peter O'Toole

Annabella Sciorra

Luke Perry

Talia Shire

REVILL, CLIVE: Wellington, NZ, Apr. 18, 1930.

REY, ANTONIA: Havana, Cuba, Oct. 12, 1927.

REYNOLDS, BURT: Waycross, GA, Feb. 11, 1935. Fla. State U.

REYNOLDS, DEBBIE (Mary Frances Reynolds): El Paso, TX, Apr. 1, 1932.

REYNOLDS, MARJORIE: Buhl, ID, Aug. 12, 1921.

RHOADES, BARBARA: Poughkeepsie, NY, 1947.

RHODES, CYNTHIA: Nashville, TN, Nov. 21, 1956.

RHYS-DAVIES, JOHN: Salisbury, England, May 5, 1944.

RICCI, CHRISTINA: Santa Monica, CA, 1980.

RICHARD, CLIFF: India, Oct. 14, 1940.

RICHARDS, MICHAEL: Culver City, CA, July 14, 1950.

RICHARDSON, JOELY: London, Jan. 9, 1965.

RICHARDSON, LEE: Chicago, IL, Sept. 11, 1926.

RICHARDSON, MIRANDA: Southport, England, Mar. 3, 1958.

RICHARDSON, NATASHA: London, May 11, 1963.

RICKLES, DON: NYC, May 8, 1926. AADA.

RICKMAN, ALAN: Hammersmith, England, Feb. 21, 1946.

RIEGERT, PETER: NYC, Apr. 11, 1947. U Buffalo.

RIGG, DIANA: Doncaster, England, July 20, 1938. RADA.

RINGWALD, MOLLY: Rosewood, CA, Feb. 16, 1968.

RITTER, JOHN: Burbank, CA, Sept. 17, 1948. US. Cal.

RIVERS, JOAN (Molinsky): Brooklyn, NY, NY, June 8, 1933.

ROBARDS, JASON: Chicago, IL, July 26, 1922. AADA.

ROBARDS, SAM: NYC, Dec. 16, 1963.

ROBBINS, TIM: NYC, Oct. 16, 1958. UCLA.

ROBERTS, ERIC: Biloxi, MS, Apr. 18, 1956. RADA.

ROBERTS, JULIA: Atlanta, GA, Oct. 28, 1967.

ROBERTS, RALPH: Salisbury, NC, Aug. 17, 1922. UNC.

ROBERTS, TANYA (Leigh): NYC, 1955.

ROBERTS, TONY: NYC, Oct. 22, 1939. Northwestern U.

ROBERTSON, CLIFF: La Jolla, CA, Sept. 9, 1925. Antioch College.

ROBERTSON, DALE: Oklahoma City, July 14, 1923.

ROBINSON, CHRIS: West Palm Beach, FL, Nov. 5, 1938. LACC.

ROBINSON, JAY: NYC, Apr. 14, 1930.

ROBINSON, ROGER: Seattle, WA, May 2, 1941. USC.

ROCHEFORT, JEAN: Paris, France, 1930.

ROCK-SAVAGE, STEVEN: Melville, LA, Dec. 14, 1958. LSU.

ROGERS, CHARLES "BUDDY": Olathe, KS, Aug. 13, 1904. U Kan.

ROGERS, MIMI: Coral Gables, FL, Jan. 27, 1956.

ROGERS, ROY (Leonard Slye): Cincinnati, Nov. 5, 1912.

ROGERS, WAYNE: Birmingham, AL, Apr. 7, 1933. Princeton.

ROLLE, ESTHER: Pompano Beach, FL, Nov. 8, 1922.

ROLLINS, HOWARD E., JR.: Baltimore, MD. Oct. 17, 1950.

ROMAN, RUTH: Boston, Dec. 23, 1922. Bishop Lee Dramatic School.

RONSTADT, LINDA: Tucson, AZ, July 15, 1946.

ROOKER, MICHAEL: Jasper, AL, Apr. 6, 1955.

ROONEY, MICKEY (Joe Yule, Jr.): Brooklyn, NY, Sept. 23, 1920.

ROSE, REVA: Chicago, IL, July 30, 1940. Goodman.

ROSEANNE (Barr): Salt Lake City, UT, Nov. 3, 1952.

ROSS, DIANA: Detroit, MI, Mar. 26, 1944.

ROSS, JUSTIN: Brooklyn, NY, Dec. 15, 1954.

ROSS, KATHARINE: Hollywood, Jan. 29, 1943. Santa Rosa College.

ROSSELLINI, ISABELLA: Rome, June 18, 1952.

ROSSOVICH, RICK: Palo Alto, CA, Aug. 28, 1957.

ROTH, TIM: London, May 14, 1961.

ROUNDTREE, RICHARD: New Rochelle, NY, Sept. 7, 1942. Southern Ill.

ROURKE, MICKEY: Schenectady, NY, Sept. 1956.

ROWE, NICHOLAS: London, Nov. 22, 1966, Eton.

ROWLANDS, GENA: Cambria, WI, June 19, 1934.

RUBIN, ANDREW: New Bedford, MA, June 22, 1946. AADA.

RUBINEK, SAUL: Fohrenwold, Germany, July 2, 1948.

RUBINSTEIN, JOHN: Los Angeles, CA, Dec. 8, 1946. UCLA.

RUCKER, BO: Tampa, FL, Aug. 17, 1948.

RUDD, PAUL: Boston, MA, May 15, 1940.

RUDNER, RITA: Miami, FL, 1956.

RUEHL, MERCEDES: Queens, NY, Feb. 28, 1948.

RULE, JANICE: Cincinnati, OH, Aug. 15, 1931.

RUPERT, MICHAEL: Denver, CO, Oct. 23, 1951. Pasadena Playhouse.

RUSH, BARBARA: Denver, CO, Jan. 4, 1927. U Calif.

RUSSELL, JANE: Bemidji, MI, June 21, 1921. Max Reinhardt School.

RUSSELL, KURT: Springfield, MA, Mar. 17, 1951.

RUSSELL, THERESA (Paup): San Diego, CA, Mar. 20, 1957.

RUSSO, JAMES: NYC, Apr. 23, 1953.

RUTHERFORD, ANN: Toronto, Canada, Nov. 2, 1920.

RUYMEN, AYN: Brooklyn, NY, July 18, 1947. HB Studio.

RYAN, JOHN P.: NYC, July 30, 1936. CCNY.

RYAN, MEG: Fairfield, CT, Nov. 19, 1961. NYU.

RYAN, TIM (Meineslschmidt): Staten Island, NY, 1958. Rutgers U.

RYDER, WINONA: Winona, MN, Oct. 29, 1971.

SACCHI, ROBERT: Bronx, NY, 1941. NYU.

SÄGEBRECHT, MARIANNE: Starnberg, Bavaria, Aug. 27, 1945.

SAINT, EVA MARIE: Newark, NJ, July 4, 1924. Bowling Green State U.

SAINT JAMES, SUSAN (Suzie Jane Miller): Los Angeles, Aug. 14, 1946. Conn. College.

ST. JOHN, BETTA: Hawthorne, CA, Nov. 26, 1929.

ST. JOHN, JILL (Jill Oppenheim): Los Angeles, Aug. 19, 1940.

SALA, JOHN: Los Angeles, CA, Oct. 5, 1962.

SALDANA, THERESA: Brooklyn, NY, Aug. 20, 1954.

SALINGER, MATT: Windsor, VT, Feb. 13, 1960. Princeton, Columbia.

SALT, JENNIFER: Los Angeles, Sept. 4, 1944. Sarah Lawrence College.

SAMMS, EMMA: London, Aug. 28, 1960.

SAN GIACOMO, LAURA: Orange, NJ, Nov. 14, 1961.

SANDERS, JAY O.: Austin, TX, Apr. 16, 1953.

SANDS, JULIAN: Yorkshire, England, Jan 15, 1958.

SANDS, TOMMY: Chicago, IL, Aug. 27, 1937.

SAN JUAN, OLGA: NYC, Mar. 16, 1927.

SARA, MIA: Brooklyn, NY, 1968.

SARANDON, CHRIS: Beckley, WV, July 24, 1942. U WVa., Catholic U.

SARANDON, SUSAN (Tomalin): NYC, Oct. 4, 1946. Catholic U.

SARRAZIN, MICHAEL: Quebec City, Canada, May 22, 1940.

SAVAGE, FRED: Highland Park, IL, July 9, 1976.

SAVAGE, JOHN (Youngs): Long Island, NY, Aug. 25, 1949. AADA.

SAVIOLA, CAMILLE: Bronx, NY, July 16, 1950.

SAVOY, TERESA ANN: London, July 18, 1955.

SAXON, JOHN (Carmen Orrico): Brooklyn, NY, Aug. 5, 1935.

SBARGE, RAPHAEL: NYC, Feb. 12, 1964.

SCACCHI, GRETA: Milan, Italy, Feb. 18, 1960.

SCALIA, JACK: Brooklyn, NY, 1951.

SCARPELLI, GLEN: Staten Island, NY, July 1966.

SCARWID, DIANA: Savannah, GA, Aug. 27, 1955, AADA. Pace U.

SCHEIDER, ROY: Orange, NJ, Nov. 10, 1932. Franklin-Marshall.

SCHEINE, RAYNOR: Emporia, VA, Nov. 10. VaCommonwealthU.

SCHELL, MARIA: Vienna, Jan. 15, 1926.

SCHELL, MAXIMILIAN: Vienna, Dec. 8, 1930.

SCHLATTER, CHARLIE: NYC, 1967. Ithaca College.

SCHNEIDER, JOHN: Mt. Kisco, NY, Apr. 8, 1960.

SCHNEIDER, MARIA: Paris, France, Mar. 27, 1952.

SCHRODER, RICK: Staten Island, NY, Apr. 13, 1970.

SCHUCK, JOHN: Boston, MA, Feb. 4, 1940.

SCHULTZ, DWIGHT: Milwaukee, WI, Nov. 10, 1938. MarquetteU.

SCHWARZENEGGER, ARNOLD: Austria, July 30, 1947.

SCHYGULLA, HANNA: Katlowitz, Germany, Dec. 25, 1943.

SCIORRA, ANNABELLA: NYC, Mar. 24, 1964.

SCOFIELD, PAUL: Hurstpierpoint, England, Jan. 21, 1922. London Mask Theatre School.

SCOGGINS, TRACY: Galveston, TX, Nov. 13, 1959.

SCOLARI, PETER: Scarsdale, NY, Sept. 12, 1956. NYCC.

SCOTT,CAMPBELL: South Salem, NY, July 19, 1962. Lawrence.

SCOTT, DEBRALEE: Elizabeth, NJ, Apr. 2.

SCOTT, GEORGE C.: Wise, VA, Oct. 18, 1927. U Mo.

SCOTT, GORDON (Gordon M. Werschkul): Portland, OR, Aug. 3, 1927. Oregon U.

SCOTT, LIZABETH (Emma Matso): Scranton, PA, Sept. 29, 1922.

SCOTT, MARTHA: Jamesport, MO, Sept. 22, 1914. U Mich.

SCOTT-TAYLOR, JONATHAN: Brazil, 1962.

SEAGAL, STEVEN: Detroit, MI, Apr. 10, 1951.

SEARS, HEATHER: London, Sept. 28, 1935.

SECOMBE, HARRY: Swansea, Wales, Sept. 8, 1921.

SEDGWICK, KYRA: NYC, Aug. 19, 1965. USC.

SEGAL, GEORGE: NYC, Feb. 13, 1934. Columbia.

SELBY, DAVID: Morganstown, WV, Feb. 5, 1941. UWV.

SELLARS, ELIZABETH: Glasgow, Scotland, May 6, 1923.

SELLECK, TOM: Detroit, MI, Jan. 29, 1945. USCal.

SERNAS, JACQUES: Lithuania, July 30, 1925.

SERRAULT, MICHEL: Brunoy, France. 1928. Paris Consv.

SETH, ROSHAN: New Delhi, India. 1942.

SEYMOUR, JANE (Joyce Frankenberg): Hillingdon, England, Feb. 15, 1952.

SHARIF, OMAR (Michel Shalhoub): Alexandria, Egypt, Apr. 10, 1932. Victoria College.

SHANDLING, GARRY: Chicago, IL, Nov. 29, 1949.

SHATNER, WILLIAM: Montreal, Canada, Mar. 22, 1931. McGill U.

SHAVER, HELEN: St. Thomas, Ontario, Canada, Feb. 24, 1951.

SHAW, SEBASTIAN: Holt, England, May, 1905. Gresham School.

SHAW, STAN: Chicago, IL, 1952.

SHAWN, WALLACE: NYC, Nov. 12, 1943. Harvard.

SHEA, JOHN: North Conway, NH, Apr. 14, 1949. Bates, Yale.

SHEARER, HARRY: Los Angeles, Dec. 23, 1943. UCLA.

SHEARER, MOIRA: Dunfermline, Scotland, Jan. 17, 1926. London Theatre School.

SHEEDY, ALLY: NYC, June 13, 1962. USC.

SHEEN, CHARLIE (Carlos Irwin Estevez): Santa Monica, CA, Sept. 3, 1965.

SHEEN, MARTIN (Ramon Estevez): Dayton, OH, Aug. 3, 1940.

Bronson Pinchot

Madeleine Stowe

Christopher Plummer

SHEFFER, CRAIG: York, PA, 1960. E. StroudsbergU.

SHEFFIELD, JOHN: Pasadena, CA, Apr. 11, 1931. UCLA.

SHELLEY, CAROL: London, England, Aug. 16, 1939.

SHEPARD, SAM (Rogers): Ft. Sheridan, IL, Nov. 5, 1943.

SHEPHERD, CYBILL: Memphis, TN, Feb. 18, 1950. Hunter, NYU.

SHERIDAN, JAMEY: Pasadena, CA, July 12, 1951.

SHIELDS, BROOKE: NYC, May 31, 1965.

SHIRE, TALIA: Lake Success, NY, Apr. 25, 1946. Yale.

SHORT, MARTIN: Toronto, Canada, Mar. 26, 1950. McMasterU.

SHOWALTER, MAX (formerly Casey Adams): Caldwell, KS, June 2, 1917. Pasadena Playhouse.

SHUE, ELISABETH: S. Orange, NJ, Oct. 6, 1963. Harvard.

SHULL, RICHARD B.: Evanston, IL, Feb. 24, 1929.

SIDNEY, SYLVIA: NYC, Aug. 8, 1910. Theatre Guild School.

SIEMASZKO, CASEY: Chicago, IL, March 17, 1961.

SIKKING, JAMES B.: Los Angeles, Mar. 5, 1934.

SILVA, HENRY: Puetro Rico, 1928.

SILVER, RON: NYC, July 2, 1946. SUNY.

SILVERMAN, JONATHAN: Los Angeles, CA, Aug. 5, 1966. USC.

SIMMONS, JEAN: London, Jan. 31, 1929. Aida Foster School.

SIMON, PAUL: Newark. NJ, Nov. 5, 1942.

SIMON, SIMONE: Marseilles, France, Apr. 23, 1910.

SIMPSON, O. J. (Orenthal James): San Francisco, CA, July 9, 1947. UCLA.

SINATRA, FRANK: Hoboken, NJ, Dec. 12, 1915.

SINBAD (David Adkins): Benton Harbor, MI, Nov. 10, 1956.

SINCLAIR, JOHN (Gianluigi Loffredo): Rome, Italy, 1946.

SINDEN, DONALD: Plymouth, England, Oct. 9, 1923. Webber-Douglas.

SINGER, LORI: Corpus Christi, TX, May 6, 1962. Juilliard.

SINISE, GARY: Chicago, Mar. 17. 1955.

SKELTON, RED (Richard): Vincennes, IN, July 18, 1910.

SKERRITT, TOM: Detroit, MI, Aug. 25, 1933. Wayne State U.

SKYE, IONE (Leitch): London, England, Sept. 4, 1971.

SLATER, CHRISTIAN: NYC, Aug. 18, 1969.

SLATER, HELEN: NYC, Dec. 15, 1965.

SMIRNOFF, YAKOV (Yakov Pokhis): Odessa, Russia, Jan. 24. 1951.

SMITH, CHARLES MARTIN: Los Angeles, CA, Oct. 30, 1953. CalState U.

SMITH, JACLYN: Houston, TX, Oct. 26, 1947.

SMITH, KURTWOOD: New Lisbon, WI, Jul. 3, 1942.

SMITH, LANE: Memphis, TN, Apr. 29, 1936.

SMITH, LEWIS: Chattanooga, TN, 1958. Actors Studio.

SMITH, LOIS: Topeka, KS, Nov. 3, 1930. U Wash.

SMITH, MAGGIE: Ilford, England, Dec. 28, 1934.

SMITH, ROGER: South Gate, CA, Dec. 18, 1932. U Ariz.

SMITH, WILL: Philadelphia, PA, Sept. 25, 1968.

SMITHERS, WILLIAM: Richmond, VA, July 10, 1927. Catholic U.

SMITS, JIMMY: Brooklyn, NY, July 9, 1955. Cornell U.

SNIPES, WESLEY: NYC, July 31, 1963. SUNY/Purchase.

SNODGRESS, CARRIE: Chicago, IL, Oct. 27, 1946. UNI.

SOLOMON, BRUCE: NYC, 1944. U Miami, Wayne State U.

SOMERS, SUZANNE (Mahoney): San Bruno, CA, Oct. 16, 1946. Lone Mt. College.

SOMMER, ELKE (Schletz): Berlin, Germany, Nov. 5, 1940.

SOMMER, JOSEF: Greifswald, Germany, June 26, 1934.

SORDI, ALBERTO: Rome, Italy, June 15, 1919.

SORVINO, MIRA: NYC, 1970.

SORVINO, PAUL: NYC, Apr. 13, 1939. AMDA.

SOTHERN, ANN (Harriet Lake): Chicago, IL, Aug. 28, 1943.

SOTO, TALISA: Brooklyn, NY, 1968.

SOUL, DAVID: Chicago, IL, Aug. 28, 1943.

SPACEK, SISSY: Quitman, TX, Dec. 25, 1949. Actors Studio.

SPACEY, KEVIN: So. Orange, NJ, July 26, 1959. Juilliard.

SPADER, JAMES: Buzzards Bay, MA, Feb. 7, 1960.

SPANO, VINCENT: Brooklyn, NY, Oct. 18, 1962.

SPENSER, JEREMY: Ceylon, 1937.

SPRINGFIELD, RICK (Richard Spring Thorpe): Sydney, Australia, Aug. 23, 1949.

STACK, ROBERT: Los Angeles, Jan. 13, 1919. USC.

STADLEN, LEWIS J.: Brooklyn, NY, Mar. 7, 1947. Neighborhood Playhouse.

STALLONE, FRANK: NYC, July 30, 1950.

STALLONE, SYLVESTER: NYC, July 6, 1946. U Miami.

STAMP, TERENCE: London, July 23, 1939.

STANG, ARNOLD: Chelsea, MA, Sept. 28, 1925.

STANLEY, KIM (Patricia Reid): Tularosa, NM, Feb. 11, 1925. U Tex.

STANTON, HARRY DEAN: Lexington, KY, July 14, 1926.

STAPLETON, JEAN: NYC, Jan. 19, 1923.

STAPLETON, MAUREEN: Troy, NY, June 21, 1925.

STARR, RINGO (Richard Starkey): Liverpool, England, July 7, 1940.

STEEL, ANTHONY: London, May 21, 1920. Cambridge.

STEELE, BARBARA: England, Dec. 29, 1937.

STEELE, TOMMY: London, Dec. 17, 1936.

STEENBURGEN, MARY: Newport, AR, 1953. Neighborhood Playhouse.

STEIGER, ROD: Westhampton, NY, Apr. 14, 1925.

STERLING, JAN (Jane Sterling Adriance): NYC, Apr. 3, 1923. Fay Compton School.

STERLING, ROBERT (William Sterling Hart): Newcastle, PA, Nov. 13, 1917. UPittsburgh.

STERN, DANIEL: Bethesda, MD, Aug. 28, 1957.

STERNHAGEN, FRANCES: Washington, DC, Jan. 13, 1932.

Kevin Pollak

Elaine Stritch

Jonathan Pryce

Victoria Tennant

Randy Quaid

Debra Winger

Aidan Quinn

Irene Worth

STEVENS, ANDREW: Memphis, TN, June 10, 1955.

STEVENS, CONNIE (Concetta Ann Ingolia): Brooklyn, NY, Aug. 8, 1938. Hollywood Professional School.

STEVENS, FISHER: Chicago, IL, Nov. 27, 1963. NYU.

STEVENS, KAYE (Catherine): Pittsburgh, July 21, 1933.

STEVENS, MARK (Richard): Cleveland, OH, Dec. 13, 1920.

STEVENS, STELLA (Estelle Eggleston): Hot Coffee, MS, Oct. 1, 1936.

STEVENSON, PARKER: Philadelphia, PA, June 4, 1953. Princeton.

STEWART, ALEXANDRA: Montreal, Canada, June 10, 1939. Louvre.

STEWART, ELAINE: Montclair, NJ, May 31, 1929.

STEWART, JAMES: Indiana, PA, May 20, 1908. Princeton.

STEWART, MARTHA (Martha Haworth): Bardwell, KY, Oct. 7, 1922.

STEWART, PATRICK: Mirfield, England, July 13, 1940.

STIERS, DAVID OGDEN: Peoria, IL, Oct. 31, 1942.

STILLER, BEN: NYC, 1966.

STILLER, JERRY: NYC, June 8, 1931.

STIMSON, SARA: Helotes, TX, 1973.

STING (Gordon Matthew Sumner): Wallsend, England, Oct. 2, 1951.

STOCKWELL, DEAN: Hollywood, Mar. 5, 1935.

STOCKWELL, JOHN (John Samuels, IV): Galveston, TX, Mar. 25, 1961. Harvard.

STOLER, SHIRLEY: Brooklyn, NY, Mar. 30, 1929.

STOLTZ, ERIC: California, Sept. 30, 1961. USC.

STONE, DEE WALLACE (Deanna Bowers): Kansas City, MO, Dec. 14, 1948. UKS.

STORM, GALE (Josephine Cottle): Bloomington, TX, Apr. 5, 1922.

STOWE, MADELEINE: Eagle Rock, CA, Aug. 18, 1958.

STRAIGHT, BEATRICE: Old Westbury, NY, Aug. 2, 1916. Dartington Hall.

STRASBERG, SUSAN: NYC, May 22, 1938.

STRASSMAN, MARCIA: New Jersey, Apr. 28, 1948.

STRATHAIRN, DAVID: San Francisco, Jan. 26, 1949.

STRAUSS, PETER: NYC, Feb. 20, 1947.

STREEP, MERYL (Mary Louise): Summit, NJ, June 22, 1949. Vassar, Yale.

STREISAND, BARBRA: Brooklyn, NY, Apr. 24, 1942.

STRITCH, ELAINE: Detroit, MI, Feb. 2, 1925. Drama Workshop.

STROUD, DON: Honolulu, HI, Sept. 1, 1937.

STRUTHERS, SALLY: Portland, OR, July 28, 1948. Pasadena Playhouse.

SUMMER, DONNA (LaDonna Gaines): Boston, MA, Dec. 31, 1948.

SUTHERLAND, DONALD: St. John, New Brunswick, Canada, July 17, 1935. U Toronto.

SUTHERLAND, KIEFER: Los Angeles, CA, Dec. 18, 1966.

SVENSON, BO: Goreborg, Sweden, Feb. 13, 1941. UCLA.

SWAYZE, PATRICK: Houston, TX, Aug. 18, 1952.

SWEENEY, D. B. (Daniel Bernard Sweeney): Shoreham, NY, 1961.

SWINBURNE, NORA: Bath, England, July 24, 1902. RADA.

SWIT, LORETTA: Passaic, NJ, Nov. 4, 1937. AADA.

SYLVESTER, WILLIAM: Oakland, CA, Jan. 31, 1922. RADA.

SYMONDS, ROBERT: Bistow, AK, Dec. 1, 1926. TexU.

SYMS, SYLVIA: London, June 1, 1934. Convent School.

SZARABAJKA, KEITH: Oak Park, IL, Dec. 2, 1952. UChicago.

T, MR. (Lawrence Tero): Chicago, IL, May 21, 1952.

TABORI, KRISTOFFER (Siegel): Los Angeles, Aug. 4, 1952.

TAKEI, GEORGE: Los Angeles, CA, Apr. 20, 1939. UCLA.

TALBOT, LYLE (Lysle Hollywood): Pittsburgh, Feb. 8, 1904.

TALBOT, NITA: NYC, Aug. 8, 1930. Irvine Studio School.

TAMBLYN, RUSS: Los Angeles, Dec. 30, 1934.

TARANTINO, QUENTIN: Knoxville, TN, Mar. 27, 1963.

TAYLOR, DON: Freeport, PA, Dec. 13, 1920. Penn State U.

TAYLOR, ELIZABETH: London, Feb. 27, 1932. Byron House School.

TAYLOR, RENEE: NYC, Mar. 19, 1935.

TAYLOR, ROD (Robert): Sydney, Aust., Jan. 11, 1929.

TAYLOR-YOUNG, LEIGH: Washington, DC, Jan. 25, 1945. Northwestern.

TEAGUE, ANTHONY SCOOTER: Jacksboro, TX, Jan. 4, 1940.

TEAGUE, MARSHALL: Newport, TN.

TEEFY, MAUREEN: Minneapolis, MN, 1954, Juilliard.

TEMPLE, SHIRLEY: Santa Monica, CA, Apr. 23, 1927.

TENNANT, VICTORIA: London, England, Sept. 30, 1950.

TERZIEFF, LAURENT: Paris, France, June 25, 1935.

TEWES, LAUREN: Pennsylvania, 1954.

THACKER, RUSS: Washington, DC, June 23, 1946. Montgomery College.

THAXTER, PHYLLIS: Portland, ME, Nov. 20, 1921. St. Genevieve.

THELEN, JODI: St. Cloud, MN, 1963.

THOMAS, HENRY: San Antonio, TX, Sept. 8, 1971.

THOMAS, JAY: New Orleans, July 12, 1948.

THOMAS, MARLO (Margaret): Detroit, Nov. 21, 1938. USC.

THOMAS, PHILIP MICHAEL: Columbus, OH, May 26, 1949. Oakwood College.

THOMAS, RICHARD: NYC, June 13, 1951. Columbia.

THOMPSON, EMMA: London, England, Apr.15, 1959. Cambridge.

THOMPSON, FRED DALTON: Laurenceberg, TN, Aug. 19, 1942

THOMPSON, JACK (John Payne): Sydney, Australia, Aug. 31, 1940.

THOMPSON, LEA: Rochester, MN, May 31, 1961.

THOMPSON, REX: NYC, Dec. 14, 1942.

THOMPSON, SADA: Des Moines, IA, Sept. 27, 1929. Carnegie Tech.

THOMSON, GORDON: Ottawa, Canada, 1945.

Alan Rickman

Eric Roberts

Roy Scheider

Vincent Spano

THORSON, LINDA: Toronto, Canada, June 18, 1947. RADA.

THULIN, INGRID: Solleftea, Sweden, Jan. 27, 1929. Royal Drama Theatre.

THURMAN, UMA: Boston, MA, Apr. 29, 1970.

TICOTIN, RACHEL: Bronx, NY, Nov. 1, 1958.

TIERNEY, LAWRENCE: Brooklyn, NY, Mar. 15, 1919. Manhattan College.

TIFFIN, PAMELA (Wonso): Oklahoma City, OK, Oct. 13, 1942.

TIGHE, KEVIN: Los Angeles, Aug. 13, 1944.

TILLY, MEG: Texada, Canada, Feb. 14, 1960.

TOBOLOWSKY, STEPHEN: Dallas, Tx, May 30, 1951. So. Methodist U.

TODD, BEVERLY: Chicago, IL, July 1, 1946.

TODD, RICHARD: Dublin, Ireland, June 11, 1919. Shrewsbury School.

TOLKAN, JAMES: Calumet, MI, June 20, 1931.

TOLO, MARILU: Rome, Italy, 1944.

TOMEI, MARISA: Brooklyn, NY, Dec. 4, 1964. NYU.

TOMLIN, LILY: Detroit, MI, Sept. 1, 1939. Wayne State U.

TOPOL (Chaim Topol): Tel-Aviv, Israel, Sept. 9, 1935.

TORN, RIP: Temple, TX, Feb. 6, 1931. UTex.

TORRES, LIZ: NYC, 1947. NYU.

TOTTER, AUDREY: Joliet, IL, Dec. 20, 1918.

TOWSEND, ROBERT: Chicago, IL, Feb. 6, 1957.

TRAVANTI, DANIEL J.: Kenosha, WI, Mar. 7, 1940.

TRAVIS, NANCY: Astoria, NY, Sept. 21, 1961.

TRAVOLTA, JOEY: Englewood, NJ, 1952.

TRAVOLTA, JOHN: Englewood, NJ, Feb. 18, 1954.

TREMAYNE, LES: London, Apr. 16, 1913. Northwestern, Columbia, UCLA.

TREVOR, CLAIRE (Wemlinger): NYC, March 8, 1909.

TRINTIGNANT, JEAN-LOUIS: Pont-St. Esprit, France, Dec. 11, 1930. DullinBalachova Drama School.

TSOPEI, CORINNA: Athens, Greece, June 21, 1944.

TUBB, BARRY: Snyder, TX, 1963. AmConsv Th.

TUCKER, MICHAEL: Baltimore, MD, Feb. 6, 1944.

TUNE, TOMMY: Wichita Falls, TX, Feb. 28, 1939.

TURNER, JANINE (Gauntt): Lincoln, NE, Dec. 6, 1963.

TURNER, KATHLEEN: Springfield, MO, June 19, 1954. UMd.

TURNER, TINA (Anna Mae Bullock): Nutbush, TN, Nov. 26, 1938.

TURTURRO, JOHN: Brooklyn, NY, Feb. 28, 1957. Yale.

TUSHINGHAM, RITA: Liverpool, England, Mar. 14, 1940.

TUTIN, DOROTHY: London, Apr. 8, 1930.

TWIGGY (Lesley Hornby): London, Sept. 19, 1949.

TWOMEY, ANNE: Boston, MA, June 7, 1951. Temple U.

TYLER, BEVERLY (Beverly Jean Saul): Scranton, PA, July 5, 1928.

TYRRELL, SUSAN: San Francisco, 1946.

TYSON, CATHY: Liverpool, England, 1966. Royal Shake. Co.

TYSON, CICELY: NYC, Dec. 19, 1933. NYU.

UGGAMS, LESLIE: NYC, May 25, 1943. Juilliard.

ULLMAN, TRACEY: Slough, England, Dec. 30, 1959.

ULLMANN, LIV: Tokyo, Dec. 10, 1938. Webber-Douglas Acad.

UMEKI, MIYOSHI: Otaru, Hokaido, Japan, 1929.

UNDERWOOD, BLAIR: Tacoma, WA, Aug. 25, 1964. Carnegie-Mellon U.

URICH, ROBERT: Toronto, Canada, Dec. 19, 1946.

USTINOV, PETER: London, Apr. 16, 1921. Westminster School.

VACCARO, BRENDA: Brooklyn, NY, Nov. 18, 1939. Neighborhood Playhouse.

VALANDREY, CHARLOTTE (Anne Charlone Pascal): Paris, France, 1968.

VALLI, ALIDA: Pola, Italy, May 31, 1921. Academy of Drama.

VALLONE, RAF: Riogio, Italy, Feb. 17, 1916. Turin U.

VAN ARK, JOAN: NYC, June 16, 1943. Yale.

VAN DAMME, JEAN-CLAUDE (J-C Vorenberg): Brussels, Belgium, Apr. 1, 1960.

VAN DE VEN, MONIQUE: Holland, 1957.

VAN DEVERE, TRISH (Patricia Dressel): Englewood Cliffs, NJ, Mar. 9, 1945. Ohio Wesleyan.

VAN DOREN, MAMIE (Joan Lucile Olander): Rowena SD, Feb. 6, 1933.

VAN DYKE, DICK: West Plains, MO, Dec. 13, 1925.

VAN FLEET, JO: Oakland, CA, Dec. 30, 1919.

VANITY (Denise Mathews): Niagara, Ont., Can, 1963.

VAN PALLANDT, NINA: Copenhagen, Denmark, July 15, 1932.

VAN PATTEN, DICK: NYC, Dec. 9, 1928.

VAN PATTEN, JOYCE: NYC, Mar. 9, 1934.

VAN PEEBLES, MARIO: NYC, Jan. 15, 1958. Columbia U.

VAN PEEBLES, MELVIN: Chicago, IL, Aug. 21, 1932.

VANCE, COURTNEY B.: Detroit, MI, Mar. 12, 1960.

VARNEY, JIM: Lexington, KY, June 15, 1949.

VAUGHN, ROBERT: NYC, Nov. 22, 1932. USC.

VEGA, ISELA: Mexico, 1940.

VELJOHNSON, REGINALD: NYC, Aug. 16, 1952.

VENNERA, CHICK: Herkimer, NY, Mar. 27, 1952. Pasadena Playhouse.

VENORA, DIANE: Hartford, CT, 1952. Juilliard.

VERDON, GWEN: Culver City, CA, Jan. 13, 1925.

VERNON, JOHN: Montreal, Canada, Feb. 24, 1932.

VEREEN, BEN: Miami, FL, Oct. 10, 1946.

VICTOR, JAMES (Lincoln Rafael Peralta Diaz): Santiago, D.R., July 27, 1939. Haaren HS/NYC.

VINCENT, JAN-MICHAEL: Denver, CO, July 15, 1944. Ventura.

VIOLET, ULTRA (Isabelle Collin-Dufresne): Grenoble, France.

VITALE, MILLY: Rome, Italy, July 16, 1928. Lycee Chateaubriand.

VOHS, JOAN: St. Albans, NY, July 30, 1931.

VOIGHT, JON: Yonkers, NY, Dec. 29, 1938. Catholic U.

VON DOHLEN, LENNY: Augusta, GA, Dec. 22, 1958. UTex.

VON SYDOW, MAX: Lund, Sweden, July 10, 1929. Royal Drama Theatre.

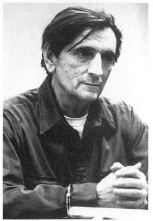
Harry Dean Stanton

Daniel Stern

Fisher Stevens

David Strathairn

WAGNER, LINDSAY: Los Angeles, June 22. 1949.

WAGNER, ROBERT: Detroit, Feb. 10, 1930.

WAHL, KEN: Chicago, IL, Feb. 14, 1953.

WAITE, GENEVIEVE: South Africa, 1949.

WAITE, RALPH: White Plains, NY, June 22, 1929. Yale.

WAITS, TOM: Pomona, CA, Dec. 7, 1949.

WALKEN, CHRISTOPHER: Astoria, NY, Mar. 31, 1943. Hofstra.

WALKER, CLINT: Hartfold, IL, May 30, 1927. USC.

WALLACH, ELI: Brooklyn, NY, Dec. 7, 1915. CCNY, U Tex.

WALLACH, ROBERTA: NYC, Aug. 2, 1955.

WALLIS, SHANI: London, Apr. 5, 1941.

WALSH, J.T.: San Francisco,. CA. Sept. 28, 1943.

WALSH, M. EMMET: Ogdensburg, NY, Mar. 22, 1935. Clarkson College, AADA.

WALSTON, RAY: New Orleans, Nov. 22, 1917. Cleveland Playhouse.

WALTER, JESSICA: Brooklyn, NY, Jan. 31, 1944 Neighborhood Playhouse.

WALTER, TRACEY: Jersey City, NJ, Nov. 25, 1942.

WALTERS, JULIE: London, Feb. 22, 1950.

WALTON, EMMA: London, Nov. 1962. Brown U.

WARD, BURT (Gervis): Los Angeles, July 6, 1945.

WARD, FRED: San Diego, CA, Dec. 30, 1942.

WARD, RACHEL: London, Sept. 12, 1957.

WARD, SELA: Meridian, MS, July 11, 1956.

WARD, SIMON: London, Oct. 19, 1941.

WARDEN, JACK (Lebzelter): Newark, NJ, Sept. 18, 1920.

WARNER, DAVID: Manchester, England, July 29, 1941. RADA.

WARNER, MALCOLM-JAMAL: Jersey City, NJ, Aug. 18, 1970.

WARREN, JENNIFER: NYC, Aug. 12, 1941. U Wisc.

WARREN, LESLEY ANN: NYC, Aug. 16, 1946.

WARREN, MICHAEL: South Bend, IN, Mar. 5, 1946. UCLA.

WARRICK, RUTH: St. Joseph, MO, June 29, 1915. U Mo.

WASHINGTON, DENZEL: Mt. Vernon, NY, Dec. 28, 1954. Fordham.

WASSON, CRAIG: Ontario, OR, Mar. 15, 1954. UOre.

WATERSTON, SAM: Cambridge, MA, Nov. 15, 1940. Yale.

WATLING, JACK: London, Jan. 13, 1923. Italia Conti School.

WAYANS, DAMON: NYC, 1960.

WAYANS, KEENEN, IVORY: NYC, June 8, 1958. Tuskegee Inst.

WAYNE, PATRICK: Los Angeles, July 15, 1939. Loyola.

WEATHERS, CARL: New Orleans, LA, Jan. 14, 1948. Long Beach CC.

WEAVER, DENNIS: Joplin, MO, June 4, 1924. U Okla.

WEAVER, FRITZ: Pittsburgh, PA, Jan. 19, 1926.

WEAVER, MARJORIE: Crossville, TN, Mar. 2, 1913. Indiana U.

WEAVER, SIGOURNEY (Susan): NYC, Oct. 8, 1949. Stanford, Yale.

WEDGEWORTH, ANN: Abilene, TX, Jan. 21, 1935. U Tex.

WELCH, RAQUEL (Tejada): Chicago, IL, Sept. 5, 1940.

WELD, TUESDAY (Susan): NYC, Aug. 27, 1943. Hollywood Professional School.

WELDON, JOAN: San Francisco, Aug. 5, 1933. San Francisco Conservatory.

WELLER, PETER: Stevens Point, WI, June 24, 1947. AmThWing.

WENDT, GEORGE: Chicago, IL, Oct. 17, 1948.

WEST, ADAM (William Anderson): Walla Walla, WA, Sept. 19, 1929.

WESTON, JACK (Morris Weinstein): Cleveland, OH, Aug. 21, 1924.

WETTIG, PATRICIA: Cincinatti, OH, Dec. 4, 1951. TempleU.

WHALEY, FRANK: Syracuse, NY, July 20, 1963. SUNY/Albany.

WHALLEY-KILMER, JOANNE: Manchester, England, Aug. 25, 1964.

WHEATON, WIL: Burbank, CA, July 29, 1972.

WHITAKER, FOREST: Longview, TX, July 15, 1961.

John Travolta

John Turturro

Ben Vereen

Elijah Wood

WHITAKER, JOHNNY: Van Nuys, CA, Dec. 13, 1959.

WHITE, BETTY: Oak Park, IL, Jan. 17, 1922.

WHITE, CHARLES: Perth Amboy, NJ, Aug. 29, 1920. Rutgers U.

WHITE, JESSE: Buffalo, NY, Jan. 3, 1919.

WHITELAW, BILLIE: Coventry, England, June 6, 1932.

WHITMAN, STUART: San Francisco, Feb. 1, 1929. CCLA.

WHITMORE, JAMES: White Plains, NY, Oct. 1, 1921. Yale.

WHITNEY, GRACE LEE: Detroit, MI, Apr. 1, 1930.

WHITTON, MARGARET: Philadelphia, PA, Nov, 30, 1950.

WIDDOES, KATHLEEN: Wilmington, DE, Mar. 21, 1939.

WIDMARK, RICHARD: Sunrise, MN, Dec. 26, 1914. Lake Forest.

WIEST, DIANNE: Kansas City, MO, Mar. 28, 1948. UMd.

WILBY, JAMES: Burma, Feb. 20, 1958.

WILCOX, COLIN: Highlands, NC, Feb. 4, 1937. U Tenn.

WILDER, GENE (Jerome Silberman): Milwaukee, WI, June 11, 1935. UIowa.

WILLIAMS, BILLY DEE: NYC, Apr. 6, 1937.

WILLIAMS, CARA (Bernice Kamiat): Brooklyn, NY, 1925.

WILLIAMS, CINDY: Van Nuys, CA, Aug. 22, 1947. KACC.

WILLIAMS, CLARENCE, III: NYC, Aug. 21, 1939.

WILLIAMS, DICK A.: Chicago, IL, Aug. 9, 1938.

WILLIAMS, ESTHER: Los Angeles, Aug. 8, 1921.

WILLIAMS, JOBETH: Houston, TX, Dec 6, 1948. Brown U.

WILLIAMS, PAUL: Omaha, NE, Sept. 19, 1940.

WILLIAMS, ROBIN: Chicago, IL, July 21, 1951. Juilliard.

WILLIAMS, TREAT (Richard): Rowayton, CT, Dec. 1, 1951.

WILLIAMSON, FRED: Gary, IN, Mar. 5, 1938. Northwestern.

WILLIAMSON, NICOL: Hamilton, Scotland, Sept. 14, 1938.

WILLIS, BRUCE: Penns Grove, NJ, Mar. 19, 1955.

WILLISON, WALTER: Monterey Park, CA, June 24, 1947.

WILSON, DEMOND: NYC, Oct. 13, 1946. Hunter College.

WILSON, ELIZABETH: Grand Rapids, MI, Apr. 4, 1925.

WILSON, FLIP (Clerow Wilson): Jersey City, NJ, Dec. 8, 1933.

WILSON, LAMBERT: Paris, France, 1959.

WILSON, NANCY: Chillicothe, OH, Feb. 20, 1937.

WILSON, SCOTT: Atlanta, GA, 1942.

WINCOTT, JEFF: Toronto, Canada, 1957.

WINDE, BEATRICE: Chicago, IL, Jan. 6.

WINDOM, WILLIAM: NYC, Sept. 28, 1923. Williams College.

WINDSOR, MARIE (Emily Marie Bertelson): Marysvale, UT, Dec. 11, 1924. Brigham Young U.

WINFIELD, PAUL: Los Angeles, May 22, 1940. UCLA.

WINFREY, OPRAH: Kosciusko, MS, Jan. 29, 1954. TnStateU.

WINGER, DEBRA: Cleveland, OH, May 17, 1955. Cal State.

WINKLER, HENRY: NYC, Oct. 30, 1945. Yale.

WINN, KITTY: Washingtohn, D.C., 1944. Boston U.

WINNINGHAM, MARE: Phoenix, AZ, May 6, 1959.

WINSLOW, MICHAEL: Spokane, WA, Sept. 6, 1960.

WINTER, ALEX: London, July 17, 1965. NYU.

WINTERS, JONATHAN: Dayton, OH, Nov. 11, 1925. Kenyon College.

WINTERS, SHELLEY (Shirley Schrift): St. Louis, Aug. 18, 1922. Wayne U.

WITHERS, GOOGIE: Karachi, India, Mar. 12, 1917. Italia Conti.

WITHERS, JANE: Atlanta, GA, Apr. 12, 1926.

WONG, B.D.: San Francisco, Oct. 24,1962.

WONG, RUSSELL: Troy, NY, 1963. SantaMonica College.

WOOD, ELIJAH: Cedar Rapids, IA, Jan 28, 1981.

WOODARD, ALFRE: Tulsa, OK, Nov. 2, 1953. Boston U.

WOODLAWN, HOLLY (Harold Ajzen-berg): Juana Diaz, PR, 1947.

WOODS, JAMES: Vernal, UT, Apr. 18, 1947. MIT.

WOODWARD, EDWARD: Croyden, Surrey, England, June 1, 1930.

WOODWARD, JOANNE: Thomasville, GA, Feb. 27, 1930. Neighborhood Playhouse.

WORONOV, MARY: Brooklyn, NY, Dec. 8, 1946. Cornell.

WORTH, IRENE (Hattie Abrams): Nebraska, June 23, 1916. UCLA.

WRAY, FAY: Alberta, Canada, Sept. 15, 1907.

WRIGHT, AMY: Chicago, IL, Apr. 15, 1950.

WRIGHT, MAX: Detroit, MI, Aug. 2, 1943. WayneStateU.

WRIGHT, ROBIN: Dallas, TX, Apr. 8, 1966.

WRIGHT, TERESA: NYC, Oct. 27, 1918.

WUHL, ROBERT: Union City, NJ, Oct. 9, 1951. UHouston.

WYATT, JANE: NYC, Aug. 10, 1910. Barnard College.

WYMAN, JANE (Sarah Jane Fulks): St. Joseph, MO, Jan. 4, 1914.

WYMORE, PATRICE: Miltonvale, KS, Dec. 17, 1926.

WYNN, MAY (Donna Lee Hickey): NYC, Jan. 8, 1930.

WYNTER, DANA (Dagmar): London, June 8. 1927. Rhodes U.

YORK, DICK: Fort Wayne, IN, Sept. 4, 1928. De Paul U.

YORK, MICHAEL: Fulmer, England, Mar. 27, 1942. Oxford.

YORK, SUSANNAH: London, Jan. 9, 1941. RADA.

YOUNG, ALAN (Angus): North Shield, England, Nov. 19, 1919.

YOUNG, BURT: Queens, NY, Apr. 30, 1940.

YOUNG, CHRIS: Chambersburg, PA, Apr. 28, 1971.

YOUNG, LORETTA (Gretchen): Salt Lake City, UT, Jan. 6, 1912. Immaculate Heart College.

YOUNG, ROBERT: Chicago, IL, Feb. 22, 1907.

YOUNG, SEAN: Louisville, KY, Nov. 20, 1959. Interlochen.

ZACHARIAS, ANN: Stockholm, Sweden, Sweden, 1956.

ZADORA, PIA: Hoboken, NJ, 1954.

ZERBE, ANTHONY: Long Beach, CA, May 20, 1939.

ZIMBALIST, EFREM, JR.: NYC, Nov.30, 1918. Yale.

ZUNIGA, DAPHNE: Berkeley, CA, 1962. UCLA.

OBITUARIES

GEORGE ABBOTT, 107, one of the theatre's most prominent directors, died of a stroke on January 31, 1995 at his home in Miami Beach. Among his stage credits are *On Your Toes*, *Pal Joey*, *High Button Shoes*, *Call Me Madam*, *Wonderful Town*, *Fiorello!*, and *A Funny Thing Happened on the Way to the Forum*. On screen he directed such films as *Why Bring That Up?*, *The Sea God*, *My Sin*, and *Too Many Girls*, and co-directed *The Pajama Game* and *Damn Yankees*. Survived by his wife, a sister, 2 granddaughters, a grandson, and 6 great-grandchildren.

AL ADAMSON, 66, B-movie director, was found buried under the flooring of his house in Indio, CA, on Aug. 2, 1995. He had been reported missing for more than five weeks. His films include *Hell's Bloody Devils*, *Dracula vs. Frankenstein*, *Blood of Dracula's Castle*, *Blood of Ghastly Horror*, and *The Naughty Stewardesses*. No survivors reported.

MAXENE ANDREWS, 79, member of the popular 1940s singing trio The Andrews Sisters, died of a heart attack in Hyannis, MA, on Oct. 21, 1995. With sisters LaVerne (who died in 1967) and Patti she recorded such hits as "Hold Tight," "Beer Barrel Polka," "Boogie Woogie Bugle Boy," and "Rum and Coca-Cola." They appeared as themselves in such movies as *Argentine Nights*, *Buck Privates*, *In the Navy*, *Hold That Ghost*, *Give Out Sisters*, *What's Cookin'?*, *How's About It?*, *Follow the Boys* (1944), *Hollywood Canteen*, *Moonlight and Cactus*, *Swingtime Johnny*, and *Road to Rio*. In addition to her younger sister she is survived by a daughter, a son, an adopted daughter, a foster son, and 1 grandchild.

RICK AVILES, 41, Manhattan-born actor and comedian, best known for his role as the hired killer in *Ghost*, died of heart failure on Mar. 17, 1995 in Los Angeles. His other movie credits include *Cannonball Run*, *Mystery Train*, *The Godfather Part III*, *Green Card*, *The Saint of Fort Washington*, *Carlito's Way*, and *Waterworld*. Survived by his parents, 2 sisters and a brother.

TONY AZITO, 46, Manhattan-born screen, stage and TV actor, best known for playing the loose-limbed police sergeant in the Broadway revival of *The Pirates of Penzance* and its subsequent film adaptation, died of AIDS on May 26, 1995 in New York City. His other movies include *Private Resort*, *Moonstruck*, *Bloodhounds of Broadway* and *The Addams Family*. Survived by his mother, a sister, and 3 brothers.

THOMAS BECK, 86, 1930s film actor died in Miami Shores, FL, on Sept. 23, 1995. His movies include *Charlie Chan in Egypt*, *Charlie Chan at the Opera*, *White Fang* (1936), *Under Two Flag*, *Seventh Heaven* (1937), *Heidi* (1937), and *The Family Next Door*. No reported survivors.

VIVIAN BLAINE (Vivian Stapleton), 74, Newark-born screen, stage and TV actress, best remembered for playing Adelaide in the original 1950 Broadway production and 1955 film version of the musical *Guys and Dolls*, died of congestive heart failure on Dec. 9, 1995, in Manhattan. Following her 1942 film debut in *Through Different Eyes*, she was seen in such movies as *Jitterbugs*, *Greenwich Village*, *Something for the Boys*, *Nob Hill*, *State Fair* (1945), *Three Little Girls in Blue*, *Skirts Ahoy*, *Public Pigeon No. 1*, *The Dark*, and *Parasite*. Her three marriages ended in divorce. No survivors.

RALPH BLANE, 81, lyricist who, with composer Hugh Martin, wrote the songs for one of Hollywood's best loved musicals, *Meet Me in St. Louis*, producing the hits "The Trolley Song," "Have Yourself a Merry Little Christmas," and "The Boy Next Door," died at his birthplace of Broken Arrow, OK, on Nov. 13, 1995. His work was heard in such other films as *Best Foot Forward*, *Easy to Wed*, *Good News* ("Pass That Peace Pipe"), *Summer Holiday*, *One Sunday Afternoon*, *My Dream Is Yours*, *Athena*, and *The Girl Rush*. Survived by his son.

JULIAN BLAUSTEIN, 82, film producer, died on June 20, 1995 at his home in Beverly Hills, CA. Among his movie credits are *Broken Arrow* (1950), *Mister 880*, *The Day the Earth Stood Still*, *The Outcasts of Poker Flat*, *Don't Bother to Knock*, *Desiree*, *Storm Center*, *Cowboy*, *Bell Book and Candle*, *The Wreck of the Mary Deare*, and *Khartoum*. Survived by his wife, a son, a daughter, and 4 grandchildren.

Janet Blair

Robert Bolt

EDWIN BLUM, 89, Atlantic City-born screenwriter died on May 2, 1995 in Santa Monica, CA. His credits include *The Adventures of Sherlock Holmes*, *The Canterville Ghost*, *Down to Earth*, and *Stalag 17*. Survived by his wife, a daughter, a son, and 4 grandchildren.

ROBERT BOLT, 70, British screenwriter and playwright who won Oscars for his work on the films *Doctor Zhivago* and *A Man for All Seasons* (from his play), died on Feb. 20, 1995, at his home near Petersfield, Hampshire, England. He had been suffering from heart trouble. His other scripts include *Lawrence of Arabia*, *Ryan's Daughter*, *Lady Caroline Lamb* (which he also directed), *The Bounty*, and *The Mission*. Survived by his wife, actress Sarah Miles, and 4 children.

PHILIP BORSOS, 41, Canadian film director died of leukemia January of 1995 in Vancouver. His credits include *The Grey Fox*, *The Mean Season*, *One Magic Christmas*, and *Far From Home: The Adventures of Yellow Dog*. No reported survivors.

JEREMY BRETT (Peter Jeremy Huggins), 59, British screen, stage, and TV actor, who found his greatest fame portraying Sherlock Holmes in a series of mysteries for the BBC, died of a heart failure on Sept. 12, 1995, in London. His film credits include *War and Peace* (1956), *The Wild and the Willing*, *My Fair Lady* (as Freddy Eynsford-Hill), *Nicholas and Alexandra*, and *The Medusa Touch*. Survived by a son from his first marriage to actress Anna Massey.

Philip Borsos

Jeremy Brett

Rosalind Cash

Elisha Cook, Jr.

Peter Cook

Gary Crosby

LILLIAN BRONSON, 92, character actress died on Aug. 1, 1995 in San Clemente. Her films include *Family Honeymoon*, *The Hucksters*, and *Spencer's Mountain*. No reporter survivors.

PHYLLIS BROOKS (Phyllis Weiler), 80, Idaho-born screen and stage actress of the 1930s and 1940s died at her home in Cape Neddick, ME, on Aug. 1, 1995. Her credits include *I've Been Around*, *You Can't Have Everything*, *Rebecca of Sunnybrook Farm* (1938), *In Old Chicago*, *Charlie Chan in Honolulu*, *Slightly Honorable*, *The Shanghai Gesture*, *Lady in the Dark*, *The Unseen*, and *Dangerous Passage*. She retired from show business after her marriage in 1945. Survived by 2 sons, 2 daughters, a brother, and 8 grandchildren.

ROSALIND CASH, 56, Atlantic City-born screen, stage, and TV actress, died of cancer on Oct. 31, 1995, in Los Angeles. Her movie credits include *Klute*, *The Omega Man*, *Hickey and Boggs*, *The New Centurians*, *Melinda*, *Uptown Saturday Night*, *Cornbread Earl and Me*, *The Monkey Hustle*, *Wrong Is Right*, *The Adventures of Buckaroo Banzai*, *The Offspring*, and *Tales From the Hood*. One of the original members of the Negro Ensemble Company, she was also a regular on the daytime serial "General Hospital." Survived by a sister and 2 brothers.

JACK CLAYTON, 73, British film director who received an Oscar nomination for his first feature, *Room at the Top*, died on Feb. 25, 1995, in Slough, England. He had been suffering from heart and liver problems. His six other credits are *The Innocents*, *The Pumpkin Eater*, *Our Mother's House*, *The Great Gatsby* (1974), *Something Wicked This Way Comes*, and *The Lonely Passion of Judith Hearne*. Survived by his wife, actress Haya Harareet.

ELISHA COOK, JR., 91, San Francisco-born screen, stage and TV actor who became one of the industry's most prolific character players, appearing in over 100 films, died in Big Pine, CA, on May 18, 1995. Among his movies are *Pigskin Parade*, *Love Is News*, *They Won't Forget*, *Newsboys' Home*, *Submarine Patrol*, *Tin Pan Alley*, *Love Crazy*, *The Maltese Falcon* (perhaps his most famous role, as Wilmer, the Gunsel), *I Wake Up Screaming*, *Phantom Lady*, *Up in Arms*, *Dark Waters*, *Dillinger* (1945), *Cinderella Jones*, *The Big Sleep* (1946), *The Long Night*, *The Gangster*, *The Great Gatsby* (1949), *Don't Bother to Knock*, *Shane*, *I the Jury* (1953), *The Killing*, *Chicago Confidential*, *Baby Face Nelson*, *House on Haunted Hill*, *Platinum High School*, *One-Eyed Jacks*, *Black Zoo*, *The Haunted Palace*, *Rosemary's Baby*, *The Great Northfield Minnesota Raid*, *Blacula*, *Electra Glide in Blue*, *The Black Bird*, *The Champ* (1979), *1941*, *Carny*, *Tom Horn*, and *Hammett*. No immediate survivors.

PETER COOK, 57, British actor, writer and comedian, formerly a member of the satirical revue *Beyond the Fringe*, died of a gastrointestinal hemorrhage on Jan. 9, 1995 in London. Originally partnered with Dudley Moore, Cook made his film debut with him in 1966's *The Wrong Box*. There followed such films as *Bedazzled* (which he also co-wrote), *Monte*

Carlo or Bust (Those Daring Young Men in Their Jaunty Jalopies), *The Bed Sitting Room*, *The Rise and Rise of Michael Rimmer* (also writer), *The Hound of the Baskervilles* (1977; also co-writer), *Yellowbeard* (also co-writer), *Supergirl*, *The Princess Bride*, *Without a Clue*, and his last, *Black Beauty*, in 1994. Survived by his third wife and 2 daughters from his first marriage.

HOWARD COSELL (Howard William Cohen), 77, controversial sportscaster who spent fourteen years as commentator on ABC's "Monday Night Football," died of a heart embolism in Manhattan on Apr. 23, 1995. He made appearances as himself in the films *Bananas*, *The World's Greatest Athlete*, *Two Minute Warning*, and *Broadway Danny Rose*. Survived by 2 daughters and 6 grandchildren.

JOHN CRAVEN, 79, New York City-born film, stage, and TV actor, best know for creating the role of George in the original 1938 production of *Our Town*, died on Nov. 24, 1995 at his home in Salt Point, NY. His movie credits include *The Human Comedy*, *Dr. Gillespie's Criminal Case*, *The Purple Heart*, *Friendly Persuasion*, and *Ocean's Eleven*. The son of actor Frank Craven, he is survived by his wife, 2 sons, a daughter, and 3 grandchildren.

GARY CROSBY, 62, screen and TV actor, died of lung cancer on Aug. 24, 1995, in Burbank, CA. The eldest son of performer Bing Crosby he made his screen debut in 1942 playing himself in his father's film *Star Spangled Rhythm*. His other movies include *Holiday for Lovers*, *A Private's Affair*, *Mardi Gras*, *Girl Happy*, and *The Night Stalker*. On TV he was a regular on the series *Adam-12*. Survived by a son and his brother, Philip.

SEVERN DARDEN, 65, improvisational comedian and actor, one of the founders of Chicago's Second City troupe, died of heart failure at his home in Santa Fe, NM, on May 26, 1995. His movie credits include *Luv*, *Dead Heat on a Merry-Go-Round*, *Planet of the Apes*, *The President's Analyst*, *They Shoot Horses Don't They?*, *The Hired Hand*, *The Last Movie*, *Real Genius*, *In God We TruSt*, *Why Would I Lie?*, and *Back to School*. Survived by his wife and a son.

KATHERINE DeMILLE, 83, Canadian born screen actress, the adopted daughter of director Cecil B. DeMille, died of Alzheimer's disease on Apr. 27, 1995. Her films include *Viva Villa*, *Call of the Wild* (1935), *Ramona*, *Blockade*, *Reap the Wild Wind*, *The Story of Dr. Wassell*, and *Unconquered*. Survived by her children from her marriage to actor Anthony Quinn.

CHARLES DENNER, 69, French actor, perhaps best known for starring in Francois Truffaut's *The Man Who Loved Women*, died of cancer in Dreux, France on Sept. 10, 1995. His other films include *Landru*, *Life Upside Down*, *The Sleeping Car Murder*, *The Two of Us*, *The Bride Wore Black*, and *Such a Gorgeous Kid Like Me*. No reported survivors.

CY ENDFIELD, 80, Pennsylvania-born film director who relocated to Britain following the 1950s blacklisting period, died on Apr. 16, 1995, at his home in Shipston-on-Stour, Warwickshire, England of unspecified causes. His credits include *Gentleman Joe Palooka*, *Tarzan's Savage Fury*, *Hell Drivers*, *Mysterious Island*, *Zulu*, and *Sands of the Kalahari*. Survived by his wife and 2 daughters.

ED FLANDERS, 60, Minneapolis-born screen, stage, and TV actor, died of a self-inflicted gunshot wound to the head at his home in Denny, CA, on Feb. 22, 1995. He won a Tony Award for *A Moon for the Misbegotten* and an Emmy for his role on the series "St. Elsewhere." His movies include *The Grasshopper*, *MacArthur*, *Twinkle Twinkle Killer Kane (The Ninfth Configuration)*, *True Confessions*, *The Pursuit of D.B. Cooper*, and *Bye Bye Love*, released posthumously. No reported survivors.

ART FLEMING, 70, New York City-born actor and game show host, died of pancreatic cancer on Apr. 25, 1995 at his home in Crystal River, FL. He served as host of the quiz shows "Jeopardy!" (the original run of the series from 1964–1974) and "College Bowl," and appeared in such features as *A Hatful of Rain*, *MacArthur*, and *Airplane II: The Sequel*. Survived by his wife, a daughter, a sister, 2 stepchildren, and 5 grandchildren.

FRIZ FRELENG (Isadore Freleng), 89, Kansas City-born animator who helped create some of the classic Looney Tunes cartoons, died in Los Angeles on May 26, 1995. He received Academy Awards for the short films *Tweety Pie* (1947), *Speedy Gonzalez* (1955), *Birds Anonymous* (1957), *Knighty Knight Bugs* (1958), and *The Pink Phink* (1964). Survived by his wife, 2 daughters, and 4 grandchildren.

Alexander Godunov

Harry Guardino

Ed Flanders

Eva Gabor

GALE GORDON, 89, New York City-born screen, TV, and radio actor, best known for his frequent work opposite Lucille Ball, died of cancer on June 30, 1995, in Escondido, CA. After guesting frequently on "I Love Lucy" he was a regular on Miss Ball's three subsequent series, "The Lucy Show," "Here's Lucy," and "Life With Lucy." His movie credits include *Rally 'Round the Flag Boys*, *Don't Give Up the Ship*, *Visit to a Small Planet*, *All in a Night's Work*, *All Hands on Deck*, and *The 'Burbs*. His wife had died a few weeks earlier. Survived by a sister.

ELEANORE GRIFFIN, 91, Hollywood screenwriter, who won an Academy Award for her work on *Boys Town*, died in Woodland Hills, CA, on July 26, 1995. Her other films include *St. Louis Blues*, *A Man Called Peter*, *Good Morning Miss Dove*, and *One Man's Way*. No reported survivors.

HARRY GUARDINO, 69, New York City-born screen, stage, and TV actor, died in Palm Springs, CA, on July 17, 1995, of lung cancer. His movies include *Sirocco*, *The Big Tip-Off*, *Houseboat*, *Pork Chop Hill*, *The Five Pennies*, *Five Branded Women*, *King of Kings* (as Barabbas), *Hell Is for Heroes*, *The Pigeon That Took Rome*, *Rhino!*, *The Adventures of Bullwhip Griffin*, *Madigan*, *Lovers and Other Strangers*, *Red Sky at Morning*, *Dirty Harry*, *They Only Kill Their Masters*, *Capone*, *St. Ives*, *The Enforcer* (1976), *Rollercoaster*, *Goldengirl*, and *Any Which Way You Can*. Survived by his wife, 3 sons, a daughter, 2 brothers, 2 sisters, and 1 grandson.

EVA GABOR, 74, Budapest-born screen and TV actress, best known for her role on the long-running TV sitcom *Green Acres*, died of respiratory distress and other complications on July 4, 1995 in Los Angeles. Among her movie credits are *The Last Time I Saw Paris*, *Artists and Models*, *Don't Go Near the Water*, *My Man Godfrey* (1957), *Gigi*, *A New Kind of Love*, and *The Rescuers* (as the voice of Miss Bianca). She is survived by her mother, her 2 sisters, including actress Zsa Zsa Gabor, and 2 step-daughters from her fourth marriage.

MICHAEL V. GAZZO, 71, actor and playwright, best known for his 1955 Broadway drama *A Hatful of Rain*, died of complications from a stroke on Feb. 14, 1995, in Los Angeles. As an actor he received an Oscar nomination for *The Godfather Part II*, thereafter appearing in such movies as *Black Sunday*, *Fingers*, *King of the Gypsies*, *The Fish That Saved Pittsburgh*, and *Back Roads*. Survived by his wife, daughter, 2 sons, a sister, a brother, and 3 grandchildren.

ALEXANDER GODUNOV, 45, former Russian ballet dancer who defected to the U.S. and later turned to acting died at his West Hollywood home of heart failure caused by acute alcoholism on May 18, 1995. Following his movie debut in *Witness* he acted in *Die Hard*, *The Runestone*, *Waxworks II*, and *North*. No reported survivors.

Phil Harris   Tom Helmore

Michael Hordern   John Howard

ALBERT HACKETT, 95, New York City-born screen and stage writer who authored more than 30 screenplays with his first wife and collaborator Frances Goodrich, died of pneumonia in Manhattan on March 16, 1995. Among their credits are *The Thin Man* (Oscar nomination), *Naughty Marietta*, *Ah! Wilderness*, *After the Thin Man* (Oscar nomination), *Rose Marie*, *The Firefly*, *Lady in the Dark*, *It's a Wonderful Life*, *The Pirate*, *Easter Parade*, *Summer Holiday*, *In the Good Old Summertime*, *Father of the Bride* (Oscar nomination), *Seven Brides for Seven Brothers* (Oscar nomination), *The Long Long Trailer*, and *The Diary of Anne Frank* (based on their Pulitzer Prize and Tony Award-winning play). Ms. Goodrich died in 1984. Hackett is survived by his second wife.

PHIL HARRIS, 91, Indiana-born actor, singer, and bandleader, died at his home in Rancho Mirage, CA, on Aug. 11, 1995. Best known for his radio work with Jack Benny and, later, with his wife Alice Faye, he was seen in such movies as *Melody Cruise*, *Man About Town*, *Buck Benny Rides Again*, *Here Comes the Groom*, *The High and the Mighty*, *Anything Goes* (1956), *Goodbye My Lady*, *The Wheeler Dealers*, and *The Cool Ones*. His voice was heard in three Disney animated features: *The Jungle Book* (as Baloo the Bear, singing the Oscar-nominated "The Bare Necessities"), *The Aristocats*, and *Robin Hood*. In addition to Faye, he is survived by 2 daughters, 4 grandchildren, and 2 great-grandchildren.

Burl Ives

TOM HELMORE, 91, British screen, stage, and TV actor, died on Sept. 12, 1995, in Longboat Key, FL. His films include *Let's Do It Again* (1953), *Lucy Gallant*, *Trouble Along the Way*, *Designing Woman*, *The Tender Trap*, *Vertigo*, and *The Time Machine*. Survived by a daughter.

TED HOOK, 65, dancer, film extra, and restaurant owner, died of pneumonia at his home in Manhattan on July 19, 1995. He appeared in such movies as *By the Light of the Silvery Moon*, *Torch Song Trilogy*, and *Lean on Me*. He ran the New York restaurants Backstage and Onstage. Survived by his mother, and his sister.

SIR MICHAEL HORDERN, 83, British screen, stage, and TV character actor, a familiar face in countless international productions, died of kidney disease in Oxford, England on May 2, 1995. Starting in films in 1939 he appeared in such movies as *Mine Own Executioner*, *Passport to Pimlico*, *A Christmas Carol* (Scrooge), *Tom Brown's School Days*, *The Story of Robin Hood*, *The Card* (The Promoter), *The Warriors* (The Dark Avenger), *Alexander the Great*, *The Man Who Never Was*, *Sink the Bismark!*, *El Cid*, *Cleopatra* (1963), *The V.I.P.s*, *The Yellow Rolls-Royce*, *Genghis Khan*, *The Spy Who Came in From the Cold*, *Khartoum*, *A Funny Thing Happened on the Way to the Forum*, *The Taming of the Shrew*, *How I Won the War*, *The Jokers*, *I'll Never Forget What's 'is Name*, *Where Eagles Dare*, *The Bed Sitting Room*, *Anne of the Thousand Days*, *The Pied Piper*, *The Possession of Joel Delaney*, *Theatre of Blood*, *The Mackintosh Man*, *Lucky Lady*, *The Slipper and the Rose*, *Joseph Andrews*, *Gandhi*, *The Missionary*, *Yellowbeard*, *Lady Jane*, and *Dark Obsession (Diamond Skulls)*. He was knighted in 1983. Survived by a daughter.

Nancy Kelly   Patric Knowles

JOHN HOWARD (John Cox), 82, screen and TV actor, whose noted roles include playing Ronald Colman's brother in *Lost Horizon* and Katharine Hepburn's fiancee in *The Philadelphia Story*, died of heart failure on Feb. 19, 1995, at his home in Santa Rosa, CA. Other credits include *Soak the Rich*, *Bulldog Drummond Comes Back*, *Prison Farm*, *The Invisible Woman*, *The Mad Doctor*, *I Jane Doe*, *The Fighting Kentuckian*, *The High and the Mighty*, and *Unknown Terror*. He retired from acting in the 1970s to become a teacher. He is survived by his wife, 2 sons, and 2 daughters.

HARRY HURWITZ, 57, New York City-born film director and writer, died of heart failure while awaiting a heart transplant on Sept. 21, 1995, in Los Angeles. His movies include *The Projectionist*, *Richard*, *Safari 3000*, and *That's Adequate*. Survived by his wife and 3 sons.

BURL IVES, 85, Illinois-born screen, stage, and TV performer, one of the country's most beloved folk singers, as well as an outstanding actor, died of complications of mouth cancer on Apr. 14, 1995, at his home in Anacortes, WA. In 1958 he played his two greatest film roles, rancher Rufus Hannassey in *The Big Country* (for which he won the Academy Award as best supporting actor), and Big Daddy in *Cat on a Hot Tin Roof* (repeating

Priscilla Lane

Viveca Lindfors

his stage role). His other pictures include *Smoky* (debut, 1946), *Green Grass of Wyoming*, *So Dear to My Heart*, *East of Eden*, *A Face in the Crowd*, *Desire Under the Elms*, *Our Man in Havana*, *The Spiral Road*, *Summer Magic*, *Ensign Pulver*, *The Brass Bottle*, *Blast-Off (Those Fantastic Flying Fools)*, *The McMasters*, *Just You and Me Kid*, *White Dog*, and *Two-Moon Junction*. Survived by his second wife, a son, 2 stepsons, a stepdaughter, and 5 grandchildren.

DOROTHY JEAKINS, 81, San Diego-born costume designer, who won the very first Academy Award for best costume design, for *Joan of Arc*, in 1948, died in Santa Barbara, CA, on Nov. 21, 1995. She received additional Oscars for *Samson and Delilah* and *The Night of the Iguana*, while her other credits included *The Greatest Show on Earth*, *My Cousin Rachel*, *The Ten Commandments*, *Elmer Gantry*, *The Misfits*, *The Music Man*, *The Sound of Music*, *Reflections in a Golden Eye*, *The Molly Maguires*, *Catch-22*, *The Way We Were*, and *The Dead*. Survived by 2 sons and a half-brother.

NANCY KELLY, 73, Massachusetts-born screen and theatre actress, best known for her Tony Award-winning role as the tormented mother of a homicidal child in *The Bad Seed*, died of a diabetes-related illness on Jan.

Ida Lupino

2, 1995, at her home in Bel Air, CA. She repeated her role in the 1956 film version of *The Bad Seed* earning an Oscar nomination. Her other films include *Submarine Patrol*, *Jesse James*, *Stanley and Livingstone*, *He Married His Wife*, *One Night in the Tropics*, *Scotland Yard*, *Parachute Batallion*, *To the Shores of Tripoli*, *Women in Bondage*, *Tarzan's Desert Mystery*, *Show Business*, *The Woman Who Came Back*, and *Murder in the Music Hall*. Survived by her daughter and 3 granddaughters.

PATRIC KNOWLES (Reginald Lawrence Knowles), 84, British screen and stage actor who played second leads in many Hollywood films after settling there in 1936, died on Dec. 23, 1995, in Woodland Hills, CA. Among his movies are *The Charge of the Light Brigade* (1936), *The Patient in Room 18*, *The Adventures of Robin Hood* (as Will Scarlett), *It's Love I'm After*, *The Sisters*, *Another Thin Man*, *How Green Was My Valley*, *The Wolf Man*, *The Strange Case of Dr. Rx*, *Frankenstein Meets the Wolf Man*, *Hit the Ice*, *Crazy House*, *Kitty*, *Of Human Bondage* (1946), *Monsieur Beaucaire*, *Ivy*, *Three Came Home*, *Flame of Calcutta*, *Khyber Patrol*, *Band of Angels*, *Auntie Mame*, *The Way West*, *The Devil's Brigade*, *Chisum*, and *Terror in the Wax Museum*. Survived by his wife, a son, a daughter, 4 grandchildren, and a great-grandchild.

Louis Malle

ALEXANDER KNOX, 88, Canadian-born screen, stage, and TV actor, best known for his Academy Award-nominated role as President Woodrow Wilson in the 1944 bio-pic *Wilson*, died of bone cancer on April 25, 1995, in Northumberland, England. Among his other film credits are *The Four Feathers* (1939), *The Sea Wolf* (1941), *This Above All*, *The Commandos Strike at Dawn*, *None Shall Escape*, *Sister Kenny* (which he also co-wrote), *The Judge Steps Out* (also co-writer), *The Night My Number Came Up*, *The Vikings*, *The Two-Headed Spy*, *The Wreck of the Mary Deare*, *Oscar Wilde*, *The Longest Day*, *In the Cool of the Day*, *Crack in the World*, *Mister Moses*, *Khartoum*, *Accident*, *You Only Live Twice*, *How I Won the War*, *Nicholas and Alexandra*, *Gorky Park*, and *Joshua Then and Now*. Survived by his wife, and a grandson.

HOWARD KOCH, 93, New York City-born screenwriter, best known for his Oscar-winning script of *Casablanca*, died in Kingston, NY, on Aug. 17, 1995. His other credits include *The Sea Hawk*, *The Letter*, *Sergeant York*, *Mission to Moscow*, *Rhapsody in Blue*, *No Sad Songs for Me*, *The War Lover*, *Loss of Innocence*, and *The Fox*. Survived by his wife, a daughter, a son, 5 grandchildren, and 2 great-grandchildren.

Dean Martin

PRISCILLA LANE (Priscilla Mullican), 76, Iowa-born screen actress who starred in such notable films as *Brother Rat*, *Four Daughters*, *The Roaring Twenties*, and *Arsenic and Old Lace*, died on Apr. 4, 1995, in Andover, MA, following a brief illness. Starting as a singer with Fred Waring she made her debut in *Variety Show*, followed by such other movies as *Men Are Such Fools*, *Cowboy From Brooklyn*, *Yes My Darling Daughter*, *Daughters Courageous*, *Dust Be Me Destiny*, *Four Wives*, *Three Cheers for the Irish*, *Four Mothers*, *Blues in the Night*, *Saboteur*, *The Meanest Man in the World*, and her last, *Deadline at Dawn*, in 1948. She retired from the screen after marrying. Her sisters, also actresses, were Rosemary Lane (who died in 1974), and Lola Lane (who died in 1981). Survived by 2 daughters, 2 sons, and 6 grandchildren.

VIVECA LINDFORS (Elsa Viveca Torstensdotter Lindfors), 74, International screen and TV actress, died from complications from rheumatoid arthritis on Oct. 25, 1995, in her birthplace of Uppsala, Sweden. After debuting in Swedish films she made her American debut in 1948 in *To the Victor*. Her other screen credits include *Adventures of Don Juan*, *Night Unto Night*, *No Sad Songs for Me*, *Dark City*, *Four in a Jeep*, *The Raiders*, *Moonfleet*, *The Halliday Brand*, *I Accuse!*, *The Tempest*, *The Story of Ruth*, *King of Kings*, *No Exit*, *These Are the Damned*, *An Affair of the Skin*, *Sylvia*, *Puzzle of a Downfall Child*, *The Way We Were*, *Welcome to L.A.*, *A Wedding*, *Voices*, *The Hand*, *Creepshow*, *The Sure Thing*, *Misplaced*, *The Linguini Incident*, *Stargate*, and *Last Summer in the Hamptons*. Survived by a daughter and 2 sons, one of whom is actor Kristoffer Tabori, from her marriage to director Don Siegel, and 4 grandchildren.

ARTHUR LUBIN, 96, Los Angeles-born film and TV director, who helmed several comedies starring Abbott & Costello and Francis the Talking Mule, died in Glendale, CA, on May 11, 1995. Among his films were *Buck Privates*, *Hold That Ghost*, *Eagle Squadron*, *Phantom of the Opera* (1943), *Ali Baba and the 40 Thieves*, *Queen for a Day*, *Francis*, *Francis Goes to the Races*, *Rhubarb*, *It Grows on Trees*, *The First Traveling Saleslady*, *Escapade in Japan*, *The Incredible Mr. Limpet*, and *Hold On!* No reported survivors.

Doug McClure   Butterfly McQueen

IDA LUPINO, 77, London-born screen, stage, and TV actress, who became the first woman to successfully make the transition from star to leading director, died of cancer on Aug. 3, 1995 at her home in California. Following her 1933 debut in the British film *Her First Affair* she later went to Hollywood where her pictures included *Search for Beauty*, *Peter Ibbetson*, *Anything Goes* (1936), *Yours for the Asking*, *Artists and Models* (1937), *The Lone Wolf Spy Hunt*, *The Adventures of Sherlock Holmes* (1939), *The Light That Failed*, *They Drive by Night*, *High Sierra*, *The Sea Wolf* (1941), *Out of the Fog*, *Ladies in Retirement*, *The Hard Way* (1943), *Life Begins at 8:30*, *Thank Your Lucky Stars*, *Hollywood Canteen*, *Devotion*, *Escape Me Never*, *Roadhouse*, *Lust for Gold*, *Woman in Hiding*, *Women's Prison*, *The Big Knife*, *While the City Sleeps*, *Junior Bonner*, *The Food of the Gods*, and her last, *My Boys Are Good Boys* in 1978. Her directorial credits include *Outrage* (which she also wrote), *Hard Fast and Beautiful*, *The Hitchhiker* (also writer), *The Bigamist*, and *The Trouble With Angels*. Survived by a daughter from her marriage to the late actor Howard Duff.

JEFFREY LYNN (Ragnard Jeffrey Lynn), 89, Massachusetts-born screen, stage, and TV actor, died on Nov. 24, 1995, in Burbank, CA. Following his debut in the 1938 film *Four Daughters* he was seen in such movies as *Yes My Darling Daughter*, *The Roaring Twenties*, *The Fighting 69th*, *All This and Heaven Too*, *Four Mothers*, *Black Bart*, *A Letter to Three Wives*, *Up Front*, and *Tony Rome*. Survived by his third wife, a daughter, 7 stepchildren, 3 sisters, 2 brothers and 17 grandchildren.

Donald Pleasence

LOUIS MALLE, 63, French director-writer, whose notable works include *Murmur of the Heart* (Oscar nomination for screenplay) and *Atlantic City* (Oscar nomination for direction), died of lymphoma at his home in Beverly Hills, CA, on Nov. 23, 1995. Among his films as director (on which he often served as writer and/or producer) are *Elevator to the Gallows*, *The Lovers*, *A Very Private Affair*, *The Fire Within*, *Viva Maria*, *Calcutta*, *Lacombe Lucien*, *Pretty Baby*, *My Dinner With Andre*, *Crackers*, *Au Revoir les Enfants/Goodbye Children*, *May Fools*, *Damage*, and his last, *Vanya on 42nd Street*, in 1994. He is survived by his wife, actress Candice Bergen, their daughter, a son by actress Gila von Weiterhausen, and a daughter by actress Alexandra Stewart.

DEAN MARTIN (Dino Crocetti), 78, Ohio-born screen and TV actor-singer who became one of the most popular entertainers of his time, died of acute respiratory failure on Dec. 25, 1995, at his home in Beverly Hills, CA. For the first part of his career he was teamed with Jerry Lewis, appearing in sixteen successful comedies including *My Friend Irma* (their debut, in 1949), *At War With the Army*, *That's My Boy*, *Jumping Jacks*, *The Caddy*, *Money From Home*, *Living It Up*, *You're Never Too Young*, and *Hollywood or Bust* before the duo split in 1956. Afterwards he continued to succeed as a recording artist and nightclub entertainer while establishing himself as a reliable actor in such movies as *The Young Lions*,*Some Came Running*, *Career*, *Rio Bravo*, *Who Was That Lady?*, *Bells Are Ringing*, *Ocean's Eleven*, *All in a Night's Work*, *Sergeants 3*, *Toys in the Attic*, *Who's Been Sleeping in My Bed?*, *Four for Texas*, *What a Way to Go*, *Robin and the 7 Hoods*, *Kiss Me Stupid*, *The Sons of Katie Elder*, *The Silencers*, *Murderers' Row*, *Bandolero*, *Five Card Stud*, *Airport*, *Showdown*, and *The Cannonball Run*. His hit TV series "The Dean Martin Show" ran from 1965 to 1974, while his best-selling singles included "That's Amore" and "Everybody Loves Somebody Sometime." Survived by 2 sons and 4 daughters.

DOUG McCLURE, 59, California-born screen and TV actor perhaps best known for his starring role on the long running western series "The Virginian," died of lung cancer at his home in Sherman Oaks, CA, on Feb. 5, 1995. His feature film credits include *The Enemy Below, South Pacific, Gidget, Because They're Young, The Unforgiven, Shenandoah, Beau Geste* (1966), *The King's Pirate, The Land That Time Forgot, At the Earth's Core, Humanoids From the Deep, The House Where Evil Dwells, Cannonball Run II, 52 Pick-Up,* and *Maverick.* Survived by his wife, 2 children, his mother, and a brother.

BUTTERFLY McQUEEN (Thelma McQueen), 84, Florida-born screen, TV, and stage actress, who won screen immortality playing the maid Prissy in *Gone With the Wind,* died on Dec. 22, 1995, in Augusta, GA, after being critically burned when she tried to light a kerosene heater in her home. The actress, who drifted in and out of acting while indulging in social work, also appeared in such movies as *Cabin in the Sky, Flame of Barbary Coast, Mildred Pierce, Duel in the Sun, The Phynx, Amazing Grace,* and *The Mosquito Coast.* No reported survivors.

JOHN MEGNA, 42, New York City-born film and TV actor, who played Dill in the 1962 film version of *To Kill a Mockingbird,* died of AIDS on Sept. 4, 1995 in Los Angeles. His other films include *Hush...Hush Sweet Charlotte, Blindfold, Go Tell the Spartans, Smokey and the Bandit II,* and *The Cannonball Run.* Survived by 2 sisters, one of whom is actress Connie Stevens, and a brother.

LEWIS MELTZER, 84, Hollywood screenwriter died of pneumonia on Feb. 23, 1995, in Albuquerque, NM. His credits include *Golden Boy, The Lady in Question, Once Upon a Time, Along the Great Divide, The Man With the Golden Arm,* and *Autumn Leaves.* Survived by his second wife, 2 sons, his brother, 2 daughters, and 2 grandchildren.

PATSY RUTH MILLER (Patricia Ruth Miller), 91, silent film actress, best known for playing Esmeralda opposite Lon Chaney in the 1923 version of *The Hunchback of Notre Dame,* died at her home in Palm Desert, CA, on July 16, 1995. Her other films include *Camille, Omar the Tentmaker, Oh What a Nurse!, Why Girls Go Back Home, Broken Hearts of Hollywood, The White Black Sheep, So This Is Paris, Wolf's Clothing, Painting the Town, We Americans, Beautiful but Dumb, The Sap,* and her last, *Quebec,* in 1951. She left acting to become a writer. Survived by a son, 2 stepchildren, 7 grandchildren, and 2 great-grandchildren.

Frank Perry   John Smith

ELIZABETH MONTGOMERY, 62, Los Angeles-born screen and TV actress, best known for her starring role in the TV sitcom "Bewitched," died at her home in Los Angeles on May 18, 1995, following a bout with cancer. The daughter of the late actor Robert Montgomery, she appeared in only a handful of theatrical films: *The Court-Martial of Billy Mitchell, Johnny Cool, Who's Been Sleeping in My Bed?,* and *How to Stuff a Wild Bikini.* Survived by her husband, actor Robert Foxworth, and 3 children from an earlier marriage to producer William Asher.

GILBERT MOSES, 52, Cleveland-born film and stage director, died at his Manhattan home on Apr. 14, 1995, of multiple myeloma. His two movie credits were *Willie Dynamite* and *The Fish That Saved Pittsburgh.* Survived by his companion, his mother, 2 daughters, 2 brothers, and 4 sisters.

ESTHER MUIR, 92, film and stage actress died in Mount Kisco, NY, on Aug. 1, 1995. Among her movies credits are *A Dangerous Affair, So This Is Africa, The Bowery, Fury, A Day at the Races* (in which she was wallpapered by the Marx Brothers), *City Girl, Stolen Paradise,* and *X Marks the Spot.* In the 1950s she became a California real estate developer. Her first marriage, to choreographer-director Busby Berkeley, ended in divorce, as did her second, to producer/composer Sam Coslow. Survived by her daughter and 2 grandchildren.

Lana Turner

EIJI OKADA, 75, Japanese actor best known to U.S. audiences for his starring role in the 1959 film *Hiroshima Mon Amour,* died on Sept. 14, 1995, in Japan. His other credits include *Until the Day We Meet Again, Woman of the Dunes, The Ugly American* (his only American film), *She and He,* and *This Transient Life.*

TESSIE O'SHEA, 82, British screen, stage, and TV actress-singer, died of congestive heart failure in 1995, at a nursing home in Leesburg, FL. Best known for her appearances on the English music hall circuit and London stage she also was seen in such films as *The Way Ahead, London Town, The Shiralee, The Russians Are Coming the Russians Are Coming, The Best House in London,* and *Bedknobs and Broomsticks.* No immediate survivors.

JOHN PATRICK, 90, Kentucky-born writer who won a Pulitzer Prize for his 1953 play *The Teahouse of the August Moon,* was found dead on Nov. 7, 1995, in Delray Beach, FL, a suicide. In addition to adapting *Teahouse,* his other film scripts included *Three Coins in the Fountain, Love Is a Many-Splendored Thing, High Society,* and *Les Girls.* No reported survivors.

FRANK PERRY, 65, New York City-born motion picture director who received an Oscar nomination for his debut effort, *David and Lisa,* died of prostate cancer in Manhattan on Aug. 29, 1995. His other credits are *Ladybug Ladybug, The Swimmer, Last Summer, Trilogy, Diary of a Mad Housewife, Doc, Play It as It Lays, Man on a Swing, Rancho Deluxe, Mommie Dearest* (which he also co-wrote), *Monsignor, Compromising Positions, Hello Again,* and his last, *On the Bridge,* a documentary journal on his own bout with cancer. Survived by his third wife and 2 brothers.

Ginger Rogers

Genevieve Tobin   Willard Waterman

DONALD PLEASENCE, 75, British film, stage, and television actor, died on Feb. 2, 1995, at his home in St. Paul de Vence in the south of France. He had been recovering from heart surgery performed a few months earlier. His many motion pictures include *Stowaway Girl, A Tale of Two Cities* (1958), *The Two-Headed Spy, Look Back in Anger, Battle of the Sexes, Circus of Horrors, Sons and Lovers, No Love for Johnnnie, Hands of Orlac, Lisa (The Inspector), The Caretaker, The Great Escape, Dr. Crippen, The Hallelujah Trail, Fantastic Voyage, Cul-de-Sac, Eye of the Devils, The Night of the Generals, You Only Live Twice, Will Penny, The Madwoman of Chaillot, Soldier Blue, THX-1138, The Pied Piper, Innocent Bystanders, Wedding in White, Tales That Witness Madness, The Mutations, Escape to Witch Mountain, Hearts of the West, The Devil Within Her, The Last Tycoon, The Eagle Has Landed, Telefon, Halloween, Dracula, Escape From New York, Alone in the Dark, Prince of Darkness, Hanna's War, Shadows and Fog,* and *The Advocate.* Survived by his fourth wife, and 5 daughters.

GINGER ROGERS (Virginia Katherine McMath), 83, Missouri-born screen and stage actress-dancer who became one of Hollywood's legendary performers through her ten musical teamings with Fred Astaire, died of natural causes at her home in Rancho Mirage, CA, on April 25, 1995. Her 1930 debut in *Young Man of Manhattan,* was followed by such movies as *The Sap From Syracuse, Follow the Leader, The Thirteenth Guest, You Said a Mouthful, 42nd Street, Gold Diggers of 1933, 20 Million Sweethearts, Romance in Manhattan, Stage Door, Having Wonderful Time, Vivacious Lady, Bachelor Mother, Fifth Avenue Girl, Primrose Path, Lucky Partners, Tom Dick and Harry, Roxie Hart, Tales of Manhattan, The Major and the Minor, Once Upon a Honeymoon, Lady in the Dark, I'll Be Seeing You, Weekend at the Waldorf, Magnificent Doll, Storm Warning, We're Not Married, Monkey Business* (1952), *Dreamboat, Forever Female, Black Widow* (1954), *The First Travelling Saleslady, Oh Men! Oh Women!,* and her last, *Harlow,* in 1965. She received the 1940 Academy Award as best actress for *Kitty Foyle.* With Astaire she co-starred in *Flying Down to Rio, The Gay Divorcee, Roberta, Top Hat, Follow the Fleet, Swing Time, Shall We Dance, Carefree, The Story of Vernon and Irene Castle,* and *The Barkleys of Broadway.* Her five marriages, including those to actors Lew Ayres and Jacques Bergerac, and director William Marshall, all ended in divorce. No survivors.

RALPH ROSENBLUM, 69, film editor, died of heart failure at his Manhattan home on Sept. 4, 1995. His credits include *A Thousand Clowns, The Pawnbroker, The Night They Raided Minsky's, Goodbye Columbus, Take the Money and Run, Sleeper,* and *Annie Hall.* Survived by his wife, a daughter, a son, and a brother.

MIKLOS ROZSA, 88, one of Hollywood's most prolific composers, died on July 27, 1995 in Los Angeles following a stroke. He won Academy Awards for his work on *Spellbound* (1945), *A Double Life* (1947), and *Ben-Hur* (1959). He scored such other films as *Thief of Baghdad* (1940), *Lydia, That Hamilton Woman, Five Graves to Cairo, So Proudly We Hail, Double Indemnity, The Lost Weekend, A Song to Remember, The Killers* (1945), *The Strange Loves of Martha Ivers, The Asphalt Jungle, Quo Vadis, Julius Caesar* (1953), *Knight of the Round Table, Tribute to a Bad*

Man, *Lust for Life, Tip on a Dead Jockey, King of Kings* (1961), *El Cid, The VIPs, The Green Berets, The Private Life of Sherlock Holmes, Fedora, Time After Time,* and *Dead Men Don't Wear Plaid.* Survived by his wife, a daughter, a son, a sister, and 3 granddaughters.

ALLAN SCOTT, 88, New Jersey-born screenwriter whose credits include the Astaire-Rogers musicals *Top Hat, Follow the Fleet, Swing Time,* and *Shall We Dance,* died on Apr. 13, 1995, in Santa Monica, CA. He also received credit on such movies as *Quality Street, Skylark, So Proudly We Hail, The Fourposter,* and *The 5000 Fingers of Dr.T.* Survived by his daughter, actress Pipa Scott, his son, and 4 grandchildren.

MADGE SINCLAIR, 57, Jamaica-born screen, stage, and TV actress, who won an Emmy Award for the series "Gabriel's Fire," died on Dec. 20, 1995, in Los Angeles, of leukemia. Her movie credits include *Conrack, Cornbread Earl and Me, I Will I Will...for Now, Star Trek IV: The Voyage Home, Coming to America,* and *The Lion King* (as the voice of the Lion Queen, Sarabi). Survived by her husband, her sons, her mother and a sister.

JOHN SMITH (Robert Van Orden), 63, screen and TV actor, best known for starring in the western TV series "Cimarron City" and "Laramie," died of cirrhosis of the liver on Jan. 25, 1995, at his home in Los Angeles. His movies include *Going My Way, The High and the Mighty, We're No Angels, Ghost Town, The Bold and the Brave, Friendly Persuasion, Island of Lost Women, Circus World,* and *Waco.* No reported survivors.

TERRY SOUTHERN, 71, Texas-born screenwriter and novelist who received Oscar nominations for collaborating on the scripts of *Dr. Strangelove* and *Easy Rider,* died of respiratory failure on Oct. 29, 1995, in Manhattan. His other film credits include *The Loved One, The Cincinnati Kid, Barbarella,* and *The Magic Christian.* Survived by his son and his companion.

KATHERINE SQUIRE, 92, screen and stage actress, died on March 29, 1995, in Lake Hill, NY. Her credits include *The Story on Page One, Song Without End, Lolly Madonna XXX,* and *When Harry Met Sally.* Survived by three stepdaughters.

ROBERT STEPHENS, 64, British screen, stage, and TV actor, who starred in Billy Wilder's 1970 film *The Private Life of Sherlock Holmes* as the great detective, died in London on Nov. 12, 1995. He had undergone a liver and kidney transplant and suffered rejection problems. Acclaimed for his West End work in such plays as *The Royal Hunt of the Sun, The Seagull,* and *King Lear,* his movie credits included *A Taste of Honey, The Small World of Sammy Lee, Cleopatra* (1963), *Morgan!, Romeo and Juliet* (1968; as The Prince), *The Prime of Miss Jean Brodie, Travels With My Aunt* (the last two with then-wife Maggie Smith), *Luther, The Duellists, Empire of the Sun, Wonderland (The Fruit Machine), Henry V* (1989), *The Bonfire of the Vanities, The Pope Must Die, Searching for Bobby Fischer,* and *The Secret Rapture.* He was knighted in early 1995. Survived by his fourth wife and 4 children including actor Toby Stephens.

GRADY SUTTON, 89, Tennessee-born screen, stage, and TV character actor, a notable comic foil to W.C. Fields in such films as *Man on the Flying Trapeze* and *The Bank Dick,* died in Woodland Hills, CA, on Sept. 17, 1995. Following his debut in the 1925 film *The Mad Whirl* he was seen in dozens of movies including *The Freshman* (1925), *Let's Go Native, Movie Crazy, Hot Saturday, The Story of Temple Drake, College Humor, Alice Adams, Valiant Is the Word for Carrie, My Man Godfrey* (1936), *Pigskin Parade, Stage Door, Waikiki Wedding, Turn Off the Moon, Vivacious Lady, Alexander's Ragtime Band, You Can't Cheat an Honest Man, It's a Wonderful World, Torrid Zone, Lucky Partners, Somewhere I'll Find You, The More the Merrier, The Great Moment, Dragonwyck, Since You Went Away, A Royal Scandal, Since You Went Away, Anchors Aweigh, Dead Reckoning, My Wild Irish Rose, White Christmas, Living It Up, The Chapman Report, My Fair Lady, Myra Breckinridge,* and *Support Your Local Gunfighter.* No reported survivors.

GENEVIEVE TOBIN, 93, New York City-born screen and theatre actress, died on July 31, 1995, in Pasadena, CA. Following her 1930 debut in *A Lady Surrenders* she appeared in such movies as *One Hour With You, Cohens and Kellys in Hollywood, Pleasure Cruise, I Loved a Woman, Dark Hazard, Uncertain Lady, Kiss and Make Up, The Goose and the Gander, Broadway Hostess, The Petrified Forest, The Great Gambini, Dramatic School, Zaza,* and her last, *No Time for Comedy,* in 1940. She married director William Keighley in 1938; he died in 1984. Survived by her sister.

LANA TURNER (Julia Jean Mildred Frances Turner), 75, Idaho-born screen and TV actress, one of Hollywood's most glamorous stars of the 1940s and 1950s, died on June 29, 1995, in Los Angeles. She had been receiving treatment for throat cancer. Allegedly discovered by a reporter at a Hollywood ice cream parlor she made her initial impact in a small role in *They Won't Forget* then went on to stardom in such features as *Love Finds Andy Hardy*, *Ziegfeld Girl*, *Dr. Jekyll and Mr. Hyde* (1941), *Honky Tonk*, *Johnny Eager*, *Somewhere I'll Find You*, *Slightly Dangerous*, *Marriage Is a Private Affair*, *Week-End at the Waldorf*, *The Postman Always Rings Twice*, *Green Dolphin Street*, *Cass Timberlane*, *Homecoming*, *The Three Musketeers* (1948), *A Life of Her Own*, *Mr. Imperium*, *The Bad and the Beautiful*, *Latin Lovers*, *The Prodigal*, *Sea Chase*, *The Rains of Ranchipur*, *Diane*, *Peyton Place* (Academy Award nomination), *Another Time Another Place*, *The Lady Takes a Flyer*, *Imitation of Life* (1959), *Portrait in Black*, *Bachelor in Paradise*, *Who's Got the Action?*, *Madame X* (1966), and *Bittersweet Love*. Seven times married and divorced she is survived by her only child, daughter Cheryl Crane.

BENAY VENUTA (Benvenuta Rose Crooke), 84, San Francisco-born screen and stage actress, best known for her Broadway work in such shows as *Anything Goes*, *By Jupiter*, and *Hazel Flagg*, died of lung cancer on Sept. 1, 1995, at her home in Manhattan. Her film credits include *Annie Get Your Gun*, *The Fuzzy Pink Nightgown*, *Call Me Mister*, and *Bullets Over Broadway*. Survived by 2 daughters, and 5 grandchildren.

WILLARD WATERMAN, 80, screen, TV and stage character actor, died of bone marrow disease on Feb. 2, 1995, at his home in Burlingame, CA. Best known for starring in "The Great Gildersleeve" on TV, he was seen in such films as *Riding High* (1950), *Three Coins in the Fountain*, *How to Be Very Very Popular*, *Hollywood or Bust*, *Auntie Mame*, and *The Apartment*. Survived by his wife, 2 daughters, and 3 granddaughters.

DAVID WAYNE (Wayne McKeekan), 81, Michigan-born screen, stage, and TV actor, died of lung cancer on Feb. 9, 1995, at his home in Santa Monica, CA. After receiving the very first Tony Award given for a musical performance, for *Finian's Rainbow*, he made his film debut in 1949's *Portrait of Jennie*. His subsequent credits include *Adam's Rib*, *The Reformer and the Readhead*, *M* (1951), *As Young as You Feel*, *Up Front*, *Wait 'Til the Sun Shines Nellie*, *With a Song in My Heart*, *We're Not Married*, *O. Henry's Full House*, *Down Among the Sheltering Palms*, *How to Marry a Millionaire*, *The Tender Trap*, *Three Faces of Eve*, *The Sad Sack*, *The Last Angry Man*, *The Andromeda Strain*, *Huckleberry Finn*, *The Front Page* (1974), *The Apple Dumpling Gang*, and *Finders Keepers*. Survived by his twin daughters, and 2 grandchildren.

MARY WICKES (Mary Isabelle Wickenhauser), 85, sardonic character actress of screen, stage, and TV, died on Oct. 22, 1995, in Los Angeles. She made her film debut in 1941 recreating her stage role of the nurse, Miss Preen, in *The Man Who Came to Dinner*. Thereafter she was seen in such movies as *Now Voyager*, *Who Done It?*, *How's About It?*, *Happy Land*, *Higher and Higher*, *June Bride*, *On Moonlight Bay*, *I'll See You in My Dreams*, *The Story of Will Rogers*, *The Actress*, *By the Light of the Silvery Moon*, *Good Morning Miss Dove*, *Dance With Me Henry*, *Don't Go Near the Water*, *It Happened to Jane*, *The Music Man*, *Who's Minding the Store?*, *Dear Heart*, *How to Murder Your Wife*, *The Trouble With Angels*, *Where Angels Go Trouble Follows*, *Snowball Express*, *Postcards From the Edge*, *Sister Act*, *Little Women* (1994), and *The Hunchback of Notre Dame* (as the voice of one of the gargoyles). No reported survivors.

CALDER WILLINGHAM, 72, Atlanta-born screenwriter and novelist, died of lung cancer on Feb. 19, 1995, in Laconia, NH. His film credits include *Paths of Glory*, *The Vikings*, *One-Eyed Jacks*, *The Graduate* (for which he received an Academy Award nomination), *Little Big Man*, and *Rambling Rose* (based on his novel). The 1957 movie *The Strange One* was based on his novel *End as a Man*. Survived by his wife, 5 children, a brother, a sister, and 5 grandchildren.

WOLFMAN JACK (Robert W. Smith), 57, Brooklyn-born disc jockey, died of a heart attack at his home in Belvidere, NC. He had just returned from an extensive tour to promote his autobiography *Have Mercy! Wolfman Jack*. He played himself in the 1973 film *American Graffiti* and also acted in such movies as *Motel Hell*. Survived by his wife, his son, and his daughter.

David Wayne

Mary Wickes

INDEX